Timber and Building Construction

The Proceedings of the Ninth Annual Conference of the
Construction History Society

Queens' College, University of Cambridge, 1-3 April 2022

Edited by

James W P Campbell
Nina Baker
Michael Driver
Michael Heaton
Natcha Ruamsanitwong
Christine Wall
David Yeomans

Published by The Construction History Society
1 Scroope Terrace
Cambridge
CB2 1PX

www.construction.co.uk

© 2022, First Edition
ISBN 978-0-9928751-8-3

Copyright © by the Construction History Society
All rights reserved. These proceedings may not be reproduced. In whole or in part, in any form without permission from the Construction History Society

Formatting and layout by Natcha Ruamsanitwong
First printed by Lulu print on demand for the Construction History Society

Proceedings of the Ninth Construction History Society Conference
edited by James W P Campbell, Nina Baker, Michael Driver,
Michael Heaton, Natcha Ruamsanitwong, Christine Wall, David Yeomans

THE SEVENTH ANNUAL CONSTRUCTION HISTORY SOCIETY CONFERENCE

Organised by:

The Construction History Society
in association with Queens' College, Cambridge

Held by:

Queens' College, University of Cambridge &
The Department of Architecture, University of Cambridge

Organising Committee

Chair: James W P Campbell
Secretary: Natcha Ruamsanitwong
Treasurer: Jonathan Lee

Scientific Committee

Chair: David Yeomans
Secretary: Natcha Ruamsanitwong
James Campbell
Nina Baker
Michael Driver
Mike Heaton
Christine Wall

Editorial Committee

Chair: James W P Campbell
Secretary: Natcha Ruamsanitwong
Nina Baker
Michael Driver
Michael Heaton
Christine Wall
David Yeomans

In memory of Thelma Seear

Acknowledgements

The preparation of any conference takes an enormous amount of time and effort on behalf of a large number of people. I am hugely grateful to all those who have assisted in the planning of this, Eighth Annual Construction History Society Conference in the second year of this global pandemic. In particular, I would like to thank Natcha Ramitsanitwong who gathered all the abstracts, sent them out for review and worked so hard to put these proceedings together, coordinating the formatting on her own. David Yeomans as chair of the Scientific Committee again took on the unenviable task again of managing the scientific committee. I am as always grateful for his sage advice and I would like to thank him and all the other members of that committee for their efforts in reviewing all these proposals. Once the papers were in the editorial committee took over and went painstakingly through every paper. Any errors remaining are my fault not theirs.

I would like to thank all those staff of the Architecture Department and Queens' College, in the University of Cambridge who agreed to host this conference, without whose aid none of this would be possible. I would like to thank all those members of the Committee of the Construction History Society who give their time so generously to the society without any form of remuneration. They are Michael Driver, Michael Heaton, Will Maclean, Nicholas von Behr, Michael Tutton, Nina Baker, Andrew Jackson, Jonathan Lee, and the journal editors Christine Wall, Hermann Schlimme, Inge Bertels and Will Mclean, ably assisted by Angharad Hart (Editorial Secretary) and Karey Draper (Book Reviews). Without their support the Society would not function.

This year, as last year, we have a session on water supply in memory of Thelma Seear. Thelma was founder of the Fountain Society and left a substantial legacy to Queens' for the study of Architecture and History of Art and for the promotion of the study of fountains. We are seeking to start that process by including various papers in this conference looking at the broader topic of water supply. The conference was entirely paid for by a generous donation from the Seear Fund. We hope Thelma would have approved. Most of all I would like to thank the contributors to this book without whose papers none of this would be possible.

James W P Campbell
2022

Contents

Preliminaries

Campbell, James WP. Introduction i

Keynote Lecture

Holzer, Stefan M. How to erect a large timber roof truss 3

Middle Ages

Lengenfeld, Jonas The complex masonry of the Schönburg Castle Keep chimney system (1201 CE) in the context of contemporary examples 23

Wendland, David & Gielen, Mark The Design and Construction of the Vaults in Notre-Dame in Paris and the Development of Medieval Vaulting and Stereotomy: Surveys, Analyses and Experiments 39

Maira-Vidal, Rocío English Master Builders in The Iberian Peninsula in The 13th Century: The Construction of The Sexpartite Vaults of Lincoln Cathedral and Their Influence on The Monastery of Las Huelgas Reales in Burgos 57

The Sixteenth Century

Nazari, Soheil & Mahmoudnejad, Amirhossein Documentation and Analysis of The Free-Handed Vaulting Technique at The Toor Caravanserai, Iran 75

Yeomans, David & Riall, Nicholas Tudor King Post Roofs 89

Contents

Song, Lei & Campbell, James WP.	The Depiction of Water Technology in Ramelli's Le Diverse et Artificose Machine and Its Influence on Engineering Treatises in China in the 17th Century	101

The Seventeenth and Eighteenth Centuries

Knobling, Clemens	From model to reality – a case study on the timber bridge of Baden (CH)	117
Gantner, Martin	Innovation and Tradition: 'Signature' roof constructions and master builder's networks in the late eighteenth and early nineteenth centuries in in the catholic regions of central, northern and eastern Switzerland	129
Schmitt, Rebecca Erika	Geometric design and construction of a Late Baroque brick vault: Kilian Ignaz Dientzenhofer's Benedictine Church of the Holy Cross and St. Hedwig at Legnickie Pole	143
Romano, Lia & Falcone, Marika	Wooden vaults in Naples between survey and construction knowledge: the case of the church of Santa Maria Egiziaca all'Olmo	157
Motta, Martina	The Wood Sector and the King's Works. A Different Perspective for the Study of 18th Century Royal Construction Sites in the Kingdom of Sardinia	171
Prosser, Lee	Some Experimental Trussed Floors at Kensington Palace, London	185
Vandenabeele, Louis	The Paduan ties of Poleni	197
Diaz, Martina & Vandenabeele, Louis	The eighteenth-century timber trade towards the Basilica of St Anthony in Padua through archives, shipping marks and dendrochronology	209
Mair, Raimund	The Renovation of the Waterworks at the Rotes Tor in Augsburg by the Well Master Caspar Walter	221

The Nineteenth Century

Prisco, Gian Marco	Iron bridges and the influence of international models in 19th century Spanish architecture	237
Bill, Nicholas A.	From Carpentry Manuals to Engineering Textbooks (1792 – 1870)	249
Chrimes, Mike	Thomas Telford and the construction of Canal Tunnels 1794-1830	261
Hays, Benjamin J.	Water for the University: An Early History of the University of Virginia's Water supply, 1817-1885	275
Franz, Hannah & Rinke, Mario & Lepretre, Emilie & Dieng, Lamine	The gap between theory, practice and regulations in design criteria for iron and steel structures in 19th century France: the example of train sheds	287
Russnaik, Kylie	Timber Roof Structures of 19th-century Casinos in Switzerland	301
Jacobs, Jamie	Pugin's role as Superintendent of Woodcarving	315
Maissen, Manuel	Early Iron Bridges in Switzerland 1850-1875: A Primer	329
Melsens, Sarah & Sahasrabudhe, Chetan	Technical Writings as Political: Building Manuals and Pattern Books From British India (1880-1947	343

Early Twentieth Century

Korensky, Vladimir	Early Reinforced Concrete Shells in Russia	361
von Behr, Nick	The patent war between François Hennebique and Armand Considère: competing reinforced concrete systems in 'fin de Belle Époque'	373

Contents

France

Reyniers, Lara & Van de Voorde, Stephanie & Wouters, Ine	Capturing the Practice of Deconstruction in Brussels (1903 – 1939): Photographic Heritage Collections as A Starting Point for Construction History	387
Haddadi, Roshanak & Rinke, Mario	National, traditional, scientific – the formation of a multifaceted early glulam identity	397
Ladinski, Vladimir B.	Contribution of Early Women Architects in North Macedonia	411
Angillis, Jelle & Bertels, Inge	Voices from the Post-War Belgian Building Industry: A Study of a General Contractor and its Involvement in Building Practices via Oral History	427
Kuban, Sabine	The Livestock Auction Hall in Riedlingen – Regional Timber Construction in the 1930s in the South-West of Germany	439
Lucente, Roberta & Canestrino, Giuseppe	Technical manuals in the years of Reconstruction after World War II in Italy: Mario Ridolfi and the "Manuale dell'Architetto".	453

Late Twentieth Century

Marfella, Giorgio	Alfred Picardi and the Tubular Structure of Chicago's Standard Oil Building: Engineering for Holistic Efficiency	469
Schmid, Benjamin & Weber, Christiane	From physical to digital – the form-finding and measuring models of the Mannheim Multihalle	485
Burchardt, Jørgen	Systems for Standardised Precast Concrete Elements: The Case of the Larsen & Nielsen System	497
Frommelt, Konrad M.	Algorithm or experience – The search for objective design methods for serial structures in the GDR	515

Greco, Laura & Spada, Francesco	The Palazzo Galbani by Eugenio and Ermenegildo Soncini and Pier Luigi Nervi (1956-59). A case of building prefabrication in Milan	529
Parein, Marylise & Wouters, Ine & Van de Voorde, Stephanie	Fibre Cement Slates: An Industry Reinventing Itself (1970-2000)	541
Ferreira Crevels, Eric	A Joint of Many Worlds: Entangled Stories in Battaile en Ibens's 78+ Construction System in Timber	551

James W.P. Campbell

Introduction

This is a ninth volume in the series of books published by the Construction History Society containing the proceedings of the international conferences held at Queens' College, Cambridge in April each year. This year, 2022, is the third year that has been disrupted by the global pandemic (called at the time COVID-19). Learning from last year's conference this conference was again being held in hybrid format, with a live audience in Queens' and a small number presenting online. The last volume contained a series of chapters on the Trades and Professionalism in Construction History. This conference carried the theme of timber in building construction, although this was loosely interpreted and the papers cover a wide range of topics in Construction History. One session was also devoted to water supply in memory of Thelma Seear (see acknowledgments above). The papers have been arranged chronologically as far as possible, although obviously many papers span ranges of dates and longer periods. In total there are 40 papers including the two keynotes all of which are printed here.

Keynote Lectures

This year's theme was timber in building construction, with two keynote lectures. The first delivered by David Yeomans on King Post Roofs in England can be found in the appropriate chronological section. The second, by Stefan Holzer, cover the general problem of erection of roofs, looking at the general issues involved in lifting large trusses into position and propping them in place temporarily until they could be permanently fixed. It is common today to hear about the importance of off-site prefabrication as a modern building technique, but as this paper reminds us, off-site production is as old as building itself and creates as many problems as it solves.

Conference Papers

Each year I comment on how the papers in these volumes cover a very board range of subjects ranged under the umbrella term of "Construction History". In choosing timber as subject I had expected a broad spread of papers across different time periods but actually the papers were tightly bunched in later period with a strong European bias. The overall distribution is roughly as follows:

Time Period	Papers Covering this Period	
	Number	Percentage
Medieval World	3 papers	(8%)
15-16th century	3 papers	(8%)
17th Century	2 papers	(5%)
18th Century	7 papers	(18%)
Nineteenth Century	9 Papers	(23%)
Twentieth century	15 papers	(38%)
Number of Papers in Volume = 40		

Table. 1 Table showing distribution of papers in this volume by period

This was far from a normal year and travelling is still highly curtailed and this is perhaps reflected in the numbers.

Introduction

The COVID virus is still widespread although vaccination and changes in the virus itself have meant that restrictions on travel are very gradually being lifted. However several years of restrictions have meant that researchers have been restricted in access to sites and travel and also to archives and libraries that are still only just beginning to open up and subject to delays and limits on numbers. All of this has placed huge restrictions on what people have been able to do and meant that researchers have inevitably had to stick to subjects close to home or that could be done resources available. There is a glimmer on the horizon in terms of travel opening up and restrictions beginning to be lifted but there is still a long way to go. One encouraging move has been the foundation of Asian Construction History Network which seeks to bring together colleagues from Turkey to Japan, looking at the rich international connections that were forged along the "Silk Road" routes that flourished across the centuries but are often overlooked, and the more recent extraordinary developments in building construction. We hope this network will start sending many more papers from parts of the globe currently sadly under-represented.

Middle Ages

In previous years I have used the title Medieval World for this section, signalling that the very notion of Middle Ages is really only a Western European phenomenon. However the three papers form this period are distinctly European and all look at the peculiar problems of Gothic Vaulting. Jonas Lengenfeld has used modern computer surveying to provide us with an inside view of the chimneys of Schönburg Castle, while David Wendland, Mark Gielen and Rocio Maira-Vidal look at the problems of stereotomy inherent in Notre Dame, and Lincoln and its connection to a monastery in Burgos.

Sixteenth Century

The first paper in this section continues the study of vaulting, looking at Caravanserai in Iran. The two other papers look at problems of transference. The 1500s were a period of marked change brought on by technical innovation and its transference through the new mode of moveable-type printing in Europe that created by the 1500s a publishing boom. Technical books began to appear and ideas that had previously been restricted to particular geographical regions could be spread across the globe. Roof structures began to be drawn and copied across countries. David Yeomans has shown in his books how Inigo Jones took Italian roofing ideas and brought them to England and how texts played a crucial role in this process but certainly details of the trusses that resulted were peculiarly English. In his keynote lecture David shows how he and Nicholas Riall have managed to trace these details back to earlier Tudor roofs, proving that these were pre-existing forms used in native design which were adopted into later roofs based on the Italian designs to produce a peculiarly English hybrid. My own paper with Lei Song looks again at the surprising story of how Ramelli's intriguing textbooks informed Chinese manuals of the time on water supply.

The Seventeenth and Eighteenth Centuries (1600-1800)

The theme of timber in architecture comes out perhaps most strongly in the section on the seventeenth century and eighteenth century. This section also shows the range of interests in Construction History: Clements Knobling shows use the timber bridge in Baden and the wonderful models that survive. Lee Prosser looks at wooden floors while Martiona Diaz and Louis Vandenebeele look at timber supply and timber marks.

The Nineteenth Century (1800-1900)

The nineteenth century is always a popular period. As Nicholas Bill in his paper on Carpentry Manuals shows, it is the period when structural calculations are introduced and the full potential of iron realised. Steel and concrete first appear in this period. There are two papers on iron bridges in this year's conference and one on iron in railway sheds.

Early Twentieth Century 1900-1950

As usual the twentieth century attracted more papers than any other justifying splitting it in two this year. The first half century encompasses the emergence of concrete and steel as dominating materials in large scale structures and this is reflected in the papers. We have two papers in this section looking at the rival concrete systems, as well as papers on women in architecture, photography, glulam structures and technical manuals.

Late Twentieth Century 1900-2000

The last section brings us almost up to date. Again the materials in the buildings studied in these papers varied and included fibre cement slates, tubular steel, precast concrete and timber. It is particularly interesting to see two papers this year tackling the use of models, both mathematical and physical, for testing out ideas. In general we do not encourage papers from later than 2000 because it is difficult to get historical distance but as we slide towards 2030 this will inevitably change.

Concluding Remarks

Planning a conference this year has been more challenging than previously. While the initial problems of COVID over the last few years have involved lockdowns, the last 6 months emerging from lockdowns and dealing with waves of rising infection rates and closures and ever-changing rules and regulations has still been extremely difficult to navigate and brought a level of uncertainty and difficulty to anything involving forward planning. It is also only six months since the last conference. As we look forward to the holding the tenth conference next year, I remain hugely grateful to all those who helped me prepare for this year's conference without whose help none of this would be possible.

James W.P. Campbell
Conference Chairman
Construction History Society
April 2022

Keynote Lecture

How to erect a large timber roof truss

Stefan M. Holzer
Professor, Chair of Construction History and Building Archeology, Eidgenössische Technische Hochschule Zürich

Abstract

For centuries, roof trusses were assembled from individual timber members prepared on the ground and subsequently lifted into place and joined together one by one. However, the development of wide-span roofs sometimes prohibited this member-by-member erection strategy. Large roof trusses, which came increasingly into use during the 18th century, either required a supporting structure for erection, or lifting of larger pre-assembled parts of the final truss. Naturally, hoisting and assembly devices have rarely left a trace. Moreover, iconographic and written sources also provide only scant evidence on the erection procedures. The present paper collects what can be drawn from the scattered evidence and shows that erection procedures and devices applied to assemble metal roof trusses during the 19th century were probably deeply rooted in carpentry tradition, and that some roofing systems required quite considerable temporary structures.

Introduction

During the last few decades, the historic evolution of timber trusses in general and roofs in particular has been investigated in detail. It is now commonly acknowledged that considerations referring to erection procedures were an important driving force behind the development of roof trussing systems. Many roof trusses were conceived in such a way as to permit incremental assembly: all the members were prepared on the ground beforehand, including fine-tuning of the joint geometries and checks for perfect fit. Once all the members of the truss were ready, they were numbered with carpenter's marks and stowed on the worksite until they would be raised. Carpenter's marks permitted easy identification of each and every member and thus enabled quick assembly on site. Short assembly times were a key consideration: an incompletely assembled truss was liable to get overturned by the wind, putting the entire undertaking at stake. Therefore, carpenters strove to decompose the roof truss into individual subsystems that were stable in themselves due to windbracing and soulaces. For example, the Central European medieval roof truss system of the «*stehender Stuhl*» essentially relied on piling up various storeys of table-like trestles. Once stabilized, these trestles could serve to support adequate temporary working platforms, enabling the lifting of the remaining members such as rafters and collar beams. At the end of the assembly process, the «*stehender Stuhl*» structure remained in the roof truss and became an integral part of it, also providing additional bracing to the finished structure. Figure 1 demonstrates the usefulness of the «*stehender Stuhl*» as a possible working platform in a photograph from a recent restoration site in Munich.

Incremental assembly helped to obviate both the need of heavy lifting devices and the need of costly scaffolding. However, during the early modern era, free spans of roof trusses approached and sometimes even exceeded the 20 metre limit. Such spans required roof truss types which were not only adapted to easy assembly, but which also met increased structural requirements. In most of the cases, carpenters resorted to built-up or «reinforced» beams and/or complex king and queen post truss designs. Roof trusses employing built-up tie-beams assembled from several parts spread over Europe from the 16th century onwards. Such trusses no longer permitted member-by-member assembly, but required some temporary support or lifting of larger units. Unfortunately, the literature of the time typically provides neither textual nor pictorial information on the actual raising procedures used with these long-span roofs.

Figure 1: Traditional roof truss with „stehender Stuhl", serving as a scaffolding for erection or dismantling, as well as permanent bracing of the roof structure (Munich, recent worksite; author)

At the same time, innovative roof truss systems were invented. It suffices to cite the Delorme system, employing arched trusses made up from a large number of short boards. These systems were promoted as particularly economic solutions since they obviated the requirement to provide large timber scantlings and particularly long tree trunks while still enabling large unsupported spans owing to the arch principle. The perceived economy of Delorme roof trusses and other arched truss systems made these innovative structures seemingly attractive to 18th century architects and engineers, and the Delorme system experienced a real «boom» around the turn from the 18th to the 19th century in France. In Germany, David Gilly and others advocated the related «curved board» system (*Bohlendach*) which had probably originated from a transfer of stone arch centring or false vault construction, to roofing. Both the Delorme system and Gilly's system were not suitable for incremental assembly on site, but rather required the pre-assembly of large parts at least of the principal trusses, on the ground. The same holds for the laminated arches which came up slightly later, in the early years of the 19th century, first in bridge building (Wiebeking and others), then also in roofing. Notably, the system invented by the French officer Amand-Rose Émy reached considerable popularity in 19th century textbooks, if restricted diffusion in actual building practice. All the laminated timber arch systems required pre-assembly on the ground, or on-site bending of the lamellas, on sturdy trestles. While the latter method was indeed applied in the construction of bridges and bridge centres, pre-assembly was evidently a way to go with roof trusses, although it required strong lifting gear or a worksite very close to the final position of the trusses.

Surprisingly, the contemporary literature on the innovative roofing systems provides almost no clue on how to address the lifting and assembly problems entailed by the sophisticated trusses. In the remainder of the paper, we will collect the scattered evidence that may be gathered from printed and archival sources.

Hoisting devices

A single softwood baulk with a typical length of 15 m and 20/30 cm scantling weighs around 500 kg. In order to lift such a load, it suffices to have a simple cranked winch providing a gear transmission ratio of around 10:1, and perhaps two operators. The winch may either be installed on top of the building to be roofed, or on the ground. At any rate, a single pulley firmly attached to a point high enough above the gutters is required and sufficient for lifting the members. Once up at the roof level, our baulk can be handled, carried around and positioned by several men without any serious issues. Lifting gets even easier when a block and tackle system is applied. While this solution requires ropes of considerable length, our baulk may even be lifted by a single operator without a windlass.

Once the tie-beams of a roof truss are in place, and temporarily covered with some boards, they provide a convenient platform for the remaining raising operations. Even the lifting gear can then be established on that platform. One of the first and very rare depictions of a building during roof erection is due to Étienne Martellange. This Jesuit priest and architect surveyed several building sites of Jesuit monasteries and churches in western and central France during the first half of the seventeenth century. When he visited the Jesuit establishment in La Flèche in 1612, one aisle of the convent was just about to be roofed (Fig. 2). The medium-sized roof truss is based on a series of trapezoidal frames. Martellange's drawing shows that the trapezoidal frames were pre-assembled on top of the building, in a horizontal position, and then lifted to the vertical by a simple crane. This crane could be described as a braced derrick without a boom. It is called an *engin* in the contemporary French literature. It is shown, e.g., in André Félibien's *Principes de l'Architecture* (first edition 1676)[1]. The machine (Fig. 3) consists of a vertical, fixed A-frame, stabilized by a backward brace. The whole structure sits on top of sleepers arranged in the shape of a «T». On top of the vertical mast in the centre of the A-frame, a small jib called *fauconneau* is pivoting on a tenon. This miniature jib allows a certain rotation and lateral displacement of the load. A similar miniature jib is already depicted on the famous *predella* by Piero di Cosimo (around 1500) now in the Ringling Art Museum (Sarasota, Florida), however, in that case on top of a gin pole. In Félibien's illustration, the load is lifted without any block-and-tackle, solely with the winch attached to the backward leg.

Figure 2: Erection of trapezoidal roof frames by means of an «engin» (Étienne Martellange, 1612)

How to erect a large timber roof truss

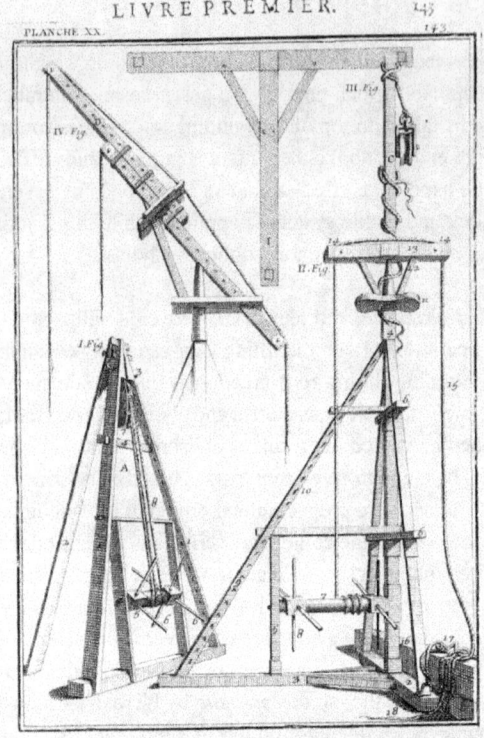

Figure 3: Lifting devices employed in France, 17th to 19th centuries (André Félibien, 1676)

The «engin» reappears in several French late 17th century construction site representations. For example, it is employed for unloading building material from ships in Lievin Cruyl's drawings (1687) of the construction site of the Pont Royal, Paris [2], and it can also be discerned on Sébastien le Clerc's famous engraving of the construction site of the Louvre colonnade (1677)[3]. The machine also shows up in the *Encyclopédie*, in the plate dedicated to hoisting devices. It is evident that the *engin* was fairly light and therefore easy to move, so that it met carpenters' needs very well. There existed also a variant with a fixed rather than turning jib [4].

However, in the long run, the *engin* was obviously replaced by a still simpler and lighter machine, the shear legs (Fig. 4). This crane type consists of an A-shaped trestle made up of two poles, which are joined at the top and spread at the bottom. The whole is held in an inclined position by means of stay ropes. Adjusting the stays allows a change of inclination and thus a limited amount of horizontal movement of the load. It is not clear how this machine entered the early modern construction site. For sure, the shearleg derrick had already been described in the ancient literature, including Vitruvius. However, the early modern translators and illustrators of Vitruvius unanimously transformed the two-legged derrick into a simple tripod, changing Vitruvius' original wording of «tigna duo» arbitrarily and misleadingly into «tigna tria». This error – which was only corrected in the late 19th century by Valentin Rose in his second edition of Vitruvius – can be traced back to the most influential early modern edition, namely, Fra Giocondo's illustrated version of 1511. Giocondo's spurious conjecture was copied by virtually all subsequent editions, and, as a consequence, all these editions also depicted a tripod (not very useful for most construction purposes) rather than a shearleg derrick. However, an isolated early proof for the use of the shearleg derrick can be found in Scamozzi. He described (1615) its use for erecting the flag masts in front of St. Mark's basilica, Venice, and he also noted its limited capability of horizontal transport [5]. Scamozzi called the machine *capra ritta*. Perhaps it is no coincidence that we find this machine in the famous merchants' and seafarers' city: The shearleg derrick seems to have survived primarily in the nautical domain, whence it may have been imported into construction during the 18th century. Anyhow it is described and depicted as a shipboard loading and unloading device in Nicolas Aubin's nautical dictionary of 1702, then called *cabre*. Later, shear legs were employed in gigantic scale in France for masting ships. In the dockyards, they were know as *bigue*. In this naval application, they were employed to lift loads as heavy as 25 tons [6]. Shearlegs got popular in bridge building in France in the 18th century, when they were employed to keep the individual members of timber centres in place during assembly. They appear alongside with *engins* and gin poles (called *écoperches*[7] in France) in the well-known bridge construction books of Régemortes (1771) and Perronet (1783/1788).

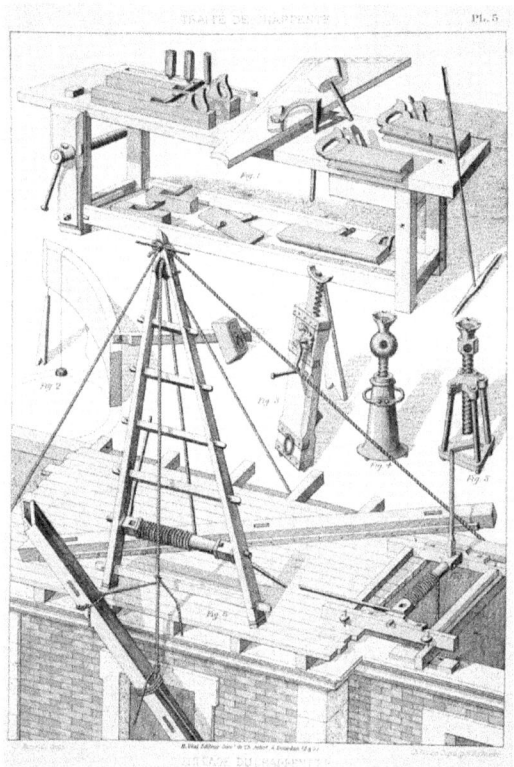

Figure 4: Shear legs employed as standard lifting device by 19th century carpenters (Louis Mazerolle, around 1900)

Erecting a bridge centre is a task similar to raising a roof truss – particularly an arched roof truss –, and the shear legs found a lot of application in roof truss erection in the 19th century, as we will see presently. Shearlegs at a smaller scale – then called *chèvre* in France – were widespread in carpentry around 1800 [8]. Joseph-Antoine Borgnis, author of a comprehensive *Traité complet de mécanique* in ten volumes, including one on *Mouvemens des fardeaux* (1818), wrote: «One set of shearlegs, or one cable-stayed mast, which is transported from one location to the next, is sufficient for erecting all vertical timber elements»[9]. By the middle of the 19th century, shearlegs had largely replaced the *engin* on construction sites, and they were depicted as standard carpenters' devices [10]. A late example is found in Mazerolle's carpentry treatise (fig. 4).[11] In Mazerolle's illustration, the shearlegs are positioned at the edge of the building to be roofed, in order to lift material from the ground. However, it seems that this was not the principal domain of the shearlegs. Rather, a very simple device was employed. It is described and depicted in Johann Andreas Romberg's carpentry treatise of 1847 (fig. 5) [12]. A long pole is fixed in a vertical position, directly in front of the building to be roofed. The pole is clamped into the ground for the lower 3 to 4 feet. The pole is not stayed by ropes, but attached to the façade by means of wooden braces. At the top end of the mast, a short jib supported by a soulace is pivoting on a tenon. This permits limited rotation of the jib. Romberg recommends this device for the hoisting of truss elements for a roof «in case it is too high above ground». Romberg's figure shows not only the mast, but also the block-and-tackle, as well as the attached load which is guided by two additional ropes attached to its ends. A very similar wall-mounted mast hoist is also depicted in Borgnis' *Traité complet de mécanique* of 1818 [13].

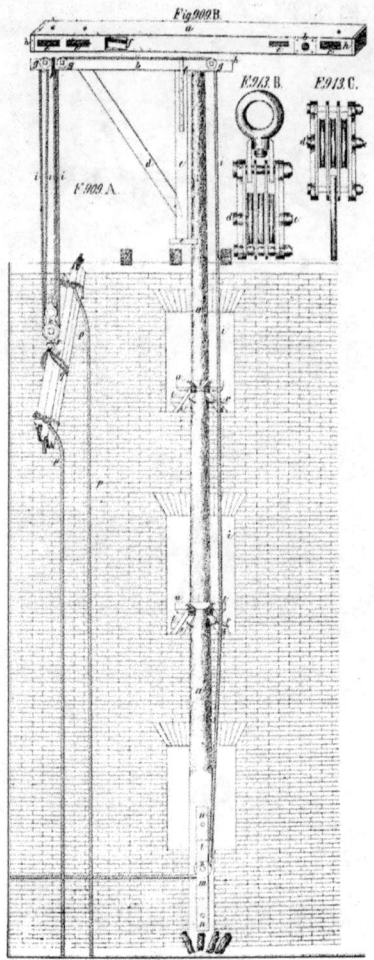

Figure 5: Simple lifting device used by carpenters (Johann Andreas Romberg, 1847)

It is obvious that the mast attached to the perimetral walls of a building and embedded in the earth was a stationary hoist. A somewhat more mobile tower is presented in the offical Prussian carpentry manual, *Vorlegeblätter für Zimmerleute*, published in the late 1820s for the internal use of the Prussian administration and then in the 1830s for the general public [14]. The lifting tower (fig. 6) is essentially the same as Romberg's lifting device, but embedded in a free-standing timber frame. The tower rests on a set of sleepers, so that the mast does not need to be imbedded into the ground. The authors of the manual claim to have used the lifting tower «on several occasions».

Stefan M. Holzer

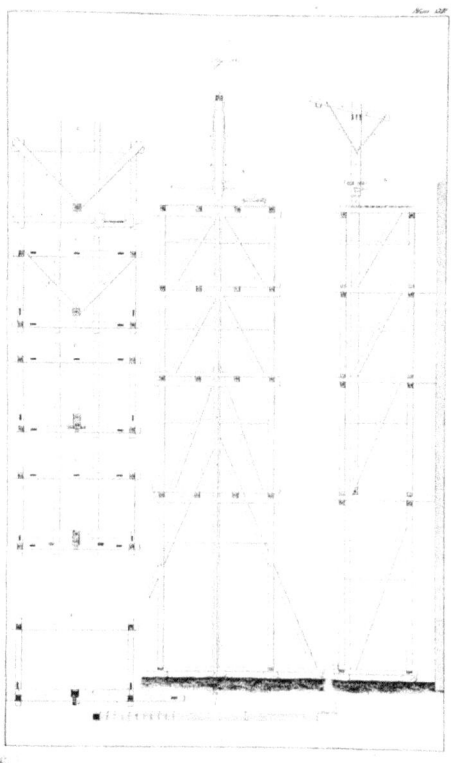

Figure 6: Carpenter's crane (Vorlegeblätter für Zimmerleute, 1835)

Lifting entire trusses or assembly on elevated platforms

Once arrived at the top of the building, the beams for the roof trusses still required considerable moving, handling and positioning. We have seen that even in Étienne Martellange's time, roof frames were partially pre-assembled in the horizontal plane and then erected. This procedure required a working platform at eaves level. In the case of the classical roof trusses with a continuous layer of tie-beams, the tie-beams provided a suitable support for such a platform, which could be created ad hoc by some boarding. However, whenever there was no continuous layer of tie-beams, a separate platform was required. A classic case for timber roof structures which called for erection with a scaffold were domes: The interior of a dome being void, there was no possibility of continuous tie-beams, and therefore, a scaffold had to be built up from the ground. This case was already mentioned by Caspar Walter in his 1769 special treatise on timber spires and domes [15]. In Paris, the erection of the timber dome of the Halle au Blé, designed by Molinos and Pronnier in a revival of Delorme's method and erected in 1784, was one of the most significant examples. The scaffolding was depicted by Krafft in his posthumous Traité des échafaudages (1856), alongside with the one for the subsequent erection of the replacement cast iron dome (after the timber one had burnt down) designed by Bélanger and erected in 1811 [16]. The latter one was also included in the lithographed plans of the École des Ponts et Chaussées (1821)[17]. The individual parts of both constructions being relatively small and light, no complicated hoisting gear was required, but the working platforms themselves probably consumed more building material than the final structure.

The domes might appear as an exceptional case. It is perhaps less evident that simple ridge roofs of considerable span required similar complex scaffolding as well. Examples are the Italian roof trusses of queen or king post types, when carried to veritably large spans. Those roofs with a large span were usually equipped with multi-part tie-beams. Typically, their tie-beams were composed of three or five parts, with a particular butt or lap joint in the centre. It is difficult to imagine that such a huge and heavy tie-beam (reaching 24.4 m in the Sala dei Cinquecento in Palazzo Vecchio, Florence, already in the middle of the 16th century) was assembled on the ground and then lifted as a whole. Likely, the assembly of the parts was achieved on scaffolding which provided at least a temporary support in the centre of the space. Unfortunately, the Italian literature of the 16-18th centuries does not provide a single hint on the erection procedures employed for these large-span trusses.

However, this lacuna is somewhat complemented by an interesting French source. During the 18th century, the Italian type of roof truss found increasing application in France. One of its most important domains in France was theatre construction. Both the auditorium and the scene of a large theatre typically required free spans approaching or transcending 20 m. An important Italian precedent – the roof of the *Teatro Argentina* in Rome, erected in 1731, purportedly by the famous Vatican master Nicola Zabaglia –, had been surveyed by the French architect Gabriel-Martin Dumont, and published in engravings in the early 1760s. This roof served as an example for many wooden theatre roofs built in Paris in the early 19th century, as may be observed by reviewing the plans in the two carpentry treatises of Jean-Charles Krafft (1805 and 1822). One of them was the *Théâtre de l'Académie Royale de Musique*, better known by its popular designation, *Opéra Le Pelletier* (the building was located in Rue Pelletier). This theatre was erected in a hurry when the former *Opéra* of Paris, the so-called *Théâtre des Arts* in Rue Richelieu, had been unexpectedly closed down after the assassination of the Duc de Berry in front of it. The new opera house was designed by François Debret (1777–1850) and opened in 1821. Original plans for the structure have been conserved in a folder created by Charles Rohault de Fleury (1801–75), who was one of the later (1846–61) architects-in-chief of the *Académie Royale de Musique*. This folder is now in the Musée Carnavalet, Paris. One of the drawings [18] carries an approval signature by Debret, proving that the plan is the original design plan; the other drawings are identical in size and format and can therefore be attributed to the same hand. Two of the plans show the transverse and longitudinal sections of the theatre, including the scaffolding (Figs. 7 and 8)[19]. The roof was essentially a king-and-queen post truss, very similar to the roof of the *Teatro Argentina*, the timber posts being replaced by iron stirrups in their lower parts. The tie-beam consisted of three parts of comparable length, joined by vertically arranged lap joints of the zigzag „Jupiter joint" type. These joints were secured by iron straps and wooden lugs.

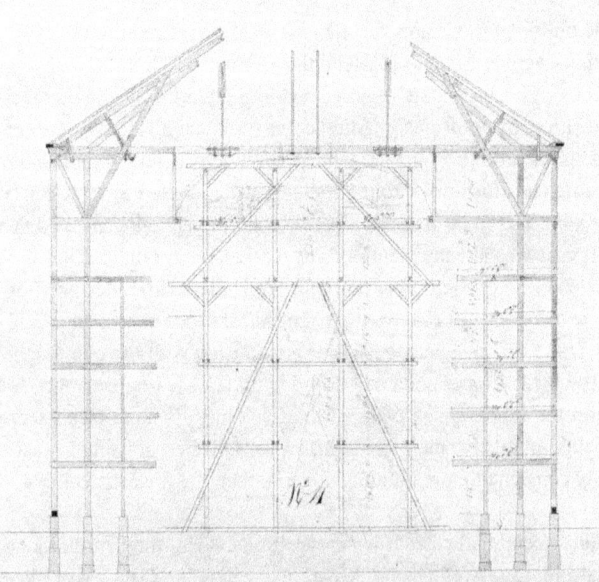

Figure 7: Transversal section of the scaffolding used to erect the roof of the Opéra Le Pelletier, Paris, in 1821 (Musée Carnavalet, Paris, D.13865-29)

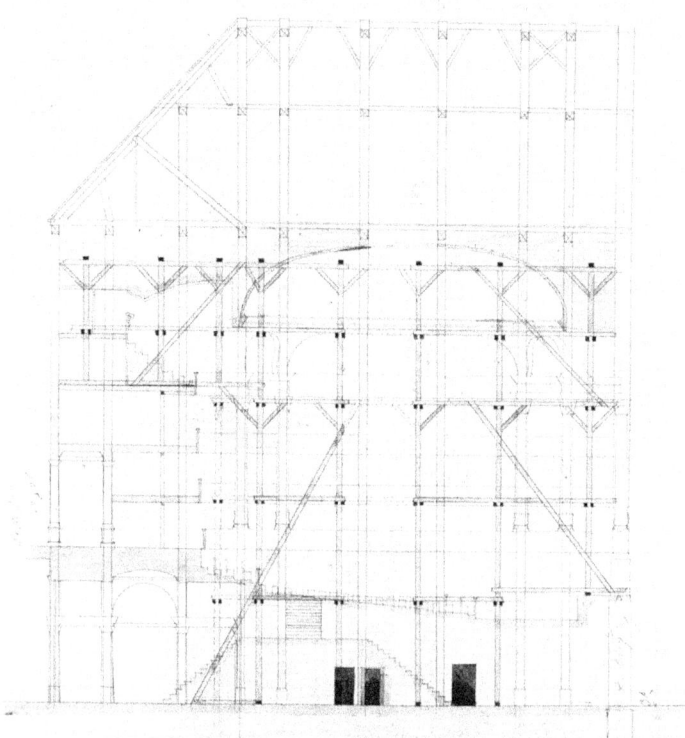

Figure 8: Longitudinal section of the scaffolding used to erect the roof of the Opéra Le Pelletier, Paris, in 1821 (Musée Carnavalet, D.13865-30)

The section drawings show the whole interior of the auditorium filled with a huge scaffold with five platform levels. Structurally, the scaffold comprises two storeys, a high lower one and a low top one. The scaffold is made from squared timber and held together by twin braces, which are presumably attached to the posts by iron bolts. This was the standard form of the scaffold in Paris at the time [20]. The plans do not include joint details, but it can be assumed that the soulaces which provided wind-bracing to the structure were probably attached to the posts by mortice-and-tenon joints. The scaffolding was not restricted to a single bay or a few bays of the theatre roof, but filled the entire building, as is evident from the longitudinal section. To a modern viewer, it may seem strange that the amount of timber consumed by the scaffolding is probably at least as great as that employed in the roof. However, it needs to be remembered that such sturdy scaffolding could later also be employed to apply the decoration to the interior of the theatre, and that the squared timber – unscathed but for the mortices – could easily be re-employed for subsequent use. Some years later, the resulting economical advantage of scaffolding made with reusable squared timber over simple rope-bound pole scaffoldings was also acknowledged in England [21].

In the first half of the 19th century, many innovative roof truss types came up which dispensed with the tie-beam: roofs of the revived Delorme type, David Gilly's roofs, Emy's laminated arches and Ardant's polygonal arches. Unless the respective buildings were essentially «roof only» structures, these new truss types also called for extensive scaffolding. Fortunately, the erection procedures for some of these roofs have been described in the literature of the time.

The Gilly roofs employed a similar structure as the Delorme structures. They were made up of several layers of short boards cut to a circular shape, arranged on edge to form the arch, and nailed together. Typically, the Gilly arches were erected as a whole or in two halves, as can be observed in situ in preserved roofs. Erection of a half or complete arch plus some bracing was no easy task, although Gilly himself of course tried to downplay the effort required [22]. August Ferdinand Triest's (1768–1831), a pupil of David Gilly and editor of the last two volumes of Gilly's famous 4-volume *Land-Bau-Kunst*, published a tripartite monograph on cost estimates which includes details on the erection procedures required for the Gilly roofs. Triest reports that the roof-only riding hall in Berlin-Charlottenburg was completely assembled on the ground, and then lifted to the vertical by carpenters standing on a multi-storey trestle scaffolding [23]. His description was also accompanied by an illustration (Fig. 9). Triest stressed that the simple trestle scaffolding saved the effort of constructing a full-fledged scaffold in squared timber with carpentry joints, and that the *ad hoc* scaffold was easy to move. To the modern viewer, the stacked trestles may appear rather unsafe, but stacked trestle scaffolding was not uncommon in the 18th and 19th centuries. Triest's illustration was even copied almost unchanged to the official *Vorlegeblätter für Zimmerleute* edited by the Prussian administration of public works [24].

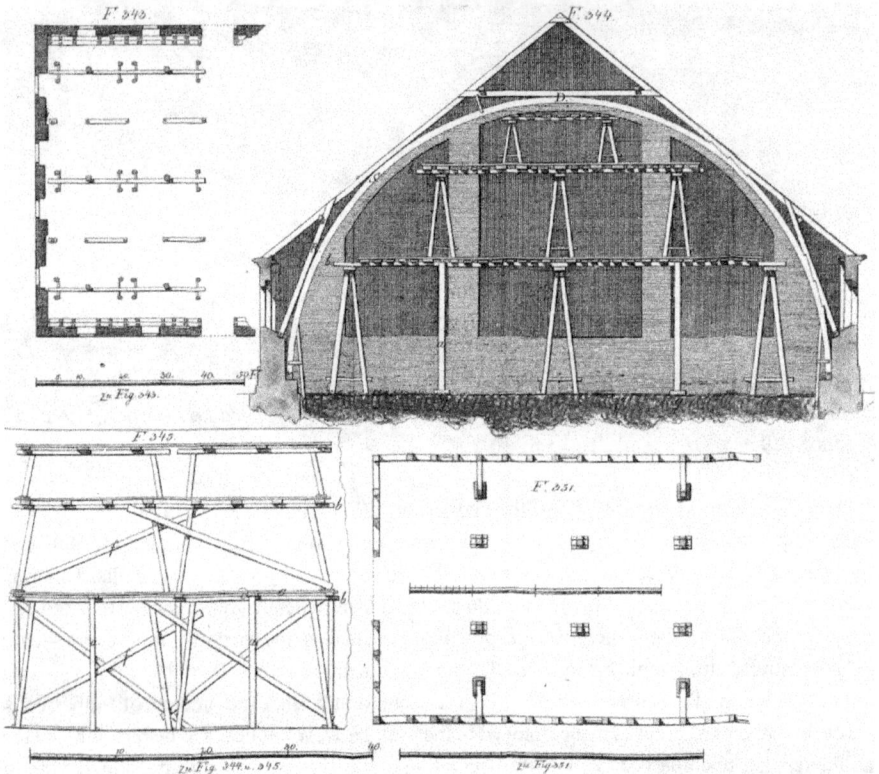

Figure 9: Erection of a roof truss for a riding hall in Berlin-Charlottenburg, employing trestle scaffolding (August Ferdinand Triest, 1809)

An interesting picture showing the lifting of large pre-assembled parts of an arched roof structure is contained in the *Nouvelle Collection de 530 dessins*, lithographed at the *École des Ponts et Chaussées* in Paris, for the use of its students, in 1825 (Fig. 10) [25]. It shows the erection of the arched trusses of a covered dock at Rochefort, in 1821. Close inspection of the drawing reveals that the timber arch supporting the roof is made up of short curved pieces that are connected by mortice-and-tenon joints (not an Émy arch). Although the author of the drawing, the *ingénieur attaché aux travaux maritimes* Louis Marie Jacques Duhamel (1773–1849), calls the lifting machines *cabre* (shearlegs), they are clearly of the *engin* type. Two of them are employed to fix the uprights of the frame, while the central one serves to lift the entire pre-assembled roof structure, complete with its arch, rafters, and radial braces.

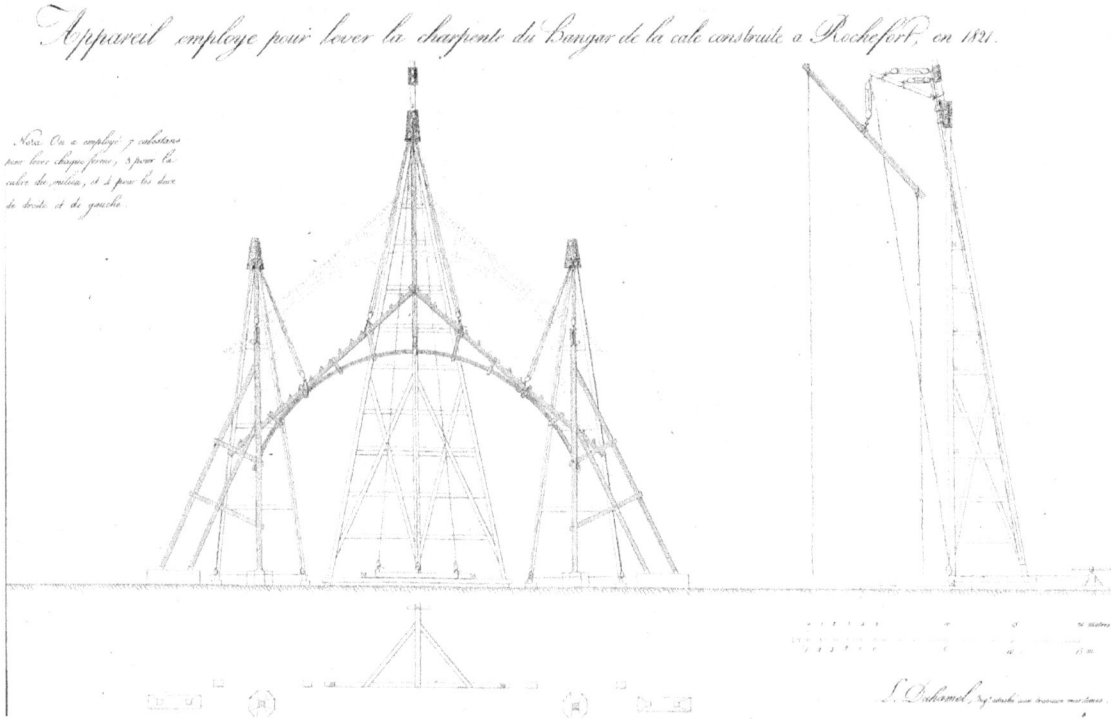

Figure 10: Erection of the timber trusses of a covered dock in Rochefort in 1821 (Nouvelle Collection de dessins relatifs à l'art de l'ingénieur, 1825)

A moving roller-mounted platform for the assembly of a similar arched roof truss over a riding hall in Saint-Germain was depicted in Jean Charles Krafft's Traité des échafaudages (Fig. 11).[26] Although this monograph on scaffolding and temporary works appeared only posthumously in 1856, the roof truss dates probably to the same period as the aforementioned dock shed at Rochefort, like most of Krafft's other examples. The assembly of a roof truss on high masonry walls added some further complication to the erection process. Either, there had to be a working platform at eaves level where the roof trusses could be assembled and then finally erected, or the entire truss had to be lifted into place in a single action from the ground (implying the use of heavy lifting gear), or, finally, a more traditional member-by-member assembly had to be chosen. Obviously, the carpenters opted for the third choice in Krafft's example, as can be guessed from the absence of a lifting device on Krafft's drawing. This method was applicable only if the roof truss consisted of a limited number of medium-size elements that could be joined in situ with relative ease. Unfortunately, Krafft's text does not provide any details on the process. Nevertheless, the moving assembly platform clearly foreshadows the auxiliary structures employed later in the 19th century for erecting large iron trusses.

How to erect a large timber roof truss

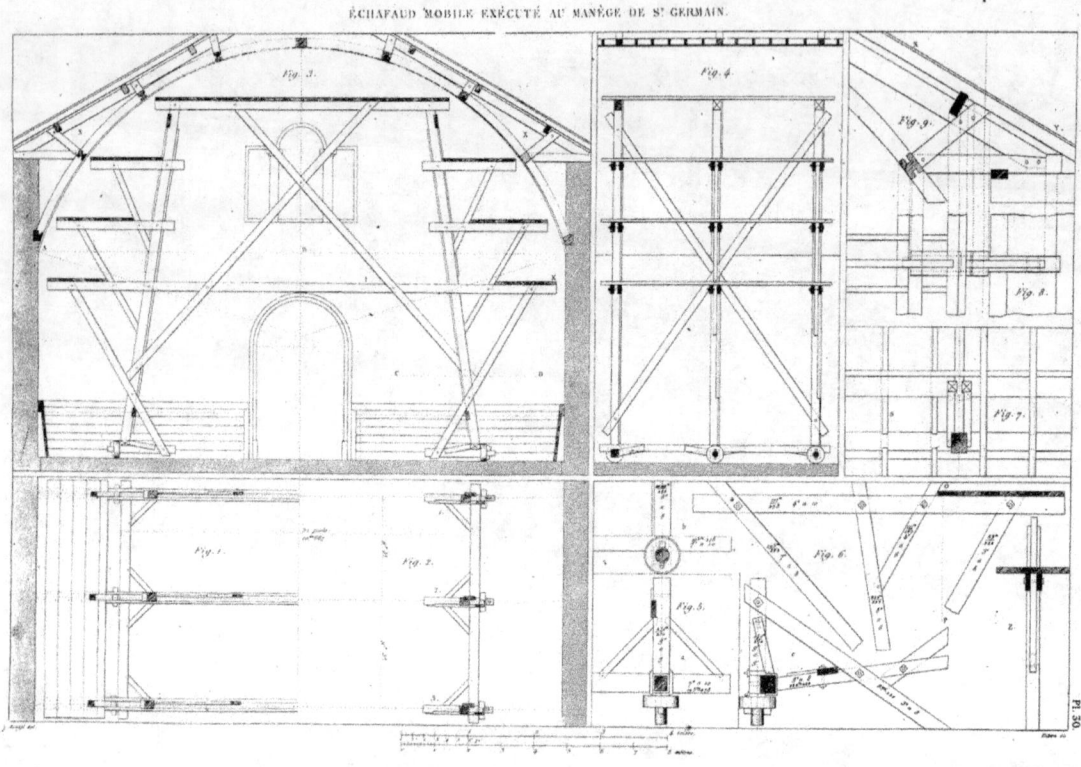

Figure 11: Erection of the timber trusses of a riding hall in Saint-Germain-en-Laye near Paris (Jean-Charles Krafft 1822)

When colonel Amand-Rose Émy invented his system of laminated arches made from horizontally stacked boards, bent to arch form, in 1819, realized for the first time in the riding hall of the barracks in Marac near Bayonne (1825), with a span of 21 metres, he faced the same problems as the builders of the other arched trusses: «Being unable to lift the entire trusses, I had prepared a movable scaffolding which was easy to assemble and disassemble, which carried a vertical centring, exactly identical to the one which was used to compose the trusses on the horizontal assembly floor. This scaffolding [...] consisted of two parallel trusses made from pine boards, distant from each other 2 metres, which had six levels of tie-beams carrying working platforms, so that all levels of the roof truss could be reached easily»[27]. This scaffolding was set up on four trestles and stabilized in its upright position by stay cables and struts. The laminated arches which had been assembled on the horizontal floor were then taken apart again, each piece individually mounted to the centring-scaffolding, and reassembled there. It is clear that this labour-intensive process led to a very protracted erection and could not be the last word if the system was to be a success. In the second riding hall of the Émy system, built in 1826 in Libourne (Gironde), Émy left it to his attendant, Jean-Joseph Chayrou, to find a more efficient erection method: «Our worksite was established on a temporary platform at the level of the eaves of the roof to be built. The platform extended over the whole width of the riding hall, and half of its length, i.e. it measured 22 metres by 24 metres. On that platform, 24 feet above the ground, the arched trusses were drawn and assembled»[28]. The trusses had to be rotated by 90 degrees before erection since they had to be laid out lengthwise on the assembly platform. For erecting the roof trusses, three shearlegs were established atop the assembly high platform [29]. Furthermore, since that platform extended only along half the length of the hall, the upright trusses were then stored at one end of the hall, only to be shifted to their final location in the end of the assembly process. In this step, they were kept in the vertical plane by stay ropes, and moved horizontally on small roller cars. Even with this improved procedure, the assembly of the 14 trusses took 72 days with a workforce of 15, much longer than the erection of any traditional truss. Naturally, Émy himself tended to downplay the problems in his 1828 monograph on the new system, and even Chayrou did not insist on the inherent difficulties in the erection, but the editor of the military journal which had published Chayrou's report added a note: «Even this new procedure does not appear very advantageous to us, since it costs a lot to build the assembly floor at 8 m above the ground. Furthermore, it requires the moving of materials, which should be avoided, and it proved to be difficult to assemble the last trusses. We believe that the assembly should have taken place on the floor of the riding hall. [...] The trusses could have been lifted employing cable-stayed masts, which are much used in this country, and easier to use than the shearlegs»[30].

Nevertheless, the use of the elevated assembly platform had a certain success. Even for the so-called Ardant trusses, which proved to be a better alternative to the rather work-intensive and not very stiff laminated arches, similar erection techniques were employed. The Ardant truss is also an arched truss, but the arches are formed by a polygonal arrangement of struts rather than laminated boards. They have only recently become known under the designation of Ardant because their mechanical performance was compared to the Émy trusses in a famous 1840 monograph, but were already in use in France in the 1820s [31]. The process of erecting such a truss is shown in another figure in the 1825 *Nouvelle Collection de dessins* of the *École des Ponts et Chaussées* (fig.13)[32]. The drawing shows the erection of the roof of a dock in Cherbourg on the Channel. Incidentally, cable-stayed masts rather than shearlegs were employed here.

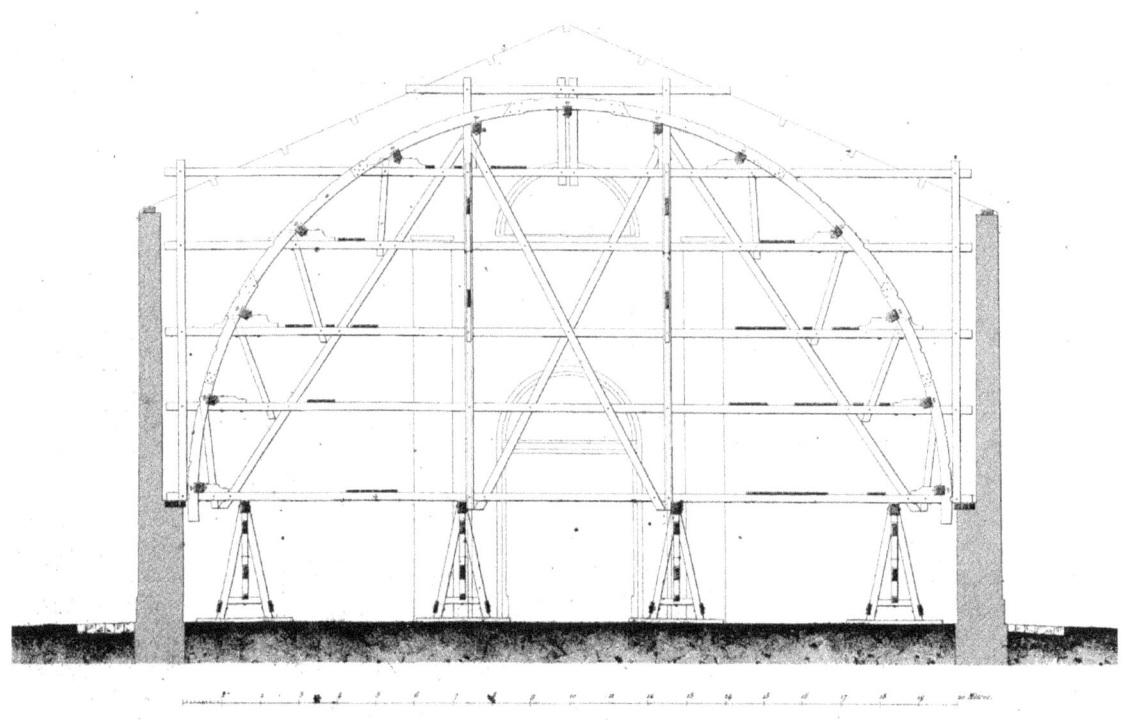

Figure 12: Erection of a roof truss with a laminated timber arch in Marac in 1825 (Amand-Rose Émy, 1828)

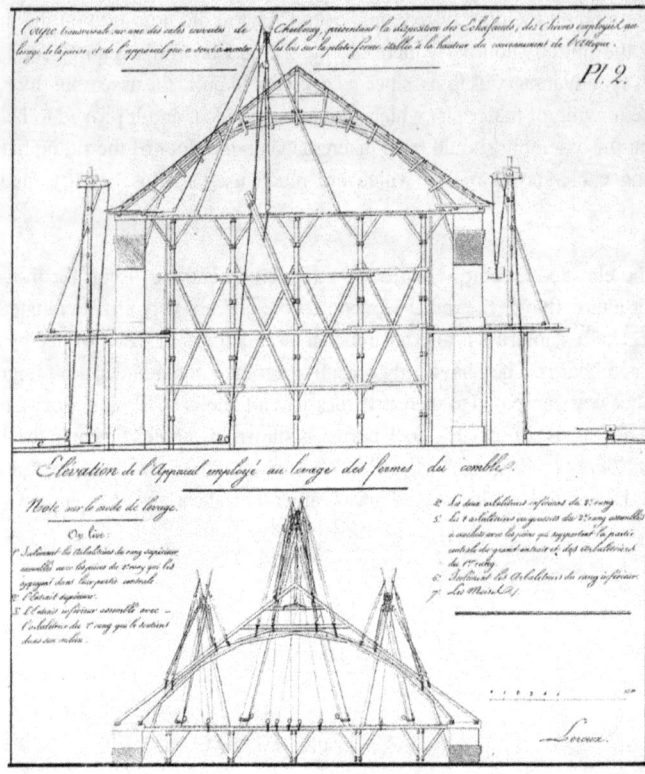

Figure 13: Erection of an «Ardant truss» in Cherbourg (Nouvelle Collection de dessins relatifs à l'art de l'ingénieur, 1825)

Conclusion

The present paper has outlined the historical development of the assembly procedures of timber roof trusses. Whereas traditional roof trusses owed much of their design to erection and assembly considerations, novel truss configurations were tried during the early 19th century whose layout was dictated by structural considerations rather than worksite practicalities. Many of these new systems called for the lifting of pre-assembled substructures or even entire trusses. The main lifting machines involved in roof truss erection were then shearlegs and cable-stayed masts. However, the lifting capacities and height of these machines typically limited the size and complexity of the trusses that could be erected without major hassle. Often, elaborate platforms had to be established at the level of the roof. Some contemporary reports and drawing show impressive temporary structures which consumed almost as much timber as the final roof trusses, putting in doubt the purported savings in material and expense of the novel truss systems. The methods developed for the erection of complicated timber roof trusses translated directly to the assembly of iron roofs around the middle of the 19th century.

References

[1] A. Félibien, *Des principes de l'architecture, de la sculpture, de la peinture et autres arts qui en dépendent*, Paris: Coignard, 1676, pl. XX on p.139. Pertaining text on p.126.
[2] Bibliothèque nationale de France, département Estampes et photographie, RESERVE FOL-VE-53 (H).
[3] For a copy, see, e.g.: Bibliothèque nationale de France, RESERVE QB-201 (170)-FT4. The copper plates still exist and are occasionally employed to produce fresh imprints.

[4] J.-A. Borgnis, *Traité complet de mécanique appliquée aux arts. Mouvemens des fardeaux,* Paris: Bachelier, 1818, p.268 and pl. 7.

[5] V. Scamozzi, *L'idea della architettura universale,* Venice: Valentino, 1615, vol. 2, p.368: «Si può far ancor questa machina con duoi alberi armati, & annodati in cima, & allargati da'piedi, chiamandola Capra ritta, e si governa con le sarti, e si ordisce con le taglie, & argana, & ordito di taglie. Con questa machina levano, e rimettono i stili, ò antenne dinanzi alla Chiesa di San Marco qui in Venetia; vero è, che ella si può piegare se non all'innanzi, & all'indietro; ma non cosi à destra, e sinistra da'lati.»

[6] See, e.g., Borgnis (note 4), pp. 244–246.

[7] See, e.g., Borgnis (note 4) p.243.

[8] Borgnis (note 4) p.246: «Les charpentiers et les maçons font un très-grand usage des chèvres dans l'érection des bâtimens.»

[9] Borgnis (note 4), p.286: «Une chèvre, ou une écoperche, que l'on transporte successivement d'un lieu à un autre, suffit pour élever et placer toutes sortes des pièces de bois verticales.»

[10] E.g., J. Claudel and L. Laroque, *Pratique de l'art de costruire,* Paris: Carilian-Goeury, 1850, pp. 122–123: «On lui donne la préférence sur les chantiers de construction, à cause de son prix moins élevé et de la facilité avec laquelle on peut la transporter et l'établir en un lieu quelconque.»

[11] L. Mazerolle, *Traité théorique et pratique de charpente,* Dourdan: Juliot/Vial, s.d. [around 1900], here part 1, plate 5.

[12] J.A. Romberg, *Die Zimmerwerks-Baukunst in allen ihren Theilen,* 2nd ed., Leipzig: Romberg, 1847, col. 448–449.

[13] Borgnis (note 4), plate 8.

[14] Königliche technische Deputation für Gewerbe (ed), *Vorlegeblätter für Zimmerleute in 37 lithographirten Tafeln mit Erläuterungen,* 2nd ed., Berlin: Schenk & Gerstäcker, 1835, pp. 14–15 and plate 23.

[15] C. Walter, *Zimmerkunst,* Augsburg: Veith, 1769, p.32: «Eine Arbeit die selten vorzukommen pfleget, und worzu gewiß großer Fleiß, sowohl bei dem Anlegen des Wercksatzes, als bey dem Abbinden der Bogen, und Schifter-Gesperr auch Anordnen eines Gerüstes, so auch mit Holtz verbunden werden muß, als dessen man by dem Aufstellen bey dieser Art von Kupplen oder Kugelhelme höchst benöthiget ist.»

[16] J. Ch. Krafft, *Traité des échafaudages,* Paris: Roret, 1856, p.3 and plate 18 for the scaffold of 1784 and p.2 and plates 16–17 for the scaffold of 1811.

[17] Ch. Bérigny (ed), *Collection de 350 dessins, relatifs à l'art de l'ingénieur,* Paris: École Royale des Ponts et Chaussées, 1821.

[18] Musée Carnavalet, inventory number D.13865-11: «bon pour Exécution». The museum attributes the plans to Rohault de Fleury. The roof truss seen on the plans is almost identical to the drawings of the structure published in: J. Ch. Krafft, *Traité de l'art de la charpente, théorique et pratique. Part 6: Construction des théâtres,* Paris: Auteur, Firmin Didot, Rey & Gravier, et al., 1822, plate 20, here called Opéra Provisoire.

[19] Musée Carnavalet, Paris: D.13865-29, transversal section; D.13865-30: longitudinal section.

[20] For more information on the history of scaffolding, see: S. M. Holzer, *Gerüste und Hilfskonstruktionen im historischen Baubetrieb. Geheimnisse der Bautechnik,* Berlin: Ernst & Sohn, 2021, here pp. 57–61.

[21] Th. Grissell, „Scaffolding for large erections", *The Civil Engineer and Architect's Journal,* vol. 11 (1845), p.106: «The cost was one-half, and sometimes one-third, of the ordinary type of scaffold, if the loss by the rotting and destruction of poles and cords was taken into account.»

[22] D. Gilly, *Handbuch der Land-Bau-Kunst,* 5th ed., Braunschweig: Friedrich Vieweg, 1822, vol. 2, p.193, gives a short explanation, according to which the first thing to be erected is the ridge purlin, temporarily supported by some suitable poles (fig. 152 in Gilly's book). Then, from each side, the half-arches are set in until the roof is complete and the temporary poles can be removed.

[23] A.F. Triest, *Grundsätze zur Anfertigung richtiger Anschläge welche die Land-Baukunst in sich begreift,* vol. 3, Berlin: Kunst- und Industrie-Comptoir, 1809, p.562: «Stellt man Rüstböcke nicht zu weit aus einander, und belegt sie mit starken Brettern, so leisten sie selbst bei Errichtung hoher Dächer vorzügliche Dienste, wie z. B. beim Bau der neuen Königl. Reitbahn in Charlottenburg der Fall war, bei der die 30 Fuß hohen Sparren des Bogendachs *ohne verbundene* Rüstung nur auf guten Rüstböcken gerichtet wurden, und wodurch das Geschäft sehr erleichtert ward, indem ein solches Bockgerüste leichter, als ein verbundenes Gerüst, zu translociren ist.»

[24] Vorlegeblätter (note 14), plate 21.

[25] B. Brisson (ed), *Nouvelle collection de 530 dessins ou feuilles de textes relatifs à l'art de l'ingénieur,* Paris: École Royale des Ponts et Chaussées, 1825, part 2, no. 161 (no pagination).

[26] Krafft 1856 (note 16), plate 30.

[27] A.-R. Émy, *Description d'un nouveau système d'arcs pour les grandes charpentes*, Paris: Carilian-Goeury, 1828, p.8.
[28] J.-J. Chayrou, „Notice sur l'éxécution de la nouvelle charpente de M. le colonel Émy au quartier de cavalerie de Libourne", *Mémorial de l'Officier du Génie*, vol. 10 (1829), pp. 31–51, here p.38.
[29] Émy (note 27), p.10.
[30] Chayrou (note 28), p.51, „Apostille du directeur".
[31] P. Ardant, *Études théoriques et expérimentales sur l'établissement des charpentes à grande portée,* Metz: Lamort, 1840.
[32] Brisson (note 25), part 2, no. 162 (no pagination), plate 2.

Middle Ages

The complex masonry of the Schönburg Castle Keep chimney system (1201 CE) in the context of contemporary examples

Jonas Lengenfeld
Department of construction history, Brandenburgische Technische Universität Cottbus-Senftenberg
Cottbus, Germany

Abstract

High Medieval chimneys, although often the focal point of contemporary representative buildings, are rarely a topic of construction history. More often they appear in art or architectural history where they are discussed regarding their style and ornamentation. It is however worthwhile to examine these important representative objects with the tools of the construction historian. In them, we can find important information regarding the contemporary craftsmanship and skills. Based on extensive first-hand examinations and building archaeology this paper aims to discuss the planning and building process of the highly complex cut-stone chimney system in the keep of Schönburg Castle (1201 CE) using new methods of reverse engineering.

The Tower of Schönburg Castle

On the southern bank of the Saale River, five kilometres east of the episcopal city Naumburg, Schönburg castle sits enthroned on a red sandstone cliff. Its tower or *Bergfried* which houses the chimney system was erected at the beginning of the thirteenth century and is situated in the inner baily of the larger castle complex dating back at least to the twelfth century [1]. (Fig. 2)

The keep, built over a circular plan of 9.63 metres in diameter, reaches a height of 29.82 metres measured from the recent day ground surface up to the battlements. The conical brick spire was erected in a younger phase of construction. The walls, up to 2.95 metres thick, which the chimney flue crosses diagonally, are constructed with a triple shelled masonry. (Fig. 3) A core of layered quarried red sandstone masonry laid in lime mortar is clad by an inner and outer ashlar facing laid in proper pseudoisodomic courses. The ashlars are cut precisely following the curvature of the wall surfaces with their faces hewed by the pick hammer in such a skilled manner that the well-preserved parts of the surface appear completely smooth.

While the quality of the faces and the stringently conducted pseudoisodomic masonry, running around the tower in 82 carefully levelled courses, are unmatched in contemporary regional towers of comparable size, these are far from the only exceptional features. The bed joints of the inner and outer shell share the same height, which is almost complete in the lower sections and still maintained in many places of the higher sections. (Fig. 3)

This is not structurally necessary, as the facing walls are separated by the quarry stone core – even though the few samples we have from the core masonry suggest that the quarry stone core was erected simultaneously, corresponding to the ashlar facing walls. It is most likely that the correspondence between the height of the courses of the outer and inner shell provides evidence for the planning process. Presumably, a specific height was chosen for every course. Based on this decision the necessary number of ashlars for both facing walls with their specific curvature were then produced, stored, and laid accurately on the building site.

The complex masonry of the Schönburg Castle Keep chimney system (1201 CE) in the context of contemporary examples

This requires the communication of relevant information as well as sophisticated planning and logistics. Qualities and processes that are better known from major building projects conducted by important cathedral lodges or *Bauhütten* during this time. Some of the best researched examples of which can be found in the big churches built in the Île-de-France during this era [2].

Figure 1: Fireplace in the first storey viewed from the entering corridor. (R. Wieczorek)

Figure 2: View from the western bank of the saale river upon the inner Baily and Tower of the Sch nburg. (R. Wieczorek)

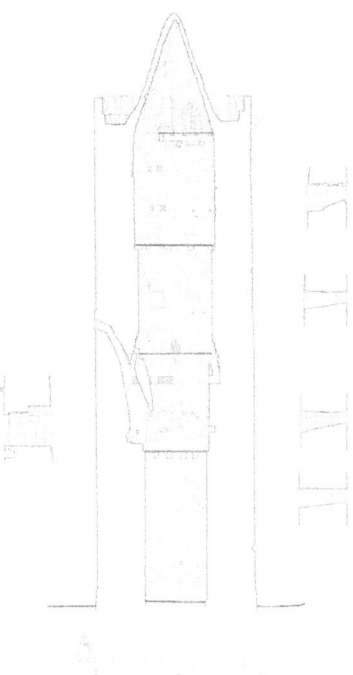

Figure 3: Section of the Tower or Bergfried. The thin lines indicate the height of the courses. Left and right the corridor and windows are shown. Notice the flue leading diagonally trough the wall (author)

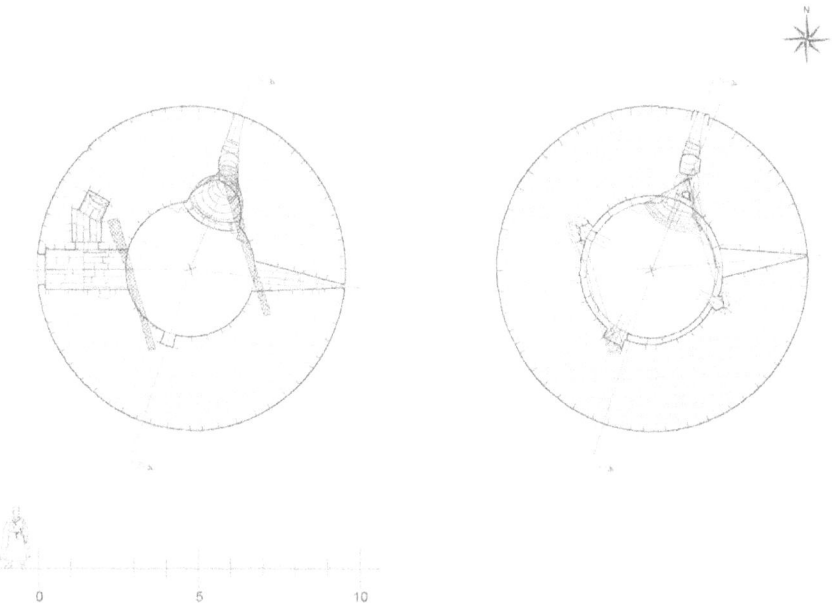

Figure 4: Floorplan of the first storey (left) upwards view with features of the ceiling visible. Floorplan of the second storey (right) downwards view on chimney hood channels within the wall. (author)

The complex masonry of the Schönburg Castle Keep chimney system (1201 CE) in the context of contemporary examples

The Kemenate

Internally the tower is split into four storeys plus the later one added with the spire. A slit window can be found on each floor orientated in a different direction. All ceilings are constructed as wooden joists resting on a wall recess between each storey. The only exception of this is the ceiling above the typically high ground floor. Its four massive oak beams (0,30 x 0,40 metres in cross section), which are embedded into the facing walls, were likewise planned to carry a heavy screed floor resting on them and the recess in the wall atop.

This situation allowed the opportunity to use dendrochronology from this ceiling to establish the *terminus post quem* regarding the erection of the tower. The preserved sapwood dates to the summer of 1201. This makes an installation dating from the autumn of 1201 onwards most likely [3].

The storey above these beams is the main floor of the tower and functioned as the entrance floor as well. Formerly access to the tower was granted through a portal in the west wall of the first storey. As its threshold lies 8.80 metres above the ground level it has to be assumed that it was accessible over a wooden bridge from one of the ruined adjacent buildings, most likely the palace. (Fig. 12) The said portal (1.85 metres high) is covered by a round arch precisely following the curvature of the outer shell of the tower on the outside. The adjacent corridor leading trough the 2.78-metre-thick wall is covered by a straight arch in the form of a gable and subsequently by a higher barrel vault. Both are carefully hewn and laid in a planned style. (Fig. 3) In the north wall a round arch portal leads into a small Garderobe. It is covered by a straight arch in the area of the possible door and a barrel vault above the toilet shaft [4]. (Fig. 4) The whole construction is remarkably complex and lavish compared to other contemporary castles. Even the corridor in the imperial castle tower at Wimpfen is constructed in a simpler style [5]. The barrel vault above the inner part of the corridor ends in a 2.3metre-high round arch portal leading to the room. Its face is once again following the cylindrical shape of the room facing creating a complicated spatially curved arch.

When entering the circular room measuring 4.00 metres in diameter and 5.39 metres in height the view is drawn to the fireplace in the northeaster section of the wall constructed from fair-faced masonry. (Fig. 1) Above a semi-circular fire room and resting upon lavish early gothic capitals, a shallow segmental arch with spatial curvature spans 1.6 metres wide across the fireplace. Cut from limestone and consisting of two corbels and a keystone. it supports the mantelpiece. This complex structure in the form of a beehive reaches all the way up to the ceiling. Its elegant connection to the walls with a narrow joint bearing witness to excellent craftsmanship. Inside the chimney, the mantelpiece describes the same figure at an increased recline this time merging with the cone shaped back wall of the chimney. This results in a drop-shaped cross section of the smoke hood that raises questions. (Fig. 3) The 7-metre-long flue carries on crossing diagonally through the wall before finally exiting from the wall at a height of 16,2 m above the ground through a 60 cm high opening with the shape of a gable crowned by the remains of an early gothic finial.

This complex chimney system, the planned flooring and the elaborate fireplace inside the first floor allow us to designate this room as a *Kemenate*: the German term deriving from the Latin *caminus* = fireplace that was used in the high medieval era to describe a heated room [6]. This room could be heated either by a tiled stove, air heating or an open fireplace. In representative buildings however, the latter played an important role. Especially in the public hall of the palace, a big and elaborately designed open fireplace had pride of place [7]. Remains of huge mantelpieces often reaching through several storeys, like in the ruins of the *Palas* at Münzenberg castle (ca. 1150-1174) (Fig. 5) [8], or the lavish ornamented columns, corbels and decorative plates of the fireplace at the imperial *Palas* in Gelnhausen Palatinate (ca. 1170) [9], give us a hint how important fireplaces and chimneys were for the medieval individual. The fireplace in the hall of Wildenburg castle (1190) possibly even found its way into the courtly poetry of Wolfram von Eschenbachs Parzival (1200-1210) [10]. The corbels of this example weighing approximately five metric tons demonstrate which structural tasks were taken on for this status symbol. (Fig. 6) This approach often made the chimney systems the most complex stone components of secular buildings like at Schönburg.

Figure 5: North wall of the palace (Palas) at Münzenberg castle (1170). The remains of the chimney flue and Mantelpiece reaching trough two storeys dominate the wall. (author)

Figure 6: The chimneys of Wildenberg castle (1190-1200) and Besigheim castle (1220-1230) (from left to right). (author)

The complex masonry of the Schönburg Castle Keep chimney system (1201 CE) in the context of contemporary examples

The Chimney

The chimney itself presents the main source for this paper. (Fig. 7) Its fire room is defined by the courses one to seven of the chimney back wall. The bottom of the fire room is situated 0.36 metres above the recent day floor level. Like the chimney and the tower facings, the fire room is constructed from red sandstone ashlars hewed finely with a pick hammer as fair-faced masonry. They are laid in tidy pseudoisodomic courses that match internally but do not correspond with the bed joints of the inner tower facing. The fact that these two systems are consistent within themselves, but incompatible with each other, suggests that the fireplace, like other more complex parts (window of the first floor, portals) was produced by specialists in advance of the building process. It was then fitted in when the tower reached the appropriate height for installation. This explains the use of smaller atypical ashlars around the fire room that were used to fit both parts together. (Fig. 1/8) This practice is well known in the construction of cathedrals but rarely documented in castles [11].

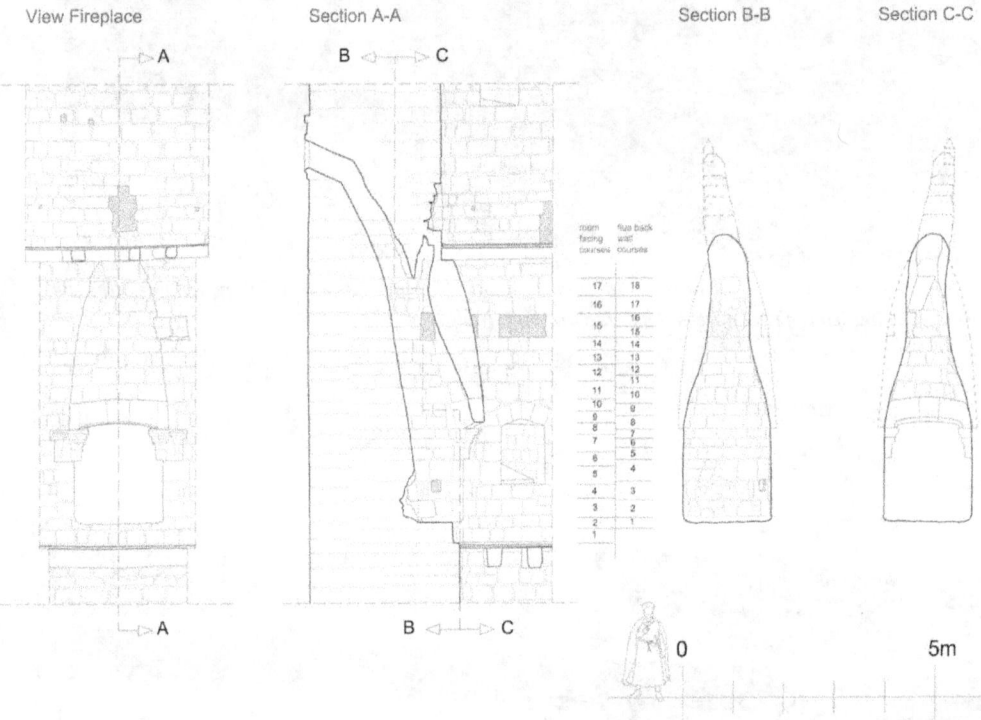

Figure 7: View and cut sections of the chimney system in the Tower of Schönburg castle. Note the levels of the different bed joints shown on the table. (author)

The plan of the fire room is unclear today since a large portion of its back wall was destroyed by the heat of a fire as the shell-like stone surfaces indicate. However, it was possible to reconstruct its former shape from building archaeological findings on its floor. Based on these results the courses one and two described a semicircle with a radius of 0.88 metres. The centre of this circle is positioned in the middle of a line between the corner stones of the fire room. From the bed joint above course two upwards the back wall of the fireplace as well as the flue up to course 18 is inclined constantly at approximately 80° leading through the wall.

Courses four and three maintain the diameter of the semicircle while following the inclination of the back wall. The centre of the circles thus shifts in a parallel manner. Above course four the height of the courses is reduced significantly. A possible reason for this is that these courses do not feature the representative corner stones like courses two three and four. These stones forming the frame of the fireplace communicate between the circle of the fireplace and that of the room. Likewise, in an attempt to obtain a straight edge, they show a relatively big height of 0.32 to 0.41 metres. (Fig. 1/7)

Atop these corner stones' 1.58 metres above the floor rest two lavish early gothic limestone capitals with a complicated cornice. Regarding the profile of the cornice and the quality of the work they are comparable to those in the eastern parts of Naumburg Cathedral, although their layout and construction is more complex. While appearing monolithic at first sight, they consist of three blocks. (Fig. 8) The first block maintains the ground shape of the corner stones and features a chalice capital above the corner and a console facing the room with the edge. Atop this block the cornice blocks follow, coming to the same the height as course seven. The first cornice block picks up the form of the fire room wall and forms the cornice above the chalice capital. While the second forms the cornice above the console which features a different profile. Presumably in an attempt to prevent a visible joint on the face of the stones: the butt joint is angled facing into the second cornice stone. (Fig. 8)

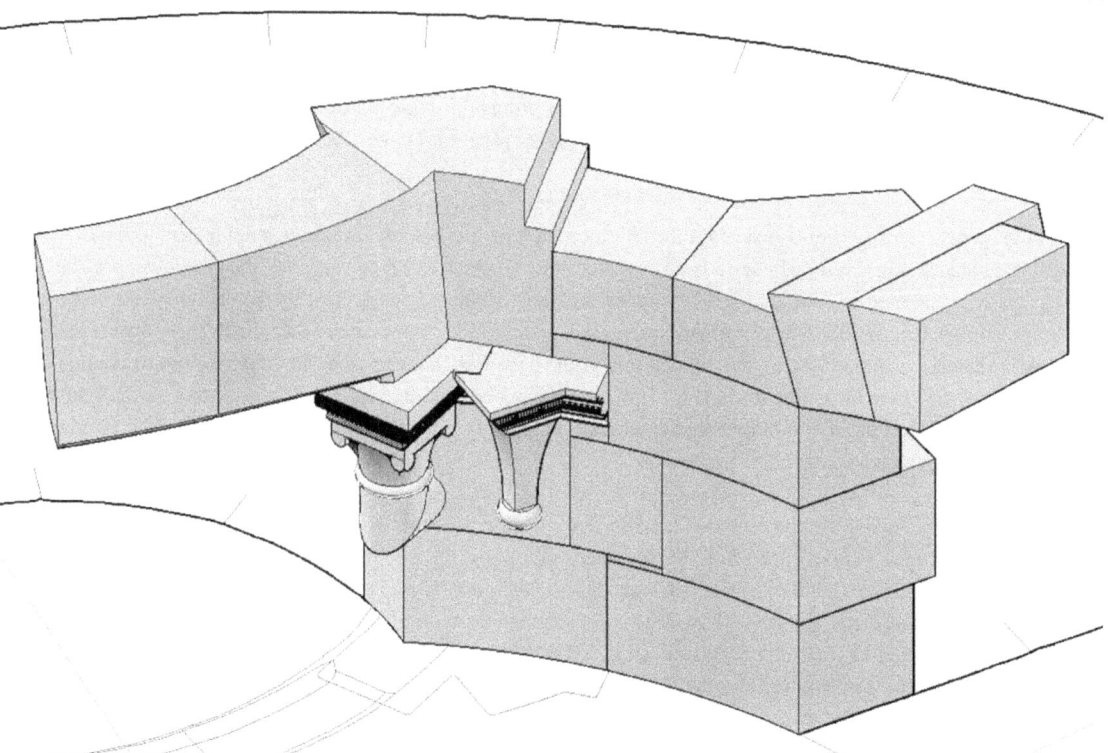

Figure 8: Isometric detail of the wall east of the chimney with corbel capital and masonry shell. Note the complex geometry's of the corbel and the corner stones.

The complex masonry of the Schönburg Castle Keep chimney system (1201 CE) in the context of contemporary examples

Above the cornices at a height of 2.17 metres rests a shallow segmental arch consisting of two corbels and a keystone. Like the capitals, cornices and the arches of the portals it was not crafted from red sandstone but limestone. The reason for this is that limestone's finer structure is better suited for the fine masonry needed for these special parts. This theory is further supported by the fact that the faces of these stones are much more processed than those of the red sandstone ashlars. They were hewn two times by the *Fläche* or *Steinbeil* = stone axe (fourteenth century designation) an axe like iron tool with a straight edge of 4-6 centimetres. This special method of hewing the stone twice became fashionable in the late Romanesque – early gothic period [12].

The corbels and the eastern corbel in particular are the most complex stones in the tower. With a weight of up to 700 kg their bounding box is the heaviest as well. They react to no less than six constraints: namely the radius of the room shell, the inner shell of the chimney, the room facing of the curved mantel piece, the chimney facing of the mantle and finally the geometries of the spatial bend arch. Even small mistakes would lead to problems with the other constraints making these stones a true masterpiece.

Furthermore, during examinations regarding the chimney arches intrados it became evident that it cannot be described by a single curve. Apparently, the intrados of all three components are described by individual circles. The axis on which the centre of these circles are placed form a fan-like structure. This allows the intrados of each stone to be marked on its face more easily. The slight wavey line resulting from this method is too small to be seen by the uneducated eye. It was possible to detect this geometry with a modern Scan to CAD Software (Geomagic) that was used to geometrically analyse the chimney system. Due to its specialized form-analysing tools it allows for a more exact geometrical analysis than those conducted by hand or CAD Programs. For further reading regarding this topic please read the publication in this endnote [13]. It is worth mentioning that neither on these most complex parts nor on the well planned ashlars could any masons mark be found on a visible face.

Behind the corbels starting with course eight the chimney shaft or flue begins. It measures 5.5 meters to the exit out of the wall, but since the flue above course 18 is inaccessible and of a much easier construction than the lower part we going to focus on these 2.8 metres. The back wall, meaning the parts which are not defined by the mantel piece, resembles a semi-circular plan. (Fig. 9) But contrary to the fire room the radii of the courses are reduced with every course leading it to shrink in diameter while following the defined line of the back wall. This leads to the organic form of the flue in the cross section when viewed from the front. (Fig. 7) The bed joint above course 14 is the first one that corresponds to the bed joints in the mantel piece and inner tower face alike. Potentially this marks the spot up to which the fireplace and back wall were pre-fabricated off the building site.

The front of the flue facing the room above the chimney arch is closed by the mantel piece. The feature cut from red sandstone resembling a beehive intersecting the cylinder of the tower face dominates the room. Normally the inside of the mantel would follow in a parallel course but instead it displays an increased recline towards the flute. The first course is still describing a base circle similar to that of the hood's face in the room (0.99 metres) leading to an elliptical ground plan meeting the smaller circle of the back wall. (Fig. 10) But the second and third course show a stronger decline and merge with the circle of the back wall. From the bed joint above course three the mantel and the back wall form a closed circle with a radius of 0.52 metres.

Jonas Lengenfeld

Figure 9: View up the chimney flue from the fire room. Note the highly complex geometry and the second channel. (R. Wieczorek)

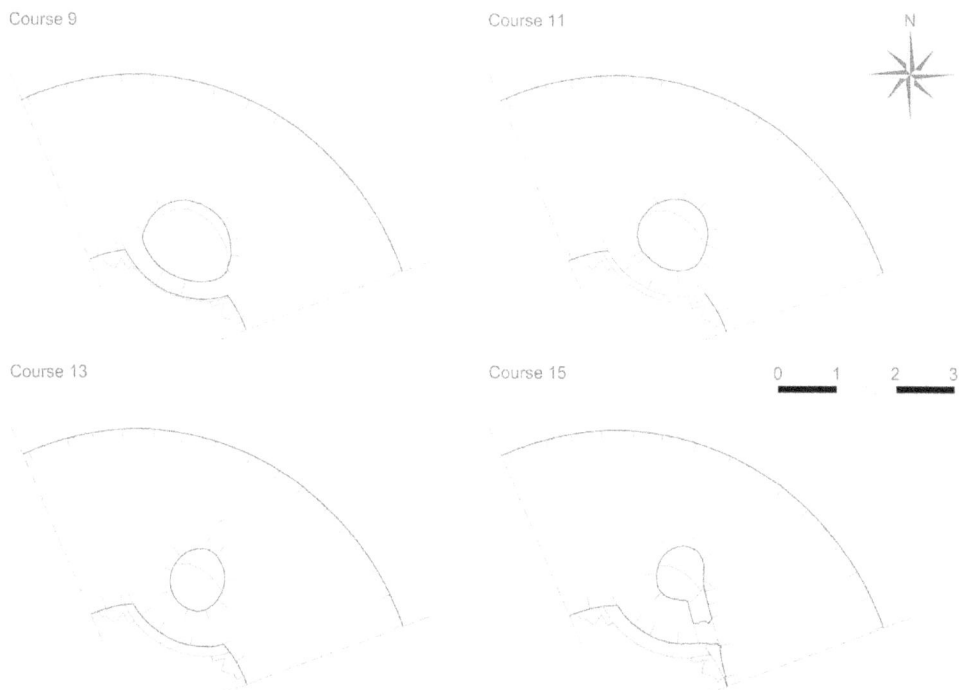

Figure 10: Horizontal Section trough the mantel and flue. Shown are the Bed joints above four courses of the chimney Back wall (left to right top to bottom). (author)

The complex masonry of the Schönburg Castle Keep chimney system (1201 CE) in the context of contemporary examples

We do not know what lay behind the builder's intention to decouple the shape of the chimney shaft and the outer form of the mantle. Perhaps it was the wish to build a more representative mantle. This intention, however, brought challenges. The ashlars of the mantle have to react on the different internal and external geometries and get deeper with every course. In the first course, this task was fulfilled with stones that simultaneously formed the room and flue face of the fireplace while their underside had to even out the round extrados of the chimney arch. (Fig. 7) On top of that, the ashlars of the mantle were not pre-made but fitted on site according to the courses of the inner tower facing. This is particularly evident on the first two courses of the mantle in the flue and the first course inside the room. Here the craftsman had to even out a height difference of seven centimetres within a span of 1.8 metres which occurred during the building process of the room facing. They solved this problem by arranging the height of the stones in the manner of a five stepped stairway. Although this looks strange in the plan, it is not visually apparent when examining the structure.

Only the first course of the mantle is constructed by ashlars reaching from the room to the flue. Above the first course the mantle was executed in a double shell masonry as the butt joints and insights show.

The described method of erecting the mantle in a relatively late stage seems common according to my research up to this point. It is unusual though that, with two exceptions on the eastern joint, all ashlars of the outer mantle shell bind into the facing of the room. Most contemporary examples like Münzenberg castle and Besigheim castle feature mantles that were built in front of the wall connected only by a few anchor stones. (Fig. 5/6)

The outer face of the mantle itself can be described by a circle with a radius of 16.94 metres describing the vertical curve and a second circle with a radius of 1.50 metres describing the horizontal curve of the first bed joint underneath course one. (Fig. 11) Thus every ashlar is curved horizontally and vertically. In contrast to the fire room however the horizontal radius is not fixed thus leading its geometrical centre to wander following the vertical face. Instead, every bed joint features a different radius that all share the same centre. This centre can be defined by a vertical line starting where the bed joint between courses nine and ten meets the back wall of the chimney. (Fig. 11) The back wall of the chimney thus once again acted as a focal point for its design.

Course six of the mantle's front marks the beginning of a different geometry. Its outer face is described by a circle with a radius of 5.99 metres describing the vertical curve while the horizontal one described by circle with a radius of 1.44 metres. The radius of the horizontal circle was kept for the following bed joints. The builders changed from a system of concentric circles to a system of steady circles which were moved to form the desired inclination. The reason for this could be a kind of rationalisation. Despite its great accuracy and refinedness, the concentric method was also time consuming especially for the planner. Due to the different radii every bed joint needed a new template that had to be defined and produced. By simply shifting the same radius multiple times, the builders saved material and time. Further while still using the same tools the faces of the ashlars above course six of the mantles were crafted less properly. The bigger mortar joints between the room face and the mantle, though, are not signs of poor work. As stated earlier, the ashlars of the mantle bind into the wall while those of the wall are running against them. To meet this geometry, the ashlars of the room facing have to feature thinner and pointier sides with every course. At the top of the mantle it became impossible to solve this problem using ashlars. The missing part is therefore filled with a mortar joint expanding from course to course. (Fig. 1)

This rationalisation, however, is accompanied by similar features which appear above the bed joint of course 14. The stone changes from a red sandstone to a more yellowish type that occurs in the chimney as well as on the inner and outer face of the tower. Above this bed joint only four red ashlars can be found on the mantle that may have been already produced as the change was decided. Further the mortar joints of above this mark are simple flush joints while every joint in the lower part of the tower, including those in the uninhabitable ground floor are adorned with a groove (*Pietra Rasa*). (Fig. 1) Together this can be seen as a certain break within the design of the tower. Although not a complete break since it was still finished to the battements and the chimney was completed as well.

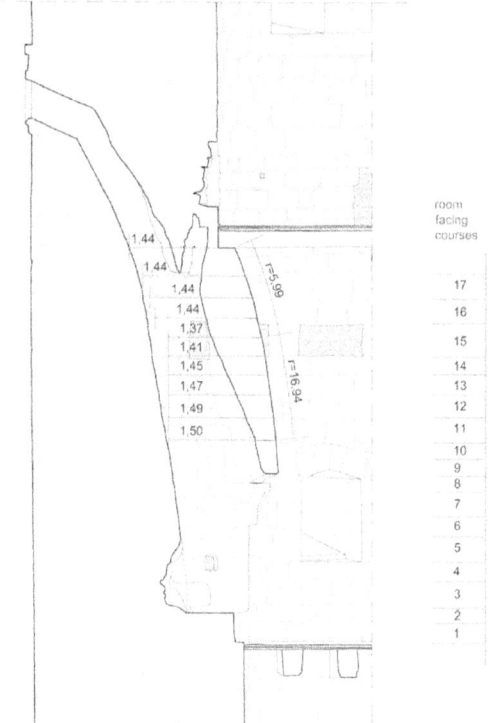

Figure 11: Section trough the chimney System (A-A) showing the horizontal and vertical radii of the outer face of the mantle. (author)

The obvious height difference in the courses above this mark, though, is likewise not directly linked to this rationalisation. Mantle and flue are intersected by channels above Course 14. Based on the finding of 0.2-metre-wide beam imprints on their floor they were constructed for a temporary wooden structure which was probably used during the building process. The structure consisted of two horizontal beams placed parallel to each other, their middle running tangential along the inner face of the wall. From their heads reaching deep into the wall, four beams rose upwards in the direction of the tower centre, their channels ending in the next storey. (Fig. 1/4) It likely would have resembled a trestle frame of four times four metres in span with a significantly greater height. Possibly a crane which was set upon the rising wall at this point. This would explain the bigger and heavier ashlars of the faces from this course on. The workmen surely planned to close this temporary channel in the last stages of the construction. But this didn't happen, the horizontal channel puncturing the mantle and the vertical one arising from the flute weren't closed until the 19th or early 20th century as the findings of sawn stone and a thick layer of organic material between these deposits and the medieval floor indicates. It seems the finishing touches were not executed and the chimney was never used during the Middle Ages.

When erecting the possible crane, it was nevertheless still intended to build and use it. The last 2.7 metres of the chimney flue were constructed in the significantly less complex form of a rectangular channel leading through the wall at an angle of 26 degrees. It finally exits the wall with an angle of 67 degrees' through a 60 cm high opening with the shape of a gable crowned by the remains of an early gothic finial. Together with the capitals, this is the only architectural ornament of the tower, both of which are found on the chimney.

The complex masonry of the Schönburg Castle Keep chimney system (1201 CE) in the context of contemporary examples

Design and building process

Based on these findings it is possible to formulate a theory about what the design and building process of the chimney system might have looked like. Although Schönburg castle has not been archaeologically surveyed, the findings on the preserved *enceinte* and documents of the nineteenth century suggest that space within the baily was very limited. (Fig.12) Even if the eastern part was vacant a maximum of 600 square metres (30 x 20) was available of which 73m² would been needed for the tower not including potential scaffoldings. This space is not large enough to accommodate the necessary infrastructures (workshops, storage space, etc.) of a cathedral lodge. Planning and prefabrication of the components probably took place at one or more other locations. After receiving the building order, the timber was cut, the building site was selected, and the preparations began. The chimney was designed together with the tower with the aim of creating a representative effect. Its back wall (up to course 14), the fire room and the arch were prefabricated early in the construction process, the latter by particularly talented workers. It was still unknown what height the courses of the first floor would have. The following spring, work began on the tower shaft. In midsummer or autumn, the prefabricated components were fitted into the fabricated masonry. The weight of the corbels made a crane a necessity. For the laying of the keystone a false work was erected under the fireplace. Based on the now known course heights, the stones of the mantle were designed and adapted to the existing masonry on site. Mantle and inner wall were executed together up to course 14. During the winter break, the quarry was changed, and the processes rationalised. The crane, now moved to the top of the wall, helped accelerate construction in 1203. The tower was completed but the chimney was never used for unknown reasons.

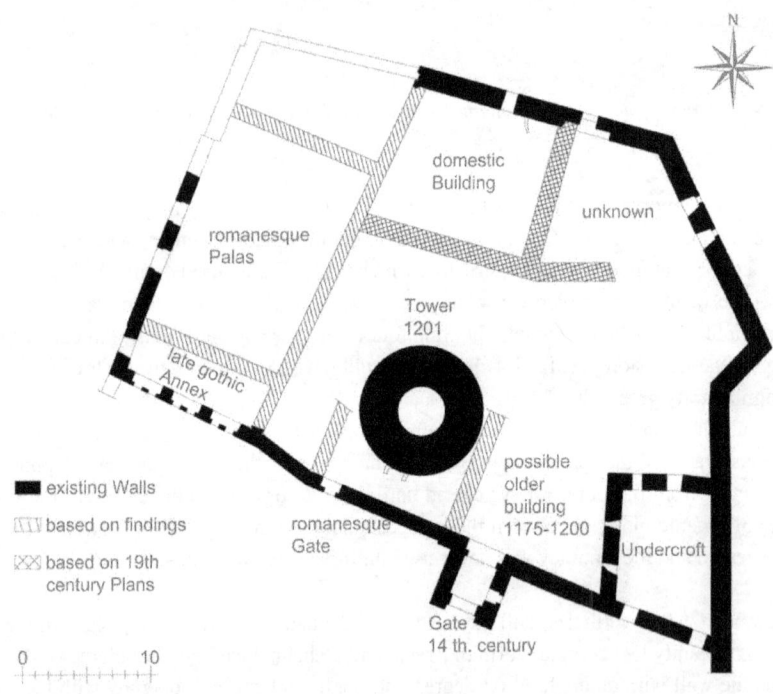

Figure 12: Floorplan of Schönburg castles inner baily. (author)

Client and Masons

The written sources do not tell us who planned to warm himself at this fireplace, nor whom was instructed to design and build it. But judging from the finds it is possible to formulate a thesis. Representative chimneys in towers are not uncommon at this time. But in towers of comparable size, they normally lack decoration and often consist of a simple niche with a flue above like in the neighbouring castle of Saaleck. (Fig. 13) Even the bigger residential towers of financially potent clients like the *Bergfried* III of Neuenburg castle (1180) reach neither size nor quality of the example in Schönburg [14]. (Fig. 13) In its refined artistic construction and size, it satisfies the demands of elite culture. A similar elaborate but less complex chimney in a relatively small tower can be found in the palace of the Margraves of Baden in Besigheim (1220-30) [15]. (Fig. 6) It can be assumed that the clients at Schönburg were at least similarly wealthy elites. The families of the *Edelfreie* and episcopal Naumburg Ministerials associated with the castle in the later twelfth and early thirteenth centuries do not seem to have lived up to this claim [16]. It can therefore be assumed that the bishops of Naumburg, who are documented to have had a knight in the castle in 1217 and to have owned it in the fourteenth century at the latest, were the clients [17].

Based on the results of dendrochornology, it can then be assumed that Berthold II, a partisan of the Hohenstaufen dynasty, commissioned the construction [18]. A possible reason which occurred earlier in the same year 1201 could be the change of his mighty territorial neighbour the Landgrave of Thuringia to the rival faction of the Welfs during a power struggle within the Holy Roman Empire [19]. When this opponent was beaten by the emperor and finally openly subjected in 1204 the need for a defensive tower with a representative room was possibly no longer present [20].

Figure 13: The chimneys in Bergfried III of Neuenburg castle (1180) and the tower of Saaleck castle (1200) (left to right). (author)

The complex masonry of the Schönburg Castle Keep chimney system (1201 CE) in the context of contemporary examples

The question remains who planned and built the tower for the bishop. The high level of planning required in the areas of construction technology and construction operations, as well as the confident handling of complex design techniques such as the concentric chimney mantel and the spatially curved arches, required an experienced lodge. In addition, the quality of the workmanship and the desire to work on complex systems such as the chimney arch or the vaultings of the access corridor speak in favour of highly specialised experts who tend to work on a supra-regional basis. This is supported by the unusually early use of Gothic forms in this region. Against this background, it seems reasonable to assume that the workers of the then newly built Naumburg Cathedral were the creators of this small masterpiece. Furthermore, this would explain where the craftsmen went after not finishing the last stages of the tower and where to locate the workshops. Initial investigations at Naumburg Cathedral seem to confirm the assumption based on similar construction methods and tool marks as well as the lack of Masons marks.

Conclusion

As demonstrated chimneys were a central object of feudal representation in the High Middle Ages. Due to their importance, a great deal of planning and material resources were invested in them. This means that new and complex building techniques can be found on these objects. Their study is therefore not only useful for increasing knowledge in this field but also promises to provide insights into historical construction methods and processes as a whole especially regarding the construction of thick stone walls.

Acknowledgements

This paper is an excerpt of my doctoral research project "The development of chimneys in High Medieval Central European residential buildings in construction and function" which is under way at the Brandenburg University of Technology supervised by Prof. Dr.-Ing. D. Wendland. If I was able to arouse your interest, I am thankful for any hint regarding potentially well preserved or complex chimneys of the said era and place. I would like to thank the staff of the *Denkmalamt* Naumburg and the honorary janitors of Schönburg castle securing the access to the tower. The survey at Schönburg was conducted with the assistance by J. Gebler and L. Wehrle. Professional Photos were taken by R. Wieczorek.

Furthermore, I thank R. Schmitt for supporting me with many useful information's regarding the Saale area and in particular for the results of the dendrochronology carried out by T. Eißing. Last but not least I have to thank S. Krüger the archivist of Besigheim. A special thanks goes to A. Burns for proofreading this article and Prof. Dr. phil. U. Fauerbach who made this doctoral project possible.

References

[1] R. Schmitt, 'Zur Geschichte und Baugeschichte der Schönburg, Burgenlandkreis', *Burgen und Schlösser in Sachsen-Anhalt - Mitteilungen der Landesgruppe Sachsen-Anhalt der Deutschen Burgenvereinigung e.V.*, vol.12, 2003, pp.15-79.
[2] The works of D. Kimpel are still authoritative in this Field, L. Calstelfranchi, (ED), Die Baukunst im Mittelalter, Solothurn 1995. D. Kimpel, *Struktur und Wandel der mittelalterlichen Baubetriebe*.
[3] Results handed out by R. Schmitt, dating carried out by Dr.-Ing. T. Eißing (Otto Friedrich University Bamberg) (2013).
[4] J. Lengenfeld, D. Wendland, 'Die Planung der komplexen Werksteinkonstruktion im Bergfried der Schönburg – das Werk eines Naumburger Meisters', *proceedings Fünfte Jahrestagung der Gesellschaft für Bautechnikgeschichte, Zürich* 2021. Petersberg: Michael Imhof (forthcoming).
[5] F. Arens, *Die Königspfalz Wimpfen*. Berlin: Deutscher Verlag für Kunstwissenschaften, 1967. Table 75.
[6] W. Koch, *Baustilkunde*. Gütersloh: Bertelsmann Verlag, 2006. p.459.
[7] J. Lengenfeld, D. Wendland, (Note 4)

[8] B. Jost, *Burgruine Münzenberg*. Regensburg: Schnell und Steiner, 2000. p.48.

[9] T. Biller, *Kaiserpfalz Gelnhausen*. Regensburg: Schnell und Steiner, 2015. p.48.

[10] W. von Eschenbach, *Parzival*. Ditzingen: Philipp Reclam, 1981. p.392.

[11] D. Kimpel, (Note 2)

[12] P. Völkle, *Werksteinplanung und Steinbearbeitung im Mittelalter*. Ulm: Ebner Verlag, 2016. p.78.

[13] J. Lengenfeld, D. Wendland, (Note 4)

[14] R. Schmitt, 'Schloß Neuenburg bei Freyburg/Unstrut. Amerkungen zur Baugeschichte der Vorburg', *Burgen und Schlösser in Sachsen-Anhalt - Mitteilungen der Landesgruppe Sachsen-Anhalt der Deutschen Burgenvereinigung e.V.*, vol.12, 2003, pp.150-177

[15] H. Maurer, 'Die Türme des Markgrafen Hermann V. im Rahmen stauferzeitlicher Wehrbau-Architektur', *Oberrheinische Studien*, vol.24, 2005, p.126.

[16] H. Helbig, *Der wettinische Ständestaat - Untersuchungen zur Geschichte des Ständewesens und der landständischen Verfassung in Mitteldeutschland bis 1485*. Köln, Wien: 1980. pp.159-163.

[17] R. Schmitt, (Note 1), p.17.

[18] Max-Plank-Institut für Geschichte, (Ed.) *Germania Sacra - Historisch Statistische Beschreibung der Kirch des Alten Reiches. Die Bistümer der Kirchenprovinz Magdeburg*. Berlin, New York: 1998. pp.785-790.

[19] A. Frölich, 'Herrschaftsstrukturen und Herrschaftslegitimation in der Literatur - Der Thüringer Landgrafenhof unter Hermann I', (Ph.D. thesis, Johann Wolfgang Goethe-Universität zu Frankfurt am Main, 2007), (unbuplished), http://core.ac.uk/download/pdf/14500418.pdf, pp.30-36.

[20] A. Fröhlich, (Note 1,8), p.34.

The Design and Construction of the Vaults in Notre-Dame in Paris and the Development of Medieval Vaulting and Stereotomy: Surveys, Analyses and Experiments

David Wendland, Mark Gielen
Brandenburgische Technische Universität Cottbus-Senftenberg

Abstract

Among the many innovative church constructions in the Ile-de-France during the twelfth century that immediately followed the ground-breaking new building of the abbey church of Saint-Denis, the high vaults in the cathedral of Notre-Dame in Paris mark a turning point – both in sheer dimensions and in their quality of execution as stone constructions. On the other hand, some solutions in design and construction that can be observed in these vaults remain unique within the dynamic development of Gothic vaulting in the great cathedrals built in the following years. On closer view it turns out that the general design of the vault as well as its construction details are hardly understood until now, mainly because they have been overlooked in a unifying perspective on Gothic architecture coined by the idealistic view of the Gothic Revival in the nineteenth century. Further, the particular relation between vault design and stereotomy needs to be clarified, and its significance needs to be understood.

Introduction

After the severe damage and partial destruction of the high vaults in Notre-Dame in Paris in the devastating fire in April 2019, in view to the upcoming interventions a thorough and detailed understanding of this structure is necessary – defining the significance and historical value in regard to the particular design, building technology, and relation between form and construction. The questions arising in regard to consolidation, repair and partial reconstruction can be expected to be far more detailed and precise than usual in research on construction history or even in building archaeology. On the other hand, the damaged state gives way to some observations that wouldn't be possible on intact buildings. Moreover, already in preliminary studies carried out so far, a number of open research questions have emerged, regarding in particular the developments in the geometric design of vaults and in stone planning during the middle-ages in Central Europe, as well as issues of knowledge transfer in a broader geographic context.

Our research in progress [1] addresses the issues of design, planning, stonemasonry and building by means of practical experiments carried out on large scale (Fig. 1). These are based on the available information and preliminary observations on the building [2], the results will have to be cross-linked with archaeological investigations on the building. In the following, we will discuss some correlations with the interpretation of the few existing sources and the developing knowledge on practices of design and planning in medieval architecture and vault construction.

In the development of the Gothic rib vault regarding architectural design, construction system and geometric concept, the first essential steps are attributed to Norman church buildings of the eleventh century, where the cross vaults in the aisles in addition to the transversal arches that separate the bays were provided with stone ribs along the diagonal groins [3]. In the second quarter of the twelfth century, vaults with major spans were built over the naves of some larger church buildings with rib systems that combined the scheme of transversal arches with the figure of the cross vault: uniting two bays of diagonal arches within one compartment of transverse arches in Durham Cathedral, or spanning transverse arches also in the middle of the bay in the sexpartite vaults of the abbey churches in Caen. In the geometry of the vault, the ribs

The Design and Construction of the Vaults in Notre-Dame in Paris and the Development of Medieval Vaulting and Stereotomy: Surveys, Analyses and Experiments

form the primary feature: by principle, they describe circle segments in vertical planes; the surfaces of the vault are adapted to these curves [4].

Figure 1: Experiments on the construction of the vaults in Notre-Dame in scale 1:3 (January 2022).

Immediately in the succession of these prominent high vaults of the Norman realm, the new parts of the abbey church of Saint-Denis were built, starting with the western narthex around 1135 [5]. In this innovative architecture with outstanding programmatic claim, the vaults play an essential role. While the construction of the ribs is similar to that in the previous examples – instead of arch voussoirs, rectangular blocks are used that are profiled on the intrados – the new conspicuous feature is the exposed stone masonry of the shells built with a carefully devised pattern. The courses are arranged parallel to the ridge, or to be more precise, the bed joints describe lines between the ribs that are equidistant to the straight ridge line of every shell (Fig. 2). Only in the lower portions, the masonry courses deviate from this regular pattern.

The high vaults of Saint-Denis from the twelfth century, surely sexpartite vaults with the same regular pattern of exposed stone in the webs, no longer exist, neither do their immediate successors in the cathedrals of Sens and Noyon [6]. A significant further step of innovation can be seen in the vaults of the nave of Saint-Maurice in Angers [7], 1149-53, where the shells are also built in fine dressed stone blocks, while presenting a concave shape with pronounced double curvature. These "domical vaults" are cross vaults on large square bays with ridges that, like the ribs, describe vertical circle segments – and so do the bed joints of the vault masonry. The perfection of the stonework in these curved surfaces built with perpendicular blocks is remarkable.

In the cathedrals of Laon and Paris, both started in the 1160s, the high vaults once more combine the motif of concave shells in perfectly dressed exposed stonework with the pattern of the sexpartite vault. The effort of creating curved surfaces that display perfect regularity in the stonemasonry was obviously of special importance to the builders. A challenging question for us is how this design could be defined and translated to working instructions, how the planning and assembly was accomplished. This regards issues of technical knowledge and on the historical development of applied geometry. A deeper insight will be essential also for gaining a thorough understanding of the significance of this architecture.

Figure 2: Abbey church Saint-Denis, vault in the narthex.

The high vaults in Notre-Dame

Within this dynamic development of increasing effort in geometric complexity along with perfection of the stonemasonry in the vaults, Notre-Dame in Paris stands out also for its sheer dimensions: the high vaults have a clear height of ca. 33 metres and a span of over 13 metres. The vaults in the choir, the inner bays of the transept arms, and the nave are formed as sexpartite vaults with bays of an approximately square plan, each corresponding with two bays of the aisles. The choir was vaulted before 1186, the eastern part of the nave before 1200, the western bays in the early thirteenth century [8]. There are some differences in the design among these three building phases, our study focuses on the eastern bays of the nave [9].

The sexpartite vault combines a system of transverse arches corresponding to the arcade of the aisles with the scheme of the cross vault, where the diagonal arches spanning two compartments create the double-size bays of the nave (Fig. 4). Although the design of all ribs is similar, the transverse ribs have a greater section – suggesting that they were conceived as being the principal structural feature of the vault. The geometric design of the vault, in contrast, is in first place based on the cross ribs, which have a semi-circular elevation. This leads to a significant increase of the rise of the diagonal arches and determines the level of the central keystone in the summit. The transverse arch in the middle of the bay also has a semi-circular elevation, but is stilted in order to reach the central keystone: above the abaci at the impost level, the rib first rises vertically over little less than 2 metres until the curvature starts. The other transverse arches that separate the bays start at the common springing level: their elevation is defined as autonomous two-centre pointed arches, apparently with a determined ratio 3/5 of span and radius. The formeret or wall ribs seem to be determined by the span and radius ratio of 2/3; although strongly stilted, their summits remain far below the level of the vertex of the bay. The ridges of the shells of the vault are a priori defined by circle segments as well, which like the curves of the arches are inscribed in vertical planes, with a common radius presumably devised to be equal to the width of the nave. In direction towards the clerestories, their curvature is continuous: the centre is located in the middle of the bay. Descending from the summit, they determine the level of the ridges of the formerets, thus having an important impact in the design of the clerestory. In longitudinal direction, the ridge curves, having the same curvature, are inserted between the given endpoints at the central keystone and the summits of the transversal arches between the bays, resulting in a discontinuous course longitudinal to the nave.

Figure 3: The high vaults in Notre-Dame in Paris: eastern bays of the nave (2009).

All this means before all, that the superelevation of the summit of the bay due to the semi-circular diagonal ribs, is a main determinant of the shape of the vault and directs most features of the geometric design. Hence, as opposed to a regular sequence of transverse arches, which is still present in the plan, the spatial curve system of the vault is in first place determined by the high rising diagonal arches: the *ogives*. This term, which denotes the cross ribs and apparently refers to the matter of "rising", first appears around 1230 in Villard de Honnecourt's "Lodge Book" and in several sources thereafter [10].

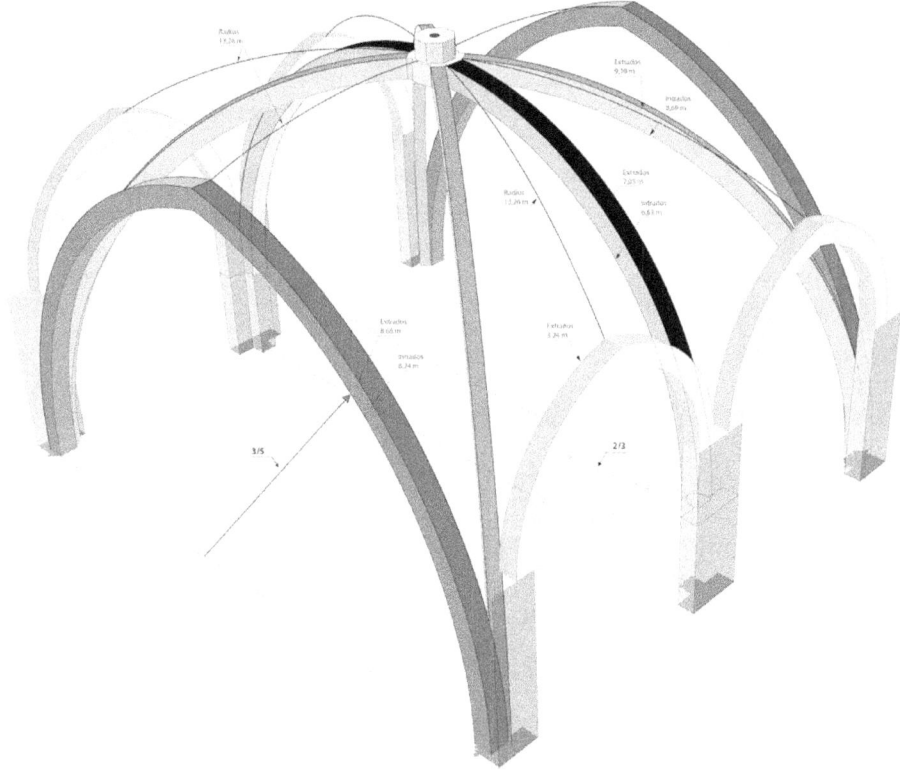

Figure 4: Geometric design of the rib system in the high vaults in Notre-Dame, eastern part of the nave.

Construction details, planning and building

The ribs are built from stone elements that comprise only the visible part under the vault surface, hence, they are connected with the masonry shells only by a continuous mortar joint. These elements are not carved as arch voussoirs, but as rectangular blocks – unlike the common image of Gothic rib vaults, but similar to the earlier predecessors mentioned above (Fig. 2) and contemporary examples. The carved profile on the intrados still resembles very much the original envelope block, and the curvature of the arch is produced only within the mortar joints. For the construction process and planning, this means that the rib elements could be produced in series without taking into account the exact curvature of the rib. Although not uniform in height, due the standard profile they could be assembled directly from the palette like masonry blocks. Only the last piece of every rib directly under the keystone had to be cut ad hoc to the right length.

In contrast, the keystones are elements that needed to be specifically carved according to the general design of the vault. The central keystones are very large and heavy workpieces that, unlike the ribs, are embedded in the shell of the vault and emerge on the extrados. Their volume therefore includes in vertical direction the thickness of the shell, the height of the rib profile, plus the sculptural element on the lower side, and in the horizontal dimensions the branches of the connecting ribs: the envelope block must have measured over 1 metre in height and ca. 1.26 metres in both horizontal edges. Planning and carving of these stone elements not only included the intersection of the rib profiles in their approach to the central ring, but also their directions in plan which is not exactly square but rectangular. They are stereotomic items that could be produced only on the basis of detailed information upon the general design of the vault – produced in a full-scale drawing and transmitted by means of templates [11].

The Design and Construction of the Vaults in Notre-Dame in Paris and the Development of Medieval Vaulting and Stereotomy: Surveys, Analyses and Experiments

The keystones of the single arches also had to be carved with the radial beds that for their definition referred to the general design. However, this could be done even without needing a full-scale drawing, if the arch was designed with a defined ratio of span and radius. For this, a procedure requiring only a square, carried out directly on the workpiece, is shown in Villard de Honnecourt's "lodge book". This instruction belongs to a passage in the book where procedures of setting-out as well as planning media like templates are described. In our experimental reconstruction, the procedure turned out to be practical and reliable (Fig. 5). Such possibility of simplifying the stone-planning may have motivated the use of arches with defined ratio, as we suppose in the reconstruction of the vault design.

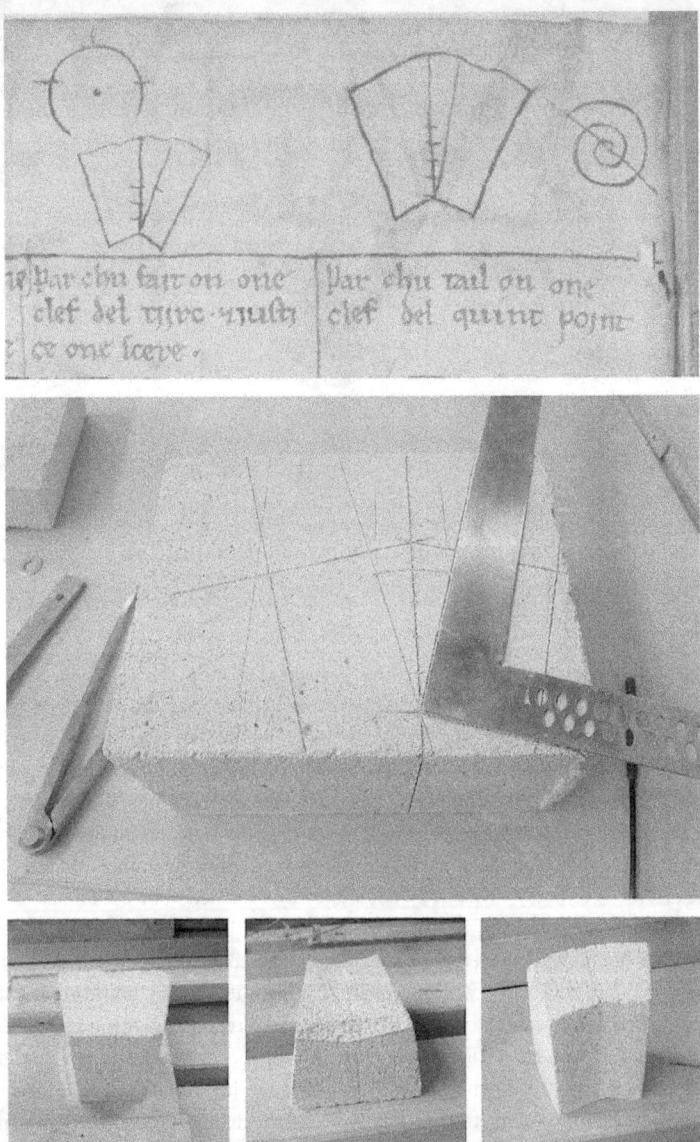

Figure 5: Instruction for carving the keystone of an arch with defined ratio of length and span, in Villard de Honnecourt's "Lodge Book" (Paris, BNF, ms. fr 19093); application in a rib keystone and in a ridge stone of the vault.

In the construction process the ribs and keystones had to be assembled upon a temporary supporting structure, designed according to the general project of the vault by means of appropriate planning media. There is no comprehensive information about these structures from sources or from archaeological evidence. Nevertheless, from previous research on late Gothic structures [12] it is possible to develop hypotheses that correlate well with the design principles of the vault: In the experiments, a system of vertical posts under the keystones to which the centring arches made of boards cut according to the curvature of the ribs were mounted, turned out to be practical. This structure, erected on a temporary floor at the springing level on which the geometric system could be established *in situ* in full scale, also facilitates the information flow from design to execution.

The starting points of the ribs were already fixed when the clerestories were built. Hence, the assembly starts with positioning the keystones according to the centre of the bay defined within the real boundary conditions of the building (Fig. 6). Then the centring arches can be adjusted precisely to the rib branches of the keystone. After that, the ribs can be built on the centring arches.

Figure 6: Experiments on the construction process: For the assembly of the ribs, first the keystone is positioned, then the centring is adjusted, enabling a precise connection of the ribs.

As the ridges of the shells appear straight in plan and describe the defined curvature in the elevation, it must be supposed that they were directed by centring arches similar to those of the ribs, produced according to the design described above (Fig. 7, top). For building the masonry shell of the vault, geometric guidance and support was needed, although a complete formwork was probably not necessary and could have even caused difficulties in the execution of the exposed masonry. In the vaults of Saint-Denis (Fig. 2), the linear courses could be built on straight laths fixed to the ribs – this support for every course had to be maintained until the vault was closed. In the curved courses of the concave shells in Notre-Dame, instead of laths, centring arches had to be used for every single course. Here, due to the curvature, they were only needed to support the unfinished courses and could then be taken out (Fig. 7).

We discussed the geometric properties of the masonry pattern elsewhere [13]. By principle, the courses must be aligned according to the curve of the ridge. This requires guiding their position – however, an absolute definition cannot be provided due to the changing heights of the courses and also due to the cumulating errors when the masonry is built up from the bottom to the top. In the experiments we used a system of marks based on equidistant lines that was established starting from the ridge line downwards and gave indication on the general direction of the courses in every portion of the shell (Fig. 7, top).

While the shells, despite their double curvature and with all the perfection of the joint pattern, are executed as block masonry with serial prismatic elements, the ridges are made with special stones that have the shape of keystones: stereotomic elements that have to be carved according to their position. These ridge stones are a rather singular phenomenon: While the linear ridges of the vaults in the narthex of Saint-Denis simply show a joint, these special rib stones appear in the concave shells of the vaults in Angers – along with the increasing perfection of the dressed stone surface and the introduction of the arched curvature of the ridges and the single courses. After Notre-Dame, these special stone elements disappear: the ridges in the vaults of the Cathedral of Reims are built also with special elements of a different type, and in the later development these elements seem to disappear altogether.

Although these special stones had to be produced upon precise instructions drawn from the design of the vault, we suppose that they were standardized and could be carved according to the keystones of the transversal and *formeret* arches. Here again, the effort of planning could be considerably reduced by using the procedure described in Villard's "Lodge Book" (Fig. 5) – in any case, this element gives strong emphasis to the aim of perfection in the stone surfaces of the vault.

Figure 7: Experiments on the construction process: Top, application of guiding marks for the masonry pattern. Centre, building of the courses upon single centrings. Bottom, double centring for the last course and the ridge stones – here a different procedure from the one shown in figure 1 is experimented.

The Design and Construction of the Vaults in Notre-Dame in Paris and the Development of Medieval Vaulting and Stereotomy: Surveys, Analyses and Experiments

Some considerations on the development of structural, geometric and architectural design of vaults in the context of early Gothic

For a thorough understanding of the design, planning and construction of the high vaults of Notre-Dame, two aspects are of particular importance. One is the development of stone planning, taking into account also the information transfer from design and construction, and the use of media related to it. While the built object is the principal information source on this matter, the observations made can be correlated with very few written or graphic sources that can be critically revised upon this research. The other is the development of the geometric and structural design of vaults.

As to the geometric design of vaults, there is a fundamental difference between the cross vault as it developed in the Roman Antiquity, which is defined by intersecting cylindrical surfaces creating groins that describe elliptic curves, and the Gothic vault which is determined by the curves that are defined a priori as circle segments, to which the surfaces of the vault are adapted [14]. The first concept has the advantage of geometrically defined surfaces that facilitate the planning particularly in ashlar vaults, but it also has important disadvantages: the difficulties related to the elliptic arches and, foremost, the necessity of having a square plan in order to avoid spatial curves at the cross groins. In the second case, the arches due to their elementary geometric description bring no difficulty at all for planning and for communicating the design specifications, and there are no limitations to the plan of the vault. The only inconvenience is the greater geometric complexity in the surfaces, which however can be overcome in practice by rather simple means, for instance with ruled surfaces spanned between the arches.

The ground-breaking invention of this new concept of vault geometry is usually attributed to the early rib vaults, from which, as mentioned above, a direct succession can be drawn to the evolution of the prominent early Gothic vaults in the Ile-de-France. It appears plausible to assume that in a rib vault all the effort of planning as well as the main temporary support during construction is necessarily focused on the stone ribs. However, this long-established notion is now challenged by accurate surveys and geometrical analyses of the shape of some vaults of earlier date.

In fact, recent analyses carried out in the church of St. Pantaleon at Cologne by Heckner and Meyer [15] showed that the cross vaults in the western part of the structure, dating from the tenth century, the curves defining the boundary arches as well as those of the diagonal arches all describe circle segments. Direct evidence shows that the vault was built on a formwork of wooden planks, which according to the shape of the vault surface must have been fixed upon centrings along the walls and the diagonal groins.

Our surveys in Speyer Cathedral give a similar picture of the geometric design of curves and surfaces [16]. The groin vaults in the aisles, dating from the mid-eleventh century, were the first cross-vaults built in monumental scale in Central Europe after the fall of the Roman empire (Fig. 8): they span 8.46 m and reach a clear height of 14.46 m. Already the fact that the plan of the bays is not square but rectangular shows that their geometric concept cannot be based on the antique scheme of intersecting cylindrical surfaces [17]. The geometric analyses of the scan data confirm that the design of theses vaults actually correspond with the concept we associate with Gothic vaulting (Fig. 9).

The bays are defined by semi-circular arches in the four sides upon a common springing level: transverse arches separating the bays and *lesenes* integrated in the arcade and outer wall, all in exposed stone. The transverse arches are higher than the wall arches due to their greater span. The boundaries of the vault describe semi-circles with the same radii as the stone arches but are slightly elevated. The surfaces of the vault are plastered – in particular the extra plaster applied to highlight the groins creates some problems for the analysis of the survey. Nevertheless it is clear that the groins describe circle segments in vertical planes. The design is rather straight-forward: the centres of the bays are placed on the same level as the boundaries in longitudinal direction (only in some cases slightly lower), and the elevations of the four diagonal arches are defined by the upper end point with horizontal tangent and the starting point in the corner, creating surbased segment arches (Fig. 9). The vault surfaces can be in principle described as being generated with straight lines tended between the curves at the groins and boundaries – hence, it can be supposed that the shells were built on a wooden formwork. We may assume that also in this case the temporary supporting structure consisted of a central pole erected on a wooden platform with diagonal centrings on which the planks of the formwork were mounted.

Figure 8: Vault in the aisle of Speyer Cathedral, eleventh century. The cross vaults on rectangular plan are designed with defined curves over the groins, like in Gothic vaults.

Analysing the shape of the vault surface, the straight lines in the shells in longitudinal direction can easily be observed. Particularly interesting is the profile of the ridges in transverse direction, which descend from the centre to the lower arches on the sides (Fig. 9, centre): while completely straight in the middle and lower portions, they show a concave curvature in the vicinity of the summit. In fact, if the ridge lines described straight lines descending directly from the summit to the boundary arches, near the summit they would remain below the level of the diagonal groins, resulting convex surfaces in the uppermost parts of the ridges – a problem that was described by scholars in the nineteenth century [18]. It is obvious that the builders of these vaults were aware of this problem and solved it systematically: according to the survey we suppose that an extra linear element was inserted in longitudinal direction between the diagonal centrings near the summit. Hence, not only for their great dimensions and sound construction, but also for the geometric expertise they show, we can conclude that the early cross vaults in Speyer cannot be considered just as some first attempt or experiment: rather, the "Gothic" scheme of vault design was already well established in the eleventh century.

Speyer Cathedral, promoted by the Emperors of the Salian dynasty and in its time the largest church in Central Europe, in the transept built ca. 1080-1105, contains another ground-breaking vault construction [19]. The two bays, approximately square in plan, each have a ribbed cross-vaults with the huge span of ca. 14 metres and a height of over 30 metres (Fig. 10). The ribs of dressed stone have rectangular section; there is no keystone, but one rib is continuous while the other two half-ribs are set against it. The elevations of the diagonal ribs clearly describe circle segments (Fig.11) – they are somewhat surbased, in contrast to the perfectly semi-circular boundary arches, but nevertheless have a considerable rise over their summits. The difference in respect to the vaults in the aisles is more than obvious: instead of defining the central summit level with the transverse arches creating very flat diagonal groins, here the elevations of the diagonal ribs, in analogy to the other arches in dressed stone, are nearly semi-circular (although actually it may not have been determined geometrically, but by an absolute measure given for the height of the summit). Hence, this design decisively gives rise to the diagonal stone rib – according to the idea of *ogive* discussed above.

The Design and Construction of the Vaults in Notre-Dame in Paris and the Development of Medieval Vaulting and Stereotomy: Surveys, Analyses and Experiments

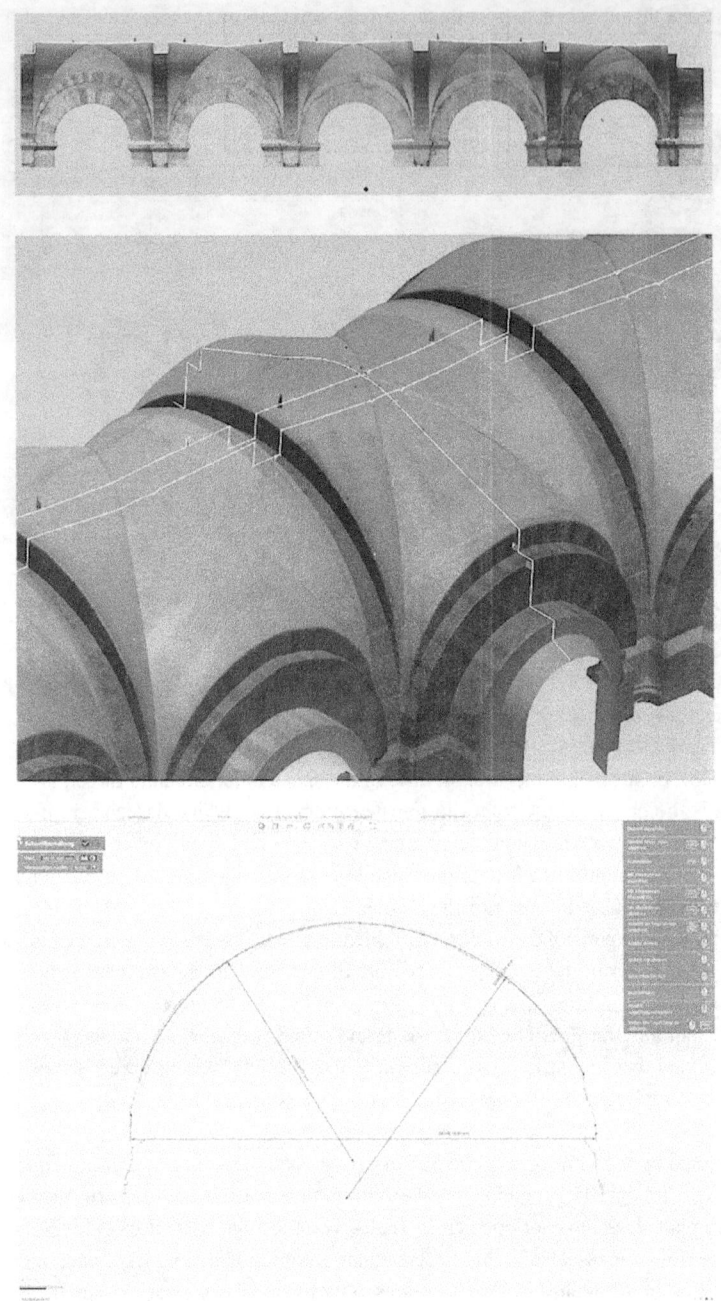

Figure 9: Geometric analysis of the cross vault in the aisle of Speyer Cathedral: the longitudinal ridges are straight and in most cases horizontal; the surfaces of the transverse shells are also defined by straight generating lines, avoiding the geometric problems that would occur near the summit; the groins are defined by circle segments in vertical planes.

Figure 10: Speyer Cathedral, rib vault in the transept.

The shape of the vault surface (Fig. 11) shows greater complexity than in the aisles, surely also due to the fact that in the formwork the great distance between the diagonal and boundary arches required additional centrings. In any case, the difficulties given by the inclination of the ridges rising to the summit of the vault are well mastered, and it can be definitely stated that the surfaces are not spherical but generated between the pre-determined curves of the arches.

The high vaults in the nave of Speyer Cathedral from the late eleventh century unfortunately no longer exist in the original. As rebuilt in the seventeenth century, they are cross vaults with diagonal groins in approximately square bays, each comprising two bays of the aisles, separated by transverse arches like in the vaults in the aisles built some decades earlier. As the remaining original transverse arch shows, they surely reproduce the original dimensions: 13,90 metres free span, 33 metres in height – which probably corresponds to 14 feet span and 100 feet height. From a historical point of view, a comparison between the high vaults in Speyer with those in Notre-Dame of Paris, built hundred years later, may be surprising. But it could be more than mere coincidence that the section of the nave in the great cathedral of the Emperor and in the cathedral of the King of France have the same dimensions.

The Design and Construction of the Vaults in Notre-Dame in Paris and the Development of Medieval Vaulting and Stereotomy: Surveys, Analyses and Experiments

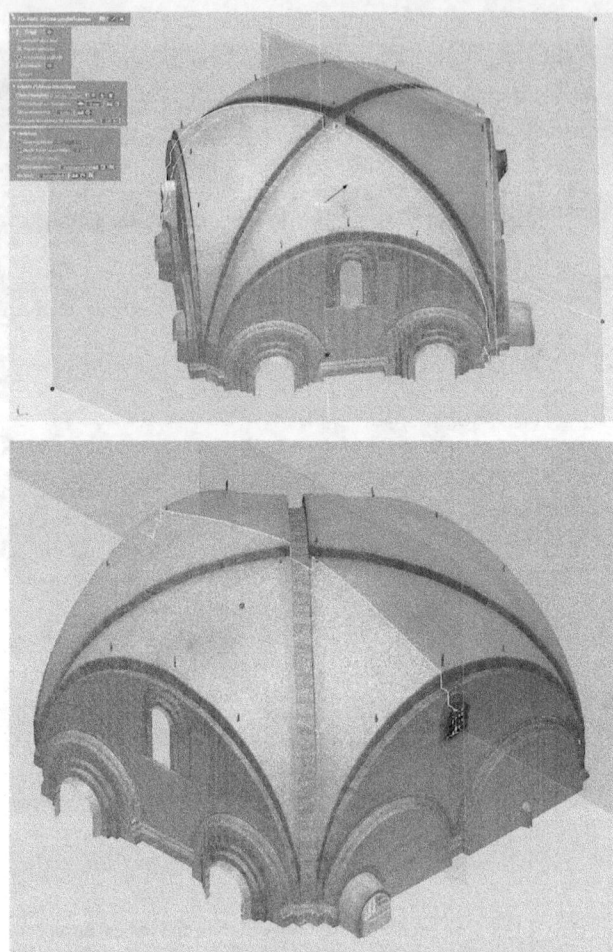

Figure 11: Geometric analyses of the vault in the transept, late eleventh century: the elevation of the ribs as well as of the boundaries describe circle segments and are nearly semi-circular; the surfaces are not spherical, but determined by the boundary curves.

Conclusions

For these considerations about the geometric concept of the vaults, which is essential for the architectural and structural design of these buildings and which, as we have seen, must be discussed in a much broader context than it has been done in previous research, the built objects are the only source of information. This underlines the importance of preserving the original structures – in particular in the vaults of Notre-Dame in Paris, all remaining parts must be maintained because they are historical documents of primary value, and reconstruction of the destroyed parts must be kept to the minimum and carried out with the greatest respect for the original. For this, thorough knowledge on the original structure, its design and building process is essential – these processes and practices determined its shape and every detail. It will still require a lot of scientific research.

This applies not only to the shape of the vaults and to the construction details, but also to the characteristics of the stonework that are intrinsically related to the intensions of the builders as well as to the practices of stone planning as application of knowledge in practical mathematics. Again, the built object is literally shaped by historical knowledge and working practice, and at the same time it is a source for understanding this knowledge and theses practices in history. Until now, little of all this is understood – what has become more that obvious already in the preliminary studies presented here, however, is that many features of the high vaults in Notre-Dame differ substantially from uniform image of the Gothic vault as it has been coined in the modern reception.

While from the preliminary research and from the considerations made above, the high vaults of Notre-Dame are positioned in a broadened context, we can also state a distinctive characteristic feature of the early Gothic church architecture in the Ile-de-France: This can be seen in the intrinsic relation between vault design and stone planning – like for instance in the effort of creating the regular pattern in the shells and of adding the specially tailored ridge stones. The exposed stonework, with the search for perfection or the aspiration for giving notion of perfection in the greatest complexity, is a guiding theme in the regional and geographic context (Fig. 12), and in particular a principal motif in the architecture of Notre-Dame. Elsewhere we sketched a possible interpretation as to the significance of this architecture [20], and we could also show the relation of the exercises described in Villard de Honnecourt's "Lodge Book" – the only known source on the practices of stone planning in the context of Gothic architecture and, as we have seen, correlating with the tasks and solutions we can find on the building – with the contents of the treatises of stereotomy that appear only centuries later [21].

This distinct feature, incidentally, was to remain an essential characteristic and a strong tradition in the architecture of this region way beyond the middle-ages, as the immense efforts of artful stereotomic solutions in the early modern Parisian architecture impressively demonstrate.

Figure 12: Advanced stereotomy in the abbey church of Saint-Martin-des-Champs in Paris, first half of twelfth century.

The Design and Construction of the Vaults in Notre-Dame in Paris and the Development of Medieval Vaulting and Stereotomy: Surveys, Analyses and Experiments

Acknowledgements

The experiments described here are carried out at the BTU at Cottbus by the authors with the collaboration of Juliane Henkel, Leo Koppe, Vladimir Korensky, Heike Bücherl and Jonas Lengenfeld. We wish to thank Dr Veronique Vergès-Belmin, Laboratoire de Recherches des Monuments Historiques (LRMH) in Champs-sur-Marne, for giving the opportunity to examine samples of fallen stones from Notre-Dame, as well as Pascal Prunet, Architecte en Chef des Monuments Historiques, for providing valuable information on the building. The laser scans in Speyer Cathedral were carried out in 2019 by Jonas Lengenfeld and Soheil Nazari, the geometric analyses have been performed by the authors. We thank the Architect to Speyer Cathedral, Hedwig Drabik M.A., and the Dombauamt Speyer for their support and kind permission.

Where not otherwise noted, all illustrations are by the authors.

References

[1] D. Wendland, "La construction et la stéréotomie des voutes médiévales de Notre-Dame : Les procédures pour la coupe de pierre dans les coques de double courbure au contexte de la histoire de la géométrie appliquée", proposed in the framework of the *Chantier scientifique CNRS Notre-Dame*.
[2] D. Wendland, M. Gielen, V. Korensky, "The construction and Stereotomy of the medieval vaults in Notre-Dame: Planning, stone-cutting and building of the double-curved shells", v. 2 pp. 333-340 in J. Mascarenhas-Mateus and A. Paula Pires (eds), *History of Construction Cultures*, Leiden: Balkema, 2021.
[3] P. Frankl, *Gothic Architecture* (1962), rev. by P. Crossley, New Haven: Yale Univ. Pr., 2001; N. Nußbaum, S. Lepsky, *Das gotische Gewölbe: Eine Geschichte seiner Form und Konstruktion*, Darmstadt: WB, 1999.
[4] This basic principle was already described by the scholars who in the nineteenth century established the modern scientific research of medieval architecture, in particular in the seminal essay by Robert Willis: "On the construction of the vaults in the middle-ages", *Transactions of the Royal Institute of British Architects*, 1. 1842, pp. 1-69. See also W. Müller, *Grundlagen gotischer Bautechnik*, München: Deutscher Kunstverlag, 1990.
[5] S. M. Crosby, *The Royal Abbey of Saint-Denis from Its Beginnings to the Death of Suger, 475-1151*. Yale Univ. Pr., 1987. D. Kimpel, R. Suckale, *Die gotische Architektur in Frankreich 1130-1270*, München: Hirmer, [1985] 1995.
[6] Kimpel, Suckale (Note 5); Nußbaum, Lepsky (Note 3).
[7] Frankl, *Gothic Architecture* (Note 3); Nußbaum, Lepsky, (Note 3) p. 109.
[8] C. Bruzelius, "The Construction of Notre-Dame in Paris", The Art Bulletin 69 (4) 1987: pp. 540-569; A. Erlande-Brandenburg, *Notre-Dame in Paris: Geschichte, Architektur, Skulptur*. Freiburg/Basel/Wien: Herder, 1992 [1991]; Nußbaum, Lepsky, (Note 3) p. 70.
[9] The considerations on the vault design are based on publications by Rocío Maira, who carried out a laser scan in this area, while arriving at a different interpretation: R. Maira, "Bóvedas sexpartitas. Los orígenes del gótico", Dissertation, Universidad Politécnica de Madrid, 2016; R. Maira, "The Evolution of the Knowledge of Geometry in Early Gothic Construction: The Development of the Sexpartite Vault in Europe", *International Journal of Architectural Heritage*, 11 (7), 2017, pp. 1005–1025; and elsewhere. Moreover, we recur to the drawings prior to the transformations in the 19th century in Erlande-Brandenburg 1992 (Note 8).
[10] For *ogive*, occasionally also spelled *augive*, cf. H. Hahnloser, *Villard de Honnecourt: kritische Gesamtausgabe des Bauhüttenbuches ms. fr 19093 der Pariser Nationalbibliothek* (2nd rev. and augm. ed.), Graz: Akad. Druck- u. Verlagsanstalt, 1972. p. 170-71, 380. We find the reference to lat. *augere* by far the most convincing explanation of this term. In the medieval sources, the term refers solely to the diagonal ribs of vaults, while its use for "pointed arch" is inexistent at least until the sixteenth century.
[11] For the procedure in complex late Gothic stone elements cf. D. Wendland, F. Degenève, "How to order fitting components for looping ribs: Design procedures for the stone members of complex Late Gothic vaults", pp. 159-170 in J. Campbell et al. (eds), *Building Histories: The Proceedings of the Fourth Conference of the Construction History Society*, Cambridge 2017; D. Wendland, *Steinerne Ranken, wunderbare Maschinen: Entwurf und Planung spätgotischer Gewölbe und ihrer Einzelteile*. With contributions by M. Aranda Alonso, A. Kobe and M.J. Ventas Sierra, Petersberg: Imhof, 2019.

[12] Wendland, *Steinerne Ranken*, (Note 11). See also D. Wendland, M. J. Ventas Sierra, "Zum Bau figurierter Gewölbe – eine Anleitung im Werkmeisterbuch des Rodrigo Gil de Hontañón", pp. 244-72 in S. Bürger, B. Klein (eds), *Werkmeister der Spätgotik: Personen, Amt und Image*, Darmstadt: WB, 2010.

[13] Wendland, Gielen, Korensky (Note 2); D. Wendland, *Lassaulx und der Gewölbebau mit selbsttragenden Mauerschichten. Neumittelalterliche Architektur um 1825-1848*. Petersberg: Imhof, 2008.

[14] See Note 4. On the research history Wendland, *Lassaulx* (Note 13). Among the early scholars, in particular Ungewitter emphazises that the geometric concept of Gothic vaults is not necessarily linked to the architectural style and pointed arches, but can be perfectly associated with semi-circular arches: G. G. Ungewitter, *Lehrbuch der gothischen Constructionen*, Leipzig: Weigel, 1859-1864.

[15] U. Heckner, H. Meyer, "Was macht das Holz im Gewölbe? Spuren von Bau- und Lehrgerüsten am Westbau von St. Pantaleon in Köln", lecture at the symposium *Lehrgerüste und Gewölbe-Bau* (C. Voigts, S. Holzer), ETH Zurich, 4 October 2021.

[16] The survey of the remaining medieval vaults in Speyer by laser-scanning was carried out in autumn 2021.

[17] The idea that the design of these vaults is based on cylinders has been stated many times in the scientific literature, although it is clearly visible from the shape of the groins that this cannot be true.

[18] First by J.C. von Lassaulx in 1846, later by K. Mohrmann. Wendland, *Lassaulx* (Note 13).

[19] For the dating and construction details: D. v. Winterfeld, "Die Rippengewölbe des Domes zu Speyer", *Jahrbuch des Vereins für christliche Kunst in München*, 12.1988, pp. 101-112; D. v. Winterfeld, "Offene Fragen der Bauforschung zum Speyrer Dom", pp. 135-157 in M. Müller, M. Untermann, D. v. Winterfeld (eds), *Der Dom zu Speyer. Konstruktion, Funktion und Rezeption zwischen Salierzeit und Historismus*, Darmstadt: WBG, 2012.

[20] Wendland, Gielen, Korensky (Note 2).

[21] Wendland, *Steinerne Ranken* (Note 12). See also J. Lengenfeld, D. Wendland, "Die Planung der komplexen Werksteinkonstruktion im Bergfried der Schönburg – das Werk eines Naumburger Meisters", in proceedings *Fünfte Jahrestagung der Gesellschaft für Bautechnikgeschichte Zürich 2021*. Petersberg: Michael Imhof (forthcoming).

English Master Builders in The Iberian Peninsula in The 13th Century: The Construction of The Sexpartite Vaults of Lincoln Cathedral and Their Influence on The Monastery of Las Huelgas Reales in Burgos

Rocío Maira-Vidal
Institute of History. Spanish National Research Council (IH-CSIC)

Abstract

Lincoln Cathedral represents one of the most interesting examples of sexpartite vault construction (1210-50). This type of vaulting was used to cover a variety of spaces in the building generating diverse structures with a common feature: diagonal ribs in the shape of pointed arches. This feature makes their geometric design unique in England, while in the rest of Europe there are only seven similar examples, four of them located on the Iberian Peninsula. The geometric system used in Lincoln marked a very significant development in ribbed vault construction. The overall thrust of the structure was reduced, and the assembly process simplified while providing greater volumetric flexibility to adapt to the space to be covered.

The Monastery of Las Huelgas in Burgos was built by Alfonso VIII and his wife Eleanor Plantagenet, daughter of Henry II of England and Eleanor of Aquitaine. While the royal charter founding the monastery, granted in 1187, still survives, the construction commencement date is not clear. Some researchers conclude that it was as late as the first half of the thirteenth century. My analysis allows me to affirm that construction cannot have begun before the second quarter of the thirteenth century and that the technology used was probably imported into the Iberian Peninsula by the master builder who worked on Lincoln Cathedral. However, the evolution detected in the techniques used in the Spanish monastery when compared to those of the English cathedral would indicate that the new stone cutting methods being implemented were those that were in the early stages of development in France in the thirteenth century, implying the presence of two master builders, the other being of French origin.

Geometric and construction features of European sexpartite vaults

Sexpartite vaults are typical of the early Gothic. They were mainly used between the second half of the twelfth century and the first half of the thirteenth century. My doctoral thesis focused on the study of their geometry and construction, for which I previously identified the vaults remaining in Europe in order to carry out an in-depth analysis of those found in France, Spain, England, Germany, Switzerland and Italy [1]. The case-by-case analysis was based on measurements taken using total station, laser scanner and photogrammetry (Fig. 1). Sexpartite vaults were mostly built with two semi-circular diagonal ribs with their centres on a level with the impost [2]. Of the 119 cases studied, pointed geometries were used for the diagonal ribs in just eight buildings, built between the twelfth and thirteenth centuries: Lincoln Cathedral, three French buildings and four Spanish buildings located in the northern and central areas of the Iberian Peninsula. The buildings located in France date from the latter third of the twelfth century. These isolated examples are the Abbey of Sainte-Croix in Bordeaux, the Abbey of Saint-Georges in Boscherville and the Church of Sainte Madeleine in Vézelay and they did not have a major impact in France, despite the enormous subsequent expansion of the typology [3]. Two of the Spanish examples, the Collegiate Church of Santa Maria de Roncesvalles and the Church of San Saturnino in Pamplona, belonged to the Kingdom of Navarre and two, Cuenca Cathedral and the Monastery of Las Huelgas Reales in Burgos, belonged to the Kingdom of Castile. The French churches set a precedent, yet they were built more than half a century before the other buildings, which are all contemporary to each other. These findings suggest a transfer of

English Master Builders in The Iberian Peninsula in The 13th Century: The Construction of The Sexpartite Vaults of Lincoln Cathedral and Their Influence on The Monastery of Las Huelgas Reales in Burgos

construction knowledge between the Kingdom of England and the Iberian Peninsula in the first half of the thirteenth century.

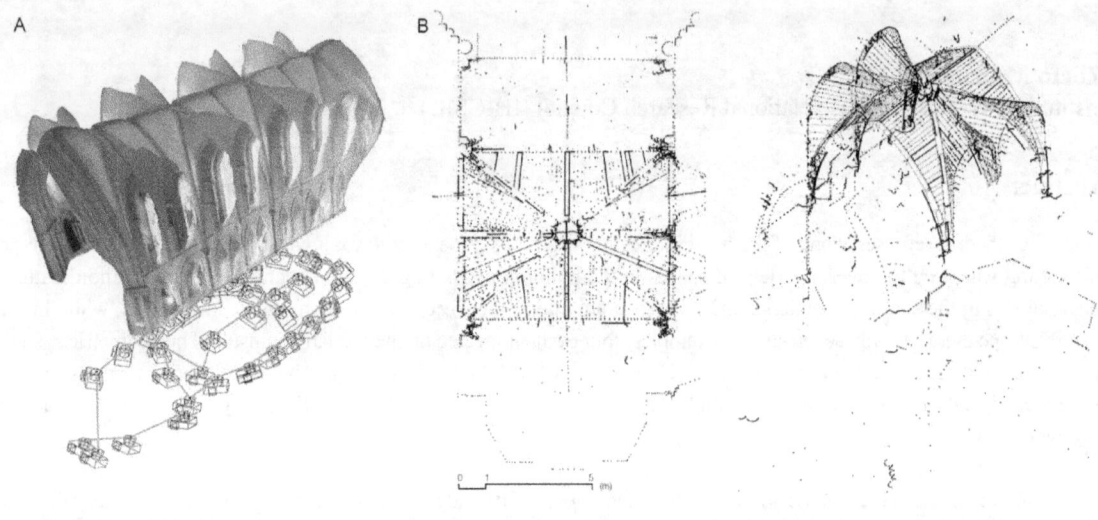

Figure 1: Photogrammetric and laser total station measurements in Lincoln Cathedral (A) and in the Monastery of Las Huelgas Reales de Burgos (B). Author's models.

From the thirteenth century onwards, construction techniques such as the use of *tas-de-charges* on the vault supports and the use of the bevel for stone cutting, developed significantly and were implemented quite quickly. In older sexpartite vaults, the ribs converged on their support as separate elements, acting as springers. *Tas-de-charges* emerged in the early thirteenth century [4]. At the Monastery of Las Huelgas Reales de Burgos (Spain, after 1220), Cuenca Cathedral (Spain, 1225) and the Church of Notre Dame de Dijon (France, 1220-40), the supports consist of *tas-de-charges* that are remarkable for their configuration and size. They are made up of one or two curved, very high stones, while the traditional solution for these joints comprise a larger number, usually five or six, of short and straight stones placed on top of one another [5]. We also observed that these three examples and eight more French vaults are the only cases where the bevel had been used as a cutting tool. Two of the French structures date back to the twelfth century while the other examples were built in the thirteenth century. In all other European sexpartite vaults, the *voussoirs* were cut with a set square, so they are not curved but rather straight. Specialised stonemasons with a sound knowledge of the construction innovations that were being developed at that precise point in time were required for the use of a bevel.

Despite the considerable distance that separates these three European regions, Lincoln, Dijon, Burgos and Cuenca, some researchers, such as Street [6], Lambert [7] and more recently Palomo [8], have observed stylistic similarities and historical aspects that provide a link between these works. Sculpture and decorative details could easily be reproduced by itinerant craftsmen who had visited one, or more, of the buildings. However, the geometry and construction systems employed required specific technical knowledge, which suggests that the same master builder or stone workshops would have been involved in the construction of these buildings, where the techniques used were unique and advanced for the time in which they were executed. Having observed these techniques, we can confirm this relationship, which other disciplines had already been suggesting (Fig. 2).

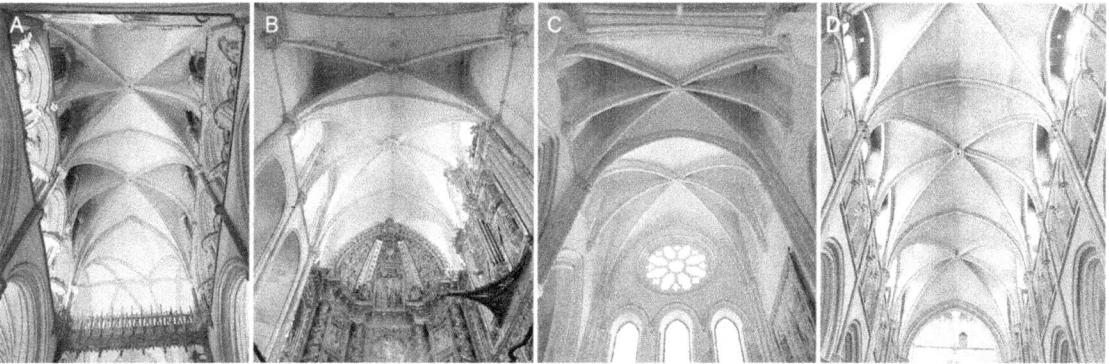

Figure 2: Sexpartite vaults in Lincoln Cathedral (eastern transept, A), the Monastery of Las Huelgas Reales de Burgos (B), Cuenca Cathedral (transept, C) and the church of Notre Dame de Dijon (D). Author's photographs.

New contributions to the sexpartite vault from the master builder at Lincoln Cathedral

The origin of the sexpartite vault goes back to twelfth century France, where numerous examples can be found. It subsequently spread throughout the rest of Europe, from the thirteenth century onwards, but its use was still rare and scattered [9]. In England, it was only used in five buildings: St. Peter's Norman Church in Tickencote (1160) and in Canterbury, Rochester, Lincoln and Durham cathedrals (in the Chapel of the Nine Altars). The only English sexpartite vaults that reproduce French geometric designs are found in Canterbury Cathedral [10]. The design of those located above the choir is the same as the design used for the vaults at Cathedral of Sens, the master builder's place of origin [11]. Those covering the arms of the transept were built based on the geometry of the Cathedral of Notre Dame de Paris, also designed by William de Sens before he abandoned his work there. His successor, of English origin, employed different geometries in the rest of the eastern end of the cathedral, taking the first steps toward what were to be typical English examples of perpendicular Gothic, which were subsequently used in the sexpartite vaults of Rochester [12].

Lincoln Cathedral has traditionally been regarded as an example of the English school, as pointed out by Viollet Le Duc himself [13]. However, the geometry of its sexpartite vaults, where all the ribs are pointed arches, differs from the other English examples (Fig. 3). In the sanctuary of Canterbury Cathedral and in Rochester Cathedral the diagonal ribs are semi-circular or flattened, and the geometry of the remainder varies, with pointed, semi-circular or flattened ribs [14]. Lincoln's Norman Cathedral collapsed in 1185 after a minor earthquake [15, 16, 17, 18]. The new geometry used in its reconstruction could have arisen from the need to find more stable structures by considerably reducing the horizontal thrust (Fig. 4). It would also have provided greater flexibility for the design, since the height of the boss could be determined at will as it did not depend on the diameter of the diagonal ribs, which are not semi-circular. In the case of the eastern transept in Lincoln Cathedral the boss is 2.35 metres higher than it would have been if its ribs had been semi-circular, while in the western transept it is 0.70 metres higher. This feature allows the walls to be higher, letting more light into the building. The pointed geometry also makes it possible to adapt the vaulting more easily to the floor plan, shaping more slender structures where the proportion of the wall ribs stands out as very high in relation to the span they cover. The bilobed or asymmetrical pointed arch shapes of these ribs are unusual in continental Gothic.

English Master Builders in The Iberian Peninsula in The 13th Century: The Construction of The Sexpartite Vaults of Lincoln Cathedral and Their Influence on The Monastery of Las Huelgas Reales in Burgos

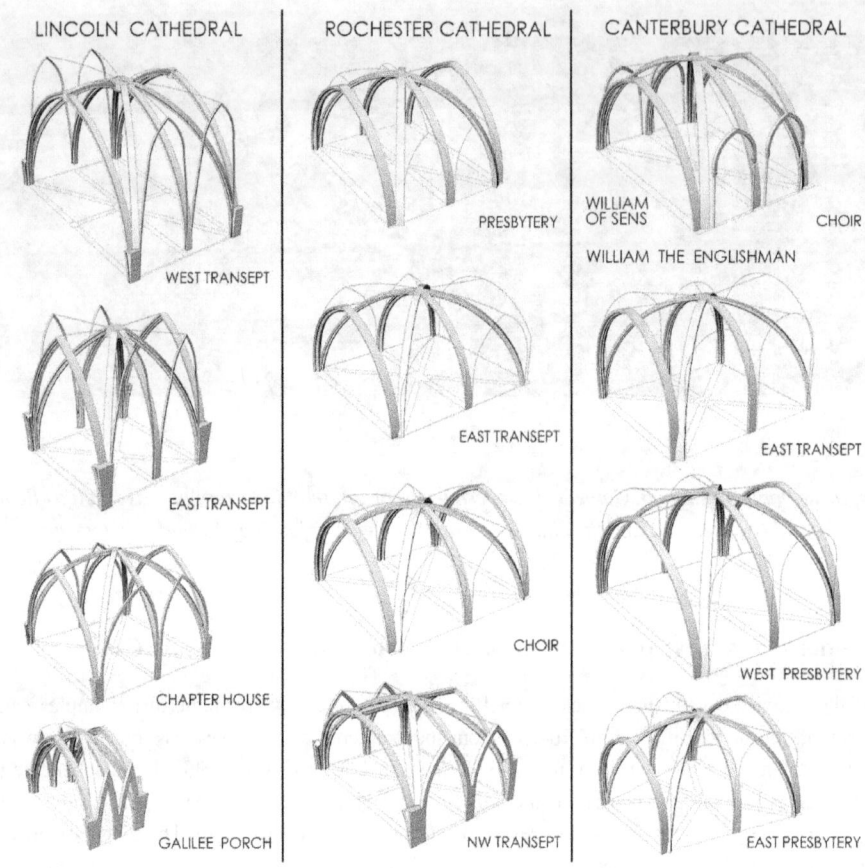

Figure 3: English sexpartite vaults. Author's models.

Figure 4: Sexpartite vaults in Lincoln Cathedral (A eastern transept, B western transept, C chapter house and D Galilee Porch). Author's photographs.

In continental Gothic, the sexpartite vaults present in a building share a common geometry regardless of the space to be covered. On the other hand, in England vaults differ depending on where they are located inside the building, thus enriching the cathedral's space which is perceived as a distinct series of areas with different structural and compositional features. The diagonal ribs in the vaults of Lincoln Cathedral are pointed and their centres are level with the impost. The difference between the vaults covering the different parts of the building arises from the proportion of the vault plan dimensions and from the geometry of the other ribs. The central rib and the transverse ribs are also pointed, and their centres are level with the impost or stilted to a greater or lesser degree, depending on each case. The original designs of the transept vaults are particularly striking since the support of their central ribs is located at a higher level than the other ribs and the ridge ribs descend towards the central boss and are (sometimes) even curved.

All the ribs of the vault except the wall ribs, are standardised in the sexpartite vaults at Lincoln Cathedral. In order to design them with the same curvature, the master builder stilted the ribs from the impost, adding between 20 and 85 centimetres. This system made it possible to use the same type of centring to build the different ribs, simplifying assembly and reducing the cost. In the vaults of the transepts, both the transverse and the central ribs were stilted in order to reach the desired height using the same curvature as the diagonal ribs. The central rib in the western transept vaults was stilted above the level of the impost that supported the diagonal and transverse ribs, although this central rib is flattened in relation to its level of support, which is higher than the impost of the other ribs (Fig. 5). Only the central rib in the vaults of the chapter house and over the Porch of Galilee is stilted. The centres of the other ribs remain on the level of the impost (Fig. 6). This system of standardisation based on small stilts was imported from France, although in the French examples the ribs were raised slightly less, approximately one foot (30 cm).

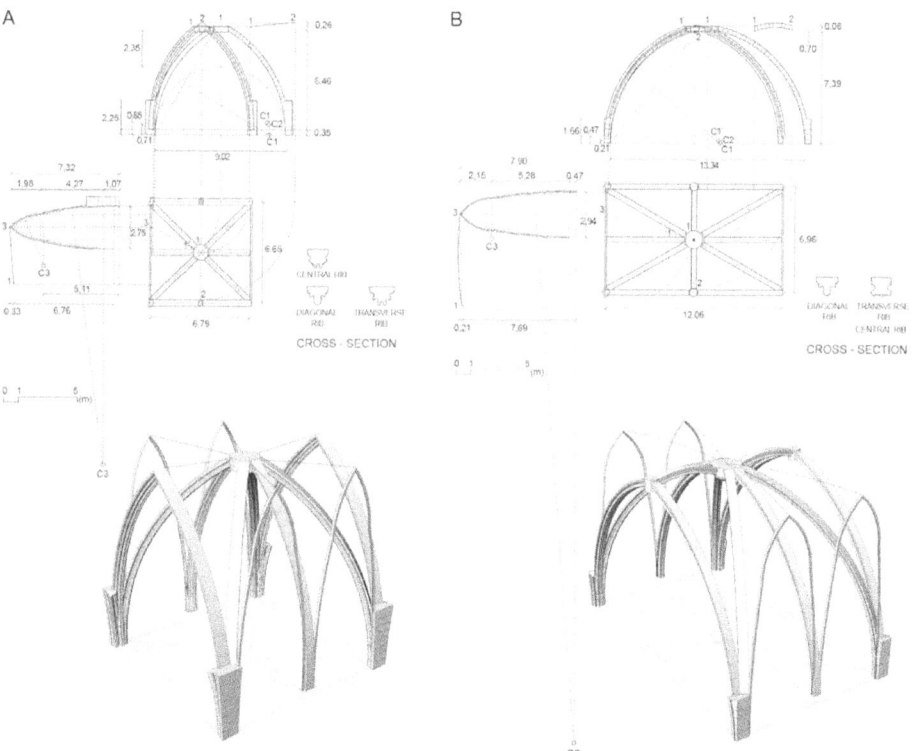

Figure 5: Geometric design and 3D model of the vaults over the eastern (A) and western (B) transepts of Lincoln Cathedral. Author's drawings.

English Master Builders in The Iberian Peninsula in The 13th Century: The Construction of The Sexpartite Vaults of Lincoln Cathedral and Their Influence on The Monastery of Las Huelgas Reales in Burgos

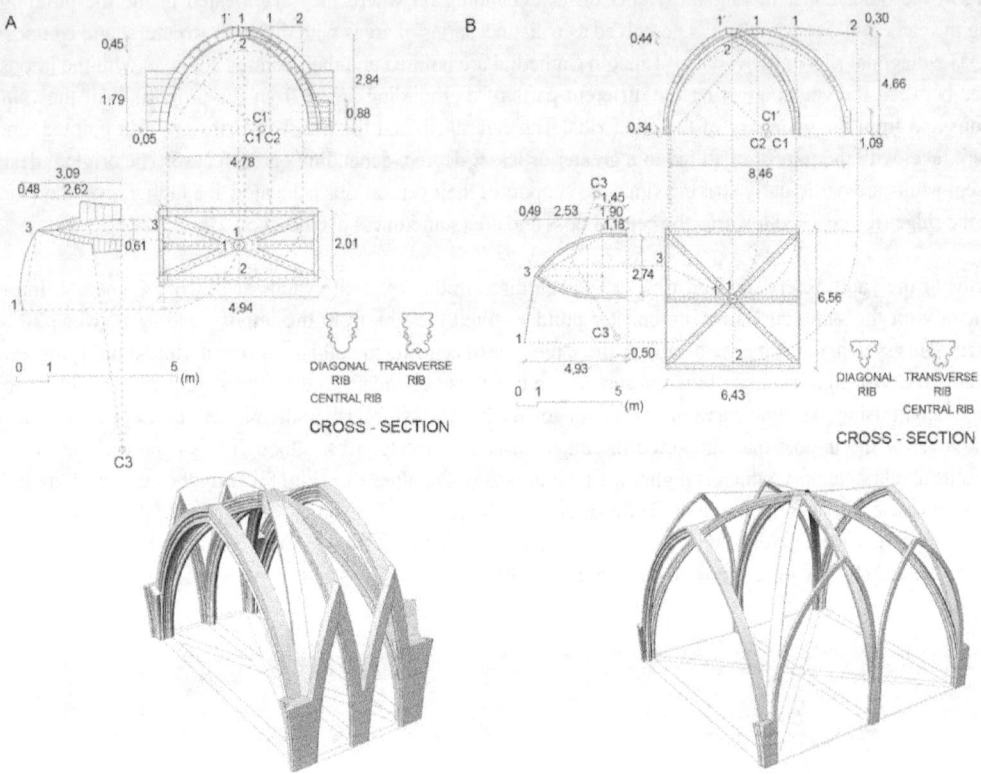

Figure 6: Geometric design and 3D model of the vaults over the Galilee Porch (A) and the chapter house (B) of Lincoln Cathedral. Author's drawings.

Lincoln Cathedral and the Canterbury Cathedral choir vaults, designed by William de Sens, are the only two examples among the English sexpartite vaults where French standardisation was employed. In the transept of Canterbury Cathedral, designed by William de Sens and built by William the Englishman, standardisation is partial, only being used for the transverse and central ribs, and it was not implemented using small stilts since the ribs were raised more than a metre and a half above the impost. In the sexpartite vaults of the Canterbury Cathedral sanctuary and in Rochester Cathedral, to achieve their standardisation the ribs were tilted forward. Standardisation is partial in both buildings where only some ribs share the same curvature, constituting the origin of typical English standardisation [19], which is not found at all in Lincoln. The use of French standardisation in Lincoln Cathedral is very significant given that this method was rare in England, as the analysis of data shows. Speculation has arisen about the possible French origin of the master builder of Lincoln Cathedral [20]. He would definitely have trained in French workshops or had some relationship with the construction trends that came from France. He may even have known about earlier French examples, such as the Abbey of Saint-Georges in Boscherville, located on the French coast opposite Great Britain, near Caen. There is no doubt that he had a good knowledge of French standardisation and of the sexpartite vault, which must have driven him to implement new designs for this typology in the English cathedral. But the original design and compositional freedom at Lincoln, very different from French constructions, could indicate his English origin.

English master builders on the Iberian Peninsula: Lincoln geometries exported to Burgos and Cuenca

The arrival of Queen Eleonor Plantagenet on the Iberian Peninsula must have given rise to an exchange of artistic influence between the kingdoms of England and Castile in the latter decades of the twelfth century and the early decades of the thirteenth century. Lincoln Cathedral, the Monastery of Las Huelgas Reales de Burgos and Cuenca Cathedral provide evidence of the technical knowledge transfer between the two regions. Previous research undertaken in other disciplines, mainly based on stylistic and formal analysis, establishes a relationship between these buildings [21]. Palomo and Ruiz Souza argue that the master builder Richard of English or Aquitaine origin, could have participated in the Burgos monastery until his departure in 1203. According to their study, much of the building would have been completed by 1214, before the monarchs died [22]. The transept at Cuenca Cathedral was built toward the end of the first quarter of the thirteenth century, also by a foreign master builder whose place of origin is unknown [23]. Palomo affirms that Cuenca Cathedral was influenced by France and England, finding similarities with Canterbury Cathedral and the Church of Notre Dame de Dijon [24].

Based on my geometrical analysis, I can not only confirm the relationship between Lincoln, Cuenca and Burgos, but also suggest new hypotheses for the construction dates of the cenobium at Burgos. The geometric similarities between the different vaults indicate that the same master builder or workshops were involved in the three buildings. Sexpartite vaults were usually built over sections that were almost square, rectangular proportions being rare. In Lincoln Cathedral, the vaults built over the western transept and those covering the Galilee Porch are markedly rectangular, especially in the latter case, where the distance between the support walls is almost 2.5 times greater than the length of the short side of the vault. The vaults of the transept at Cuenca Cathedral and of the Monastery of Las Huelgas Reales are also rectangular, although less obviously so (Table 1). In the case of Cuenca Cathedral, the constraints of the plot may have given rise to this feature, since it is assumed that this was the location of the mosque before the city was conquered [25]. The vaults at Cuenca and Burgos share the same type of geometry as the English cathedral, where all the ribs are pointed arches. The use of this particular design allows us to confirm the relationship between these three buildings (Fig. 7).

Table 1: Proportion and height of sexpartite vaults in the study cases.

	Construction date	Plan (width x length) (m)	Height of the boss from the floor (m)	Height of the boss from the impost line (m)
Lincoln Cathedral (western transept)	1210	12.06 x 6.96	21.84	7.39
Lincoln Cathedral (eastern transept)	1220-40	6.79 x 6.65	20.87	6.71
Lincoln Cathedral (chapter house)	1220-35	6.43 x 6.56	12.32	4.66
Lincoln Cathedral (Galilee Porch)	1240-50	2.00 x 4.94	7	2.84
Monastery of Las Huelgas Reales de Burgos (sanctuary)	After 1220 *	8.12 x 6.37	16	5.35
Cuenca Cathedral (transept)	1225 *	8.94 x 6.47	19.50	6.65
Notre Dame de Dijon	1220-40	8.20 x 8.20	18.06	4.95

*Dates proposed by the author

English Master Builders in The Iberian Peninsula in The 13th Century: The Construction of The Sexpartite Vaults of Lincoln Cathedral and Their Influence on The Monastery of Las Huelgas Reales in Burgos

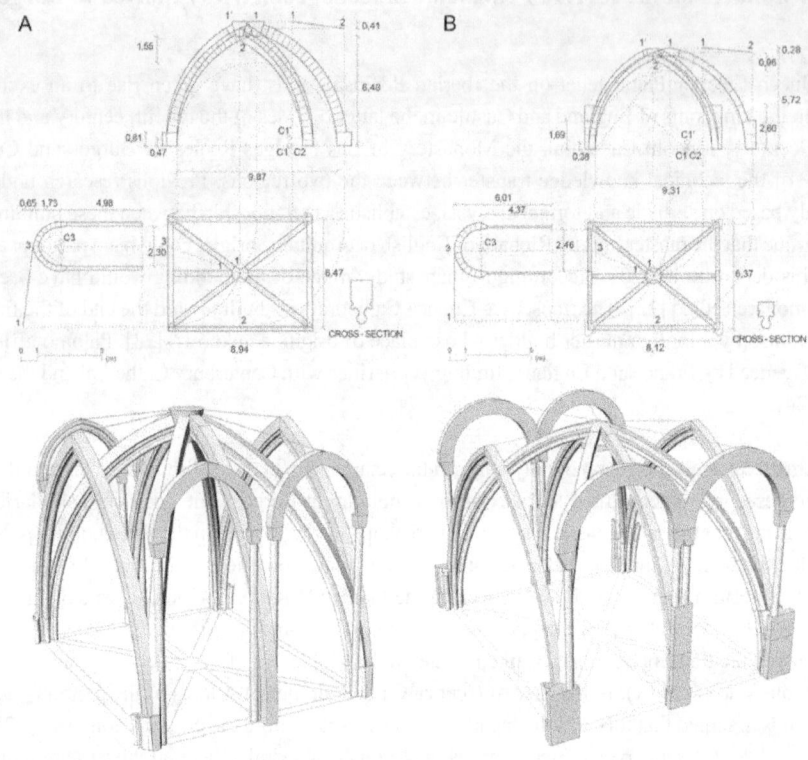

Figure 7: Geometric design and 3D model of the vaults over the transept of Cuenca Cathedral (A) and the Monastery of Las Huelgas Reales de Burgos (B). Author's drawings.

The same standardisation system was also used for the ribs in all three cases, using small stilts. My in-depth study of Spanish sexpartite vaults enabled me to affirm that the method of standardisation used in the High Middle Ages on the Iberian Peninsula was the French method and its use therefore does not indicate that the English master builder of Lincoln had participated. However, the standardisation of the transept of Cuenca Cathedral shows a particular characteristic that differentiates it from the French examples, relating it more to English techniques. The difference lies in the stilt used for the central rib, which enabled it to reach the height of the boss with the same curvature as the other ribs. This stilt, measuring nearly half a metre, far exceeds the usual 30 cm found in examples located in France (Fig. 7). The same occurs in Lincoln, where this stilt is also much longer. In addition, the design used in the sexpartite vaults of Cuenca Cathedral differs according to their location: eastern end, transept or nave. This characteristic is typical of English Gothic. Construction in Cuenca may have lasted throughout the thirteenth century, which could explain the heterogeneity of the designs, while in Lincoln the spaces covered with sexpartite vaults would have been built in under fifty years.

When comparing the stereotomy, we found similarities in the size of some elements such as the bosses, where the central sculpted component is particularly voluminous and the perimeter arms very short (Fig. 8). However, the differences are more significant than the similarities: the *tas-de-charges* and the *voussoirs* were cut using more advanced stonemasonry techniques in the Spanish examples, implying that the technological transfer must have come from Lincoln to the Iberian Peninsula. Had the technological transfer taken place in reverse, there would be evidence of these stonemasonry techniques in the English cathedral as well as the same geometry (Table 2). The *tas-de-charges* of Las Huelgas Reales de Burgos comprise one or two very high stones and the rib *voussoirs* are extraordinarily long, some even nearly one and a half metres in length. The *voussoirs* in Cuenca Cathedral are smaller but they are also curved. This type of stonework was executed using a bevel, a tool that allowed the stones to be cut with the same curvature as the arch. In Lincoln they are shorter, between 25 and 35 cm, and were cut without curvature. Their *tas-de-charges* were built by placing seven or eight short, straight pieces on top of one another (Fig. 9). Sexpartite vaults were usually built using straight stones cut with a set square, a technique that was gradually abandoned in favour of the bevel from the thirteenth century onwards [26].

Figure 8: Comparison of bosses in Lincoln Cathedral (A), the Monastery of Las Huelgas Reales de Burgos (B) and Cuenca Cathedral (C). Author's photographs.

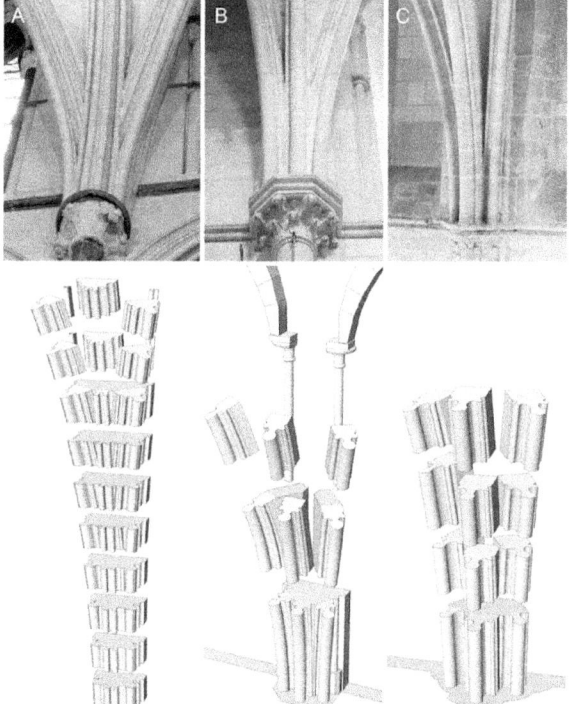

Figure 9: Comparison of the tas-de-charges of the corner supports in Lincoln Cathedral (A), the Monastery of Las Huelgas Reales de Burgos (B) and Cuenca Cathedral (C). Author's drawings and photographs.

Table 2: Voussoirs, tas-de-charges and webs size in the studied vaults.

	Voussoir length (cm)	Webs length x width (cm)	Height of each tas-de-charge / Total height of tas-de-charges from impost line (cm) / Number of blocks
Lincoln Cathedral (western transept)	32-36 (straight voussoirs)	No data	Corner tas-de-charges 33 / 166 (5 blocks)
Lincoln Cathedral (eastern transept)	26-30 (straight voussoirs)	30-40 x 15 Medium size stone blocks and small slabs	Corner tas-de-charges 28 / 225 (8 blocks)
Lincoln Cathedral (chapter house)	25-30 (straight voussoirs)	15-20 x 10 Small slabs	Corner tas-de-charges 27 /109 (4 blocks)
Lincoln Cathedral (Galilee Porch)	18-30 (straight voussoirs)	No data	Central tas-de-charge 18 / 88 (5 blocks) Corner tas-de-charges 26 / 179 (7 blocks)
Monastery of Las Huelgas Reales de Burgos (sanctuary)	80-145 (curved voussoirs)	80-314 x 20 Long prismatic stones	Central tas-de-charge 130 / 260 (2 blocks) West corner tas-de-charges 84 / 167 (2 blocks) East corner tas-de-charges 118 / 118 (1 blocks)
Cuenca Cathedral (transept)	22-50 (curved voussoirs)	30-100 x 20 Medium size stone blocks	Corner tas-de-charges 81 / 81 (1 block)
Notre Dame de Dijon	35-60 (curved voussoirs)	No size data Medium size stone blocks	Central tas-de-charge 233 / 233 (1 block) Corner tas-de-charges 78 / 156 (2 blocks)

French influence on the implementation of new stone cutting techniques at Las Huelgas Reales de Burgos and in the transept at Cuenca Cathedral

The length of the *voussoirs* at the Monastery of Las Huelgas Reales de Burgos makes the stereotomy unusual. To date, I have not found any other sexpartite vault that has been built using stones ranging from 0.80 to 1.45 metres in length. Las Huelgas Reales represents a unique case in Europe. The *tas-de-charges* of its central supports were executed using two very high stones, rising to 2.60 metres from the support. The four corners consist of one or two stones placed one on top of the other, each approximately one metre high (Figs 9-10). The weight of these stones was considerable, which would have complicated lifting them to the height of assembly (Table 2). These characteristics indicate that the master builder had significant expertise in organising and designing the infrastructure and logistics for construction.

The stereotomy of Cuenca Cathedral is less developed. Most of its voussoirs do not exceed 30 cm in length, which led me to conclude, erroneously in my first analysis, that a bevel had not been used in this case. However, some voussoirs are longer, approximately half a metre in length, and their tas-de-charges are as high as 0.81 metres. These stones are curved and were cut using a bevel (Table 2). It appears that mixed techniques were used in this case. It is possible that each block removed from the quarry would have been a different size and the smaller ones would have been used for cutting the shorter voussoirs, while larger blocks would have been needed for the rest. The use of mixed techniques is strange and perhaps responds to a lack of expertise in the cutting method and its associated advantages. These vaults do not have tas-de-charges on the central supports but do have them in the corners. The solution used for this joint, based on a single very high tas-de-charge, reproduces the system used at Las Huelgas on a smaller scale (Fig. 9). However, here the stonemasonry and configuration are not as well developed and the tas-de-charge is not as high as the solution at Burgos, preventing the advantages of this type of support from being fully exploited. Higher tas-de-charges reduce the thrust of the vaults since they are cut to lie horizontally. Structurally they function like walls, generating vertical thrust. Horizontal thrust begins where the tas-de-charges end and the inclined bed joints of each rib's individual voussoirs begin. Therefore, higher tas-de-charges reduce the thrust of the structure. The construction techniques present in Las Huelgas Reales were used at Cuenca Cathedral, although to a lesser degree of development, and imply that a master builder with some, but not a full, knowledge of these new systems must have participated. The master builder concerned had probably been involved in the construction of Las Huelgas and tried to reproduce the techniques learned there, but with less success.

The perfection and delicacy of the solutions of Las Huelgas Reales de Burgos indicate the participation of experienced master builders who imported new stone cutting techniques that were unknown up till then on the Iberian Peninsula. In Europe, there is only one other case with similar stereotomic solutions: the Church of Notre Dame de Dijon. The tas-de-charges of these French vaults were also solved using one or two curved stones, depending on whether they were central or corner supports, placed on top of each other. The central tas-de-charge reaches heights up to 2.33 metres while each of the two stones that make up the corner tas-de-charges are approximately 0.78 metres high and are divided into two symmetrical halves. The voussoirs are also curved pieces cut with a bevel, although unlike the voussoirs of Las Huelgas Reales they do not exceed 0.60 metres in length (Table 2). This establishes the French example as a precedent to the one at Burgos. Probably the master builders of Dijon, who were very familiar with the new vault construction systems that were beginning to be implemented, exported these solutions to Las Huelgas Reales de Burgos, where they developed them to the full (Fig. 10).

English Master Builders in The Iberian Peninsula in The 13th Century: The Construction of The Sexpartite Vaults of Lincoln Cathedral and Their Influence on The Monastery of Las Huelgas Reales in Burgos

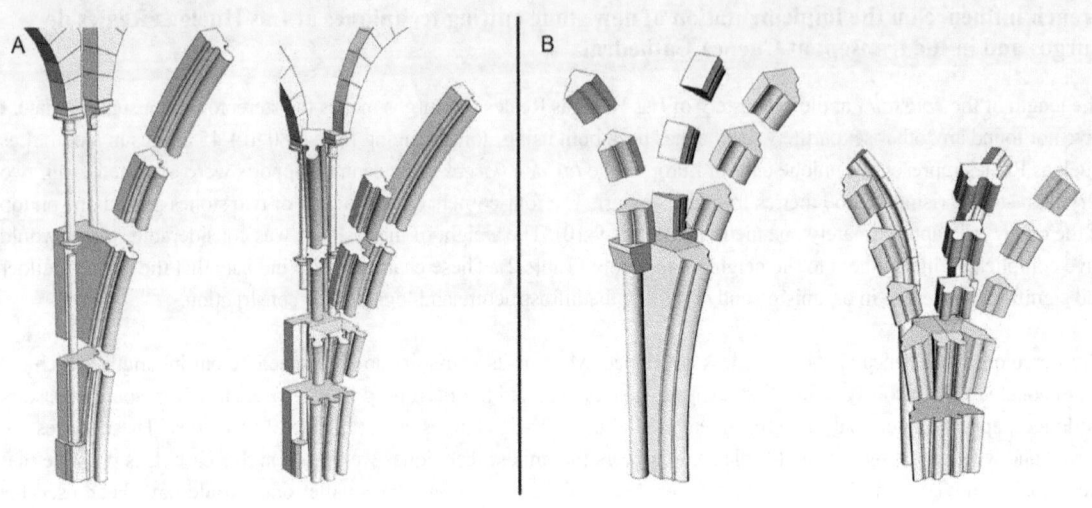

Figure 10: Comparison of the tas-de-charges in the Monastery of Las Huelgas Reales de Burgos (A) and the church of Notre Dame de Dijon (B). Author's drawings.

Robert Willis claimed that the webs in early cross-ribbed vaults were smaller in contrast to later structures [27]. The webbing that remains exposed in Lincoln Cathedral enabled me to affirm that very small stone blocks were used, in some cases small slabs. In the Church of Notre Dame de Dijon and in Cuenca Cathedral the webbing stones are a medium size, which is normal in early cross-ribbed vaults. On the other hand, the web surfaces of Las Huelgas Reales de Burgos were built with long prismatic stones between 0.80 and 3.14 metres in length. This is again an original and unique solution, where the stones were lintelled between the support ribs and their enormous size and slender proportions complicated stonemasonry and assembly.

Construction knowledge transfer in the Middle Ages: Conclusions

The comparative study of the evolution of construction systems in different European buildings provides the opportunity to analyse how technical knowledge developed and expanded in Europe. Political relationships between the different territories and the itinerant nature of master builders and workshops contributed to a heterogeneous expansion of the use of new techniques. The innovative construction systems that developed almost simultaneously in regions located far apart allows connections between the different buildings to be established.

The English master builder of Lincoln Cathedral developed a new geometric typology for the sexpartite vault, which allowed the thrust to be reduced and the vault to adapt better to the space. The original and heterogeneous designs, characteristic of English Gothic, make this construction very different from the few earlier French examples dating from the latter third of the twelfth century. These older designs had no subsequent impact on the French sexpartite vault typologies, which are completely different from the Lincoln example. The unique design of the English cathedral and the use of French standardisation with larger-than-usual stilts, suggest that Lincoln's master builder was of English origin, although his training would have been influenced by French techniques. His later participation in the construction of the

Monastery of Las Huelgas Reales de Burgos enabled this new geometric solution to be imported to the Iberian Peninsula, promoting its expansion throughout other areas in the Kingdom of Castile and the Kingdom of Navarre. The stereotomy that was used at Las Huelgas de Burgos places this Spanish monastery at the forefront of the stone cutting techniques employed in the thirteenth century, far superior to those used at Lincoln Cathedral. Innovation in stone cutting processes began in France in the thirteenth century. The fact that both techniques converge in the monastery gives support to my findings concerning the direction of transmission of new construction knowledge: from England and France to the Iberian Peninsula. This fact is of particular importance when determining the possible date of commencement of construction at the Monastery of Las Huelgas Reales de Burgos, which must have been later than the beginning of construction at Lincoln and Dijon and definitely after 1220.

Acknowledgments

This work is funded by the project *Construction innovations in the Middle Ages: origins, development and transmission of new technologies in Western Europe (11th-13th centuries).* National Research Challenge Grant, Spanish Ministry of Science and Innovation, PID2020-119583RJ-100, pi Rocío Maira Vidal.

References

[1] R. Maira Vidal, 'Bóvedas sexpartitas. Los orígenes del gótico' (Ph.D. thesis, Universidad Politécnica de Madrid, 2016).
[2] R. Maira Vidal, 'The evolution of the knowledge of geometry in Early Gothic construction: the development of the sexpartite vault in Europe', *International Journal of Architectural Heritage*, vol. 11, no 7, 2017, pp. 1005-1025.
[3] R. Maira Vidal, 'Expansion et développement des voûtes sexpartites en France: différences typologiques selon les régions' pp. 1101-1111 in G. Bienvenu, M. Monteil, H. Rousteau-Chambon, (Eds), *Construire! entre Antiquité et Époque contemporaine. Actes du 3e congrès francophone d'histoire de la construction,* Nantes 2017, Paris: Picard, 2019.
[4] R. Maira Vidal, 'Evolution of construction techniques in the Early Gothic: comparative study of the stereotomy of European sexpartite vaults using new measurement systems', *Journal of Cultural Heritage*, vol. 28, 2017, pp. 99-108.
[5] ibid.
[6] G. Goddard King, George Edmund Street: unpublished notes and reprinted papers, *The Hispanic Society of America*, 1916.
[7] E. Lambert, El arte gótico en España, Madrid: Editorial Cátedra, 1985.
[8] G. Palomo Fernández, La Catedral de Cuenca en el contexto de las grandes canterías catedralicias Castellanas en la Baja Edad Media. Tomos I y II, Cuenca: Diputación de Cuenca, 2002.
[9] Maira Vidal, (Note 2).
[10] R. Maira Vidal, 'Two masters, two methods. First steps towards English standardisation in the construction of the sexpartite vaults in Canterbury Cathedral' pp. 97-109 in J. Campbell, N. Baker, M. Driver, (Eds), *The history of building trades and professionalism. Proceedings of the eighth conference of the Construction History Society*, Cambridge: The Construction History Society, 2021.
[11] J. Foyle, *Architecture of Canterbury Cathedral*, London: Scala Publishers, 2013. pp.76-95.
[12] Maira Vidal, (Note 10).
[13] J. S. Alexander, 'Was the builder of the 'crazy vault' Reaction and response in the thrirteen century at Lincoln Cathedral' pp. 391-419 in N. NicGhabhann, D. O'Donovan, (Eds), *Mapping new territories in art and architectural history: essays in honour of Roger Stalley*, Turnhout: Brepols, 2021.
[14] Maira Vidal, (Note 10).
[15] N. Bennett, 'Setting and History', in *Lincoln Cathedral. A journey from past to present*, London: Third Millennium Publishing, 2010. pp. 14-31.
[16] M. Lucas, 'The crossing, transepts and screen', in *Lincoln Cathedral. A journey from past to present*, London: Third Millennium Publishing, 2010. pp. 62-79.

[17] N. Bennett, 'The cloister and the Chapter House' in Lincoln Cathedral. A journey from past to present, London: Third Millennium Publishing, 2010. pp. 96-109.

[18] P. Buckler, 'The Galilee Porch' in Lincoln Cathedral. A journey from past to present, London: Third Millennium Publishing, 2010. pp. 128-165.

[19] Maira Vidal, (Note 10).

[20] Alexander, (Note 13).

[21] H. Karge, 'La arquitectura gótica del siglo XIII' pp. 543-599 in L. García, (Dir.), *Historia de la Ciencia y de la técnica en la Corona de Castilla*, I, Edad Media, Salamanca: Junta de Castilla y León, 2002.

[22] G. Palomo Fernández, J.C. Ruiz Souza, 'Nuevas hipótesis sobre las Huelgas de Burgos. Escenografía funeraria de Alfonso X para un proyecto inacabado de Alfonso VIII y Leonor Plantagenêt', *Goya*, 316-317, 2007, pp. 21-44.

[23] M. Muñoz García, 'Interpretación arqueológica de una catedral gótica' pp. 95-104 in F. Menor, Carlos Bustos, J.M. Conde, (Eds.), *La Catedral de Santa María de Cuenca. Tres décadas de intervenciones para su conservación*, Madrid: Fundación ACS, 2009.

[24] Palomo Fernández, (Note 8).

[25] ibid.

[26] Maira Vidal, (Note 4).

[27] R. Willis, *On The Construction Of The Vaults Of The Middle Ages*, London: The Royal Institute of British Architects, 1910.

The Sixteenth Century

Documentation and Analysis of The Free-Handed Vaulting Technique at The Toor Caravanserai, Iran

Soheil Nazari [1], Amirhossein Mahmoudnejad [2]

[1] Brandenburgische Technische Universität Cottbus – Senftenberg, Cottbus, Germany
DFG Graduiertenkolleg.
[2] University of Tehran, Faculty of Fine Arts.

Abstract

The article intends to document a neglected Caravanserai in Iran. The caravanserai is of early sixteenth century construction, a period that witnessed an evolutionary movement in road construction projects promoted by Safavids. The building is located on a previously significant road between Isfahan and Golpayegan. As a result of decades of neglects, portions of the vault infill have collapsed allowing investigation of the vaulting technique. The vaults are constructed based on free-handed technique without using centering or formwork. The analysis of this kind of vaulting has been rarely mentioned in scholarly sources. This article gives a detailed description of the material used in the construction and documents the technique of the vaulting. The vaults have been surveyed by photogrammetry, allowing use to obtain 3D model of the vaults with the actual characteristics of bricks, and geometry of the vaults.

Introduction

The Toor Carvanserai is located on the western edge of the Iranian desert Dasht-e Kavir, between latitude 33°12'39" and longitude 50°44'25", on a historic main road leading to Isfahan, and was built in the early stages of the road construction projects promoted by the Safavids dynasty (1501–1736 AD). It was an established policy of the Safavids to stage the roads that were connected with caravanserais. Primary sources put the building on the historical map of the Isfahan–Golpayegan road, a strategic highway between two historically well-known urban districts. A caravanserai was a roadside inn where travellers (caravaners) could rest and recover from the day's journey. Toor Caravanserai is first mentioned in Jean Chardin's (1643–1713 AD) travelogue [1], and was later noted by Maxime Siroux, who collected a general information on the locations and histories of Iranian caravanserais and ancient routes in the twentieth century [2].

As trade routes developed in the Safavids era, caravanserais became more of a necessity. This resulted in a network of caravanserais that stretched from east to west, connecting important cities like Herat in the east and Mashhad in the north-east to Isfahan, and from there to Sari and Rey in the north, and Tabriz in north-west. A caravanserai is a roadside inn where people travelling in groups across the dessert on camels could rest after a day's journey, particularly to ensure safety when travelling through a dangerous area. Caravanserais constitute the second largest group of buildings, after mosques, in the architectural heritage of Iran. A wide variety of architectural designs and vaulting techniques can be traced in caravanserai construction in different climates zones of Iran. Since caravanserais were constructed mostly far from the cities in the middle of deserts, architects adopted the simplest and most durable methods of construction. The construction materials of caravanserais were generally chosen according to local resources.

In the Toor caravanserai fired bricks are employed in the vaulted coverings and the walls, supported by travertine stone in the plinths. The vaulting technique is associated with free-handed vaulting [3] without formwork. This technique, frequently used in central Iranian architecture, allows construction beyond the constraints of timber or gypsum consumption as formwork. The technique is applicable to both ordinary building tasks and complex geometry as well as to construction at height or in narrow spaces. Construction of vaulting structures without formwork has been well investigated in the western architectural heritage. The possibility of constructing stone vaults without formwork is mentioned in the western technical literature from the seventeenth century [4], and detailed practical instructions were formulated in 1829 by the German architect J.C. von Lassaulx [5]. Wendland [6] focuses on traditional vault construction without formwork based on a comparative study that includes a critical review of the historical literature as well as studies of models and a gothic prototype. Maxim Siroux in the 1970s focused on Iranian ancient roads and caravanserais, and his work led to an increase in the number of known caravanserais on the current borders of Iran. Siroux suggests in his article "*Les caravanserais routiers Safavids*" that the construction technique of the domes and vaults in caravanserais demands a thorough investigation [7].

Despite the widespread use of brick vaulting without formwork in Iranian architecture, the technique demands a thorough investigation in terms of geometry and masonry pattern. As a result of decades of neglect, portions of the vault infill have collapsed in the Toor caravanserai, allowing surveys of the brick patterns and giving an insight into the vaulting techniques. This article gives a detailed description of the materials used in the monument and of the geometry of the caps, before documenting the brick vaults and offering an analytical discussion of Iranian free-handed vaulting from the perspective of construction techniques. The brick vaults are surveyed by photogrammetry, allowing us to obtain a computer-generated three-dimensional model that represents the actual characteristics of the bricks and the geometry of the vaults.

The Historic Roads of Isfahan and Caravanserais

Historical sources suggest that the construction of caravanserais dates back to the Achaemenids (550–330 BC). Since Iran was on the path of the international trade between the Far East, the Mediterranean coast and Europe, establishing safe roads and inns was necessary to meet the need for transportation and travel [8] Greek historian Herodotus wrote in his fifth book about an ancient highway, 2,500 kilometres (1,600 miles) long, that stretched from Sardis to Susa. Herodotus explains that royal stations and excellent caravanserais existed along the whole length of the Sardis–Susa road, which traversed an inhabited tract free from danger [9] Road development continued in the following centuries. After the introduction of Islam in the seventh century, under the sovereignty of the Great Seljuks (twelfth–thirteenth centuries) and the Safavids, great attention was paid to road infrastructure. The Ribat-I Sharaf caravanserai, built in 1154 in a desert area on the road between Merv and Nishapour, is one of the most exquisite caravanserais.

Isfahan province, which covers twenty-four cities, is located in the geographic center of Iran. According to the 2016 census, the province was the sixth largest and third most populous province of Iran. Located at the intersection of the north–south and east–west historic routes, the city was at the centre of military and commercial affairs. Isfahan was three times capital of Iran. After the Arab conquest of Iran in the seventh century, Isfahan grew under the Persian Buyid dynasty (930–1062 AD), and the city walls were thought to have been constructed during the reign of Buyid Amirs [10] Toghrol Beig (993–1063), the founder of the Great Seljuks of Iran, selected Isfahan as the capital of his domains in the mid-eleventh century, but the city grew in size and magnificence under his grandson, Malik Shah (r. 1073-92). After the fall of Seljuks (c.1200) Isfahan declined and was eclipsed by other cities like Tabriz. In 1327 Ibn Battuta described the city as "one of the largest cities of the Islamic world, but declining in most of the parts" [11]. The city's golden age began during the Safavids dynasty (sixteenth–seventeenth century) when, under the reign of Shah Abbas (1588–1629), the capital was moved in 1589 from Qazvin to Isfahan. The city enjoyed a privileged status under the Safavids' political hegemony in terms of budget and infrastructure. It was an established policy of the Safavids to stage the roads that connected them with caravanserais. Construction projects on the Dehagh road that connects Isfahan to Golpayegan will be considered in this paper.

Figure 1. Aerial photo of the Toor caravanserai located on the Dehagh road between Golpayegan and Isfahan. (Photo: Authors)

Dehagh road intersects with the Isfahan–Tehran highway 24 kilometers north of Isfahan. The road is identified as a historical route, joining the Iranian central plateau to a medieval geographical division by the name of Jebal [12]. Maxim Siroux mentions Dehagh road as the ancient road of Isfahan, Golpayegan and Borujerd. At least until the early eighteenth century, the road was in use by pilgrimage caravans of the Shiite holy cities of Najaf, Kerbala and Baghdad. The remaining historic constructions along the road comprise three Safavids caravanserais and numerous ruins with unidentified functions, all built in coarse masonry. From Isfahan to Golpayegan, the three caravanserais as they appear in order are the Hasanije, the Jelowgir and the Toor. The latter is the oldest and located in the village of Dor, 45 kilometers south-east of Golpayegan. According to the inscription installed on the upper side of the entrance portal of the Toor caravanserai, the construction date of the building is 1552, during the reign of the Safavid king Shah Thamasb (1524–1576). In 1679 during the reign of Shah Suleimen (1666–1694), the building was decorated and renovated. Therefore, the architectural characteristics of the Toor caravanserai demonstrate the early stage of Safavid strategies in developing roads and service infrastructure. After surveying and analyzing the architectural design of the Toor building, we shall consider one of the semi-damaged vaults as part of our argument about vaulting techniques and material used in the building.

Figure 2. The aerial view of the entrance iwan and the domed vestibule leading to the central yard of the Toor caravanserai (Photo by authors).

Architectural Canvas of the Toor Caravanserai

The building covers 2800 square metres and extends north-west to south-east. The plan of the Toor caravanserai is rectangular, 55.55m × 47.50m in dimensions. The façade covering the entire width of the north-west side of the exterior is divided by an entrance iwan flanked by four blind arched niches on each side. The portal is axially centered with a height of approximately 10.00m and a width of 4.40m followed by two cupolas leading to the yard. The generic spatial model for caravanserais in the central plateau of Iran comprises a central courtyard, here measuring 20m by 30m, surrounded by four iwans on each side and vaulted accommodation rooms facing the courtyard. The courtyard would be reached by a vestibule covered by two cupolas, one after another. The vestibule is flanked by two semi-square rooms on both sides. The two rooms were likely to have been used as storage and administration. The iwan and the vestibule provide a bypass from outside to the yard.

In the typical Persian caravanserais, the courtyard is the deciding feature for the design and architectural layout. The central yard serves as the drop-off for the caravans. The spaces surrounding the courtyard include sixteen accommodation rooms facing the yard and stalls between the rooms and exterior space. There are sixteen accommodation units around the yard, each unit consisting of an iwan on a smaller scale serving as an entrance to the rooms. The dimensions of the rooms are 3.50m × 3.80m and the ceiling of each unit is covered with a single bricked dome. The stalls create a long corridor on the four sides of the plan, making a clear distinction between the interior space of the building (the yard and the rooms) and the outside. Access to the stables is provided in each of the four corners of the square central yard.

Generally, in the architectural design of the caravanserais latrines were laid out at the end of stalls. However, no trace of latrines remains in the Toor caravanserai, but they must have been at the end of the stables. No place can be clearly identified as a kitchen, but a remnant of a chimney is visible in the vault shell of the western iwan (see Fig 1), which suggests that the space under the western vault can be identified as a kitchen.

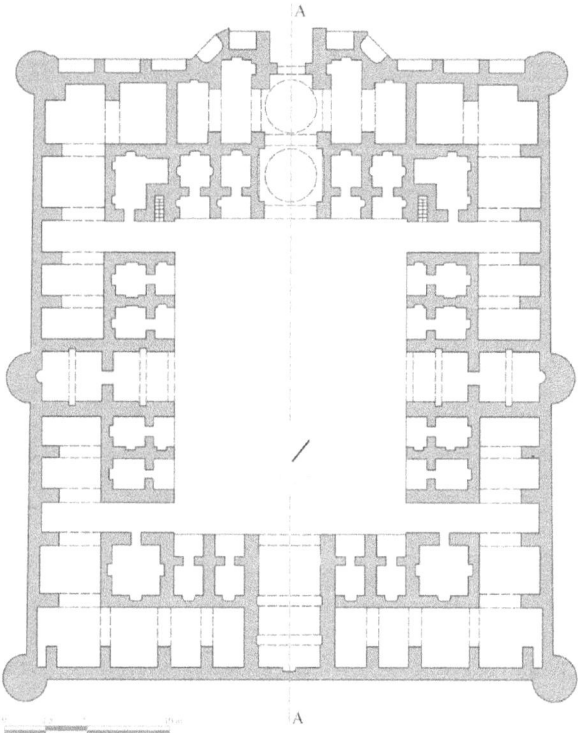

Figure 3. The plan of the Toor Caravanserai (Redraw by authors).

Six semi-circular towers are attached to the exterior walls, all in fired bricks. The roof of the building and the towers are reached by two staircases located on the northern side of the yard. The roof and the towers are not topped with crenellation, and therefore no military or defensive function can be considered for the building roof and tower. Along the A–A axis (in Fig 3), beginning at the entry iwan and terminating at the hall of the iwan on the opposite side, each side is the mirror copy of the other. The main building materials of the caravanserai are 20cm × 20cm bricks used with gypsum mortar for walls and vaults on the inner and outer sides. The iwans in the middle of four sides of the courtyard are higher in elevation and span than the flanked porches of the accommodation rooms. The only ornamental work found in the building is the vertical brick works on the uppermost edge of the iwans around the courtyard. The vertical bricks also work to identify the upper edges of the walls and as a parapet (Fig 4). In the present state, the building seems to have been deserted for a long time. Figure 1 shows that almost half of the domes are dilapidated. The collapsed portions allow for surveying and understanding of the brick patterns and technique of the vaulting and dome-making.

Vaulting Technique

The covering of the bays of the stables and the accommodation rooms are cloister vaults without the use of ribs or centering in the construction process. The vaults are constructed with a pointed profile like the arches, and the thickness of the vault shell is that of one masonry unit (20cm). The vaulting technique is called "free-handed vaulting" and is associated with laying brick units with fast-setting mortar without using formwork or centering (Wendland, 2004). The technique is used for vaults built over quadrilateral bays and to avoid considerable wooden or gypsum supports by applying self-support brick courses – typical vaulting for caravanserais.

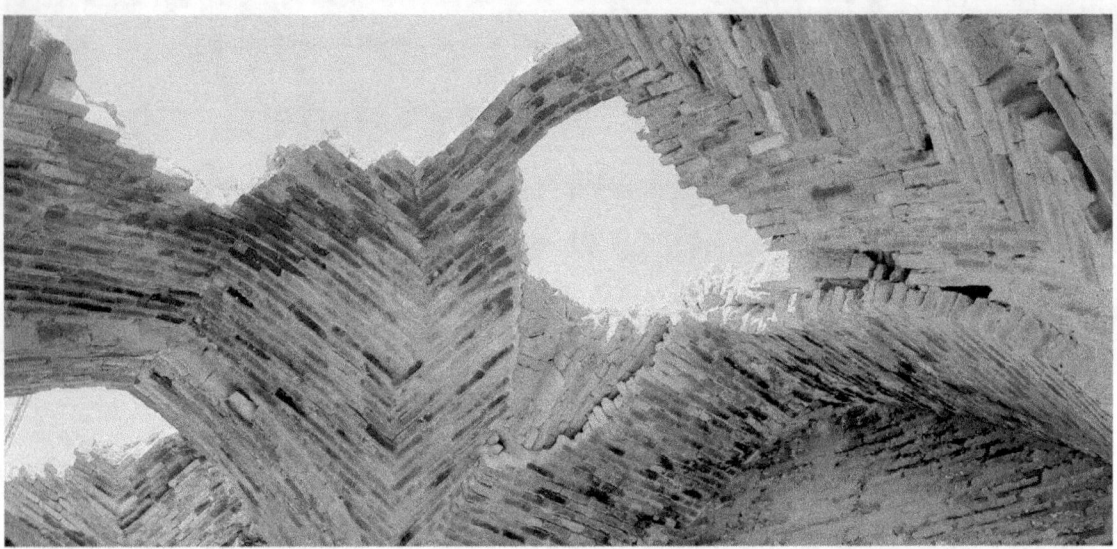

Figure 4. View of a semi-damaged vault of the caravanserai (Photo by authors).

In any review of vaults and domes built on pointed arches, the identification of the arch profile is a prerequisite. An endless variation in the form of the pointed arch in Iranian architecture is possible with the width-to-height ratio, owing to the location of the arc centers. Most pointed arches in the Iranian sphere are three or four centered. From the fourteenth century onwards, four-centered types were increasingly mainstreamed as the structural models of choice in daily constructions and medium-span vaults and domes. The most readily identified group is colloquially known in the craft as panjo haft (literally, five and seven). Determined by using an ortho-photogrammetric view, the profile of the four main iwans and the arches forming the transverses over the walls is a family member of panjo haft, namely panjo haft-e tond. In this type, as shown in Fig 5, the first center is (E), the second center is (F) and (O) is the middle point of span (OC = half of the span). The first centre would be determined by intersection of a circle with the centre of (D) and radius of (DC) with the (AD) span line. The second center is determined as the extension of (BE) when it meets the perpendicular line to (D). Another interpretation of the panjo haft derives from dividing the spring-line into seven segments. The first center is chosen on the seventh segment and the second centre is chosen on the fifth segment down the spring-line.

For the analysis of the vaulting technique, we selected three neighbouring vaults on the western edge of the building that cover the stable aisle: a relatively intact vault without any damage, a semi-deteriorated vault in which the apex is collapsed, and a third vault in which only the spandrel remained. The geometry of the vaults is designed by four concave surfaces that meet up with each other at the apex and lean over the four transverses underneath. Two of the transverses are larger in span and height. These two open to the next bays of the stable, and the other two flanking transverses, which are lower in height and width, face the exterior wall and the other transverse to the entrance vestibule of the stables. The bays are rectangular – 300cm wide and 490cm long. All the coverings and the transverses are constructed with masonry courses and fast-binding clay mortar (Gach va Khak). Bricks form the four coves and due to the curvature of the shell (profile of the shell), they are self-supporting courses.

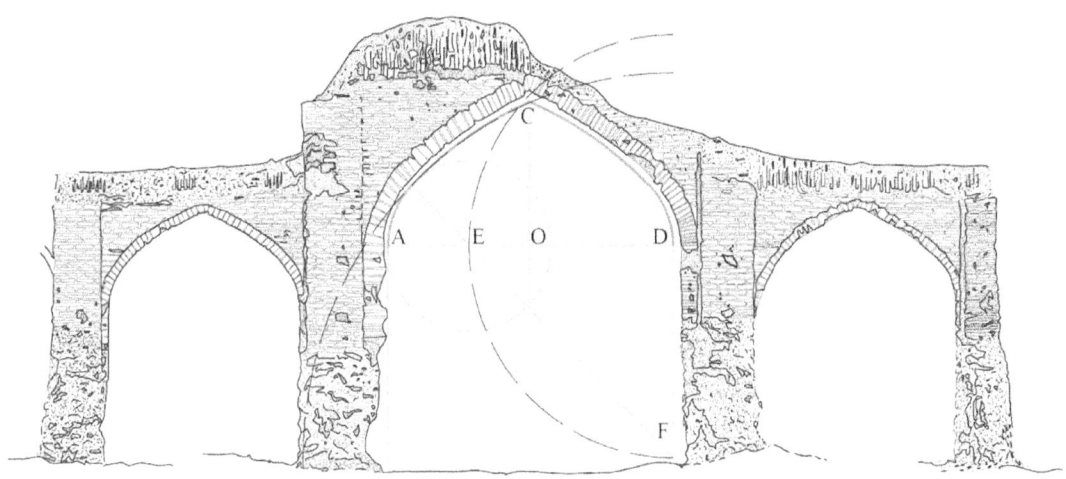

Figure 5. Photogrammetric front view of the eastern iwan and the panjo haft profile. (Photo: Authors)

The three vaults cover rectangular plans (410 × 300 cm). The vaults at the Toor caravanserai are in fact longitudinal vaults, but use a very different technique from that commonly known in the western tradition, or even middle eastern ones. Construction of the vaults can be arranged in three sequences. Laying out the bricks in the four spandrels is the first step. The courses of spandrels do not span the space yet. The first courses of the spandrels infill the corners of the rectangle and also provide the abutment for the first double-curved course that span the space. The units of bricks will be laid in place temporarily through the adhesion of the fresh gach va khak mortar until the course is completed. At the spandrels short courses occur and the units must be cut in different shapes to infill the spandrels and provide backrest for the full courses.

After the completion of the first full course, the successive courses can easily be added until the courses reach the height of the apex of the corresponding arch; hence the elevation code of the last course of first stage of the construction is the same as the pinnacle of the corresponding arch (M and N are approximately at the same level). The temporary stability of the bricks is due to the fast adhesion of the mortar and to the fact that the brick layout follows the form of an arch. As soon as the course is closed and spans the space underneath, the courses are stable due to their curvature, and do not rely anymore on mortar adhesion. In this stage, the rectangular shape of the span (ABCD in Fig 5) is inverted to the square span of EFGH. The survey shows that the spatial positions of the bed joints are tilted parallel planes up until this stage.

At the second stage of construction, the courses rise up from the four edges of the square towards the centre simultaneously, forming four coves to cover the space. The four coves consist of several double-curved courses of bricks on top of each other, which are seamed together at the edges by dovetail pattern. In fact, the dovetail pattern identifies the ridges of the coves and maintains the integrity of the coves at the ridges. The bed-joints of the courses of the coves at this stage are still tilted parallel planes. The curvature of the vault construction in the second stage follows the curvature of the first stage of the construction. The dovetail design of the bricks diagonally forms the lines EI, FJ, GK, and HL, leading to the rectangle IJKL.

Documentation and Analysis of The Free-Handed Vaulting Technique at The Toor Caravanserai, Iran

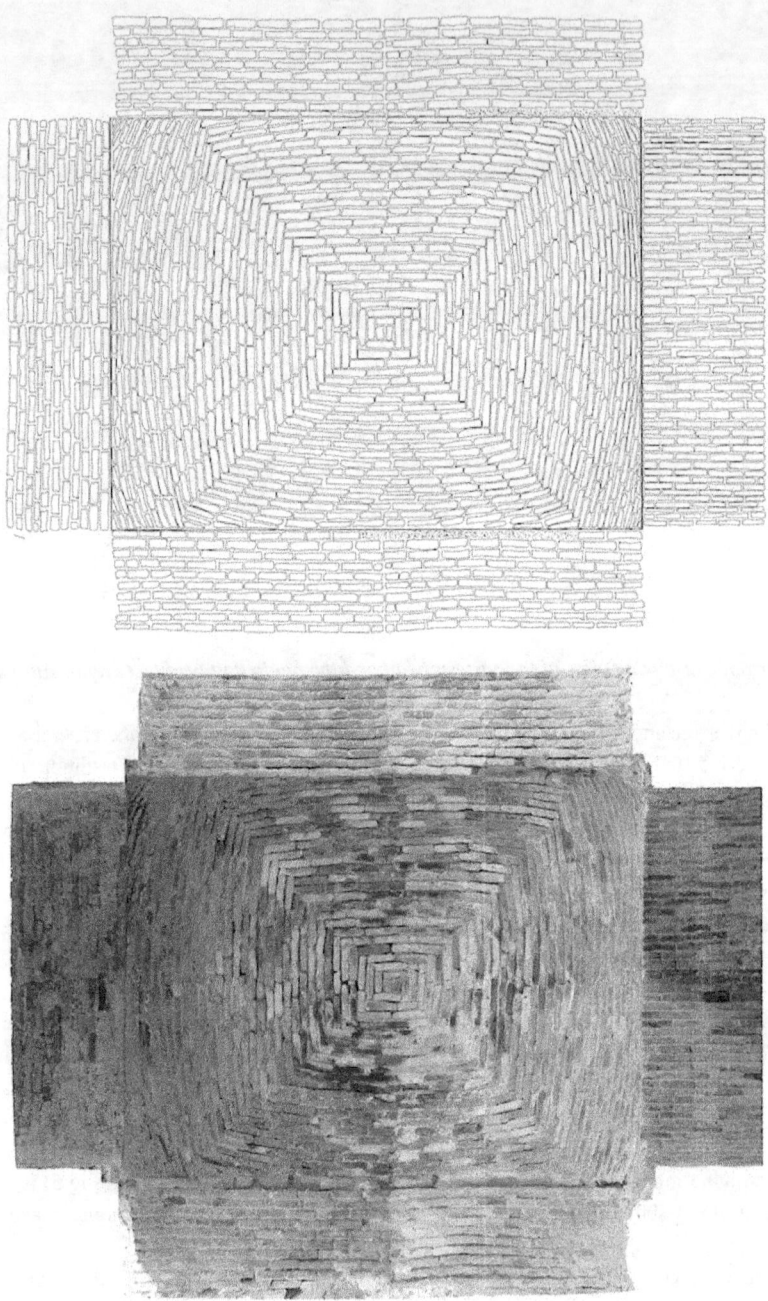

Figure 6. The arrangement of the bricks of the vaults. Drawing is extracted from photogrammetric ortho view of the vault. (Photo by authors).

Inverting the rectangular plan to the square shortens the protraction of the courses along the length and width of the rectangular span, reducing the risk of buckling of the courses before they become stiff enough. Then by inverting and proceeding the courses of the vault from the four sides of the square toward the centre, the master builder has applied an optimized solution to both cover a rectangular space and avoid the risk of buckling that is so likely for fresh courses. The dovetail pattern and possible short execution of the courses make the vaulting rather easy and stable without any support.

The final stage of construction would be capping the summit of the vault. The survey shows that up until the capping of the vault, the courses rise up according to corbelling the units and the planes of bed-joints are parallel to each other. But at the summit, where the four coves meet each other, a correction in direction of the beds occurs. This means that the profile of the vault is not a pointed arc, but is a smooth and rounded curve. The direction of the units, and consequently the bed-joints in the rectangular area IJKL, are slightly shifted toward vertical axis. So, the master builder covers the apex of the vault with courses that stand in place almost vertically – as a result, a rounded line at the summit appears.

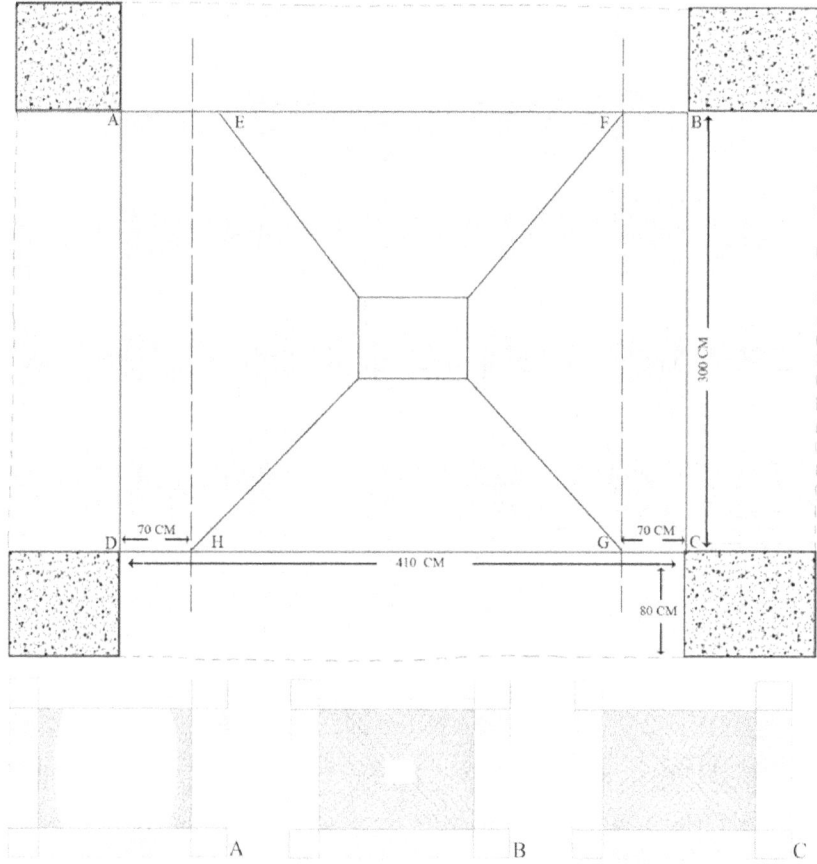

Figure 7. The construction process and design of the vault. (A), (B) and (C) illustrate the sequence of vault construction (Photo by authors).

Documentation and Analysis of The Free-Handed Vaulting Technique at The Toor Caravanserai, Iran

Every single course of this kind of vaulting must be made stable by forming an arch. As the stability of the arch is provided by its arch form, identification of the curvature (profile) of the vault shell and the layout of the masonry pattern is the key to the entire design. The profile of the vault is also a four-centred curve like the 5&7 profile of the transverses, constructed in a different manner (Fig. 8). Since the transverses have been constructed by using centering, the profile of the transverses are rigidly compatible with the geometry of 5&7. Contrary to the transverses, the vaults have been constructed without any support or centering. Thus, the profile of the vault has deformations and corrections in some degree. The two centres of the profile of the vault can be identified like the 5&7 of the transverses. The curvature of the vault constitutes two arcs of AB and BD. The arc AB is a segment of the circle with the centre of E, and the arc BD is a segment of the circle with a centre located on a vertical line down to the springing line. Since the vault has been constructed free-handed without the use of any centering at all, the profile line of the vault does not obey exactly the practical geometry of AD.

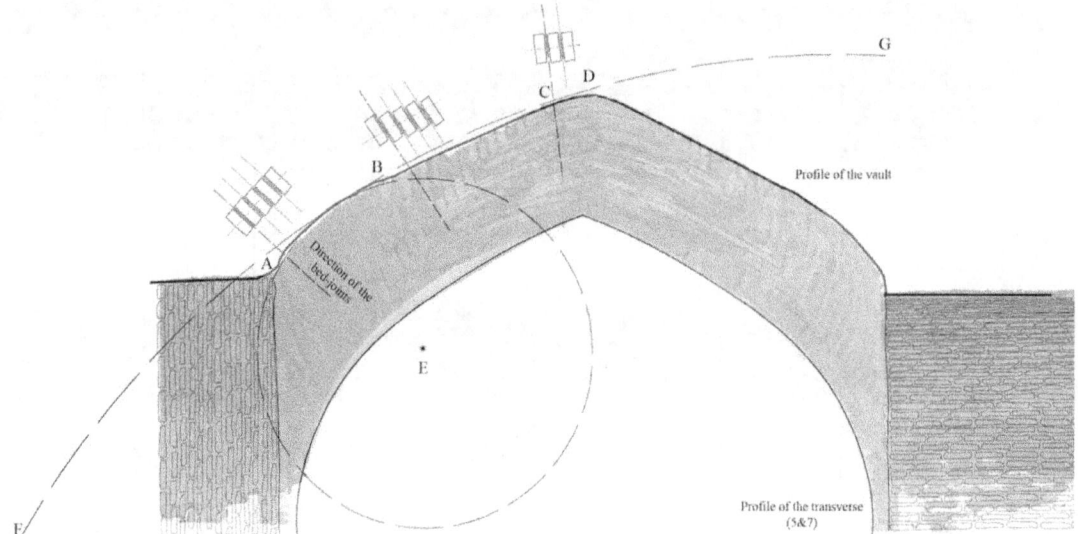

Figure 8. The section of the vault, illustrating the profile of the transverse (5&7), the profile of the vault shell, and the direction of the bed-joints (Photo by authors).

As mentioned before, the courses from spandrels up to the rectangle of the summit proceed on tilted parallel bed-joint planes. The bed-joints are parallel but not radial, because the latter demands excessive amount of mortar as the curvature of the courses increases. An excessive amount of mortar means the desirable adhesion duration between mortar and masonry units gets longer. Therefore, as masonry vaulting without any formwork is based on a fast-binding process, corbelling the units in parallel beds is preferable.

Corbelling is a technique applied in vault construction by masonry units in which the vaulting proceeds by projecting each course of bricks outward for a very short distance over the course below. Corbelling of the bricks follows the desired profile of the arch fluently without any necessary support or formwork. In this case, the bricks are laid pitched and form the courses, and the builder assembles the vault by corbelling the successive courses. The advantage of corbelling is that it helps builder to lay bricks with parallel, rather than truly radial, beds. The technique is also practised in the European sail vault.

Observations show that a considerable correction occurs in the direction of the bed-joints in some certain points of the vault shell. The courses of the springing resting directly on the transverses are laid in parallel beds and corbelling at this stage is negligible (Fig. 8). The courses rise up till they form the shoulder of the arch (AB arc in the Fig. 8). As long as the layout of the brick starts with a dovetail pattern, in the second stage of the construction (B in the Fig. 8) the courses proceed by corbelling the masonry units. At this point the beds are still parallel but with a slight divergence rather than the courses of the springing. This means the master builder has corrected the direction of the beds after a certain degree (almost 37° - B to C in Fig. 8) to be able to form the intended profile of the vault (Fig. 8). The courses that run corbelled and in parallel beds between 37° and nearly 90° of the span line form the voussoir of the vault. The direction of the bed-joints changes at the summit where the units are laid almost vertical in place.

Figure 9. Left: Vault construction without using formworks in Iran (Photo: Perkins Ward). Right: the 3d view of the vault (Photo: authors).

As previously mentioned, the transverses have been built with using centring. The method of using centering to construct ribs or transverses is known as "Lenge gachi" in Iranian traditional architecture vocabulary. Iranian arches, especially the multi centered five and seven families, have complex geometry. Therefore, these arches are difficult to implement without centering or formwork. A particular Iranian solution is to build a gypsum centering rib, to use as a model and guide. To build the gypsum centring rib, firstly, a full scale of the front view of the desired arch, in this case panjo haft-e tond (Fig. 5), is sketched on the ground. By placing bricks on the sketched lines with 10-18 cm space in between a mold is formed. The mold is then filled with gypsum slurry. Sand is often poured into the mold to prevent the gypsum rib from sticking to the ground. Before the slurry gets dried off, date palm tree fibers or bamboo stems were placed into the mold frame to increase the tensile strength of the gypsum. Three different types of brick work pattern can be identified in Iranian architecture: 1. Pitched, 2. Radial and 3. Tile [13].. Generally, pitched brickworks have been employed mostly for load-bearing elements. Since the transverses of the bays in the caravanserai bear the load of the vault and also provide the abutment for the first courses, and the bricks have been arranged in pitched-works (Fig 10).

Figure 10. The view of the transverse and the start point of the dovetail pattern of the vault (Photo: authors).

Conclusion

In this study we have described the construction of brick vaults of the Toor caravanserai. The building is located on the historic main road between Isfahan and Golpayegan, on the western edge of the Iranian desert. The building suffers from damage to its coverings, plinths and walls due to decades of neglect. The collapsed portions allowed us to investigate and document the vaulting technique. The surveys show that the vaults have been erected without using any support or formwork. The technique was used in the construction of caravanserais in remote areas to accelerate building and in response to the lack of wooden or plaster formworks. In order to shorten the length of the courses and reduce the risk of buckling of the fresh courses, the builder has inverted the rectangular space to a square by proceeding with the vaulting from two short edges of the rectangular plan. In this way, the number of full courses that transverse the whole span is reduced to a minimum. After squaring the span, the courses are raised up from four sides of the square and are jointed together diagonally in a dovetail pattern. The direction of the plane of the bed-joints is the key in projecting the courses. As a result of corrections from the springing to the summit, the directions are diverse in different parts of the vault shell.

Acknowledgment

Soheil Nazari greatly appreciates for the advice given by Prof. David Wendland, professor of construction history at the Brandenburg University of Technology.

References:

[1] John Chardin, *Travels of John Chardin into Persia and the East India.* London: Mofes Pitt, 1686.
[2] Maxime Siroux, *The ancient ways of Isfahan and their buildings.* Tehran: Iranian National Ancient Monument Preservation Organization, 1978.
[3] David Wendland, Traditional Vault Construction Without Formwork: Masonry Pattern and Vault Shape in the Historical Technical Literature and in Experimental Studies, *International Journal of Architectural Heritage*, Vol.1, 2007, pp.311-365.
[4] Roland Besenval, *Technologie de la Vôute dans l'orient amcien.* Paris: Editions Recherche sur les civilisations, 1984.
[5] David Wendland, 'A case of Recovery of a Medieval Vaulting Technique in the 19th century: Lassaulx's vaults in the Church of Treis' pp. 2107-17 in S. Huerta, (Ed.), *Proceeding of the First International Congress on Construction History*, Madrid 2003, Madrid: Instituto Juan Ferrera, 2003.
[6] David Wendland (note 3).
[7] Maxime Siroux, Les caravanserais routiers Safavids, *Iranian Studies*, vol.7, 1974, pp. 348-375.
[8] Roman Girshman, *Iran Parthians and Sassanians - the Art of Mankind.* London: Thames and Hudson, 1962.
[9] Herodotus, and G. C. Macaulay, *The history of Herodotus.* London: Macmillan, 1914.
[10] Lisa Golombek, Urban Patterns in Pre-Safavid Isfahan, *Iranian Studies*, vol.7, 1974.
[11] Ibn Battūta, *The Travels of ibn Battuta to Central Asia.* Reading (UK): Ithaca Press, 1999.
[12] Ibn Rasteh, *Al-A'laq al-Nafisa. Trans. H. Gharachanlu.* Tehran: Amirkabir, 1987.
[13] Soheil Nazari, 'The practical geometry of Persian ribbed vaults: A study of the rehabilitation of the Kolahduzan Dome in the Tabriz historic bazaar' pp. 439-446 in João Mascarenhas-Mateus and Ana Paula Pires (Ed.), Proceedings of the Seven International Conference on Construction History, Lisbon, Portugal, 12-16 July 2021.

Tudor King Post Roofs

David Yeomans, Nicholas Riall
Independent Scholars

Abstract

The king post and queen post trusses that became common during the eighteenth century are known to date from their introduction into England from Italy in the seventeenth century. However several roofs with king post trusses have been recognised that date from the mid-sixteenth century. These share with the later trusses the flared or joggled head at the top of the king post to receive the principal rafters, a system not found elsewhere and which must therefore be an English invention. One of these is in what was the gatehouse to a palace built near Bletchingley. Two more are in the roof structures of part of Lacock Abbey. The date of these and their similarity to details later adopted by Inigo Jones for his king post roofs raises the question of whether this system was developed by carpenters of the Office of Works, and whether there might be other roofs using this type of structure. A third roof was set over the Council chamber of the Queen's House in the Tower of London, with a fourth but somewhat different roof to be found over the nave of St David's cathedral, Pembrokeshire. All these roofs plus a fifth at Hampton Court palace have been dated through dendrochronology.

The paper will provide details of the Bletchingley and Lacock roofs, which essentially have king posts inserted into what are otherwise clasped purlin and collar braced roofs in order to support floors. Possible connections with carpenters of the King's Office of Works will be explored.

Introduction

Although medieval roofs in France and Germany used king posts in tension the practice was never adopted in England until much later. The side purlin roofs, which eventually superseded the trussed rafter roofs, initially relied upon large tie beams to carry struts in compression that assisted the principal rafters. In the south of England the clasped purlin roof became common by the sixteenth century. It seems to be generally accepted that these purlin roofs, relying upon large scantling timbers for both the purlins and principal rafters, derived from cruck construction, which was widely distributed in Britain [1]. Shallow pitched roofs relied upon strutting from the tie beams while for more normal 48° pitches crown post roofs and clasped purlin roofs became popular [2]. It was only in the seventeenth century that a new form of king post truss was introduced into England from Italy to frame the shallower pitched roofs and cope with the larger spans that were wanted for the new styles of architecture. This type was introduced first by Inigo Jones who had visited the country and then developed by Christopher Wren who drew upon an Italian book on mechanics [3].

It has been something of a surprise, therefore, to find a number of king post roofs dating from the sixteenth century, particularly as these all show the same form of king post, flared or joggled at the top to receive the principal rafters. This is not a feature found in French or German roofs (nor in Italian roofs) and so the joggle must have been an English invention. This raises the possibility that when Jones and Wren introduced the Italian type of roof truss, they were also drawing on knowledge of construction that had appeared in the previous century with this uniquely English form of king post. Three of the sixteenth century roofs are similar in that they have relatively steep pitches but the reasons for incorporating a king post in tension are rather different. Indeed it seems as if the earliest of these three might not have needed a post in tension although the other two did. A fourth king post roof certainly did need a post in tension and is the most enigmatic of them, being radically different from the others.

Council chamber, Queen's house, Tower of London

Hewett says of the roof of the council chamber at the Tower of London that "Three bays of this roof survive in a mutilated condition, and a hypothetical reconstruction of it is shown . . ." [4] He has a drawing of the roof structure and a detail drawing of which he says "The jointing of the roof frames is highly complex . . ." Figure 1 is a drawing showing his reconstruction and based on his drawing, while Figure 2 shows a more or less complete truss that survives forming the gable. Within the room the king posts have been cut below the collars, the queen struts removed and the tie beams have been cut away leaving stubs at the wall. Loss of the queen posts also meant loss of the curved braces between them and the purlins; evidence for those braces being long mortices still clearly visible in the purlins. However there simply cannot have been the curved braces between the principal rafters and the purlins as suggested by Hewett and shown dotted in Figure 1. There are mortices in the principals but no corresponding means of connecting the braces to the purlins. The inference must be that there were downward braces to the wall plate, but it is now not possible to see enough of the wall plate to verify that.

Unfortunately there has been more than one episode of mutilation. Removal of the tie beam must have occurred when the present floor was inserted into the original room but there has clearly been later work. The stubs of the tie beams are not original and the posts and wall plates have been cut back. The posts have been cut back to the centre-line of the pegs that held the tie beam braces and the marks of some mechanical tool can be clearly seen on the faces of the wall plates. The detail that we can see are the mortices in the posts for the braces to assist the tie beams, although the posts have been cut back to the centre-line of the fixing pegs.

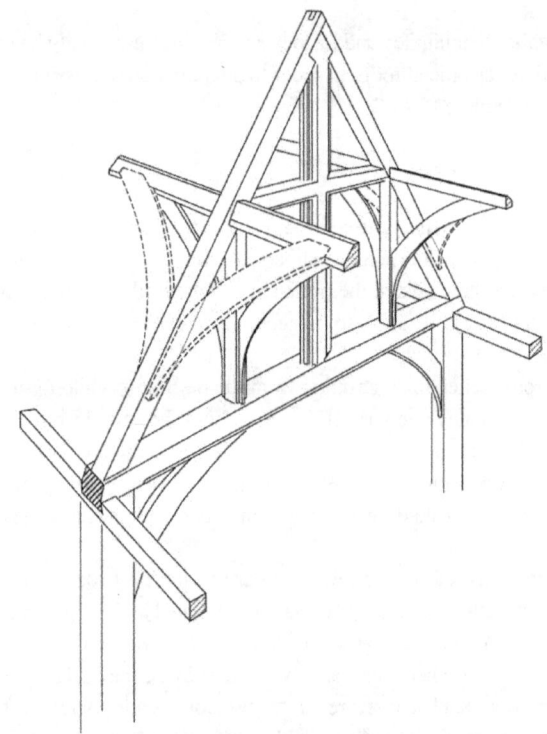

Figure 1: Queen's House, Tower of London. Roof of the Council Chamber, Reconstruction after Cecil Hewett

Setting aside questions raised about the reliability of Hewett's details, what we can be sure about is the use of a king post with joggles; although whether it was necessary for this king post to actually be in tension is a moot point. It seems most likely that it was designed as much for visual effect as for structural necessity. The trusses incorporate the collar and queen struts that carpenters would have been familiar with at that time and also uses braces between wall posts and tie beam that would have assisted the latter. That being so we have no reason to assume that the king post was seen as structural in spite of the joggled head and it might well have been seen as a 'decorative' feature of the roof.

Figure 2: Gable wall of the council chamber (photo. David Yeomans).

The collars would provide adequate assistance to the principals and if not, and the queen posts carried some compressive force, the braces between the tie beam and the main posts of the building would have helped to relieve the tie beam of any bending. The only thing we can be certain of is that the carpenters who built this roof were well aware of the details necessary for a king post in tension, i.e. the joggled head. We know that James Nedeham carried out some of the work and it has been suggested that "the new roof and floor of the queen's great chamber were built . . . by other London carpenters of standing" [5]. While Salzman reproduces a contract with Thomas Hall and John Kynge for three new houses at the Tower that specifies the scantlings of timbers to be used in the floor and walls, all that it says of the roof is that it should have "good and sufficient rafters . . . according to the proporcion of the same howse" [6]. Of course this is not the same part of the building and the roofs of these houses were probably common rafter roofs. We have no other contracts but several carpenters involved at that time who were Masters of the Carpenters' Company [7].

Lacock Abbey

The roofs at Lacock Abbey are much simpler, rather utilitarian, and much more likely to have used the king posts to deliberately carry tensile forces. Lacock Abbey was acquired by Sir William Sharington following the Dissolution and converted by him into a country house. The king post trusses that are there clearly date from the work carried out by Sharington when he built the Stable Court. The roof of the east side has a king post, a high collar and two pairs of purlins (Fig. 3); the purpose of the structure is to support a floor as well as the roof covering. A refinement of the carpentry is the treatment of the collars, which are carefully curved at their ends and with long tenons morticed into the principals with three fixing pegs. Longitudinal stability is ensured by curved wind braces between the principals and upper purlins, visible in Figure 4, although these were not used in all bays.

The height of the collars was necessary to facilitate movement within the roof space as it is clear from a number of features that it was used as accommodation of some kind, possibly sleeping quarters for members of the household. There is a garderobe within the adjacent roof above the north side of the Stable Court. Light is provided by dormer windows with the gable of the dormers framed with clasped purlins.

Structurally, the purpose of the king posts is simply to assist the tie beams to which they are fixed with pegged mortice and tenon joints. One can see the necessity of this given the relatively long span of a little over 6m and the load from the attic floor. However, there is no attempt to use the king post in a structural arrangement to assist the principal rafters; that is entirely dealt with by the collars.

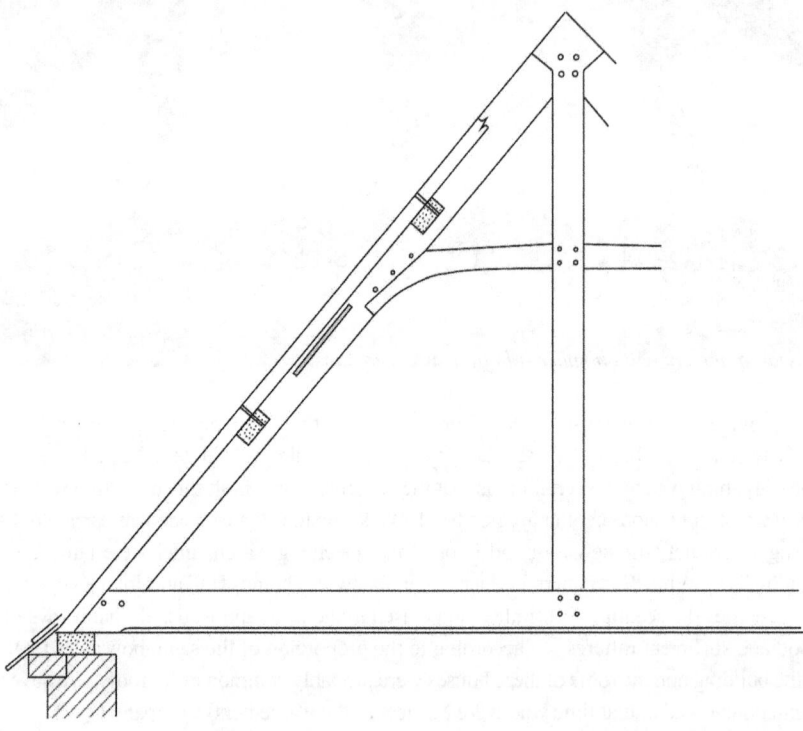

Figure 3: Drawing of the king post truss at Lacock Abbey based on an original drawing possibly by Harold Brakspear, architect and archaeologist.

Figure 4: Interior of the roof at Lacock Abbey (photo. Nicholas Riall).

Place Farm, Bletchingley

The third roof is far more complex and the king post was not strictly to solve a roofing problem. What is now a private house at Place Farm, Bletchingley, was originally the gate-house to a Tudor palace. The property was part of the divorce settlement on Anne of Cleves, but this was rented by Thomas Cawarden, who was almost certainly responsible for the building that we now see, although this is a fraction of the buildings that were there [8]. It is clear from the brickwork on the front elevation that the building has been much altered, but the outline of the original archway through which one might have ridden into the courtyard of the palace still survives. But with the ground floor now much higher than it was originally, there have been extensive alterations to the plan of the building. Nevertheless, the main timbers of the original roof survive and it is possible to reconstruct the form that it once took.

The roof is of five bays and there was originally access into an end bay of the attic via a staircase. The surviving timbers of the attic floor, although altered, show that this was not a small stair but one that could have been regularly used. Steps would then have led through a doorway formed in one of the roof trusses into the central bay, where there was square floor set above the basic attic floor level and arranged diagonally within that bay. The evidence for that is a large spine beam carried by the king posts of two roof trusses, with mortices for the floor joists and the diagonal beams, which no longer survive (Figs. 5 & 6). The interpretation is that there was originally a belvedere projecting through the roof from which members of the household would presumably have been able to watch the hunting in the grounds of the palace. What is striking about this arrangement are the king posts that support this spine beam, which are additional to what is otherwise a clasped purlin roof, albeit one that has two collars and two pairs of purlins rather than the usual one.

The king posts have joggled heads so that they might be supported by the principal rafters, and are joined to the tie beam with mortice and tenon joints. Each king post has a bracket formed towards its foot in order to support the floor beam. These posts must have been cut from a prodigious pieces of timber, because they had to be wide enough at the top to accommodate the joggles and wide enough in the other direction to accommodate the brackets. What they share with the other two king post roofs described above is that the king posts have no function in assisting the principal rafters, unlike the king post trusses that were to appear in the seventeenth century. Assisting the principal rafters remained the task of the collars, which these king posts had to interrupt.

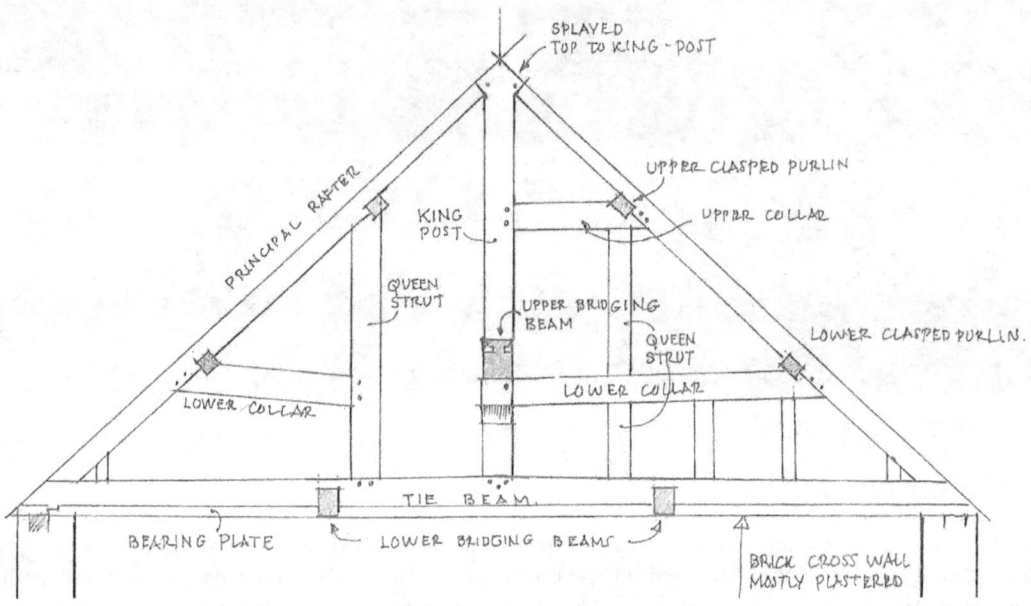

Figure 5: Elevation of frame 4 of the roof of Place Farm (Bletchingley Palace). Courtesy Nye Saunders.

Regrettably we know little of the commissioning of this building nor of the carpenters who worked on the framing. Cawarden, given his role as Master of Revels, would certainly have had access to carpenters working for the Office of Works. That would account for the use of king posts clearly designed to work in tension. What is curious about the roof is the combination of what at the time would have been a sophisticated structure, i.e. the king post in tension, with what is otherwise a very traditional roof form, the clasped purlin, albeit one with two pairs of purlins. Thus for both Place Farm and Lacock we have king posts designed for a specific purpose, but inserted into what was otherwise a very traditional roof.

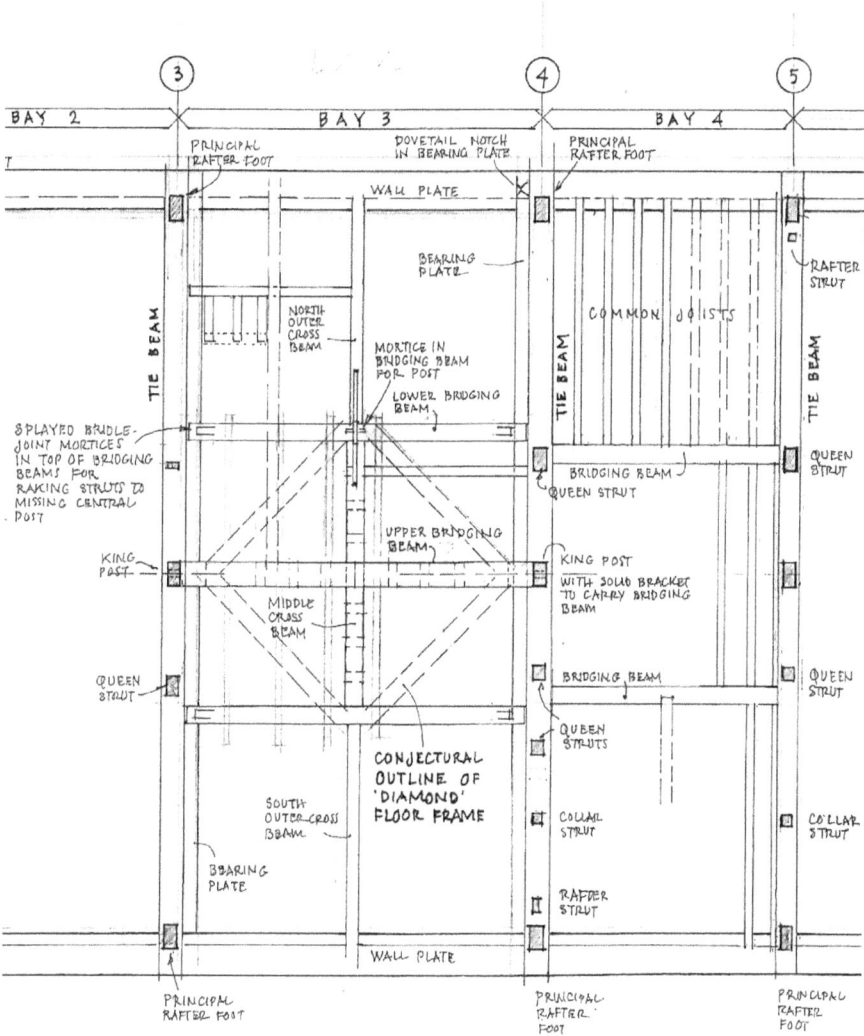

Figure 6: Part plan of the attic of Place Farm (Bletchingley Palace). Courtesy Nye Saunders.

St David's Cathedral

The roof at St David's is the most enigmatic of these four. Originally the nave roof had a steep pitch, as can be seen from its trace against the wall of the tower, and the transept roofs still have this steep pitch. However the present nave roof, constructed between 1530 and 1540, is a very shallow pitch and carries below it an ornate decorative ceiling based on a series of pendants with tracery arches between them. Whether the installation of the ceiling was the occasion for rebuilding the structure or it was the other way round we do not know. However, there might well have been concern for the original roof as the nave columns have a distinct outward lean, which might well have been seen as being exacerbated by thrusts from the original roof, although we also know that the building had foundation problems.

Tudor King Post Roofs

The shallow pitched roof has king posts with flared heads against which the principal rafters thrust, these being notched into the tie beams at their outer ends. The king posts connect with the tie beams with dovetail joints, as do two other posts, which are also dovetailed into the principals. All these posts are of paired timbers and were clearly designed to be in tension, placed to assist the tie beams above the decorative pendants. The posts are further joined to the tie beam with metal straps, which Caroe has suggested are medieval [9]. However they are much more likely to date from the time when either John Nash or George Gilbert Scott worked at the cathedral.

Unlike the other three roofs described here, this is not the adaptation of a well known roof form by the insertion of king posts but a working out of how to assist a long spanning tie beam carrying a load other than its own weight. With dovetailed ends, the king posts and the posts above the pendants were clearly seen by the carpenters as being in tension.

Figure 7: Roof of St. David's Cathedral, Pembrokeshire. Royal Commission on Historic Monuments of Wales.

This example is more difficult to understand than the others because there is no clear reason why a shallow pitch should have been adopted for such a long span. Flat lead roofs were commonly used in church roofs and the structure treated decoratively, as later celebrated in the nineteenth century by the Brandons [10]. However, their spans were sufficiently small, and there was no suspended decoration, so that they could rely upon large tie beams and/or arch braces. In contrast, at St. David's a king post in tension was needed to assist such a long spanning tie beam, and the secondary posts also needed to be in tension to take the weight of the decorative ceiling. This roof shows the clearest understanding of the structural behaviour of king post trusses; and it is a pity that we know nothing of the carpenters involved, although it seems likely that such an important work might well have involved carpenters from London, and hence those associated with the Office of Works.

Great Watching Chamber, Hampton Court

Information on the Great Watching Chamber at Hampton Court has been provided by Lee Prosser of Historic Royal Palaces. This is a shallow pitched roof somewhat like that at St David's. However it is of smaller span and does not have the same kind of loads on the tie beams, which are massive. It differs from the others in that the joggle at the top of the king posts to receive the principals is formed by cutting into a very wide timber forming the post (Fig. 8). Moreover each truss has two struts between tie beam and principals added close to where there were original purlins. This has been dated by both documents and tree ring dating to 1535 [11]. In this case we have a roof truss with something of the form of a king post truss but with no necessity for the post to act in tension.

Figure 8: Head of king post of a truss above the Great Watching Chamber, Hampton Court (photo. Lee Prosser, Historic Royal Palaces)

Discussion and conclusions

Whilst there is some documentary evidence for these roofs, placing them all in the sixteenth century, tree-ring dating provides additional, and usually the only reliable dating information. The overall picture is that these roofs date from between the mid 1530s to the mid 1540s, although there seems to be no clear-cut dates for the St David's roof. However, we hardly need precise dates for our purpose here, which is to assess the level of knowledge and understanding of king posts in tension. The roofs that carpenters built using joggled king posts would have depended upon the opportunity they had for building long span roofs and the need for tensile king posts. We can see that most clearly at Bletchingley where a clasped purlin roof would have been adequate but for the need to support a floor above tie beam level.

Unlike the seventeenth century king post trusses, where we can assume some knowledge of Italian roof design, this is hardly possible for these sixteenth century roofs. Neither Barbaro's nor Serlio's book on architecture, which illustrated king post roofs, was published till 1550 and the only record of English carpenters or architects travelling to Italy before Inigo Jones is John Shute. The most likely source for the idea of king posts in tension, which was not a technique commonly used in England, was France although the way in which it was used there was quite different from the way in appears in the roofs described here. We can see from Hoffsummer's extensive catalogue of roofs in Belgium and Northern France that purlin roofs there took a quite different form from that in England [12]. Roofs were generally of steeper pitch and rather than using principal rafters of large scantling, as common in England, the French added a sub-rafter under a normal common rafter with small scantling purlins held between the two. These sub-rafters were then tenoned into the king posts, providing a simple means of supporting them, while inclined struts from the post took load from the purlins. What we seem to have in these English examples (if we assume that the St. David's roof was built by English carpenters) is the French idea of a post in tension adapted to suit what is otherwise English carpentry, i.e. carpentry using large scantling timbers rather than the small sizes used in France. However, in all of the English examples the post was not used to carry load from the purlins and so does not fall within the normal development roof structures.

The transmission of ideas from France and its dissemination among English carpenters can be explained by English carpenters working in France or by French carpenters working in England. There were military campaigns in France under Henry VIII for which carpenters travelled to France and there were carpenters of various nationalities working on Henry's Nonsuch Palace. Carpenters would work closely together and so ideas could be easily transmitted. Contracts of the period show the close working of carpenters of the Office of Works and the apprentice system would have guaranteed the passing on of new techniques and so their dissemination.

The English king posts in tension were supported at their tops by a pair of large scantling principal rafters. If these had been simply tenoned into the king posts the joints would have been relying upon the pegged tenons to transmit the forces. The splayed or joggled top was a more effective means of transmitting the downward pull of the king post into the principals. What we have is a French structural arrangement modified to suit English practice. Moreover both the Lacock and Bletchingley roofs have other features of English roofs so that the king posts used in order to support floors were simply inserted into what were otherwise simply collar strutted principals or clasped purlin roofs.

With only a small number of roofs of the period presently known to have king posts in tension, the question that remains is how widespread at the time was knowledge of this kind of structure. We have assumed awareness of French construction, and a spread of that amongst London carpenters associated with the Office of Works. We hope that a number of these roofs having been found will be encouragement for others to recognize similar roofs if found so that a better picture of the appearance of this type of structure may be developed.

Acknowledgements

We would like to thank the staff of the National Trust, Emma Hitchings and Dr. Andy Cochrane, for giving us access to the roofs at Lacock, Lee Prosser of Historic Royal Palaces and the Constable of the Tower for access to the Tower of London, Nye Saunders Architects for the use of their drawings.

References

[1] F. Charles, *Medieval Cruck-Building and Its Derivatives: A Study of Timber-Framed Construction Based on Buildings in Worcestershire*. London: Society for Medieval Archaeology, 1967; N.W. Alcock, P.S. Barnwell, and M. Cherry, *Cruck Building: A Survey*. Rewley House Studies in the Historic Environment 11. Donington: Shaun Tyas, 2019.
[2] J. Walker, ed, *The English Medieval Roof, Crown Post to King Post.* Essex: Essex Historic Buildings Group, 2011.
[3] D. Yeomans, *The Trussed Roof: Its History and Development*. Aldershot: Scolar Press, 1992.

[4] C. Hewett, *English Historic Carpentry.* Chichester: Phillimore, 1980. p.187

[5] *The History of the King's Works,* Colvin, H.M., D.R. Ransome, John Summerson, Vol III, London: Her Majesty's Stationary Office, 1963 (1975 repr), p.267.

[6] L.F. Salzman, *Building in England down to 1540.* Oxford, 1952, p. 581.

[7] King's Works, p.267n.

[8] H. Ellis, 'Extracts from the Proceedings of the Privy Council', in *Archaeologia*, 18 (1817), pp.131-32.

[9] A. Caroe, D.R, *Old Churches and Modern Craftsmanship.* Oxford, New York & Toronto: Oxford University Press, 1949.

[10] R. Brandon, and J. Arthur Brandon, *Open Timber Roofs of the Middle Ages*. London: Batsford, 1860.

[11] L. Prosser, personal communication.

[12] P. Hoffsummer, (ed.). *Les Carpentes Du XIr Au XIXe Siècle, Typologie et Évolution En France Du Nord et En Belgique*. Cahiers Du Petriomoine 62. Paris: Monum, Éditions du patrimoine, 2002 – translated by Nathaniel Alcock et al. as *Roof Frames from the 11th to the 19th Century. Typology and Development in Northern France and in Belgium.* Turnhout, Belgium: Brepols, 2009.

The Depiction of Water Technology in Ramelli's *Le Diverse et Artificose Machine* and Its Influence on Engineering Treatises in China in the 17th Century

Lei Song, James W. P. Campbell
Department of Architecture, University of Cambridge, UK

Abstract

This paper looks at Agostino Ramelli and his treatise *Le Diverse et Artificose Machine*. In particular, it categorises the hydraulic machines depicted in the treatise and his possible contribution to water lifting technology, including his depictions of cylinder pumps, rotary pumps, double-acting pumps, chain pumps, cams and cranks, and complex fountains. Most importantly, the paper then shows how Ramelli's treatise was introduced to China by the Jesuit missionaries in the seventeenth century and how it had a major influence on the depiction of hydraulic machines in Chinese engineering books in this period.

Introduction

As historians are beginning to realise, many of the inventions commonly attributed to the Industrial Revolution were in fact merely copies of earlier technologies imported from elsewhere. As more research is done it becomes clear that Medieval technology was more sophisticated than is often supposed. Archaeology plays a crucial role in broadening our understanding in the absence of technical literature. However, from the 1500s, clues to earlier technical innovations and technology of the time can be found in manuals and treatises that appeared in the Renaissance with the birth of printing. While moveable type printing was invented in 1450 in Europe it took time for the technology to become widespread and it is really only in the mid-16th century that technical manuals began to appear in print, bringing an existing manuscript tradition to a much broader audience. From 1550 a variety books started to appear, showing a variety of mechanical and technological inventions, some of which were real and some of which, as historian of technology George Basalla has noted, 'go beyond what is technically feasible [1]'.

The problem for the construction historian is thus to separate the real from the imaginary. These books include Georgius Agricola's book *De Re Metallica* (On Metals) published in 1556, Jacques Besson's *Theatrum Instrumentorum* (Theater of Machines) completed and published in 1571-2, Jean Errard's *Instruments Mathematiques Mechaniques* (1584), and Vittorio Zonca's *Novo Teatro di Machine et Edificii* published at Padua in 1607. These books were devoted to machinery and its possibilities. For example, Agricola's book was concerned with the mechanical devices employed in mining and metallurgy.

Agostino Ramelli's *Le Diverse et Artificose Machine*

The richest and best known of these mechanical treatises was Agostino Ramelli's *Le Diverse et Artificose Machine* which came out in 1588 [2]. It is a treatise of engineering contrivances and machines which contains 195 engraved plates of illustrations. The original edition was written in both Italian and French. It was only in 1976 that the book was first translated and republished in English, titled *The Various and Ingenious Machines of Agostino Ramelli: A Classic Sixteenth-Century Illustrated Treatise on Technology* [3]. In addition to the original text, the editors of this edition, Martha

The Depiction of Water Technology in Ramelli's Le Diverse et Artificose Machine and Its Influence on Engineering Treatises in China in the 17th Century

Teach Gnudi and Eugene S. Ferguson, provide a useful biographical study of the author, a pictorial inventory of the principal components of Ramelli's machines, and discussion the precedents and influences of Ramelli's works.

While Ramelli's work demonstrated a unity of pictorial style, the machines he was drawing were a mixture of entirely original creations and the technology of his time. There has even been some speculation that the manuscripts of Leonardo da Vinci (1452-1519) might have had an influence on Ramelli's machines [4]. In the early twentieth century, Payson Usher suggested that Leonardo da Vinci's manuscripts marked the 'beginning of modern treatises on hydraulics and applied mechanics' as represented in the work of Ramelli, Besson, and Zonca [5]. In 1972, after the discovery of Leonardo's manuscripts *Codex Madrid* in 1965, Ladislao Reti went through both and found eight examples of similar mechanisms in Ramelli's book and Leonardo's manuscripts [6]. For example, a similar double Noria for raising water can be found in both Ramelli's book and Leonardo's manuscript. However, it seems very unlikely that Ramelli had access to Leonardo's manuscripts (only a single copy existed) and much more likely that both were depicting machines available at the time.

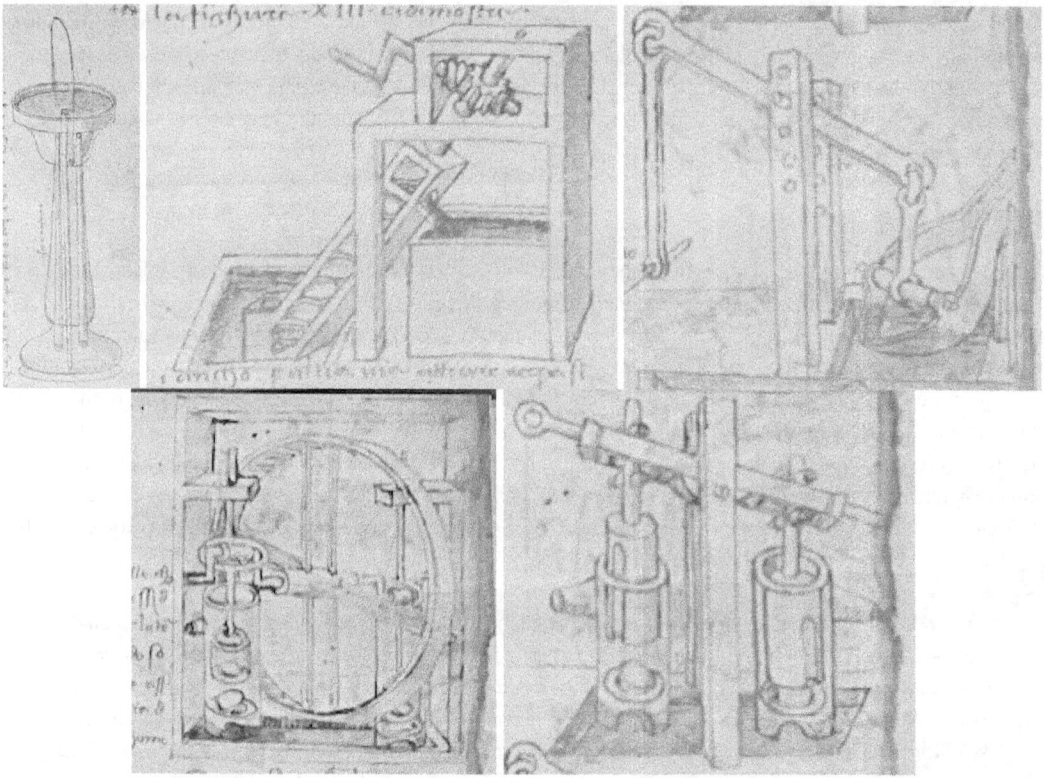

Figure 1: Water machines from Francesco di Giorgio's manuscript Trattato di Architectura: a fountain (top-left), Archimedean water screws (top-middle), hinged-pan swape (top-right), double-acting force pumps (bottom-left), double-acting hinged fan bellows (bottom).

A more likely influence is Francesco di Giorgio Martini (1439-1502) [7]. According to late historian of technology Professor Gustina Scaglia, it was possible that Ramelli became acquainted with Francesco di Giorgio's machine drawings in his twenties while doing his military service (1553-1555) at the siege of Siena [8]. Francesco di Giorgio's *Trattato di Architectura* had a great number of illustrations and texts on various pumps, mills, fountains, and water-lifting devices, which formed the basis of Ramelli's techniques (Fig. 1). In addition, architects might also have had an influence on Ramelli's designs. Gnudi and Ferguson suggested that the sense of spectacular and complexity in Ramelli's works may have benefited from the precedent architectural constructions, such as the great dome of Florence Cathedral by Filippo Brunelleschi (1377-1446) and the Vatican obelisk by Domenico Fontana (1543-1607) [9]. In spite of the similarities, Ramelli's work showed unique pictorial style and fanciful technical innovations that went beyond any of his predecessors. Without further documentary evidence we cannot determine whether or not Ramelli studied the works of Leonardo, Francesco di Giorgio or other predecessors since lost. We can however say that Leonardo, Francesco di Giorgio, and Ramelli shared the same mechanical traditions and their works illustrate the hydraulic technologies in the early modern period.

Agostino Ramelli (1531–1608?)

Despite the fact that Ramelli's book played an important role in the field of Renaissance technology, comparatively little has been written about its author. A short biography was provided by Gnudi and included in the English edition [10]. This mostly derives from Ramelli's own statements in the Preface and Dedication of his book [11]. Ramelli (1531-1608) was either born in Ponte Tresa, Switzerland, or the nearby village of Mesenzana, Italy, four years after the sack of Rome in 1527 by the Spanish troops of Charles V [12]. He went on to become a military engineer in France under the Duke of Anjou, later Henry III, King of France and Poland [13]. He was sent to draw up plans of the fortified port of La Rochelle and assisted the Catholic League in the defence of Paris in 1590 [14]. His military rank explains his title Capitano Agostino Ramelli on the title page (Fig. 2). The frontispiece (Fig. 2) shows Ramelli was holding a pair of spring dividers above a fortification miniature while his other hand resting on a helmet. The portrait represents his two areas of expertise: mathematics and war. He was described by his French peer Ambroise Bachot as "a true Daedalus as architect and the Archimedes of our age [15]".

Figure 2: The cover page (left) and frontispiece (right) of Ramelli's book.

The Contents of Ramelli's Le Diverse et Artificose Machine

In *Le Diverse et Artificose Machine*, the water-related machines range from the utilitarian (pumps, water wheels, mills) to the imaginative (automatic fountains and a book-wheel). Based on the classification of devices in the English translation of the book [16], there are 110 water-raising devices, 21 grain mills, 10 cranes, 7 machines for dragging heavy objects, 2 machines for raising excavated earth, 2 cofferdams, 4 fountains and bird calls, one book wheel, 15 military bridges, 14 military screw jacks and breaking devices, 4 military hurling engines, and one gunner's quadrant. Among all the devices, four types of prime movers were shown: 110 used manpower (56%), 65 waterpower (33%), 9 horsepower (5%), and 3 windpower (2%). Water was thus a key power source for his inventions and indeed before the invention of steam power the key source of power for industry.

Each plate of the machines in the book was supplemented with the textual explanation given in two languages side by side. The Italian text was printed in Italic letters and the French translation was in Roman letters. It was not uncommon to publish a bilingual work within the same volume. Besson did the same. The choice of languages reflects Ramelli's career and origins. His efforts to present his text in two commonly-used languages made his work readily available to the majority of the European engineers and combined with its rich illustrations ensured it popularity in the sixteenth century.

What makes this book distinct from its counterparts is that the plates were illustrated in such great detail that machines could actually be constructed from them. The text is written to be purely practical and full of mechanical descriptions without any historical or personal asides. Having said that, it is still difficult to reconstruct them based on the book because of a lack any dimensions or specific materials. Ramelli's was criticised for this by his rivals. In his treatise *Les Raisons des forces mouvantes* (1615), the architect and engineer Salomon de Caus dismissed Besson and Ramelli's existing works as 'machines invented on paper' ('machines par eux inventées sur le papier') that could have failed to function practically, urging readers to purchase his book instead [17].

The sequence of presentation in Ramelli's book follows a certain logic: machines of similar function are put in sequence, from the simplest to the most complex ones which combine or improve earlier devices (Plates 1-2, 5-6, 7) [18]. The presentation of drawings was innovative. Ramelli used the cutaway views to display the component parts in his machines, fore-runners of modern 'exploded view' (eg.Plates 5, 53, 185). He also used cutaway views in the machines themselves in Plates 15, 54 and used "phantom views" to display the structure of components (the inner tube) in Plate 98.

In terms of the contents of the book, Ramelli seemed more fascinated by the hydraulic technologies than machines of war, despite his training as a military engineer. Over half of the mechanical inventions in this book were concerned with lifting, distributing, and displaying water, including a variety of pumps, fountains, water wheels, and water screws. His major contribution was arguably in water lifting technology, including cylinder pumps, rotary pumps, double-acting pumps, chain pumps, cams and cranks, and complex fountains, which will be illustrated in detail in the following sections.

Innovations of Water Technology in Ramelli

Cylinder Pumps with Crankshafts

In England, pumps and water scoops seem to have first appeared in the 1500s. The first known pumped system in England was installed by Peter Morice, a Dutch engineer driven by an undershot water wheel under one of the arches of London Bridge in 1582. Later five arches were being used to pump Thames's water to a high square tower at the bridgehead from which it was distributed by gravity [19]. Ramelli's treatise thus seems to be ahead of his time in terms of the pumps. Of the 110 water-raising devices that were described in this treatise, there were various kinds of water pumps: force pumps, lift pumps, bellows pumps, oscillating wing pumps, rotary pumps, paternoster chain pumps, and Archimedean screws.

Ramelli's book is the first known piece to depict a four-cylinder pump operated by a single crank-shaft as shown in Plate 5 (Fig. 3). Following the water-driven machine in Plate 5, Ramelli depicted a similar kind of machine with variations, a two-cylinder encased pump with crankshaft which was man-powered. The water-raising device in Plate 5 operated with the help of a river. When cog B turns cage gear C, the crankshaft D causes the four rods to move pistons up and down, so that the water rises through pipes L M N O to pipes T V X Y and finally into receptacle Z from which it is carried through channel or pipe K. Where the crankshaft enters the cases (shown as P Q R S) a seal is required to maintain the pressure and the piston must also include a valve to allow water to flow through it. Ramelli depicted three alternative piston valves in the cutaway views on the left.

The use of crankshafts in encased water-lifting devices was a relatively new innovation. Man harnessed water in prehistoric times. A wide range of basic machine components were used by the Greeks and Romans, including gears, chains, linkages, pistons, and pulleys. Yet the crank does not seem to have appeared in the West until the ninth century A.D. The earliest example of the use of cranks was found in the Chinese Han dynasty no later than 200 AD [20]. The earliest evidence of a compound crank and connecting-rod in Renaissance Italy was found in Mariano di Jacopo Taccola's manuscript, but the sketch was mechanically defective [21]. Ramelli successfully integrated cranks and connecting-rods into hydraulic machine designs and depicted eighteen examples in his treatise.

Figure 3: Plate 5 (left) shows a four-cylinder encased pump with a crankshaft. Plate 6 (right) shows a two-cylinder encased pump with a crankshaft.

The Depiction of Water Technology in Ramelli's Le Diverse et Artificose Machine and Its Influence on Engineering Treatises in China in the 17th Century

Rotary Pumps

Ramelli described and illustrated the first known rotary pumps, which were probably his most significant contribution [22]. It was the original kinematical solution that should be attributed to Ramelli. No rotary pumps are found among Leonardo's extant works [23]. Ramelli depicted thirteen original designs of rotary pumps (Plates 38-40, 51-53, 93, and 105-109). The water-lifting machine in Plate 38 (Fig. 4) is a sliding-vane rotary pump. When the wheel turned, vanes create a void at the inlet port and draw liquid in, which is transferred from inlet to discharge port as the vanes slid into slots. Another different type of rotary pump, the gated-lobe rotary pump, is shown as A in Plate 40 (Fig. 4). These rotary pumps transfer a certain volume of fluid through a rotating mechanism by using the actions of rotating vanes, screws, or gears whose teeth are fitted into each other to work precisely. This sort of rotating system creates a partial vacuum to draw the liquid into the pump. Most of Ramelli's rotary pumps were variations on the gated lobe pump.

Figure 4: Plate 38 (left) and Plate 40 (right) depicts the rotary pumps.

Link Chain Pumps

The link chain pump was a type of primitive pumping mechanism that has been used in China for three thousand years [24]. The Dutch carried the early chain pumps from China to Europe. The link chain pumps consisted of open troughs which were tilted in sequence to empty into each other by a system of linking rods to form a continuous conveyor. Ramelli's Plates 95 and 96 show the apparatus that could have been used (Fig. 5). Ladislao Reti's has suggested that the water-raising machine built by Juanelo Turriano which was built about 1580 to supply water to the city of Toledo in Spain worked on this principle [25].

Figure 5: Plate 95 shows the link chain pump.

Pumps using Archimedean Screws

Some of Ramelli's images depict Archimedean water screws, one of the earliest hydraulic devices. Also known as Egyptian screws, the mechanism was first described by Archimedes c. 234 BC and records suggest that he was describing existing water screws or screw pumps in Hellenistic Alexandria, Egypt that has been used before the third century BC [26]. By definition, Archimedean screws as water pumps are equipped with gears to transfer water from a low-lying body to a higher ditch, as such water is pumped by turning a screw-shaped surface inside a pipe.

Ramelli shows multiple combinations of transmission mechanisms using Archimedes screws Plates 45-48 show two kinds of water wheels, four different schemes of transmitting power from the first mover to the train of Archimedean screws, and six different gear configurations [27]. Plate 46 is the only one to include a section of the screw. This one was based on two helical blades. Furthermore, two types of wheels were used as the first mover. In Plates 45, 46, and 48, the machines used the noria as part of the lifting system. As shown, the undershot wheel, as the first mover, transferred the force of the stream to the two sets of radial paddles or vanes, which filled the central set of water-lifting buckets and carried the water to the top of the wheel. There was nothing particularly novel about the use of noria. They are simply water wheels driven by a running stream where the power of the stream is used to lift water in the wheel to a higher level where it discharges into a channel or tub. They are shown in many of Ramelli's plates. Here however the noria is used to

The Depiction of Water Technology in Ramelli's Le Diverse et Artificose Machine and Its Influence on Engineering Treatises in China in the 17th Century

lift the water into a tank which is then emptied by an Archimedes screw. In Plate 47, the machine is driven by a horizontal waterwheel driving three screws to draw the water from the spring to the top receptacle.

Fountains

Ramelli depicted a high level of complexity in his designs of three fountains shown in Plates 184-186 (Fig. 6). Bedini has suggested that these fountains may have been influenced by Hero's *Pneumatics* [28]. However, Gnudi and Ferguson Hero's have pointed out that the *Pneumatics* had only been published a few years before Ramelli's book and it was unlikely that he could have developed such an elaborately decorated and complex fountain in so short a time. Gnudi and Ferguson also provided a detailed description of the fountains' mechanisms:

> The pressure exerted by the water standing in pipe I on the air in the lowest chamber V provides the impetus to cause the water in compartment Q to flow upward through pipe H into the upper vase E F. The proportions of the pipes would have to be such that the pressure in I was sufficient to lift the water through H.
>
> Water flows out of the revolving pipes because they are arranged as siphons. They revolve because their outlet nozzles are pointed in a direction that employs the reactive force of the water, as it issues from the nozzles, to push tangentially and thus turn the pipe assembly [29].

The operations of these fountains were based upon a subtle application of hydraulic principles. The cross-section in Plate 185 shows the internal system, which was identical to the fountain in the preceding plate. The serpentine-shaped pipes are designed to acted as siphons to draw the water up, while the internal system relies on the different levels of air and water pressure to keep the water circulating. According to Ramelli's description, this fountain was designed to be displayed on a banquet table and could be filled with perfumed water so guests could enjoy the fragrance, or simply wash their hands.

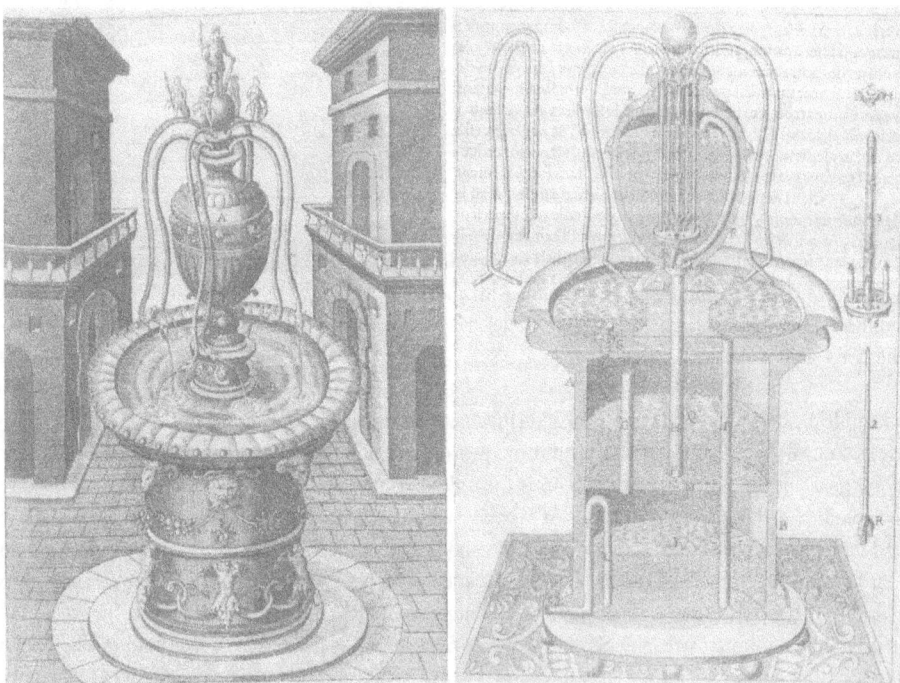

Figure 6: Plate 184 (left) and Plate 185 (right) show the elevation and section of a fountain design.

Transfer of Images of European Hydraulic Machines to China

Ramelli's book was undoubtedly influential in the West but what is more surprising is the fact that it was extensively copied soon after its publication in the Far East. At the end of the sixteenth century, Jesuit missionaries took a number of machine books into China and these formed the basis for three Chinese engineering books: *Tai Xi Shui Fa* (Hydraulic machinery of the West) by Sabatino de Ursis and Xu Guangqi (1612)[30], the *Qi Qi Tu Shuo* (Illustrations and explanations of wonderful machines) by Johann Schreck and Wang Zheng (1627)[31], and the *Zhu Qi Tu Shuo* (Diagrams and explanations of a number of machines) by Wang Zheng (1627)[32]. The original title of *Qi Qi Tu Shuo* was *Yuan Xi Qi Qi Tu Shuo Lu Zui* (The best diagrams and explanations of wonderful machines of the Far West), which was later simplified to its present form. All three books had an emphasis on hydraulic devices.

Qi Qi Tu Shuo was the first Chinese translation of a work that introduced Western machine engineering to China. It was a collaboration work by Wang Zheng (王徵 1571-1664) and Johann Schreck, also Terrenz or Terentius, or his Chinese name Deng Yuhan (鄧玉函 1576-1630). Johann was a remarkable German Jesuit missionary who has received little scholarly attention [33]. He was a friend of Galileo and one of the earliest members of the Accademia dei Lincei, the prestigious European scientific institution in Rome. In this book, Johann was credited with dictating the original western texts to Wang and Wang was responsible for illustrating European machines in a Chinese pictorial style and formulating Johann's interpretations into written Chinese [34]. Wang expressed his wish to provide public benefit and his attempt to select 'the most pragmatic, convenient, and delicate' machines to depict in the book [35]. In so doing, *Qi Qi Tu Shuo* played an important part in introducing new hydraulic techniques to China and later to Japan and Korea.

The preface of *Qi Qi Tu Shuo* named several western engineers [36]. Wang considered Archimedes as the great engineer for building the water screws, which was renamed in Chinese as the 'dragon-tail car' (Long Wei 龙尾). The preface also mentioned other engineers who he believed to be the creative people who understood the principles of thousands of machines, including Agricola (Geng Tian), Simon Stevin (Xi Men), and Ramelli (La Mo Li) [37]. Several historians have compared Ramelli's plates with the diagrams in *Qi Qi Tu Shuo*. The first scholar to note the resemblance was H. Th. Horwitz who pointed out that the diagrams were inaccurate and contained technical misunderstandings while the texts were more accurate reproductions of the originals. The most informative study was conducted by Joseph Needham in his monumental *Science and Civilization in China*. He provided a comprehensive list of machines described and illustrated in the Chinese books produced under Jesuit influence, identifying sources including Besson, Ramelli, Zonca, Vitruvius, and Francesco di Giorgio [38]. While it is true that certain pictures in these Jesuit books were directly reproduced from Western works, it does not necessarily mean that the ideas they contained were new in the Chinese history of technology.

Qi Qi Tu Shuo consists of three volumes with the first two forming the theoretical basis of the mechanical works. The third volume contains 54 machines in twelve sections: machines for weight raising (Qi Zhong 起重), weight hauling (Yin Zhong 引重), weight-raising by turning (Zhuan Zhong 转重), water lifting (Qu Shui 取水), grinding-mills (Zhuan Mo 转磨), saw-mills for wood (Jie Mu 解木), saw-mills for stone (Jie Shi 解石), a vertical stamp mill (Zhuan Dui 转碓), a revolving bookcase inspired by Ramelli (Shu Jia 书架), the Vitruvian anaphoric clock (Shui Ri Gui 水日晷), mechanical cable ploughing (Dai Geng 代耕), and force pumps for fire-fighting (Shui Chong 水铳)[39].

In particular, the section on machines for water-lifting in *Qi Qi Tu Shuo* contains nine diagrams of machines. Some of these machines already had a prototype in *Tai Xi Shui Fa* (Fig. 7), which offered detailed diagrams on its components and construction principles. It was the first time these basic devices had been depicted Chinese engineering books and many diagrams were identical to those in early printed versions of Vitruvius (the original illustrations had been lost but translators of early printed versions provided their own)[40]. These devices include: the Archimedean water screws called Long Wei (龙尾), which literally means 'Dragon's tails'; the piston pumps called Heng Sheng (恒升); the double-acting force pumps or double cylinder piston water pumps known as Yu Heng (玉衡). These prototypes can be seen in the machines in the *Qi Qi Tu Shuo*.

The Depiction of Water Technology in Ramelli's *Le Diverse et Artificose Machine* and Its Influence on Engineering Treatises in China in the 17th Century

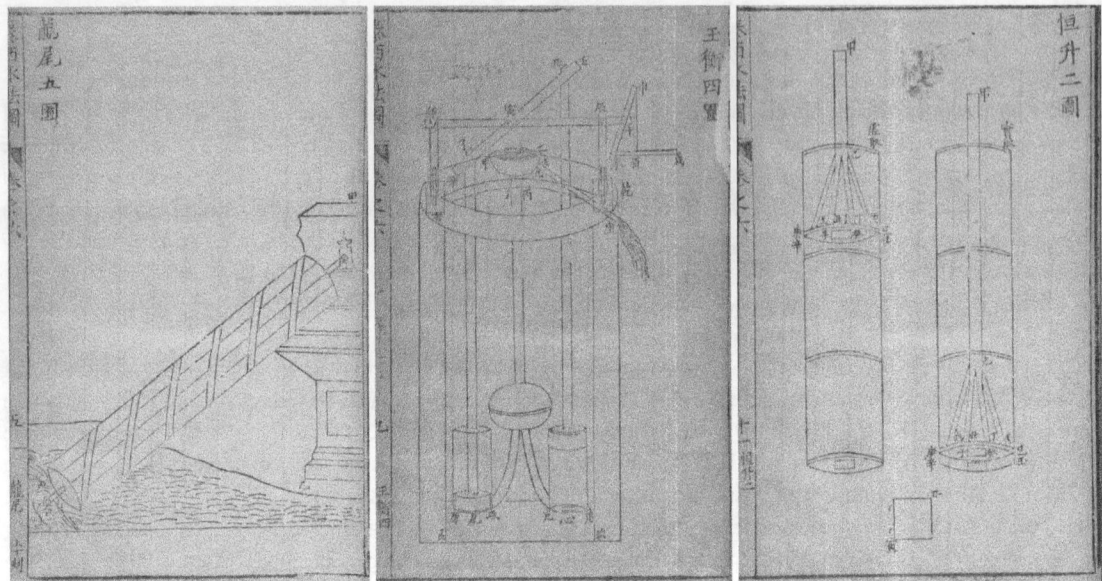

Figure 7: Illustrations from Tai Xi Shui Fa: the Archimedean water screws (left), Yu Heng (middle), and Heng Sheng (right).

When comparing the diagrams in *Qi Qi Tu Shuo* with the plates in Ramelli's book, it can be seen that *Qi Qi Tu Shuo* reproduced the plates directly (Fig. 8). The first diagram in *Qi Qi Tu Shuo* depicts a machine of Archimedean water screws with a vertical water wheel to simultaneously move three screws. This machine undoubtedly resembles Ramelli's Plate 45. The second diagram also depicts Archimedean water screws reproduced from Ramelli's Plate 47 but with a horizontal water wheel. However, the structure of the Chinese horizontal water wheel is illustrated inaccurately; the configuration of the blade is not clearly drawn. The third diagram shows the manpowered piston water pump similar to Ramelli's Plate 61. The fourth diagram shows a water wheel driven by a Dutch horizontal-axis tower-type windmill similar to Ramelli's Plate 73. The sixth diagram is a double swape lifted and lowered automatically by an obliquely cut conical cam rotated by a horizontal water-wheel. Needham pointed out that it was a reproduction from Besson [41]. The ninth diagram is a rotary water pump that is the same as Ramelli's Plate 109.

The Chinese diagrams can also compared with the illustrations in Francesco di Giorgio's manuscripts. The seventh diagram is a hinged-pan swape that is similar to a machine drawn in Francesco di Giorgio's manuscripts (Fig. 1). The eighth diagram illustrates the manpower double cylinder piston water pump, with two-throw crankshaft working in rings or eyes on the piston rods, operated by a drum treadmill. The simple form is different from Ramelli's plates and also resembles a piston water pump in the sketch from Francesco di Giorgio's manuscripts (Fig. 1).

Based on the comparative study above, one can see that the two Jesuit engineering books, *Qi Qi Tu Shuo* and *Tai Xi Shui Fa*, for the first time introduced five European water technologies into China. These included the Archimedean screws, the Ctesibian double-acting force pump, the Dutch vertical tower-type windmills, the double swape worked by a rotating conical cam, and rotary water pumps.

Figure 8: A comparison of plates from Ramelli (top row) and diagrams in Qi Qi Tu Shuo (bottom row).

Conclusion

The illustrations in Ramelli's book show many functional hydraulic machines that were either developed from existing devices or later constructed from his ideas. Ramelli's innovation combined many readymade components or machines in new ways. Simple piston pumps, Archimedean water-screws, noria water wheels, and chains of buckets and rosary pumps were machines long in use. Ramelli's new inventions, such as the four-cylinder water pumps, rotary pumps, and double-acting piston pumps, reflected the book's significance as the culmination of Renaissance technological usage and the beginning of further development. These innovations were later introduced in China by Jesuit missionaries and contributed to the development of water technology in the Far East. Of these Jesuit contributions, *Qi Qi Tu Shuo* was published thirty years after its European prototypes, which probably makes it the best reflection of contemporary western technologies. The extent to which Ramelli's machines reflected current practice or were largely exercises in imagination will no doubt remain disputed but what we do know is that the principles Ramelli was illustrating were real strategies for lifting water so it seems likely that he was depicting inventions he had seen or made himself, albeit with a certain artistic license, making him an important source for all construction historians, but one that should be used with due caution.

The Depiction of Water Technology in Ramelli's Le Diverse et Artificose Machine and Its Influence on Engineering Treatises in China in the 17th Century

References

[1] George Basalla, The Evolution of Technology, Cambridge Studies in the History of Science (Cambridge University Press, 1989), p. 67.

[2] Agostino Ramelli, Le diverse et artificiose machine / del capitano Agostino Ramelli... Nellequali si contengono uarij et industriosi mouimenti, degni digrandissima speculatione, per cauarne beneficio infinito in ogni sorte d'operatione. Composte in lingua italiana et francese (Paris: sn, 1588).

[3] Martha Teach Gnudi and Eugene S. Ferguson, The Various and Ingenious Machines of Agostino Ramelli (London, 1976).

[4] Ferguson, in his introduction in the English edition of Ramelli's book, has shown the similarities between Ramelli's drawings and the illustrations in Leonardo's manuscripts. See Gnudi and Ferguson, The Various and Ingenious Machines of Agostino Ramelli, 1976, p. 34-35.

[5] Abbott Payson Usher, A History of Mechanical Inventions / Abbott Payson Usher., Rev. ed. (First edition in 1929) (New York: Dover, 1988), p. 327.

[6] Ladislao Reti, 'Leonardo and Ramelli', Technology and Culture, 13.4 (1972), 577–605 (p. 580).

[7] Gnudi and Ferguson, pp. 33–35; Gustina Scaglia, 'Leonardo Da Vinci's Drawing in the Pierpont Morgan Library: Its Travels from Milan to La Rochelle (1519-1572)', Arte Lombarda, 113/115 (2-4), 1995, 27–36 (p. 32); Ladislao Reti, 'Francesco Di Giorgio Martini's Treatise on Engineering and Its Plagiarists', Technology and Culture, 4.3 (1963), 287–98 <https://doi.org/10.2307/3100858>; Francis C. Moon, The Machines of Leonardo Da Vinci and Franz Reuleaux: Kinematics of Machines from the Renaissance to the 20th Century (Springer Science & Business Media, 2007), p. 153.

[8] Gustina Scaglia, p. 31.

[9] Gnudi and Ferguson, p. 33.

[10] Gnudi and Ferguson, p. 24.

[11] His birth year, place of birth and much other information derived from the cover page of his book by Dr. Gnudi.

[12] See Dr. Gnudi's biographical study of the author and Note 2 in The Various and Ingenious Machines of Agostino Ramelli, 1987.

[13] Gnudi and Ferguson, pp. 13–14.

[14] Gnudi and Ferguson, p. 13.

[15] Martha Teach Gnudi, 'Agostino Ramelli and Ambroise Bachot', Technology and Culture, 15.4 (1974), 614–25 (p. 619).

[16] Gnudi and Ferguson, p. 27. I owe this classification to Eugene S. Ferguson.

[17] Salomon de Caus, Maria Nugent, and donor DSI Burndy Library, Les raisons des forces mouuantes auec diuerses machines tant vtilles que plaisantes : aus quelles sont adioints plusieurs desseings de grotes et fontaines (A Francfort : En la boutique de Jan Norton, 1615) <http://archive.org/details/raisonsdesforce00Caus> [accessed 28 November 2021]; Luke Morgan, Nature as Model: Salomon de Caus and Early Seventeenth-Century Landscape Design (University of Pennsylvania Press, 2007), p. 127.

[18] Gnudi and Ferguson, p. 26.

[19] C J MERDINGER, p. 284.

[20] Joseph Needham, Science and Civilisation in China: Volume 4, Physics and Physical Technology, Part 2, Mechanical Engineering (Cambridge University Press, 1965), pp. 118–19.

[21] Lynn Townsend White, Medieval Technology and Social Change: Lynn White, Jr, Acls Humanities E-Book (London: Oxford University Press, 1962), p. 113 <http://hdl.handle.net/2027/heb.01086> [accessed 30 November 2021].

[22] Gnudi and Ferguson, p. 549.

[23] Ladislao Reti, 'Leonardo and Ramelli', p. 603.

[24] F. W. Robins, The Story of Water Supply / by F.W. Robins. (London ; New York: Oxford University Press, 1946), p. 43.

[25] Ladislao Reti, 'El Artificio de Juanelo en Toledo', 1967, pp. 3-46. Cited from Gnudi and Ferguson, pp. 552–53.

[26] B. A. Stewart and Terry A. Howell, Encyclopedia of Water Science (New York: Marcel Dekker, 2003), p. 759; Joseph Oleson, Greek and Roman Mechanical Water-Lifting Devices: The History of a Technology (Toronto: University of Toronto Press, 1984), p. 23.

[27] Gnudi and Ferguson, p. 550.

[28] Silvio A. Bedini, 'The Role of Automata in the History of Technology', Technology and Culture, 5.1 (1964), 24–42 (p. 25).

[29] Gnudi and Ferguson, p. 558.

[30] Sabatino De Ursis and Guangqi Xu, Tai xi shui fa, Tian xue chu han (China: sn, 1628).

[31] Joannes Schreck and Zheng Wang, Qi qi tu shuo: san juan / Deng Yuhan kou shu ; Wang Zheng yi hui. Xin zhi zhu qi tu shuo / Wang Zheng zhu. (China]: Lai lu tang, 1627).

[32] Needham, pp. 211–22.

[33] For the recent studies on Johann's biography, please see Claudia von Collani editor and Erich Zettl editor, Johannes Schreck-Terrentius SJ: Wissenschaftler und China-Missionar 1576-1630 / hrsg. von Claudia von Collani und Erich Zettl., Missionsgeschichtliches Archiv ; Bd. 22 (Stuttgart: Franz Steiner Verlag, 2016).

[34] Schreck and Wang.

[35] See the preface in Johannes Schreck and Zheng Wang, Yuan xi qi qi tu shuo lu zui. 3 juan 远西奇器图说 3 卷 (Zhang Pengfen, 1627) <http://nbn-resolving.de/urn:nbn:de:bvb:12-bsb00075643-2> [accessed 7 December 2021].

[36] The original text in the preface is: "大名人亚希默得， 新造龙尾车、小螺丝转等器，又能记万器之所以然。今时巧人之最能明万器之理者，一名未多，一名西门，又有绘图刻传者，一名耕田，一名刺墨里。此皆力艺学中传授之人也。"

[37] Needham, p. 213.

[38] Needham, pp. 215–18.

[39] Needham, p. 220. This article follows Needham's translation of the sections' titles in Qi Qi Tu Shuo.

[40] Michela Cigola and Yibing Fang, 'Traces and Echoes of De Architectura by Marcus Vitruvius Pollio in the Work of Xu Guangqi in 17th Century China', Frontiers of Mechanical Engineering, 11.1 (2016), 3–11.

[41] Needham, p. 220.

The Seventeenth and Eighteenth Centuries

From model to reality – a case study on the timber bridge of Baden (CH)

Clemens Knobling
Institute of Construction History and Preservation (IDB), ETH Zurich, Switzerland

Abstract

In the Swiss town of Baden, there is a bridge over the river Limmat which was built in 1810 by Blasius Balteschwiler, one of the most successful bridge builders of the period. It replaces a bridge dating from 1650, which had been one of the widest spanning bridges of the time. The original appearance of both bridges is known through contemporary models and drawings. Not only do the models themselves represent an important evidence for construction history, but show the early use of a "rod polygon" structure in a bridge. A drawing of the bridge of Baden can also be found in the collection of Swiss bridges in John Soane's Museum. Here, however, there are some inconsistencies that need to be investigated.

Another model from the 19th century, which can be found next to the old models in the historical museum of Baden, may date from the time of reconstruction. It is quite remarkable due to the use of a timber arch, but was not realised in favour of Balteschwiler's design.

This contribution is part of an ongoing research on Swiss timber bridges. It shows how important historical models can be in this context.

Introduction

In the Swiss town Baden in the canton of Aargau, several important traffic routes cross: routes from the Alps, from the Lake Constance, from Basel and from Zurich cross the river Limmat here. There has been a bridge here since Roman times, when Baden became famous for its thermal baths. The exact location of the Roman bridge is unknown, but it was further downstream than the present one.

Baden is situated at a narrow ford of the river Limmat between two steep mountain ridges, making it a place of strategic importance. The town was therefore always well-fortified, even more when the it finally became an embattled place in the confessional conflicts of the 16th to 18th centuries. Two castles existed in medieval times, one on a hill above the city and one below, next to the river. The lower castle was still fortified with bastions in the 18th century. Today, only a tower with the bridge gate is preserved. The unusually steep approach to the bridge in the narrow valley still points out its former importance as an easily controlled bottleneck (Fig. 1).

Evidence for the medieval bridge construction in Baden is sparse. The earliest known bridge was built here in the 13th century. [1] A second one had to be built after a flood in the 15th century. It was a covered bridge on wooden trestles. An early depiction can be found in the veduta from Edlibach's chronicle of 1505 [2], which shows the bridge standing on pillars next to the castle and another gate tower on the town side.

This was destroyed or demolished and another bridge was built by 1568/69, [3]. It is this which is depicted in an engraving by Merian from 1642, which shows it standing on three trestles (Fig. 2). Struts supported the tie beams from each bay.

From model to reality – a case study on the timber bridge of Baden (CH)

In 1647, one of the trestles got damaged [4], and was replaced by a stone pillar. However, the new pillar sank in the floods shortly after its erection, so the Baden council decided to build a new bridge without piers. [5]

Figure 1: Baden and the bridge over the river Limmat. Picture: Clemens Knobling

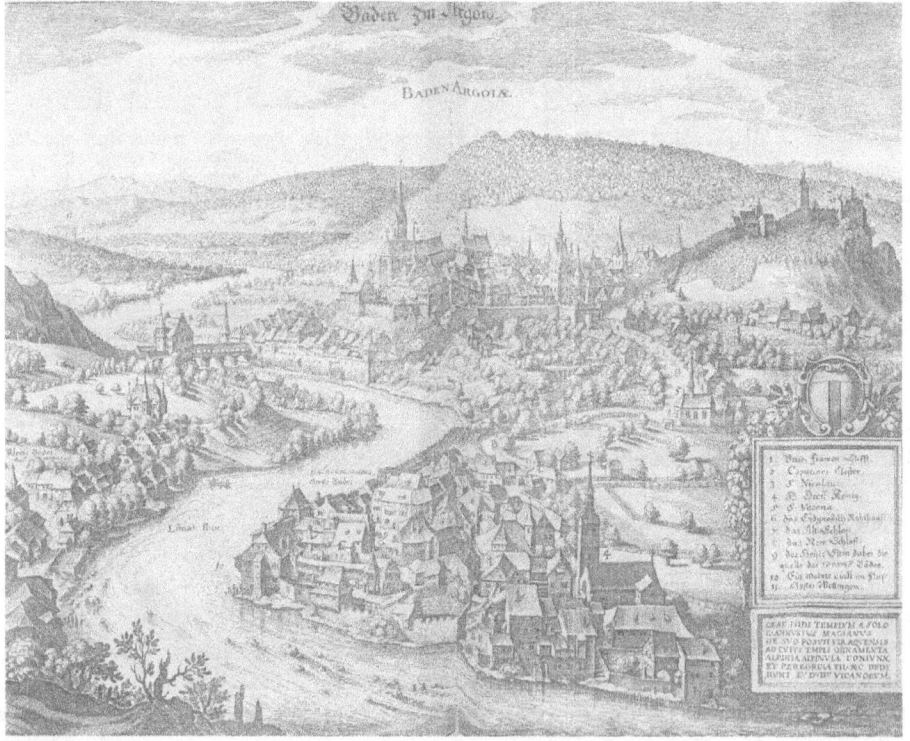

Figure 2: Engraving of Baden with the Bridge of 1568/69 by Matthäus Merian, 1642

The first bridge without intermediate supports from 1650

The council of the city of Baden commissioned the two master carpenters Hans Schüep and Michael Egger [6] to build the new bridge. They were first to set up a wooden model and submit it for assessment (Fig. 3, 4). They designed it with what was then the widest span in Switzerland, no less than 38 m. [7] Despite these considerable dimensions, the construction was completed in only four months. The two builders had to provide a guarantee that the bridge would last for 101 years. [8] They succeeded but, after 149 years of service, the bridge was destroyed by the retreating French army under General Masséna in 1799.

Two models of the 17th century bridge have been preserved in the Baden Historical Museum. They are both very similar, just different in scale and some details. It can probably be assumed that one of them is the model that had to be submitted to the town council for assessment before construction. [9] Furthermore, two also almost identical plans of the bridge have been preserved in the state archives of Basel (Fig. 5). Based on these drawings and models, we can form a clear idea of the shape and construction of the bridge.

The models of the bridge

It is remarkable that there are two very similar models, showing differences only in minor details. It can be assumed that both models were built for the erection of the bridge, maybe by the same builder, but obviously in close succession. One model is slightly smaller (scale approx. 1:35) (Fig. 3) than the other (scale approx. 1:25) (Fig. 4). The models still have a "raw" appearance – the larger one even more so – but they certainly served as working models to consider ideas and explain them to the laymen of the council. Even though the proportions of the individual parts seem to be somewhat inadequate, the models demonstrate the principal design ideas clearly, and the relatively coarse execution indicates that the models were built, and possibly rebuilt, quickly. At least one of them was made by the master builders Schüep and Egger themselves, as proven by an archival document which records that a model was commissioned by the city council of Baden though we do not know which one.

The main structure of the model bridges in modern terms could be described as a triple rod polygon. In the smaller one, the individual rods are straight, in the larger model they are partly curved. The curved elements seem to run through two bays of the bridge, that means they are interrupted at every second queen post. In the smaller model, the elements of the polygon are butt jointed each queen post. In both models, two main structures build a load bearing wall next to the roadway. In the large one, a strutted frame complements the rod polygon. In the smaller one also the inner supporting structure is a rod polygon, but with just slightly inclined straining beams. The roadway is slightly curved in the small model and horizontal in the large model. A wind bracing is only shown in the larger model just below the roadway. The smaller model contains no wind bracing. There are also differences in the roof. The principal trusses of both roof structures are stiffened with scissor braces. In the smaller model, however, the principal trusses are situated much closer together, which seems more realistic. Secondary trusses are missing in both cases. A longitudinal bracing in the roof is only shown in the small model by means of diagonal struts between the truss and the ridge purlin. In the large model this is completely missing, probably for reasons of abstraction.

The builders obviously planned the bridge without tie beams, there being not necessary due to the connection of the rod polygon with the massive abutment. The larger model shows a horizontal beam below the roadway, but this is probably only intended to indicate the lower edge of the cladding. However, it cannot be ruled out that this is a hint of a tie beam, which was then not executed over the entire model. There are no straining beams of the strutted frames, expected below the roadway. This is most likely a simplification of the model.

From model to reality – a case study on the timber bridge of Baden (CH)

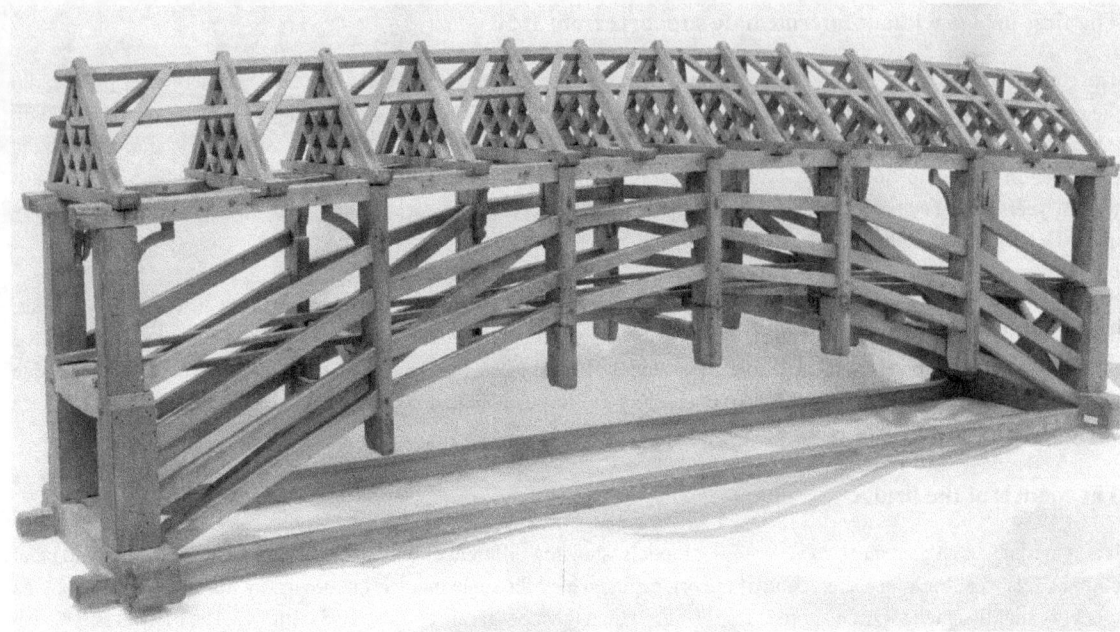

Figure 3: Small model of the bridge of 1650, Historisches Museum Baden. Picture: ETH, S. M. Holzer

Figure 4: Large model of the bridge of 1650, Historisches Museum Baden. Picture: ETH, S. M. Holzer

The drawings of the bridge

When comparing the models with the two almost identical drawings (Fig. 5), some notable differences can be observed. Due to the individual, arch-shaped beams, the construction looks more like a hybrid of a rod polygon and a true arch. One must assume that the drawing shows the queen posts in section, i.e. that the real elements of the rod polygon (or arch) ran centrally through the queen posts. The single elements each extend over two bays of the construction, so they are butted at every second queen post. However, the construction drawn does not appear to be stiff, nor are there any additional braces between the queen posts. A true arched structure would be eventually be built in 1766 in neighbouring Wettingen by Hans Ulrich Grubenmann. [10] The toothed arch in that bridge acts as a single, monolithic component by friction-locked lamellae.

Possibly, the representation of the polygon as an arch in the Baden drawings was intended to reassure the viewer: the arch was always considered to have an extraordinary load-bearing capacity. [11] Possibly this was advantageous for the presentation of the bridge design.

The bridge in the drawings has a horizontal beam - this could represent a tie beam or the roadway. The latter is argued by the fact that the design models do not have a tie beam either. The roof construction is shown in more detail in the drawings, e.g. by a longitudinal bracing with St. Andrew's crosses in the plane of the roof covering between the principal trusses.

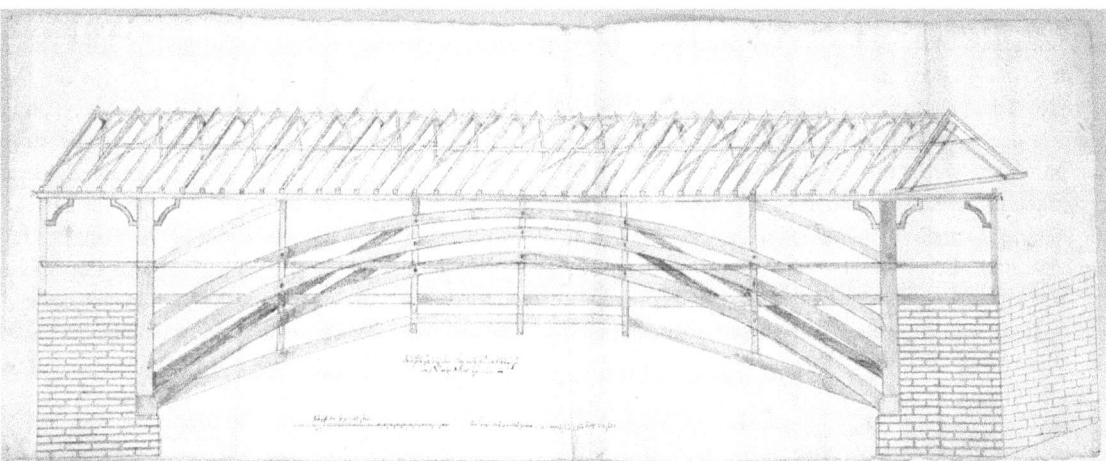

Figure 5: Drawing of the bridge of Baden from 1649 (Staatsarchiv Basel-Stadt, Planarchiv, A1,99)

The inner supporting structures of the load bearing wall are only shown schematically. As in the large model, these can be recognised as strutted frames, but doubled.

The colour scheme of the drawing cannot be clearly deciphered. The different colours may have been intended to indicate the different structures within the overall construction, thus improving the clarity of the plan. Below the drawing there is a written specification of the types of wood to be used for the individual building components, indicating that the plans were made still in the planning phase.

Since the bridge was destroyed, we can only guess the extent to which the drawings and models corresponded to reality. The rod polygon of the models, especially that of the small one with straight elements, seems to be a more realistic solution than the one shown in the drawings. But a rod polygon structure constructed using curved beams would have been possible. The bridge over the river Glatt - once in Glattbrugg, later moved to Rümlang - built in 1767 by Johannes Grubenmann, has a rod polygon of curved beams. [12] However, this was composed of two layers of thick beams and therefore appeared much more solid than the fragile arches of the drawing shown here.

In summary, it can be assumed that the small model is nearest to the final form and most closely reflects the final state of the master builders' design. In terms of the rod polygon and the roof construction, it appears to be more careful and detailed than the larger model.

With all the findings from the drawings and models, the presumed appearance of the bridge of 1650 can be summarised as follows: the bridge structure was constituted by the superposition of different trusses. The main structure was a triple rod polygon. It supported five queen posts each. The individual rods of the polygon were butted against the queen posts. These in turn were composed of two parts in order to enclose the longitudinal tie beam. Further structures complemented the overall construction: a strutted frame supported the tie beam from the abutments, further strutted frames reached from the abutments to the inner queen posts. Another diagonal bracing was placed between the outer queen posts. Also the inner struts of the strutted frames served as bracing. All the elements - strutted frames and rod polygon – were combined in the typical "load-bearing wall" or trussed girder.

Classification of the bridge

The bridge shown in the models and drawings represents the earliest known use of a rod polygon in Swiss bridge construction. An even earlier rod polygon in combination with a strutted frame in a bridge was documented in 1598 by Heinrich Schickhardt in the South Tyrolean town of Klausen. [13] The oldest surviving example of a rod polygon in Swiss bridge construction is the Rehetobel Bridge, built around 1700. [14] The bridge at Baden thus closes a major gap and proves the use of this construction in Switzerland before the 18th century. The famous bridge over the Rhine at Schaffhausen, which was built in 1758 by Hans Ulrich Grubenmann, also used rod polygons, which was, by then, one of the preferred methods of construction for large spans. With the construction of the Wettingen bridge (1766, Hans Ulrich Grubenmann), the true timber arch composed of interlocking lamellae was added to the range of available bridge construction techniques. Unfortunately, our knowledge of wooden bridge construction in the 18th century is still incomplete due to major losses. Too many important examples, like the Baden bridge, perished in the turmoil of the wars after the French Revolution. A research project on Swiss timber bridges, which has been applied for by the author, is intended to remedy this through research in the archives.

A contemporary drawing of the Baden Bridge in John Soane's Museum

Lastly the archive of John Soane's collection contains a puzzling representation of the Baden bridge (Fig. 6). The drawing is a copy of an original made in 1792 by John Augustus Hervey, eldest son of the Anglican Bishop of Derry, Frederick Hervey [15], and engraved by Cristoforo Dall'Acqua from Vicenza. [16] The date of the drawing suggests that the bridge should be the same one as the one represented by the Baden models and archival sources. However, the drawing shows an entirely different structure. For example, the rod polygon is missing completely and the load-bearing wall consists only of a triple queen post truss and a central strutted frame. Thus, although some elements are vaguely reminiscent of the drawings from the archives and the models, the essential parts (including the rod polygon) are missing. Perhaps Hervey did not want to depict all the elements of the bridge. However, this is unlikely, especially since other bridges with rod polygons have also been depicted completely. [17] Does the drawing from the Bishop of Derry's collection, the originals of which are mostly lost, therefore lead to doubts about the correctness of Schüep's and Egger's models and drawings? This seems unlikely as the models were part of the commissioning of the builders. [18] David Yeomans has pointed out, and further cross-checking with historical treatises supports this [19], that drawings are often confused with those elsewhere and wrongly titled. [20] Moreover, some of the drawings from Hervey's collection are less accurate than those produced by Soane himself. [21] We must therefore assume that the drawing of the Baden Bridge in John Soane's museum is either incorrect - it would be possible that one of the two copying processes resulted in a wrong allocation (in which case the inscription would be wrong). Furthermore, the proportions of the drawing and the relatively weak supporting structures would argue against a bridge with a 38 meters span. The above-mentioned research project on Swiss timber bridges will attempt to clarify the (few) unclear attributions in the collection of the John Soane's Museum by comparing them with the still preserved stock and sources from Swiss archives.

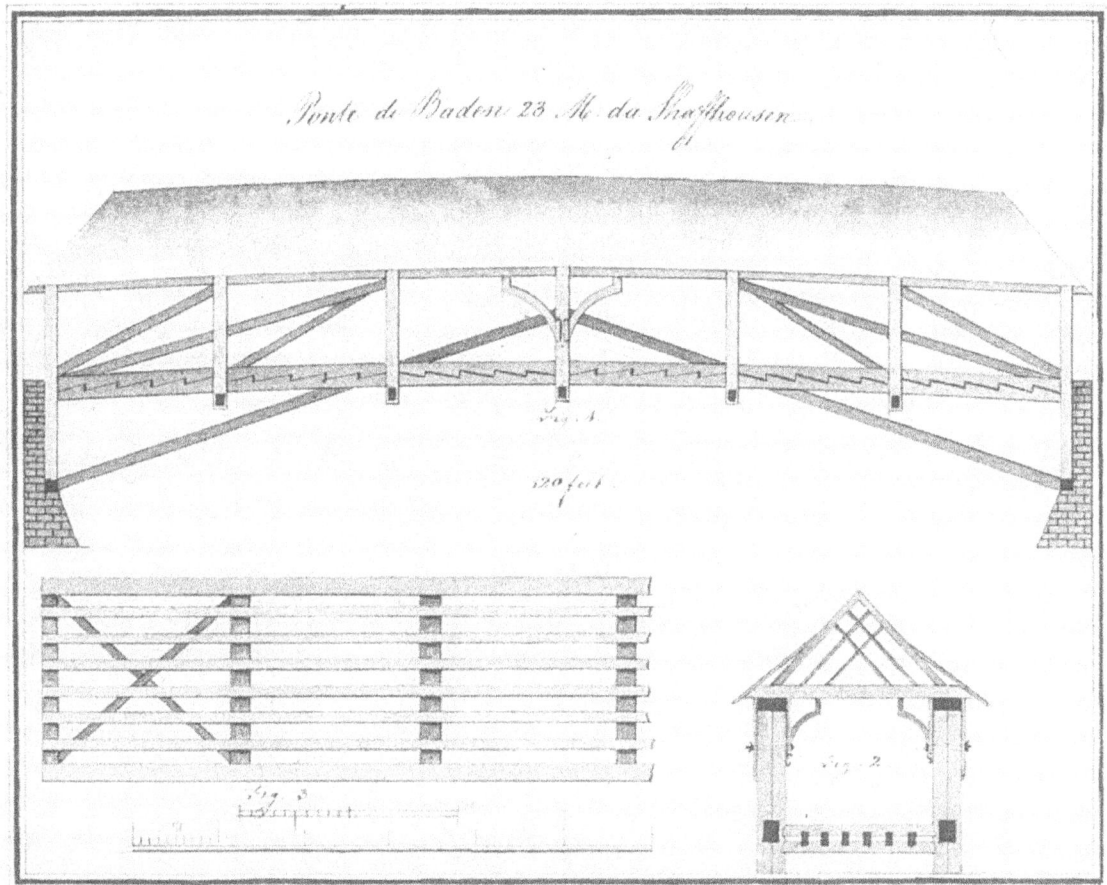

Figure 6: Copy of an engraving of the Bridge of Baden by Cristoforo Dall'Acqua after a drawing of John Augustus Hervey, 1792 (Sir John Soane's Museum London, taken from Maggi and Navone 2003, see Note 16)

The bridge of 1810

After the destruction of the bridge in 1799, the people of Baden had to deal with a temporary bridges for a few years. In 1802, Johannes Grubenmann, a relative of the more famous Hans Ulrich Grubenmann, submitted four designs for a new bridge, but the projects were not realized for lack of money. [22] In 1806, timber was cut for the new bridge. [23] In

From model to reality – a case study on the timber bridge of Baden (CH)

1807, the Zurich master craftsman Conrad Stadler was asked for a design. Finally, the local master builder Lang also submitted a design model without commission. The municipality requested another design from master builder Blasius Balteschwiler. The projects by Stadler, Lang, Balteschwiler and another project by Johannes Grubenmann were finally judged by a commission of experts. Their decision was unanimously in favour of Balteschwiler's design. At that time, Balteschwiler had already successfully constructed a considerable number of timber bridges, such as the ones in Olten, Rheinau, Rheinfelden and Laufenburg, establishing his authority. [24] Construction began in October 1809 and was completed after one year.

Balteschwiler was able to reuse the masonry abutments of the previous structure. He did not copy the rod polygon of the predecessor bridge, nor did he follow the example of other recently built timber arch bridges in the surrounding area [25], e.g. in Mellingen (J. Ritter, 1794), Wettingen (H. U. Grubenmann, 1766, also destroyed in 1799) or Lucerne (J. Ritter, 1803). Instead, he built the bridge from multiple superimposed strutted frames. Their straining beams are interlocked by toothing. The struts are attached to the tie beam with abutting joints and do not reach the abutments. Instead, the interlocked tie beams are connected directly to the abutments by separate braces (Fig. 7). Seven pairs of doubled queen posts support the tie beam and embrace the diagonal struts of the trusses. The cross girders are attached to the queen posts below the tie beams with bolts. Diagonal struts stiffen the joint and shorten the free span of the 7.30 m wide cross girders. The queen posts are connected by straining beams and soulaces in a portal-like manner underneath the roof (Fig. 8). The ridge purlin of the roof is also braced by struts. The hexagonal design of the ridge purlin, composed of two interlocking beams, facilitates the connection of the struts lying diagonally in the roof layer. This is a typical element in Swiss timber bridge construction of this era.

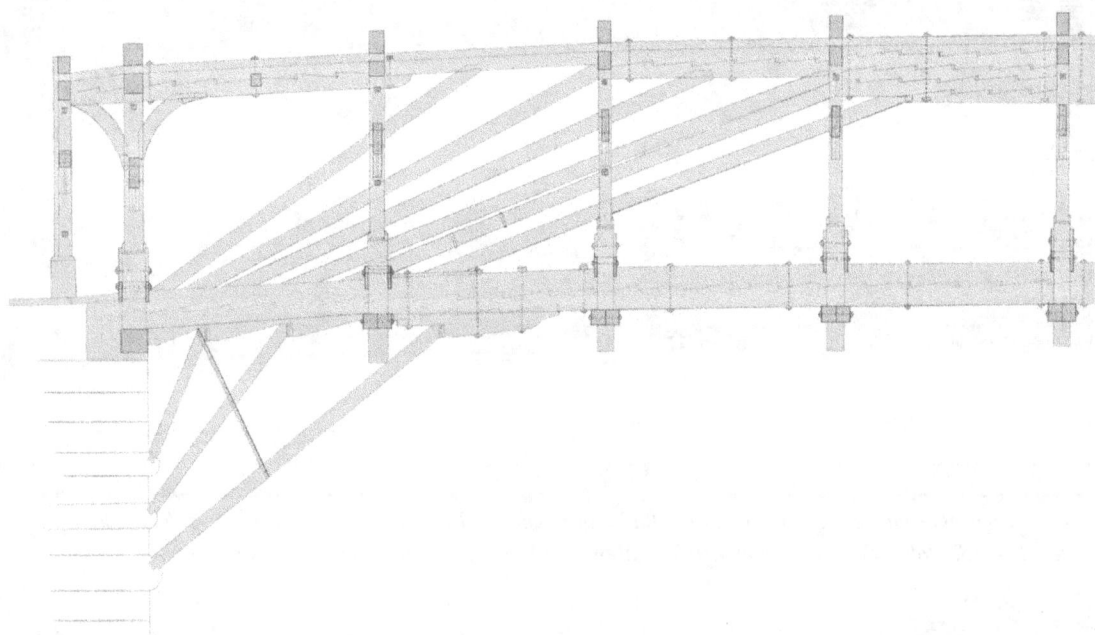

Figure 7: Measured drawing of the Bridge of Baden built in 1810 (ETH Zurich: V. Desponds, J. Fischbacher, F. Schwartz, L. Zehnder)

Figure 8: Bridge of Baden, built in 1810. Picture: Clemens Knobling

The wind bracing in the form of St. Andrew's crosses is attached to the cross beams below the roadway. The queen posts and the straining beams are made of oak. The remaining components are made of softwood.

The simplicity of the construction suggests a very rational approach taken by Balteschwiler, which also took into account the long-term maintenance of the bridge. The experts praised the fact that the construction consisted of only a few elements, which they expected to be particularly durable – easing future maintenance. Repairs were apparently only necessary underneath the roadway. All in all, the solid bridge is an impressive testimony to Balteschwiler's skills and knowledge in timber construction. Many similar structures can be found in his work, such as the bridge in Wettingen (Fig. 9), built in 1818 to replace Grubenmann's structure, which was destroyed in 1799. [26] The similarity of this bridge to the Baden bridge makes it more than likely that it was designed by the same master. The Wettingen bridge also has the same span [27] and is also based on the basic system of the queen post truss with interlocked tie beams. However, the struts of the central trusses are extended to the abutments. It is not known what led Balteschwiler to move away from the Baden design at this point.

From model to reality – a case study on the timber bridge of Baden (CH)

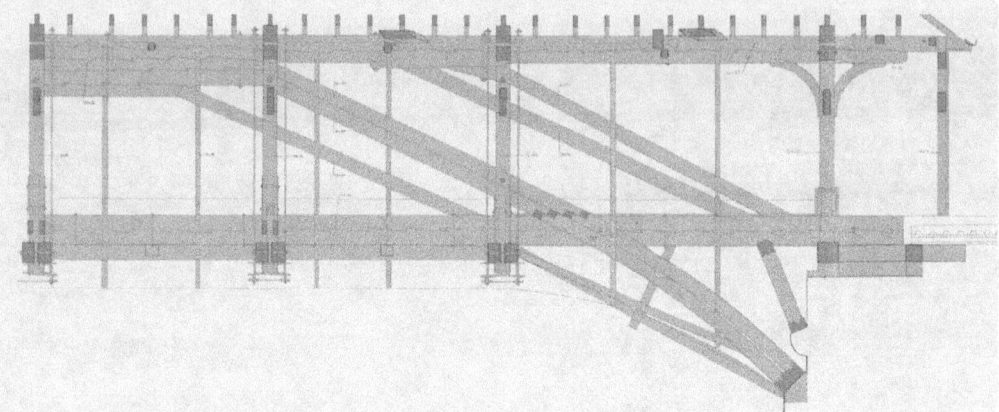

Figure 9: Measured drawing of the Bridge of Wettingen built in 1818 (ETH Zurich: J. Oehler, S. Weber, E. Oberndorfer, A. Moroder, G. Maag)

A span of nearly 40 meters sets a limit for a construction made of queen post trusses and strutted frames. Therefore, Balteschwiler's bridges are among the widest examples of this kind. In the first half of the 19th century, the true timber arch, modelled on Grubenmann's bridge in Wettingen, became the preferred method of constructions with a wider span – for example at the Wintersey bridge in the Emmental with a span of 59.5 meters.

A further model in the Historical Museum of Baden

A further model of a timber bridge (Fig. 10) can also be found in the Historical Museum of Baden, together with the other models of the bridge of 1649/50. Its origin is unknown and there are no detailed descriptions. The details of the design indicate that the model probably also dates to the early 19th century. It can be assumed that it is also related to the Baden Bridge. The dimensions would be approximately correct. If the model is compared to the span of the Baden river crossing of 37 m, then its scale would be about 1:30.

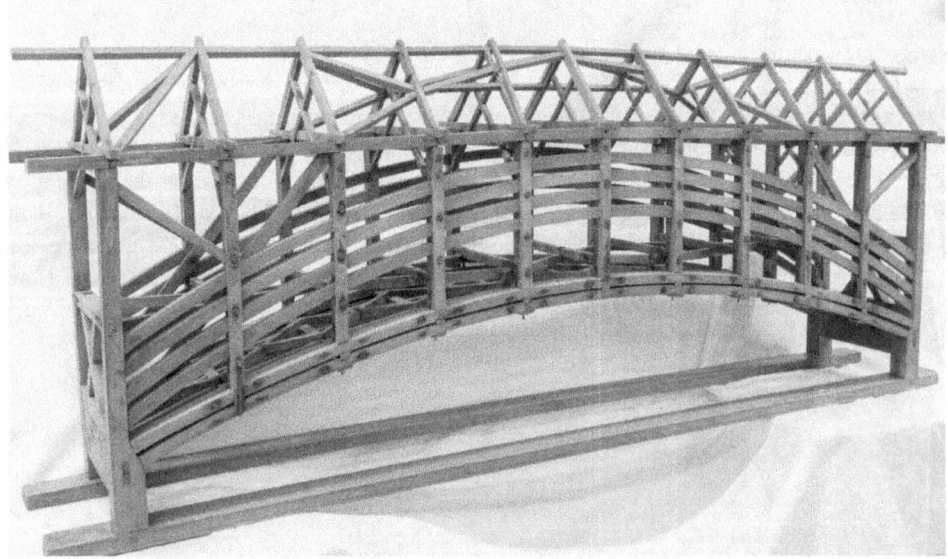

Figure 10: Model of a bridge, probably 19th century, Historisches Museum Baden. Picture: ETH, S. M. Holzer

It is quite likely that this could be the model made without commission by the local master builder Lang in 1807. [28] However, this cannot be proven.

The construction of the proposed bridge is quite unusual. The load-bearing walls are each formed by four arches, each of which is enclosed by twin queen posts. A two-layer wedged wooden arch forms the lower end of the load-bearing wall and takes up the cross bracing. The queen posts consist of two beams each, a stronger one on the inside and a slimmer one on the outside. Both elements are connected to each other by iron screws. The inner elements have notches for the four arches. The individual segments of the arch are obviously butted at these points. It is quite likely that the builder intended a butt joint at each queen post - thus the main structure would not be considered a layering of true arches, but rather a fourfold rod polygon of four. A bridge structure in this form is a special case in the history of bridge construction, which gives the model a certain significance. If it is indeed Lang's model, the contemporary experts also seem to have regarded this construction as a curiosity, and decided not to commission him to build it, awarded the contract instead to Balteschwiler's simpler and much more rational design. Nevertheless, the model bears witness to the importance of arches and rod polygons in the thinking about the timber construction at the time.

Conclusion: models of Swiss timber bridges

The numerous surviving models of Swiss timber bridges will be studied within the framework of the above-mentioned future research project. Most of these were made before the actual bridge was built. They therefore allow conclusions to be drawn about the design ideas of the builders. In numerous cases, only the models of the bridges still exist, while the original structures have long since disappeared. An example of this is the impressive wooden model of the Wettingen bridge by Hans Ulrich Grubenmann. [29] It is kept in the Civil Engineering Office of the Canton of Aargau in Aarau. The model does not correspond to the drawings of the bridge - for example those of Sir John Soane, who knew the bridge from his own experience, and Jean Charles Krafft. The bridge in the model appears to span a much wider distance than the original (60 m) - an impression that is perhaps created by the larger number of queen posts. The wind bracing of the model bridge is also very elaborated. Not much is known about the model. It can be assumed that it was used - if it was created at all by Grubenmann - to successfully bid for the construction contract.

Numerous other models are still waiting to be discovered and scientifically analysed. They will hopefully contribute to our understanding of the fascinating subject of Swiss wooden bridges and provide further insight sinto the state of knowledge and planning methods of their builders at the time.

References

[1] P. Hoegger, *Die Kunstdenkmäler des Kantons Aargau. Volume VI: Der Bezirk Baden I*, Basel: Birkhäuser, 1976. p. 81
[2] J. Killer, 'Die Holzbrücken von Baden und Umgebung', *Badener Neujahrsblätter*, 10 (1934), pp. 19-33.
[3] Hoegger, (Note 1), p. 81
[4] Killer, (Note 2), p. 31
[5] Hoegger, (Note 1), p. 81
[6] Hoegger, (Note 1), p. 81
[7] J. Killer, 'Die Familie der Balteschwiler von Laufenburg', *Vom Jura zum Schwarzwald: Blätter für Heimatkunde und Heimatschutz*, 46-48 (1972-74), pp. 3-62.
[8] Hoegger, (Note 1), pp. 81-82.
[9] Hoegger, (Note 1), p. 83
[10] W. Stadelmann, *Holzbrücken der Schweiz: ein Inventar*, Chur: Bündner Monatsblatt, 1990, p. 76
[11] S.M. Holzer, 'Der Bogen im Dach', *Bautechnik*, 84, vol. 2 (2007), pp. 130-146.

[12] J. Killer, *Die Werke der Baumeister Grubenmann*, Zürich: Gebrüder Leemann & Co., 1959, pp. 48-50

[13] S. M. Holzer, *Hölzerne Brücken in der Schweiz*, unpublished Script, Zürich: Institute of Construction History and Preservation, 2021

[14] E. Steinmann, *Die Kunstdenkmäler des Kantons Appenzell-Ausserrhoden, Volume II: Der Bezirk Mittelland*, Basel: Gesellschaft für Schweizerische Kunstgeschichte, 1980. pp. 66-70.

[15] P. de la Ruffinière du Prey, 'Eighteenth-century English sources for a history of Swiss wooden bridges', *Zeitschrift für schweizerische Archäologie und Kunstgeschichte = Revue suisse d'art et d'archéologie = Journal of Swiss archaeology and art history*, 36 (1979), pp. 51-63.

[16] A. Maggi and N. Navone (eds.), *John Soane and the wooden bridges of Switzerland. Architecture and the culture of technology from Palladio to the Grubenmanns* (Archivio del Moderno, Accademia de Architettura, Università della Svizzera Italiana & Sir John Soane's Museum, London), Mendrisio: Archivio de Moderno, Accademia de Architettura, Università della Svizzera Italiana, 2003

[17] de la Ruffinière du Prey (Note 15), p. 54, Fig. 3

[18] Hoegger, (note 1), p. 83

[19] The author thanks Stefan M. Holzer

[20] D. Yeomans, 'Soane and Swiss bridges', *Construction History*, 19 (2003), pp. 47-63.

[21] P. de la Ruffinière du Prey, (Note 15), p. 56.

[22] Hoegger, (Note 1), p. 82

[23] Killer, (Note 2), p. 32

[24] Killer, (Note 7), pp. 3-34.

[25] Hoegger, (Note 1), p.86

[26] P. Hoegger, *Die Kunstdenkmäler des Kantons Aargau. Volume VIII: Der Bezirk Baden III, Das ehemalige Zisterzienserkloster Marisstella in Wettingen*, Basel: Wiese, 1998, pp. 378-383.

[27] The former bridge of Grubenmann in Wettingen had a span of 60 meters. For the new bridge, the span is shortened by a pillar in the water, connected the bank of the river by another bridge. It is likely that the span was shortened for economical reasons to reuse the Baden bridge design with just a few modifications.

[28] Hoegger, (Note 1), p. 86

[29] Killer (Note 12), p. 40

Innovation and Tradition: 'Signature' roof constructions and master builder's networks in the late eighteenth and early nineteenth centuries in in the catholic regions of central, northern and eastern Switzerland

Martin Gantner
Institute of Construction History and Preservation (IDB), ETH Zurich, Switzerland

Abstract

This paper focuses on timber roofs of catholic single nave churches in central, northern and eastern Switzerland between 1600 and 1850. The second half of the 18th century saw a veritable building boom of rural single nave churches. In this context, architectural history has defined a regional quasi-blueprint of the typical late baroque single nave church. In central Switzerland this so called "Landkirchenschema" is mostly attributed to the two families of master builders Singer and Purtschert. In today's Canton of St. Gallen, it is Johann Ferdinand Beer, a master builder from the neighboring Vorarlberg region in Austria, who is credited to have contributed to the eastern variant of this quasi-blueprint. While this topic has been investigated by architectural history quiet excessively already, no one up to this point has systematically examined the roof structures of these churches.

The paper presents results of the development of the carpentry in terms of constructional systems as well as the differences regarding the manufacturing techniques, or, in some cases, lack thereof over the course of 250 years. Furthermore, insight can be given about different styles of construction that are strongly connected to the time and the region, the different families of master builders as well as their pupils or employees. In terms of construction, the time of the building boom in the second half of the 18th century can be put into context to what was before as well as what cam e afterwards. With a sample of a little over 100 roofs stretched over roughly 250 years, it is possible to trace innovative constructions and their impact on later structures. This gives us the opportunity to determine which innovations diffused into the general canon of construction, even become standard at some point, and which had little to none impact on subsequent structures. It is, on the other hand also possible to outline what can be considered the standard means of constructing a roof truss over a single nave church regarding several parameters such as region, time, master builder or the span of the building.

Introduction

The following research was done as part of a project funded by the Swiss National Science Foundation (SNSF) and supervised by Prof. Dr.-Ing. Stefan M. Holzer of the Institute of Construction History and Preservation (IDB) at ETH Zurich. This project on the evolution of the wide-span timber roof in northern and central Switzerland is devised into three parts. The first part investigated roof constructions between 1650 and 1850 over reformed church buildings [1]. Ongoing research deals with wide-span roofs over structures built in the second half of the nineteenth and early twentieth centuries and will include churches as well as secular building tasks such as riding halls or railway buildings [2]. This paper will present findings on the third part of the project: the roofs over catholic churches. In the course of this research, 101 roofs over mostly rural single-nave churches in central, northern and eastern Switzerland have been surveyed and documented. These structures date from shortly after 1600 to roughly 1850.

Especially the second half of the 18th century saw a building boom in churches. Central Switzerland and today´s Canton of St. Gallen were and still are predominately rural areas and the aforementioned building boom resulted in the development of a certain type of church in terms of parish churches. The so called *Landkirche* (country church) of the

Innovation and Tradition: 'Signature' roof constructions and master builder's networks in the late eighteenth and early nineteenth centuries in in the catholic regions of central, northern and eastern Switzerland

18th century is typically a single-nave building with a narrower presbytery that is flanked by the church tower on one side and the sacristy on the other. The inside bears the typical stucco-decoration and large ceiling paintings (Fig.1). Several master builders are credited for developing the blueprint for this type of rural church: In central Switzerland this so called *Landkirchenschema* is mostly attributed to Jakob Singer and Niklaus Purtschert [3]. In today's Canton of St. Gallen, it is Johann Ferdinand Beer, a master builder from the neighbouring Vorarlberg region in today's Austria, who is credited to have contributed to the eastern variant of this quasi-blueprint [4].

Figure: 1 Entlebuch (Canton of Lucerne), parish church St. Martin, interior overview, Photo: M. Gantner.

The liegenderstuhl as a construction principle

All the surveyed roofs are based on the traditional *liegenderstuhl* construction. This system within a common rafter roof had been around since at least the early fifteenth century and is believed to have been developed in southern Germany [5]. By the sixteenth century, the construction method became standard for roofs over churches as well as secular buildings. By the early eighteenth century, a certain standardization had taken place. The typical *liegenderstuhl* for the baroque and neo-classical period consists of different construction elements (Fig. 2). A first distinction can be made between two different types of trusses within the roof: the principal truss with a *liegenderstuhl* and the secondary truss without a *liegenderstuhl*. The secondary truss consists of two rafters, one or more collar beams and a tie-beam. The main elements of the *liegenderstuhl* can be found in the primary trusses: two collar struts and a straining beam, not unlike a trestle frame, form a substructure under the rafters and the collar beam. This is the actual *liegenderstuhl* which is braced with soulaces. The principal trusses are connected to each other with longitudinal beams, one on the upper end (collar plate) and one on the bottom end (lower plate) of the collar struts. Both the collar plate and the lower plate are connected to the collar strut using mortise and tenon joints. Both usually have a distinctive pentagonal shape to ensure optimal contact with the other members of the structure. While the collar plate, albeit in various shapes, was found in all the surveyed roofs, some constructions lack a lower plate. In addition to these longitudinal members of the *liegenderstuhl*, most of the roofs have noggin pieces and a form of wind bracing that are situated between two principal trusses. Also, king or queen posts are standard for the constructions at least from the eighteenth century onward.

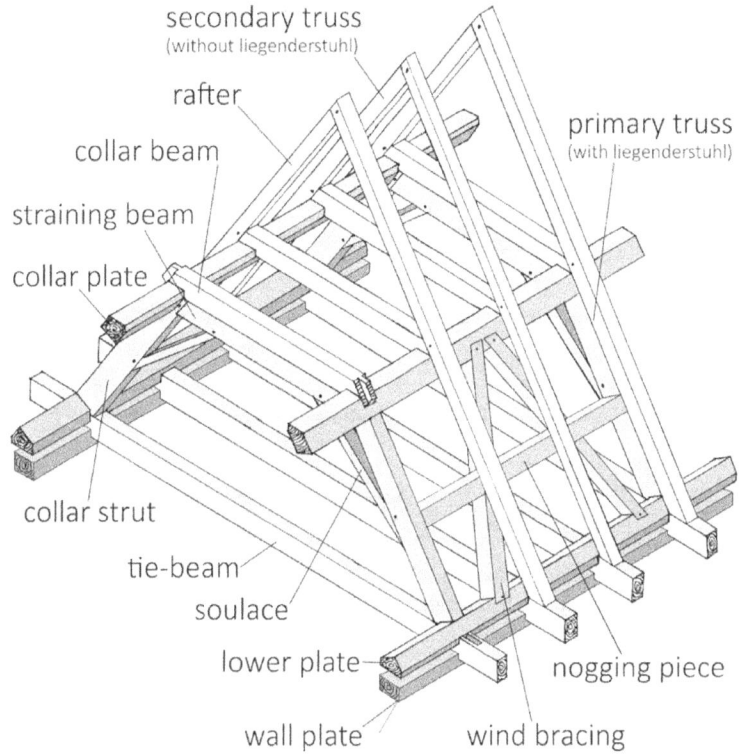

Figure 2: Schematic of a liegenderstuhl with its different elements, S. M. Holzer (with additions).

Tradition

The building trade in the eighteenth century was similarly organized throughout southern Germany and the German speaking part of Switzerland. After the decision had been made to build a new parish church, a couple of master builders would submit plans as well as cost estimates out of which the most suitable, and more often than not the cheapest, was chosen. The following building contract was normally drawn up as a *Generalakkord* [6]. This means the master builder took up all works in stone, wood, glass and iron as a whole. In some instances, he even had to take care of all the decoration such as stucco and ceiling paintings. The various tasks would be divided among the respective workers of the crew or the master builder would give out subcontracts to carpenters, masons, smiths and so on. Depending on the master builder, his crew would comprise a more or less steady group of people. It seems that in central Switzerland, the stonemasons and carpenters were regularly regional workers, while Johann Ferdinand Beer always recruited his crew from his home in the Vorarlberg [7]. The congregation was usually obliged to provide services and bring the materials to the building site.

Innovation and Tradition: 'Signature' roof constructions and master builder's networks in the late eighteenth and early nineteenth centuries in in the catholic regions of central, northern and eastern Switzerland

The building season normally lasted from spring to autumn. Since the walls of these rural baroque churches, unlike gothic architecture, are simply double shell rubble stone without a lot of intricate stone carving, the shell of most of the churches could be finished within one season [8]. Most recorded erections of the roof took place in September or October, the latest being November. The roof was prepared on a timber yard that was more or less close to the building site. The findings show that the timber was handled when still fresh and the carpenter's marks where cut before the timber had dried out. Based on original plans as well as from the surveyed roofs, it is safe to say that, at least from the middle of the eighteenth century onward, it was normally the master builder who decided on the roof construction. This is even more astonishing because almost all of these master builders were stonemasons or masons by trade.

Jakob Singer (1718-1788) and Niklaus Purtschert (1750-1815) in central Switzerland

For the seventeenth and early eighteenth centuries, there are no master builders who can be linked to more than one of the surveyed churches. This is mostly owing to the lack of historic sources. With the building boom in the middle of the eighteenth century, this starts to change. Two master builders started to dominate the building trade in central Switzerland. Jakob Singer, originally from Forchach in northern Tyrol in today's Austria, was a stonemason [9]. There is evidence that in the 1740s, he and his brother Johann Anton worked in central Switzerland as part of a group of traditional seasonal workmen. Soon thereafter Jakob settled in the town of Lucerne; his brother followed shortly after. Until his death in 1788, Jakob Singer built at least eight of the churches that were surveyed for the project. Jakob's son Josef Singer followed his father into the building trade.

Around 1770, another family of master builders started to gain popularity. As early as the late seventeenth century, the Purtschert family can be traced in the north-western part of today's Canton of Lucerne, near the famous monastery of St. Urban. The family originally came from the Vorarlberg and seems to always have been working in the building trade [10]. In fact, it is believed, that the Purtschert's relocation to central Switzerland had something to do with construction work on the monastery of St. Urban. Members of the Purtschert family collaborated with Jakob Singer. Whether Singer was teaching some of the Purtschert is debated [11]. Niklaus Purtschert was the most successful master builder of the family. At least for some years he studied in Paris and, from the late 1770s until his death in 1815, he completed nine of the surveyed churches. Niklaus Purtschert was city foreman (*Steinwerkmeister*) in Lucerne.

Architectural history has always made a close connection between Jakob Singer and Niklaus Purtschert [12]. These links become even more apparent when we take a look at their roof constructions. The system applied by Jakob Singer is a rather simple *liegenderstuhl* (Fig. 3) [13]. The collar plate as well as the lower plate have the typical pentagonal shape. For spans up to around 15 meters, a single storey construction was chosen. In addition to this, a single king post is located in every principal truss. The upper end is braced to the collar beam. A longitudinal beam that is placed above the tie-beams passes through the lower ends of the king posts. Two storeys of *liegenderstuhl* were applied over churches with langer spans. The nave of the parish church in Cham (Canton of Zug) is 17.19 meters wide and was erected in 1784. The *liegenderstuhl* is constructed very similarly to the ones with a narrower span. The only difference is that the second storey has a rectangular collar plate which is rather uncommon for Jakob Singer. In order to account for the larger span, Jakob Singer also used a triple system with one king post that is flanked by two queen posts. The upper end of the king post shows the typical bracing while the queen posts have the distinctive longitudinal beam that passes through the lower end of the members. The wind bracing was in some roofs done with simple diagonal beams. In other instances, it is carried out in an 'A' or 'V' shape. All roofs have noggin pieces which are located in the storey of the *liegenderstuhl* and connect two principal trusses.

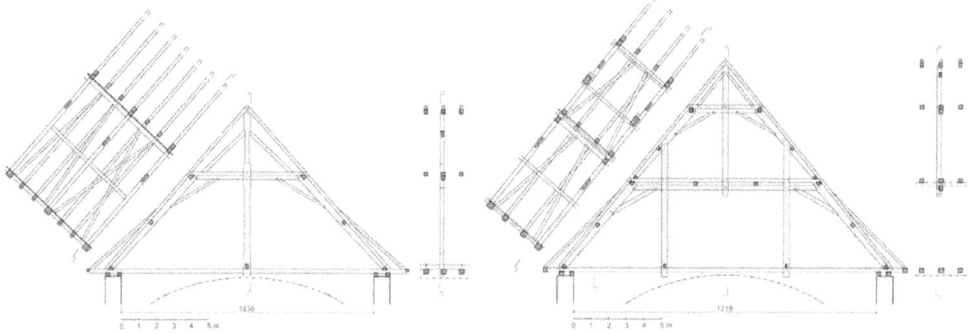

Figure 3: Two roofs over churches planned by Jakob Singer. Left: Triengen (Canton of Lucerne), erected 1788. Right: Cham (Canton of Zug), erected 1784. M. Gantner.

Niklaus Purtschert's roofs are very similar to the ones planned by Jakob Singer (Fig. 4). The liegenderstuhl as well as the system of king and queen posts are virtually the same. Up to a span of 16 meters, the trusses are designed as single storey. The churches in Ruswil (erected 1783) and Schüpfheim (erected 1806, both Canton of Lucerne) span 17.73 meters and 19.37 meters, respectively. Both have a two storey liegenderstuhl and a triple system of king and queen posts. The lower plates and the collar plates on all of Niklaus Purtschert's roofs are shaped pentagonally and the longitudinal beams are passed through the lower ends of the posts [14]. The wind bracing is typically carried out in an 'A' or 'X' shape. The roof in Ruswil was erected one year before the one in Cham. Therefore, it is fair to say that Jakob Singer was probably inspired by Niklaus Purtschert's design. Regarding the overall system of the liegenderstuhl and the king posts, it was evidentially Niklaus Purtschert who took over the construction from Jakob Singer. But the roofs over the churches by Niklaus Purtschert differ in one major regard. In all of Purtschert's constructions, a select few of the trusses are equipped with cross braces. The lower ends are connected to the masonry of the nave, while the upper ends are lap jointed to the liegenderstuhl and the rafters. These trusses are evenly distributed over the roof of the nave so that only every second or third truss has cross braces (Fig. 5).

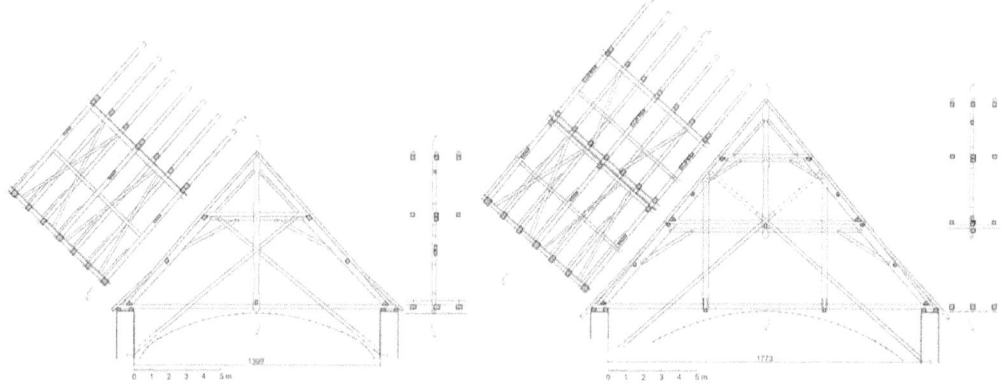

Figure 4: Two roofs over churches planned by Niklaus Purtschert. Left: Entlebuch (Canton of Lucerne), erected 1778. Right: Ruswil (Canton of Lucerne), erected 1783. M. Gantner.

Innovation and Tradition: 'Signature' roof constructions and master builder's networks in the late eighteenth and early nineteenth centuries in in the catholic regions of central, northern and eastern Switzerland

Figure 5: Entlebuch (Canton od Lucerne), parish church St. Martin, overview of the roof, erected 1778. Photo: M. Gantner.

The master builders in central Switzerland who took over after Jakob Singer and Niklaus Purtschert had died, not only carried forward the blueprint of the country church, but also continued to apply very similar roof constructions. For Josef Singer, Jakob's son, this is not much of a surprise. Other builders such as the brothers Josef and Franz Händle and Jost Kopp are known to have worked as foreman or carpenter for the Singer and Purtschert. There they must have picked up the roof systems. The brothers Händle, both stone masons, originally came from Tyrol. Jost Kopp was a carpenter from Beromünster in the Canton of Lucerne and was one of the few master builders not primarily trained in the stone working trades.

Johann Ferdinand Beer (1731-1789) under the employment by the prince-abbot of St. Gallen

Very similar to central Switzerland, a building boom in country churches also occurred in the east. The northern Part of today's Canton of St. Gallen was governed by the prince abbot of the monastery that gave the region its name. To ensure the spiritual well-being of his subjects, in the early seventeenth century the abbot installed an office which supervised the parishes in that regard [15]. Head of that office was the 'Offizial'. From 1759 to 1785, this post was held by Iso Walser, who actively promoted the building of new churches. As a master builder, Walser almost always employed Johann Ferdinand Beer. Beer was based in the Vorarlberg in today's Austria and lead a workshop that undertook the traditional seasonal travel to work abroad [16]. He always recruited his team from his home region.

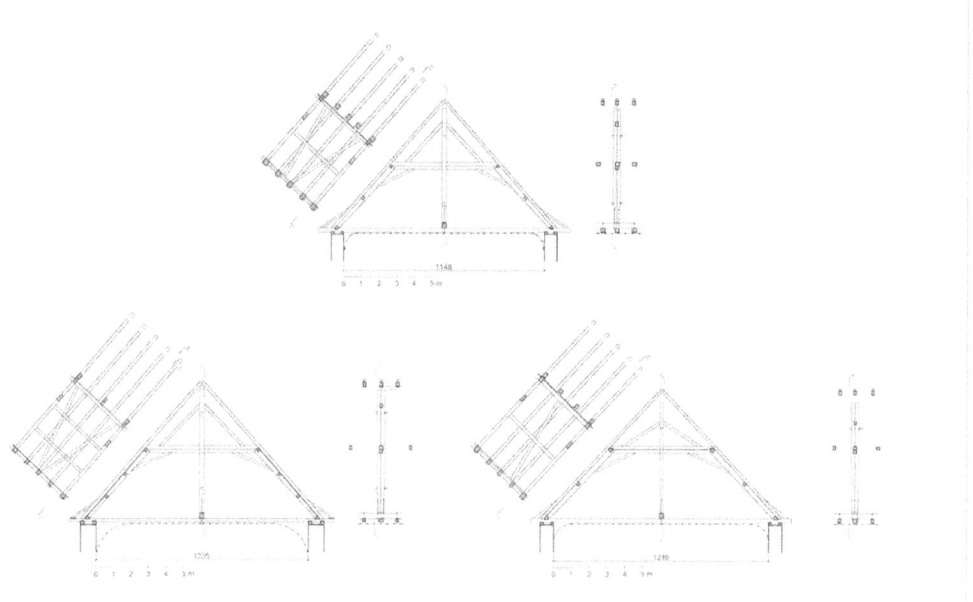

Figure 6: Three roofs over churches by Johann Ferdinand Beer (all Canton of St. Gallen). Top: Berg, erected 1775/1776. Bottom left: St. Fiden, erected 1777/1778. Bottom right: Untereggen, erected 1783. M. Gantner.

The surveyed roofs over churches built by Johann Ferdinand Beer show that he too always applied a particular construction system (Fig. 6). It is still within the framework of the liegenderstuhl and at first glance, does not seem do differ too much from the roofs that we already seen in central Switzerland. The lower plates and the collar plates normally have a pentagonal shape. Only in the two smallest roofs in Wildhaus and Hemberg, a rectangular collar plate was documented. This is probably due to their spans of just around 10 meters [17]. The wind bracing in the roofs were constructed diagonally as well as in an 'A' or 'V' shape. The most distinctive feature of Beer's roof constructions are the king posts. These always consist of two members which enclose the elements of the liegenderstuhl, namely the collar beam and the straining beam, parallel to the ridge line. The two members of the king post are secured by wooden bolts. The upper end is braced to the collar beam. Most of the time, the lower end is connected to the longitudinal beam over the tie-beam using a mortise and tenon joint. In addition to that, an iron stirrup strap that runs through the longitudinal beam and around the tie-beam is bolted to the kingpost (Fig. 7).

After Johann Ferdinand Beer's health had started to decline in the 1780s, other master builders were contracted to build two churches. These roofs also hold a lot of similarities to the constructions planned by Johann Ferdinand Beer. Especially the king posts are done in almost exactly the same fashion. Iso Walser stepped down from the post as 'Offizial' in 1785 [18]. The events of the French Revolution also had a great impact on today's Switzerland. The prince abbot of St. Gallen was stripped of his secular powers and the monastery was temporarily dissolved. The end of the *Ancien Régime* in 1803, mediated by Napoleon himself, led way to the fist iterations of the Swiss State that was finally founded in 1848 as the modern Swiss Confederacy. While the boom could be upheld in other regions, the building of new country churches in the northern part of today's Canton of St. Gallen where the prince abbot and the 'Offizial' had such a big impact on the building trade, came to a halt.

Innovation and Tradition: 'Signature' roof constructions and master builder's networks in the late eighteenth and early nineteenth centuries in in the catholic regions of central, northern and eastern Switzerland

Figure 7: Berg (Canton of St. Gallen), parish church St. Michael, erected 1775/1776. King post consisting of two members, secured by a wooden bolt. M. Gantner.

Innovation

For the second half of the eighteenth century, it can be said that the most successful master builders in central as well as eastern Switzerland had a particular standard system of roof constructions as far as single-nave country churches are concerned [19]. These constructions are very well rooted in the traditional carpentry and the construction methods of what is widely considered as a baroque *liegenderstuhl* [20]. It is the way that certain elements of the construction are made and combined that distinguish these quasi-standard or 'signature' roofs for each master builder. The collar plates, the lower plates, the wind bracing and most of all the system of the king and queen posts are highly specific for the different people. But this not to say that there was no strive for innovative construction during the investigated period. Three examples of innovation will be presented in the following paragraph. They all differ in approach as well as success as far as subsequent implementation is concerned.

The roof over the parish church in Beckenried (Canton of Nidwalden) was erected in 1790 or shortly thereafter [21]. The master builder for the church was Niklaus Purtschert. The roof over the nave is constructed as a single storey *liegenderstuhl* with a single row of king posts (Fig. 8). At first glance, the roof in Beckenried looks like a typical roof for Niklaus Purtschert. The principal trusses nos. 3, 5 and 7 are equipped with cross braces that reach from the masonry of the nave to the collar struts of the *liegenderstuhl*. Only the construction of the wall plate is done differently. Instead of two wall plates located on the edges on either of the walls, there is an additional short joist. On top of these joists, similar to wall plates, there lies a second pair of longitudinal beams. The actual tie-beam sits on that second layer of wall plates.

The aim of this construction was obviously to create more height for the vault. The ceilings of these country churches in the eighteenth and early nineteenth centuries were always done in wood. In central Switzerland it is normally a barrel vault with lunettes. In northern and eastern Switzerland, flat ceilings are more common. It is therefore not surprising that the double layered wall plate gets incorporated into all of the surveyed roofs in central Switzerland up to 1850, whereas in northern or eastern Switzerland it is nowhere to be found. Not only Niklaus Purtschert continued to implement the detail, virtually all master builders active in central Switzerland took up the double layered wall plate almost immediately after it was introduced in Beckenried in 1790 or shortly thereafter (Fig. 9).

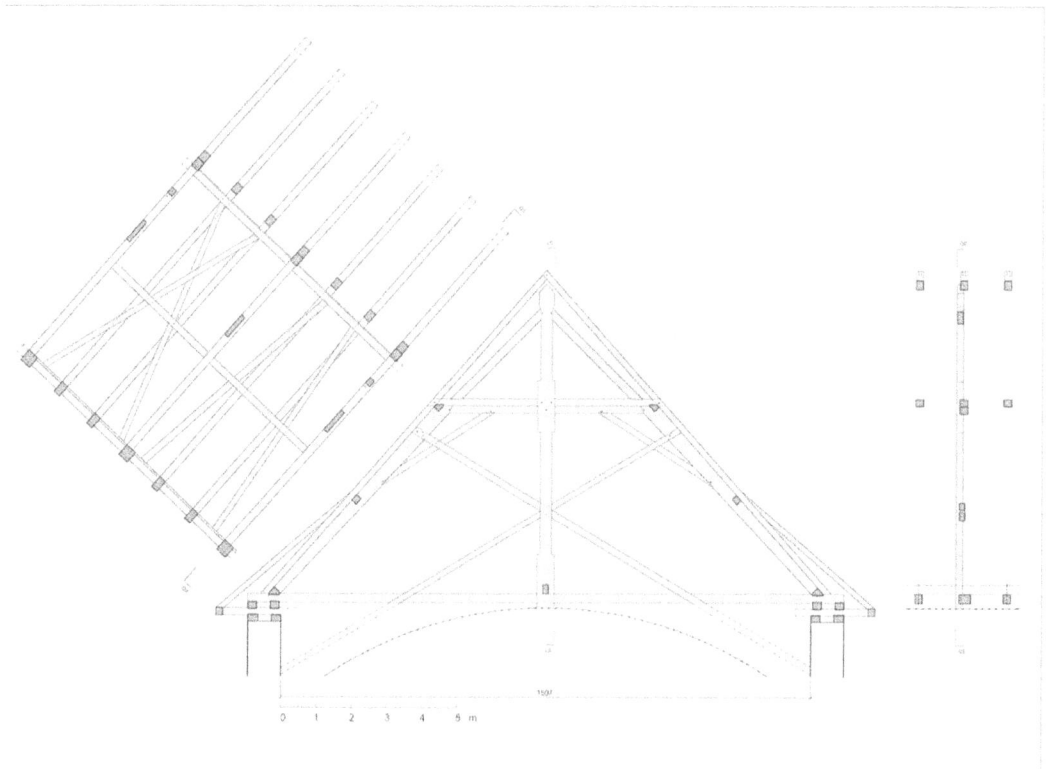

Figure 8: Beckenried (Canton of Nidwalden), parish church S. Heinrich, erected 1790 or shortly thereafter. Cross section of truss no. 3. First iteration of the double layered wall plate. M. Gantner.

Other innovative constructions can be traced to the 1830s. This is the time when the combination of the *liegenderstuhl* with purlins became more common. Although ridge purlins have been documented fairly often in the seventeenth and eighteenth centuries, these purlins in the early nineteenth century are situated lower between the rafters and the *liegenderstuhl* [Fig. 10]. Johann Keusch, a master builder from the southern region of today's Aargau seems to have implemented this combination regularly, although other roofs have been surveyed where a similar system was applied. Around the same time, the roof pitches in general start to get flatter as the neo-classical architecture and its decoration finally got a foothold in these rural churches. The goal behind these purlins is to accommodate the *liegenderstuhl* to these flat roof pitches since the collar struts need a certain steepness to connect to the collar plates as well as to the lower plates. The combination between the *liegenderstuhl* and middle purlins only start to occur towards the end of the investigated period. It will be interesting to see if and how this continues to be implemented in roofs after the middle of the nineteenth century.

Innovation and Tradition: 'Signature' roof constructions and master builder's networks in the late eighteenth and early nineteenth centuries in in the catholic regions of central, northern and eastern Switzerland

Figure 9: Isenthal (Canton of Uri), parish church St. Theodul, erected 1821 or shortly before (Plans by Jakob Natter, around 1806). Detail of the double layered wall plate. Photo: M. Gantner.

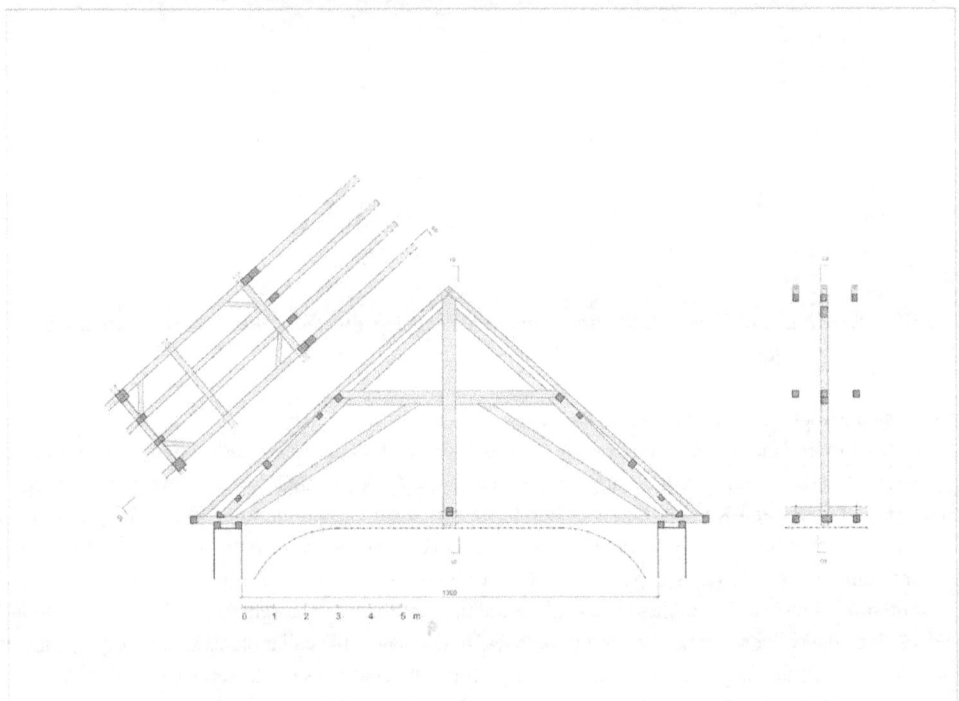

Figure 10: Waltenschwil (Canton of Aargau), parish church St. Nikolaus, erected 1837. Cross section of truss no. 5. Combination of the liegenderstuhl with purlins. M. Gantner.

The last innovative construction method can be linked to one specific master builder. Fidel Obrist was based in the town of Rheinfelden in the northern part of the Canton of Aargau [22]. In the 1820s, he built three churches near his home, before he was contracted to two parish churches in the Canton of Lucerne. In 1831 or shortly before, the roof in Emmen was erected and in 1835, or shortly thereafter, the new church in Malters was covered by its roof [23]. Both churches span over 16 meters in their naves. Malters, with a clear span of 20.74 meters, is the biggest church surveyed in the project. Both roofs are not really based on the *liegenderstuhl* in the traditional sense. The principal trusses are constructed with collar struts that, much like principal rafters, reach up to the apex where they support a ridge purlin [Fig. 11]. Two layers of collar beams are connected to these principal rafters and braced with soulaces. All these connections are done with mortise and tenon joints. To support the wide span, a triple system of king and queen posts is lap jointed to the principal rafters as well as the collar beams. These tension posts are secured in the transverse direction by braces which form a four-part polygonal arch. Purlin-like beams between the rafters and the principal rafters, as well as additional longitudinal beams that run through the king and queen posts, and an 'A' shaped wind bracing, stiffen the roof in the longitudinal direction. It remains unclear where Obrist drew the inspiration for this kind of construction. Similar principles could not be found, neither in the surveyed roof within the whole project nor in other wide-span constructions that were studied. It is interesting to see that both roofs in Emmen as well as Malters are constructed with the double layered wall plate.

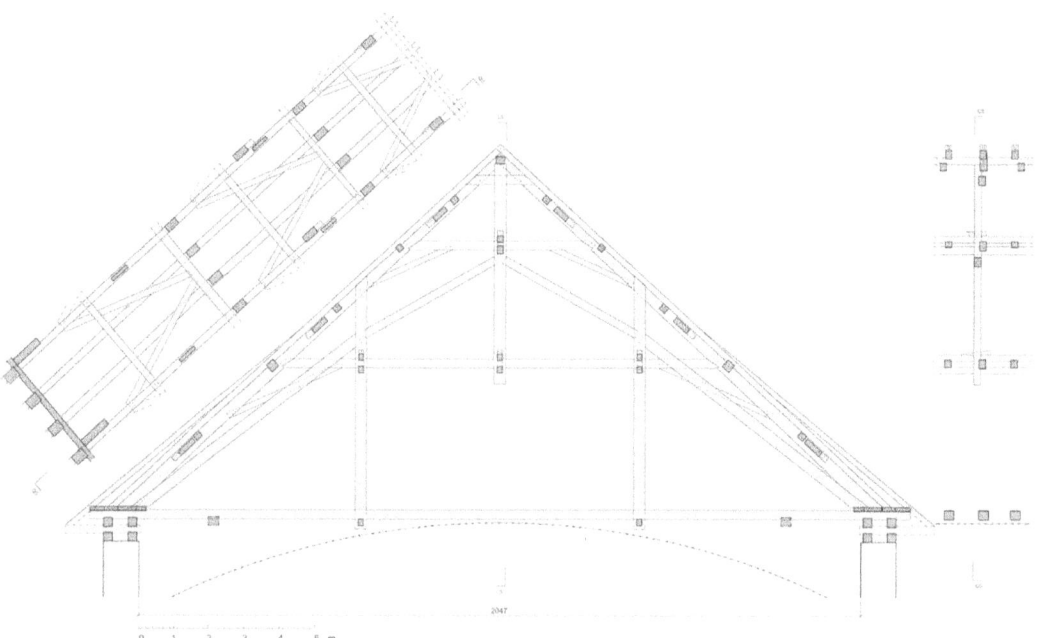

Figure 11: Malters (Canton of Lucerne), parish church St. Martin, erected 1835 or shortly before. Cross section truss no. 3. Fidel Obrist's system with principal rafters did not find any succession.

Innovation and Tradition: 'Signature' roof constructions and master builder's networks in the late eighteenth and early nineteenth centuries in in the catholic regions of central, northern and eastern Switzerland

While the effect of the introduction of the purlins to the *liegenderstuhl* has to be determined by further surveys of roofs from the second half of the nineteenth century, the other two innovations that were presented here have very different success stories. Niklaus Purtschert's double layered wall plate was almost immediately adopted by all of the master builders in central Switzerland. Even Fidel Obrist implemented the system in his two church roofs in Emmen and Malters. The roofs that he built earlier in the Canton of Aargau, did not have this kind of construction. Fidel Obrist's invention on the other hand, did not find any successors. Emmen and Malters remain the only roofs that were constructed with this particular system. This might be because the system was regarded as too elaborate or unnecessarily complex since it affected nearly everything in the roof. Niklaus Purtschert's invention on the other hand, only modified one part of the construction that could be implemented by anyone. In addition to that, Niklaus Purtschert was a prominent figure in his time. He was city foreman of Lucerne and most of the master builders that were active in the early nineteenth century were former employees of Purtschert. Fidel Obrist in contrast, was not rooted locally and, for all we know, not as well-known as a master builder. The network between the master builders in central Switzerland already became apparent when discussing the roof systems of Jakob Singer and Niklaus Purtschert. It may very well have been this network that continued into the early nineteenth century as well as the fact that it is quiet an elaborate construction, that prevented Fidel Obrist's innovative system from broader success.

Conclusions

Especially in the second half of the eighteenth century, the surveyed church roofs of some of the master builders show a high level of standardization. Such 'signature' roof constructions can be defined for the master builders Jakob Singer, Niklaus Purtschert as well as Johann Ferdinand Beer. It is interesting to see that the collaboration in the 1770s between the families Singer and Purtschert resulted in very similar roof constructions. The only main difference is the use cross braces in certain of the principal trusses in the roofs of Niklaus Purtschert.

Johann Ferdinand Beer's most characteristic feature are the king posts consisting of two members. These are always secured by wooden bolts. All of the three major master builders for catholic single nave churches in the second half of the eighteenth century have adopted a fairly traditional construction system. In general, all these roofs can be referred to as typical baroque constructions. Next to the cross braces implemented by Purtschert, it is mostly the system of the king post that is most distinctive for the different builders.

Beside this rather traditional approach to church roofs, there are some instances where innovative construction could be observed. Niklaus Purtschert introduced the double layered wall plate around 1790 and it almost instantly was adopted by all of the other master builders in central Switzerland until 1850. The combination of the liegenderstuhl with purlins became somewhat common around 1830. It will be interesting to see if and how this is carried over to the second half of the nineteenth century. Finally, Fidel Obrist's approach to the roof using a system of principal rafters did not find any successors. His two roofs in Emmen and Malters remain the only examples for this rather elaborate experiment.

References

[1] J. Schäfer, '*Dachkonstruktionen. Die Entwicklung frühneuzeitlicher Holztragwerke zwischen 1650 und 1850 im reformierten Kirchenbau der Deutschschweiz*'. (Ph.D. Thesis ETH Zürich, 2021).
[2] For details on the research project see https://holzer.arch.ethz.ch/en/research/doktorate/russnaik-kylie.html (Consulted on 10th February 2022).
[3] H. Horat, *Die Baumeister Singer im Schweizerischen Baubetrieb des 18. Jahrhunderts*. Luzern/Stuttgart: Rex, 1980, pp. 50-86; 213-217.
[4] J. Grünenfelder, 'Beiträge zum Bau der St. Galler Landkirchen unter dem Offizial P. Iso Walser 1759–1785' in *Schriften des Vereins für Geschichte des Bodensees und seiner Umgebung*, vol. 85, 1967, pp. 179-187.

[5] T. Eissing, *Kirchendächer in Thüringen und dem südlichen Sachsen-Anhalt, Dendrochronologie - Flösserei – Konstruktion.* Altenburg: Reinhold, 2009, p. 154.

[6] H. M. Gubler, Zunftwesen und Organisation der Ausbildung und Tätigkeit, in W. Oechslin (Ed.), *Die Vorarlberger Barockbaumeister, Ausstellung in Einsiedeln und Bregenz zum 250. Todestag von Br. Caspar Moosbrugger.* Einsiedeln: Benziger, 1973, p. 20.

[7] Grünenfelder, St. Galler Landkirchen (Note 4), p. 127.

[8] ibid.

[9] Horat, Baumeister Singer (Note 3), pp. 23-31; H. Horat, 'Singer, Jakob', in Historisches Lexikon der Schweiz (HLS): https://hls-dhs-dss.ch/de/articles/019931/2011-07-13/ (Consulted on 7th February 2022).

[10] H. Horat, *Das Baubuch von Ruswil 1780-1801.* Luzern/Stuttgart: Rex, 1984, p. 47; H. Horat, 'Purtschert, Niklaus', in Historisches Lexikon der Schweiz (HLS): https://hls-dhs-dss.ch/de/articles/019913/2011-11-03/ (Consulted on 7th February 2022).

[11] A. Reinle, *Die Kunstdenkmäler des Kantons Luzern, vol. VI.* Basel: Birkhäuser, 1963, P. 356; Horat, Baumeister Singer (Note 3), p. 220.

[12] Both master builders are credited for the development of the blueprint for the country church ('*Landkirche*') in central Switzerland. The common term which refers to said blueprint is '*Singer-Purtschert-Schema*'.

[13] As far as the surveyed roofs are concerned, his overall system of the roof truss was applied for the first time in the early 1770s. For the churches in Ettiswil and Altishofen (both Canton of Lucerne) Jakob Singer submitted the plans. The buildings were carried out by Johann Jakob Purtschert, Niklaus' father, while Singer was occupied with a different project. See Reinle, Kunstdenkmäler Luzern (Note 11), p. 365. Jakob Singer although, applied this standard roof system in all of his future projects.

[14] In Ruswil the longitudinal beams are located underneath the tie-beams. In Schüpfheim the beams are above the tie-beams, which is the more common method.

[15] Grünenfelder, St. Galler Landkirchen (Note 4), pp. 9-10.

[16] H. Horat, 'Beer, Johann Ferdinand', in Historisches Lexikon der Schweiz (HLS), Online: https://hls-dhs-dss.ch/de/articles/019822/2002-05-03/(Consulted on 8th February 2022).

[17] Wildhaus and Hemberg are both located in today's Canton of St. Gallen and span 9.27 meters and 10.10 meters, respectively.

[18] Grünenfelder, St. Galler Landkirchen (Note 4), p. 22.

[19] Surveys on hall churches by the Singer and Purtschert as well as on a central plan church by Johann Ferdinand Beer show that multiple construction principles also were carried over to these other building tasks.

[20] Compared to constructions in southern Germany, the roofs of Jakob Singer, Niklaus Purtschert and Johann Ferdinand Beer mostly follow the established principles of traditional carpentry. For examples see S. Holzer; B. Köck, *Meisterwerke barocker Bautechnik, Kuppeln, Gewölbe und Kirchendachwerk in Südbayern.* Regensburg: Schnell & Steiner, 2008, pp. 69-93.

[21] H. Achermann, *Die Beckenrieder Sakrallandschaft.* Lindenberg: Kunstverlag Josef Fink, 2003, pp. 5-6.

[22] E. Koller, Zur Baugeschichte der Pfarrkirche Fislisbach, in *Badener Neujahrsblätter*, vol. 44, 1969, pp. 103-104.

[23] Reinle, Kunstdenkmäler Luzern (Note 11), pp. 26-28; B. Hennig/A. Meyer, *Die Kunstdenkmäler des Kantons Luzern*, vol. II, Neue Ausgabe. Bern: Gesellschaft für Schweizerische Kunstgeschichte, 2009, pp. 310-312.

Geometric design and construction of a Late Baroque brick vault: Kilian Ignaz Dientzenhofer's Benedictine Church of the Holy Cross and St. Hedwig at Legnickie Pole

Rebecca Erika Schmitt
DFG Research Training Group 1913 "Cultural and Technological Significance of Historic Buildings"
Chair of Construction History, Brandenburg University of Technology Cottbus-Senftenberg, Germany

Abstract

This paper investigates the case study of Kilian Ignaz Dientzenhofer's church of St. Hedwig in the Polish region of Silesia. The building, a popular pilgrimage church, is known in the history of art and architecture as a Late Baroque jewel with a curious design and famous frescoes. While the shape of the building and its vault has led to different interpretations in the past, its geometry has not yet been analysed on a reliable basis. Moreover, the construction of the brick vault has not yet been subject to scientific research. In order to investigate these aspects, a 3D laser scan of the vault's extrados and intrados was utilised as the primary source. The 3D model generated from the scan not only enabled the detailed description of structural ribs, brick patterns and construction details on the extrados, but also made a geometrical analysis using reverse geometric engineering possible. The results show a geometric design of the vault surfaces as well as double-curved arches based on simple plane circle segments. This clear geometric definition of the vault is associated with a remarkable simplicity of construction method and centering. In the context of other vault designs by members of the Dientzenhofer professional circle of master builders and architects, the vault of St. Hedwig can be seen as both a continuation and an improvement in terms of geometric design and construction details.

St. Hedwig at Legnickie Pole

The former Benedictine church of the Holy Cross and St. Hedwig is located in the heart of a monastery complex at Legnickie Pole in the Polish region of Silesia (Fig. 1). The building is a Late Baroque *Gesamtkunstwerk*, consisting of architecture, sculpture and painting of the highest artistic standard [1]. The project, which was intended to support the re-Catholisation of the region, was initiated by Othmar Zinke (1663–1738), the resourceful abbot of Břevnov, a Benedictine archabbey on the outskirts of Prague with supervision over several other monasteries. The abbot hired a group of Bohemian craftsmen he had worked with before, making St. Hedwig's a Bohemian work on Silesian soil [2]. The architect Zinke chose for his monastery project was Kilian Ignaz Dientzenhofer (1689–1751), the son of Christoph Dientzenhofer (1655–1722), who had built two other monasteries for Zinke but had died a year earlier. The design for St. Hedwig bears many similarities to the works of the father Christoph, and uncles Johann and Georg, who were also successful architects and builders but worked in Germany. The Dientzenhofers' designs, especially their vaults, are known for their complex geometries and free-moving forms, which were often associated with the Italian Baroque designs of Borromini and Guarini. The design of the young Kilian Ignaz was in no way inferior to that of his older relatives, making St. Hedwig an early major work of the architect, whose artistic legacy would later surpass even that of his relatives.

Geometric design and construction of a Late Baroque brick vault: Kilian Ignaz Dientzenhofer's Benedictine Church of the Holy Cross and St. Hedwig at Legnickie Pole

Figure 1: The façade of St. Hedwig

Building history

In 1703 abbot Zinke acquired the land in Legnickie Pole with the intention of building a monastery, but construction of the monastery buildings could not begin until twenty years later, in 1723 [3]. Work on the church then began in 1727 and the consecration took place in 1731. The frescoes were completed in 1733 by the famous Bavarian artist Cosmas Damian Asam (1686–1739) [4]. Only a few years later, in 1740, Silesia became part of Prussia and the connection with the Bohemian Benedictines was severed. While the monastery buildings were converted for different uses in the following centuries, the church retained its function and appearance. Restorations were carried out in 1932/33, in the mid-1980s [5], and recently in the course of the church's designation as a Basilica Minor in 2014. Today, the building is a popular pilgrimage church and tourist destination.

Description

The church is symmetrically situated between the two wings of the monastery; only the front façade with its two towers is visible from the street. The interior consists of several spaces lined up along a longitudinal axis (Figs 2, 4-5). The curved walls and the vault above give the impression of a series of intersecting ovals. The first oval is the entrance under the organ gallery, located longitudinally between the two towers. The high and wide nave has an oval shape, resembling an elongated hexagon aligned along the main axis. There are four chapels in a lenticular shape on the concave sides at the diagonal points of the hexagon. The chapels are separated from each other by wall pillars. Another transverse oval follows before the axis ends in the rounded choir.

Figure 2: Inside view of St. Hedwig

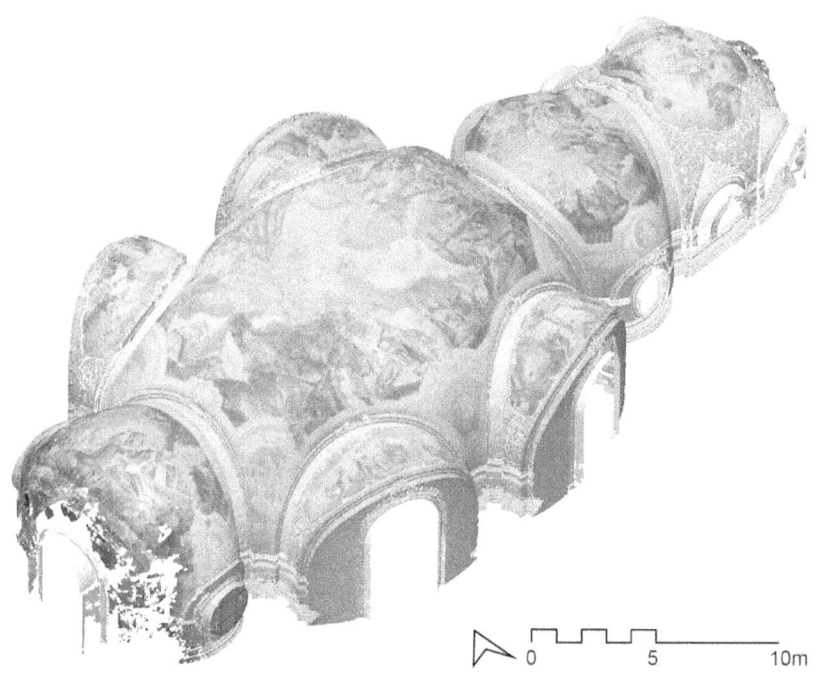

Figure 3: The intrados as a triangulated mesh model (isometric top view)

Geometric design and construction of a Late Baroque brick vault: Kilian Ignaz Dientzenhofer's Benedictine Church of the Holy Cross and St. Hedwig at Legnickie Pole

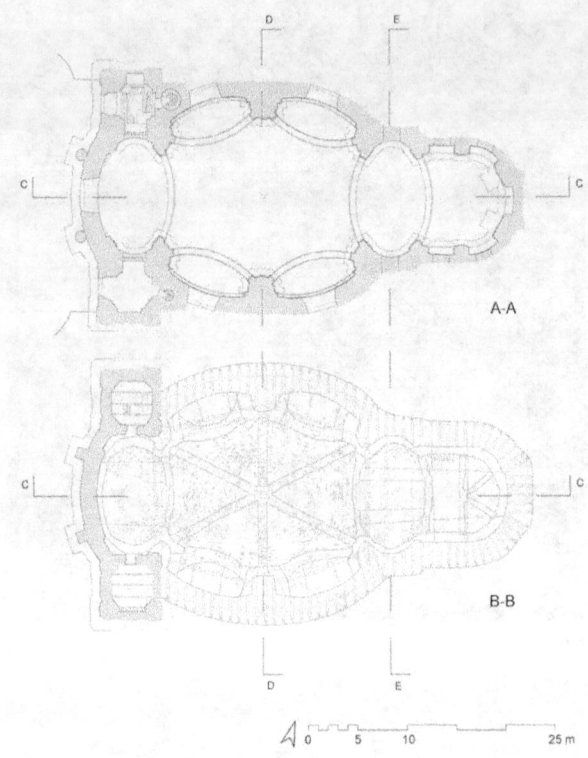

Figure 4: Horizontal sections of the vault: intrados (A–A, view from below) and extrados (B–B, view from top)

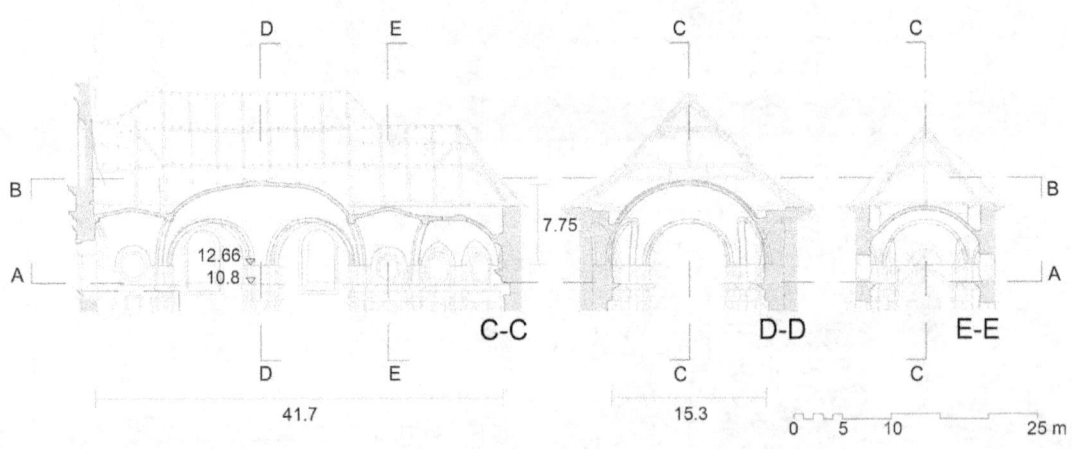

Figure 5: Longitudinal section (C–C), cross section through main vault (D–D) and choir vault (E–E)

The interior is spanned by a domed vault that picks up on the oval shapes of the ground plan. The different regions of the vault are separated by double-curved arches. The large central vault, convex on a longitudinal plan, rests together with the arches on the six wall pillars. This baldachin system of a vault on pillars, seemingly detached from the walls, was also used by Christoph Dientzenhofer for his most important works. The vault is covered with frescoes painted by Asam, which together with sculptures, paintings and the architecture form a *Gesamtkunstwerk* with a complex iconography [6].

Previous research

For a long time, St Hedwig was not sufficiently appreciated by architectural research and was only briefly mentioned in relevant publications, a situation that has only changed in recent decades. While aspects of the vault construction have not been mentioned at all and the vault's geometric design was not specifically mentioned, the geometric basis of the design of the church as a whole has been discussed by many authors. In addition to the complex shape of the building, the inconsistency and obvious errors of the available plans [7], as well as the loss of the original building plans during the Second World War [8], may also have been reasons for this debate.

It has been suggested that the design of the building's nave was simply based on a hexagon with concave sides [9]. Jan Wrabec, to whom we owe most publications about the building [10], initially described the design as being based on ellipses [11]. Christian Norberg-Schulz, in contrast, proposed a graphical analysis of the design of St. Hedwig, concluding that the nave is formed by the interpenetration of two circles along one axis, with the architect generally using ovals as auxiliary structures [12].

Method

In 1991 Wrabec wrote that a final confirmation of the theories about the underlying geometry of St. Hedwig's design could only come from an "ideal survey, but this is difficult to imagine" [13]. Thirty years later, a method using millions of single measurements comes close to such an ideal and is already common practice: 3D laser scanning.

In November 2021, a Leica RTC360 LT was used to scan the interior of the church and the roof. The data obtained was not only used to draw accurate plans of the entire building (Figs 4-5), but also to learn more about the geometric design and construction of the vault. The analysis of the shape of the intrados of the vault as it was executed was possible with reverse geometric engineering. To do this, the triangulated mesh model (Fig. 3) was divided into its individual regions, and geometrically defined curves and surfaces were fitted to these regions as accurately as possible. These hypotheses were then verified by analysing the deviation between the scanned model and the ideal curves and surfaces. The deviation between measured and modelled surfaces was visualised by colour coding and the deviation between measured and modelled curves by needle diagrams (Figs 7-8, 10-11).

A vault's deviation analysis is always influenced by factors other than the original building design. Typical vault deformations such as a slight sagging of the apex, deviations during the construction process, and slight changes of the intrados' surface due to repainting and restoration have to be taken into account as well as error tolerances in the measurement (in this case 2.9 millimetres at 20 metres). For these reasons, the results must be discussed, put into context, and presented in a disprovable way [14].

Construction and geometric design

The vault of St Hedwig (Figs 4-5) has a total length of 41.7 metres. The cornice ends 10.8 metres above the floor, above which follows a 1.86 metre high vertical wall section with plaster decoration before the actual springing of the vault. The maximum internal vault height from this point is 7.75 metres. While the lower half of the vault merges into the outer wall, the upper half extends into the roof. This upper half reveals the construction of the vault on the extrados (Fig. 6).

Geometric design and construction of a Late Baroque brick vault: Kilian Ignaz Dientzenhofer's Benedictine Church of the Holy Cross and St. Hedwig at Legnickie Pole

The vault is accurately built of bricks of uniform size (30 x 15 x 7.5 centimetres). The mortar joints have a thickness of 1–2 centimetres. The thickness of the masonry shell is about 34 centimetres, corresponding to the length of a brick plus 1 centimetre of plaster on the extrados and 3 centimetres on the intrados. Apart from the main vault, the rest of the vault is covered by a layer of mortar. The masonry shell has structural ribs on the extrados. During a repair in the twentieth century, a concrete ring beam was inserted around the main vault, as well as several tie rods anchoring it to the outer wall.

The geometric design of the building, based on circular arches (with a radius of about 9.8 metres) combined into oval shapes arranged along a longitudinal axis, is evident in the plans (Figs. 4-5) [15]. The design of the vault translates these two-dimensional forms into three-dimensional bodies separated by double-curved arches. The horizontal and vertical (longitudinal and transversal) sections and projections of these shapes provide an initial insight into the form, which is refined by subsequent modelling and deviation analyses. Together with the observation of construction details, these analyses also enable hypotheses about the construction process of the vault.

The main vault

The main vault, measuring 19.3 x 15.3 metres, covers the nave. The canopy-like vault rests on six wall pillars and is framed by six double-curved arches. As a result of the removal of the mortar covering of the main vault's extrados (presumably during a structural restoration), the header bond pattern of the brick masonry is clearly visible (Fig. 6). The brick courses in the vault are arranged in continuous circumferential courses that adapt to the concave shape, up to a point of about 60° inclination (measured from the springing). From there, in the upper part of the shell, the masonry pattern is adjusted to forming perfectly circular ring courses. Six ribs on the extrados run radially from the six corners to the peak where they meet. These ribs, which are interlocked with the rest of the masonry and also follow its ring courses, are about 88 centimetres wide and protrude 15 centimetres, or half a brick high, from the surface of the vault. The ribs are bricked alternately in stretcher and header bond courses. At the apex of the vault is a circular opening 30 centimetres in diameter, closed off from above and below (and incorporated into the Asam fresco as a church clock). A patch of mortar in the eastern part of the main vault suggests that a bricked-in wooden beam was removed here, possibly during the repair measure.

Figure 6: The extrados of the main vault, north-east corner

To understand the geometric definition of the vault shape and to get clues about the centering, it is necessary to analyse the plane sections and projections of the scan where geometric features can be encountered. The horizontal projection of the main vault (Fig. 7a) shows the vault edges based on the adjacent double-curved arches. The corners of the hexagonal shape are 27.5° from the transverse line. The cross-section at the widest point (Fig. 7b) shows a relatively large deviation of 10 centimetres as opposed to a perfect semicircle. The longitudinal section (Fig. 7c) shows a small deviation (< 2 centimetres) from the circular arcs in the lower area. The upper portion is best described by two lines that rise slightly towards the apex. The transition from arc to line occurs at 60° inclination. Similarly, a diagonal section through the vault (Fig. 7d) shows almost perfect circular sections up to 60° and lines rising above. Based on circular arcs in the lower part and rising lines in the upper part (Fig. 7e), the vault can be modelled with a loft command (a surface is spanned between defined curves, Fig. 7f). This model has a maximum deviation of 10 centimetres for a span of 21.7 metres (Fig. 7g).

One can imagine the construction process as follows: wooden centering in the shape of circular arcs was placed on these diagonal, longitudinal and transverse lines and the vault was built up to 60°, with the extrados ribs above the centering. The upper part of the vault was vaulted using simple planks that spanned from the centering to a central post. This area was built with a much shallower angle and circular courses.

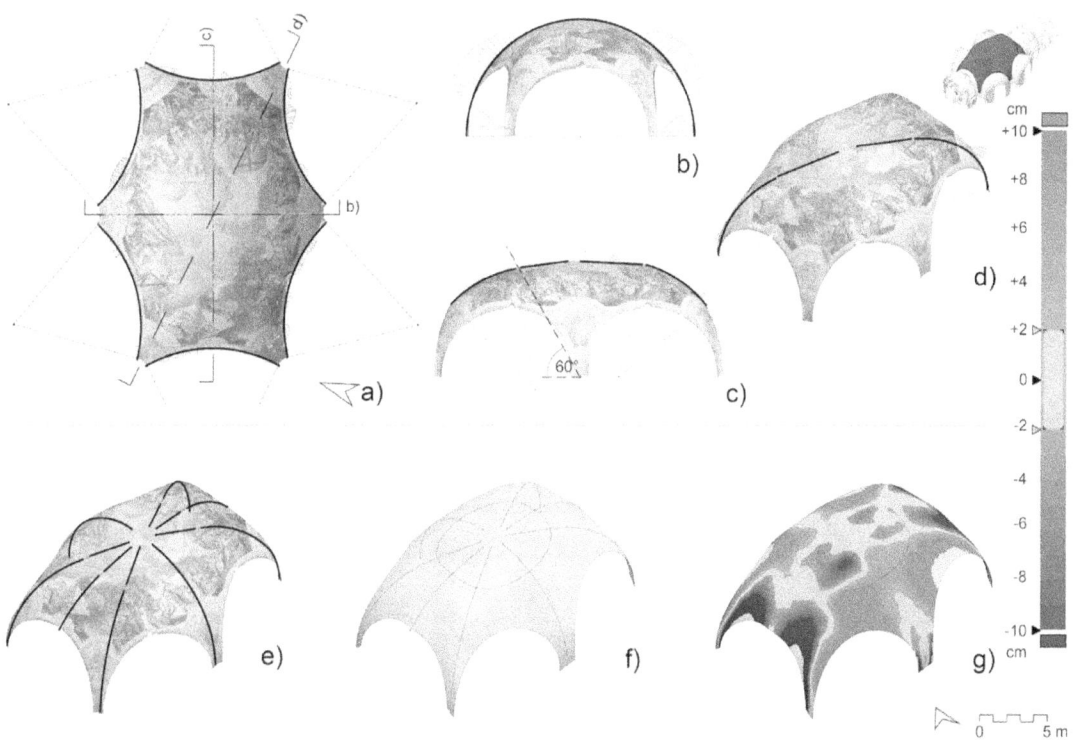

Figure 7: Geometric design of the main vault: a)–d) horizontal, transverse, longitudinal and diagonal projections; e) curves defining the geometry; f)–g)_ modelled vault surface and its deviation from the measured surface. The deviation from the measured points is shown in a colour scale.

Geometric design and construction of a Late Baroque brick vault: Kilian Ignaz Dientzenhofer's Benedictine Church of the Holy Cross and St. Hedwig at Legnickie Pole

The vaults with an oval projection

Along the longitudinal axis in the east and west, two vault areas with an oval projection adjoin the main vault. These vaults, above the organ gallery and between the main and choir vault, both measure approximately 11.35 x 7.1 metres. Circular windows cut into the vault in the lower, vertical wall area. Their extrados surfaces are covered with mortar, but the header bond pattern of the bricks is visible at a few places. The bricks are laid in rounded courses with a dovetail seam along the longitudinal axis of the building (the transverse axis of the oval vaults).

The vault between the main and choir vaults shows its oval shape in the horizontal projection (Fig. 8a). The four ideal circle segments with two different radii that form the oval show a maximum deviation of 6 centimetres from the measured data. The longitudinal projection (Fig. 8b) shows curves closely resembling circular arcs for the apex of the vault (maximum deviation 4 cm), only the area around the window openings deviates. The transverse projection (Fig. 8c) shows that the ridge curve can be described by rising straight lines towards the peak. The vault is delimited by the two double-curved arches on the long side and the two incising window openings on the narrow side, which also follow a double curvature (Fig. 8d). These arches, together with the arc and the lines of the apex, define the geometry of the vault (Fig. 8e).

During the construction process, a centering in the shape of a semicircle was probably used for the apex of the vault in the longitudinal direction and simple boards were used in the transverse direction, which were attached to this wooden arch.

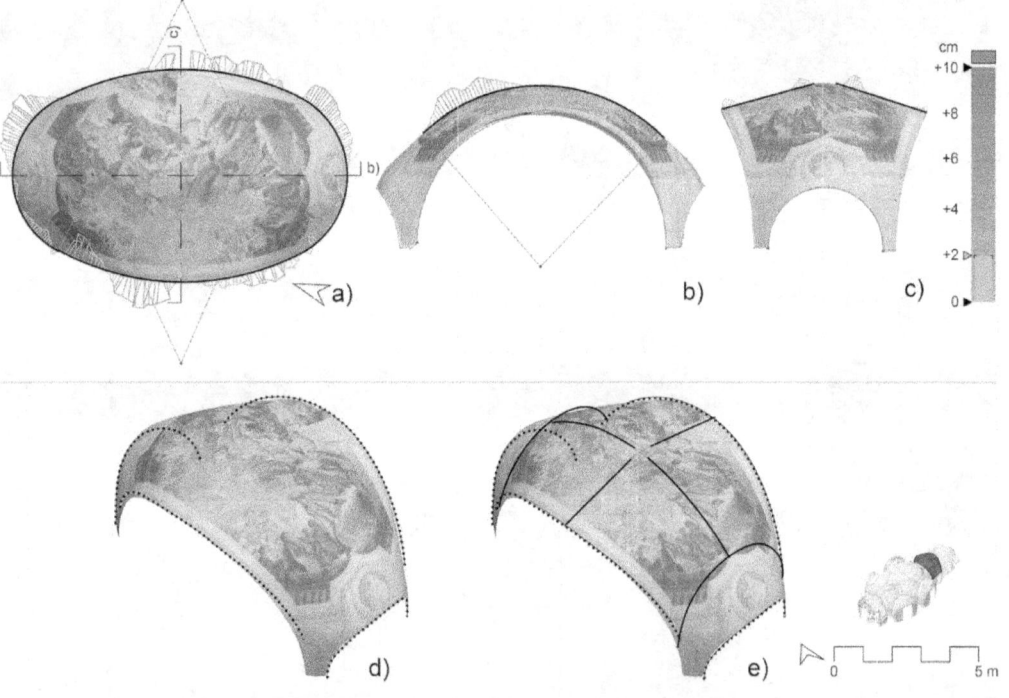

Figure 8: Geometric design of the vault between main and choir vaults: a)–c) horizontal, transverse and longitudinal projections; d) double curves (dotted lines) defining the edges; e) apex curves defining the geometry. The deviation from the measured points is shown in a colour scale.

The choir vault

The vault above the choir, approx. 7.40 x 9.30 metres, consists of a barrel-shaped area that merges into the flat rounded end of the apse. Five lunettes intersect the vault surface above the circular windows and the niche of the high altar, their edge is highlighted with stucco. At the extrados, the header bond of the bricks and their continuous, seamless ring courses are visible underneath the mortar. The rounded, almost quarter-spherical, part of the choir vault has four extrados ribs, which match the ribs of the main vault but are more irregularly bricked and taper towards the peak (40–60 centimetres width). Two of these ribs, merging at the apex, are placed across the vault where the barrel-shaped section merges into the rounded section. Two others are placed in such a way that they divide the rounding into three equal parts. The geometry of the choir vault is defined by circular arcs for longitudinal- and cross- sections.

The double-curved arches

Seven arches, curved in their horizontal as well as their vertical projections, divide the different regions of the vault from each other. Three of them, with a span of 8.13–8.25 metres, are located in the longitudinal axis of the building, while four arches with a slightly smaller span of 7.91–8.01 metres are located along the outer walls of the central hexagon. All that can be seen of their extrados is that their bricks are laid mostly with a header bond transverse to their direction of span. All the double-curved arches were attached to wooden beams with two iron bands about 5 centimetres wide (Fig. 9). One end of the iron bands is bricked in, the other one nailed to the beam. The double-curved arches are suspended against their bending towards the edge of the vault. The iron bands of the two arches adjacent to the intermediate vault are connected, but this connection seems to have been changed during the repair works.

Figure 9: The extrados of the vault above the organ gallery: iron band (front left), and modern fixtures (concrete ring beam on the left, tie rod in the back)

Geometric design and construction of a Late Baroque brick vault: Kilian Ignaz Dientzenhofer's Benedictine Church of the Holy Cross and St. Hedwig at Legnickie Pole

The double-curved arches of St. Hedwig (in this example, the one next to the choir vault) follow very closely simple circular arcs in their horizontal (Fig. 10a, maximum deviation less than 2 centimetres) and vertical (Fig. 10b, maximum deviation 4 centimetres) projections. The particular shape of the arches is defined geometrically by the spatial curves describing their edges. These spatial curves can be modelled by extruding the planar curves from the respective projection plane horizontally and vertically (Fig. 10c,d), and intersecting the resulting cylinder surfaces (Fig. 10e). The surface of the arch can be modelled by spanning a surface between the two edges with a loft command (Fig. 10f). The deviation between the modelled and measured surfaces is about 8 centimetres, indicating a sagging apex (Fig. 10g).

The iron bands attaching the arches to wooden beams were used during construction to prevent the double-curved arches from tilting inward before the main vault, keeping them in place, had been erected.

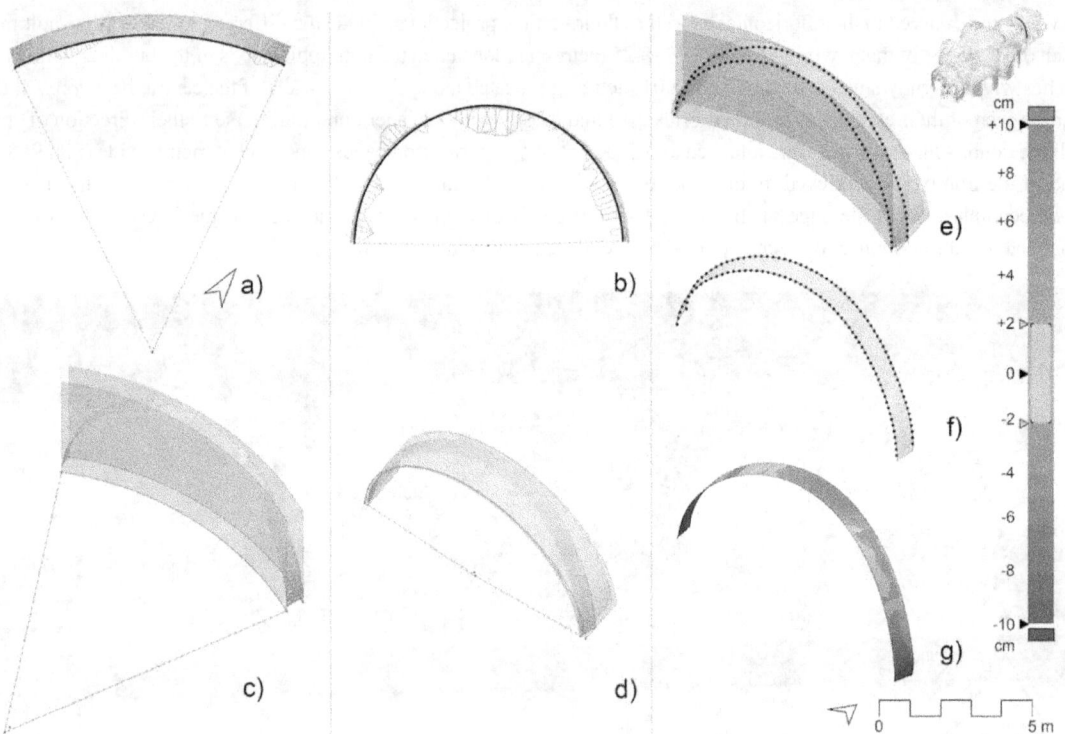

Figure 10: Geometric design of the double-curved arch (next to the choir vault): a)–b) horizontal and vertical projections; c)–d) surfaces extruded from plane curves; e) intersection curves (dotted lines) of surfaces; f)–g) modelled surface between the intersection curves and its deviation from the measured arch. The deviation from the measured points is shown in a colour scale.

The lunette vaults

The four lunette vaults are defined by the curves of the double-curved arches and the outer wall to which they adjoin. They correspond to rounded barrel vaults with a slightly raised apex. Although their extrados is mostly covered with mortar, it can be seen that they were built with a header bond in courses parallel to their short side, which merge into the courses of the double-curved arches.

Similar to the double-curved arches, the lunette vaults (in this example the south-eastern one) follow circular arcs in their horizontal and vertical projections (Fig. 11a-b, maximum deviation 5 centimetres). Their shape can be recreated by extruding these circular arcs (Fig. 11c-d), intersecting the resulting surfaces (Fig. 11e) and creating a loft surface between the intersection curves (Fig. 11f; because of the raised apex area, an additional arc with the same radius but 14 cm higher position in between the two curves is required for modelling). The resulting deviation between modelled and measured surfaces is about 4 centimetres (Fig. 11g).

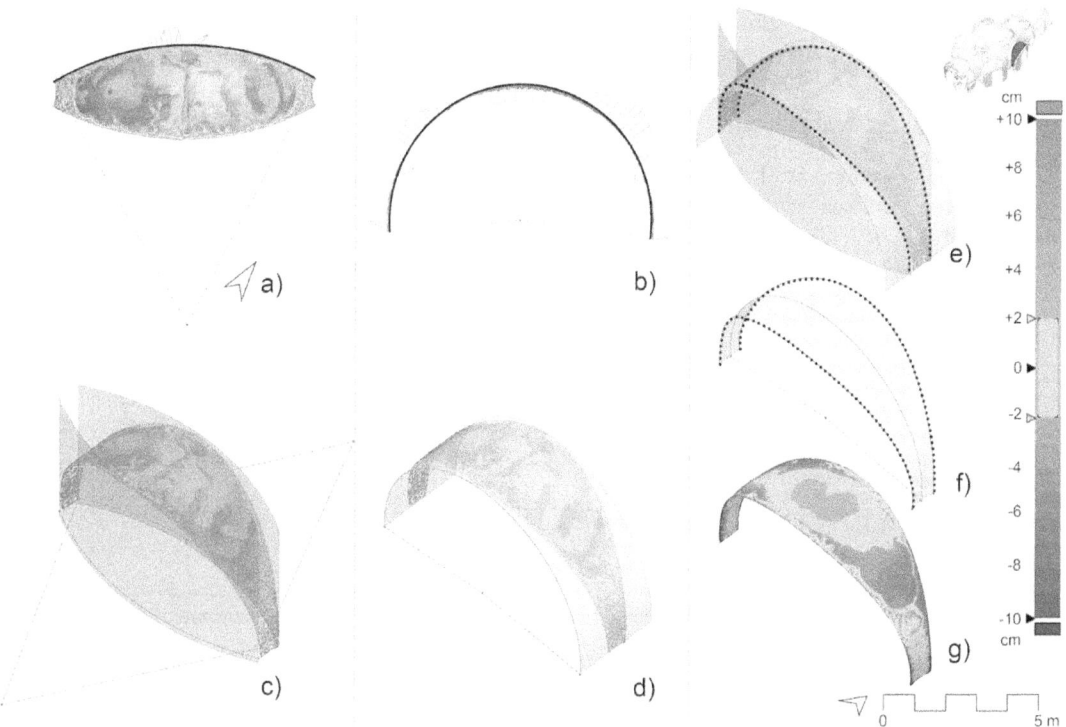

Figure 11: Geometric design of the (south-eastern) lunette vault: a)–b) horizontal and vertical projections; c)–d) surfaces extruded from plane curves; e) intersection curves (dotted lines) of surfaces; f)–g) modelled surface between the intersection curves and its deviation from the measured arch. The deviation from the measured points is shown in a colour scale.

Theoretical and historical context

The results concerning the geometric design of St. Hedwig must be considered in their theoretical and historical context. Looking at the geometry of the vault, the frequent use of double-curved arches is striking. Spatially curved forms were a common feature in Early Modern treatises on architecture and stereotomy [16], such as the practical *Le premier tome de l'architecture* by Philibert de l'Orme, (1567) [17], but also the more theoretical *Architettura Civile* by Guarino Guarini (1737) [18]. These spatial curves were also part of a common practice in building crafts, a standard task dating back to Late Gothic design practices and traditions that had not yet died out in Bohemia [19]. Kilian Ignaz Dientzenhofer probably made his design for St. Hedwig under these various influences.

Not only double-curved arches, but also oval shapes in general, were an essential part of the designs of other members of the Dientzenhofer family and of the architects and builders in their professional circle. Johann Dientzenhofer's Banz Abbey Church (1710–18), for example, has a design based on circle and oval arcs for its general shape, but also for its double-curved arches [20]. The same applies to several buildings by Balthasar Neumann, who was in close contact with Johann, for example the pilgrimage church Vierzehnheiligen (1742–72) with its design of oval arcs or the Residence Church in Würzburg (1732–43), with oval and circle arcs [21]. The recourse to these forms, the frequent use of double-curved arches, and construction details such as the extrados ribs all indicate a common knowledge base about geometry and construction in the Dientzenhofer environment. While Kilian Ignaz's designs are generally somewhat simplified, more often using for example circular arcs instead of oval arcs, they are clearly an advance on the concepts already established by this group. This is also in line with the general research opinion that sees Kilian Ignaz's churches as further developments of Guarinesque spatial concepts [22], and as simplifications of the designs of his father Christoph [23].

Conclusion

Kilian Ignaz Dientzenhofer's St. Hedwig's is remarkable not only for its extraordinary architecture and art, but also for the elegant geometric design and well-thought-out construction details of its brick vault. The three-dimensional design of the vault is based entirely on simple planar circle arcs arranged to form elaborate double-curved arches and complex-looking vault surfaces. Uncomplicated two-dimensional shapes are used to maximum effect to create refined forms with simple geometric definition. The laser scanning-based analysis of form and the observation of construction details provide insight into the vault construction process, such as the use of straightforward centering based on circular arches and simple planks. Compared to other Dientzenhofer designs, the double-curved arches are not only based on a reduced geometric design of circular arcs, but also have added construction details such as the iron bands, suggesting an intensive examination of possible weaknesses in the traditional design. As a result, St. Hedwig's can be considered not only part of a significant group of sacred architectural works, but possibly even as an improvement in the areas of geometry and construction.

Acknowledgements

This paper is part of the author's doctoral research project, "Vault Architecture of the Dientzenhofer Family and their Professional Circle in the Context of Applied Geometry and Stereotomy", which is underway at the DFG Research Training Group 1913 at Brandenburg University of Technology under supervision by David Wendland.

I wish to acknowledge the kind support of the officials of the church of the Holy Cross and St. Hedwig, who enabled my survey in Legnickie Pole during a week in October 2021: Rev. Dr. Stanisław Szupieńko, Conservator of Monuments of the Bishop's Curia of Legnica, and Rev. Wlodzimierz Gucwa, priest of St. Hedwig. I also thank Teresa Lipczyńska for assisting me before, during and after the survey.

References

[1] J. Wrabec, 'Trzy tropy w Legnickim Polu' in Stowarzyszenie historyków sztuki, (Ed.), *Sztuka Baroku: Materiały sesji naukowej ku czci śp. profesorów AdamaBochnaka i Józefa Lepiarczyka*, Kraków: Wydawnictwo Klubu Inteligencji Katolickiej, 1991, p. 143.
[2] H. Dziurla, 'Silesian Monasteries as the Centres of "Bohemian" Baroque Art' in M. Kapustka, J. Klípa, A. Kozieł, P. Oszczanoswki, V. Vlnas (Eds), *Silesia: A pearl in the Bohemian crown*, Prague: Národní galerie v Praze, 2007, p. 241.
[3] J. Wrabec, *Barokowe kościoły na Śląsku w XVIII wieku: Systematyka typologiczna*, Wrocław: Zakład Narodowy Im. Ossolińskich, 1986, p. 92.

[4] G. Münch, *Kloster und Kirche Wahlstatt: Eine Führung*, Breslau: Frankes Verlag und Druckerei / Otto Borgmeyer, 1941, p. 10.

[5] B.F. Menzel, *Abt Othmar Daniel Zinke und die Ikonographie seiner Kirchen in Brevnov - Braunau - Wahlstatt*, St. Ottilien: Eos Verlag Erzabtei St. Ottilien, 1986, p. 91.

[6] T. Hladík, V. Vinas, M. Vondráčková, 'Sub Umbra Alarum. The relationship between Bohemian and Silesian Baroque art in the light of cultural investments of Czech aristocracy and Catholic church' in M. Kapustka, J. Klípa, A. Kozieł, P. Oszczanoswki, V. Vlnas (Eds), *Silesia: A pearl in the Bohemian crown*, Prague: Národní galerie v Praze, 2007, p. 230.; Wrabec (Note 1), pp. 146ff.; Menzel (Note 5).

[7] J. Wrabec, 'Unbestimmtheit und Innovation der Kirche des hl. Kreuzes und der hl. Hedwig in Wahlstatt (Legnickie Pole)' in M. Bogade (Ed.), *Transregionalität in Kult und Kultur: Bayern, Böhmen und Schlesien zur Zeit der Gegenreformation*, Wien: Böhlau Verlag, 2016, p. 129.

[8] J. Wrabec, *Dientzenhoferowie czescy a Śląsk*, Wrocław: Zakład Narodowy Im. Ossolińskich, 1991, p. 38.

[9] H.G. Franz, *Studien zur Barockarchitektur in Böhmen und Mähren*, Brünn: Rudolf M. Rohrer, 1943, pp. 37–39

[10] Wrabec (Notes 3, 7, 8)

[11] Wrabec (Note 3), p. 94; in his later writings he joined Norberg-Schulz in his interpretation of the geometric concept: Wrabec (Note 7), p. 136.

[12] C. Norberg-Schulz, *Kilian Ignaz Dientzenhofer y el barroco bohemio*, Barcelona: Oikos-Tau, 1993, p. 73.

[13] "idealny pomiar, który jednak trudno sobie wyobrazić", Wrabec (Note 8), p. 41.

[14] D. Wendland, 'Arches and Spirals: The Geometrical Concept of the Curvilinear Rib Vault in the Albrechtsburg at Meissen and Some Considerations on the Construction of Late-Gothic Vaults with Double-Curved Ribs' in R. Carvais, A. Guillerme (Eds), Nuts & bolts of construction history: Culture, technology and society, Fourth International Congress on Construction History, Paris, 3–7 July 2012. Paris: Picard, 2012.

[15] Chapter "Previous research"; Norberg-Schulz (Note 12), p. 73; Wrabec (Note 7) p.136.

[16] R.E. Schmitt, D. Wendland, 'The geometric design of the "Guarinesque" vaults in Banz and Vierzehnheiligen in relation to the treatises of stereotomy' in J.M. Mateus, A.P. Pires (Eds), History of Construction Cultures: Proceedings of the 7th International Congress on Construction History, July 12-16, 2021, Lisbon, Portugal. Volume 2. Boca Raton: CRC Press, 2021, p. 376.

[17] P. de L'Orme, *Le premier tome de l'architecture*, Paris: Fédéric Morel, 1567.

[18] G. Guarini, *Architettura civile*, Turin: Appresso Gianfrancesco Mairesse, 1737.

[19] J. Wrabec, 'Ambicje, materiał i konstrukcja: Dialog pomiędzy zleceniodawcą, Architektem i wykonawcą w czasach baroku', in E. Basiul, P. Birecki, J. Raczkowski (Eds), *Album Amicorum. Między Wilnem a Toruniem: Księga pamiątkowa dedykowana prof. Józefowi Poklewskiemu*, Torún: Wydawnictwo Naukowe Uniwersytetu Mikołaja Kopernika, 2008, p.405.

[20] Schmitt (Note 16), p. 373.

[21] R.E. Schmitt, D. Wendland, 'Untersuchung der geometrischen Konzeption der Gewölbe der Basilika Vierzehnheiligen auf Basis von 3D-Scanningdaten im Kontext der Stereotomie', Gesellschaft für Bautechnikgeschichte (Eds), Tagungsband der Fünften Jahrestagung der Gesellschaft für Bautechnikgeschichte, 10.-12. Juni 2021, Zürich. In preparation.

[22] Norberg-Schulz (Note 12), p. 163; Wrabec (Note 7) p. 128.

[23] J. Wrabec, 'Bohemian Stream in Silesian Baroque Architecture', M. Kapustka, J. Klípa, A. Kozieł, P. Oszczanoswki, V. Vlnas (Eds), *Silesia: A pearl in the Bohemian crown*, Prague: Národní galerie v Praze, 2007, p. 308.

Wooden vaults in Naples between survey and construction knowledge: the case of the church of *Santa Maria Egiziaca all'Olmo*

Lia Romano, Marika Falcone
Department of Architecture, Università degli Studi di Napoli Federico II

Abstract

This paper deals with the wooden vault of the church of *Santa Maria Egiziaca all'Olmo*, interlacing historical data with outcomes of field research through an interdisciplinary work. The study analyses the individual parts composing the vault through the critical reading of documents preserved in the Neapolitan archives, a series of comparisons with other coeval wooden vaults and the analysis of the results of the geometric survey [1].

Introduction

Vaults made of wooden ribs and reeds spread throughout the Italian peninsula with numerous variations since the sixteenth century. The need to create lightweight structures, not necessarily walkable, led to the definition and adoption in distant contexts of a construction system that has its roots in Roman technical culture. Although, for obvious reasons of preservation, no Roman wooden vault has survived to the present day, traces of holes in the ancient walls – as in the case of Pompeii and Herculaneum – allow us to hypothesise a *longue durée* of the technique, which, however, appears to come to a standstill during the Middle Ages.

According to the current state of studies, wooden and reeds vaults did not emerge in the Neapolitan context till the second half of the sixteenth century [2]. During the Middle Ages wood was a well-established choice as construction material for floors and trusses. In this respect, the 1521 translation of Vitruvius' treatise may have played a pivotal role in the revival of light building techniques and paved the way towards the adoption of wooden vaults in construction. However, it was the eighteenth century that saw the greatest proliferation of these types of vaults in Naples. In the aftermath of the strong earthquakes that struck the city in the late seventeenth and early eighteenth centuries, wooden vaults started being preferred to the common heavy vaults in yellow tuff in view of their intrinsic lightness.

The case of the church of *Santa Maria Egiziaca all'Olmo* in Naples should be framed in this context and period. (Fig. 1) Its vault made up of wood and reeds is an exceptional case due to its elliptical layout, made more complex by the presence of many overlapping layers at the extrados of the vault. The research activity has been focused on the development of a methodology for the analysis of this case-study, conducted with an interdisciplinary approach, between survey activities and historical-constructive studies, under the guidance of Profs. Massimiliano Campi and Valentina Russo of the Department of Architecture of the University of Naples Federico II [3].

In view of the complexity and poor accessibility of the vault, combining the results of the geometric survey with the information derived from the historical investigation has been a clear requirement for the analysis of the vault. The geometric survey, carried out by means of digital photogrammetry, has allowed the identification of dimensional and colorimetric characteristics as well as the exact position and size of the wooden elements of a significant portion of the vault, otherwise not detectable with traditional methods. This experience has highlighted the limits of the technologies currently available for surveying these structures, thus posing new research questions.

Wooden vaults in Naples between survey and construction knowledge: the case of the church of Santa Maria Egiziaca all'Olmo

Figure 1: Naples, Church of Santa Maria Egiziaca all'Olmo: view of the church and the vault.

The church and the vault: a brief historical overview

The church of *Santa Maria Egiziaca all'Olmo* is part of a large monastery founded in 1342 in one of the poorest neighbourhoods of the city to house repentant prostitutes. The structure is the result of numerous interventions carried out over the centuries and was built on a chapel, under the name of *Santa Maria di Cerleto*, which existed before the foundation of the monastery [4].

Between the end of the sixteenth century and the beginning of the seventeenth century, the church and monastery underwent major restoration works [5], but the intervention that gave the structure part of its current configuration dates back to the 1680s. The nuns, who belonged to the high aristocracy of the Kingdom of Naples, were eager to celebrate the social role of the monastic community in the city and to give the complex greater magnificence, displaying a new strategy of persuasion towards the lay community, a result of the Counter-Reformation. The lavish decorations and furnishings were, in fact, used as a tool for religious propaganda.

The project was entrusted to the architect Dionisio Lazzari [6] who, between 1683 and 1688, worked on the transformation of the church and the layout of the small square in front of it. It should be pointed out that the current urban situation, not dealt with in this essay, is the result of a significant urban evisceration carried out at the end of the nineteenth century [7].

Lazzari's work was drastically interrupted by the violent earthquake that struck the city in 1688 and by his death in 1689. Work continued under the direction of other architects and engineers until the first half of the eighteenth century [8]

Dionisio Lazzari, in order to integrate the church with the surrounding medieval secular buildings, rejected the solution of a monumental façade. The interior space was conceived following the Baroque trends of the period. The single nave was designed on an elliptical plan with five rooms on each side, three of which were used as chapels. The altar area was covered by a dome accentuating the development of the major axis of the ellipse. Regarding the idea of the nave on an elliptical plan, Lazzari was certainly influenced by the experiments carried out in the first half of the seventeenth century by Fra Nuvolo in the church of San Carlo all'Arena, which was undoubtedly an important reference [9].

The original vault covering the nave, of which no trace remains today, was probably designed as a heavy tuff structure, similar to the one in the church of *San Carlo all'Arena*. According to some historiographic hypotheses, it was probably visible from the outside [10]. This vault was set on a portion of masonry (ring), a partial trace of which is still visible today. The work carried out at the end of the twentieth century, which involved raising the structure with the construction of a high reinforced concrete kerb, overlapped the pre-existing structure, leaving only the impost of the original vault visible in some parts.

The vault collapsed for unknown reasons in 1742. In that year, the deed drawn up by the Neapolitan notary Giovan Battista Cantilena [11] informs us that a large part of the church had collapsed and that the task of drawing up a new project and rebuilding the structure had been entrusted to the architect Michelangelo de Blasio [12]. The document is extremely interesting in that it provides information on the materials to be used. As for the vault, it was planned to build it with a structure of wood and reeds. The sudden collapse probably induced the architect to create a false vault, lighter than the existing one, which would not weigh too heavily on the new walls [13].

It should be noted that in the same year the choir vault of the church of Santa Maria Regina Coeli in Naples also collapsed and was rebuilt in 1743 using wood and reeds. Although in that case the geometry of the structure was different; the two vaults have in common not only the material and partly the dimensions, but also the presence of an imposing wooden support structure, probably built in different periods. (Fig. 2)

Figure 2: Naples, Church of Santa Maria Egiziaca all'Olmo (on the left); Church of Santa Maria Regina Coeli, choir (on the right): view of the extrados of the vault and the supporting structure.

Wooden vaults in Naples between survey and construction knowledge: the case of the church of Santa Maria Egiziaca all'Olmo

Unfortunately, the above-mentioned deed does not go into more detail on the new vault and does not provide explanatory drawings of the structure. Instead, a drawing of the new wooden truss was attached to the document, which presents two peculiar aspects: the structure was based on a continuous wooden kerb, which was unusual in the local construction practice, and it was reinforced, in the lower part, by two inclined beams whose ends were embedded in the masonry [14]. (Fig. 3)

No subsequent transformation or consolidation of the wooden vault is known. It was slightly damaged by the earthquake of 1805 [15] and apparently unaffected by the work on the church roof carried out in 1944, after the bombing of World War II, and following the devastating earthquake of 1980 [16]. The latter restoration intervention which took place between 1986 and 1989, was not very respectful of the historical background and included the construction of a massive concrete kerb and the replacement of the old wooden trusses with new steel elements. Although the bills of quantities do not describe the work carried out in detail, a visual analysis of the vault shows that it was consolidated with steel tie rods, which connected the various parts of the roof and of the vault.

Of the old wooden truss, only the horizontal tie beams have been left *in situ*, resting in some places on wooden supports, and in others, embedded in the concrete kerb. The discontinuous wooden bearing plates could represent the trace of what remains of the continuous kerb designed in 1742 by the architect Michelangelo de Blasio. Unfortunately, the presence of many overlapping layers, not easily datable, undermines the comprehension and the study of the structure.

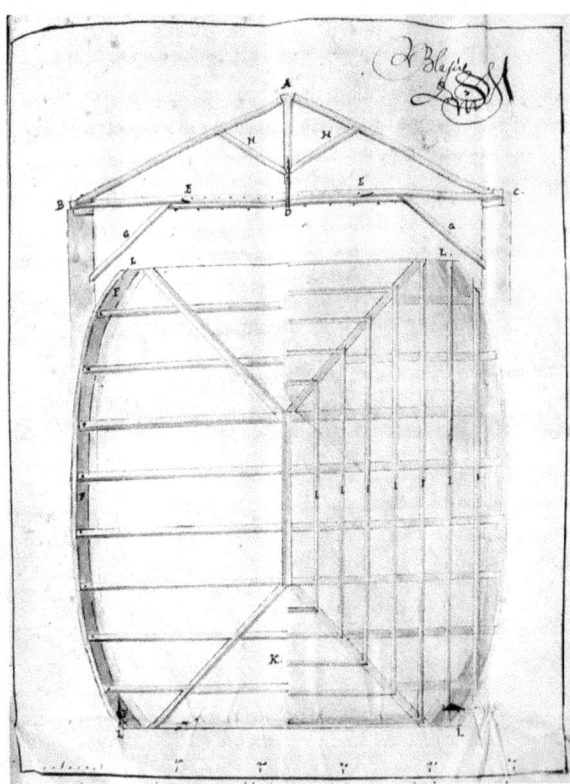

Figure 3: M. de Blasio, project of the new wooden roof, 1742 (from Borrelli (note 13, p. 51, ASNA)

The wooden vault between survey and knowledge

The phase of knowledge and analysis of the vault, of its morphological, dimensional and geometric characteristics, developed from survey drawings. This has allowed us to know and support the analysis of the changes that have occurred over time [17]. The wooden vault of the *Santa Maria Egiziaca all'Olmo* has a very complex architectural structure, which determined the need to plan the survey phases accurately. It required a collection of heterogeneous data that led to the creation of a digital database that describes the current state of conservation [18].

The articulated form of the wooden vault has required careful planning of the survey phases, both in terms of the use of technological instruments and data management procedures. With these premises, it was appropriate to identify suitable tools to overcome the environmental conditions of the object of study, outlining the survey campaign in detail and choosing the most suitable method for studying the elements of the vault. This has been an opportunity to test protocols for the use and management of relevant technologies.

The survey operations have been preceded by various inspections, necessary for a direct knowledge of the object and following the assessment and conformation of the area to be surveyed. In the operational approach that characterized the survey and the subsequent phases, the research has addressed in the first instance the problem relating to the accessibility of the wooden vault as it is placed at a height of 17.34 metres from the entrance to the church. Therefore, it has been essential to study the church as a whole and the access points to the extrados of the vault. It can be reached through two openings located at the upper ends of the nave, from the side of the dome (at a height of 17.34 metres) and from the entrance pronaos (at a height of 15.50 metres), currently being restored. In the latter case it was not possible to proceed with the acquisition phases of the metric data but, through the visual analysis and the photographic survey, it has been possible to deduce useful information for comparison with the portion of the vault actually surveyed. (Fig. 4)

Figure 4: Naples, Church of Santa Maria Egiziaca all'Olmo: view of the extrados of the vault from the two openings (side dome on the left; side pronaos on the right).

The only point of collection of data for the survey, in fact, is a window (1.20 metres x 1.50 metres) located on the side of the dome accessible from the sacristy. From this space there are several flights of stairs, very narrow, without resting landings and handrails that culminate on an outdoor terrace at a height of 10.66 metres. Then, two wall ladders, one composed of five rungs, the other of ten rungs, has allowed us to reach the height. (Fig. 5)

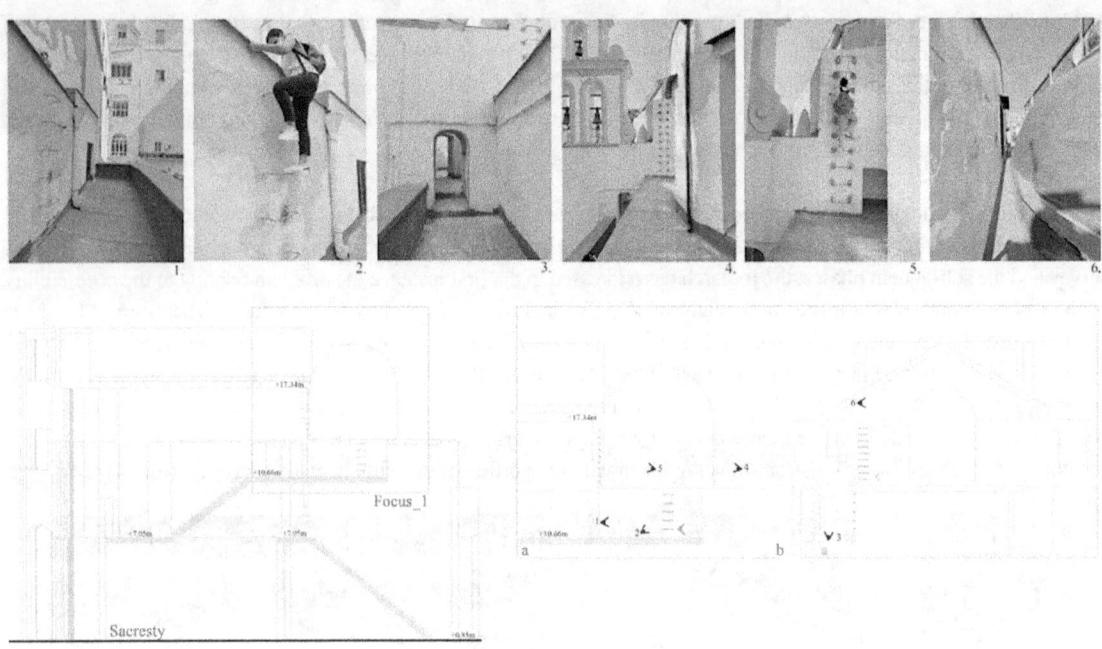

Figure 5: Diagram showing the environmental criticalities of the survey.

Through a very narrow space of 0.30 meters between the dome and the vault it has been possible to reach the opening from which the extrados of the vault is visible, protected by a two-pitched roof. On the basis of these limitations, as regards the survey phases, the methodology of digital photogrammetry was chosen. Among the survey techniques that in recent decades have profoundly transformed the methods of data acquisition and restitution, digital photogrammetry is certainly one of the most interesting. Thanks to the new Structure from Motion (Sfm) applications, this technique allows the acquisition of a three-dimensional product, which is fundamental for the purposes of documentation, analysis and representation. The result is a three-dimensional model with levels of accuracy similar to those generated with active optical sensors *(range-based)* as laser scanner, Lidar, etc. In the field of Cultural Heritage, the use of the methodology based on passive optical sensors *(image-based)* is increasingly widespread, considering the need to couple the accuracy of the metric data with a colorimetric representation capable of expressing the qualities of the object [19].

The points of the station would not have been sufficient, and it was not possible to use 3D and 2D targets fundamental for the alignment between the scanning positions during data processing. The tools used were therefore a professional reflex camera and a smartphone, two practical, inexpensive, small and easily transportable objects. In addition to the difficulties already described, particular attention was paid to the data acquisition phase as the window is placed at a higher level than the extrados of the vaults. It was not possible to integrate the direct metric survey on the elements of the vault to scale the three-dimensional model obtained from photogrammetry. The window space and other measurements taken in situ were used as a reference. At the same time, the highly variable lighting conditions required the planning the photographic shots in order to avoid areas of shadow and overexposed areas in the captured images. Furthermore, the reduced acquisition space has not allowed a view of the vault as a whole but only a small portion, which has been used as a guide to reconstruct the remaining part by analogy. A second photogrammetric survey has been carried out for the interior of the church.

Data has been collected through photographic acquisitions with a Nikon D5000 digital SLR. To guarantee a sufficient amount of information, it was decided to use both a parallel and convergent axis acquisition technique producing an average overlap between the images acquired for the different datasets of about 70 percent. Then, 38 frames were taken using a digital camera, with manual mode, without the use of flash and with a focal length of 18 millimetres.

The complexity of the vault has required a second survey phase aimed at determining an integrative model of the missing parts. Not being able to lean out further from the window, after the first photo shot, with the integrated camera of the smartphone, Iphone12PRO, two videos were recorded. In this case, a special telescopic rod for photographic purpose has been used with an extension ranging from 0.70 metres to 1.50 metres. This telescopic rod, with the smartphone mounted at the end using the anchor support, has made it possible to record videos, capturing further information. At the same time, an additional photogrammetric survey was carried out inside the church using the same instrumentation and acquisition technique. Through this survey, the intrados of the elliptical vault was outlined.

Once the data acquisition phase was completed *in situ*, the processing phase has been carried out with the aid of two photogrammetric programs. From the first program, 3D Zephir, the frames from the videos shot have been extracted while from the second, Agisoft Metashape, all the data have been processed in a single workflow [20]. The Self-Calibrating Bundle Adjustment of the photogrammetric application automatically oriented the images. The SfM algorithms has allowed the simultaneous estimate of the three-dimensional structure of the scene (Structure) and the position of the camera (Motion), i.e. the internal and external orientation parameters of the camera.

With these premises, and following the consolidated photogrammetric processing, after the alignment of the frames, the first step obtained has been a sparse cloud of 47,755 points. Once the alignment was correct, the dense cloud was created with the thickening of the dimensional and colorimetric points. From the dense cloud of 47,140,749 points, the polygonal model of 3,142,715 faces and 7,340 vertices was generated, which was reconstructed by organizing the points of the cloud into polygonal mesh surfaces. In this case, the model has been enriched with attributes capable of describing the surface aspects, restoring the visual apparatus of the artifact. Once the polygonal model was obtained, it has been possible to generate the final model through the texture from which the orthophotos for the redesign of the vault were extrapolated. The data was then combined to identify all the elements and reconstruct the form of the vault. (Fig.6)

The same methodological process was also conducted for the survey of the extrados of the vault. In this case, 125 images were acquired.

The difficulties of the data acquisition phases have not allowed the overall reconstruction of the wooden vault but the dimensional and colorimetric information obtained from the survey operations, albeit limited, has been fundamental for the definition of the individual elements and for the hypotheses of chronological reconstruction. On the basis of the survey carried out, in fact, it has been possible to analyse the elements in their three-dimensional form. Subsequently, this information has been isolated with representative methods at multiple levels of detail, and at various scales of representation. (Figs 7, 8, 9)

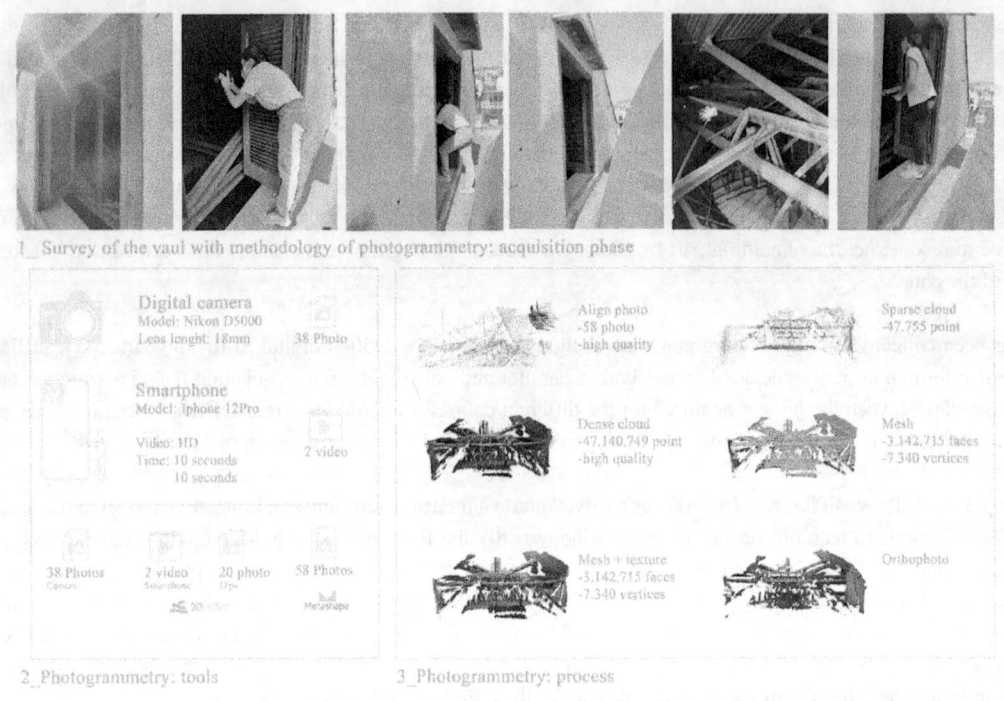

Figure 6: Acquisition, processing and elaboration of data obtained by photogrammetric survey.

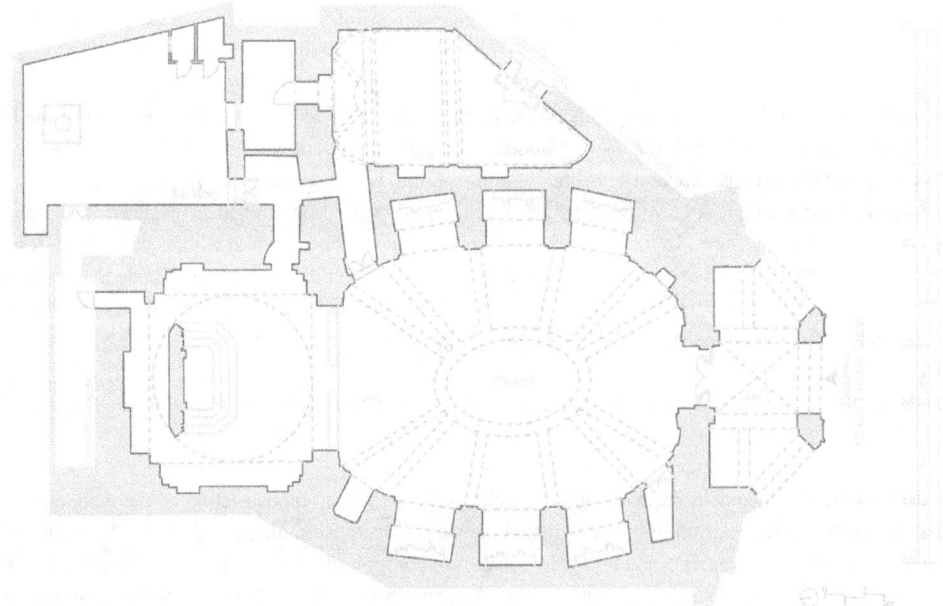

Figure 7: Naples, Church of Santa Maria Egiziaca all'Olmo: plan.

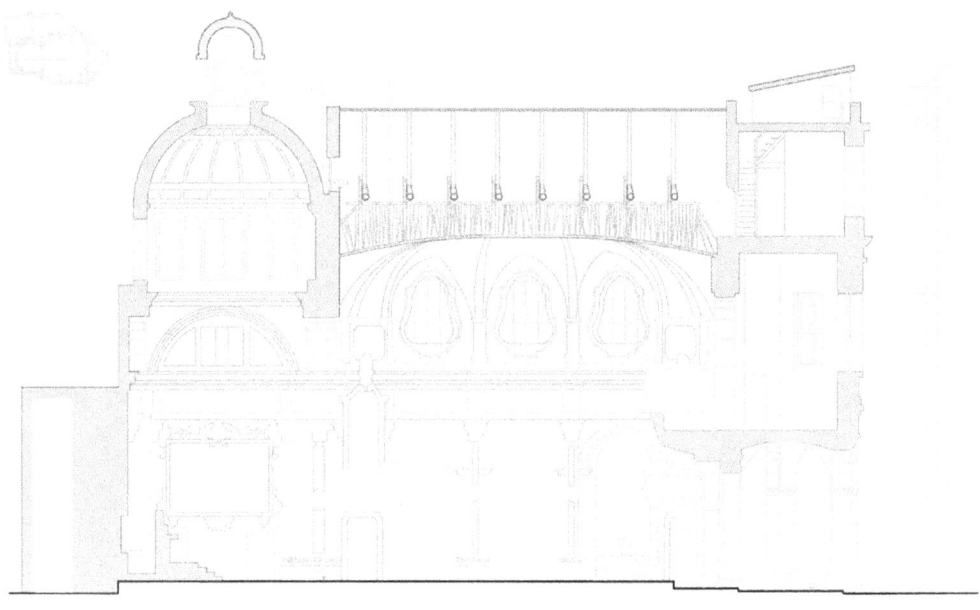

Figure 8: Naples, Church of Santa Maria Egiziaca all'Olmo: longitudinal section.

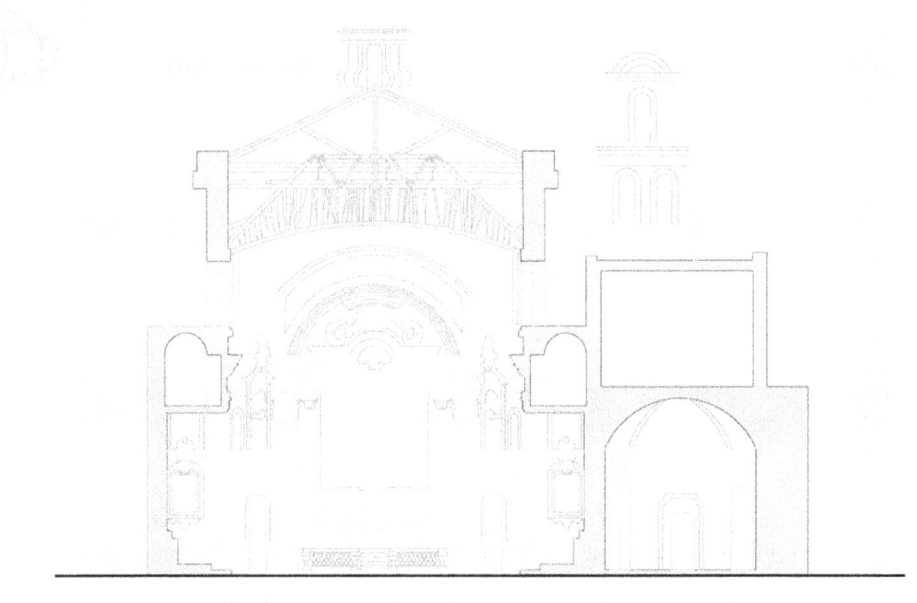

Figure 9: Naples, Church of Santa Maria Egiziaca all'Olmo: cross section.

Wooden vaults in Naples between survey and construction knowledge: the case of the church of Santa Maria Egiziaca all'Olmo

Starting from the traditional elaborations in plan and section, drawn up from the orthophotos, the multiple distinguishing marks of the wooden vault have been highlighted. These representations have been of fundamental importance for understanding and cataloguing the 'dense forest' of beams and ribs, determining precise metric, geometric and colorimetric information for each element. (Fig. 10)

Figure 10: Naples, Church of Santa Maria Egiziaca all'Olmo: construction detail. 1) steel truss; 2) wooden reticular support structure; 3) tie-beam of the existing truss; 4) suspension elements; 5) wooden kerb; 6) wooden vault (ribs, restoni and reeds)

Construction features: parts of the vault and nomenclature

In order to correctly describe and interpret the parts that make up the vault of the church of *Santa Maria Egiziaca all'Olmo*, a comparison should be made with other Neapolitan wooden structures in order to frame the case under investigation in a wider context.

The eighteenth and nineteenth century technical literature on the Neapolitan area provides an initial and only partial vision of the wooden vaults, both in terms of the methods of execution and the parts making up the structures. For this reason, it has been necessary to start from the material data, combining field investigations with the interpretation of technical descriptions found in archive documents.

Construction features of wooden vaults in Naples

An initial, and only partial, direct and indirect investigation [21] has allowed the proposal of an initial outline of the various elements that constitute Neapolitan wooden vaults. Constants and variations in construction have been identified and the different parts making up the vaults have been catalogued. In a schematic and general view, starting from the extrados towards the intrados, it is possible to find the presence of:

1. a support structure, called armaggio;

2. a load-bearing framework of the vault consisting of curved profiles, called centine (ribs) coupled and nailed or held together by metal bands. Orthogonal to the shaped ribs are set transverse elements with a rectangular cross-section and a stiffening function, called restoni/listoni. In archival documentation, the ribs are also called fogliette or felle [22];

3. suspension elements to the truss or floor, known as ginelle or catinelle;

4. the coating. This can be made of woven reeds (canniccio), wooden sticks (called cerchj) or wooden boards;

5. plaster on the intrados.

Neapolitan wooden vaults, unlike those found in other regional contexts in Italy, are almost never self-supporting, except in rare cases where the room to be covered is extremely small. This is the case of some rooms in the historical flat of the Royal Palace of Naples, with a span of about three metres. In most cases, however, they are suspended from a support structure (listed in n.1 above) which may take one of three forms:

- a floor from which the vault is suspended;

- an inter-floor structure independent of the floor and consisting of equidistant beams, with their ends embedded in the masonry, to which the vault is connected;

- Lastly, a structure placed at roof level and autonomous with respect to the truss of the pitched roof. Supporting structures that are independent of floors and roofs are safer from a structural point of view. Connecting the vault to a floor that can be walked on or that is subject to possible vibrations could lead to localised stresses, undermining the equilibrium of a wooden vault.

The data available from direct surveys have been combined with indirect sources, in particular bills of quantities, mainly from the nineteenth century, and rates, such as *Tariffa del Genio*, dated 1838 [23]. According to this last one, woven reeds (*canniccio*) had to be made of large dry canes, crushed and tied with wooden sticks placed in squares of about 50 centimetres. The canes had to be covered with a layer of mortar about one centimetre thick.

The wooden vault of the Church of Santa Maria Egiziaca all'Olmo

The peculiarity of the church of Santa Maria Egiziaca all'Olmo lies in the complex support structure from which the vault is suspended. Observing the roof system of the church from top to bottom, thanks to the metric survey carried out, it has been possible to catalogue the different parts structurally connected to each other (Fig. 10):

- the steel roof, dating from the interventions after the 1980 earthquake (1989) and built to replace the existing wooden trusses;

- Tie-beams of the existing wooden trusses, without any structural function, resting in some places on wooden bearing plates and, in others, drowned in the recent reinforced concrete kerb;

- the wooden reticular support structure, consisting of rectangular section profiles, doubled, and connected by bolted metal plates. No information is available on the dating of this structure. Visual analysis of the wood and the nodes suggests that it may have been added or modified after the construction of the vault. In order to confirm this hypothesis, it would be advisable to carry out dendrochronological investigations and tests on the wood species;

- *ginelle/catinelle* (suspension elements) with the function of suspending the underlying wooden vault from the reticular structure. Such elements show a non-constant section and are nailed both to the ribs of the vault and to the base beam of the reticular structure;

- the actual wooden vault consisting of ribs, in some places doubled, placed at a distance between centres of about 40 centimetres and stiffening elements (*restoni*) fitted at right angles (distance between centres of about 35 centimetres). (Fig. 11) At the present time, the coating of the vault is not visible from the extrados due to a thick layer of dust. It is assumed, however, on the basis of historical data that it is made of reed.

It is worth emphasising that along the supporting walls of the vault there is a kerb consisting of wooden beams of circular cross-section placed one after the other and resting on beam bearing plates placed on the masonry. This wooden kerb serves as a support for a system of beams to which the suspension elements of the vault are attached. The grid of beams is only present at the ends of the elliptical area and serves as a support to the vault in the parts with the greatest curvilinear section. (Fig. 12)

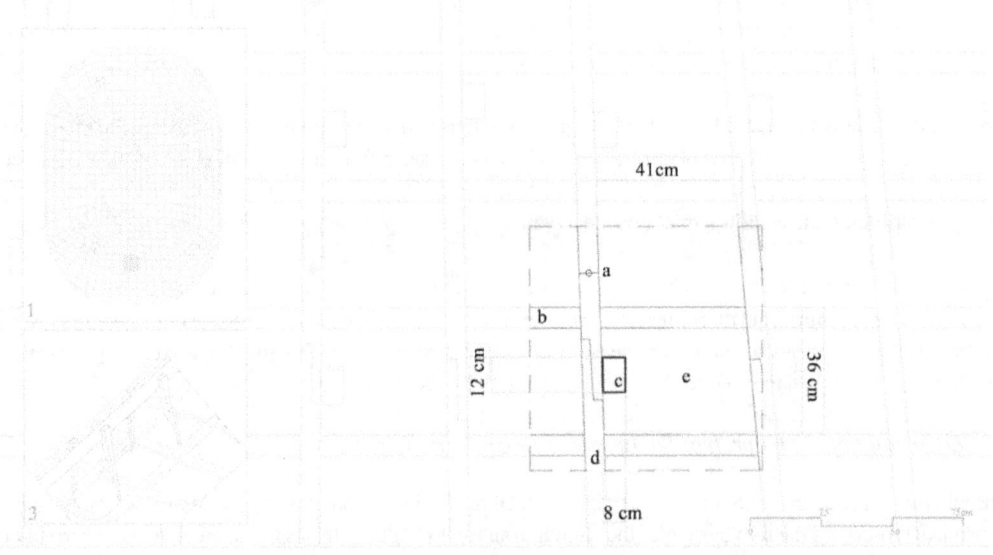

Figure 11: Naples, Church of Santa Maria Egiziaca all'Olmo: 1) hypothetical carpentry plan; 2) planimetric detail of the surveyed portion; 3) schematic drawing of the suspension elements (ginelle)

Figure 12: Naples, Church of Santa Maria Egiziaca all'Olmo: view of the wooden kerb.

At present, as already mentioned, a series of consolidations are visible, probably carried out between the second post-war period and the end of the 1980s. These are tie rods and hooping systems made of thin iron cables with the function of consolidating the connection between the support structure and the ribs. In addition, after the 1980 earthquake, the original truss tie beam and the reticular support structure were attached to the new metal truss by means of steel brackets. These interventions made the truss, the reticular support structure and the vault closely connected, thus modifying the original structural scheme that foresaw, for obvious safety reasons, the total autonomy of the vault with respect to the roof.

Conclusions

This paper represents the first result of a research in progress on the vault of the church of the *Santa Egiziaca all'Olmo* and, in broader terms, on the wooden vaults in the Neapolitan context. The experience carried out on the case study has made evident the need to combine historical research and direct knowledge of the building. Further innovative no-contact surveys and targeted investigations on the wooden parts could, in the future, support the hypotheses on the chronological transformations of the structure (dendrochronology and/or 14C.) and provide new findings. For example, the identification of the tree species could help to understand if the choice of the wood was mainly based on the mechanical properties or on the availability in the forest of the region. This combination of information and different expertise could open up new and stimulating fields of research.

References

[1] Although the present paper is the result of a common research, L. Romano authors paragraphs 2 and 4, whereas M. Falcone authors paragraph 3. Introduction, conclusions, drawings and photos (2021) are by both the authors.

[2] V. Russo, L. Romano, F. Marulo, 'Volte ad incannucciato nel cantiere storico napoletano. Risultati da una ricognizione in progress', *Archeologia dell'Architettura*, XXV, 2020, pp. 87-102.

[3] The survey and the study of the construction features was carried out as part of a Bachelor thesis at the Department of Architecture of the University of Naples Federico II, 2021 (student: Stefania Argenziano, tutors. V. Russo, M. Campi, L. Romano).

[4] L. Di Lernia, 'Un episodio del tardo barocco: la chiesa di S. Maria Egiziaca all'Olmo' pp. 201-216 in G. Cantone (Ed.), Barocco napoletano, II, Roma: Istituto poligrafico e Zecca dello Stato, Libreria dello Stato, 1992.

[5] Di Lernia (note 4), p. 205; G. B. D'Addosio, 'Documenti inediti di artisti napoletani del XVI e del XVII secolo', *Archivio storico per le Province napoletane*, n.ro 46, year 7, 1921, pp. 383-395.

[6] R. Mormone, 'Dionisio Lazzari e l'architettura napoletana nel tardo Seicento', *Napoli nobilissima*, VII, pp. 158-167.

[7] G. Alisio, *Napoli e il Risanamento. Recupero di una struttura urbana*. Napoli: Edizioni Scientifiche Italiane, 1980.

[8] Di Lernia (note 4), pp. 206-211; Naples, State Archive (ASNA), *Corporazioni religiose soppresse*, vol. 5175.

[9] G. Amirante, 'La pianta centrale nell'architettura barocca e tardo barocca napoletana', *Opus*, 12, 2014, pp. 185-200.

[10] Mormone (note 6), p. 164.

[11] G. G. Borrelli, 'Aggiunte alla veste settecentesca della chiesa di Santa Chiara a Napoli', *Confronto. Studi e ricerche di storia dell'arte europea*, no.3, 2020, pp. 35-57; ASNA, *Archivi dei Notai del XVIII secolo, Notaio Giovan Pietro Cantilena*, scheda 480, prot. 17, 349r-355r

[12] O. Cirillo, 'Esercizi barocchi, geometria e misura nell'attività di Michelangelo de Blasio' pp. 481-495 in A. Gambardella (Ed.), Ferdinando Sanfelice. Napoli e l'Europa, Napoli 1997, Napoli: Edizioni Scientifiche Italiane, 2004.

[13] L. Romano, *Volte leggere. Saperi e magisteri costruttivi tra Napoli e l'Europa*. Firenze: Nardini, 2021.

[14] The drawing is published by Borrelli (note 11, p. 51) but it is no more attached to the related deed (ASNA).

[15] Naples, Diocesan Archive, *Vicario delle Monache*, b. 280D

[16] Naples, Archive of the 'Soprintendenza Archeologia, Belle Arti e Paesaggio per il Comune di Napoli', b.17/344

[17] M. Campi, A. di Luggo, R. Picone, P. Scala, (Eds), *Palazzo Penne a Napoli tra conoscenza, restauro e valorizzazione*. Napoli: Arte'm, 2018, pp. 31-36.

[18] A. C. Alabiso, M. Campi, A. di Luggo, *Il patrimonio architettonico ecclesiastico di Napoli- Forme e spazi ritrovati*. Napoli: artstudiopaparo, 2015, pp.17-31.

[19] L. De Luca, *La fotomodellazione architettonica*. Palermo: Dario Flaccovio Editore, 2011, pp. 19-29.

[20] P. M. Cabezos-Bernal, P. Rodriguez-Navarro, T. Gil-Piqueras, 'Documenting paintings using gigapixel sfm photogrammetry', *Int. Arch. Photogramm. Remote Sens. Spatial Inf. Sci.*, XLVI-M-1, 2021, pp. 93-100.

[21] Russo, Romano, Marulo, (note 2), pp. 87-102.

[22] ASNA, *Opere Pie-Spirito Santo*, fs. 48, ff. 218 recto; ASNA, *Ministero degli Affari Interni*, II versamento, b. 3602bis, n. 10.

[23] Corpo Reale del Genio, *Piazza di Napoli. Tariffa de' prezzi de' lavori che si eseguono dal Corpo Reale del Genio nelle fortificazioni e negli edifici militari di detta piazza*, Napoli 1838.

The Wood Sector and the King's Works. A Different Perspective for the Study of 18th Century Royal Construction Sites in the Kingdom of Sardinia

Martina Motta
Politecnico of Turin

Abstract

This paper presents new perspectives of the 18th century royal construction sites in the Kingdom of Sardinia. The object of the research is to broaden the investigation of the construction site to include the construction material of larch wood, which was used in the buildings' carpentry. Studying the construction site and focusing on techniques of extraction, logistics chains and territorial modifications, show how much the events of architecture are intertwined with the physical environment and its exploitation.

Introduction

What relationship links the construction site in Early Modern Europe to the territory of provenance of its building materials? This is the question we want to answer in this text, taking into consideration a specific territory, and a material, wood, which is among the most common and most indispensable for the operation of a construction site.

To try to answer this question, it is essential to redefine a working method on archival sources related to the construction site. Until today, historiographical research has mostly focused on the time of construction, and therefore on the facts of the construction site in situ [1]. Attention was therefore paid, above all, to documents related to the assembly operations of the building, including the instructions given by the designers - engineers and architects. This last source contains a vast amount of information on the requirements of the materials provided to the construction site and on the subjects involved, the skills required, the techniques, and times of execution of the assignments [2].

However, to shed light on what happens "before" the actual construction, and "elsewhere" from the construction site, it is necessary to consider more heterogeneous sources, both institutional and local, produced in the places of extraction or production of materials, and by different actors.

This is what has been done in our case study, to see how the events of some 18th century construction sites in Piedmont (then part of the ancient Italian state of the Kingdom of Sardinia) are intertwined with those of the woods providing the timber.

On the one hand, we considered, at the State Archives of Turin, the fund of the "State Company of Buildings and Fortifications" (*Azienda di fabbriche e fortificazioni*), which contains documentary series on civil and military public works, such as contracts, budgets, and accounts, starting from 1685. At the same time, through the study of the "Hunting and Forests" (*Cacce e foreste*) fund, we collected royal licenses, reports on the state of the woods, and edicts for their conservation. The examination of these institutional sources was then integrated with local archival sources: the municipal archives of Salbertrand, Chiomonte, Exilles, and Oulx of the Upper Susa Valley. These sources were essential in reading the facts from the perspective of the communities and therefore of the territories of extraction of timber. The "Community Registry", "Consular accounts", "General accounting", "State of the woods and forest of the community", "Quarrels and

The Wood Sector and the King's Works. A Different Perspective for the Study of 18th Century Royal Construction Sites in the Kingdom of Sardinia

Litigation" sections of these archives reveal important testimonies about the processes triggered by the construction site and provide us with a complex and multi-actor picture of how woods could function in the eighteenth century, increasingly conditioned by the needs of the state.

State construction and the conquest of the woods

Figure 1: Encyclop die [...] par MM. Diderot, et D'Alembert (1770). The word 'forest' was conceived according to the public utility: useful plants include 'crops', 'weeds' those that compete with and insects that feed on leaves are 'parasites'. (ASTO, Biblioteca Antica, T.III.1 - 15).

The first half of the 18th century represented for the Kingdom of Sardinia and Piedmont a period of great transformations in the field of construction and urban planning, both civil and military. The great wars started by Vittorio Amedeo II [3] involved an enormous consumption of timber. Beams, poles, bundles, but also timber for lime kiln fuel, served to power the military infrastructure: peripheral fortresses, such as Fenestrelle, Brunetta, and Exilles, on the Franco-Piedmontese border,[4] and urban fortifications, such as the system of bastions and military quarters in Turin, the Kingdom's capital. After the Turin siege of 1706 and the conclusion of the wars at the beginning of the 18th century, work on the fortifications continued, but important non-military construction sites also opened. New urban policies lead to the opening of dozens of new construction projects: infrastructure, such as canals and the third expansion of the capital city, and architectural construction sites. In 1713, the architect Filippo Juvarra was called to Court, and we owe to him the design of all major interventions of the following two decades [5]. Within 30 years, most sites of the Savoy court were either renewed or built from scratch: the buildings around the castle square, the offices for the Royal Secretariats, the Teatro Regio, the court archives, the Royal Academy. At the same time, the system of suburban residences, the so-called "crown of delights" [6] was extended in the Turin belt, to celebrate the prestige of the royal dynasty and its capital city.

To meet the needs of this large number of construction sites and operations in terms of wooden resources, the General Agency of Buildings and Fortifications, to which the jurisdiction and competencies on the construction sites belonged, promoted a general reform of the rules and practices regarding wood materials. Although this reform concerned the whole Kingdom, the area we chose to observe, as it was the more directly affected, is that of the Alpine valleys closest to the capital, Turin [7].

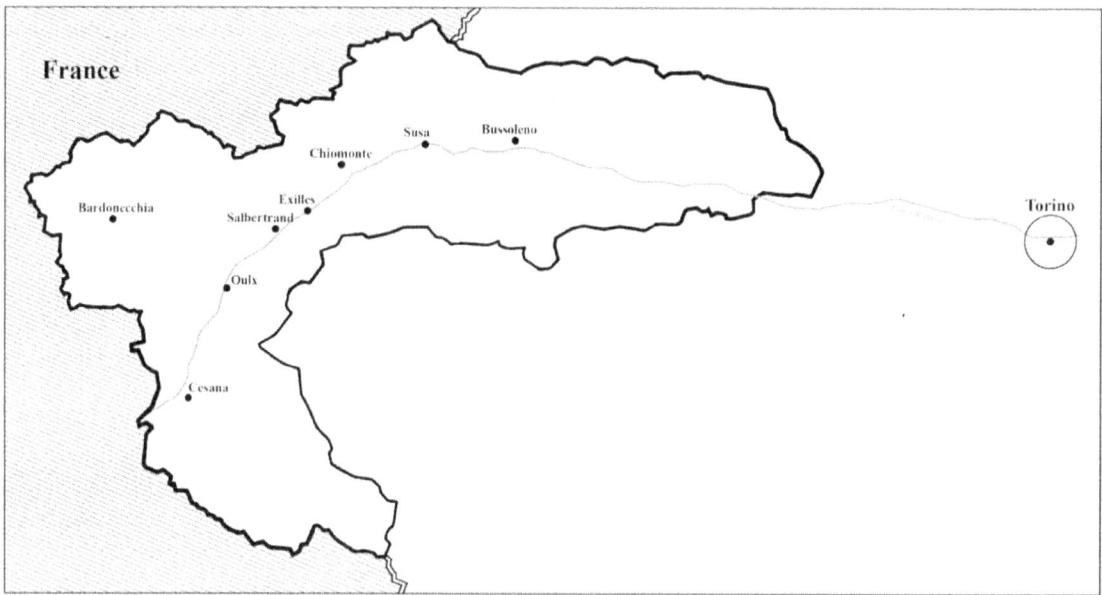

Figure 2: The Upper Susa Valley extends over 50 km in an east-west direction from the French border to the outskirts of Turin. The Dora Riparia river, a tributary of the Po, flows through the valley. (Author).

These valleys had been part of the French province of the Dauphiné until 1713. However, they were also part of a more ancient, largely self-governed entity, the *Republic of the Escartons,* that France had slowly incorporated, but not yet cancelled. Since the year 1343 all woods - together with the uncultivated lands, pastures, and waters - in the *Escartons* were subject to *bandi* ("bans") defined by the local communities, which regulated their exploitation and planned the forms of use in a logic of self-organization [8]. For centuries, in addition to providing timber, the woods had represented a complex economic cycle for the communities: the collection of herbs and wild fruits, charcoal, grazing of the undergrowth, complementary fodder reserve, components of the soil fertilization cycle [9]. The change of government of the valleys on the Italian side of the Alps, incorporated into the Kingdom of Sardinia in 1713, radically changed the fate of these forests. From a multiple and collective resource, they became an externalized economic resource, focused on timber in all its possible uses.

The new political and economic conception is expressed with radical clarity by the 1782 report of the *Intendant* of the province of Susa, Galeani Napione di Cocconato. The *Intendant* argued "that the communities should not possess woods, nor pastures [10]". It was his view that woods and pastures should have been sold to private individuals, whose more vigilant and enlightened eye would have made them bear fruit for the benefit not only of the direct owners but of the whole state. Napione also severely criticized the traditional uses of the woods, seen as a cause of their devastation, and denounced the high consumption of timber for local uses. "Almost everything is made of wood," - he wrote - and the peasants "use plants to build walls, embankments, buildings, houses, planks, canals, fences, and barriers around possessions, instead of hedges." The official went so far as to suggest a law prohibiting the construction of wooden houses in the Upper Valley.

The Wood Sector and the King's Works. A Different Perspective for the Study of 18th Century Royal Construction Sites in the Kingdom of Sardinia

Although only a few of the measures advocated by Napione were put in place before the end of the ancient regime, the renewal of the tools for the control and management of the woods by the state authority throughout the 18th century was radical. The regulatory reform required, to be effective, a series of census and survey initiatives. Their immediate need is testified by a letter from the Intendant Gullier of October 2, 1719 (preserved in the *Memoirs for the prohibition of the cutting of tall woods in the Valleys on this side of Monginevro, purchased with the Treaty of Utrecht*). Gullier complained about the absence of forestry rules and stressed the importance of a survey that would provide "a specific designation of the situations, Regions, places, denominations, and extent of the places where the Woods are, of their quality, easiness or difficulty to extract them, abusiveness of cutting them, and in the extraction of pitch, grape or turpentine [11]".

Figure 3: S.B. Nicolis di Robilant, De l'utilit et de l'importance des voyages [...] (1790). Important scientific expeditions were promoted by the Savoy State to seek and map natural resources during the eighteenth century. (Biblioteca Reale Torino, Storia Patria, 945/1-2).

The action of reform in terms of resources and wooded territories was to be organized into three main lines of action, intertwined with each other:

- The assessment of the forest situation through the drafting of accurate statistical surveys, which served to know the demographic and economic consistency of local communities. The first of these comprehensive investigations dates to 1741. The most complete investigation, called "General Statistics", [12] took place between 1750 and 1753.

- The promotion of topographic survey expeditions, performed by the technicians of the Office of Royal Topography. These operations led to the production of "maps of the woods" (*Carte dei boschi*). Though these new maps were used for the more general purpose of mapping the mineral resources of the Alpine valleys, they also recorded the woodland cover in those areas. The maps of the woods were a major step towards the reinterpretation of the common woods in a state-owned perspective. Emblematic of the objectives of this type of paper is the title of the memorandum attached to the map of the woods of Exilles [13], of 1739-40:"Description of the Typographic Chart of the woods and thickets, and explanation of the quantities of plants, their qualities, of what diameter, and to that work are suitable, in which territory they find themselves woods and thickets, which roads can be practiced to lead the woods to the Fort, as the assets, villas, or houses in case of cutting by slipping of the snows, or avalanche" [14].

- The drafting of new legislation, incorporated into the Royal Constitutions of 1729 and then reiterated in 1770. It was to be defined by Adolfo de Béranger, considered the founder of Italian forestry, as the "most advanced" forestry legislation in Italy, as it was inspired by criteria of public utility and economic governance of the territory [15]. The local, rural bans had been more conservative than innovative: the organization of local economic life was linked to the management of natural resources to defend the territory, considered an indispensable basis for the survival of the community. The laws of the state followed completely different logics.

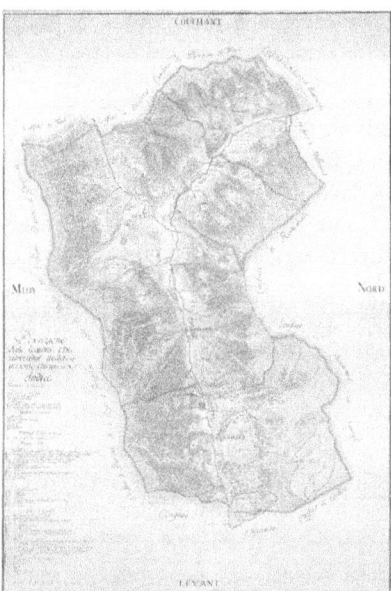

Figure 4. Exilles - Pianta topografica colla descrizione delle regioni (circa 1740). The "wood maps" were the Kingdom's cartographic tool dedicated to mapping the forest species useful for construction and other purposes. (AT-OeStA/KA Kriegsarchiv Wien, Kartensammlung, B..VII.a.242).

The Wood Sector and the King's Works. A Different Perspective for the Study of 18th Century Royal Construction Sites in the Kingdom of Sardinia

Timber from the Upper Susa Valley to Turin

The abundance of timber in the woods of the Upper Susa Valley, in particular in the territories of Chiomonte, Exilles, Salbertrand, Oulx and Sauze d'Oulx, located in the hydrographic basin of the Dora Riparia, was convenient to serve some of the main construction sites of the Kingdom of Sardinia. While three major forts of the State were actually placed within the valleys, the proximity to Turin facilitated the use of timber in the construction sites in the capital, thanks to an active network of connections to the Piedmontese plain: by land with the Royal Road or *Strada di Francia*, and by river with the Dora Riparia.

Attempting to quantify the hectares of woods that existed in these areas is difficult. However, it is possible to reconstruct a summary picture through the tools that the state put into practice once the territories had been annexed: statistics, surveys, cadastral surveys. The General Statistics [16] showed that there were 47,330 '*giornate*' [17] in the Province of Susa, with the Upper Valley counting 600 *giornate* of woods in Chiomonte, 800 in Exilles and Salbertrand, and the other 20 communities that divided only 2,500.

Figure 5: Pianta dimostrativa del fiume Dora con tutte le diramazioni (1700). The portion of the map shows the course of the Dora River from Susa and the Brunetta fortress, to the city of Turin. (Archivio Storico Citt di Torino, TD 12.1.3).

Two construction sites, that of the Basilica of Superga and the Teatro Regio, are examined here. Through their documentation we will try to discuss some issues related to the woods and the territory. The years concerning the provision of the building materials for these buildings (roughly between 1720 and 1721, for Superga, and 1738-40 for the Teatro Regio) are particularly interesting to us, as they run parallel to the drafting and first applications of the new legislation on forestry, published in the Royal Constitutions of 1729.

The Buildings and Fortifications fund record a considerable movement of timber from the Upper Susa Valley to Turin between 1720 and 1721. The town of Susa is mentioned as an intermediate stop and the hill of Superga as the destination. Other intermediate stops that are mentioned are near the city: timber was unloaded at the Monte dei Cappuccini, and then continued by road towards the hill of Superga, as in a payment of April 1725 made to the Wood Master Domenico Cantone, who "provided, conducted, paid oak or larch beams for the Superga dome scaffolding from the riverbank to the hill of Convento Cappuccini" [18]. The reference to the river is an indication of a movement by water wherever possible, an issue to which we will return. As for the origin of the timber, the payments for Superga specifically mention Salbertrand. On July 6, 1720, the Entrepreneur Franco Toscanello was "paid for conducting beams, joists and other timber from the mountains of Salbertrand and its surroundings to Susa". In 1721, another payment went to Giovanni Tomaso Prunotto, who performed "the collection of timber from Salbertrand to Superga" [19].

We know from multiple sources that Salbertrand was the community that possessed the most abundant woods in the entire Upper Susa Valley, with the wooded area covering more than two-fifths of the total surface of the commune, 90% of it covered with tall trees. The areas now called Gran Bosco and Piccolo Bosco of Salbertrand, were described by the previously mentioned 1739 map, as rich in larch trees, respectively 22,000 and 14,000 specimens excluding young trees and saplings. These wooded lots became in the 18th century the most important source of income for the community. In addition to construction sites in the capital, they supplied the military forts of Brunetta and Exilles.

From these same woods also came the timber for the construction of the Teatro Regio. In theatrical architecture, the demanding roofs above the hall and the stage required particularly long beams. The woods of Exilles, Salbertrand, Oulx and Beaulard, in the autumn of 1738 were inspected to "recognize woods suitable for the construction of the roof of the above-mentioned theater" [20]. We also have submissions of the Master Builders Michele Antonio Perrone and Giovanni Battista Coletto "for the provision of 38 beams of larch" from the "woods of Salbertrand" [21].

Bringing particularly long beams downstream was a difficult task. We have information about the infrastructure works in the Upper Valley necessary to make the timber transport from the mountains to the city more efficient. Lord Buttis, Treasurer of Susa, was reimbursed in 1739 "for the repair of roads for the transit of timber to be used for the Teatro Regio roof" [22]. In addition to the roads, attention was paid to the Dora River along its entire course. On the one hand, the upper tract of the Dora was crossed by wooden bridges, which sometimes had to be reinforced. On the other hand, the river was used for the flow of timber in many sections and in the lower valley. In the report of the Intendant Napione, we read about his intention to rectify the Dora River, "if not totally at least partially", including the gorges of the upper section, such as the Sère la Voute passage between Exilles and Salbertrand. While for "the wooden bridges that currently exist (...) it is advisable to repair them immediately with new timber" [23]. This echoes the recording in 1739 of a "repair of the bridge over the Dora River for the passage of sand carts for the construction of the royal Secretariats, Theater and new timber warehouses" [24].

The wood seen from the construction site. Larch, workers, experts, conservatori

Larch has always been a source of timber of great interest for its important physical and structural characteristics. This quality of wood has excellent strength and good stability, thanks to the hardness of the wood. It has high mechanical capabilities, due to resinous heartwood and durable and compact wood, and an excellent ratio between elasticity and resistance. In Piedmont, it was routinely used for highly stressed construction elements and, thanks to its particular length, with logs up to 25-30 m, for wide span roofs and beams (unlike the fir, used in boards for floors or internal structures). As the demand for this high-performance wood increased, the woods of the Susa Valley could correspond with a relevant production capacity, as the larch was the dominant species, with its dominance increasing over time. In the 49 wooded areas surveyed in the 1740s in the Upper Susa Valley, about 400,000 larches were counted (of which over 41% on the territory of Oulx, 9% Savoulx, 19% Beaulard, while Salbertrand and Exilles account for about 15% and 16% of the total), against 16,210 firs, 75,500 pines, 300 beeches, and just under 3,450 chestnut trees [25].

For the Basilica of Superga we have proof of the use of larch for the main scaffolding of the dome, the so-called Ponte reale, and for the supporting elements for the construction of the ribbed dome itself. The site accounts and contracts provide information on the workers and their different roles, from supply to transport to actual assembly of these complex temporary structures. Pietro Giovanni Audifredi, of the "Diretione Fabrica di Superga e Misuratore et Estimatore", carried out an estimate of the "beams and planks for the scaffolding of the dome" [26]. The entrepreneurs Mochino and Fenoglio took care of "366 dozen poplar planks for the Ponte Reale" [27]. The Master Woodworker Bernardo Garterio was paid for "the construction of the Ponte reale and wooden scaffoldings"; the Wood Masters Carlo Matteo Rondolotto, for "beams planned for the dome scaffolding" [28]. Domenico Cantone had "provided and (...) conducted a quantity of oak and larch wood beams without defects for the scaffold of the dome of the church (...) of Soperga" [29].

The Wood Sector and the King's Works. A Different Perspective for the Study of 18th Century Royal Construction Sites in the Kingdom of Sardinia

For the construction of the Teatro Regio, reference is made to the use of Alpine timber in the wide span structure of the roof: experts were sent "to recognize woodlands suitable for the construction of the roof (...) of the above-mentioned theater"; later recordings repeatedly refer to "the passage of beams for the construction of the roof of the theater" [30]. These documents show the general awareness that timber was at the center of a "supply chain" extending from the building itself, to the mountain forests. It passed from hand to hand and involved different professionals and jurisdictions.

The attention to the wooden species and to the use of the forests was manifested in the role of the "*conservatore*", an official who dealt with the maintenance of the species of interest, constantly "threatened" by local uses. The *conservatore* could be called by the Company of Buildings and Fortifications to make assessments on the availability of wood and timber. Pierre Francois Syord, former *Castellano Reale* of the Valleys of Exilles, Oulx, Cesana, received on June 19, 1738 the assignment of *conservatore* of "Woods and Forests in the Contours of Exilles". His duty was to "take care of and guard, pending the distance of 6 miles in the circuit of said Fort of Exilles, over the conservation of them Forests, and Woods to the mind of the Edicts and General Constitutions" [31].

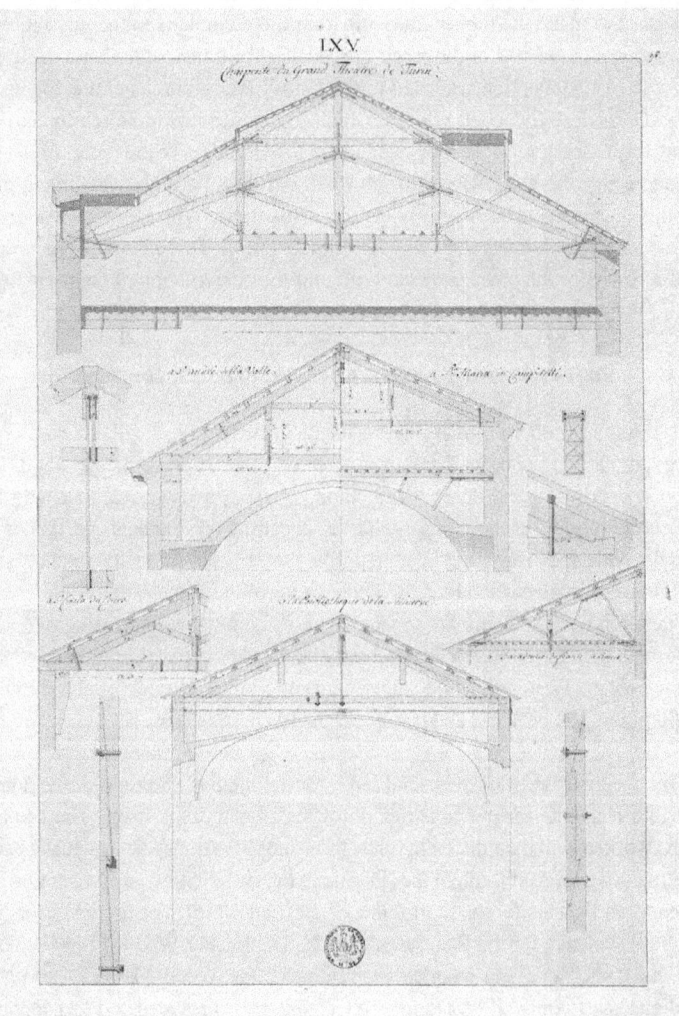

Figure 6: Charpente du Grand Theatre de Turin (1700-1800). (Collection P.-A. P ris – Dessins, vol.482, no.96).

178

In this logic, numerous payments for the in situ inspections of the forests emerge in the accounts. If we refer to the construction of the Theater, in 1739 (a year after the appointment of Syord) we read of payments to Gabriel Griemberger and Giovan Francesco Chianea, for "vacancies made for the designation of forests, and woods in the Valley of Exilles and surroundings" [32]. In the accounts of the community of Salbertrand, the field surveys increase, as is the case of the double expertise by Michel Arlaud, "expert appointed by the Community to the estimation of woodcuts on its territory, to be employed at the Royal Theatre" and of a Signor Serein, "other expert for the Royal Fortifications", who drew up discordant assessments [33].

The woods as a theater of conflict

From the examination of the documents, we have widespread evidence that the requirements of the construction site, followed upstream to the woods, had become a frequent reason for conflict [34]. The application of the new laws on forestry imposed harsh changes on the customs of the local community. Tanners were prohibited from peeling or ruining any type of tree, or damaging plants for the collection of resins. The inhabitants could obtain wood only in two limited periods, from 10 to 20 June and from 20 to 30 September [35]. The administrators were then obliged to watch and control so that no young ("green") plants, of high trunk or *di bella vista* ("good-looking") were cut, but only dry ones, and trees with defects. Grazing was forbidden in some woods and the cutting and transport of wood could not be carried out at night. The wood cut and coming from the municipal lands could not be sold, and in case of theft, private homes could be searched by the authority.

Figure 7: G. De Galard, Resin extraction (1818). The extraction of resin was banned by some of the new state regulations. (Creative Commons).

The Wood Sector and the King's Works. A Different Perspective for the Study of 18th Century Royal Construction Sites in the Kingdom of Sardinia

A number of registers (Registres des permissions de coupes de bois) are conserved, where local inhabitants asked for permission to use timber from areas reserved for the Royal Service, for individual needs, such as the repair of their home: "Joseph Richard and Maurice Alloys (...) each need fifteen pieces of larch wood to begin the re-establishment of their house"[36] is a typical petition.

Each prohibition was associated with a penalty, and the numerous fines collected are recorded in the annual municipal budgets. Among the most common cases, we read of accusations and penalties to the inhabitants who were caught cutting down trees without the permission of the intendant in charge. A lawsuit in the community of Chiomonte concerned the case of Matteo Noli and Claudio Ollivero, who were accused of theft "of woods already cut and existing on the ground", "exceeding the quantity agreed for the enterprise of the formation of palisades for the fortress at La Brunetta"; timber for which "they had not presented the justifications to this office" [37].

Illegal cutting would especially occur in border areas, with communities suing each other, or suing private owners about the use of land on the borders of the municipal territory, who often sold wooded lots intended for civil and military construction sites. In 1731 the community of Exilles sold the timber of the *Bois Noir* and the *Bois Paries* in the *Forêt du Tours* to the companies that produced lime mortar for the fort of Exilles, causing problems with the owners of the neighboring lands within the municipality of Chiomonte. In March 1781, the inhabitants of the community of Chiomonte, "who have from time immemorial to today quietly owned a quarter of the woods of common use, called Pariers Soir Tours" [38], accused Lord Antoine Jaquet of having granted "without any right, nor declaration made to the council" to Lord Antoine Arlaud of Salbertrand, the right "to cut in this area 66 larch trees" on behalf of the Royal Office.

Moreover, it must be considered that the presence of officials belonging to the state apparatus, combined with the presence of military authorities, inevitably put communities in a subordinate position. Syord suggested keeping an eye on representatives of the newly acquired land communities by operating a strict control over their meetings, as he believed their grievances and deliveries to be lies [39]. Reciprocally, the local administrators proved reluctant to collaborate in the investigations between 1750 and 1753, with the Intendant saying to them: "since the information given by people of this caliber contained nothing but gross lies, addressed to cover what the incomes of their territories were (...).. These villains still retain a lot of wildness, but when the discourse turns towards their own interest, they understand it wonderfully, and they are subtle and cunning" [40].

It must be added in this regard, that the state often broke its own rules. In Napione's (albeit biased) report, he complained about the lack of consideration for the rules of cutting demonstrated "by the contractors of barracks and fortifications" [41], as well as by the "forest guards, vile people, to whom a man of probity and honor would not give any credit", whose behavior caused friction with local communities. These considerations are echoed in local documents. In the years of the construction of the Royal Theatre, the consul of Salbertrand, Rey, went to Exilles to formulate a formal protest in front of the castellan Syord for the woods cut for the Royal Service without permission [42].

The extraction and transport of timber on behalf of the royal service, not infrequently caused damage to the local inhabitants. In the case of the Teatro Regio, numerous damages, and requests for compensation against the state by the inhabitants of Bussoleno, a town mid-way between Salbertrand and Turin, are recorded. We read for example of a request for 160 lire to cover the damage to two buildings that were demolished for the "transit of the beams for the construction of the roof of the theater" [43]. In September 1720, at the height of the construction of Superga, a payment to Mathias Bonnot had been made at Salbertrand, "to visit the faults and damages caused on the right side of the valley ("a la droitte du pays") by the cutting or dragging of pieces of wood for the Royal Service" [44].

Figure 8: Stage perspective of Teatro Regio (1761) in B. Alfieri, Il nuovo regio teatro di Torino apertosi nell'anno 1740. (Archivio Storico Teatro Regio di Torino, tav.XI).

The centuries-old experience, embodied in local rules and practices, of mountain communities regarding the link between deforestation, erosion, and landslides, was facing a crisis. The Rural Regulations of Salbertrand, published around 1600 and still presented to the Piedmontese administration around 1750, had carried their recommendations for centuries: "no one will cut down any live or dry trees, remove and take away the bark, in forests and woods or other common places and banned ones" [45]. These rules could become extremely specific, managing separately different areas, patches of wood, or rocky slopes, and reacting to natural events. In Eissard, where a landslide had damaged the plain called Pascal, "no one will be allowed to cut any quality wood, whether for the general public or for the conservation of the properties being close & below" [46]. The Article 90 is about the Valley of the pont Ventoux, where "no one may cut, extract, raise bark from the woods" for the "defense of the river" [47].

As the valleys passed under the new government, the competence for the solution of these environmental issues theoretically fell upon the state. And yet, the problems connected to the status of these territories as part of a contested border region became immediately clear. Even before the official annexation to the Kingdom of Sardinia, the petitions of 1710 [48], presented by the communities to the King, had listed numerous damages caused to the forests by military troops. In these early decades, unregulated deforestation along the streams caused landslides, avalanches and floods or worsened their effects, ultimately encouraging the great flood of 1728 that devastated the Upper Valley, destroying villages at Sauze of Cesana, Oulx, Gad near Oulx and Champbons of Exilles. The floods further deteriorated the woods, and a new felling was necessary to rebuild the houses, bridges and roads [49].

The Wood Sector and the King's Works. A Different Perspective for the Study of 18th Century Royal Construction Sites in the Kingdom of Sardinia

Conclusion

This study of the construction site with a polycentric approach has led to different considerations about how the construction site establishes a relationship with the territory. This approach was, in part, made possible through documentary extracts which are usually kept distinct from traditional historiography.

A consideration that emerges strongly, is the complex impact that the construction site and its needs impose on the places from where the resources are extracted. The creation of topographic maps, the rectification of a river, the impediment of traditional uses, the preservation of some species of trees at the expense of others, environmental phenomena such as landslides, are all examples of how at different scales and in different contexts, the construction site and its logistics chain have their own impact on the territory of the building material they use.

According to an inverse perspective, the territory, and its progressive transformation over time, have influenced and influence the events of the construction site. Both natural factors, such as the presence of a forest or that of a river, and anthropogenic factors, such as the construction of a road or the destruction of a bridge, determine the choice of that specific territory by the body responsible for construction. The proximity of the site to the supply of materials was fundamental in ancient regime.

Finally, the construction site turns out to be a source of conflict. The documentation by the state, of repressive actions or the establishment of officials in charge on the territory, shows how the authority placed itself above the specific needs of the local communities, causing repercussions in legal, economic, social and environmental terms. The intersection of local testimonies is a confirmation of this.

The re-reading of consolidated themes in the historiographical debate related to the construction sites of architecture, opens new research questions, such as environmental history, trying to relate the history of construction and the history of the environment [50]. Recontextualising the architecture with all the events leading up to the construction, provides an essential point from which the roots of the environmental issues can be examined more thoroughly.

References

[1] For the construction site of Basilica di Superga, see: G. Gritella, 'La cupola della chiesa juvarriana di Superga a Torino. Analisi della struttura e indagini sulle fasi costruttive', *Palladio. Rivista di Storia dell'Architettura e Restauro*, vol.IV, no.7, June 1991; N. Carboneri, La Reale chiesa di Superga di Filippo Juvarra 1715-1735, Torino: Ages arti grafiche, 1979; C. Palmas, La Basilica di Superga. Restauri 1989-1990, Torino: Allemandi & C., 1990. For Teatro Regio, see: A. Bellini, Benedetto Alfieri, Milano: Electa Editrice, 1978; L. Tamburini, Storia del Teatro Regio di Torino. L'architettura dalle origini al 1936, Torino: Cassa di Risparmio di Torino, 1982.
[2] Istruzione data da S.A.R. al Consiglio dell'artiglieria, fabbriche e fortificazioni, in F. A. Duboin, *Raccolta per ordine di materie delle leggi, editti, manifesti, ecc., pubblicati dal principio dell'anno 1681 sino agli 8 dicembre 1798 sotto il felicissimo dominio della Real Casa di Savoia (...)*, 1834, vol.VIII, section X, book VII, pp.559-562.
[3] Vittorio Amedeo II took part in the War against France (1690-1696) and in the War of the Spanish Succession (1700-1713). A. Barbero, Storia del Piemonte. Dalla preistoria alla globalizzazione, Torino: Einaudi, 2008.
[4] For the Piedmontese military forts, see: M. Minola, Fortificazioni nell'arco Alpino, Pavone Canavese: Priuli & Verlucca, 1998; M. Vigilino Davico, Fortezze alla moderna e ingegneri militari del ducato sabaudo, Torino: CELID, 2005; F. Barrera, I Sette Forti di Exilles. Metamorfosi architettonica di un complesso fortificato, Torino: Museo nazionale della montagna Duca degli Abruzzi, 2002; F. Barrera and A. Magnaghi, Il Forte di Exilles nell'intervento di ricupero della Regione Piemonte, Milano: Istituto Italiano dei Castelli, 1987.

[5] V. Comoli, Itinerari juvarriani, Torino: CELID, 1995; G. Griseri and A. Romano, (Eds.), Filippo Juvarra a Torino. Nuovi progetti per la città, Torino: Cassa Risparmio Torino, 1989; V. Comoli Mandracci V. and A. Griseri, (Eds.), Filippo Juvarra: architetto delle capitali da Torino a Madrid 1714-1736, Milano: Fabbri, 1995.

[6] "Crown of delights" is the name given to the series of royal residences for leisure and entertainment built between the sixteenth and seventeenth century around Turin. See G. Sgarzini, Residenze sabaude: Corona di delizie, Istituto poligrafico e Zecca dello Stato, Roma: Libreria dello Stato, 2008.

[7] The contribution particularly focuses on the Upper Susa Valley, an alpine valley located in the western Piedmont, bordered on the west by France.

[8] D. De Franco, La difesa delle libertà. Autonomie alpine nel Delfinato tra continuità e mutamenti (secoli XVII-XVIII), Milano: Franco Angeli, 2016; M. Riberi, 'Il Trattato di Utrecht e le autonomie locali nelle Alpi occidentali: il caso della République des Escartons', in G. Mola di Nomaglio and G. Milano, (Eds.), *Utrecth 1713. I trattati che aprirono le porte d'Italia ai Savoia. Studi per il terzo centenario*, Torino: Centro Studi Piemontesi, 2014; W. Ferrari and D. Pepino, Escartoun, la federazione delle libertà – Itinerari di autonomia, eresia e resistenza nelle Alpi occidentali, Valsusa: Tabor, 2013, M. Armiero, 'Commons and Forests', in M. Armiero and M. Hall, (Eds.), *Nature and History in Modern Italy*, Ohio: University Press, 2010; L. Berardo and R. Comba, (Eds.), Uomini, risorse, comunità delle Alpi Occidentali (metà XII - metà XVI secolo), Proceedings, Ostana, 21 Oct. 2006.

[9] On the banned woods of the Eastern Alps, see: A. Lazzarini, La trasformazione di un bosco. Il Cansiglio, Venezia e i nuovi usi del legno (secoli XVIII-XIX), Belluno: Isbrec, 2006; G. Bonan and C. Lorenzini, 'Common Forest, Private Timber: Managing the Commons in the Italian Alps', *Journal of Interdisciplinary History*, vol.51, n.4, Summer 2021. On woods in southern Italy, see: M. Armiero, 'La ricchezza della montagna. Il bosco dalla sussistenza al superfluo', *Meridiana*, n.44, 2002, pp.65-96.

[10] Archivio di Stato di Torino, Sezioni Riunite, Controllo generale di finanze, m.393, *Informative de' signori intendenti del Piemonte sulla Natura dei Boschi*.

[11] ASTO, Sezione Corte, Materie economiche, Caccia e boschi, m.1, f.17.

[12] ASTO, Sezione Corte, Paesi in genere per provincia, Susa, m.91, f.18, *Ragionamento Generale sopra la Provincia di Susa...*

[13] Österreichisches Staatsarchiv-Kriegsarchiv Wien, Kartensammlung, B.VII.a. 242, *Exilles - Pianta topografica colla descrizione delle regioni*.

[14] P. Sereno, 'Una carta inedita settecentesca dei boschi d'Exilles (Alta Valle di Susa)', in P. Caroli, P. Corti and C. Pischedda, (Eds.), *L'agricoltura nel Piemonte dell'800: atti del seminario in memoria di Alfonso Bogge (Torino 2 dicembre 1989)*, Torino: Centro Studi Piemontesi, 1989.

[15] A. Bérenger, 'Dell'assoluta influenza delle foreste sulla temperatura atmosferica', *Giornale di Economia forestale*, 1871-1872.

[16] ASTO, Sezione Corte, Paesi in genere per provincia, Susa, m.91, f.18, *Ragionamento Generale sopra la Provincia di Susa...*

[17] The *giornata piemontese* (Piedmontese workday) was an ancient agricultural measurement, where 1 *giornata* was equivalent to 3,810 m².

[18] ASTO, Sezioni Riunite, Camera dei conti di Piemonte, Fabbriche, Artiglieria e Munizioni da Guerra, Conti 1721, *Fabrica della chiesa di Soperga*.

[19] ASTO, Sezioni Riunite, Camera dei conti di Piemonte, Fabbriche, Artiglieria e Munizioni da Guerra, Conti 1720, cap. 361; Conti 1721, *Fabrica della chiesa di Soperga*, cap.329; 336; 337.

[20] ASTO, Sezioni Riunite, Camera dei conti di Piemonte, Fabbriche, Artiglieria e Munizioni da Guerra, Conti 1738.

[21] ASTO, Sezioni Riunite, Camera dei conti di Piemonte, Fabbriche, Artiglieria e Munizioni da Guerra, Contratti 1739.

[22] ASTO, Sezioni Riunite, Camera dei conti di Piemonte, Fabbriche, Artiglieria e Munizioni da Guerra, Contratti 1739.

[23] ASTO, Sezioni Riunite, Controllo generale di finanze, m.393, *Informative de' signori intendenti del Piemonte sulla Natura dei Boschi*.

[24] ASTO, Sezioni Riunite, Camera dei conti di Piemonte, Fabbriche, Artiglieria e Munizioni da Guerra, Conti 1739, cap.140.

[25] Sereno P., *Una carta inedita settecentesca...*
[26] ASTO, Sezioni Riunite, Camera dei conti di Piemonte, Fabbriche, Artiglieria e Munizioni da Guerra, Conti 1721, *Fabrica della chiesa di Soperga*.
[27] ASTO, Sezioni Riunite, Camera dei conti di Piemonte, Fabbriche, Artiglieria e Munizioni da Guerra, Conti 1725, cap.235.
[28] ASTO, Sezioni Riunite, Camera dei conti di Piemonte, Fabbriche, Artiglieria e Munizioni da Guerra, Conti 1725, cap.226; Conti 1721, cap.263; 339.
[29] ASTO, Sezioni Riunite, Camera dei conti di Piemonte, Fabbriche, Artiglieria e Munizioni da Guerra, Conti 1721, *Fabrica della chiesa di Soperga*.
[30] ASTO, Sezioni Riunite, Camera dei conti di Piemonte, Fabbriche, Artiglieria e Munizioni da Guerra, Conti 1738; Conti 1739, cap. 140; Contratti 1739.
[31] ASTO, Sezioni Riunite, Camera dei conti di Piemonte, Patente Controllo Finanze, Reg.14, f.37, 19 giugno 1738.
[32] ASTO, Sezioni Riunite, Camera dei conti di Piemonte, Fabbriche, Artiglieria e Munizioni da Guerra, art.183, Conti 1739.
[33] Archivio comunale di Salbertrand (ASAL), Parcellaire 1739.
[34] The conflicts between the state and local communities in Upper Susa Valley have been studied by R. Sibille, 'Comunità, comunisti, comunaglie e liti per la terra nelle alte Valli della Dora', A. Dotta and R. Sibille, (Eds.), *Comunità e gestione dei boschi nelle Valli di Oulx e Pragelato. Dalla Grande Charte al Consorzio Forestale Alta Valle di Susa*, 2013, vol.18, Salbertrand: Ecomuseo Colombano Romean. For a wider context, see: K. Pluymers, No Wood, No Kingdom Political Ecology in the English Atlantic, University of Pennsylvania Press 202; K. Matteson, Forests in revolutionary France: conservation, community, and conflict, 1669-1848, Cambridge: University Press, 2015.
[35] ASTO, Sezione Corte, Paesi in genere per provincia, Pinerolo, m.81, f.11
[36] Archivio comunale di Oulx (AOUL), Beni comunali, Stati dei tagli, m.15.
[37] Archivio comunale di Chiomonte (ACHI), Cause e liti, m.152.
[38] ACHI, Cause e liti, m.152.
[39] ASTO, Sezione Corte, I Archiviazione, Provincia di Susa, Valli di Bardonecchia, Cesana e Oulx, m.6, *Memoria formata dal Castellano Syord continente uno Stato in detaglio delle Valli d'Oulx, Issiglio, Cesana, Bardoneschia e le loro dipendenze*.
[40] ASTO, Sezione Corte, Materie economiche, Caccia e boschi, m.1, f.21, *Relazione sui tributi delle Valli del Delfinato, state acquistate a S.M. mediante il Trattato di Utrecht*.
[41] ASTO, Sezioni Riunite, Controllo generale di finanze, m.393, *Informative de' signori intendenti del Piemonte sulla Natura dei Boschi*.
[42] ASAL, Parcellaire 1739.
[43] ASAL, Compte consulaire 1720.
[44] Bandi campestri di Salbertrand, art.51, *Deffence de couper bois ez hermes*.
[45] Bandi campestri di Salbertrand, art.71, *Serve & ban en la Coste de Patarel*.
[46] Bandi campestri di Salbertrand, art.78, *Serve des bois de l'Essart & autres lieux*.
[47] Bandi campestri di Salbertrand, art.90, *Serve de bois au Pinet des Plans*.
[48] V. Coletto, 'Giuramenti e suppliche delle Comunità della Valle della Dora tra il 1709 e 1713', *La Rafanhauda*, vol.4, 2013, p.43.
[49] G. Roddi, 'L'indondazione del 1728 in Valsusa e la Prevostura di Oulx', *Segusium*, vol. XVIII, Dec. 1982, no.18, pp.65-79.
[50] For the relationship between architecture and the environment in history, see: P. Rahm, Histoire naturelle de l'architecture: Comment le climat, les épidémies et l'énergie ont façonné la ville et les bâtiments, Paris: Editions du Pavillon de l'Arsenal, 2020.

Some Experimental Trussed Floors at Kensington Palace, London

Lee Prosser
Curator – Historic Buildings. Historic Royal Palaces

Abstract

Renovation and strengthening measures in two of the principal State Apartment rooms at Kensington Palace in 2021-22 revealed a novel and early attempt at creating a trussed floor system. These rooms, constructed for King George I in 1719-21 reflect the only royal commission for the amateur architect William Benson, who had ousted Sir Christopher Wren from the surveyorship of the royal works and assumed the title himself. Three rooms were created with large spans of between 37 and 40 feet (11 and 12 metres), designed for court occasions, gatherings and dancing. A clear problem with weight and span resulted in an attempt to create a series of shallow trussed principals using complex carpentry with flitches, iron bolts and large locking bars or through-tenons with tusks. The construction bears the hallmarks of experimentation, which was ultimately ineffective. Such early attempts anticipated forms found in the carpentry manuals published a generation later, but are rarely encountered in practice. This paper will describe the floors and attempt to understand the methodology of their form and the reasoning behind their construction.

Introduction

Historic floor structures are much neglected in the field of construction history because they are fairly orthodox but unlike roofs are rarely exposed for interrogation. Serlio and others depict ingenious methods for spanning large spaces with shorter timbers, but generally in England such sophistication is rarely seen and spanning large spaces often relies simply on the dead weight and inherent strength of substantial timbers. At Kensington Palace, the floor structures normally comprise large principal joists which span fairly small or long, narrow rooms. These are linked by secondary joisting, often attended by an integrated ceiling joist arrangement for lower floors. Such simplicity is surprising, as under the influence of Wren and Hawksmoor, together with the master-carpenter Matthew Banks, Kensington typifies the rapid development and refinement of the king-post roof form, but the abundant supply of imported softwood timber may have been an inhibitor to innovation where fairly modest floors were concerned [1]. Only with the creation of much larger rooms in the early 18th century did any consideration of longer spans arise.

Background

Kensington Palace, lying in the west of London has been a royal residence since 1689, when the joint monarchs King William III and Queen Mary II purchased a Jacobean courtier's mansion and commissioned Sir Christopher Wren to transform it by enlargement and modification into a fitting, if private royal residence located at the edge of the royal hunting ground of Hyde Park [2]. Wren, assisted by his clerk of works Nicholas Hawksmoor added new galleries, state rooms and accommodation for the monarchs and courtiers as well as adapting or rebuilding other areas to create kitchens and necessary service areas (Figure 1). For thirty years the palace was an occasional residence, favoured by the later Stuart monarchs; Queen Mary II (d.1694), King William III (d.1702) and Queen Anne (d.1714) all died there. In 1714 it also found favour with the new Hanoverian monarch George I, but it was a house rarely without problems. In December 1717, Wren was directed by the Office of Works to carry out a survey of Kensington, as some of the king's houses were found to be "very much out of Repair, and require speedy care to be taken of them" [3]. Early the next year the clerk of works Henry Joynes drew up a list of problems. The old Jacobean core of the palace was found to be in poor condition and complete demolition and replacement was recommended [4]. The survey occurred at a crucial moment, as at the end of April 1718, the elderly Wren, together with Hawksmoor were ousted by William Benson (1682-1754), an amateur architect who contrived to have himself appointed to the coveted position of surveyor-general of the King's Works through political patronage. His tenure, of less than fifteen months was disastrous; accusations of incompetence and antagonism dogged him from the outset before he was effectively dismissed in turn [5]. However his brief period in office coincides with the last substantial phase of enlargement of the palace and both he and his assistant surveyor, the architect Colen Campbell (1676-1729) must have been responsible for the form and structure of the new wing.

Figure 1: View of Kensington Palace

Following the condemnation of the old core, in June 1718, King George I approved a new plan to replace it, comprising three grand rooms on the upper floor, mirrored by smaller private accommodation below.[6] A plan enrolled in the Works accounts at the National Archives depicts the three rooms with their basic measurements (Figure 2).[7] The new wing spread further than the compact footprint of the old house, expanding to fill recessed gaps on both east and west sides which had defined corner pavilions added by Wren in 1689. Architecturally the new wing is Palladian with a pedimented frontispiece and Venetian window providing a unifying link between the two pavilions, both of which were subsequently rebuilt by John Nash in 1812 (Figure 3). The new rooms are now known as the King's Privy Chamber, the Cupola Room and the King's Drawing Room and form part of a suite of state rooms of increasing importance found in most European palaces and essential to the protocol of the royal court. The Cupola Room is an anomaly however, being an 'extra' room positioned in the middle of the sequence and not found elsewhere. However, it remains the grandest and most theatrical space as a cube of 37 square feet (11 metres) with a high, coved ceiling and painted and gilded panelling (Figure 4). An estimate of £5827 was presented to the Treasury in August 1718 and work is presumed to have begun immediately. It is known that the old Jacobean house was demolished over the winter of 1718-19, exactly a century after its construction.

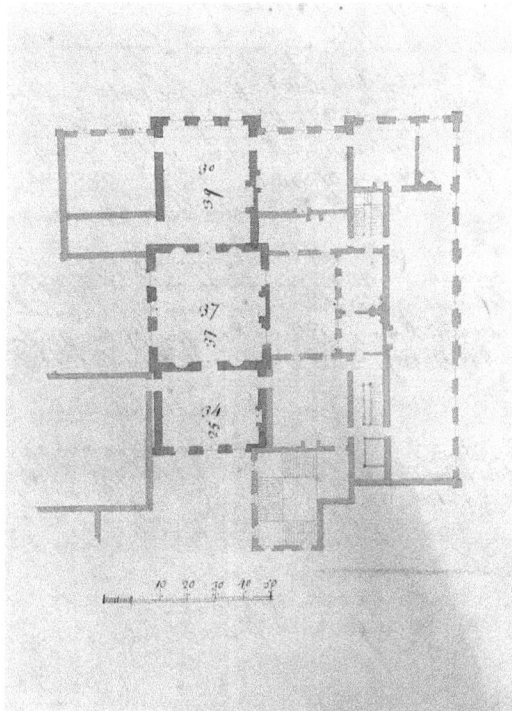

Figure 2: Plan of the new building in the National Archives

Figure 3: East front with central pedimented range of 1719-21

Figure 4: The Cupola Room

The new block was probably substantially finished as a shell by December 1719, with all structural works complete by the summer of 1721. Benson had departed in July 1719 mid-way through construction to be succeeded by Thomas Hewett. By January 1722 only the flooring remained to be laid as on the 10th of that month, the Board of Works reported that 5122 feet of "clean, dry deals", were "wanting to finish in the upper storey" [8]. The deals had been procured, as "wee have found out a fit parcell of very extraordinary Boards and at a very reasonable price, being mostly 18, 20, 22 and 30 feet long". However, the merchant, James Bolton of Southwark would not part with them without ready money and the Treasury was asked to release £320.2s.6d [9]. The rooms remained rather plainly fitted up until 1724 when William Kent was commissioned to paint the ceiling and panelled walls, and the sculptor Michael Rysbrack provided a large marble bas-relief over the fireplace [10]. During the last months of the reign, in March 1727, orders were given to replace the earlier clean deals with oak and 36 bushells of cockle shells were also delivered as insulation and sound-proofing [11].

Architecturally, the rooms are highly significant as the first notable commission by the architect, artist and landscape gardener William Kent. Panelled walls are painted with fictive pilasters, military trophies and relieved by marble door-cases and niches which house gilded statues. The ceiling is partly of tromp l'oeil form, depicting a Roman coffering system similar to the dome of the Pantheon around a huge central Garter star to glorify the new Hanoverian dynasty. The adjoining King's Drawing Room is no less lavish, with red silk damask hung on the walls above oak dado panelling, beneath a painted ceiling (Figure 5).

Figure 5: The King's Drawing Room

Kensington Palace is now managed by Historic Royal Palaces, the charitable trust which cares for unoccupied or quasi-royal residences including the Tower of London, Hampton Court Palace, Kew Palace, the Banqueting House at Whitehall and Hillsborough Castle in Belfast. Over the past ten years, the King's State Apartments have undergone a gradual restoration, reinstating where possible the original decorative schemes and finishes present in the 1720s, including wide oak floorboards following the original pattern. This has offered an opportunity for structural analysis and during 2020 and early 2021, the floors of the Cupola Room and King's Drawing Room were lifted in order to strengthen, clean and install new cabling. Removal of the old Ministry of Works floor boards exposed a system of flitching and shallow trussing of the principal joists in a manner unlike any other structural characteristics of the palace. The floors were drawn and examined over a period of some months as small areas were opened up [12]. As a result the floors were never entirely exposed at one time.

The Cupola Room

The floor of the Cupola Room is framed with two substantial east-west joists lying on the north and south sides of the room, spanned by three secondary north-south joists, thus framing a square at the centre of the room (Figure 6). The timber is all of softwood, most probably of Swedish origin as has been consistently found by analysis elsewhere at Kensington. In addition there is a system of regular subsidiary joisting of smaller scantling to allow the running of firrings across the top at the level of the principals for floor boarding, and slender ceiling joisting below. These lesser joists also radiate from the larger members to the walls where a substantial span is not required. The ceiling joists extend in long lengths, cogged under and nailed to the underside of the joisting and periodically attached with slip-tenons. The original firrings were all removed and replaced by regular softwood members in 1898 when the boarding was replaced, but the spike- and peg-holes for these remain visible (Figure 7). The newer firrings were additionally given small side-fillets which supported cut-up remnants of early 18th century softwood floorboards to form packing or pugging. This is a feature of the floors elsewhere in the palace. No trace of the cockle shells recorded in the 1720s were found in either room, suggesting that the lath and plaster of the lower ceilings has all been replaced.

Some Experimental Trussed Floors at Kensington Palace, London

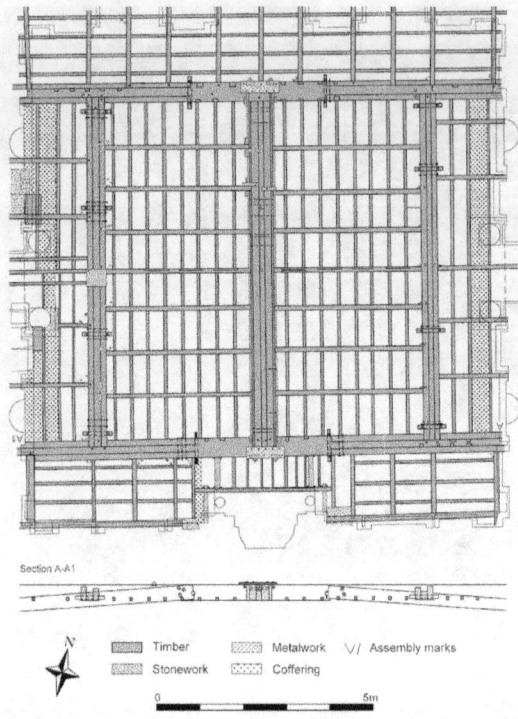

Figure 6: Plan of the Cupola Room floor

Figure 7: Part of the Cupola Room floor exposed in 2021

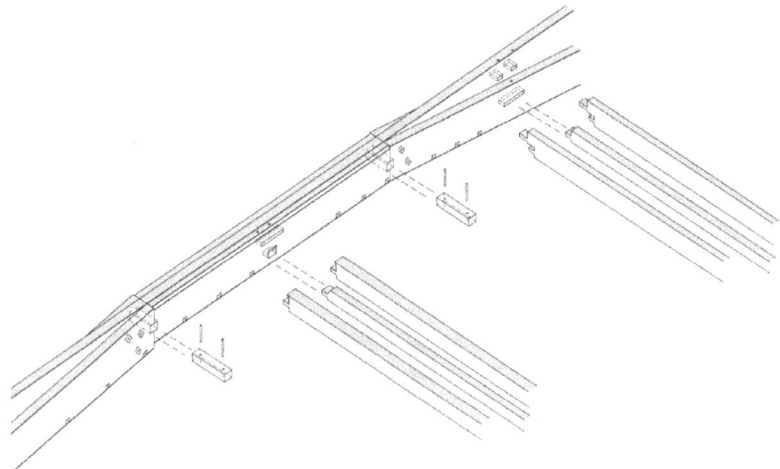

Figure 8: Exploded view of the main Cupola Room floor truss-like joist

Superficially, the form of the flooring system appears fairly conventional, but the main joists are framed as trusses and their secondary companions are flitched, likewise to create a rudimentary and shallow form of truss. The larger joists comprise robust squared baulks of softwood, 16 inches wide by 14 inches deep (0.41 x 0.36m), chamfered slightly on the upper edge, which remain at full size for a central ten-foot length (3m), before being reduced in width on either side to six inches (0.15m), the shortfall then made good with a sandwich of outer timbers which slope downwards at a shallow angle so that close to the outer wall, the upper edge of these timbers is flush with the lower edge of the main beam, the rest descending below the soffit into the room below before engaging with the wall (Figure 8). The solution to the problem of timbers impinging into the lower room was to hide them within a coffer, with columns possibly forming some ancillary structural support where the trussing members meet the main beam. Early 18th century references to the 'four pillar room' may refer to this first floor space, now known as the Red Saloon.

Structurally, the truss is held together by several methods, including locking bars, iron bolts and the abutments of the subsidiary joisting, but no strapping is present. At the junction of the trussing member with the main beam, a through-tenon or locking bar of oak, some three inches (0.07m) square is slotted cleanly and precisely through all three elements and clasped with a tusk tenon, thus keeping the timbers tightly wedged together (Figure 9). Nearby, large iron bolts are countersunk into the timber and secured with threaded nuts and washers.

The three secondary north-south joists are also trussed, but in a different manner. A central six-inch softwood member is clasped by outer members of five inches in width (0.13m), secured with the same combination of locking bars at crucial junctions, together with clusters of bolts. Each has four square locking bars, contrasting with the principals, where only two are found. The main difference in construction is that here, the outer members continue straight, whilst the central timber is cut into thirds, with the outer parts descending on either side in the manner of a truss within the sandwich of the outer members. This creates some complexity at the junction with the principal joists. In the eastern and western joists, the outer flitches have to be tenoned into both the main, central part of the joist and its trussed member, by now diminished to half the height of the joist with a staggered tenon arrangement (Figure 10). The central flitched joist is tenoned only into the principal, but the use of long slip-tenons give some clue as to the construction sequence, discussed below. This central flitched joist has consistently given cause for concern, and from the outset, an extra pair of plank-like timbers was added to each side, crudely nailed on but cut to accommodate the existing square pegs and the lesser joisting. This central joist is thus an extraordinary sandwich of five timbers.

Figure 9: Detail of the locking bar, tusk tenon and iron bolts

Figure 10: Mortice junction of the north-south flitch with the main joist

The King's Drawing Room

The adjoining room to the east was marginally less of a structural challenge for the carpenters, having a span of just 30 feet (9m) for its two principal joists. These are aligned north-south on either side of the central fireplace (Figure 11). The scantling is a little larger at 17 inches in width (0.43m), but like the Cupola Room, the outer third at each end was reduced in width to six inches, with added trussing pieces introduced in the manner of the principal jointing of the Cupola Room. However, here the locking bar is absent, and the joint, not being so tight, is instead secured with packing pieces, all bolted together with clusters of two or three bolts, inserted counter to each other. Like the Cupola Room, the truss thus required a hanging coffer in the room below, together with columns positioned at the junction of the trussing member, though it is not known if these are original or later introductions. Two subsidiary east-west joists are present, but these are not flitched, though they still need the staggered mortice and tenon arrangement at the point where they abut the trussing members of the principals. As in the adjoining room, a series of commons, traces of firrings and extended slender ceiling joists with slip-tenons are present.

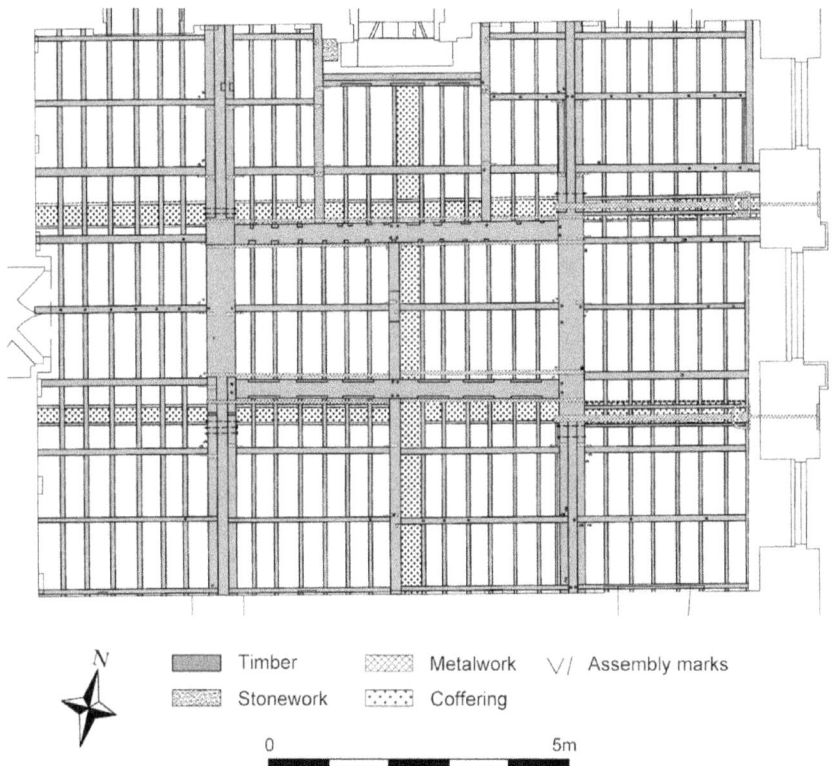

Figure 11: Plan of the floor of the King's Drawing Room

Observations

The form and complexity of the carpentry and other observations allow us to suggest the sequence in which the Cupola Room floor was installed. Where visible, good sequential assembly marking in Roman numerals survive in both rooms – particularly to the lesser jointing and is entirely conventional. Moreover, the principals and their abutting members on the flitched subsidiaries are also marked with "N" or "S" denoting their geographical location, suggesting the careful preparation of all members in the framing yard beforehand. Presumably the principals were installed with the raising of the brick shell, having lower pockets in the brickwork for the truss-like descending pieces, and a conventional pocket for the main part of the joist. However, the careful positioning of the locking bars, which are precisely cut, suggests everything laid out beforehand, though whether the joist was raised ready-made in this manner is open to question. Recent strengthening necessitated the removal of several of the locking bars which could be drawn out easily once cut, suggesting that they were not so much structural as a guide for assembly before the bolts were driven through. Their position at the junction of the trussing pieces on the main joists also makes little sense, as the added member could disengage easily without the presence of the bolts. The key to understanding the installation of the secondary north-south flitched joists appears to be indicated by the use of a long slip-tenon, which allowed the outer members of the flitch to be slotted in, followed by the insertion of the central flitch and the installation of the central outer descending pieces, presumably aided by support from below, before being locked into place by the square oak bars and then bolted. This also suggests that the central joist was the last to be framed, allowing the lesser joisting to be installed at the same time.

Later structural interventions

Loading of the Cupola Room floor has posed problems since the 18th century. In modern times, precise surveys show that the centre of the room forms a dish with the centre of the floor some 0.1m below the level of the outer walls. This was remediated by placing a large clock at the centre of the room, thus preventing gathering in the centre and avoiding too much stress on the deflecting floor. However, the survey also exposed a number of more recent structural interventions. By far the most interesting is iron strapping installed on the eastern side of the King's Drawing Room, of unknown date, but perhaps either 18th century or at the latest, part of Nash's work in the first decade of the 19th century. It is clearly not primary with the build. On the east side, large straps have been added to tie the building into the outer gable wall. These are some four inches (0.1m) thick and wrap around the principals at the junction of the truss-like members before terminating close to the outer wall with a large stirrup, which continues through the wall to a rectangular pattress plate, recessed into the outer brickwork and visible in Figure 3. This may suggests some structural movement, or perhaps concerns about the outer facade. It is known that the outer face of one of Wren's adjoining pavilions collapsed in 1807 and was repaired by John Nash and John Yenn in the years following.

Within the Cupola Room, a reversed truss arrangement was installed in 1898 by the addition of two large bolted plates of iron over the outer, central part of the principal joists as a matrix for two tension rods running alongside the central flitched joist and fixed to a small bracket on the underside, which exerts a twisting force on the principals. Ultimately it proved as ineffective as the earlier measures. Elsewhere, brackets fixing the subsidiaries are also much in evidence, several marked with the name of the foundry, 'Burbach' in Germany, which allows us to date these interventions to a wholesale restoration of the palace in 1898, when the old Ministry of Works oak floors were laid. Some later brackets, marked with 'Dorman Long', must be post-war introductions.

Discussion

Our understanding of the Cupola Room and King's Drawing Room floors is limited by a lack of adequate documentation – no pay books or accounts other than occasional warrants survive to document the involvement of particular carpenters or anything of the process of resolving issues around span and loading. On his dismissal, Benson also made off with a large collection of plans and other documents, which the Office of Works was never able to recover, and is now lost. Most historians of the palace are in agreement that Wren would not have been involved in the design and execution of the new range, which is clearly attributed to William Benson. We might also consider his assistant Colen Campbell in the same way that much of Kensington's existing architecture was actually more likely defined by Hawksmoor rather than Wren as Hawksmoor was the clerk on site, drawing up plans and overseeing the works from day to day. Both Benson and Campbell are architects whose structural approach has not been studied but analysis of some of their surviving commissions might yield results. Midway through the work, his successor Thomas Hewett (1656-1726) came onto the scene and so there is a small chance of involvement by him. One intriguing link to Wren however, is a comparison to his work at the library of Trinity College, Cambridge.[13] Here, he dealt with issues of loading, particularly beneath heavy bookcases by forming a rudimentary truss in exactly the same manner as we see at Kensington – the reduction of a large baulk with trussing side pieces, though these are numerous and short in span by comparison and may have been more effective (Figure 12). Elsewhere, Wren was more conservative. At Hampton Court he supported some floors from long straps of iron suspended from the roof trusses, embedded in stud walls as architecturally, a properly trussed floor would have altered proportions and lead to unsatisfactory results or a reduction in usable space.

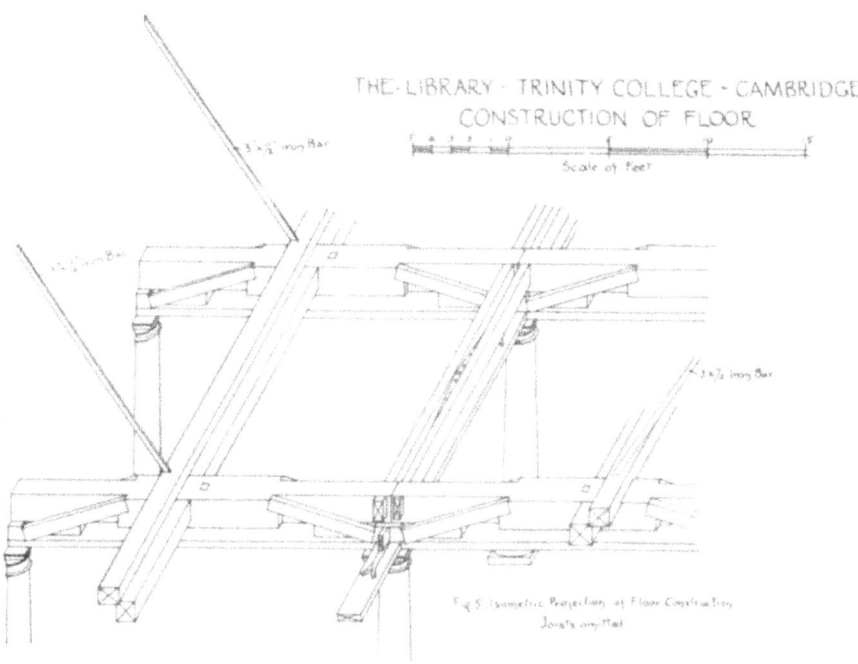

Figure 12: Detail of the floor of Trinity College Library Cambridge as drawn by Fletcher (1923)

The solution at Kensington appears to be a clever idea, but betrays a lack of knowledge of the actual performance of trusses. It begs the question why a third principal was not used to span the centre of the room, but three overly complicated flitches were employed instead. Presumably by having three shorter, on-end timbers combined in a truss-like form, an idea of greater cumulative strength was conceived thus avoiding the risk of deflection by longer timber. The curious use of a descending inner truss-like member for these flitches may have been to prevent complexity with the jointing of the subsidiary joisting, which could be double-tenoned into straight pieces of timber without the difficulties of slope and staggering of joints which the flitched joists had to navigate at their junction with the principals.

Knowledge of trussing was becoming widespread from the later 17th century, and by the time of the publication of Price's carpentry manual some fifteen years later the idea of trussing a beam for a floor was introduced as an option for the first time in print. More actual examples need to be studied to understand whether this kind of presentation in carpentry manuals was based on actual practice or merely clever promotion of hypothetical ideas but the existence of actual trussed floors, however rudimentary may indicate a certain knowledge of them. The role of the carpenter is also an important consideration. It has been suggested before that the refinement of the trussing of the roofs at Kensington, may have been a collaboration between Wren and Hawksmoor with Matthew Banks, his master-carpenter, who would have put into practice some of Wren's ideas of improving and refining the truss. Sadly we cannot name individual carpenters at this date. The last master-carpenter with a link to Wren was John Churchill, who had died in 1715. He was followed in office by Grinling Gibbons, a carver and not a practising carpenter, reflecting the transformation of the office into a more administrative role. It may be that credit for this approach must fall to Benson and Campbell, with the carpenters left to work out the details.

So far as we know, Wren's only foray into a trussed floor was at Trinity in 1695, so whether there are others to be discovered, they are clearly very rare. The floors of the Cupola Room and the adjoining Drawing Room clearly pushed the boundary of technological possibilities in the early 18th century and continue to exercise structural engineers today. To solve the problem once and for all, the most recent solution has been to flitch the flitches, this time with modern steel in order to solve the perennial problem of long span and heavy loading.

Acknowledgement

Many thanks to Tansy Collins for digitising the original drawings

References

[1] See Prosser, Lee 'The Roofs of Kensington Palace' Association for Studies in the Conservation of Historic Buildings vol 32 (2009), 1-14.
[2] Fryman, Olivia 2018 Kensington Palace: Art, Architecture and Society. Yale, New Haven.
[3] TNA Work 6/7, fo.34.
[4] TNA LC 5/157, fo.68. TNA Work 4/1, 3 Jan., 5, 6 and 14 Feb. TNA Work 6/7, fo.34.
[5] His surrender of office on 17th July 1719 is recorded in TNA T54/25 fo.305.
[6] TNA Work 6/7, fo.68.
[7] ibid, fo.69.
[8] TNA Work 4/2, f.53.
[9] TNA Work 6/7, ff.198-9; AO1/2450/156; TNA T 1/241, no.12i.
[10] TNA Work 4/3, 18 June 1725; Work6/15, fo.103; LC 5/158, fo.366; T 1/254, no.2a and b.
[11] TNA Work 4/3, 2, 9 and 30 March, 20 April, 9 May 1727; LC 5/159, fo.525; AO1/2452/160-1.
[12] Drawings and the final reports will be lodged with the curatorial archive at Historic Royal Palaces.
[13] Fletcher, Henry M. 'Sir Christopher Wren's Carpentry. A note on the library at Trinity College, Cambridge'. Journal of the Royal Institute of British Architects 1923, pp 388-391.

The Paduan ties of Poleni

Louis Vandenabeele
Institute of Construction History and Preservation (IDB), ETH Zurich, Switzerland

Abstract

The mathematician Giovanni Poleni (1683-1761) went down in the history of construction for analysing the damage to St Peter's dome and stabilising the structure with iron ties in 1743, as related in his *Memorie istoriche della gran cupola del tempio vaticano* (1748). Less known are his reports on the stability of the Basilica of St Anthony in Padua, the city where he was working as a professor from 1709 to his death. From 1720 onwards, Poleni was frequently called into the basilica to evaluate existing structures, guide repairs and comment on new constructions. Based on archival research and on-site surveys, this contribution focusses on the interventions of Poleni involving tie rods and complex masonry structures. Firstly, his assessment of deformed arches and pre-existing iron ties in 1726 and 1733. Secondly, the reinforcement of the base of the southern tower with several iron ties after it was heavily damaged by fire in 1749. This study on Poleni's work in Padua sheds new light on the background of his most famous feat of engineering and on the transfer of responsibility from practical men to scientists in 18th-century Italy.

Introduction

The life of marquis Giovanni Poleni (1683-1761) is intimately linked to the city of Padua (Veneto) and its university, where he was appointed to the chair of astronomy in 1709, of mathematics in 1719, of experimental philosophy in 1739 and of nautical studies in 1756. He was also professor of physics from 1715 and he acquired an experimental laboratory in 1738. Next to his scientific works which Poleni published on the topics of archaeology and architecture from 1735 onwards, his most famous publication in this field is the *Memorie istoriche della gran cupola del tempio vaticano* (1748).

Reflecting his interest in architecture, Poleni was frequently consulted by the *Veneranda Arca di Sant'Antonio*, the city's board in charge of the maintenance of the Basilica of St Anthony (since 1396). His numerous interventions and his long letters inventoried in the *Archivio Sartori* (1983) were firstly evoked by Negri (1986), showing the continuous involvement of Poleni from 1720 to 1755 [1]. Although his role in the preservation of the basilica is a known fact [2], there have been no further investigations on his structural assessments and their on-site implementations.

As part of an ongoing research project on the Basilica of St Anthony in Padua supervised by Prof. Stefan M. Holzer and financed by the Swiss National Science Foundation (SNSF), this contribution focusses on Poleni's assessments of masonry structures and the use of ties in the basilica. Based on new archival research and recent on-site surveys (laser scanning and thermography), three main interventions of the mathematician on arches (1726, 1733) and towers (1749) are discussed, positioned in the church's history of repairs, and related to precise surveys. Moreover, this series of works spanning over two decades help to put into context his most famous intervention at St Peter's in 1743.

The main arches

13th-century wooden ties

The western part of the basilica, largely erected between the 1230s and the 1260s, is covered by six domes composed of masonry shells and timber structures. The brick cupolas have an ogival profile and a circular base inscribed in a square, the sides of which measure some 14.5 m; they are delimited by four arches and supported by as many pillars. On the exterior of the nave, the thrust of the arches is absorbed by massive buttresses containing a network of corridors and staircases. On the interior, the base of the arches was originally connected by wooden ties removed between 1652 and 1750. Fortunately, they are still visible on an engraving by Giacomo Ruffoni dated circa 1700 (Fig. 1). As further discussed, a second higher level of wooden ties had already been removed earlier.

Figure 1: View of the transept before the removal of the wooden ties. Engraving: Giacomo Ruffoni, circa 1700.

The removal of the lower ties started in 1652 and 1655 when at least 5 beams placed under the arches forming the lateral walls of the nave were sawn and taken down [3]. As a second step, in June 1726, a carpenter was asked to remove 11 ties at the feet of the arches of the nave and the crossing to improve the appearance of the church [4]. Five days later, fearful that the work might cause a collapse, the public surveyor Francesco Tentori was sent by civil authorities – offended for not being consulted – to evaluate the works and give his opinion on the ties. According to him, the ties were primarily meant as a temporary support during the construction of the arches, which was also evidenced by traces of an upper level of ties at mid height, removed long ago. Moreover, he estimated that even if they once played a structural role, it was not the case anymore due to their decay: their removal was thus safe [5].

The analysis of Poleni in 1726

Not everyone must have felt the same way, and a second opinion was immediately sought from Giovanni Poleni. In a long letter dated July 20, 1726, the mathematician exposed a series of considerations following the Vitruvian virtues of architecture, referring also to authors like Polidorio, Portenari, Scardeone, d'Aviler, Alberti, Felibien, Serlio, Palladio, Cordemoy and Scamozzi [6]. After evoking the history and the style of the basilica, he firstly pointed out that the ties were certainly not installed for aesthetical reasons (*venustas*), as they did not contribute to its majesty and symmetry. Then, he considered their potential commodity during construction and maintenance (*utilitas*). From this perspective, he stated that if that had been the case, similar ties would have been left under the domes, which are far more difficult to build and repair. After discarding beauty and commodity, Poleni concluded that the wooden ties must have "naturally" been placed for structural purposes (*firmitas*).

Firstly, he carefully examined the connections at the foot of the arches and noticed that the ties were firmly anchored with iron straps and nails. Secondly, he looked at the dimensions of the ties and, without entering into calculations, stated that the modern knowledge on the resistance of materials could demonstrate the considerable strength of such ties. In a similar way, he praised the system of arches, pillars and buttresses, which he considered perfectly adapted to the weight of the domes. With these arguments, Poleni concluded that the medieval builder – "l'Architetto" in his words – had been perfectly knowledgeable and had used ties for structural reasons.

Regarding their recent removal, Poleni explained that the wooden ties contributed to increasing the required strength of the basilica, in such a way that it could survive accidents and the ravages of time. To illustrate this safety margin, he used an example. If the total resistance provided by the arches, their supports, and the wooden ties corresponded to 100 extra "grades of strength", the ties might represent four grades. Aware of this rough approximation, Poleni added that it would be very difficult to assign the precise contribution of the ties to the resistance of the whole. He concluded by saying that the wooden ties certainly contributed to the strength of the construction, but that removing "four grades" of safety would not result in any accident because "the mercy of God will continue to keep them at a distance". After this intervention, only 10 shorter ties remained around the arms of the transept; in 1750 Poleni endorsed their removal as well [7].

15th and 16th-century iron ties

The central arch separating and supporting the two domes of the nave is of particular interest due to its long history of damage and repairs (Fig. 2). The archives indicate that a first iron tie was installed in 1483 at about a third of its height, by the mason Pietro Voltolina [8]. Yet it seemingly did not suffice: in 1547, the arch was believed to be on the brink of collapse, as indicated by cracks in the domes, arches, vaults and along the southern buttress [9]. Three master builders consulted by the Arca stated that these cracks had always been there in living memory, but that additional iron ties should still be placed. Interestingly, the experts mentioned that pairs of wooden ties had previously been cut at about half of the arch's height and that those should be replaced by irons (they are also mentioned by Tentori in 1726). A second recommendation was to add more ties in the aisles – some were already there – and make sure that the foundations of the buttresses would not be soaked by rainwater. Although the experts were not very explicit about the reason of the damage, their recommendations point towards the understanding that the arch was opening due to a weak southern buttress. One of the experts, Stefano Voltolina (possibly the son of Pietro) also mentioned that these cracks might have been caused by an earthquake (documented in Padua on January 25, 1348 [10]. In 1548, following the expertise, two additional iron ties were placed under the main arch by the mason Giacomo da Lonato [11]. All these ties consist of three segments assembled by means of scarf joints secured by straps (Fig. 3).

Figure 2: View of the nave and the reinforced arch. Picture: Louis Vandenabeele.

Figure 3: Details of the ties placed in 1483 (below) and 1548 (above) in the arch of the nave. Picture: Louis Vandenabeele.

The analysis of Poleni in 1733

Giovanni Poleni briefly mentioned the three pre-existing iron ties in his letter of 1726. However, he ignored the date on which they had been placed, only mentioning that they had obviously been installed after the construction of the arches, as shown by traces of more recent mortar [12]. Four years passed until he was asked to investigate another arch, the one separating the angel and the presbytery domes, due to three large cracks that needed to be fixed prior to the execution of wall paintings by Giovanni Antonio Pellegrini and Antonio Vicentini. This time, Poleni attempted to date the ties of the nave, saying they had likely been added after the explosion of a nearby gunpowder storage in 1617. Thus, he did not make a direct link between those ties and the displacement of the southern buttress identified in the expertise of 1547.

The mathematician sent his assessment of the cracked arch between the angel and the presbytery domes (arch 4) to the president of the Arca on May 6, 1733 [13]. After writing that arches are architectural elements that belong to mathematicians and should therefore be treated *né per conghettura né per prattica ma secondo regole certe e costanti*, he provided a careful description of the observed damage. Poleni rightfully noticed that the arch was divided by a longitudinal joint corresponding to the junction between an original western church and a posterior eastern extension. By doing so, Poleni provided what is likely the first correct identification of the division between two main building phases in the basilica, more than a century before historians started to consider the matter. He thus understood that the arch was divided into two parts built at different times. The cracks were visible on the older arch supporting two walls and a narrow staircase, the latter providing a privileged access to the extrados. Accompanied by a (lost) survey of the cracks drawn by the mason Pietro Ratti, Poleni's expertise started with an attempt to date these cracks, which he again linked to the explosion of 1617. However, he believed this could not have been too serious because no iron ties had been added then. According to his observations, the three cracks had led to a significant downward shift of two sections of the arch on which his intervention would focus.

As a guiding principle, he highlighted the importance of mortar in arches made of small blocks (as opposed to arches made of large stones) and explained that, once a crack appeared in the mortar, it could only but increase over time due to the loads continuously applied on the structure. Based on the idea of a slow yet irremediable worsening of the situation, he suggested to take some protective measures. Poleni proposed to install a temporary centring under the arch in such a way that the undamaged parts would not be affected by the intervention. This centring would be supported by a scaffolding raised from the floor of the church, as the cornices of the pillars did not provide a sufficient support (this possibility was likely inspired by similar systems previously used at St Peter's [14]). Then, referring to the ties of the nave, he proposed to attach similar iron ties in the lower part of the arch and to use these ties to stabilize the scaffolding, which could thus be lighter. To that end, the centring would be built on top of the iron ties, temporarily supported by two rows of vertical posts preventing any deflection. To repair the arch, his daring idea was to excavate its extrados starting from the narrow staircase right above it, and to rebuild the damaged parts section by section, as fast as possible. To materialise his solution and help the carpenters, Poleni provided a (lost) physical model of the centring that should be used for the arch's repair. After Poleni's proposal was approved by the surveyor Giovani Lorenzo Orsati, a large scaffolding (used also by Pellegrini) was erected under the arch and the repairs were carried out between August 1733 and March 1734 [15]. However, the iron ties proposed by Poleni were not put in place.

From St Anthony's to St Peter's

Between 1743 and 1744, Giovanni Poleni was absorbed in the assessment and repair of the dome of St Peter's in Rome, following a study by the mathematicians Thomas Le Seur, Francis Jacquier and Ruggiero Boscovich. The structural analyses and repairs of the dome with five circular ties, a major feat of engineering, were recounted in Poleni's monumental Memorie (1748) [16] and discussed at length by various scholars [17].

The Paduan ties of Poleni

Before 1743, next to a call to examine damages in a dome of the Basilica of St Mark in Venice in 1729 [18], Poleni's interventions in the Basilica of St Anthony between 1726 and 1733 provide the earliest evidence of his approach to complex masonry structures. In Padua, from the assessments of the basilica's wooden ties to the description of cracking mechanism, one can see how the mathematician still relied on empiricism and intuition when it came to architecture. Yet from the Vitruvian virtues (1726) to the regole certe e costanti (1733), Poleni progressively developed an analytical approach to engineering fed by practical cases, hence gradually building his expertise and reputation. In Padua, one can trace the foundations of his success at St Peter's: the attentive observation of structures, the attempt to understand the origin of damage, the reliance on technical literature, the use of innovative repair techniques, and the recourse to physical models. Furthermore, through the analysis of St Anthony's arches and ties, Poleni already put words on crucial issues such as safety margins and thrust forces that he would deepen later.

In Rome, the importance of the assessment forced him to improve his understanding of masonry domes. Based on a survey of the cracks with architect Luigi Vanvitelli, Poleni discarded the three-dimensional theoretical model of the mathematicians to opt for a simpler system he was accustomed to; he considered the cupola as a series of arches and drew the analogy between a chain around a dome and a tie at the feet of an arch [19]. Poleni assessed the adequacy of the dome's shape based on recent theoretical works by Robert Hooke, Philippe de La Hire and James Stirling. Yet, although he correctly applied the hanging chain theory, his approach was still empirical when it came to sizing the reinforcements [20]. Thus, whereas the assessment of St Peter's dome testifies to Poleni's finer theoretical understanding of masonry structures – a step clearly evidenced by the comparison with his previous writings on St Anthony's arches – the intervention was chiefly relying on the practical experience he had collected since the 1720s.

A modern light on the deformations of the basilica

The recent survey of the Basilica of St Anthony with a high precision laser scanner has given access to a new level of information regarding the deformation of the structures. The analysis of the circular arches supporting the domes shows a deformation due to horizontal displacements of their supports. The deformed configuration, which is most significant in the arch above the nave (arch 2), corresponds to a typical three-hinge mechanism, with a settlement at the top and an outward movement at mid-height (Fig. 5). The addition of intermediate iron ties in 1483 and 1548, above the wooden ties (removed in 1726), was thus perfectly adapted to prevent this outward deformation.

Although the horizontal displacement of the southern buttress was correctly identified as a cause of damage for the arch of the nave, a second major reason has seemingly not been identified so far, namely the vertical settlement of the nave's pillars. This ancient settlement is clearly visible at the level of the cornices marking the feet of the arches (Figs 4-5) but also on the entire pavement of the basilica (although smoothened by later refurbishments) (Fig. 6). These deformations increase towards the western pillars of the crossing (arch 3), heavily loaded by no less than three domes, among which is the higher angel dome. Hardly visible with the naked eye, asymmetrical settlements led to a height difference reaching up to 20 cm between pairs of pillars. In the nave, this significant differential settlement is also evidenced by the asymmetrical deformation diagrams of the arches, less pronounced near the most settled pillar (Fig. 5). It is worth noting that the arch between the angel and the presbytery domes (arch 4), the cornices of which were rebuilt around the turn of the 14th century, shows disruptions on its southern side seemingly corresponding to Poleni's repairs in 1733-34. The last arch supporting the presbytery dome and the vault of the choir (arch 5) is much less deformed, likely due to smaller loads and to the buttressing action of the campanile towers on each flank.

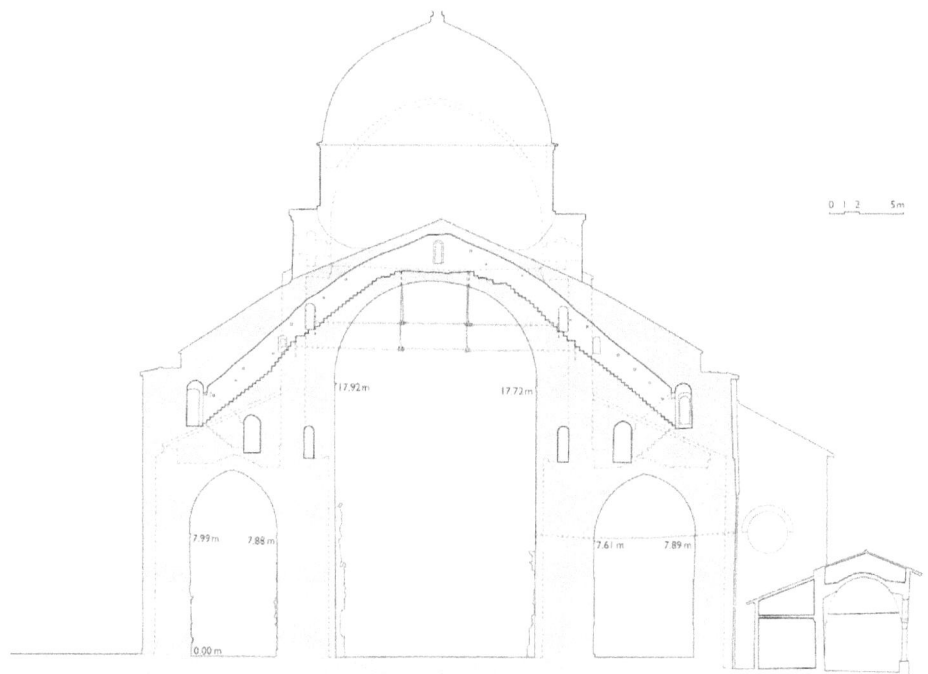

Figure 4: Section on the arch and buttress of the nave, looking east (arch 2). Drawing: Louis Vandenabeele.

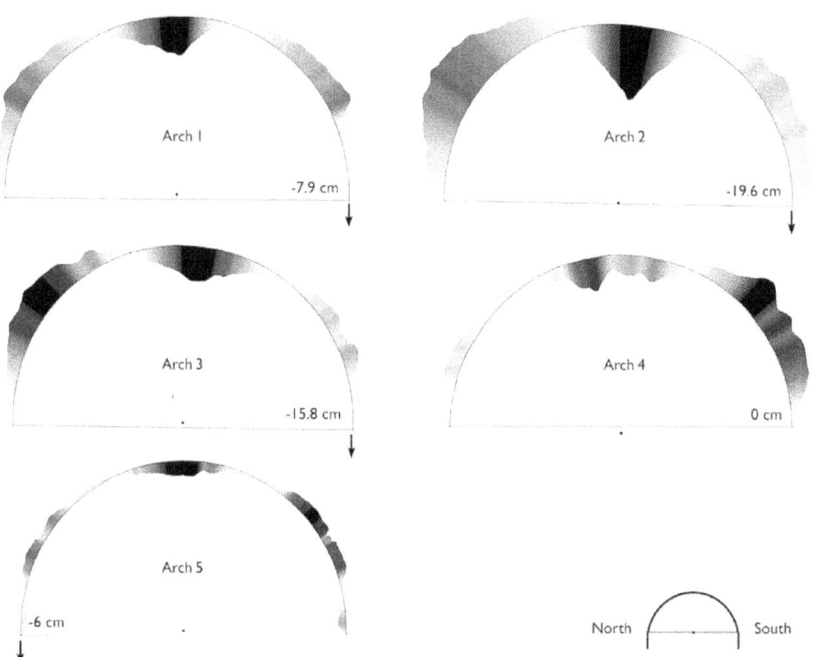

Figure 5: Deformation of the arches of the Basilica of St Anthony, sorted from West to East. Drawing: Louis Vandenabeele.

The Paduan ties of Poleni

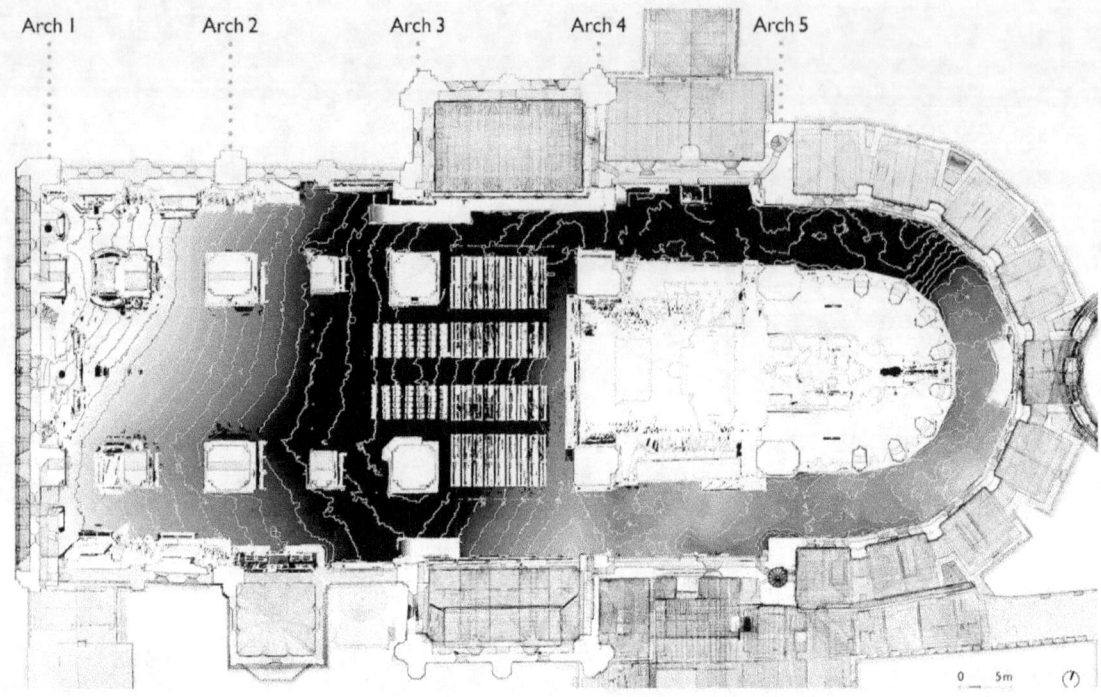

Figure 6: Plan of the basilica showing the deformations of the floor. Contour lines drawn every cm, black is low. Drawing: Louis Vandenabeele.

The southern campanile

Reinforcements after the fire of 1749

Praised all over Europe for his achievement at St Peter's and the publication of his *Memorie* in 1748, Giovanni Poleni's attention went back to Padua on March 28, 1749, when the basilica partly burned. The flames had spread from the altar baldachin to the attics, destroying four timber domes. The southern campanile burnt as well, to the point that its four bells melted. Deprived of its timber core, the brick tower was significantly damaged but did not collapse.

In charge of the reconstruction works that started immediately after the fire, Poleni visited the tower on October 1, 1749 and proposed to reinforce its damaged base with iron elements. This was not the first intervention in the history of the 70-metre high campanile, which had been rebuilt, like its twin, from mid-height on a hexagonal plan after serious damage during a storm in 1394. The original design of the towers had already been particularly precarious as they rest on arches supported by two distinct pillars at the entrance of the ambulatory (Fig. 7). Due to their exposure and bold conception, the towers required constant attention and frequent repairs over the centuries, especially with respect to the inner timber structures [21].

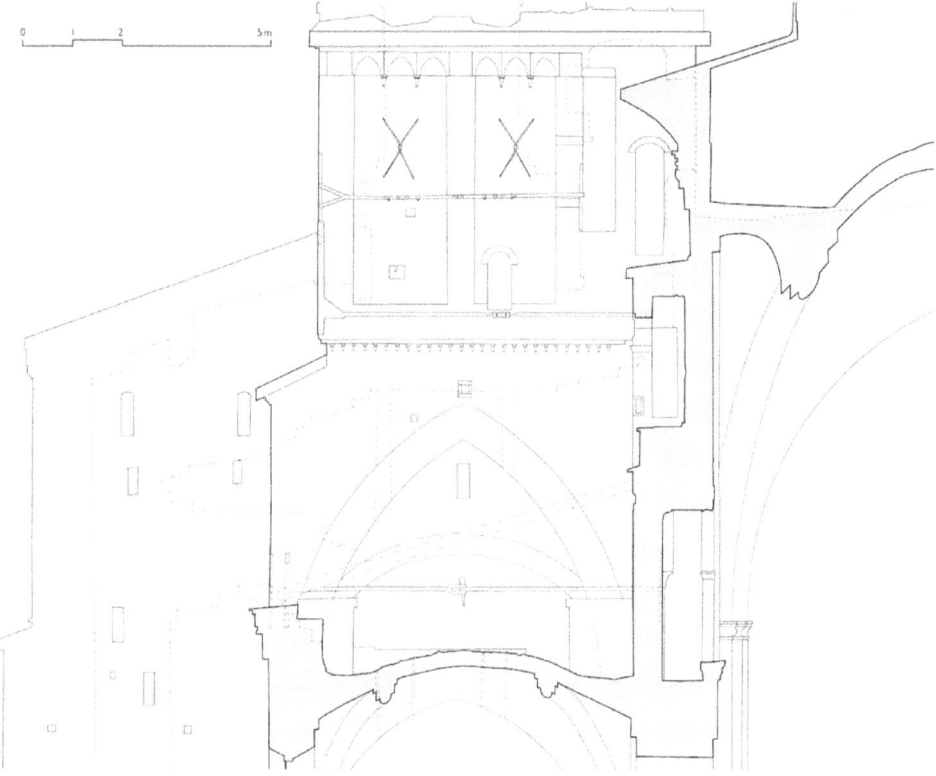

Figure 7: Base of the southern campanile, looking west. Drawing: Louis Vandenabeele.

In 1749, Poleni was thus dealing with a particularly unstable masonry structure, already partly rebuilt and now damaged by a fire that had turned its inner frame to ashes. Although only briefly mentioned in the archival documents, the intervention consisted in the repair of the brick structure by the mason Bernardo Squarzina and the addition of "many large iron chains" following Poleni's advice [22]. In the upper part, the reinforcements consisted of a main encircling strap around the tower and two smaller ties attached to iron anchors on the exterior (Fig. 8). The main strap is composed of six segments, two of which exhibit the date "1750". These segments are perfectly adapted to the existing structure and carefully assembled with four scarf joints secured with iron straps, somewhat similar to the fourth type illustrated by Rondelet (1828) (Fig. 10).

About 6 m below, at the level of the arch supporting the tower, two additional ties were placed perpendicularly to each other. Each tie is assembled with a large iron wedge in such a way that tension can be introduced through hammering (Fig. 9). Unfortunately, these ties are not dated or mentioned in the archives and thus cannot be linked with certainty to Poleni's intervention at this stage. Yet, their similarity to those used by the mathematician at St Peter's a few years earlier (with two wedges) point toward that attribution (Fig. 10). Furthermore, as the addition of iron ties was usually accompanied by brick repairs and reinforcements, a detailed examination of the surrounding masonry and a comparison with the brickwork of Bernardo Squarzina might provide a final answer to this question.

The Paduan ties of Poleni

Figure 8: Detail of the ties added in 1750 on the southern campanile. Picture: Louis Vandenabeele.

Figure 9: Detail of the (undated) tie at the base of the southern campanile. Picture: Louis Vandenabeele.

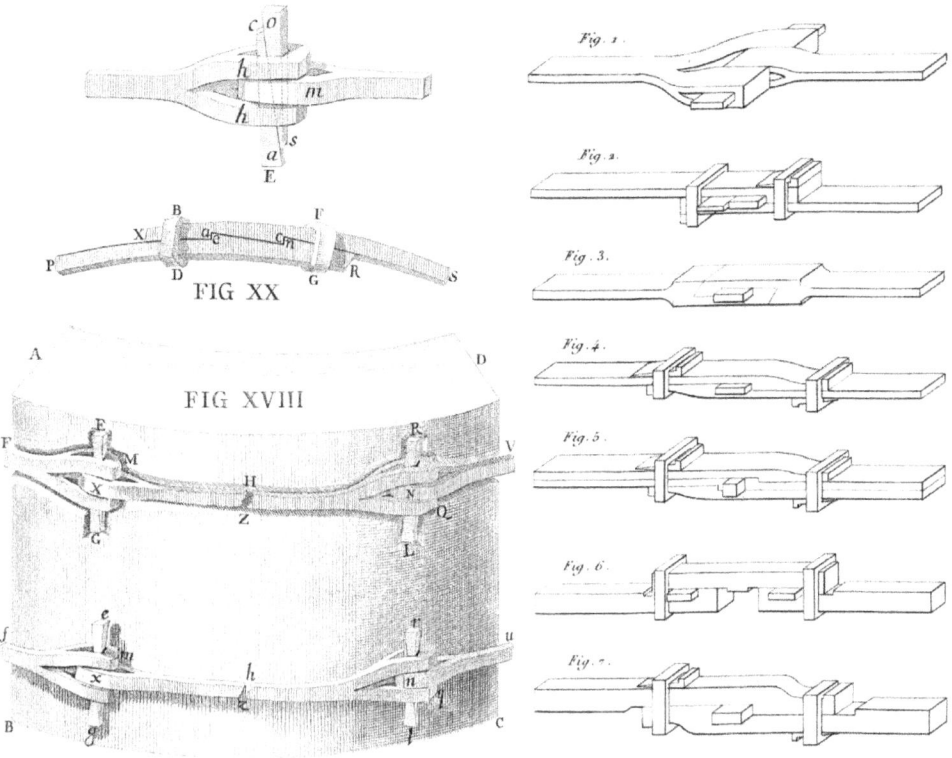

Figure 10: Left: Ties used by Poleni to reinforce the dome of St Peter. Source: Poleni, 1748. Right: Different types of joints for assembling iron ties. Source: Rondelet, 1828.

Conclusions

The works of Giovanni Poleni in the Basilica of St Anthony provide a unique insight into the mathematician's early steps into the fields of architecture and engineering. Based on archival research and on-site surveys, this contribution has shed light on the evolution of Poleni's approach to complex masonry structures based on practical cases encountered in 1726, 1733 and 1749. Before his intervention at St Peter's, his letters to the Arca reveal a rather empirical approach, although characterized by analytical thinking and references to technical literature. This long involvement at St Anthony's contributes to understanding how Poleni gained the practical experience and the reputation that lead him to his most famous feat of engineering in 1743. In the history of construction, his personal trajectory provides an early testimony of the transfer of responsibility from practical men to scientists when it came to assessing the safety of structures.

Acknowledgements

This paper is part of a research project on the Basilica of St Anthony supervised by Prof. Stefan M. Holzer (ETH Zurich) and financed by the Swiss National Science Foundation (SNSF). The author wishes to thank the Delegazione Pontificia per la Basilica di Sant'Antonio in Padova and the Veneranda Arca di Sant'Antonio for the rewarding collaboration.

References

[1] D. Negri, "Giovanni Poleni (Venezia 1683 - Padova 1761) e la fabbrica del Santo." Il Santo, no. 26, 1986, pp.493-505.
[2] V. Farinati, "Matematiche e architettura: gli interventi di Giovanni Poleni a Venezia, Padova e Roma." in P. Del Negro (Ed.), Giovanni Poleni tra Venezia e Padova, pp.80-107. Venice: Instituto Veneto di Scienze, Lettere ed Arti, 2013. E. Guidoboni, M. Berti, and C. Modena. "Le città venete e i terremoti: il caso di Padova (secc. XIV-XVI)." in E. Guidoni and U. Soragni (Eds), Lo spazio nelle città venete (1348-1509). Urbanistica e architettura, monumenti e piazze, decorazione e rappresentazione, pp.140-55. Rome: Kappa, 1997. A. Cavallari-Murat. "Giovanni Poleni e la costruzione architettonica." in Giovanni Poleni (1683-1761) nel bicentenario della morte, pp.55-93. Padua: Accademia Patavina di Scienze, Lettere ed Arti, 1963.
[3] Archivio Sartori (A.S.), Vol. 1, Basilica e convento del Santo, G. Luisetto (Ed.), Padua: Biblioteca Antoniana, 1983, pp.152-53, n. 54, 61.
[4] A.S., (Note 3) Vol. 1, p.157, n. 7.
[5] A.S., (Note 3) Vol. 1, p.154, n. 5.
[6] A.S., (Note 3) Vol. 1, pp.155-57, n. 6.
[7] A.S., (Note 3) Vol. 1, p.183, n. 33.
[8] A.S., (Note 3) Vol. 1, p.149, n. 18-19.
[9] A.S., (Note 3) Vol. 1, p.150, n. 26-29.
[10] E. Guidoboni, (Note 2).
[11] A.S., (Note 3) Vol. 1, p.152, n. 40.
[12] A.S., (Note 3) Vol. 1, pp.155-57, n. 6.
[13] A.S., (Note 3) Vol. 1, pp.167-69, n. 97.
[14] S.M. Holzer, Gerüste und Hilfskonstruktionen im historischen Baubetrieb. Berlin: Ernst & Sohn, 2021.
[15] A.S., (Note 3) Vol. 1, p.169, n. 101-105.
[16] G. Poleni, Memorie istoriche della gran cupola del tempio vaticano. Padova: Stamperia del Seminario, 1748.
[17] J. Heyman, "Poleni's Problem" In Proceedings of the Institution of Civil Engineers, vol. 84, no. 4, 1988, pp.737-59. R. J. Mainstone, "The Dome of St Peter's: Structural Aspects of its Design and Construction, and Inquiries into its Stability." AA Files, no. 39, 1999, pp.21-39. N. Marconi, "Technicians and Master Builders for Restoration of the Dome of St. Peter's in Vatican in the 18th Century: The Contribution of Nicola Zabaglia (1664-1750)." in K.-E. Kurrer, W. Lorenz, V. Wetzk (Eds), Proceedings of the Third International Congress on Construction History, pp.991-99, Cottbus: Neunplus1, 2009.
[18] V. Farinati, (Note 2).
[19] G. Poleni, (Note 16), pp.568-71.
[20] R.J. Mainstone, (Note 17).
[21] A.S., (Note3) Vol. 1, pp.123-26.
[22] A.S., (Note3) Vol. 1, p.126, n. 52-53.

The eighteenth-century timber trade towards the Basilica of St Anthony in Padua through archives, shipping marks and dendrochronology

Martina Diaz, Louis Vandenabeele
Institute of Construction History and Preservation (IDB), ETH Zurich, Switzerland

Abstract

On the night of March 28, 1749, a fire destroyed four of the eight wooden domes of the Basilica of St Anthony in Padua. The restoration of the superstructures followed immediately and was concluded in less than a year under the supervision of Giovanni Poleni, on the model of the surviving domes. Previous research on the basilica's timber domes has already revealed the commercial routes exploited by merchants from the alpine regions towards Padua between the fifteenth and nineteenth centuries. In the present contribution, the focus is put on the supply of timber for the reconstruction of the superstructures in 1749, based on archival, on-site and laboratory analyses.

As recovered in archival documents, Bortolamio Lamberti, member of a rich merchant family of Belluno settled in Venice, was commissioned to supply timber shortly after the fire. The church archives provide precise dates of timber purchases as well as lists of elements supplied by Lamberti. Moreover, shipping marks and rafting traces observed in the domes could be related to the archival findings, enabling the mapping of reconstructions and repairs in the entire building. Finally, both archival and on-site findings are discussed in the light of recent dendrochronological analyses.

Introduction

This paper is a sequel to the findings published in the Proceedings of the Eighth Annual Conference of the Construction History Society on traces of timber trades recorded in the domes of the Basilica of St Anthony in Padua (Fig.1)[1]. This research has been carried out in the scope of a doctoral thesis on the eight wooden superstructures crowning the medieval church [2], as part of a SNSF project on the thirteenth-century church supervised by Prof. Stefan M. Holzer.

In the doctoral thesis, the history of the timber superstructures was documented based on archival material, starting from fifteenth-century documents until the consolidations carried out around 2010 [3]. The most critical event was a fire that destroyed four of the eight domes on the night of March 28, 1749. Yet four timber domes were preserved - three medieval and one from the eighteen century - as confirmed by dendrochronological analyses [4].

Following a previous overview of the traces of timber rafting in the eight domes of St Anthony, this contribution focuses on the supply of timber for the reconstruction following the 1749 fire. The first part describes the state of the domes before and after the fire based on eighteenth-century archival material and recent on-site observations. The second section delves into the history of Venetian timber merchants with a focus on the Lamberti family. The last part links the merchants, the recorded marks and the reconstruction works to shed light on the dating, provenance and storage of wood supplied to the Basilica.

The eighteenth-century timber trade towards the Basilica of St Anthony in Padua through archives, shipping marks and dendrochronology

Figure 1: Drone picture of the St Anthony Basilica (picture: D. Boggian, G. Ravenna, 2021).

Eighteenth-century works on the timber domes of St Anthony

The wooden domes on top of St Anthony are composed of main bearing frames in larch, supporting shells of ribs and boards, and lead covers. Repairs and replacements took place several times, although the written sources rarely specify which elements or even which domes were involved. Eighteenth-century archives report on the decay of the superstructures since 1712 [5] and on timber purchases in 1722 for the restoration of the domes [6], implying that repairs were carried out. In 1729, the bad condition of the wooden superstructures were mentioned again [7]. However, there is no evidence of any additional works. The following warning dates back to 1743 [8] and is followed by more purchases in 1745. Those might have corresponded to interventions, but their scope is not specified. [9]. Eventually, in 1747, shortly before the fire, repairs were required in the conical structure above the crossing, even though there is no evidence that they were actually carried out [10].

When the big fire destroyed part of the church in 1749, the easternmost dome had just been built on the Relics chapel in 1739-1745, following the model of the pre-existing ones. Fortunately, the distance between the chapel and the rest of the church kept it safely out of danger. Five reports recount the spread of the fire from a baldachin in the choir and the disruptive sequence, from the domes of the choir and presbytery, to those on the crossing and the southern arm of the transept [11]. The St Anthony dome on the northern arm of the transept was providentially preserved despite being reached by flames (Fig.2). Dendrochronological analyses confirmed that the St Anthony dome and the two domes above the nave still exhibit a medieval configuration [12]. Moreover, in one of the reports mentioned above, the author specified that the visible brick shells did not collapse [13].

Figure 2: St Anthony dome, timber superstructures (picture: authors, 2019).

Two engravings depict the state of the church after the fire and after the reconstruction works. In the first, the exposed extradoses of the masonry domes are visible, without the wooden frames (Fig.3).

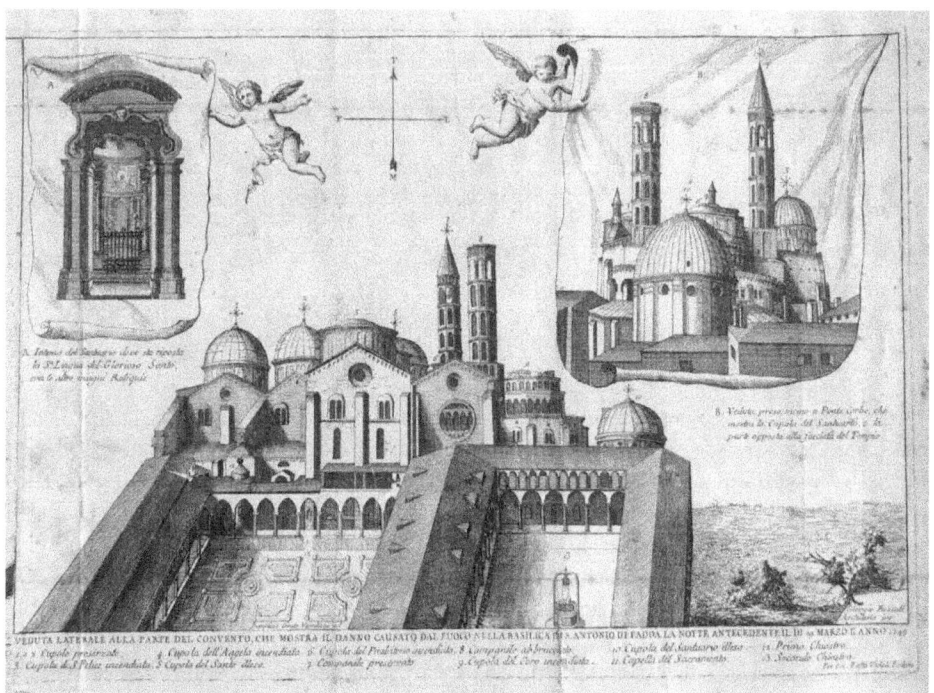

Figure 3: The Basilica roofs after the fire in 1749 (engraving G. Fossati, D. Cerato, Historical Archive of the Municipal Library in Padua, 1749).

The eighteenth-century timber trade towards the Basilica of St Anthony in Padua through archives, shipping marks and dendrochronology

This depiction confirms the version of the written sources, but a question remains concerning the partial preservation of some wooden elements. Just after the fire, Giovanni Poleni, who was director of the reconstruction site, listed the necessary operations including the preliminary removal of the wooden elements collapsed on the vaults [14]. The archives related to reconstruction of the lost roofs which lasted five months until August 1749, make no mention of reused elements. The rebuilding was carried out on the model of the medieval frames "*secondo le idee dell'antico architetto, non restare adito a nuovi pensieri*" [15]. Indeed, there is a clear analogy in terms of carpentry work, but one can also notice the lighter configuration of the new structures (Fig.4).

Figure 4: St Jacob dome, timber superstructures (picture: authors, 2019).

To better understand this reconstruction site, on-site surveys consisting of dendrochronological analyses and the record of trade marks have been carried out. Dendrochronological campaigns executed in 2021 in the angel and choir superstructures have demonstrated the presence of eighteenth-century elements felled at different dates [16]. In the Angel dome, two samples date back respectively to 1741-1766 and 1745-1754. As the estimated timespans are due to the absence of the last rings before the bark, both samples could likely refer to the reconstruction of 1749. In the choir dome, two samples with bark provided the exact same date for the felling period: autumn/winter 1727-1728. As this date turns out to be earlier than the post-fire reconstruction, the question of reused elements reemerges. One can wonder if these two struts might have been spared by the fire and were put in place again. Yet there are no traces of damage nor combustion, which would be expected on such long elements. Because almost twenty years passed between 1728 and the fire, if these elements do not belong to a previous repair campaign, they might have been stored in a merchant's warehouse or in the church.

To further explore this hypothesis, research has focused on wood supplies and merchants involved at the regional scale. Various trade marks have been recorded in the domes and illustrated in a previous contribution [17]. At this point of the research, the attention has focused on the acronym BXL, which is omnipresent in the rebuilt superstructures. Based on the finding of an original letter mentioning both the name and the acronym, one could suspect that Bartolomeo Lamberti was in charge of supplying timber for the new domes. Therefore, the activities of the Lamberti family have been investigated to check whether they would have been capable of providing such a quantity of wood, but also to shed light on storage issues.

Timber supply by the Lamberti family

Historical wooden supplies towards Padua exploited the Brenta River, downstream from the Alps or upstream from the Venetian Lagoon. In the St Anthony archive, documents unstudied so far reveal names of timber suppliers from the sixteenth century onwards. Around the mid-eighteenth century, timber for works in the Basilica of St Anthony was provided by Venetian merchants settled in different areas along the Brenta and Piave rivers or came from the deposit in Padua of the Massari family, involved in trades on behalf of Venetian merchants active upstream in Valstagna [18].

In 1745, four years before the fire, a merchant named Lamberti provided timber for unspecified works in the domes [19]. Lamberti shipped material from Venice and his business in Padua must have been important since, at the same period, he was also providing material for the roofs of the nearby Abbey of St Justina.

In a letter dated back to April 1749, one can read about Bortolamio Lamberti's willingness to supply timber for the reconstruction after the fire in the Basilica [20] (Fig.5).

Bartolomeo was a member of a family of timber traders and worked with his sons. The family had a shop in Venice and owned wood deposits and sawmills in the mountains. Their stock must have been significant since he claimed to be ready to provide all the timbers necessary for the reconstruction as early as April. This time of the year was favorable because the felling season occurred in winter and the logs arrived from the mountains to the mills during spring.

In a logbook dated 1749-1750, purchased timbers are listed for the restoration [21]. The register is sorted by dimensions; it also provides the number of used elements and their role. The biggest elements were about 14,2 m long with a diameter of 30 cm. Other long elements had a length of about 10,7 and 7,85 m while diameters varied between 21 and 24 cm. These dimensions match with the sizes of struts (about 12 m) and collar beams (about 10 m) measured on-site. Planks and thinner elements for the skeleton and the outer cover completed the provision.

Beside the mentioned documents referring to the wooden supply for the Basilica of St Anthony in Padua, the Lamberti family business is little known and a few documents have been found in the Belluno region in northeastern Veneto. The most ancient traces of the family come from the State Archive in Venice, showing that in 1641 Martin Lamberti was appointed rafting leader along the Piave River by the Venetian merchants' board [22].

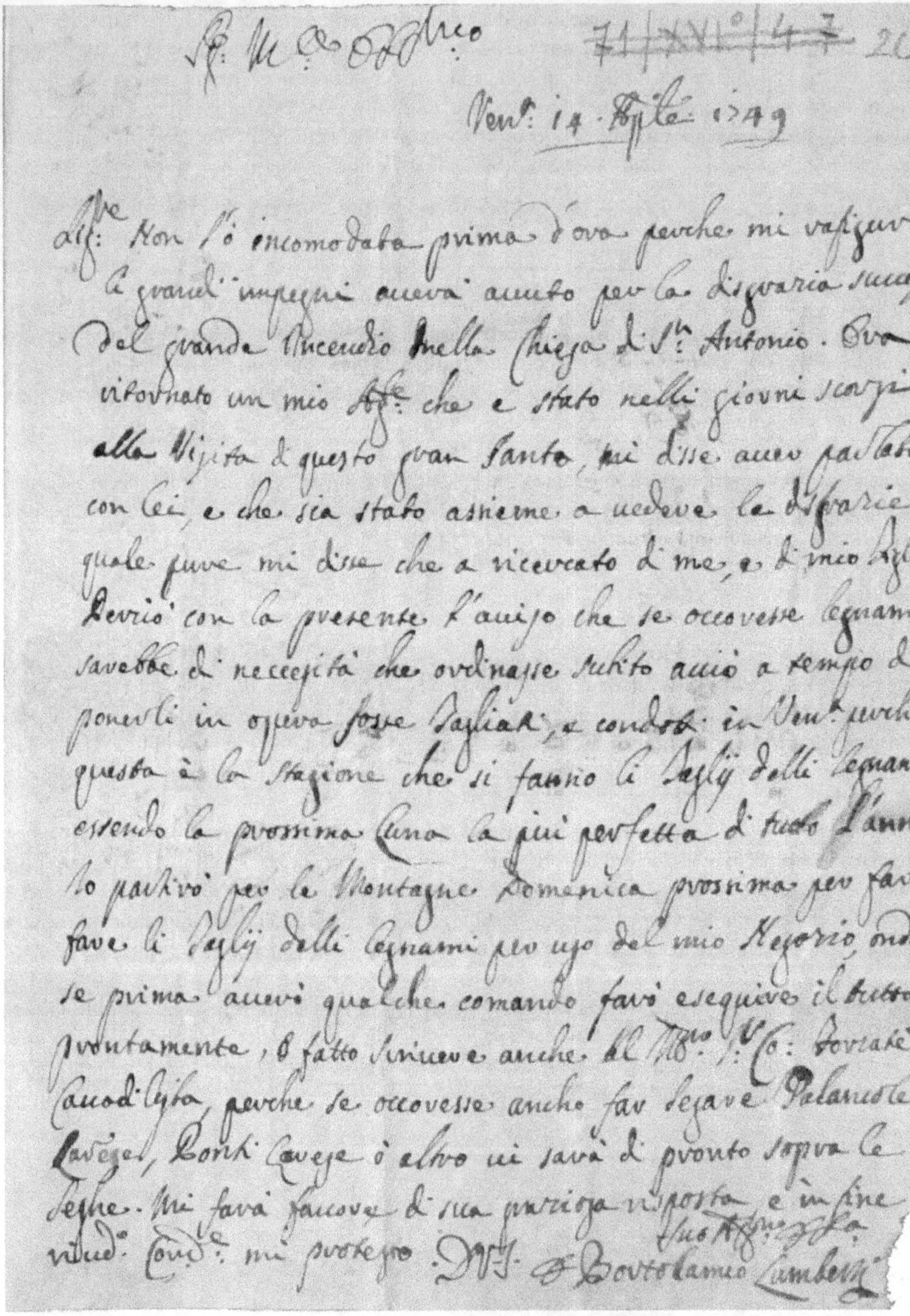

The eighteenth-century timber trade towards the Basilica of St Anthony in Padua through archives, shipping marks and dendrochronology

Figure 5: Letter on timber supply signed by Bortolamio Lamberti (picture: authors).

In the eighteenth century, the Lamberti owned mills in Meli, Villa and Bribano along the Piave. Like other merchants from Venice, Padua and the Piave valley, they also invested in the region of Fonzaso on the right side of the Brenta where they purchased and built new water sawmills [23]. Archival documents indicate that they invested there from 1709 when they bought a water sawmill [24]. At that time, Giovanni Lamberti (possibly the father of Bartolomeo) owned a sawmill close to Fonzaso, in Someda, strategically located between the Brenta and Piave Rivers [25](Fig.6).

In the eighteenth century, the Lamberti were still based in Venice, where they owned lands and wood deposits around the so-called Fondamente Nove [26]. In the first half of the nineteenth century, of the family's properties was sold. Based on these sources, it thus seems that the period 1720-1750 was very intense and that their activities decreased some decades later.

The scale of this family business and its hold on both the Piave and the Brenta leaves little doubts regarding the ability of Bortolamio Lamberti to provide large quantities of timber at a fast pace for the reconstruction of the domes, as he mentioned in the letter dated April 1749. Therefore, it is very likely that the many timbers marked BXL were indeed supplied by this Venetian merchant.

Figure 6: Central position of Fonzaso between the Brenta and the Piave river basins (drawing M. Diaz).

The eighteenth-century timber trade towards the Basilica of St Anthony in Padua through archives, shipping marks and dendrochronology

Provenance, storage and dating

Despite the investments along the Brenta River, most of the wood traded by Venetian merchants came from the Cadore and Ampezzo, two sub-alpine regions located at the northeastern corner of Veneto, bordering on Trentino Alto Adige, Friuli and Austria (Figs 7, 8). The material was floated along the Piave River, collected for sawing in water-powered mills, and rafted further down to Venice, where the Lamberti and many other merchants possessed storage grounds.

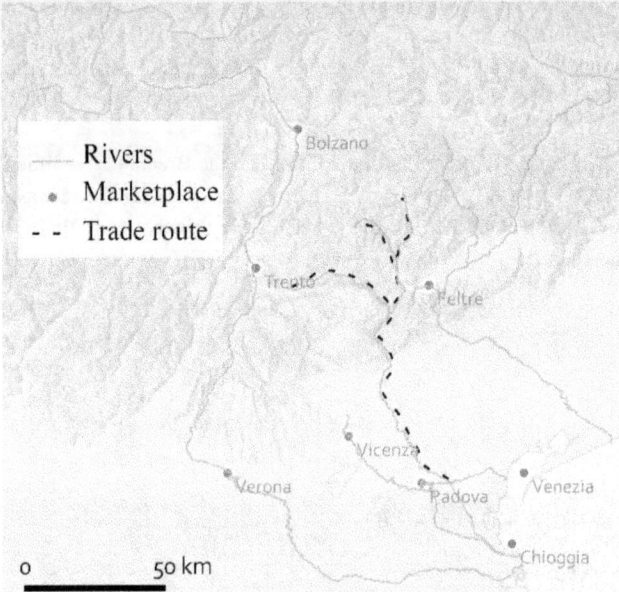

Figure 7: Trade routes along the Brenta River towards Padua (drawing M. Diaz).

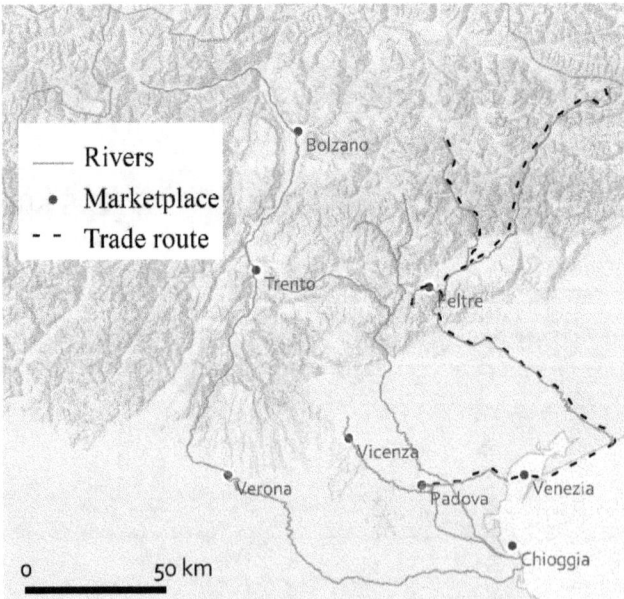

Figure 8: Trade routes along the Piave River towards Padua (drawing: M. Diaz).

For the supply of the construction site of St Anthony, it seems that the wood marked BXL came from the Piave River to Venice. Indeed, other marks visible on several beams supplied by Bartolomeo Lamberti can be related to smaller companies which were cutting trees on his behalf in Cadore, as already identified by other researchers.

Regarding the question of storage, since the struts dated 1727-28 also present the mark BXL, it is most likely that they were brought on the construction site after the fire of 1749 when Lamberti was the main supplier. On-site, this hypothesis is reinforced by the absence of damage on these elements; in the archives, the absence of important works around 1728 and the fact that Bortolamio Lamberti is only mentioned from 1745 onwards strengthen this idea. Thus, it seems that these long struts had been stored for 20 years by the Venetian merchants. Although unexpected, this result can likely be explained by the scale and the longevity of the activities of the Lamberti family.

After the reconstruction of the domes, other merchants continued to supply timber following a similar pattern. For example, nineteenth-century archives related to roof repairs mention the name of Gioachino Wiel, who provided timber in 1865 during renovations of the wooden domes [27]. The Wiel family had origins in Cadore and later settled in Venice [28] (Fig.9). At least until the 1880s, the family was rafting wood on the Piave and storing it around the Academia area.

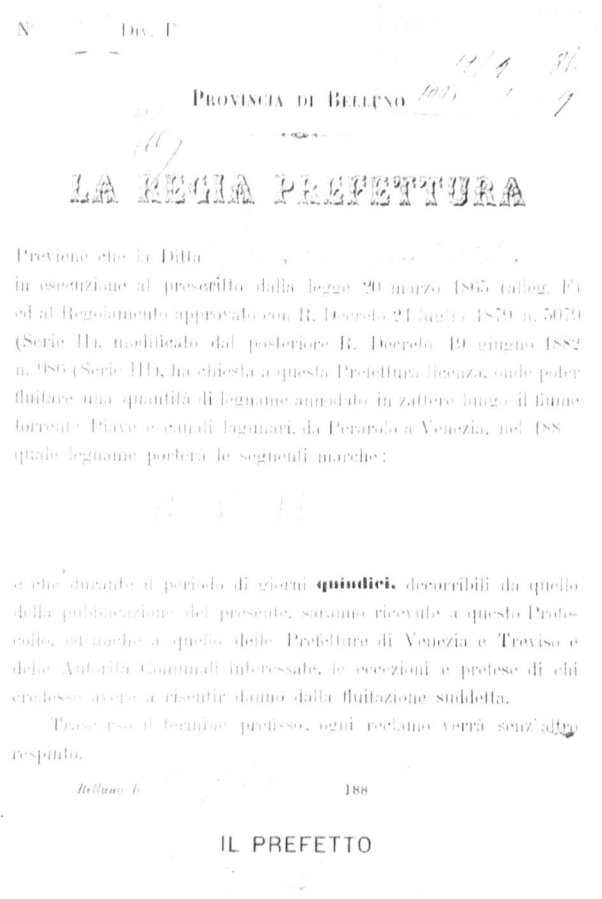

Figure 9: Authorization on timber rafting from Perarolo in Cadore towards Venice, in favor of Gioachino Wiel, (State Archive of Belluno, 1886).

Conclusion

The reconstruction of the roofs of the Basilica of St Anthony after the fire in 1749 has provided the opportunity to document timber trades towards Padua from various perspectives. Through a combination of archival evidence, shipping marks and dendrochronological results, the extent of the reconstruction and the supply of timber could be identified with precision.

These investigations have revealed the eighteenth-century connection between Padua and Venetian timber merchants. In particular, the Lamberti family provided the material after the fire of 1749, which burnt four out of eight domed roofs of the church. As Bartolomeo Lamberti could be related to the shipping mark BXL observed in the rebuilt domes, further archival research on his family reinforced this hypothesis. Moreover, additional signs on the beams marked with the acronym of Lamberti prove that they came from the Cadore region.

As the deciphering of shipping marks recorded in timber roofs is still relatively recent in Veneto, this example shows how these signs can significantly contribute to the understanding of historic buildings and their economic context. Further research in Venetian merchants' archives and the more systematic recording of these marks could greatly facilitate the characterization of old timber in this region.

Acknowledgements

This project is funded by the Swiss National Science Foundation (SNSF) and carried out in collaboration with the Pontifical Delegation for the Basilica of St Anthony in Padua. The authors thank Chiara dal Porto, from the St Anthony Archive in Padua, Dr Silvia Miscellaneo, for her support in the State Archive in Belluno, and Antonio Genova, from the historical archive of the Magnifica Comunità di Cadore.

References

[1] M. Diaz, L. Vandenabeele, S. Holzer, 'The construction of the medieval domes of the Basilica of St Anthony in Padua', pp.47-54, in J. Mascarenhas-Mateus et al. (Eds),
Proceedings of the Seventh International Congress on Construction History, Lisbon: Taylor & Francis Group, 2021.
[2] M. Diaz, 'Le sovracupole lignee della Basilica di Sant'Antonio a Padova: analisi costruttive e datazioni' (Ph.D. thesis, ETH Zurich, 2022, under review), pp.198-220.
[3] Diaz, Vandenabeele, Holzer, Padua, (Note 1) pp.47-54.
[4] Diaz, thesis, (Note 2) pp.198-218.
[5] A. Sartori, Archivio Sartori. Guida della basilica del Santo, varie, artisti e musici al Santo e nel Veneto 1989, Padova: Centro Studi Antoniani, Vol.1, p.118. Archive of the *Veneranda Arca* (ArA), '*Copie integrali dei documenti dal 1702 Ott.7 al 1713 Set.20, con copie di documenti anteriori dal 1552 mar.22, opera di Giovanni Battista Scarella, cancelliere dell'Arca dal 1692*', 18th century, series 56, c.190v. ArA, '*Copie integrali dei documenti dal 1702 ott.7 al 1713 set.20*' 10 Sept.1710, series 6.10.
[6] ArA, Payments to workers for restorations on the domes, 10 Mai 1722 – 12 Dic.1722, series 16.187, docc. 31, 49, 51,74, 83, 86.
[7] Sartori, Archivio, (Note 5), p.116.
ArA, '*Parti e Atti «Libro degli atti e parti della Veneranda Arca in Padoa. 1721, 23 giugno et finisce 1730, 27 maggio. Cancelliere il dominus Benetto Franchi*', 16 Jul.1729, series 2.27, cc.172v.
[8] ArA, '*Perizia di Stefano Codroipo, ingegnere e perito pubblico di Venezia, sui lavori di restauro da farsi nelle cupole del Santo, con annotazioni di Giovanni Poleni, presidente dell'Arca*', 5 Jul.1746, series 8.8, fasc.2, doc.11.
[9] ArA, '*Appunti e note delle spese dei materiali utilizzati per I lavori di restauro nelle cupole e nel campanile*', 1728-1746, series 8.7, fasc.3, doc.63.

[10] ArA, 'Articoli della Veneranda Congregazione dell'Arca del Santo proposti a quelli, che volessero intraprendere il ristauro da farsi alla Cupola dell'Angelo nel Tempio del Medesimo Santo)', 15 Mar.1747, series 8.8, fasc.2, docc.12.
[11] Sartori, Archivio, (Note 5), pp.170-177.
[12] Diaz, thesis, (Note 2) pp.198-220.
[13] Sartori, Archivio, (Note 5), pp.170-177.
[14] Sartori, Archivio, (Note 5), p.183; ArA, 'Lettera di Giovanni Poleni, presidente dell'Arca, al podestà di Padova per i lavori di restauro alla «cappella del Crocifisso», attuale cappella Sacro Cuore', 11 Apr.1750, series 8.8, fasc.2, doc.38.
[15] Sartori, Archivio, (Note 5), p.183.
Ara, (Note 11), doc.38.
ArA, 'Parti e Atti', 21 Jan.1747-17 Dic.1760, series 2.30, c.62.
[16] Diaz, thesis, (Note 2) pp.207-209.
[17] M. Diaz, 'Contextualisation of the Timber Trade between the Sixteenth and Nineteenth Centuries in the Basilica of St Anthony, Padua' pp.169-181 in J. Campbell, N. Baker, M. Driver et al. (Eds), Proceedings of the Eighth Conference of Construction History Society 2021. Cambridge: University Press, 2021, pp.176-177.
[18] ArA, (Note 9) doc.63.
[19] ArA, (Note 9) doc.63.
[20] ArA, 'Lettera di Bartolomeo Lamberti a Bortolo Morosini per la fornitura di legname per riparare i danni dell'incendio nella basilica del Santo', 14 Apr.1749, series 8.8, fasc.2, doc.24.
[21] ArA, 'Elenco di spedizioni e consegne di legname e ferramenta per riparare i danni dell'incendio', 5 mai-18 Sept.1749, series 17.16, Reg. cart. cc. 2v-3; 6v-7; 10v-11; 12v-13; 15v-16; 16v-17; 17v-18; 18v-19; 21v-22; 22v-23; 25v-26.
[22] R. Vianello, 'Famiglie di mercanti da legname a Venezia' in G. Caniato, (Ed.) La via del fiume dalle Dolomiti a Venezia, Caselle di Sommacampagna (VR): Cierre Edizioni, 1993. 1994, pp.306-307.
[23] B. Simonato Zasio, Taglie Bore doppie Trequarti: il commercio del legname dalla valle di Primiero a Fonzaso tra Seicento e Settecento, Fonzaso: Comune di Fonzaso and Paneveggio Pale di San Martino, 2000, p.25.
[24] Simonato Zasio, Taglie, (Note 23) p.64.
[25] Simonato Zasio, Taglie, (Note 23) pp.34, 37-38.
[26] Vianello, Venezia, (Note 22), p.306.
[27] Ara, 'Fornitura legname per manutenzione fabbriche', 24 Nov.1865-14 Mar.1896, serie 24132, doc.2038.
[28] Vianello, Venezia, (Note 22) p.309.

The Renovation of the Waterworks at the Rotes Tor in Augsburg by the Well Master Caspar Walter

Raimund Mair
Universität Innsbruck, Austria

Abstract

With three water towers and up to nine pumping stations, the waterworks at the Rotes Tor (Red Gate) was the most important facility of the historical drinking water supply of Augsburg in Germany. From 1742 onwards, the well master Caspar Walter (1701-69) subjected the works to extensive renovation. A project paper from 1744 provides a deeper insight into the work involved and the materials used.

Introduction – Augsburg's drinking water supply

Augsburg, the capital of Swabia in Bavaria, owes its emergence and prosperity in pre-industrial times to its abundance of water. As early as the Neolithic period, people settled in the area of the later upper town on the high terrace in the fork of the Lech and Wertach rivers [1]. This glacial gravel bed was also chosen for the Roman camp of Aelia Augusta as a place protected from floods and easy to defend. The ancient settlement was supplied with drinking water not only by the flowing waters, but also by numerous wells fed by a groundwater stream at a depth of about 10-13 metres [2]. The fact that it was not possible to supply the water by means of gradient water pipes due to the lack of elevations in the surrounding area only became a serious problem due to the increased population density in the late Middle Ages: the lack of a sewage system meant that the faeces from the cesspits inevitably mixed with the groundwater and contaminated it [3].

When, at the beginning of the 15th century, the city began to convert former watchtowers into water towers and set up a drinking water supply system operated by pumping stations, hygienic aspects were certainly important, but also the need to represent the emerging business location. Similar facilities were also available in other cities such as Bautzen or Lüneburg, but Augsburg was probably the chronological pioneer. As a special feature, not only were public fountains fed, from 1560 it was also possible to have a private water supply installed [4]. An expensive luxury, but one for which there were buyers in the form of wealthy merchant families such as the Fuggers and the Welsers, and which was used to finance the public water supply.

In its heyday in the mid-18th century, the decentralised system comprised nine water towers with 18 pumping stations (as of 1754) and was only replaced in 1879 with the commissioning of a central waterworks at the Hochablass on the banks of the Lech river [5].

The waterworks at the Rotes Tor (Red Gate)

According to tradition, Augsburg's first waterworks was built in 1412 at the Schwibbogentor (Schwibbogen Gate) in the south-east of the upper town. This is plausible because in the following year there are references in account books to a "prunnen Huislin" (well house) there [6].

The Renovation of the Waterworks at the Rotes Tor in Augsburg by the Well Master Caspar Walter

The plant was probably not particularly successful - sources speak of an unsuitable location and too narrow iron pipes - only four years later, the waterworks at the Haußstätter Tor, later the Rotes Tor, was built a few hundred metres away. The fact that the first project was only mentioned in the past tense from this point on suggests that it was not simply demolished but relocated in its essential components.

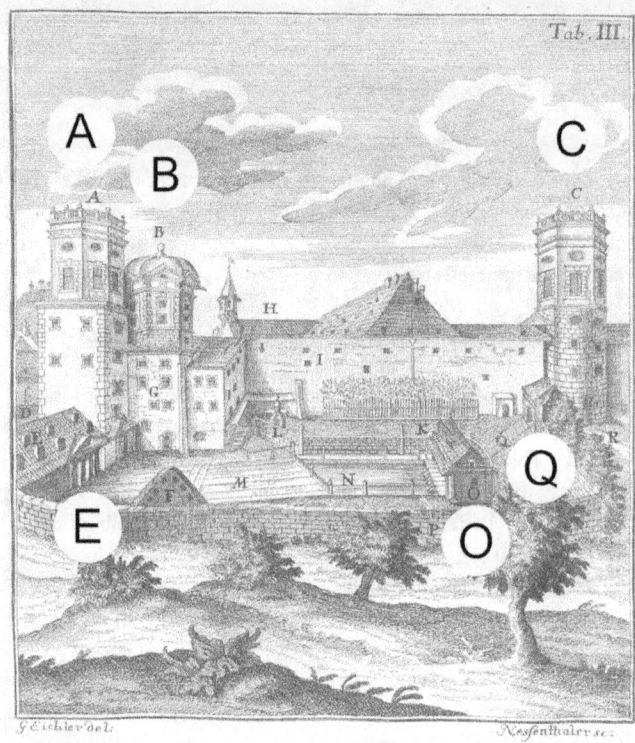

Figure 1: Waterworks at the Rotes Tor (Red Gate) (C. Walter, Anweisung vor einen jederweiligen Stadt-Brunnen-Meister des Heil. Röm. Reichs-Stadt Augspurg, Augsburg 1766. Tab. 3) with the Great Water Tower (A), the Small Water Tower (B) and the Box Tower (C).

Subsequently, the waterworks at the Rotes Tor developed into the centre of Augsburg's historic drinking water supply. It was the only facility comprising three water towers - the Großer Wasserturm (Great Water Tower, from 1416, rebuilt after a fire in 1463, raised by two storeys in 1669), the Kleiner Wasserturm (Small Water Tower, from 1470, raised by two storeys in 1559) and the Kastenturm or Spitalwasserturm (Box Tower or Hospital Water Tower, from 1599, raised by two storeys in the same year) [8]. On the upper floors of the towers there were flow-through tanks with a maximum volume of just under four cubic metres, in order to smooth out the water flow, which was pumped intermittently by the pumping technology of the time, for discharge into the pipe system. The delivery heads were between 24.8 and 28.4 metres [9].

With pipe runs of 12,800, 11,021 and 9,100 feet (about 3,800, 3,260 and 2,700 metres), they supplied a total of 358 water consumers (as of 1754) [10].

The waterworks at the Red Gate was not only a technical but also an organisational centre. The city well master responsible for the city's water supply had both his workplace and his residence there.

The Brunnenmeister (well master) Caspar Walter (1701-69)

The office of well master probably came into being at about the same time as Augsburg's first waterworks and probably evolved from the function of the Lechmeister, who had previously been responsible for all water constructions []. As far as we know today, most of the well masters were trained as carpenters - in pre-industrial times they were not only responsible for the design and maintenance, but also for the construction of the pumping stations, which were mostly made of wood. And they almost always built them, because the wooden mechanisms rotted in a relatively short time in the permanently damp environment and had to be replaced after twenty to forty years at the latest.

Caspar Walter, Augsburg's most important well master for our current understanding of the historical drinking water supply, was also a carpenter. His father's business, where he had learned his trade, was taken over by his brother and has remained in unbroken family ownership to this day.

Walter not only distinguished himself by his prudent management and technical skills, but also excelled as the most important chronicler of his profession. His most important work was the Hydraulica Augustana, a kind of travel guide to the waterworks at the Red Gate, published in 1754. In addition, however, he published numerous other printed works - instructions for the various ranks of the drinking water supply, explanations of technical water constructions as well as books on carpentry and bridge building.

From 1728 onwards, Walter was Ballier (foreman) in Augsburg's second largest waterworks, the Unteres Brunnenwerk am Mauerberg (Lower waterworks at the Mauerberg) [12]. In 1741 he was appointed to the post of municipal well master and took over the waterworks at the Red Gate, which he managed until 1768.

Once the plant had been left in a relatively desolate state by his predecessor, according to Walter, he began to subject it to a comprehensive renovation programme in 1742 [13].

Project paper and cost estimate for the year 1745

The Schwäbisches Handwerkermuseum (Swabian Craftsmen's Museum) in Augsburg houses a 24-page booklet, almost certainly dated 1744, which provides a deeper insight into the process and logistics of one section of this reconstruction work. It is addressed to the municipal building authority, and its title is somewhat incomplete: *Überschlag betreffend den Grund- und Waßer-Bau des Großen Bronnen-Thurns wie auch der zwey Ketten-Wercker in großen und Kasten Bronnen Thurn gehörig auf das 1745. Jahr* (Summary concerning the ground and water construction of the Great Water Tower as well as the two chain works in the Great Water Tower and Box-Tower for 1745). De facto, however, it sets out in twelve points the acute deficiencies of the waterworks at the Red Gate and lists all the work projected for the coming year.

Caspar Walter did not write the text himself, as can be seen from the handwriting, but signed it and therefore certainly commissioned it, if not dictated it.

In the brief introduction, reference is made to a plan drawing of the project. This can most probably be identified as a coloured plan printed in the book accompanying the UNESCO World Heritage application for Augsburg's historic water management, which was drawn by Walter himself [14]. In a cartouche in this drawing, dated February 1744, he explained - in even greater detail than in the introduction to the project paper - his basic motivation for the reconstruction, which went far beyond repair work:

The Renovation of the Waterworks at the Rotes Tor in Augsburg by the Well Master Caspar Walter

In addition to standardising the water supply for the four water wheels of the pumping stations in the Great Water Tower and in the Upper Well House with a common reservoir in the headrace and a common overflow spillway, in order to be able to quickly shut down the system in case of maintenance or accidents, a redundant alignment of the pumping system was especially important to him (Fig. 3 C/E). For this purpose, three new pumping stations were set up, two of them could be switched to different water towers.

However, a discrepancy between the drawing and Walter's description of the waterworks in the *Hydraulica Augustana* is striking: the plan shows only one pumping station in the lower well house (Fig. 1 O), but according to the *Hydraulica Augustana* a second one should have been installed there already in 1743 [15]. Since the canal for the frost-proof laying of the conduit pipes to the Box Tower (Fig. 1 Q, Fig. 3 Z) was not built until 1744, Walter must be assumed to have made a mistake here.

How important he himself saw the redesign of the waterworks at the Rote Tor in later times is shown in one of his last writings, the *Anweisung vor einen jederweiligen Stadt-Brunnen-Meister* (Instruction for every municipal well master) from 1766: The booklet not only contains service instructions and a list of the water consumers of the waterworks at the Red Gate, but also a comparison of the plant in its condition before and after the renovation (Fig. 2/3) [16].

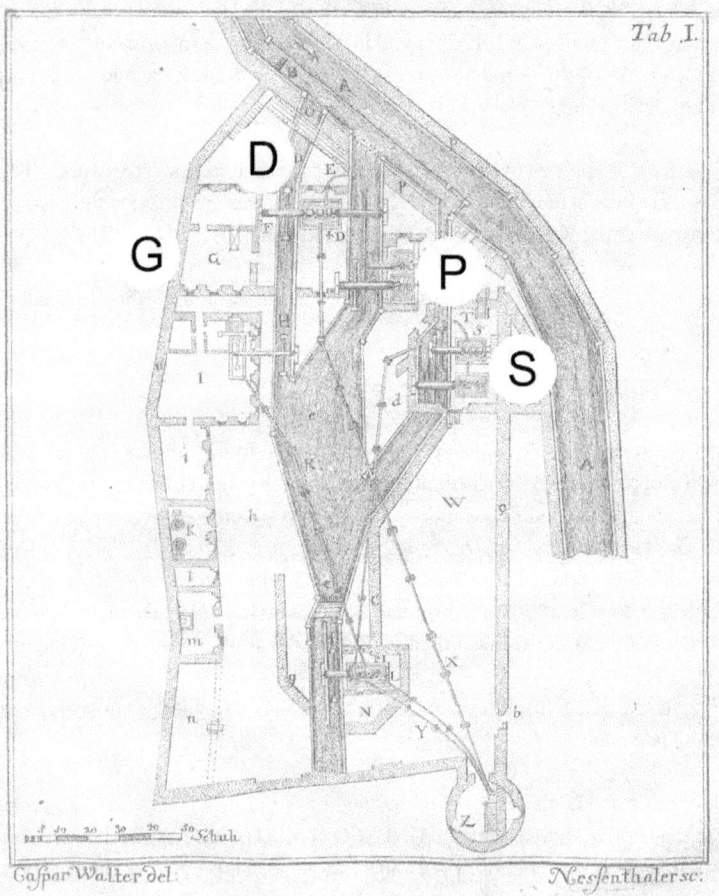

Figure 2: Waterworks at the Rotes Tor (Red Gate) (C. Walter, Anweisung vor einen jederweiligen Stadt-Brunnen-Meister des Heil. Röm. Reichs-Stadt Augspurg, Augsburg 1766. Tab. 1). Situation 1741.

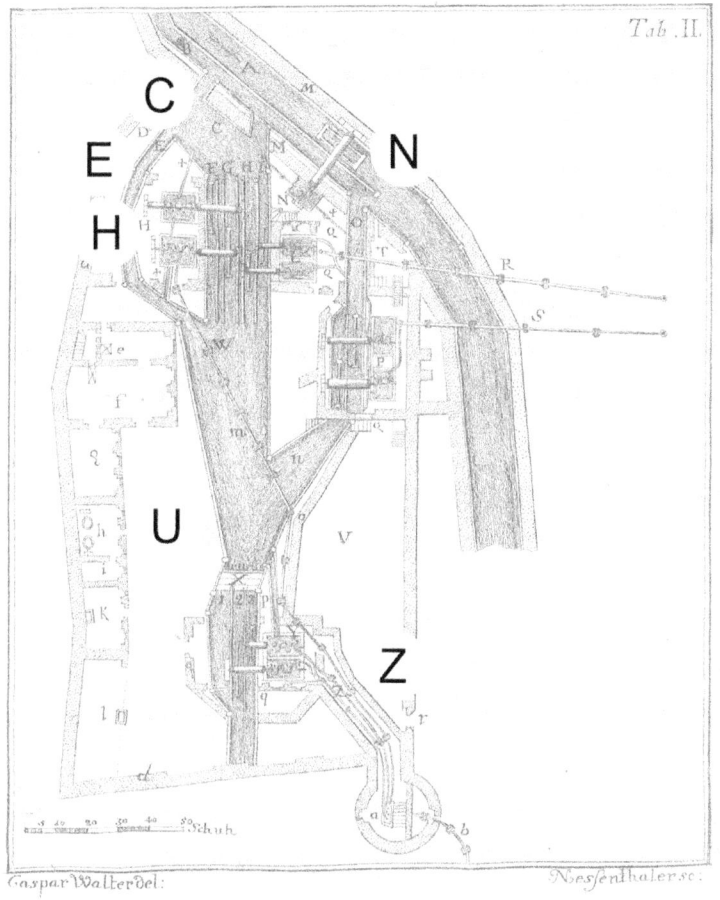

Figure 3: Waterworks at the Rotes Tor (Red Gate) (C. Walter, Anweisung vor einen jederweiligen Stadt-Brunnen-Meister des Heil. Röm. Reichs-Stadt Augspurg, Augsburg 1766. Tab. 2). Situation after renovation.

The individual sections of the project paper for the year 1745 are reproduced below only in terms of content, as a literal translation from baroque official German into English would make little sense:

Point 1

> "The so-called Stuben-rack-and-pinion pumping station (Fig. 2 D) is known to be in such a bad condition that it can no longer be dismantled and re-installed due to the damaged *Brunnenkasten* (literally translated well box, the wooden laggings of the pumping pit). It is therefore doubtful whether it would be able to continue its service through the coming winter. The same would apply to the rear crankshaft pump in the large water tower; in the case of the front one would have to fear that the crankshaft could work itself loose in the drive shaft and the water wheel would fall apart completely (Fig. 2 P)."

The Renovation of the Waterworks at the Rotes Tor in Augsburg by the Well Master Caspar Walter

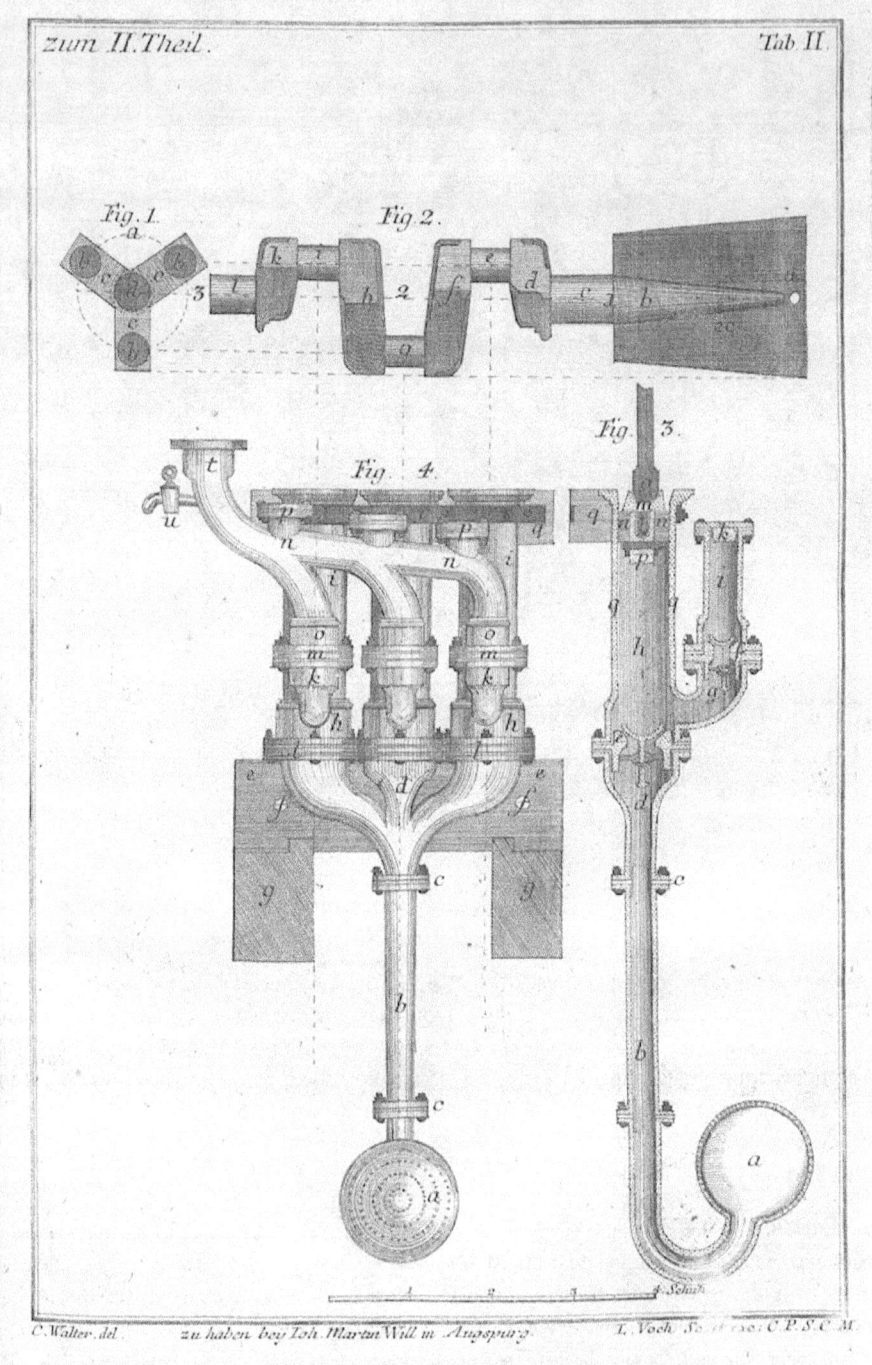

Figure 4: Crankshaft pump / crankshaft with shovel blade (C. Walter, Architectura Hydraulica, Oder: Anleitung zu denen Brunnenkünsten Vol. 2, Augsburg 1765. Tab. 2)

The frictional connection between the drive shaft and the crankshaft was usually created by a so-called shovel blade (Fig. 4). This blade - a trapezoidal iron plate - was inserted into a slot in the conical end of the shaft and clamped with three or four iron rings.

Point 2

"Therefore, let the water construction with four wheels, the large common reservoir in the headrace and the setting of the four *Brunnenkästen* be started in the coming spring."

Point 3

"Over the coming winter, everything that is necessary for this - wood, leather and metal parts for stopcocks, riser pipes and water wheels - should be prepared."

Point 4

"The four Brunnenkästen and two drive shafts are to be made at the Zimmerhof by the Lechmeister. However, the final assembly of the Brunnenkästen will only take place in the water tower, as the wall openings are too narrow for transport in the assembled state."

The Lechmeisters (Masters of the Lech river), who can be traced from 1320 onwards, were on the same level of the hierarchy as the well masters and were responsible for all water constructions (bridges, weirs, locks) apart from the drinking water supply. They were based at the Zimmerhof, the municipal building yard, near the Lech. There were workshops and material depots as well as a sawmill and the Deichelgrube, a pond in which the wooden conduit pipes were stored under water until they were used.

The concrete dimensions of the components ordered there can be seen in the cost breakdown: The drive shafts were to have a diameter of 24 inches (0.6 metres) with a length of 16 feet (4.7 metres). For the Brunnenkästen of the rack-and-pinion pumps, 50 planks with a thickness of 6 inches, a length of 8-9 feet and a width of 15-18 inches were ordered; for the Brunnenkästen of the crankshaft pumps in the Great Water Tower, also 50 planks with a thickness of 5 inches, a length of 5-7 feet and a width of 15-18 inches were ordered.

Point 5

"The roof beams and trusses of the upper well house must be renovated on the side of the large water tower as well as on that of the *Wächterstube* (guardroom) (Fig. 2 G). Since the rack-and-pinion pumps cause great vibrations, the roof structure must be additionally reinforced. In addition, the trusses of the old *Bachwerk* (creek pumping station) are to be removed, and the staircase there is to be rebuilt and covered."

The *Bachwerk* (Fig. 3 N) was a small, additional crankshaft pumping station with a stream shot waterwheel that had not existed for a long time. Since it was only refitted in 1746 – with merely two cylinders – by Caspar Walter, it finds no further mention in the present project paper.

The Renovation of the Waterworks at the Rotes Tor in Augsburg by the Well Master Caspar Walter

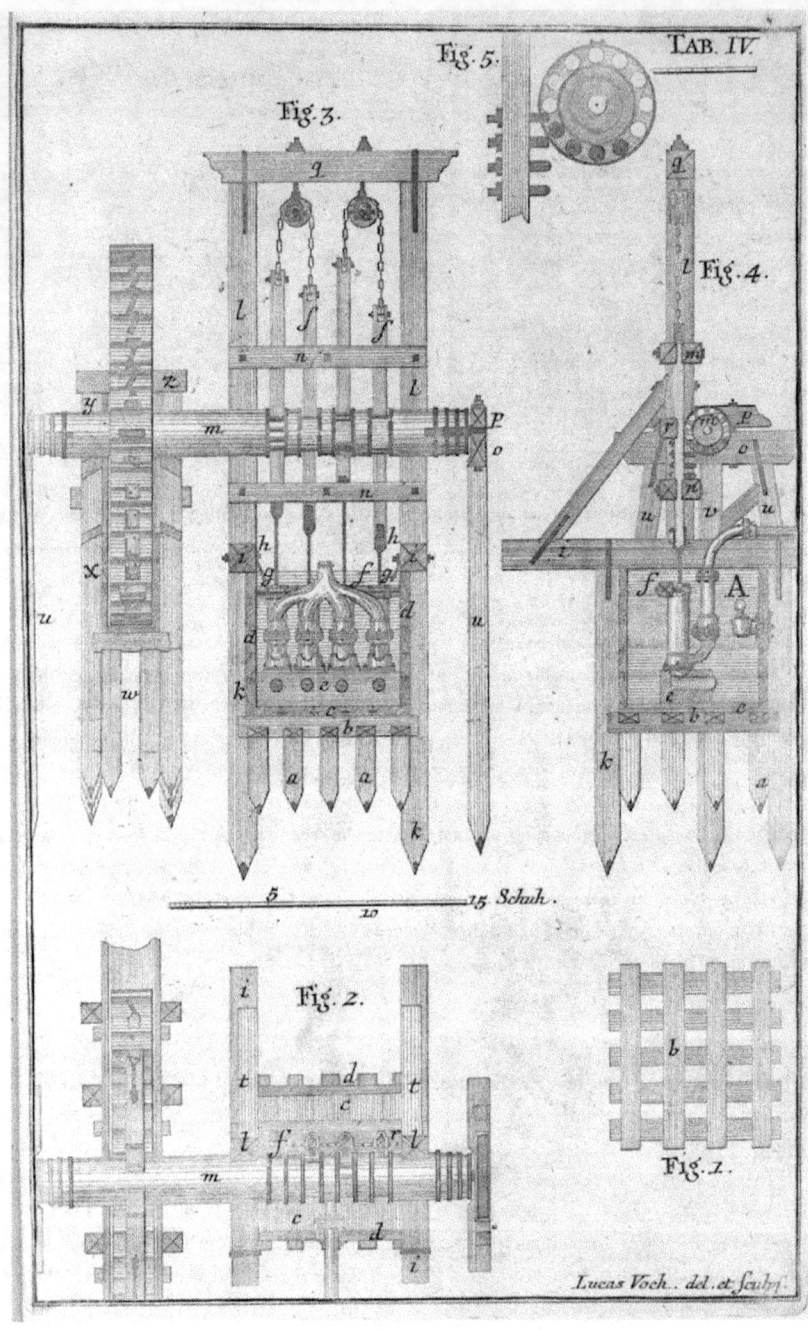

Figure 5: Rack-and-pinion pump (L. Voch, Einleitung zu der Architectura Hydraulica, Augsburg 1769. Tab. 4)

Rack-and-pinion pumps, such as those installed as reserve pumping stations in the upper well house, were cheaper to manufacture than crankshaft pumps because of the smaller proportion of iron components. However, they generated strong vibrations and were thus only moderately suitable for operation in the water towers themselves – it was not until 1744 that the last rack-and-pinion pump in the Small Water Tower had been replaced by a crankshaft pump (Fig. 2 S) [HA 16].

Point 6

"The four new water wheels and the oak planks for the common reservoir in the headrace are to be made. Gauges and patterns for the forged components of the water wheels such as bands and strut supports are to be prepared and handed over to the hammer smith so that he can make them over the winter."

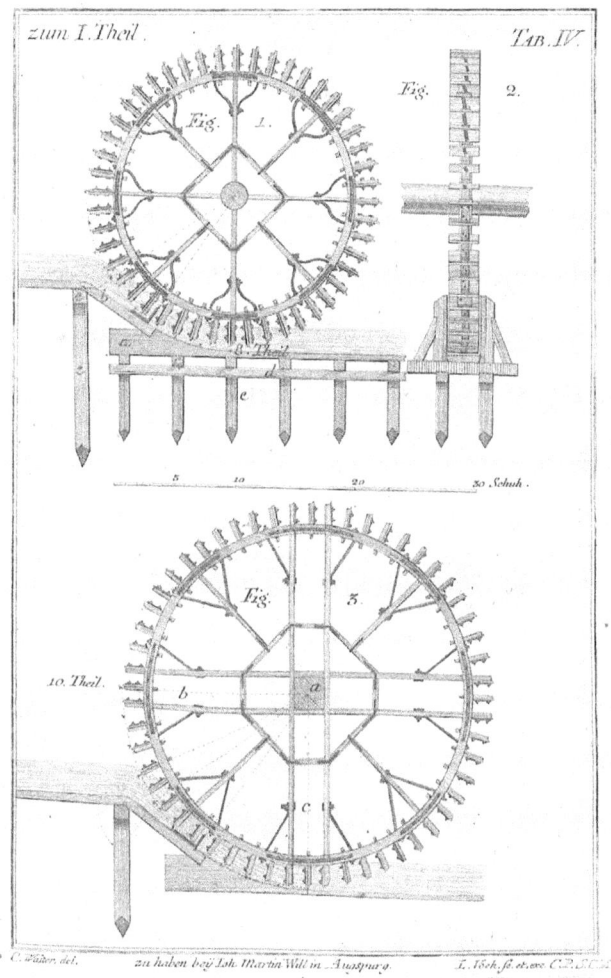

Figure 6: Water wheels (C. Walter, Architectura Hydraulica, Oder: Anleitung zu denen Brunnenkünsten Vol. 1, Augsburg 1765. Tab. 4)

The Renovation of the Waterworks at the Rotes Tor in Augsburg by the Well Master Caspar Walter

The newly made water wheels for the pumps in the large water tower had a diameter of 26 Augsburg feet (7.7 metres), those of the pumps in the upper well house of 18 feet (5.3 metres) [21]. Their exact construction is not handed down, but an example of wheels of these dimensions can be found in the first volume of Caspar Walter's *Architectura Hydraulica* (Fig. 6). The upper wheel in Lucas Voch's copperplate shows a wheel with a diameter of more than 20 feet and gives an idea of the considerable proportion of iron components.

Point 7

"Work on the great hydraulic structure was to begin at the end of March, as they would have enough to do to finish it by October."

This must have been successful, because Caspar Walter gives the construction of the common reservoir in the headrace in the *Hydraulica Augustana* as 1745 [22]. There he also describes that the newly constructed overflow spillway finally made it possible to safely drain off excess water, for example, during heavy rains.

Point 8

"The brass and lead riser pipes in the large water tower cause a lot of resistance due to their too small cross-section and would have to be recast if the pumping stations were to be repaired, as has already been done in the small water tower. However, since the pipes should remain in use over the winter, it would be better to cast new ones in the meantime and store them in the Box Tower so that they do not hinder the work."

Point 9

"As can be seen in the plan, the front rack-and-pinion pump feeds the Box Tower, while the rear one can be switched to either the Great Water Tower or the Box Tower. It is therefore necessary to cast a new brass riser pipe used for this purpose for the Great Well Tower. This, too, is to be done in the course of the winter. As for the Box Tower, the pipe of the rear plant must be connected to that of the front plant so that it can also serve as a reserve for the latter. However, this connection must be able to be shut off by a valve, otherwise the plant will not be available as a reserve for both towers." (Fig. 3 H)

Point 10

"Four large inlet valves, two for the chain works and two for the crankshaft pumps, are to be cast."

The purpose of these 150-pound inlete valves was to shut off the flow of potable water to the *Brunnenkästen* for maintenance and repair purposes [23].

Point 11

"As part of a major hydraulic engineering project at the weir near the Stadteicht, old driven piles need to be extracted. Until a new pile structure has been driven in and the Brunnenkästen at the waterworks near the Stadteicht have been rebuilt, the water conduit supplied by the latter must be fed for three months by the waterworks at the Rotes Tor as a substitute."

The Stadteicht was the municipal weights and measures office, and its tasks at that time included the calibration of beer and wine barrels. The building, torn down in 1928, was located on the Schwalllech just south of St. Ursula. Not far from it, on the city wall facing the Oberer Graben (upper moat), was a small, subordinate waterworks, which used the wet city moat, dammed by a small weir, as its works water.

Originally, there was only a well house with a two-cylinder pumping station at this location; in 1733, a crankshaft pump with three cylinders was installed [24]. It is questionable whether the interim measure announced by Caspar Walter lasted only three months, because the waterworks could not fulfil its main purpose, the supply of the lower Bäckergasse, until 1748 [25]. Before that, two old well houses had to be demolished and a new water tower about 15 metres high had to be built on the city wall.

In 1766, the waterworks supplied 16 water users via pipes of 2318 Augsburg feet (just under 690 metres) [26]. It was shut down in 1843 at the latest and demolished around 1867 after the end of the fortification obligation together with large parts of the city wall [27].

Point 12

"It would be good to obtain permission to run the riser pipes in the Great Water Tower through openings in the ceilings, as has already been implemented in the other two water towers."

Figure 7: Openings in the ceilings with riser pipes in the water towers at the Red Gate.

An explanation for this construction measure is provided by Caspar Walter himself in a detailed description of the Box Tower: With riser pipes routed along the walls, the problem was that water escaping through leaks penetrated the masonry and damaged it [28]. It can be assumed that this was a permanent condition.

It is certain that the municipal building authority gave permission for the ceilings to be broken through. The work was carried out as early as 1744 [29]. This may also have made it possible to install the new risers while the old ones were still in use (see point 8).

Conclusion

As far as can be reconstructed, all the work planned by the well master Caspar Walter for the waterworks at the Red Gate in 1745 was also carried out within the planned period. Even though Walter himself is the author of most of the chronicles in which the completion of the individual work phases is recorded, it can be assumed that his information is correct.

The renovation of the waterworks subsequently proved to be so far-sighted that the next stage of expansion, with the standardisation of the water wheels and pumping machines, was not begun until 1817 – a remarkably long period of time in the age of upheaval between crafts and engineering [30].

Today, six water towers still exist in Augsburg, and the waterworks at the Rotes Tor has been preserved as a complete ensemble – admittedly without pumping stations. The lower courtyard (Fig. 3 U) is now home to the Swabian Craftsmen's Museum, where the booklet discussed here with the projected works for the year 1745 is stored.

References

[1] B. Roeck, Geschichte Augsburgs, München: C.H. Beck, 2005. p. 9.
[2] M. Kluger, Augsburgs historische Wasserwirtschaft: Der Weg zum UNESCO-Welterbe, Augsburg: context, 2015. p. 186.
[3] M. Kluger (Note 2). p. 298.
[4] C. Walter, Hydraulica Augustana, Augsburg: Abraham Detleffsen, 1754. p. 6.
[5] C. Walter (Note 4). p. 10.
[6] D. Voigt, 'Die Augsburger Wasserwirtschaft des 14. und 15. Jahrhunderts im Spiegel der Baumeisterbücher der Reichsstadt' in C. Emmendörffer and C. Trepesch, (Eds) Wasser Kunst Augsburg. Regensburg: Schnell & Steiner, 2018. p. 55.
[7] C. Walter (Note 4). p. 5.
[8] W. Ruckdeschel, Technische Denkmale in Augsburg: Eine Führung durch die Stadt, Augsburg: Birgit Settele Verlag, 1984. pp. 25.
[9] W. Ruckdeschel (Note 8). p. 28.
[10] C. Walter (Note 4). p. 38.
[11] D. Voigt (Note 6). p. 54.
[12] B. Rajkay, 'Tiefbau mit Weitsicht – Der Brunnenmeister Caspar Walter' in C. Emmendörffer and C. Trepesch, (Eds) Wasser Kunst Augsburg. Regensburg: Schnell & Steiner, 2018. p. 127.
[13] C. Walter, Anweisung vor einen jederweiligen Stadt-Brunnen-Meister, Augsburg: Andreas Brinhauser, 1766. p. 9.
[14] M. Kluger (Note 2). pp. 214-215.
[15] C. Walter (Note 4). pp. 12-13.
[16] C. Walter (Note 13). Tab. I / II.
[17] D. Voigt (Note 6). p. 47.

[18] B. Rajkay, 'Die trockene Seite der Augsburger Wasserwirtschaft' in Stadt Augsburg (Ed.) Augsburg und die Wasserwirtschaft – Studien zur Nominierung für das UNESCO-Welterbe im internationalen Vergleich. Augsburg: context, 2017. p. 71.
[19] C. Walter (Note 4). p. 20.
[20] C. Walter (Note 4). p. 16.
[21] C. Walter (Note 4). p. 14.
[22] C. Walter (Note 4). p. 19.
[23] C. Walter (Note 4). p. 13.
[24] C. Walter, Unterricht vor einen jederweiligen Brunnen-Ballier, Augsburg: Andreas Brinhauser, 1766. p. 3.
[25] ibid.
[26] C. Walter (Note 24). p. 8.
[27] M. Kluger (Note 2). p. 272.
[28] C. Walter (Note 13). pp. 54-55.
[29] C. Walter (Note 4). p. 14.
[30] M. Kluger (Note 2). p. 220.

The Nineteenth Century

Iron bridges and the influence of international models in 19th century Spanish architecture

Gian Marco Prisco
Scuola di Specializzazione in Beni architettonici e del Paesaggio, Università degli Studi di Napoli Federico II (Italy)

Abstract

The 19th century saw the rise of socio-economic development based on scientific and industrial progress, which affected a large part of Europe in different ways. There is no doubt that innovation and technical transformations had a great influence on economic growth, as evidenced by the advent of industrial processes that invested various fields of knowledge, introducing real revolutions in transport, communications, and construction, producing technical and social advances. This situation allowed for a convergence of interests in the markets and, if on the one hand this process united a large part of European countries, breaking with a common agricultural and artisan past, on the other hand the technological gap between the different nations was evident from the start. This would soon translate into a marked industrial mobility and, consequently, into a sharing of knowledge and discoveries that characterised the culture of these years.

In the countries of Mediterranean Europe, the foreign presence was not limited to investments and the establishment of foreign companies, but translated into a series of relationships, imports of technologies and qualified 'human capital', with professionals who, especially with the introduction of iron in transport and construction, brought their know-how with them. The presence of foreign technicians in Spanish industry in the 19th century represented a real turning point in the construction of the country and its modernisation, especially in the spread of iron technologies.

The use of iron in construction became central to the architecture of this age, embodying the very essence of modernity. Its first applications involved the construction of bridges and viaducts, as a response to the challenges imposed by the limits of the territory. Throughout the time, they identified themselves -together with the railway stations - with the very image of progress, embodying the new gateways to the city and, as such, becoming playgrounds for bold experiments in technology and form. The materialisation of these ideas resulted in the affirmation of the engineer as a key figure in the construction process. In Spain, the academic training of these professionals passed through the institution, by Agustin de Betancourt, of the Escuela de Caminos de Madrid (1802), following the model of the Parisian École des Ponts et Chaussées. The influence of French and British culture in Spain went far beyond the academic sphere: the latest technological experiments reached the Iberian Peninsula through the work of Belgian, French and English engineers and construction companies who, from the second half of the 19th century, were involved in the country's most important construction sites. These technicians introduced innovative metal construction solutions - which were presented in the various universal exhibitions organised during the century - leading to a transmigration of knowledge that profoundly influenced the Spanish class of architects and engineers at the turn of the 19th and 20th centuries.

Introduction

In our culture, the nineteenth century represented more than a mere chronological reference: it embodied the birth of modernity, embracing and developing the legacy of the Age of Enlightenment through the promotion of empiricism, rationalism and science.

Iron bridges and the influence of international models in 19th century Spanish architecture

According to the studies of Kevin H. O'Rourke and Jeffrey G. Williamson [1], the first half of the nineteenth century witnessed what can be defined as the first worldwide economic globalisation. There is no doubt that innovation and technical transformations had great influence on the economic growth, as evidenced by the advent of industrial processes which invested various fields of knowledge, introducing real revolutions in transport, communications and construction, producing technical and social advances. This situation allowed a convergence of interests in lots of European countries, dealing with a common agricultural and artisanal past, but produced at the same time a technological gap between the different nations. This would soon translate into a marked industrial mobility and, consequently, into the sharing of knowledge and discoveries that characterised the culture of these years.

In Mediterranean Europe the foreign presence was not limited to investments and the establishment of foreign companies but translated into the imports of technologies and qualified 'human capital'. These professionals brought with them their know-how, something that emerged especially with the introduction of iron in transport and construction fields [2]. The presence of technicians from abroad in nineteenth century Spanish industry represented a real turning point in the evolution of the country and its modernisation, clearly evident in the construction process of iron bridges.

The aim of this research is to highlight, through its salient phases and paradigmatic architectural examples, the contribution and consequent influence exerted by the international context on Iberian engineers and iron constructions, in the overall context of the social, cultural and economic transformations experienced by Spain in the second half of the nineteenth century.

Iron constructions between statics and aesthetics

The use of iron as a building material became central to the architectural discussion from the beginning of the nineteenth century, bringing new construction techniques and processes, and inspiring a new aesthetic, made by light structural form with slender proportions [3].

As a result of the Industrial Revolution, iron in architecture and engineering reached the Iberian Peninsula, and Spain in particular, in the mid-nineteenth century. Spanish engineers enthusiastically welcomed this construction material, unlike the contemporary architectural class, as emerged in the debates of the First and Second National Congress of Architects held in Madrid (1881) and Barcelona (1888). On these occasions, the positions of the architects Josep Doménech i Estepá and Juan Torras, who defended the real possibilities of the new material in shaping the architecture of tomorrow, coexisted and clashed with theses such as that of Joaquín Bassegoda y Amigó who, while recognising the technical and economic value of iron, took a more cautious stance, warning of its necessary concealment for aesthetic reasons [4]. This debate was nothing more than the expression of questions that had already been raised in the international architectural discussion and which, once again, sharpened the encounter/clash between architecture and engineering. Viollet Le Duc, an expert in building history and an advocate of the use of iron, raised doubts about the formal and functional properties of the new material [5]: "It is not possible to obtain a healthy warm room in winter and a cool room in summer free from temperature variations with the help of iron alone. Brick walls and vaults will always have superior advantages over any other system or material. We must therefore decide to continue using bricks in many cases. Could they be combined with the iron structure? Without a doubt, but on the condition that these two construction methods retain their own characteristics, that they do not combine and then cancel each other out." Nevertheless, at first timidly, hidden behind academic and eclectic drapes, and later with all its force, naked and provocative, iron would shape the new archetypes of the industrial city.

The nineteenth century engineer, between innovation and invention

These transformations took place mainly due to the work of engineers who, breaking away from the eclectic formalisms and the question of style that dominated architecture in those years, were able to become heralds of experimentation and constructive progress.

Around 1890, while presiding over a student awards ceremony, Gustave Eiffel gave a famous speech in which he stated: "This century is the century of the engineer" [6]. Looking back to the scientific and technical transformations and economic growth, he was pleased to note the considerable differences between the early and late nineteenth century and the role that the engineer played in them. Throughout Europe they worked transforming the topography, opening roads, building railways, channelling water, developing industrial production, embodying the positivist ideal of faith in progress and scientific advancement.

France was the country which for the first time gave impetus to this professional figure. Since the mid-seventeenth century, Louis XIV's ministers focused on technical training as a mean of developing the country. In particular, the aim was to improve the network of communication routes and navigable canals in order to boost the economy of the centralised state. To this end, a unit of civil engineers, the Corps des Ponts et Chaussées, was founded in 1716, which in turn created its own school, the École des Ponts et Chaussées in 1747 [7]. From the second half of the eighteenth century, this institution defined the engineer's activity: designing and representing the works to be carried out, coordinating the necessary means and controlling their subsequent operation. The immense influence of the Ecole Polythechnique during these years was related to the fact that for the first time the task was consciously posed to establish connection between science and life, to bring about a connection between higher mathematics, physics, and applied technology. This training model, which was an example for other countries, gave rise to the figure of the modern engineer, oriented towards practice and based on a solid scientific education [8].

In Spain, at the end of the seventeenth century, engineering became part of the Enlightenment debate with the so-called Novadores Movement - literally innovators - who sought to replace conventional forms of thought, subordinated to a dogmatic truth, with knowledge obtained from reproducible empirical data. During the Habsburg period, almost all civil engineering works were carried out by military technicians, both Spanish and foreign ones, educated abroad. This situation changed with the rise of the Bourbon dinasty: the new state, modelled on the French one, required deep transformations, including the training of engineers in order to serve the Crown. As early as 1792, the Spanish engineer Augustin de Betancourt tried to organise technical higher education in his country. After training at the École des Ponts et Chaussées, he began to establish relations with England and France to acquire machines and new technologies. This patrimony would later become part of the Gabinete de Maquinas, founded by himself in Madrid and the fundamental nucleus of the later Escuela de Caminos y Canales (1802), which he conceived following the model of the similar French institution [9].

Transmigration of people and knowledge

The organisation of the national training structure during the nineteenth century was accompanied by an important number of foreign engineers, a phenomenon that allowed, where it took place, the introduction of innovative technologies and new construction solutions.

The presence of foreign engineers in the Spanish industry during these years was based on two fundamental factors. First of all, it was a response to the limitations of Iberian technical education and its professionals, who were sometimes unable to keep up with the evolution of the times [10]. In the scientific training, we witnessed then a transition phase from the previous model, centred on the creation of engineers destined to the state apparatus, to the new order of things, with the civil engineer assuming a prominent role in commerce as a consequence of industrial development.

Secondly, the presence of foreign engineers was strongly linked to the fact that a substantial part of the financial capital participating in Spanish industrialisation during the first half of this century came from other parts of Europe, particularly France, United Kingdom and Belgium. In this sense, the employment of engineers from these countries by private companies and groups was totally understandable, a sign once again of a technical, economic and cultural exportation [11].

The bridge: material and technical avant-garde

As mentioned above, the innovative spirit of men and thought in those years took the form of a new way of construction: building in iron. Contrasting the Academic praxis, iron became a symbol of progress, particularly because of its ability to permit the creation of large public spaces and overcoming the limits imposed by technology until then. In this sense, one of the construction types that best illustrated the innovative thrust of these constructions were the bridges. The evolution of this typology became paradigmatic, promising a technological utopia and a new, modern architecture.

Commonly, the origin of iron architecture coincides with the construction of the bridge over the Severn (1775-79), in Coalbrookdale (England), a well-known work by Darby, Wilkinson and Pritchard [12]. Similarly, in Spain bridge construction became the earliest field of application for the iron technology, as an answer to the challenges imposed by the limits of the territory. Once again in the history of architecture/engineering, this typology confirmed its primacy as an experimentation field to develop new ideas and solutions. The first Iberian example was the iron bridge over the Alameda de Osuna estuary in Madrid (Fig. 1), by Martín López Aguado believed to belong approximately to the 1830s [13]. In the middle years of Romanticism, the English garden of the Alameda de Osuna became step by step the backdrop for a whole series of physiocratic experiences which permitted the use of a "hard" material, such as iron, to bridge the modest flow of the estuary without condemning the passage of boats. The lightness of the composition, due to the slenderness of its elements and the almost carpentry-like character of its constructive solutions, reminded viewers of the Coalbrookedale Bridge . As well as the British example, these works had all the attraction of early experiences, focusing the attention not on the length achieved but on the adequacy and constructive possibilities of the new material offered by the Industrial Revolution.

Figure 1: The Alameda de Osuna bridge in the El Capricho Park (Madrid), Martín López Aguado, 1830s. Photo by the Darte Sidious, 2020 (wikimedia commons licence)

Throughout the years this project became seen as just the first, humble step of a long-lasting succession of monumental bridges built in the Iberian Peninsula. In the first phase these works were realized by French engineers, whose presence even preceded railway development, a field that would see them as protagonists by the mid-nineteenth century. This period embraced the use of considerable sums of money by foreign investors, who took advantage of the concessions offered by the Spanish government. The main aim – both economic and political – was to build a series of bridges over the key routes in order to improve the communication network with the capital city. One of these companies was the French one owned by Jules Seguin, who founded in Madrid the *Sociedad de Puentes Colgantes* in 1840 [14]. This firm realized various iron suspended bridges throughout the country, such as those of Fuenteduena de Tao in 1842, Arganda in 1843, and the so-called Santa Isabel, over the Gallego River in Zaragoza, in 1844. All these works were built with materials coming from France and assembled in situ under the direction of the French engineer Lamartiniere, following the model built by the same Marc Seguin in Tournon, on the Rhone, in 1825. In this scheme the wooden deck hung from iron wires, which in turn were supported by four cast-iron supports that could be moved at the base [15].

The Isabel II bridge in Seville

Indeed, the most representative work of these years was the Isabel II or Triana bridge, in Seville, (Fig. 2).

Figure 2: The Isabel II bridge (Seville), F. Bernadet and G. Steinacher, 1845-52. Photo by the author

Analysed from an urban point of view, the Sevillian iron constructions realized during these years represented centres of the city's activity, confirming the character of this architectural insertion into the needs of society. Iron came to solve difficulties in passage and covering, representing a bold sense of utility, within that category of the 'beautiful-useful' proclaimed by the refined taste of nineteenth century society. One of those key points was the connection with the Triana suburb. For hundreds of years the two banks of the Guadalquivir River, between the old Triana castle and the so called Barranco area, were crossed by a connection consisting of thirteen boats, moored with chains, supporting strong wooden planks realized by the Almohad Arabic dynasty in the 1117 [16]. Not until the beginning of the nineteenth century, was the idea of building a stable bridge to replace the fragile previous one considered, becoming firmer around 1824. The first project was commissioned by the Seville City Council to the neoclassical architect Silvestre Pérez [17], trained at the *Academia de Bellas Artes* and a pensioner in Rome. However, his proposal of a masonry bridge (Fig. 3) was held

Iron bridges and the influence of international models in 19th century Spanish architecture

back for the adoption of an iron construction scheme, as had already been tried and tested in England and France. This fact highlights the violent way in which iron burst into Spanish construction history, as a mimetic phenomenon, apart from the slow process of the Industrial Revolution, seen as a coherent whole, where the iron bridges were the physical aspect of a profound process of socio-economic transformation.

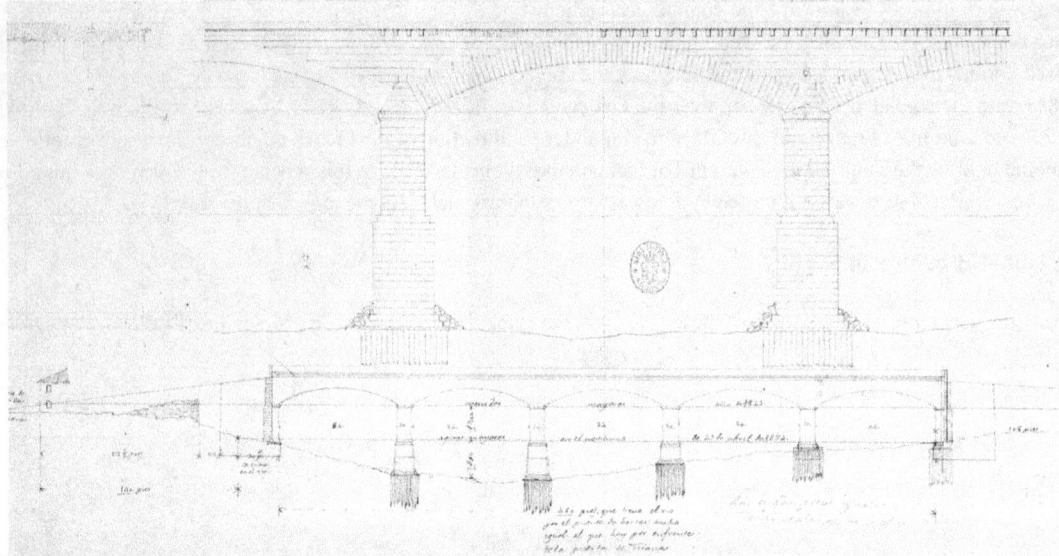

Figure 3: Fachade and cross section of the first proposition for the Isabel II bridge. Author: S. Pérez. Dib/14/27/72, Biblioteca Nacional de España, Madrid

Figure 4: The Carroussel or Saints-Pères bridge, 1834. Author: A. R. Polenceau, Photo by Hippolyte-Auguste Collard, 1883 (wikimedia commons licence).

As reported by Joaquín Guichot y Parody in 1830 [18], under the tutelage of the D. José Manuel de Arjona, the construction of a suspended bridge was first considered by Jules Segun, but in 1842 it was decided to build an iron bridge on stone piers. Built between 1845-52 by the French engineers G. Steinacher and F. Bernadet, it faithfully reproduced the model of the Carroussel Bridge (Fig. 4) realized by Antoine-Rémy Polenceau over the Seine in Paris in 1834, fig. 2. This project was published by Polonceau himself in 1839, becoming known through the explanatory tables which accompanied the text [19]. This became part of the repertories in the construction' manuals of the time (Fig. 5), increasing the already rich collection by Rondelet –edited between 1827-32 by the same Parisian publisher of Polonceau's text – or the "*Cours de construction*" (1847) by the Belgian military engineer Demanet [20], reference texts in the engineering and architecture schools of the nineteenth century.

The details of Polonceau's project were well known, as demonstrated [21] by the authors of the Triana bridge. The similarity between the Parisian model and the Sevillian one should be read not only from a formal or dimensional point of view but, above all, in the use of the complex construction system, conceived with tubular metal arches of a wooden core surmounted by circular iron elements on which the structure of the road rested (Figs 6-7).

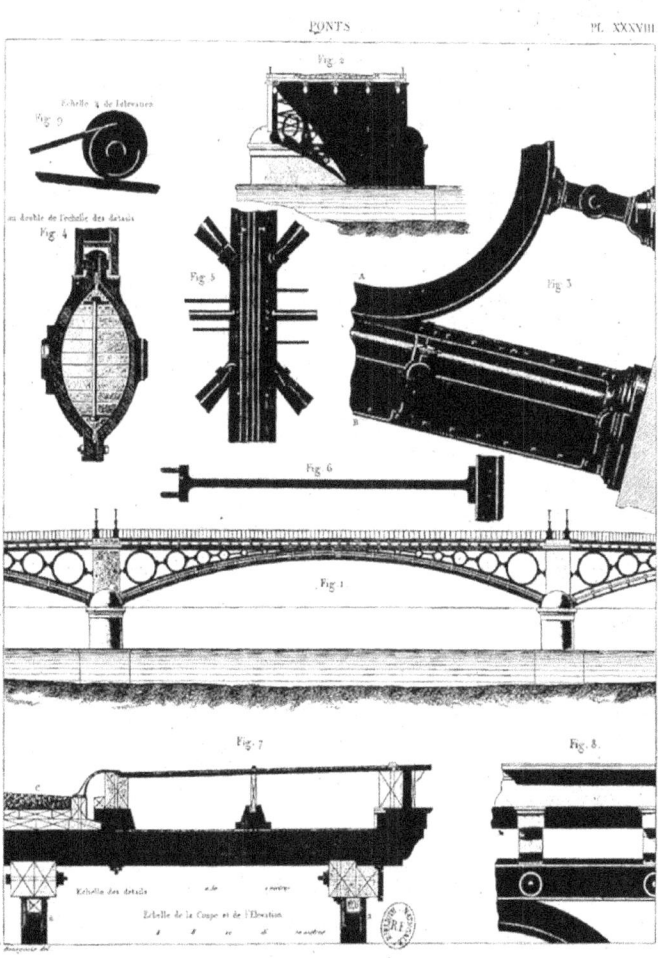

Figure 5: The Polenceau bridge system, in Vignole des charpentiers: contenant tous les d tails de la charpente en bois et en fer (3e dition), 1849, Tab. XXXIV. Author: M. Bourgeois.

Iron bridges and the influence of international models in 19th century Spanish architecture

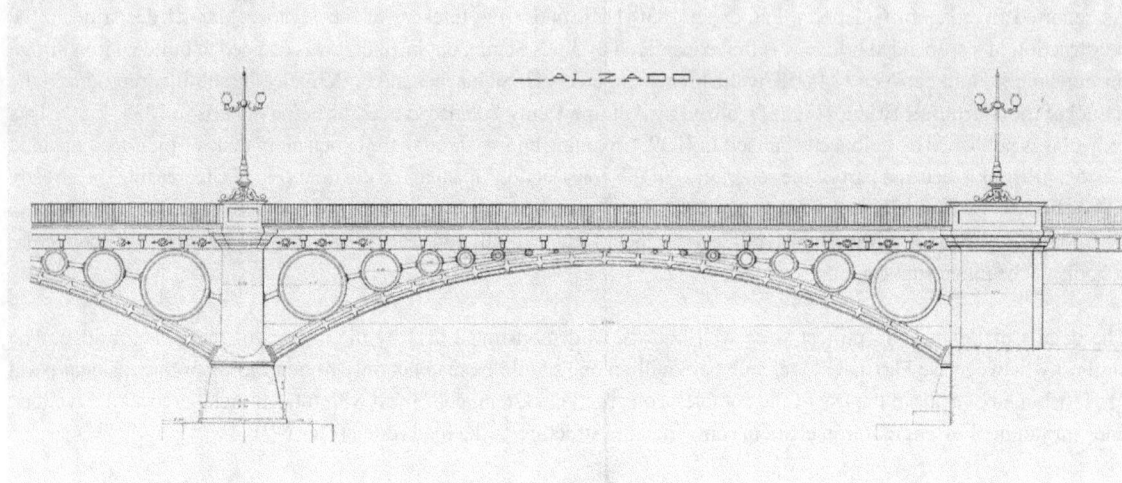

Figure 6: *Fachade of the Isabel II bridge (Seville) 'Plano de alzado, planta y corte transversal del Puente de Isabel II', 19 may 1903. Sig. 13666 .Archivo Historico provincial de Sevilla, Jefatura Prov. Carreteras, Seville*

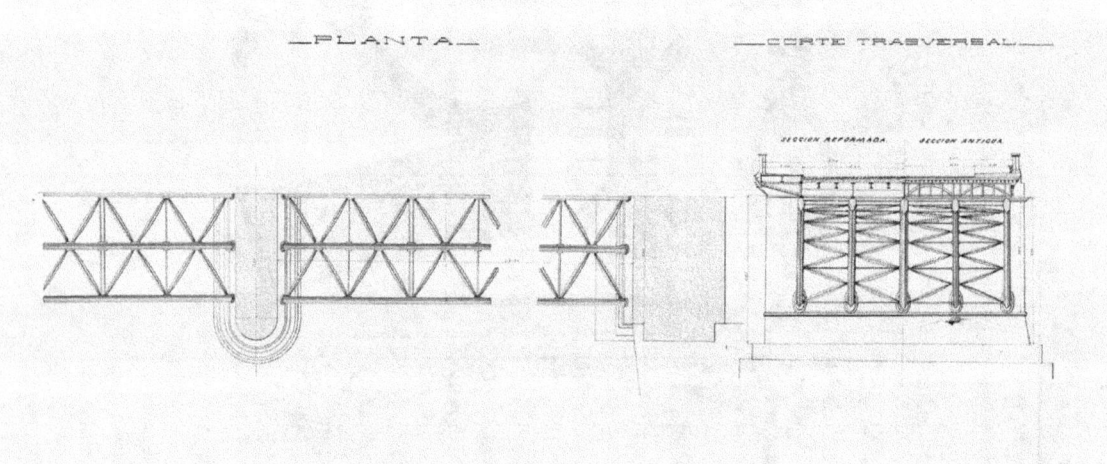

Figure 7: *Plan and cross section of the Isabel II bridge (Seville) 'Plano de alzado, planta y corte transversal del Puente de Isabel II, 19 may 1903'. Sig. 13666 .Archivo Historico provincial de Sevilla, Jefatura Prov. Carreteras, Seville*

This scheme was based on a framework of truss and secondary beams that transmitted the loads to large, lowered arches through a series of circles with different diameters placed in the spandrels (Fig. 8). Indeed, both the elegance of the achieved forms – aerial and even dynamic, thanks to the repetition of the elements – and the assembly ease of the prefabricated castings constituted an important innovation in the iron bridge construction field [22].

The iron work of the Isabel II project had a total length 136.50 meters, divided into three series of five arches supported by two central piers and two lateral abutments made of stone. The arches were made up of an external iron cylinder reinforced on the inside by a wooden core with bitumen, reaching a dimension of 43.33 metres in span – reaching 47.67

metres in the Carrousel ones – and 5 meters rise. The deck, which was repeatedly transformed to adapt it to traffic needs, was originally 16 metres wide, divided in 10 metres dedicated to road traffic and 6 metres to pedestrian use.

This bridge represented a turning point for the Spanish iron construction field, not only for the innovation of its forms, but also for the development of its construction. For the very first time in this kind of project, all the pieces were made in the Sevillian foundry of Narciso Bonaplata, using iron from the Biscayan mines of Guerezo, showing the ability reached in few years by the Iberian metal industry.

Figure 8a: The Isabel II bridge. Details of the iron structure. Photos by the author

Architecture and technical progress

The Sevillian bridge belonged to a wider policy carried out by the central government. These interventions were part of the plan for public works enacted after the first Carlist war (1833) and the *Plan General de Caretteras del Reino* (1840), which improved communications and access to the cities [23]. This impetus led to the dissemination of further models, experiencing each time the different possibilities given by the iron technology. Alongside the Polenceau scheme, were continuously introduced new ones such as the system by the French engineer Vergniais, which reconciled the suspended and rigid bridge models. This structure was made by a large cast iron arch with two other arches on the sides that ended at the top of the piers, working as a contrast to prevent any longitudinal undulating movement [24]. The scheme was initially proposed for the project of the Valladolid bridge (1852) under the direction of the aforementioned Lamartiniere (Fig. 9).

However, the 1855 Universal Exhibition saw the rise a new system: the so-called bowstring bridge, by the English engineer I.K. Brunel, in which the road surface was supported by tie rods connected to an arched structure running the length of the bridge. This innovation was enthusiastically welcomed by the Spanish construction field, choosing it as the final design in the Valladolid work (Fig. 10). Based on the model designed by Brunel himself for the Windsor Bridge in 1849, the Castellan bridge was built using Anglo-Saxon technologies and materials, supplied by the company H Porter and C. Ebro Works of Birmingham, representing one of the first cases of direct intervention of British workers in a metal construction on the Iberian soil. With the passing of time, the French engineers predominance would be overtaken by the work of British technicians, in a series of collaborations that would culminate in the creation of the railway networks in the mid- nineteenth century.

The French and British presence was fundamental in the development of key sectors of early industrialisation, especially in the construction of the railways. Their coexistence led to a division of the fields of action. Henceforth, while French engineers focused on the construction of railway complexes and stations, British engineers were mainly concerned with the design and the construction of the rail infrastructure network, including bridges and metal viaducts [25]. Despite the general distinction, there were cases where English and French engineers worked together on the same project, such as the Cordoba-Seville line, financed by the French company Savalette and built under the direction of the English engineer Joseph Lane-Manby [26].

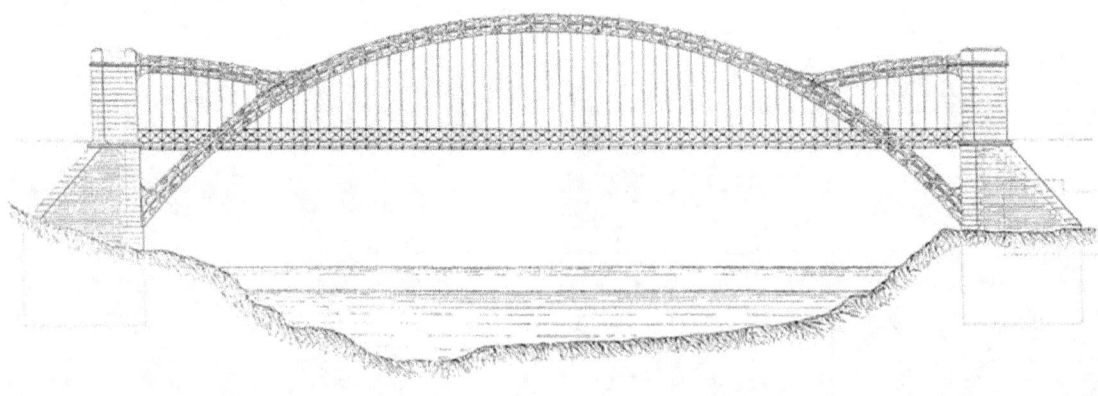

Figure 9: Project for the Valladolid Puente de Prado Bridge with the Verginais system, in Revista de Obras Publicas, Tomo II, no 5, 1854.

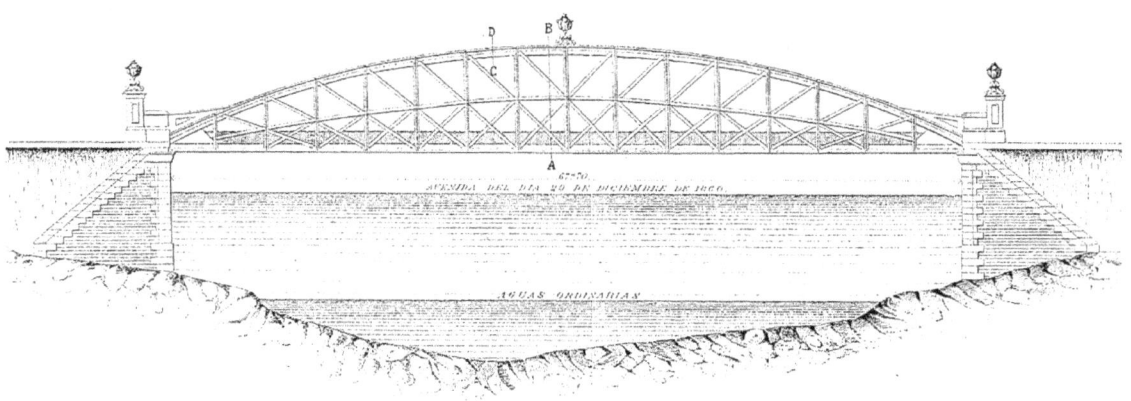

Figure 10: Project for the Valladolid Puente de Prado Bridge with the Bow-string system, in Revista de Obras Publicas, Tomo I, no 10, 1866.

Conclusions

The metal decks of the bridges and viaducts that connected cities, together with stations, markets, harbour piers and even the kiosks that embellished parks and public squares, were fundamental parts of the country's history for Spain, inseparable signs, like literature and music, of the zeitgeist of that period. As demonstrated by the bridges the design, as well as the calculation and construction of these works, lost local accents and became part of the process of international technological development. Due to the work of foreign engineers and the organisation of major events such as Universal Exhibitions, there was a real 'cultural globalisation' of the iron construction sector during the nineteenth century [27]. This transmigration of knowledge was closely linked to the dissemination of the construction manuals of the time - in which the construction systems appeared in detail, including formulas and tables for calculating the profiles, depending on the spans - and to the work of technicians and companies operating in different European countries, sharing their know-how. These experiences would leave indelible marks on the Iberian architectural culture, constituting not only material examples, as in the case of the constructions that were built, but also models of approach to questions and of overcoming the limits imposed by technology. This climate would have its closest heirs in the class of modernist architects-engineers who laid the basis of the contemporary Spanish architecture at the turn of the nineteenth and twentieth centuries. The constructive experiments of Gaudi, De Palacio and others will be the children of this international milieu which, thanks also to the economic development of the country, will gradually produce its own class of architects and engineers able to decipher the climate and the aspirations of modernity. The experience of these works appears to us fundamental in the study and conception of the future cities: they must be studied in their material and social essence, in the construction of new relationships with the urban space.

References

[1] K. O'Rourke – J. Williamson, *Globalization and History: The Evolution of a Nineteenth-century Atlantic Economy*. Cambridge (Mass): MIT Press, 2000

[2] O. Raveux, 'El papel de los técnicos ingleses en la industria metalurgica y mecánica del norte del Mediterráneo (1835-1875): una primera aproximacion', *Investigaciones de Historia Económica*, Madrid, vol. 6, no. 25, 1994, pp.92-105.

[3] G. M. Prisco, 'The Madrid-Delicias Railway Station: between formal and technological innovation in the 19th century Iberian Peninsula, *Proceedings of the Eighth Conference of the Construction History Society* (Campbell, J. et al), p. 313.

[4] P. Navascués Palacio, *Arquitectura e ingeniería del hierro en España (1814-1936)*. Madrid: Fundación Iberdrola, 2007, pp. 41.

[5] ibid, p. 95.

[6] B. Lemoine, *Gustave Eiffel*. Paris: F. Hazan, 1986, p.52.

[7] R. Castro Balaguer, 'Historia de una reconversión silenciosa: el capital francés en España, c. 1800-1936', Madrid, *Revista de Historia Industrial*, vol. 33, 2007, pp. 81-82.

[8] S. Giedion, *Building in France, Building in iron, building in ferroconcrete*. Santa Monica: Getty Center for the History of Art and the Humanities, 1995, p. 6.

[9] J. M. Cano Pavón, 'La enseñanza técnica en España y en Europa Occidental y el problema de la formación del capital humano industrial: veinticinco años de estudios'. *Revista de la Sociedad Española de Historia de las Ciencias y de las Técnicas*, vol. 26, no.56, 2003, pp. 367-398.

[10] P. Sáiz González, 'Los orígenes de la dependencia tecnológica española. Evidencias en el sistema de patentes. 1759-1900', *Historia de la tecnología en España*, Madrid: Valatenea, 2012.

[11] T. Tortella Casares, 'Una guía de fuentes sobre las inversiones extranjeras en España entre 1780 y 1914', *Revista de Historia Económica*, vol. 15, 1997, pp. 607-623.

[12] J. Heath – J. Miller, 'A history of structural defects and repairs, the Iron Bridge, Shropshire', *Proceedings of the First Conference of the Construction History Society* (Campbell, J. et al), pp. 201-08

[13] P. Navascués Palacio, *Arquitectura e ingeniería del hierro en España (1814-1936)*. Madrid: Fundación Iberdrola, 2007, pp. 41-102.

[14] J. Cárcamo Martínez, 'Jules Seguin en España: prefabricación e innovación en los puentes colgantes de Fuentidueña, Arganda, Carandia y Zaragoza construidos por el empresario francés', *Actas del Noveno Congreso Nacional y Primer Congreso Internacional Hispanoamericano de Historia de la Construcción*, vol. 1, 2015, pp. 347-356

[15] M. Seguin – C. Seguin, Diverses innovations apportées dans la construction des ponts suspendus, INP: Institut Nationelle de la Propriété Industrielle - Base Brevets du XIX siècle, 1835.

[16] J. M. Ávila Jalvo, 'El puente de Triana y su tiempo'. *Informes de la Construcción*, vol.52, no.472, 2001, pp. 5–15.

[17] S. Perez, Alzado y secciones transversal y longitudinal de un puente para Sevilla encargado por el Ayuntamiento de esa ciudad a su vuelta de Paris, en 1822, Biblioteca Nacional de España, Dib/14/27/72.

[18] J. Guichot y Parody, *Reseña histórico-descriptiva del puente de hierro de Sevilla*, Sevilla: Imprenta y litografía del Porvenir, 1852.

[19] A.R. Polonceau, *Notice sur le nouveau systéme de ponts en fonte, suivi dans la construction du pont du Carrousel*, París, Fain et Thunot, 1839.

[20] A. Demanet, *Cours de construction professé á l'Ecole Militaire de Bruxelles*. Bruxelles, Ad. Wahlen, 1850.

[21] P. Navascués Palacio, *Arquitectura e ingeniería del hierro en España (1814-1936)*. Madrid: Fundación Iberdrola, 2007, pp. 41-102.

[22] Archivo Historico provincial de Sevilla, Jefatura Prov. Carreteras, sig. 13666

[23] P. Alzóla, *Historia de las Obras Públicas en España*, Madrid: Turner, 1979, p. 359.

[24] A. Ludovico, 'Puentes colgantes según el sistema Vergniais', *La Ilustración - Periódico Universal*, Madrid, 1854, no. 263, pp. 99-100.

[25] R. Cameron, *Francia y el desarrollo económico de Europa, 1800-1914*. Madrid: Tecnos, 1971.

[26] A.Burgos Núñez – M. A. Kite, 'Plate Girder Bridges in Andalusia, 1850-1910. The Spread of an Unusual Genre of Iron Bridges', *Proceedings of the Eighth Conference of the Construction History Society* (Campbell, J. et al), p. 327.

[27] F. Capano, 'L'architettura del ferro' *I libri antichi della Facoltà di ingegneria di Napoli: nel bicentenario della Scuola di applicazione, 1811-2011* (A. Buccaro A. – A. Maglio A.), Napoli: Cuzzolin, 2013, pp.52-56.

From Carpentry Manuals to Engineering Textbooks (1792 – 1870)

Nicholas A. Bill
School of Engineering, Cardiff University / Prifysgol Caerdydd, UK

Abstract

Between 1792 and 1870, textbooks concerning structural timber underwent a dramatic change. Prior to 1792, knowledge of timber as a structural material stemmed from carpenters, some of whom produced manuals for instruction in their craft. Theory, of both the strength of materials and structural analysis was scarce, as precedence and rules-of-thumb dominated the design process. Gradually, through an increasing interest in science, changes in building practices and the growth of the engineering profession, the nature of texts evolved to resemble modern engineering textbooks.

This paper aims to demonstrate the evolution of textbooks concerning structural timber, identifying how they collectively document the development of rational design. Despite their advances, most of the nineteenth century saw outdated and incorrect material continually published by authors professing to be an authority on the subject. Authors who frequently demonstrated an ignorance of scientific developments, particularly of those in Europe. Ironically, just when the understanding of timber begins to improve it is relegated to a small section or chapter within a larger treatise on civil engineering. Although many textbooks continued to include sections on timber, there was no definitive text on timber engineering in the latter half of the nineteenth century. Early works stemming from carpentry manuals continued to be revised but were never radically altered to reflect the format and style of later engineering texts before the twentieth century.

Introduction

Before 1800, knowledge of structural timber stemmed from carpenters, some of whom produced manuals for instruction in their trade. As precedence and rules-of-thumb dominated British design processes, authors saw little merit of including the latest theories on the strength of materials or structural analysis, if they were even aware of such developments. Hence, British manuals dating between 1592 and c.1800 were typically devoid of theory.

Gradually, through changes in building practices and the growth of the engineering profession, the nature of texts evolved, which collectively document the emergence of 'scientific methods' in structural analysis. This paper presents a review of early treatise of timber published in Great Britain, documenting the transition from carpentry manuals to engineering textbooks, demonstrating the level of technical knowledge contained within.

Early Nineteenth-Century Works on Carpentry and Timber

Table 1 lists carpentry manuals and treatise on timber published in Great Britain between 1592 and 1870 [1]. Manuals published in the eighteenth century saw a dramatic improvement in the quality of illustrations and text, largely owing to developments in printing technology. Works produced c.1800 demonstrate a further improvement in quality but are also distinctly different, which can be largely attributed to a change in audience.

Table 1: British Carpentry Manuals and Books Focusing on Timber (1st Editions)

Date	Author	Title (Location: Publisher)
1651	**Stirrup**, Thomas	*The Artificer's Plain Scale: or The Carpenter's New Rule* (London)
1694	**Moxon**, Joseph	*Mechanick Exercises: or the Doctrine of Handy-Works* (London)
1733	**Smith**, James	*The Carpenters' Companion* (London)
1733	**Price**, Francis	*The British Carpenter* (London)
1738	**Salmon**, William	*Palladio Londinensis, Or the London Art of Building* (London)
1738	**Langley**, Batty	*The Builder's Compleat Assistant* (London)
1768	**Swan**, Abraham	*The Carpenter's Complete Instructor* (London)
1778	**Pain**, William	*The Carpenter's and Joiner's Repository* (London)
1792	**Nicholson**, Peter	*The Carpenter's New Guide* (London)
1797	**Nicholson**, Peter	*The Carpenter and Joiner's Assistant* (London)
1803	**Pain**, William	*The Carpenter's Pocket Directory* (London: J. Taylor)
1806	**Nicholson**, Peter	*Carpentry* (Published in: *Ree's Cyclopaedia*, Vol. 6, 1806)
1811	**Nicholson**, Peter	*Joinery* (Published in: *Ree's Cyclopaedia*, Vol. 19, 1811)
1813	**Martin**, Thomas	*Circle of the Mechanical Arts* (London: Richard Rees)
1817	**Barlow**, Peter	*An Essay on the Strength and Stress of Timber* (London: J. Taylor)
1819	**Lingard**, John	*A Philosophic and Practical Inquiry into the Nature and Constitution of Timber* (London: Evans and Ruffy)
1820	**Tredgold**, Thomas	*Elementary Principles of Carpentry* (London)
1822	**Robison**, John **Brewster**, David	*A System of Mechanical Philosophy* (Edinburgh: John Murray)
1826	**Nicholson**, Peter	*Practical Carpentry, Joinery and Cabinet-Marking* (London: Thomas Kelly)
1826	**Martin**, Thomas	*The Carpenter and Joiners' Instructor* (London: Thomas Tegg)
1835	**Turnbull**, William	*A Practical Treatise on the Strength and Stiffness of Timber* (London: John Williams)
1837	**Nicholson**, Peter	*The New and Improved Practical Builder* (London: Thomas Kelly)
1850	**Lea**, William	*Tables of the Strength and Deflection of Timber* (London: Simpkin, Marshal & Co.)
1853	**Cunningham**, Alexander	*A Few Notes and Experiments on the Stone and Timber of the Gwalior Territory* (Roorkee: Thomason Civil Engineering College)
1856	**Fowke**, Francis	*Results of a series of Experiments on the Strength and Resistance of Various Woods* (London: HMSO)
1860	**Newlands**, James	*The Carpenter and Joiner's Assistant* (London: Blackie and Son)
1867	**Fowke**, Francis	*Tables of the Results of a Series of Experiments on the Strength of British, Colonial and other Woods* (London: HMSO)

Changing Audience

A natural assumption is that carpentry manuals were written for carpenters. However, carpentry is a trade that pre-dates the printing press. Its skills were passed down from master to apprentice via practical instruction, with further knowledge of the craft developed during the journeyman period. Systems involving partial training at technical colleges, where technical literature may be consulted, are a feature of modern apprenticeships. Moreover, books were expensive and beyond the means of apprentices c.1800 [2]. Manuals may have offered value to experienced carpenters if they presented structural systems that were not frequently encountered. Therefore, carpentry manuals were more likely written for the benefit of building professionals, especially architects, who were dependent upon the trades.

Circa 1800, architecture as a profession was predominately the pursuit of gentlemen who would write on the subject or subscribe to architectural publications. Where architects were employed, they did not provide detailed drawings that would be expected of the same professionals today. Hence, there was a greater reliance upon the skill and knowledge of the clerk of works and tradesmen to produce the required details [3]. Early carpentry and building manuals were essentially pattern books, which reproduced such details in an attempt to bridge the gap in technical knowledge between building trades and design professionals, primarily for the benefit of the latter.

As such, we observe a change in authors' credentials. For example, the physicist and mathematician John Robison (1739 – 1805) wrote on carpentry to accompany his works on mechanics and materials. He described carpentry as a "liberal art" that constituted part of an engineer's learning which "distinguishes him from the workman" [4]. Later he lamented the quality of previous texts on the subject, stating that many "content themselves with instructing the mere workman, or sometimes give the master builder a few approved forms of roofs and other framings..." [5]. Moreover, when the self-styled civil engineer Thomas Martin (1791 – 1851) wrote *Circle of Mechanical Arts* (1813), his publisher noted that many craftsmen refused to help Martin with his book. It was suggested that carpenters feared the open communication of their own thoughts would expose their ignorance [6]. Regardless, there is clear evidence of a distinct departure from previous manuals aimed at tradesmen and towards instruction based upon rational means.

Peter Nicholson (1765 – 1844)

Leading this change were works of Nicholson. Described as an architect, mathematician and engineer, Nicholson authored approximately thirty books (excluding revisions) on building construction, including carpentry [7].

The Carpenter's New Guide (1792) followed his contemporaries by including joinery. Content on practical carpentry was limited, coving only three major topics: *Trussing of girders; Roofs suited for various purposes; and Story posts, and the manner of framing and piling of a bridge*. His introduction to practical carpentry featured a discussion on the comparative strength of timber in which Nicholson provided rules, with basic formula, for assessing the load on a beam. He recognised that strength was proportional to the square of the beam's depth and cited the "doctrine of mechanics" as his justification, although no derivation of beam theory ensued [8]. Nicholson latter stated that although his rules were "mathematical true" it was impossible to account for knots and other natural features that influenced the strength of timber beams. He also stated that timber was weakened by its own weight, pointing to experiments which demonstrated that timber breaks under lower loads sustained over a long time as opposed to larger weights applied instantly [9]. Nicholson was observing creep, although he failed to fully appreciate the phenomenon.

The Carpenter and Joiner's Assistant (1797) contained more theory, with extracts from French sources, on the strength of timber. Nicholson offered little original material other than practical observations. He also provided the first published account in Great Britain for the behaviour of the king post truss.

The New and Improved Practical Builder (1837) went further, including a discussion on timber bridges. Palladio's concepts were mentioned before Nicholson presented a bridge he designed over the River Clyde at Glasgow. The book also described the available timbers and their applications. Finally, on the strength of timber, Nicholson discussed the experimental work of his British contemporaries, including George Rennie (1791 – 1866), Peter Barlow, and Thomas Tredgold, in addition to French sources [10].

Nicholson's work demonstrated significant improvement in the quality of text and illustrations. Described as a leading intellect of nineteenth-century construction, Nicholson used his mathematical abilities to simplify old formulae used by architectural draughtsmen and to devise new ones [11]. His scientific approach proved highly influential, marking the emergence of a new generation of technical literature that coincided with the establishment of the engineering professions.

John Robison (1739 – 1805) and Sir David Brewster (1781 – 1868)

John Robison published numerous articles on the strength of materials in the fourth edition of the *Encyclopaedia Britannica* [12], which were later collated and annotated by fellow physicist and mathematician Sir David Brewster (1781 – 1868) in *A System of Mechanical Philosophy* (1822). These articles provide a valuable reflection on the knowledge of applied mechanics in Great Britain c.1800, but probably had limited influence on the average practitioner. Robison criticised the lack of British publications on mechanics and the content of British carpentry manuals, singling out Price's *British Carpenter* (1733) in particular [13]. The first of his four volumes included chapters on the strength of materials, carpentry, roofs, arches and centres for masonry bridges.

On the strength of materials Robison referred to the experiments of Couplet, Pitot, De La Hire, Duhamel and other of the French Academy in relation to cohesion. He referred explicitly to elasticity and ductility, providing a discussion on the plastic deformation of bodies [14].

Robison spent considerable time on cohesion, referencing the theories of Newton and Boscovich, before describing the principles of linear elastic behaviour, crediting Robert Hooke (1635 – 1703) for its discovery. Robison considers James Bernoulli's (1654 – 1705) observations on the relationship between strain and the curvature of a bar before crediting the contributions of Daniel Bernoulli (James' nephew) to the same problem [15].

Robison then discussed the strength of fibrous materials and how the values of cohesion vary in different directions, attempting to explain the anisotropic nature of timber. Several, but limited, tables of experimental values were reproduced from previous studies including, Musschenbroek and Emerson, before Robison returned to the subject of variable properties. He described the strength of different parts of the tree in which he demonstrated considerable misunderstanding, before acknowledging that scientists and engineers were far from possessing a scientific knowledge of timber [16].

Robison provided the derivation of formulae for the strength of beams in bending based upon three different hypotheses and discussed failures of previous theories [17]. Like many of his contemporaries, Robison's theory of bending of beams contained an error regarding the position of the neutral axis, which was not corrected by Brewster [18]. Despite the work of Varignon, Parent and Coulomb (to which the reader is directed!) this error in British textbooks was perpetuated, with Robison's work contributing to the confusion. However, he correctly stated that the strength of an encastré beam is twice that of a simply supported beam, before describing the conditions necessary for providing a truly encastré state. Robison also discussed the square-cube law (although he did not name it so, nor attribute such reasoning to Galileo) and its implications for design, providing an example on the effects to built-up beams and scarf joints [19].

On the strength of columns, Robison discussed Euler's theory of which he was quite critical. Following a discussion on experiments aimed at verifying Euler's theories (notable those of Musschenbroek), Robison described Euler's column theory as "erroneous" but failed to offer an alternative method of determine the strength of columns [20].

His chapter on practical carpentry omitted joinery, possibly resulting from the influence of Tredgold. Typical of contemporary texts, Robison's work was predominately descriptive with reference to a limited number of diagrams contained in plates. Some elementary analysis was provided on the equilibrium of systems of bars and straining of beams, in addition to the analysis of arches. However, the relevant analytical content is not reproduced, with reference to the original researchers instead [21]. Robison illustrated and discussed a variety of timber frameworks, including centring for masonry constructions but mainly roof trusses, reproducing designs by Inigo Jones (1573 – 1652), Sir Christopher Wren (1632 – 1723) and Nicholson. He also included a design consisting of three equilateral triangles, in an identical arrangement to a Warren girder [22].

Thomas Martin (1791 – 1851)

In 1813, Thomas Martin published his *Circle of the Mechanical Arts* [23]. Encyclopaedic in nature, its editor had hoped Martin would use Joseph Moxon's (1627 – 91) *Mechanick Exercises* (1694) as a template. Martin apparently exceeded these expectations providing a more detailed discussion on building crafts from bricklaying to plumbing, painting and even needle making [24]. Of greatest interest are his sections concerning timber.

Martin opened his section on Bridges with a brief description of bridges, their purpose and the types of materials used, before stating that design for strength and solidity should be derived by mathematical principles [25]. He noted the merits of applying the principles of trussing, as used in roofs and centres, before addressing the issue of timber decay [26]. His section on timber bridges concluded with a discussion on Palladio's bridges, and examples from Switzerland and North America.

The section on carpentry and joinery is by far the largest in the book. Typical of contemporary texts, he provided the obligatory tables of scantlings and numerous detailed plates containing trusses and joints. The origin of his entire collection is unknown, but some trusses have clearly been copied from Nicholson [27].

On the strength of materials, Martin referred extensively to European sources. He was highly critical of the lack of British sources, only having the ability to cite Emerson and Bank [28]. Martin's advocacy of scientific methods in practice and education continued following his election to the Institution of Civil Engineers in 1826. Despite this, his publications had limited mathematical content, with formula restricted to a discussion on beam theory.

Martin attempted to expand his work on carpentry with *The Carpenter and Joiners' Instructor* (1826), however, the book was flawed. With many paragraphs simply copied from his *Circle of the Mechanical Arts* (1813), Martin demonstrated considerable ignorance of the latest developments, notably Barlow's widely acclaimed treatise [29]. This draws into question when this book was actually written, or if the pseudonym of Thomas Martin had been used by someone else. Whether both publishers and readers recognised the work was flawed, it lasted only one edition and has become largely forgotten.

Peter Barlow (1776 – 1862)

Peter Barlow (1776 – 1862) produced the first major work on the strength of timber in Great Britain. Like Nicholson, Barlow was a self-educated man, who gained enough proficiency to become assistant mathematics master at the Royal Military Academy, between 1801 and 1847. At Woolwich, Barlow was commissioned by the academy's lieutenant-governor, General William Mudge (1762 – 1820), to produce information for teaching officer cadets of the Royal Artillery and Royal Engineers. His treatise *An Essay on the Strength and Stress of Timber* (1817), is the product of that commission and experimental work carried out in the royal dockyards. Obviously servicing a need, its popularity in Great Britain and her empire went far beyond military circles.

Barlow divided his treatise into four parts, with an appendix. Part I was concerned with previous studies and was further divided into four major sections: history of the strength of materials, former theories on the transverse strength and stress of beams, experiments on the transverse strength of beams, experiments on the pressure and longitudinal resistance of columns. Part II contained details of his experiments. Part III covered Barlow's theoretical deductions of which the applications were discussed in Part IV.

The book adds little to the theory of strength of materials, drawing criticism from later authors [30]. Moreover, his review of European literature demonstrated limited understanding. When discussing bending theory, Barlow (like Robison before him) failed to appreciate that the correct location for the neutral axis had been previously determined. Correcting his error in later editions, Barlow attributed the correct determination of the neutral axis to Hodgkinson, apparently unaware that Coulomb had made this correction fifty years earlier.

Despite its theoretical failings, Barlow provided the most comprehensive series of experiments on the strength of timber since Musschenbroek. However, his work was not without its flaws. Small samples sizes distorted experimental results and inhibited further understanding regarding the influence of growth and natural defects. Barlow suggested his experimental results agreed with those of Buffon, rather than Musschenbroeck and Robison, in that the heartwood was found to be the strongest. Barlow suggested that the discrepancies between studies could be attributed to the level of decay older trees experienced within the centre of their trunk [31].

The impact of Barlow's treatise was enormous. Virtually every nineteenth-century text relating to the strength of materials or applied mechanics cited his work and often reproduced his results. Undergoing successively enlarged editions, *An Essay on the Strength and Stress of Timber* (1817) remained the standard textbook on timber for half a century. Its success may owe something to the way it was written. Contemporary reviews described how the text was suitable for "practical men" [32].

Thomas Tredgold (1788 – 1829)

Tredgold received what was described as 'an ordinary education' before being apprenticed to a carpenter at age fourteen. After five years as journeyman carpenter in Scotland, Tredgold joined the London-based architectural practice of his uncle, William Atkinson (c.1774 – 1839). There he acquired an extensive knowledge of geometry, chemistry, geology and other scientific fields, as well as a reputation as a skilled engineer. This knowledge was later used to establish his own practice in 1823 [33]. Tredgold's works as an author were much more scientific in their nature, something for which he criticised previous authors.

Elementary Principles of Carpentry (1820) furthered the development of literature concerning structural carpentry, not only in its content, but for its omission of joinery and decorative elements. Written for those concerned with the construction of buildings and civil engineering works, Tredgold covered all aspects of the mechanical principles of carpentry, except descriptive geometry. In contrast with previous authors, Tredgold presented a clear design philosophy to accompany guidance on the design of building components. He divided *Elementary Principles of Carpentry* (1820) into ten distinct sections: the equilibrium and pressure of beams; the resistance of timber; construction of floors; roofs; domes; partitions; centres for bridges; timber bridges; joints; and the nature and properties of timber.

Section I on mechanics was considered "necessary to give the student an entire and comprehensive view of the science, as its several parts have a mutual influence toward the explanation and proof of each other..." [34]. Devoid of mathematics, Tredgold adopted a predominately descriptive approach, with reference to diagrams contained within plates.

When discussing the strength capacity of timber (Section II), Tredgold reproduced experimental results from British and European sources, notably France. However, it is unclear whether he actually reviewed the original French sources or relied upon abstracts produced in *Encyclopaedias* (Edinburgh, Britannica and Rees) or Barlow (1817). Regardless, he made extensive references to French sources and also published the results of his own experiments on both the stiffness and strength of timber [35].

Tredgold's discussions of theoretical topics offered limited original work and were difficult to follow, although they generally led to the correct results. To calculate the strength of beams, formulae were presented without derivation, instead Tredgold referred the reader to his sources. When considering formulae to determine the largest load a beam could sustain before fracture, Tredgold did not mention applying a factor of safety, suggesting that the expression was intended for checking purposes only. Evidently, he placed a greater importance on stiffness, arguing that "timbers are seldom exposed to strains that break them". Moreover, Nicholson cited the variable nature of timber as a barrier to deriving formulae directly applicable to all members [36].

Tredgold dedicated several pages to the design of columns [37]. He distinguished between short columns that failed in crushing and long columns that were susceptible to bending failure before providing design rules. Unlike his treatment of joists, Tredgold decided against developing design tables believing that the required sizes were dependent upon the nature of the building and therefore, determined via an assessment of the applied loads.

Section III focused on floors construction. Although some tables of scantlings were provided, these were the first to be based upon a combination of practical experience and theory, with an emphasis on controlling deflection rather than bending stress evidenced in his rules [38]. Moreover, Tredgold was unique in providing the formula used in the derivation.

Section IV and Section V on roofs and domes respectively, presented a variety of truss types with rules to determine the cross-sectional dimensions of members in King and Queen post trusses. As with floors, constants were used in rules derived from both theory and practical experience [39]. His approach demonstrates that British engineers were still some distance away from calculating loads within individual truss members. However, the Appendix included tables of scantlings for the different members within the roof trusses provided in his plates.

Section VIII contained details of timber bridges and was more detailed than any previous British book on carpentry. However, references to British bridges were minimal, instead focusing primarily on developments in Europe. This section was expanded in later editions, with the 1870 version (published after Tredgold's death) showcasing many more American examples.

Tredgold devoted Section IX entirely to joints and straps. Unlike other sections, it is devoid of theory, focussing only on providing practical advice based upon experience of different types [40]. Demonstrating his understanding of how the properties of timber affect joint design, Tredgold highlighted the importance in allowing for shrinkage and expansion, citing how quarry men use dry timber wedges later soaked with water to help break stone.

The final section (X) covered the nature and properties of timber. Where many authors failed, Tredgold defined both wood and timber, providing clear distinction between the two. His discussion centred on the structure of wood and the motion and nature of sap in trees, providing advice on the felling of trees and different seasoning techniques before covering the decay of timber and various methods of prevention. He remarked that the field was not fully understood before concluding with a discussion on the strength and classification of woods. In the first known classification system, Tredgold divided different woods into groups based upon their annual ring sizes.

The strength of Tredgold's work resides in his attempt to link theoretical and experimental studies in material science with practical applications to structures. He was arguably the most influential technical author of his generation and possibly the nineteenth century. *Elementary Principles of Carpentry* became the standard reference for the next century, with two editions published in his lifetime and a further twenty-five editions from various publishers on both sides of the Atlantic. The final version was published as late as 1946.

The Emergence of Engineering Textbooks

Engineers' Pocket Books

The compendium or engineer's pocketbook, exemplified by the works of Sir Guilford Lindsey Molesworth (1828 – 1925), owe their origins to carpentry manuals.

From Carpentry Manuals to Scientific Texts (1792 – 1870)

William Turnbull's *A Practical Treatise on The Strength and Stiffness of Timber* (1835) was written first and foremost for engineers, representing a shift from previous publications. It had no plates or figures with example structures, instead containing only tables of strengths and deflections of members. Formulae were provided but without their derivations, however, Turnbull did refer to Tredgold's experiments as his source.

William Lea followed with a similar book which was devoted entirely to timber. *Tables of Strength and Deflection of Timber* (1850) was filled with extensive tables of scantlings for red pine. Lea also provided the formulae used to generate his tables and accompanying example calculations.

Collectively, these books reflect where nineteenth-century engineers, both civilian and military, were focusing their attention: the experimental determination of mechanical properties of timber from across the British Empire. Most of their finding were published in journals, but some were published as minor treatise, including Sir Alexander Cunningham's (1814 – 93) work on timber from the Gwalior Territory of British India [41], and Captain Francis Fowke's (1823 – 65) experiments following the International Exhibitions of 1855 and 1862 [42]. Slowly, their results were reproduced, either in later editions of established works, or within newer texts that encompassed a wider content of engineering.

Textbooks for Student and Practitioners

Circa 1840, numerous textbooks appeared that were aimed towards providing some theoretical basis for study. These were typically written by emerging academics, or prominent engineers within the professional institutions, including William John McQuorne Rankine (1820 – 72).

Based upon Rankine's lectures at Glasgow University, *Manual of Civil Engineering* (1862) attempted to provide the most comprehensive volume of engineering knowledge [43]. It devoted considerable attention to timber at a time when most were concerned with iron. Throughout, Rankine demonstrated a significant improvement in the engineer's knowledge of timber science and transition towards rational design.

On the strength of materials, he devoted sub-sections to stress, strain and distinguished between working loads and fracture loads, with guidelines for factors of safety [44]. On shear, Rankine demonstrated a much greater understanding than previous authors, and explained the relationship between direct stress and shear stress [45]. On the structure and growth of timber, he delved more into its biological nature, explaining how growth affected timber properties before offering a classification system that built upon Tredgold's proposals. He then described timber from around the world and provided tables of their mechanical properties [46].

Sections were also provided on the applications of timber [47]. Numerous joints were described with accompanying sketches and advice on their design and performance. Different methods of laminating beams were also provided. On frames and trusses he opened with a discussion on bridge platforms, with guidance on how load from traffic should be transferred to the structure He continued with roof trusses before concluding with bridge trusses and centring for bridges. Trusses, lattice girders, arches, sprandrils, bowstring girders and timber piers (for trestle bridges) were all illustrated, accompanied by descriptions of their function and load resisting capability. For their analysis Rankine refers to previous theoretical sections.

Contemporary reviews of these new textbooks were frequently critical, claiming that they were too theoretical [48]. Many felt that they did not display the same approach of the 'practical man' and neglected to discuss the various non-quantifiable aspects of construction detail that have a significant effect However, Rankine's book had its supporters and was a key reference for British military engineers [49].

Ironically, just when the understanding of timber improved, it was relegated to a small section or chapter within a larger treatise on civil engineering. With the exception of perhaps Newlands, there was no definitive text on timber engineering in the latter half of the nineteenth century.

The Carpenter and Joiner's Assistant (1860) was first projected by John White, author of *Rural Architecture* (1856), who prepared the vast number of drawings. Following his death, the book was completed by James Newlands (1813 – 71), then the Borough Engineer of Liverpool. Newlands sought to expand the work into a systematic and comprehensive treatise, in which he was largely successful. Richly illustrated, its eight parts covered the full range of necessary skills and knowledge, and drew extensively from British, European, and American sources.

Summary

Written by men who were largely self-taught, these books document the transition from carpentry manuals to engineering textbooks and the emergence of a scientific approach to design.

Early works were revised but never radically altered to reflect the format and style of later engineering textbooks, nor keep pace with developments. Indeed, for most of the nineteenth century, outdated and incorrect material continued to be published. However, publishers must also share some of the blame. A contemporary review of the fifth edition Tredgold's *Elementary Principles of Carpentry* (1870), published long after his death, questioned the integrity of its publishers for publishing unverified and obsolete material for the architectural and engineering professions [50]. Such practices undoubtedly contributed to the confusion surrounding fundamental principles that continued throughout the nineteenth century.

The content omitted is just as informative as the content published. Curiously, texts seldom demonstrated the remarkable timber structures built on British railways. When examples were provided, they were frequently sourced from North America or Europe. Some caution, however, is needed when considering the implication of any material or knowledge that is absent from carpentry manuals. We noted earlier the refusal of craftsmen to help Martin write *Circle of Mechanical Arts* (1813). One must consider whether it was advantageous for any carpenter or engineer to divulge the secrets of his trade. Moreover, for those who did volunteer information with the best intentions, could they have realistically conveyed years of experience within a concise manuscript? It is possible that these individuals possessed more knowledge regarding timber than the writers were capable of articulating.

It is difficult to determine precisely how influential each publication was or how indicative the material was on the state-of-the-art other than to consider contemporary book reviews and the number of editions a particular publication underwent. Other indications are engineers notes or calculations, which are extremely scarce, or references in subsequent works.

References

[1] Those published between 1592 and 1820 have been discussed at length in: David T. Yeomans, 'Early carpenter's manuals 1592 – 1820', *Construction History*, 2 (1986), pp. 13-33
[2] James Newlands, *The Carpenter and Joiner's Assistant*. London: Blackie and Son, 1860, p. v
[3] David T. Yeomans, (Note 1), p. 29.
[4] John Robison (Collated and annotated by Brewster, David) *A System of Mechanical Philosophy,* Edinburgh: John Murray, 1822, p. 497
[5] *ibid.*, p. 497.
[6] Thomas Martin, *Circle of the Mechanical Arts*. London: Richard Rees, 1813, p. iii

[7] E. Keith Lloyd, 'Mr Peter Nicholson, the Practical Builder and Mathematician', *The Mathematical Gazette*, 66, No. 437 (Oct. 1982), pp. 203-204; D. T. Yeomans (Note 1), p. 28

[8] Peter Nicholson, *The Carpenter's New Guide.* London: 1793, p. 43

[9] *ibid*, p. 49.

[10] Peter Nicholson, *The New and Improved Practical Builder,* London: Thomas Kelly, 1837, pp. 56-80, Plates XL and XLI

[11] H. M. Colvin, *A biographical dictionary of British architects 1660 – 1840,* Gloucester: John Murray, 1978. D. T. Yeomans (Note 1) pp. 28-29.

[12] John Robison, *Encylopaedia Britannica*, 3rd Ed. Edinburgh, 1797; Supplement, 3rd Ed. Edinburgh, 1801.

[13] John Robison (Note 4), p. 370.

[14] *ibid*, pp. 372-379.

[15] *ibid*, p. 267, 383-384.

[16] *ibid*, pp. 394, 400-403 and 485.

[17] *ibid*, pp. 440-441.

[18] T. M. Charlton, *A history of theory of structures in the nineteenth century*, Cambridge: Cambridge University Press, 1982, p. 173.

[19] John Robison (Note 4), pp. 445-447.

[20] *ibid*, p. 468.

[21] T. M. Charlton (Note 18), pp. 173 – 174.

[22] John Robison (Note 4), p. 605 and Plate VIII (Figs 2, 5 and 23). T. M. Charlton (Note 18), pp. 173-174.

[23] British Library catalogue notes Thomas Martin was a pseudonym for John Farey Jr. (1791-1851)

[24] Thomas Martin (Note 6), p. iv.

[25] *ibid*, p. 33.

[26] *ibid*, p. 41.

[27] Compare Martin's Carpentry Plate II (Figs 11-13) with Nicholson's (1793) Plate 41. Similarly, Martin's Carpentry Plate II (Figs 16 and 21) with Nicholson's (1973) Plate 45 and Plate 47 respectively.

[28] Thomas Martin (Note 6), pp. 166-171.

[29] Thomas Martin, *The carpenter's and joiner's instructor in geometrical lines, the strength of materials, and mechanical principles of framed work*, London: Thomas Tegg, 1826, p. 175.

[30] I. Todhunter and K. Pearson, *A History of the Theory of Elasticity and of the Strength of Materials* (2 Vols., Cambridge, 1886, 1893)

[31] Peter Barlow, *An Essay on the Strength and Stress of Timber*. London: 1817, p.7. Point expanded upon in 3rd Ed. (1826), p. 7.

[32] *Civil Engineer and Architect's Journal*, 1, No. 2 (1837), p. 20.

[33] *The London and Edinburgh Philosophical Magazine and Journal of Science* (January 1834), p. 395.

[34] Thomas Tredgold, *Elementary Principles of Carpentry*, London: 1820, p. x

[35] *ibid*, pp. x, 40, 45- 47, 56.

[36] *ibid*, pp. 35-36.

[37] *ibid*, pp. 48-59.

[38] L. G. Booth, 'Thomas Tredgold (1788-1829): Some Aspects of his Work', *Transactions of the Newcomen Society*, 51 (1979), pp. 65-71 (p. 67).

[39] Thomas Tredgold (Note 34), pp. 72-85.

[40] *ibid*, pp. 136-148.

[41] Alexander Cunningham, *A Few Notes and Experiments on the Stone and Timber of the Gwalior Territory*. Roorkee: Thomason Civil Engineering College, 1853.

[42] Capt. F. Fowke, 'Results of a series of Experiments on the Strength and Resistance of Various Woods'. In: *Reports on the Paris Exhibition, Presented to both Houses of Parliament by Command of Her Majesty: Part 1*, London:

HMSO, 1856, pp. 402-525; Capt. F. Fowke, *Tables of the Results of a Series of Experiments on the Strength of British, Colonial and other Woods*. London: HMSO, 1867.

[43] W. J. McQuorne Rankine, *Manual of Civil Engineering*, London: Griffin, Bohn and Co., 1862.

[44] *ibid*, p. 222.

[45] *ibid*, p. 167 and 231.

[46] *ibid*, pp. 440-452.

[47] *ibid*, pp. 465-467.

[48] Critical reviews are to be found in: *Engineer*, 1 (1856), p. 57; 23 (1866), p. 203; 28 (1869), p. 56; 29 (1870), p.199. *The Mechanic's Magazine, Museum, Register, Journal and Gazette*, 37 (1842), p. 584.

[49] Favourable review contained within *The Mechanics' magazine and journal of engineering, agricultural machinery, manufactures, and shipbuilding*, 76 (1862), pp. 115-116. *Papers on subjects connected with the duties of the Corps of Royal Engineers*, XV (1866), p. 126.

[50] *The Architect*, 3 (April, 1870) pp. 174-175.

Thomas Telford and the construction of Canal Tunnels 1794-1830

Mike Chrimes
Panel for Historical Engineering Works, Institution of Civil Engineers, UK

Abstract

This paper will put Telford's work as a tunnel engineer into context in terms of the state of tunnel engineering at the time, consider how he gained knowledge in the field, his overall contribution, and its significance.

Introduction

In 1827, with work on the Second Harecastle Tunnel on the Trent and Mersey Canal nearing completion, its Engineer Thomas Telford wrote to the Proprietors: 'Having on my late inspection found it in every respect complete I am justified in asserting it the most perfect work of its kind yet executed' [1]. Telford's view, reiterated forcefully in his autobiography [2], is substantiated by a near two hundred year historical perspective. Many of the country's longest canal tunnels are no longer in use. Harecastle was built quickly to a high specification and has fared comparatively well. It appears one of a piece with his other great works. It is therefore surprising that Telford's tunnelling work has received little attention.

Table 1 makes it clear that while Telford cannot be seen as the leading tunneller of the canal age, he was involved with a number of the longest tunnels, generally as a consultant. However this begs the question how did an aspirant architect make the transition to a consultant on tunnelling within a decade. The answers lie in patronage and Telford's abilities.

Table 1: Engineers responsible for 5 or more canal tunnels in Telford's lifetime [3]

Name	Number of Tunnels (part only)	Consultancy only	Total length (Metres) Executed	Major tunnels over 1000 metres
Brindley	12 (5)	5	6400	Harecastle, Norwood
Clowes	6(5)		10100	Sapperton, Dudley 1, Lapal, Oxenhall
T Dadford jnr	10		2120	Southnet (abandoned)
Henshall	6		8900	Harecastle, Norwood, Preston Brook
W. Jessop	15 (3+)	1	12000	Blisworth, Braunston, Butterley, Greywell
Outram	5(2)		8700	Butterley, Standedge

Thomas Telford and the construction of Canal Tunnels 1794-1830

Name	Number of Tunnels (part only)	Consultancy only	Total length (Metres) Executed	Major tunnels over 1000 metres
Rennie snr	6	3	950	Advised on Harecastle, Southnet and original Strood
Telford	10 (3)	8	10600	Harecastle 2, Standedge, Strood
R. Whitworth	6	2	7900	Foulridge, Oxenhall, Sapperton

The state of canal tunnel engineering in 1793

Tunnels were built from the start of the canal age and practice was derived from the mining industry. Under Brindley, for example at Harecastle, tunnelling was facilitated by the use of horse gins and steam engines for drainage, excavation etc [4]. Hydraulic tunnels were not new: sewers and aqueducts date back millenia, and there is evidence of an early 'road' tunnel beneath the Euphrates. The construction of Malpas tunnel on the Canal du Midi in the late seventeenth century, was not 'new' but marked the start of modern canal tunnelling. By 1794 perhaps 34 tunnels had been built in Britain, many short (14 <100m; 8 100-500m), but some of greater length (11 > 1000 m), including several of great difficulty [5]. Detailed specifications were rare,[6] and when Telford began 'tunnelling' in 1793, there was no standard practice, in terms of internal diameter (height 3-5.5 metres; width 2.2-5.2 metres), thickness of linings (unlined-0.7metres), drainage methods, use of plant, numbers of shafts and their location, or use of surveying instruments. Some variations were in response to different geological formations, or mining practices, but many were driven by cost. Narrow tunnels without towpaths were the norm. Preston Brook on the Trent and Mersey can be seen as typical of the Brindley tunnels. (Fig 1) In general the longer the tunnel the more likely were ground problems, and consequently prices for the work left contractors, and the client badly exposed.

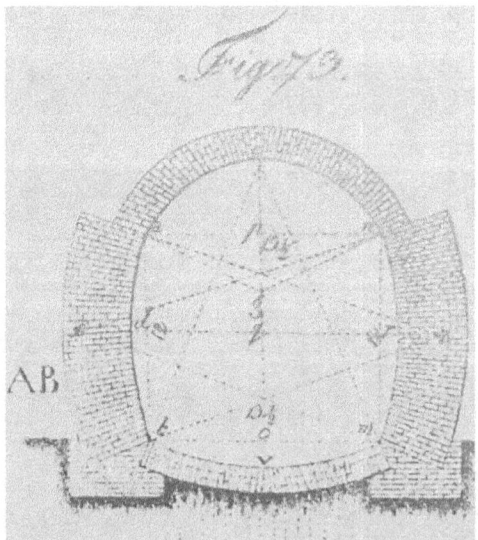

Figure 1: Cross-section of Preston Brook tunnel, from S. v. Maillard, Anleitung zu dem Entwurf und der Ausfuehrung schiffbarer Canaele, Fig 73.

Joseph Farey's article on canals, written in 1806 for an encyclopaedia, is probably the best account of practice at that time [7]. Farey described Blisworth Tunnel in some detail as it was recently constructed. It was a tunnel on which Telford reported. With a difficult history, it can be regarded as the state of art for its time, but that was a decade after Telford had started out. In summary there was mixed experience for Telford to draw on when he started out in 1793. The state of the art moved on in Telford's lifetime, and he played a role in this.

Telford's knowledge of canal tunnels

Telford's article on 'Navigation, Inland',[8] written 1814-20, demonstrates he was then aware of most canal tunnels, after 20 years experience. When he began on the Ellesmere Canal in 1793 there were no textbooks available on tunnelling. The first appeared in 1844[9]. Nothing was published before Farey [10]. By then Telford had a decade of practice. It was not until the 1820s that engineering drawings of canal tunnels were published, with which Telford was personally involved [11]. The first comparative work on canal tunnels was not published until 1841 [12]. In the absence of such literature Telford could turn to mining books, and indeed he acquired two French works, and could have consulted the libraries of Shropshire mine owners.

The position as regards canal engineering was somewhat better. A bibliography of literature on inland navigation lists 150 books, of which perhaps half were available in 1793.[13] Comparing this with Telford's Library, in the Institution of Civil Engineers, and the article he wrote on Inland Navigation c. 1820, he had copies of five key early works, while he referred to c 30 authorities in his Edinburgh Encyclopaedia article. It was a steep learning curve as his previous professional reading noted in correspondence to his friend Andrew Little related to architecture and more general science [14].

Telford is known for his tours of the UK, however his tours of Scotland in 1780, and of Southern Britain in early 1793 were focussed on his architecture [15]. While he had 20 years of construction experience, given the gaps in his knowledge of hydraulic and earth works it would not have been surprising if he had failed to make the grade.

Telford's early canal tunnels

When Telford began his career in tunnelling, standard practice had yet to evolve and many of the first generation canal engineers had passed on. His tunnel work (Table 2) will now be reviewed, concentrating on his initiation into canal engineering, and the Harecastle tunnel and its lead up.

Table 2: Telford's tunnels

Name of tunnel	Client	Dates of Telford's involvement	Length (metres)	Role	Contractor
Berwick or Preston	Shrewsbury Canal	1795-97	887	Engineer for construction	Houghton & Ford
Weston Lullingfields	Ellesmere Canal	1795-1797		Agent and Engineer	
Whitehouses	Ellesmere Canal	1796-1801	156	Agent and Engineer	Davies & Simpson

Thomas Telford and the construction of Canal Tunnels 1794-1830

Name of tunnel	Client	Dates of Telford's involvement	Length (metres)	Role	Contractor
Chirk	Ellesmere Canal	1796-1801	420	Agent and Engineer	Davies & Simpson
Ellesmere	Ellesmere Canal	1796-1804	80	Agent and Engineer	Samuel Betton & Simpson
Bosworth	Grand Union Canal	1803-1808	1057	Consultant	Pritchard & Hoof
Crick	Grand Union Canal	1803-1808	1397	Consultant	Pritchard & Hoof
Blisworth	Grand Junction Canal	1804-5	2813	Consultant	Woodhouse and Direct Labour
Standedge	Huddersfield Canal	1805-1811	4764	Consultant	Direct Labour
Paisley	Glasgow, Paisley & Ardrossan Canal	1804-1811	<100	Engineer	
Islington (& Maida Vale)	Regents Canal	1812-21	823	Consultant	Pritchard & Hoof
Falkirk	Edinburgh & Glasgow Union Canal	1815-1822	636	Consultant	John Mitchell/ Johnstone
Strood	Thames & Medway Canal	1817-1824	3595	Exchequer Bill Loan Commission Engineer	Pritchard & Hoof, & Williams
Harecastle	Trent & Mersey	1821-29	2676	Engineer	Pritchard & Hoof
Rotton Park Feeder	Birmingham Canal	1824-29	3200	Engineer	Thomas Townshend
Pennines	Chesterfield Canal extension	1824-28	<16000	Consultant	Not built
Cowley	Birmingham & Liverpool	1830-1833	630, now 74	Engineer	Provis
Coseley	Birmingham	1834-37	329	Engineer?	Townshend

Ellesmere Canal Tunnels [16]

Telford's appointment to the Ellesmere Canal [17], marked his transition from an aspirant architect to a civil engineer [18]. His responsibilities covered whatever tunnels were required [19]. William Jessop was the consulting engineer, with whom Telford conferred. There were three tunnels (Table 2). In contrast to Telford's lack of experience of tunnels, Jessop had already been responsible for at least six, with more underway, some of great length and difficulty (Table 1) and could share his experience with Telford. It is likely that before work around Chirk was started the Berwick tunnel on the Shrewsbury Canal had been completed.

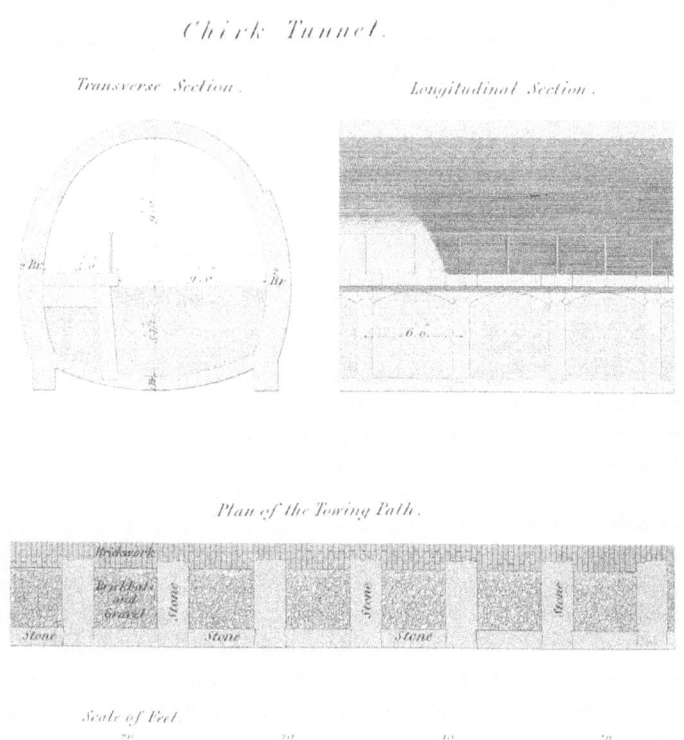

Figure 2: Chirk tunnel and towpath, from Atlas to the Life of Telford, Plate 12, ICE

Construction around Chirk began in 1796, with Telford's friend Matthew Davidson supervisor, and the tunnels were completed in 1801. Contractor William Davies was working with the mason John Simpson at Chirk. Much of the Chirk and all of the Whitehouses tunnel was carried out by cut-and-cover techniques. For the bored section at Chirk, access was from the cuttings at each end and by two shafts. A network of tramroads were laid here and Telford could see their advantages in speeding up work.

Both tunnels were 4.4m high, with 1.7m depth of waterway, and 4.3m wide, with a towpath of 1.5m width, on stone columns at 1.8m centres allowing free water flow, giving a comfortable 2.7m clearance [20]. The brickwork lining was one brick thickness (0.23m) in the invert, two bricks in the side wall up to what might be considered the springing of the arch, and one and a half bricks thick for the vault (Fig. 2). It bears a striking resemblance to the form of Harecastle tunnel build 30 years later. There was a further short tunnel built at Ellesmere. Only c 90m long, it also has an elliptical arch and towpath. There was a tunnel proposed at Weston Lullingfields, mentioned in Farey, [21] but never built.

Telford was responsible for the drawings and the specification for the tunnels [22]. It is telling that the tunnels had tow paths, a characteristic of several of Jessop's short tunnels. Telford believed the idea of tunnel towpaths originated with William Reynolds, and from his remarks the Ellesmere Canal designs would have represented an improvement in width and durability.

The work was carried out by a workforce with knowledge of local ground conditions. As Telford remarked 'in regard to earth work, I had the advantage of consulting Mr. William Jessop, an experienced engineer, on whose advice I never failed to set a proper value [23].'

Berwick Tunnel, Shrewsbury Canal [24]

Telford claimed responsibility for this tunnel [25]. Presumably he meant responsibility for construction as one of the proprietors, William Reynolds, made important contributions to the design, and work had possibly started before Telford's involvement. Josiah Clowes [26], an experienced tunnel engineer, was appointed Engineer to the Canal in 1793 and contractors were appointed on 1 January 1794. Before work began Reynolds recommended that a towpath should be included. Further modifications extending it a short distance at both ends were agreed on 5 January 1795, subject to Clowes' approval. However, he had already died, and Telford was appointed Engineer on 28 February. He would have had access to Clowes' documentation regarding the tunnel, with responsibility for its construction.

Telford, in his review of inland navigation in Shropshire, focussed on the technical innovations associated with the canal [27]. He drew attention to the advantages of the tunnel towpath. This suggests that in 1797 it had not been decided to add towpaths to the tunnels on the Ellesmere; it also makes clear that Telford was unaware of tunnel towpaths elsewhere. However his thoughts here anticipate the case he made for towpaths at Harecastle nearly 30 years later. The tunnel was 887 metres long, brick lined, and c 3m wide [28]. It was the first tunnel of any length to have a towpath, and had ventilation shafts and bell shaped approaches.

Telford's tunnels 1800-1830

The opening of the Ellesmere Canal in 1805, with the stunning cast iron aqueduct at Pont Cysyllte, consolidated Telford's reputation resulting in a number of government appointments, some with Jessop, whose clients increasingly turned to Telford. Some of Telford's best known works such as the Caledonian and Gotha canals and the Scottish and Holyhead roads did not involve tunnels, but over the next 20 years he advised on a number of tunnels. Some were not executed by Telford, like the Grand Union Canal (1804-8) [29] on which he estimated the tunnelling works at £25,690 for 1606 yards [30]. Although asked to prepare drawings for Parliament it was a scheme by James Barnes modified by Benjamin Bevan involving tunnels at Crick and Market Bosworth that was followed [31]. Telford must have been aware of subsequent problems at Crick as consultant to the Grand Junction [32].

Twenty years later Telford was consulted about an extension of the Chesterfield Canal [33]. The original proposal involved nearly 10 miles of tunnelling. Telford incurred expenditure of over £50.00 (£50,000) before it was abandoned [34].

Perhaps as an impartial expert Telford reported on the Braunston and the Blisworth Tunnel on the Grand Junction Canal (GJC), one of his mentor Jessop's masterworks, in 1805, after a chequered construction history stretching back to 1793 [35]. Telford reported as the Blisworth tunnel neared completion, to a new specification drawn up by Jessop in 1802 [36]. He must have had access to this and the method of working [37]. He would have seen the benefits of having a railroad over the line of a long tunnel to bring material on site, and the use of a large number of shafts (19), and drainage works to speed up construction. He remarked on the quality of the work in terms of materials, workmanship, and the straightness of its alignment, in contrast to the earlier Braunston. Telford would have been able to use his observations in his advice on Standedge soon after.

Standedge, Britain's longest (5210m) and highest canal tunnel also had a chequered history before Telford's advice was sought on a construction programme [38]. Work had begun under Benjamin Outram, who underestimated the difficulty of the strata [39]. There were problems with alignment, and the tunnel required lining. It was expensive, requiring much pumping and only 14 of the planned 18 shafts were completed during a decade of unsatisfactory progress which saw Outram and contractors resign.

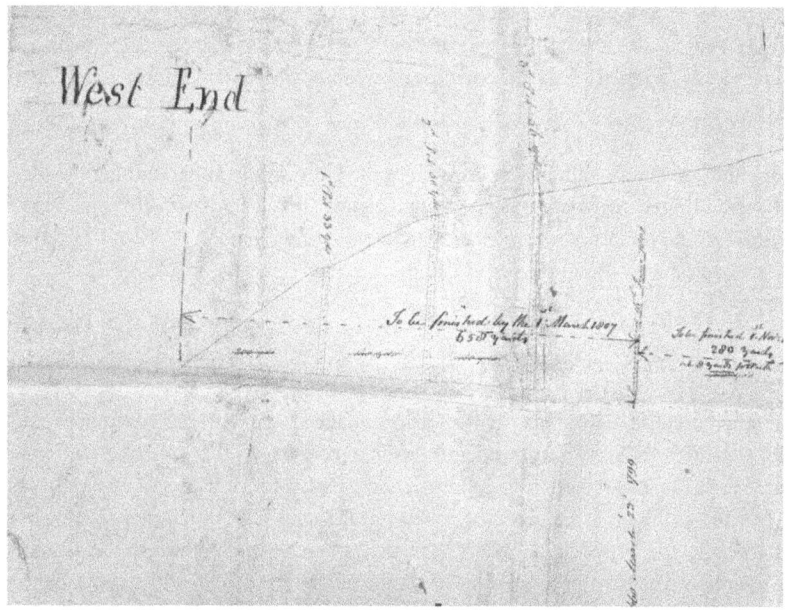

Figure 3: Longitudinal section of West end of Standedge showing Telford's dates for completion, Telford MSS, T/HU/1, ICE.

A new Act was passed in 1805, and Telford was brought in. His report was based on 'thorough knowledge of the state of the works because he had investigated everything twice',[40] with detailed estimates,[41] and a section of the tunnel on which he plotted the time to be taken for completion according to the stage of work and local geology (Fig 3) [42]. The final tunnel cost was £123,04, Telford having estimated the outstanding work in 1806 at £55290 [43].

Although the Glasgow, Paisley & Ardossan Canal (1804-11) was a minor work in Telford's oeuvre, it involved a short tunnel. In his 1805 report describing the section through Paisley he wrote: "It afterwards passes in front of the Relief Kirk and the Meeting-House into an old stone quarry, from whence there should be a tunnel for a very short distance. This, it is expected, will be done chiefly by cutting in a free-stone rock"[44]. Details of the tunnel are now lacking.

Islington and Maida Hill Tunnels, Regents Canal 1812-1820

Telford was involved with the Regents Canal as consultant to the GJC, and also as Engineer to the Exchequer Bill Loan Commission (EBLC). He and Jessop first reported in 1812. James Morgan, the canal's engineer worked closely with the contractor, Pritchard, who was responsible for Islington and Maida Hill tunnels, both without towpaths. There were problems at both and the ground proved less stable and uniform than anticipated. The Company needed funds, and appealed to the EBLC, and its Engineer, Telford. Among his papers is a drawing of the Islington tunnel showing details of the heavy falsework used to support the construction [45]. This was the basis of Charles Dupin's drawing of the canal published in 1824 [46]. Telford recommended an Exchequer loan in December 1817. In his report of June 1818 he noted that the tunnel was "Perfect the materials and workmanship excellent, and its direction perfectly straight." The canal opened in 1820. In 1821, Morgan recommended Pritchard to Telford as contractor for Harecastle tunnel [47].

Falkirk Tunnel, Edinburgh and Glasgow Union Canal, 1813-23 [48]

Telford was involved with the Union Canal from inception to completion. The Engineer was Hugh Baird who first reported in 1813, but there were objections from landowners and the Falkirk tunnel as eventually built was to deal with those of William Forbes by tunnelling through Callendar Hill [49]. Telford reported in 1815 [50]. The Act followed in 1817. Thereafter Telford negotiated with Forbes, advised the Company on the design, and procurement of the contracts, and acted as arbitrator. He also advised the EBLC to lend money, based on his inspections, reporting to them in November 1820, and early 1823.

The tunnel was 5.8m high, generally with 3.6m clearance and c 2m depth of water and 5.5m wide with a waterway of 4.1m and a 1.5m towpath. Three shafts were sunk, and a heading driven through before opening out.. Brick lined in places, with semi-circular arch portals, it was generally an exposed rock tunnel. It was a project where Telford urged additional payments to speed up work [51]. While Baird was the Engineer in charge, Telford acted as consultant throughout.

Strood Tunnel, Thames & Medway Canal 1817-24

This tunnel was important because of its length, cross-section, and the use of a transit instrument combined with sighting towers to secure its alignment [52]. It was considered the state of the art in canal tunnelling twenty years later [53]. Telford was consulted in 1817 when the proprietors turned to the EBLC for funding [54]. Initially Telford recommended a loan be refused. Despite this the investors obtained an Act in 1818, and William Tierney Clark was appointed engineer. The tunnel was 10.7m high, and 8m wide, allowing 1.5m for a towpath, and 2.4m depth of water (fig 4). The detailed specification survives among Telford's papers [55]. Many innovations were the work of the contractor Daniel Pritchard, but progress was expensive.

Figure 4: Thames and Medway Canal Tunnel, Plates 6-7, from Strickland Reports (Note 4)

Telford took a keen interest, and made detailed notes about the details of the contracts, prices, and methods in late 1822 [56]. These deliberations were for another EBLC loan, and relevant for the Harecastle tunnel planning [57]. In May 1824 Clark wrote to Telford recommending Pritchard for the Harecastle job.

Harecastle Tunnel, Trent & Mersey Canal 1822-29

The Harecastle tunnels have been cited as examples of the advance in civil engineering 1760-1830. Brindley faced perhaps his most challenging task here. The ground comprised variously hard rock, coal measures, ironstone, marl, clay and quicksand (Fig 5). His tunnel was narrow, unlined in parts, and built without a towpath [58]. The arch ring was generally 0.23m [59]. By 1820 the Canal Company faced numerous complaints about its condition, and delays in passage, and consulted Rennie who recommended a new tunnel but died in October 1821 [60]. Surprisingly his estimates did not include a towpath or provision for the working shafts.

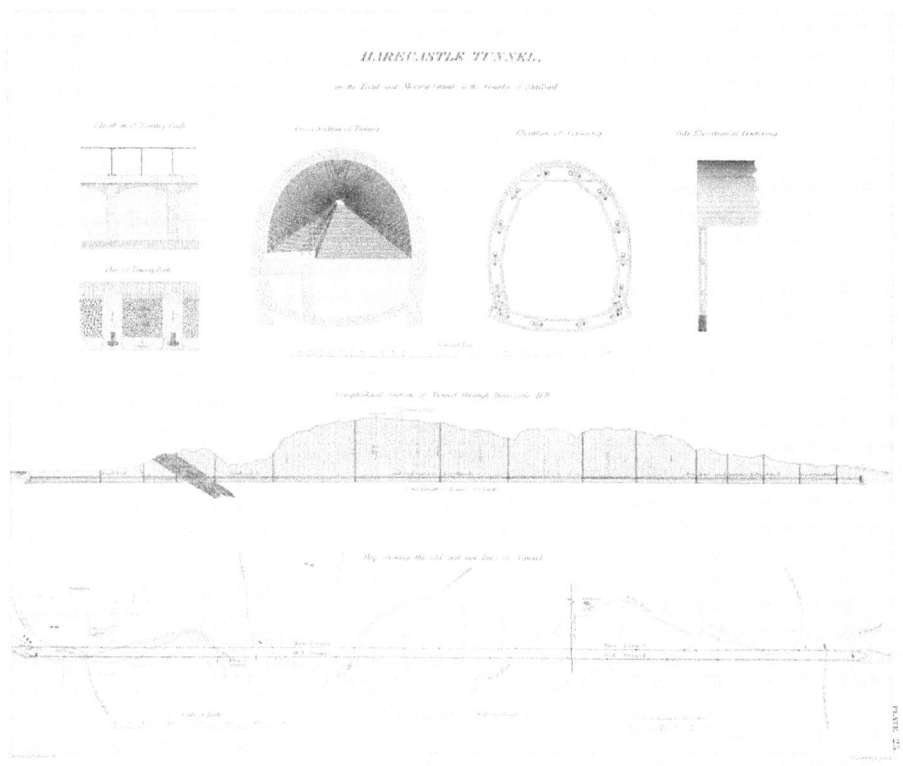

Figure 5: Harecastle tunnel, Plate 25, from Atlas to the Life of Telford, ICE

By then Telford had been approached. In early 1822 he produced his report [61]. An Act followed and in 1824 Telford was appointed Engineer. In the meantime Telford was inspecting works on the Regents and Thames and Medway canals, and was also in correspondence with the canal's Resident Engineer James Potter. He made the case for a tow path (Fig. 5), following what he considered best practice. Once the Management Committee had agreed he produced his specification, and appointed the contractors Pritchard and Hoof in July 1824.

Telford took great care in the planning. Detailed correspondence with the Committee, Contractor and resident engineer survive, with his estimates and regular reports on progress. Telford visited at least twice a year, while Potter reported in detail on progress on a monthly basis. The Contractors also kept itemised accounts on their expenditure. The tunnel opened on 30 April 1827, a remarkable achievement.

Pritchard and Hoof used easily demountable centering to speed up work. There were eventually 15 shafts, 2.7m diameter largely worked by horse gins 24 hours day, with two Boulton and Watt steam engines to keep the workings dry. There were also 12-14 air shafts. The tunnel was brick lined throughout although the shafts were not. The bricks were made from local clay or marl, a Staffordshire engineering brick, and the Barrow Lime mortar was ground in a mill modelled on one developed by Rennie. The mortar and brick mills were powered by four steam engines,. Despite some quicksand, progress was rapid with the 2447 metre tunnel completed, except for the towpath, in 550 days.

The tunnel cost £38 10s a linear yard (0.914m), compared with £3. 10s 8d for the Brindley tunnel (perhaps £12 12s 5d in 1827 project value costs). As Simms noted: a decade later 'there probably has been no Tunnel of the same length which has ever been constructed in so short a time' [62].

This, and the near contemporary Strood tunnel on the Thames and Medway Canal are probably the first major tunnels where a steady rate of progress was made from the start despite the difficult ground conditions. Telford's drawings [63], were published at the time of construction [64], and also in the Atlas to his Life. They were there to serve as exemplars to the railway engineers that followed.

Birmingham Canal, 1824-1835

Telford was involved in major improvements to the Birmingham Canal, to shorten the winding course of the Brindley era canals [65]. The reservoir built at Rotton Park was supplied by a feeder of over 4 miles, approximately half in a brick lined tunnel c 1.5 x 0.9 m in diameter [66]. Another shorter tunnel was built on the Winston Green feeder. A short tunnel was built at Coseley. It is the only canal tunnel with towpaths on both sides, a general feature of the Telford improvements. It was opened in 1835, after Telford's death.

Railway tunnels

As Engineer to the EBLC Telford reported on the Liverpool and Manchester Railway [67]. The report was critical of the engineering management and the uncertainty about the modes(s) of traction. However Telford was generally positive about the civil engineering, including Wapping tunnel, of which he possessed a detailed section [68]. Thus Telford had first hand knowledge of one of the first railway tunnels [69].

Roadworks

Road tunnels in Europe were rare after the Roman period. Telford, despite involvement with over 1000 miles of roads, did not design any. However an important feature of his road design was drainage, which included some culverts 5ft in diameter. One, specified by Sir Henry Parnell. in his *Treatise on roads,* could be a specification for a small canal tunnel [70].

Elsewhere Parnell describes Telford's approach to contractors, favouring 'liberal terms' for if 'a price …is too low…every thing is done in an imperfect way…'[71] The history of canal tunnels is littered with examples of the latter. Of course Telford's 'liberality' was framed by detailed specifications, and regular inspection. His success, with tunnel works as elsewhere, also relied on working with contractors he trusted, 'it will always be decidedly better to make an agreement with him than to advertise for tenders.' This policy was successfully followed at Harecastle.

Conclusions

Telford's tunnelling experience began in the mid- 1790s. He benefitted from the advice, and observed the work, of two of the most experienced tunnel engineers, Jessop and Clowes. Thereafter his practice reflects the essential character of his career as a civil engineer. His reputation is based in part on outstanding civil engineering structures and innovation. However it is also based upon thoroughness in terms of project preparation and management, backed by background research. This approach underpinned the success of his masterworks, and enabled him to make a positive contribution to tunnel engineering, and in the specification and management of the Harecastle tunnel set a standard for tunnel works of magnitude for the next generation of civil engineers. He demonstrated that sound tunnels could be built through difficult ground with good planning, a skilled team, and adequate finance. His achievement should not be underestimated.

References

[1] ICE, Telford MSS, T/TR/70, Telford to J. Caldwell.

[2] 'Harecastle tunnel' in T. Telford, *Life of Thomas Telford*, J. Rickman (Ed.), London: Hansard, 1838. pp.75-77, and plate 25 in Atlas to the Life, London: Payne & Foss, 1838.

[3] For information on engineers named in this article see A.W. Skempton, (Ed.) *Biographical Dictionary of Civil Engineers 1500-1830,* London: ICE, 2002.

[4] W. Strickland, *Reports on canals, railways, roads and other subjects*, Philadelphia: Carey & Lea, 1826,

[5] D. Appleby and others, *Canal tunnels of England & Wales*, Birmingham: Aylestone, 2001.

[6] P S M Cross-Rudkin, 'Canal contractors 1760-1820', *RCHS journal*, No. 207, March 2010, pp. 27-39.

[7] J. Farey, 'Canals', c. 1806, in A. Rees (comp.) *Cyclopaedia*, Vol. 6, London: Longman, 1820.

[8] T. Telford, 'Navigation, inland', in D. Brewster (comp.) *Edinburgh Encyclopaedia*, Edinburgh: Blackwood etc, 1830, vol. XV, pp. 209-315.

[9] F. W. Simms, *Practical tunnelling*, London: Weale, 1844.

[10] Farey, 'Canals', (Note 7).

[11] Strickland, Reports (Note 4), pp. 5-10, plates 4-12.

[12] L. Minard, *Cours de navigation intérieur* (2 vols.) Paris: Ecole des Ponts et chaussées, 1841, pp. 261- 272; figs. 493-563.

[13] M. Clarke, *Technology, economics, and canal development: an early technical book and what it reveals,* Market Drayton: RCHS, 2021. pp. 222-225.

[14] ICE, Letters from Telford to Andrew Little, 1 February 1786, 21 February 1788.

[15] ICE, Telford's Architectural notes, and letter from T Telford to Andrew Little, 10 March 1793.

[16] P. Brown, *Shropshire Union Canal*, Market Drayton: RCHS, 2018.

[17] TNA Rail 827-1, Minutes of Ellesmere Canal Proprietors, 27 September 1793.

[18] ICE, T. Telford, Letter to Andrew Little, 29 September 1793, and 3 November 1793.

[19] TNA Rail 827-1,- Minutes of Ellesmere Canal Proprietors, 27 September 1793, p. 12.

[20] Telford, *Life*, (Note 2) p. 47.

[21] Farey, 'Canals' (Note 10), section on 'Ellesmere canal'.

[22] ICE, Catalogue of Telford papers in Council Room, Specifications etc for Ellesmere and Chester Canal, and Bundle 25 Sundry tunnels-Thames & Medway, Ellesmere Canal and Huddersfield Canal; and Bundle 71 Ellesmere canal working drawings; Institution of Civil Engineers, (General register) Telford drawings, 3 mss vols, 2402, 'A vertical section of Tunnels of the Ellesmere Canal'.

[23] Telford, *Life* (Note 2). p. 34

[24] TNA RAIL 868/1, Shrewsbury Canal Company, Minutes of the Proprietors, 1793-1815

[25] Telford, 'Navigation, inland' (Note 7), p. 246.

[26] C. Lewis, 'Josiah Clowes (1735-1794)', *Trans. Newc. Soc*, vol. 50 1978-79 pp 155-158

[27] J. Plymley, *General view of the general view of the agriculture of Shropshire*, London: Phillips, 1803, pp. 284-316. p. 312 makes it clear that the account was written by Telford in 1797.

[28] A.R.K. Clayton 'The Shrewsbury and Newport Canals: constructional and remains', in A. Penford (Ed.) *Thomas Telford : Engineer*, London: Telford, 1980, pp. 23-40.

[29] T. Telford, *A Survey and report of the proposed extension of the Union Canal from Gumley Wharf...to the Grand Junction Canal near Buckby-wharf ...1803*, Leicester: Throsby, 1804.

[30] C. Hadfield, *Canals of the East Midlands*, Newton Abbot: David & Charles, 1970. pp. 98-104
[31] TNA RAIL 831/1-2, Grand Union Canal Minutes
[32] M. Chrimes and M. Preece, 'Groundwater lowering for Kilsby Tunnel-pumping and tunnelling, *ICE Procs. Engineering History & Heritage*, 2021, https://doi.org/10.1680/jenhh.21.00000
[33] J. Haslehurst, *Report(s) upon the proposed Grand Commercial Canal*…Chesterfield: Roberts, 1824.
[34] National Library of Scotland, D 19973, Telford MSS; Drawings listed in the ICE Drawings register (Note 39) are missing.
[35] A. H Faulkner, *The Grand Junction Canal*, Rickmansworth: Walker, 1993; C. Hadfield, and A.W. Skempton, *William Jessop, Engineer*, Newton Abbot: David & Charles, 1979. pp.110-125.
[36] T. Telford, 'Report of the General State of the Grand Junction Canal', in *Report of the General Committee of the Grand Junction Canal Company, to the General Assembly of Proprietors*, London: Brooke, 1805.
[37] TNA RAIL 830/41, Grand Junction Canal Minutes, 6 May 1802,
[38] C. Hadfield and G. Biddle, *The Canals of North West England*, Newton Abbot: David and Charles, 1970. Vol. 2, pp.322-335,
[39] R.B. Schofield, 'The construction of the Huddersfield narrow canal, 1794-1811, with particular reference to Standedge tunnel, *Trans. Newcomen Society*, vol. 53, 1981-82, pp. 17-38.
[40] T. Telford, *Abstract of the report relative to the state of the works on the Huddersfield Canal*, 29. 1. 1807.
[41] ICE, Telford MSS, T/HU/2, Estimate for finishing the Huddersfield Canal Tunnel.
[42] ICE, Telford MSS, T/HU/1, T. Telford, [Longitudinal section of Standedge tunnel]. It can be assumed there were other drawings in ICE (Note 38) Bundle 25.
[43] https://measuringworth.com
[44] T. Telford, *A Report relative to the proposed canal from the city of Glasgow to the harbour of Ardrossan, and map*, London: Barlow, 1805.
[45] ICE archives, Telford MSS, T/MI/6 Ink and wash section of Islington Canal Tunnel.
[46] C. Dupin, *Voyages dans la Grande Bratagne 1816-1820: vol. 2: Force commercials de la Grande Bretagne*, Paris: Bachelier, 1824-6.
[47] ICE, Telford MSS, T/TR/9, J. Morgan, Letter to Telford, 24 December 1821.
[48] J. Lindsay, *The Canals of Scotland*, Newton Abbot: David & Charles, 1968. pp. 66-85.
[49] H. Baird, *Additional report to the Committee of Subscribers to the Edinburgh and Glasgow Union Canal 17 October 1814*, Kelfinhead (Glasgow), 1814.
[50] ICE, Telford MSS, T/EG/.Edinburgh and Glasgow Union Canal reports and correspondence; The 1815 report T/EG/265
[51]] ICE (Note 57) T/EGU/220, Telford, draft report on Union Canal, 8 Jan 1821,
[52] Strickland, *Reports* (Note 4) pp.5-10, plates 4-10.
[53] F.W. Simms, *Public works of Great Britain*, London: Weale, 1838, Section 2: Canals etc, pp 1-4, Plates LXXXIV-VI.
[54] C. Hadfield, *Canals of southern England*, London: Phoenix House, 1955, pp 98-101.
[55] ICE, Telford MSS, T/TM/1 Thames and Medway Canal, Specification and particulars of work proposed to be done in the line of tunnel between the entrance at Higham and the Frindsbury end….
[56] ICE, Telford MSS, T/TM/2 Memorandum taken 17 December 1822.
[57] ICE, Telford MSS, T/TM/3 Thames and Medway Canal notes on Pritchard and Williams' work etc, 1822-23.
[58] A.C. Baker and M.G. Fell, *Harecastle's canal and railway tunnels*, Lydney: Lightmoor Press, 2019.
[59] ICE, Rennie Reports, Report to Proprietors of the Grand Trunk Canal, 11 September 1820,.
[60] P.S.M. Cross-Rudkin, *John Rennie*, Market Drayton: RCHS, 2022.
[61] ICE, Telford MSS, T/TR/1 etc, Trent and Mersey Canal correspondence forms the basis for what follows.
[62] F. W. Simms, *Public works*, (Note 55) pp. 4-5, plate XCII.
[63] ICE, Drawings register, 548-550, T. Telford, Plans and sections of Harecastle tunnel including centering. The plate in Simms (Note 68) was provided by Potter.
[64] Strickland, Reports (Note 4) pp.5-10, plate 11.
[65] D. Bligh and others, 'Birmingham Canal, England-a future unlocked by Telford,, *ICE Proceedings, Civil engineering*, Vol. 160, Special Issue 1, May 2007, pp. 56-60,
[66] ICE, Drawings register, 2624, T. Telford, 'Longitudinal section of the feeder from Rotton Park Reservoir to Tilford Reservoir'.
[67] T. Telford. *Liverpool and Manchester Railway…Report to the Commissioners for the Loan of Exchequer Bills. With Observations in reply by the Directors of the said Rail-way*, Liverpool: T.Kaye, 1829.

[68] ICE, Telford MSS, T/LM/31, Section of Wapping tunnel,
[69] R.H.G. Thomas, *Liverpool and Manchester Railway*, London: Batsford, 1980.
[70] H. Parnell, *A Treatise on roads…explained and illustrated by the plans, specifications, made use of by Thomas Telford Esq…*, London: Longman, 1833. p. 205
[71] Parnell, *Treatise* (Note 73). pp. 228-229

Water for the University: An Early History of the University of Virginia's Water supply, 1817-1885

Benjamin J. Hays
University Building Official and Lecturer in the School of Architecture, University of Virginia

Abstract

This paper focuses on the University of Virginia's manifold attempts, throughout the 19th century, to provide itself with "the most abundant supply" water [1]. During the early years of the university's construction, its founder Thomas Jefferson developed an early protosystem that included reliance on water collected from mountain springs. This water was carried more than half a mile to the buildings via wooden pipes. As the university transitioned from a construction site to a center for learning, its new proctor Arthur Brockenbrough updated this protosystem. He continually replaced rotting wooden pipes, constructed several additional storage cisterns, and purchased a hand-pumped fire engine. Following construction of the huge Rotunda Annex with its cast iron columns in the 1850s, a decades long attempt to convert the wooden pipe system to iron was executed by engineer Charles Ellet. Ellet's waterworks included additional storage in the form of a pond proximate to the Academical Village as well as a steam engine capable of pumping water to storage tanks located in the top of the Rotunda. A decade later, remote storage on the mountain was proposed by Green Peyton to reduce reliance on the steam engine and Rotunda attic as the means of pressurizing the overall system. By the 1880s, the university-owned water supply was deemed insufficient. Coupled with a growing realization that its inadequate sewerage system might be contaminating the water, the university joined with the City of Charlottesville to develop a remote, large capacity reservoir to meet its needs [2].

> "the greatest danger will be their overbuilding themselves by attempting a large house in the beginning, sufficient to contain the whole institution. large houses are always ugly, inconvenient, exposed to the accident of fire, and bad in cases of infection. a plain small house for the school & lodging of each professor is best. these connected by covered ways out of which the rooms of the students should open would be best. these may be built only as they shall be wanting. in fact an University should not be a house but a village. this would much lessen their first expences (sic)."
>
> – letter from Jefferson to a friend, c. 1805 [3]

Introduction

During the summer of 1817 Thomas Jefferson's long dreamt of vision for what would become the University of Virginia finally began to take shape. In June the final site for the university was chosen and the contract was executed for nearly 200 acres of land just west of Charlottesville. By July, Jefferson along with the help of two servants personally surveyed and laid out the squares of his Academical Village. The fallow field they surveyed, purchased for less than $10 an acre ($1421.25 total; see Fig. 1), would soon undergo a remarkable transformation following a series of annual building campaigns between 1818 and 1825 [4].

The extensive literature on the construction of Jefferson's Academical Village – a central green flanked by rows of student's rooms that are punctuated by professor's Pavilions and connected by his keystone Rotunda – focuses primarily on the overall planning and classical architecture of "the most ambitious and monumental architectural project" of the American 19th century (Fig. 2) [5]. Comparatively little has been written about the infrastructure required to support the

Water for the University: An Early History of the University of Virginia's Water supply, 1817-1885

new village. Specific to the focus of this paper, very few accounts discuss how the new university, underlain with sandstone having a "low capacity for holding groundwater," would be supplied with water for drinking and fire protection [6].

Primary source documents on the university's ever evolving waterworks exists in numerous archives. Many secondary sources exist as well. Frank Grizzard's dissertation *A Documentary History of the Construction of the Buildings at the University of Virginia, 1817-1828* contains several sections and an appendix dedicated to the University's earliest "Water Works and Fire Apparatus" [7]. An excellent but unpublished paper by Steven Thompson stitches together a narrative of the University's constant struggle with water supply throughout the rest of the 19th century [8]. And a recent article by Takahashi and Anderson looks at the 200-year history of "material flows" – including a short section on water supply – between the Academical Village and its "mountain" [9]. This paper relies on both primary and secondary literature, including numerous references to an excellent series of maps in order to summarize the university's attempts to secure water on its own lands between 1817 to 1885.

Early Protosystems

Work on the university's first building, Pavilion VII, started after a lengthy masonic cornerstone ceremony in late 1817. After pausing for winter, the building campaign of 1818 included commencement of a second pavilion (Pavilion III), the start of several student dormitories connected to Pavilion VII, and the continued terracing of the central green. The campaign of 1819 saw several additional pavilions take shape and an approval by the university's Board of Visitors (BOV) to supply water: "by wooden pipes from neighboring highlands" [10].

Jefferson's Protosystem

Jefferson likely understood that the location of his Academical Village did not contain adequate water supplies. The initial land purchase of 1817 shows that the university purchased not only the 43¾ acre parcel that would be the site of the Academical Village but also a non-contiguous 153-parcel labeled "Mountains" located more than half a mile to the west (Fig. 1). In an article for the *Richmond Enquirer* later that summer, Jefferson noted that the institution was located at a site "above the town of Charlottesville, high, healthy, & with good water…" [11]. The newspaper article was part of a propaganda campaign to raise funds for the nascent university and the mention of "good water" is almost certainly a reference to the springs located on the Mountain parcel rather than the shallow wells adjacent to the Academical Village.

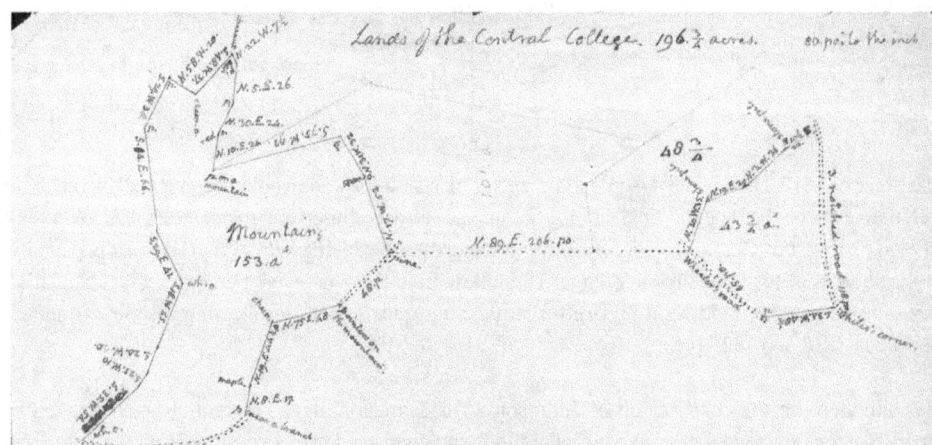

Figure 1: Lands of the Central College 196.3/4 acres. Thomas Jefferson surveyor. 1817. University of Virginia Special Collections. "Central College" was the original name for what became the University of Virginia.

By March 1819, James Dinsmore and John Perry provided the BOV with a report of several "bold good Springs" located at distances between 1100 and 1260 yards from Pavilion VII. They further stated that the springs were between six and seventy-five feet above the elevation of the Pavilion VII itself [12]. Thompson suggests Dinsmore and Perry may have been trying to determine if the water could be supplied by the force of gravity in a pressurized system [13]. However, the land between the Village and the Mountain was not a continuous downhill slope. And though wooden pipes could theoretically be pressurized using weight of water and maintaining tight joints between the timbers, the sheer number of joints required for a half-mile-long system located a remote area of central Virginia made a pressurized unlikely.

Payments for hauling and boring logs as well as trenching and laying pipe show up in university records between fall 1819 and throughout 1820. By the summer of 1820, Brockenbrough reported to Jefferson: "our pipe borers are laying down the logs...at the end of which is a reservoir, 6 by 7 feet & 5 feet deep, from whence I take water." The distances Brockenbrough reports included both a "covered ditch" as well as the logs that were simply "laid down" and given the cumulative distance, suggest that this reservoir was not located on the Academical Village in 1820 [14].

Neither the springs that were tapped nor the system of timber pipes that had been installed by the summer of 1820 were located on property owned by the university. Recognizing this, the BOV charged Jefferson and John Hartwell Cocke with purchasing at "fair valuation or reasonable price" the land situated between the Village and Mountain parcels at the same March 1819 meeting when Perry and Dinsmore reported on the mountain springs [15]. As the buildings of the Academical Village developed throughout the 1820s, the water system also grew also in complexity. Payments for casks of Roman cement as well as for digging and constructing subterranean cisterns appear in university records in 1821 and 1822. However, by summer 1824, shortly after the Rotunda was surmounted by its Delorme dome, Brockenbrough complained to Jefferson of the "present defective arrangement for the supply" of water and proposed several new strategies for dealing with the situation [16].

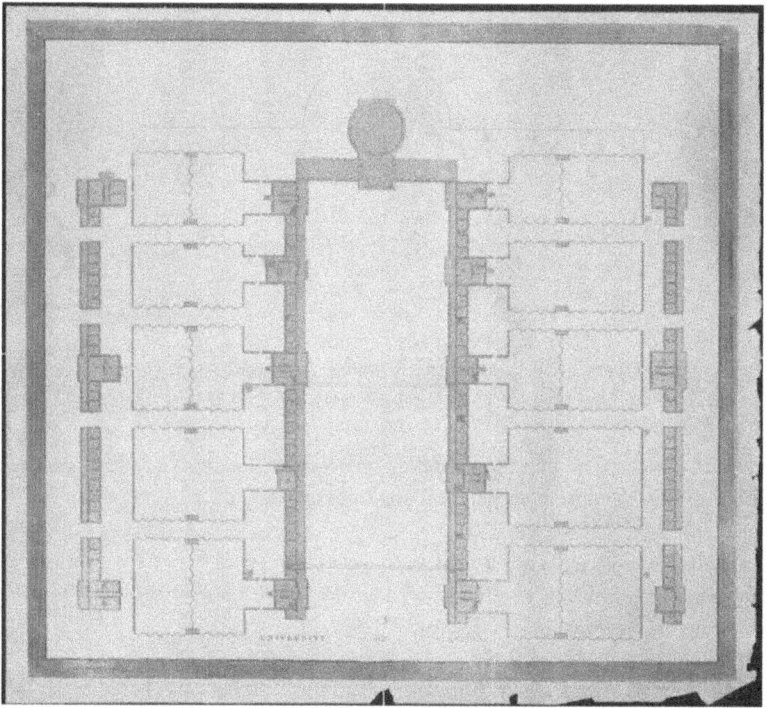

Figure 2: Engraving of the University of Virginia, showing locations of possible cisterns (the circles behind Pavilions II, V, VIII, IX, and X). 1825. University of Virginia Special Collections.

Water for the University: An Early History of the University of Virginia's Water supply, 1817-1885

Brockenbrough's Protosystem

Though Arthur Brockenbrough had been working on the construction of the university including its water supply since 1819, letters and accounts from the early 1820s suggest he was primarily executing Jefferson's water-supply vision. By 1824 however, the aging Jefferson coupled with the reality that students would finally arrive in the spring of 1825, led Brockenbrough to be increasingly vocal. In his 1824 letter to Jefferson, Brockenbrough proposed construction of two reservoirs to be located in the two north corners of the Rotunda attic. He suggested they be fed by a much larger reservoir on the university owned mountain, such that the weight of the water could "propel itself with as much power as an engine would supply" [17]. Now that the university buildings were nearly complete, Brockenbrough's primary concern was fire. Water for cooking and cleaning could come from the cisterns. His fear was that the "ensurance (sic) on the buildings" would be too great without a more comprehensive water system. Brockenbrough additionally stressed to Jefferson that university needed to finally purchase the 100 acres of land laying between the Mountain and the Village (see Fig 3). A lack of robust funds had delayed purchase of this important parcel since it was first contemplated by the BOV in 1819. In April 1825 – the month after arrival of the first 123 students – Jefferson pleaded with individual members of the Board to acquire the land before it was "forever lost" [18]. By May 1825, the parcels were at last acquired.

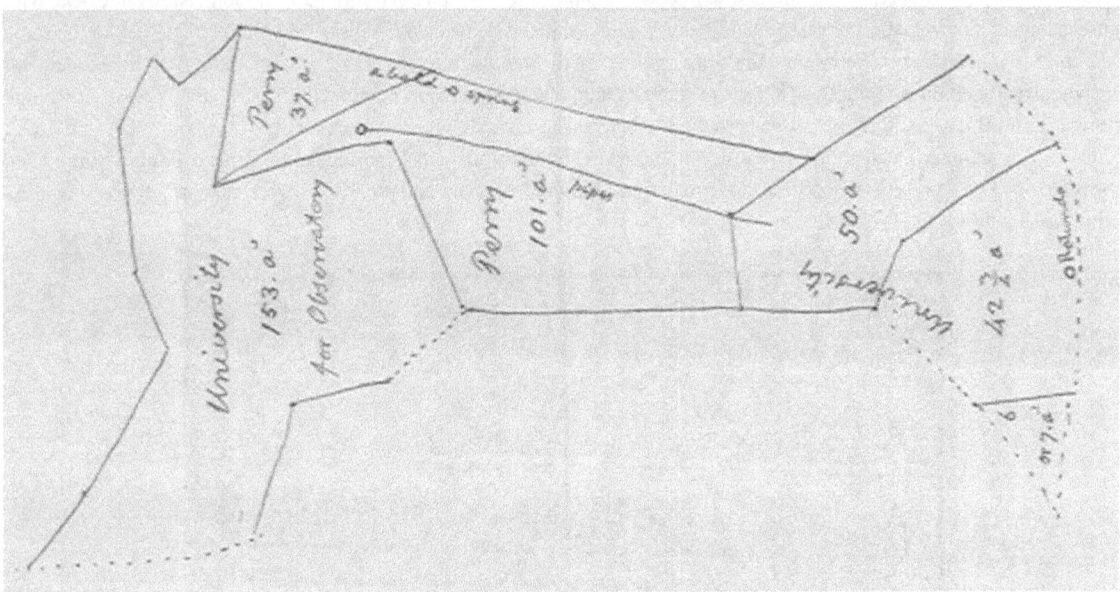

Figure 3: Lands owned by the University and John Perry. Thomas Jefferson. 1825. University of Virginia Special Collections. Note the "bold spring" and "pipes" located on Perry's tract. [19].

One year later and with less than two months to live, Jefferson described the dismal state of the water system in a letter to his friend and fellow supervising committee member John Cocke:

> "the wells and water fail…. the pipes which bring water to our cisterns must be repaired. they have rotted from too shallow covering originally. no log should lie less than 3. feet deep. this will cost more than I should be willing to risk on my own opinion. yet I believe it must be done, and immediately" [20].

In addition to their shallow depth, it appears the original timber pipes had not been bored by an individual with proper training in that unique skill set. Jefferson did not live to see changes to his protosystem; he died on July 4, 1826.

With Jefferson dead, Brockenbrough's primary liaison to the board became John Cocke. For unknown reasons, Brockenbrough modified his plan for updates to the water system from those he submitted to Jefferson in 1824. In a letter to Cocke in August, Brockenbrough proposed additional supply from the mountain as well as construction of a large cistern in his yard on Monroe Hill, "being the highest situation near the University." Brockenbrough additionally informed Cocke of an inquiry he made to Sellers & Pennock of Philadelphia with the goal of purchasing a fire engine and hose. It is possible that he abandoned the idea of pressurized water from reservoirs in the Rotunda's attic given that the building was largely complete by summer 1826 [21]. Within a year, new pipes had been laid from the Mountain to Monroe Hill, the Hydraulion engine (Fig. 4) arrived and was tested, and a large new cistern was being prepared near his house on Monroe Hill. By 1831, when Brockenbrough retired from the university, he had purchased additional hose, swivel screws, and hydrant cocks from Sellers & Pennock and continued to improve the cisterns and timber supply pipes.

Figure 4: Hydraulion by Sellers & Pennock, Philadelphia, Engraving, c. 1817-1828. Library of Congress.

Early Waterworks

Throughout the 1830s and 1840s, the university's water supply was increased by the deliberate harvesting of rainwater from buildings' roofs. Additional cisterns helped store this rainwater and were located on the east side of the Rotunda as well as the east side of the lawn. But even these additional sources of water and storage were insufficient for the growing university, especially so after construction of the huge Rotunda annex in the early 1850s (Fig. 5).

Water for the University: An Early History of the University of Virginia's Water supply, 1817-1885

Figure 5: UVA Rotunda with Annex (to the right). Photograph taken from the northeast looking southwest. The pond was located on the west side. University of Virginia Special Collections.

Ellet's Waterworks

Following completion of the Rotunda Annex, the Board of Visitors first engaged engineer Frederick Erdman (1854) and then engineer Charles Ellet (1856) to determine the "best means of providing an ample supply of water to the University" [22]. Ellet's survey includes the location of springs, streams, roads, and buildings from the Village to the east and the Mountain to the west. It additionally contains spot elevations: "marked + and − showing the difference of level in feet compared with the lowest stone step in front of the Rotunda" (see Fig. 6). On this survey, faint red linework can be seen running parallel to and just south of the natural watercourse. The red lines originate from what appears to be a large reservoir to the far left (west) on the map. Just north of the cemetery, the red line splits into two, with one heading toward Monroe Hill (labeled McCoy's) and the other terminating at a pond just east of the newly constructed Rotunda Annex. These lines represent the pressurized iron pipes of Ellet's system which filled the cistern at Monroe Hill as well as a new pond adjacent to the Annex.

In addition to the new iron supply pipes, some of the water from the new pond was pumped by a steam engine located in the Rotunda Annex into two seven-thousand-gallon tanks located in the Rotunda attic. The pressurized system imagined by Brockenbrough some thirty years earlier was finally realized. Thompson suggests the pump was a "Number 5 Worthington" and references a notebook by Professor John Staige Davis who described the pump:

> "[it] delivers about four gallons a stroke. Its ordinary rate is 35 strokes a minute. It consequently delivers about 5000 gallons an hour. It consumes 100 lbs anthracite coal or 200 lbs coke (5 bushels) per hour. It may be worked at 120 strokes per minute (delivering 28800 gallons per hour) or as slowly as 2 strokes per minute. The daily supply of water from the spring was originally estimated at 12,000 gallons and the probably daily consumption at 8000 gallons [23]."

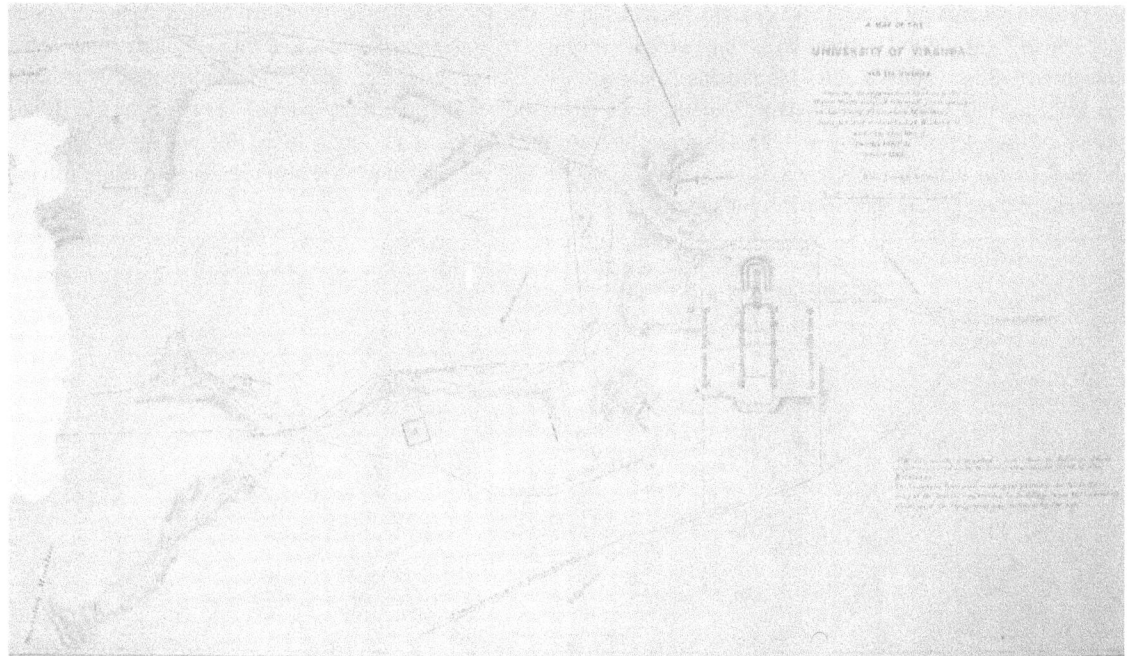

Figure 6: Map "showing the approximate location of water works" between the mountain (left) and village (right). Charles Ellet and S.A. Richardson. 1856. University of Virginia Special Collections.

Manufacturers of water pumping engines like Worthington often sought out franchises for municipal systems in the mid-19th century. It is unclear if the pump in the Rotunda was the result of such an arrangement or simply purchased directly by the University. The pipes, pond, pump, and Rotunda attic reservoirs were all installed by 1859 and that year's annual report boasts that: "for the first time…the University is supplied with water in quantities which it hoped will prove sufficient for all its purposes, and so arranged as to constitute a very complete and efficient protection against fire" [24].

Peyton's Waterworks

Within a handful of years however, the Board's annual report contained less hope. The tanks in the Rotunda attic leaked, first on the building's walls and partitions and eventually on many of the books themselves. "Plastering of the lectures halls below was loosened" by the leaking water [25]. The report additionally considered the steam engine's proximity to lecture rooms as problematic and noted the University's entirely defective system of sewerage. Two years later in 1868 the BOV reported that the Rotunda tanks "are exerting an injurious influence on the building" and proposed a new supply of water by means of a "suitable reservoir on Observatory Mountain" [26].

Green Peyton, a graduate of the civil engineering department of UVA, was named Proctor and Superintendent of Buildings and Grounds in 1867. He moved to implement the BOV's recommendations by constructing a reservoir high enough on the mountain so as to distribute water throughout the University "by gravity alone" and without reliance on the steam pump or Rotunda roof tanks. The reservoir, the outlines of which still exists in a ravine on the mountain, could hold nearly 2-million gallons of water. Additionally, the outlet pipe contained a chamber filled with 15 inches of charcoal as a means of basic filtration. A new distribution main connected the reservoir to some six fire hydrants as well as a distribution system to many of the individual buildings (see Fig. 7) [27].

Water for the University: An Early History of the University of Virginia's Water supply, 1817-1885

For reasons not entirely clear, the water tanks remained in the attic of the Rotunda. Additional leakage damaged books in the library again in 1873. An outbreak of typhoid fever caused by contamination of a well from a leaking sewer and a drought in 1881 prompted the BOV to provide Peyton with a $1000 for securing additional water supply. Peyton used the funds to "make new connections with the Rotunda tanks and refitting the steam-pump,… keeping the old [Ellet] system as a supplement to the new" [28]. Thompson suggests the Ellet era water supply to the Rotunda's pond relied on different springs than Peyton's reservoir located higher on the mountain and may have also been used to help flush the nascent sewerage system shown on Peyton's map.

Figure 7: Map of the University of Virginia showing water works (blue lines), sewers yellow lines), hydrants, fire plugs, stop cocks, and waste cocks. Green Peyton. 1870. University of Virginia Special Collections.

Bowditch's Sewer and Waterworks

The increasing university population and a growing awareness of the connection between sewerage and health caused the Board to act again. They resolved, in 1882, to "employ E.W. Bowditch or some other Sanitary Engineer…to furnish plans and specifications for the proper sewerage of the grounds and for a sufficient water supply for this purpose, and the protection of the buildings against fire" [29]. Bowditch would be supervised by William M. Thornton of the engineering department. His report was complete by late 1883 and the university secured funding by the next year to construct a system of sewers. A second report was issued in 1884 and focused on impounding a stream in the Ragged Mountains – some four miles west of the Academical Village and skirting Observatory Mountain to the south – rather than continue to increase supply using sources located on university land.

This larger water plan was executed in early 1885 as an ordinance in conjunction with the City of Charlottesville. A rock filled, earthen dam 45 feet in height and 470 feet long was to be constructed in the Ragged Mountains. The city would operate and maintain the reservoir and its 10" diameter water main and the university would pay one-seventh of the construct costs plus an annual users fee. Contracts were executed and the dam and supply line were complete before the end of the year. Even with this large, remote reservoir, growing demand within the city caused the university's supply to remain unreliable. Peyton's reservoir on Observatory Hill was thus kept as both backup and an emergency supply. By 1891 the University installed its own 6" diameter main line for its exclusive use. By the first decade of the 20th century the entire reservoir complex was expanded, increasing the reservoir's capacity from 190 million to 620 million gallons (Fig. 8) [30].

Figure 8: Photograph of the recently completed 1908 concrete dam at Ragged Mountain. University of Virginia Holsinger Collection.

Conclusion

The seven decades of water history covered by this paper – from Jefferson and Brockenbrough's protosystems in the 1810s and 1820s to Ellet, Peyton, and Bowditch's increasingly complex waterworks in the latter 19th century – parallel developments in cities throughout the United States during this period. Melosi describes the nationwide shift between 1830 and 1880 as moving from individual reliance on wells and watercourses to complex municipal enterprises dependent on specialized engineering and new powers of taxation [31]. The size and complexity of university's waterworks has continued to accelerate following the bacteriological revolution and urbanization of the late 19th and early 20th centuries in order to ensure "the most abundant supply of that element [water] for ever" [32].

Water for the University: An Early History of the University of Virginia's Water supply, 1817-1885

Acknowledgements

I am grateful to Steve Thompson who first introduced me to his excellent work on UVA's early water systems by way a guest lecture he delivered to my *History of Building Technology* course in spring 2016 [33].His material provided an overall scaffolding for this paper and has led to many fascinating exchanges over the years.

References

[1] Letter from Thomas Jefferson to individual Board of Visitor Members. April 15, 1825. *Thomas Jefferson Papers*. University of Virginia Special Collections.

[] M. Melosi. *The Sanitary City: Environmental Services in Urban America from Colonial Times to the Present.* Abridged. Pittsburgh: University of Pittsburgh Press. 2008. See in particular chapters 1 and 4. The words "protosystem" and "waterworks" in this paper follow Martin Melosi's terminology in his book *The Sanitary System*. "Protosystem" connotes a city's "original" water system while "waterworks" describes subsequent developments of later systems.

[3] Letter from Thomas Jefferson to L.W. Tazewell. January 5, 1805. *Thomas Jefferson Papers*. University of Virginia Special Collections. See also Wilson, Richard. *Thomas Jefferson's Academical Village,* p 7. Charlottesville: University of Virginia Press. 2009.

[4] F. Grizzard. "Documentary History of the Construction of the Buildings at the University of Virginia, 1817-1828." 1996. Grizzard's dissertation is not formally published. Rather it is available electronically. Citations to extensive primary sources will refer to his Chapter and *Section Titles* as well as footnote numbers, enabling subsequent readers digital access to the primary material. For Grizzard's organization of the early construction as a series of annual building campaigns, see the *Introduction*. Regarding the initial land purchase, see Chapter 1, *The Land Deal*. Hereafter referred to as Grizzard 1996. http://xtf.lib.virginia.edu/xtf/view?docId=grizzard/uvaGenText/tei/grizzard.xml

[5] Grizzard 1996, footnote 1.

[6] N. Takahashi and G. Anderson. "Downhill/Uphill: Between a Mountain and an Academical Village." *Landscript, Vol 5. Material Culture: Assembling and Disassembling Landscapes*. Jane Elizabeth Hutton, editor. 1997. Page 26.

[7] Grizzard, (Note 4).

[8] S. Thompson. "Developmental History of the University's Water Supply System." Dated July 1, 2015. Steve shared his 33-page document with me via email in 2016. I tried for years, unsuccessfully, to get Steve to publish his excellent work. Given the document's inaccessibility to researchers, wherever possible I cite Steve's primary sources.

[9] Takahashi and Anderson, (Note 6).

[10] *Minutes from the Board of Visitors of the University of Virginia*. February 26, 1819, p 10.

[11] Grizzard, **(Note 4)**, footnote 70.

[12] Grizzard, **(Note 4)**, footnote 221.

[13] Thompson, (Note 8).

[14] Grizzard, **(Note 4)**, footnote 347.

[15] Grizzard, **(Note 4)**, footnote 224.

[16] Grizzard, **(Note 4)**, footnote 639.

[17] ibid.

[18] Letter from Thomas Jefferson, (Note 1).

[19] ibid.

[20] Grizzard, **(Note 4)**, footnote 751.

[21] Grizzard, **(Note 4)**, footnote 793.

[22] *Minutes from the Board of Visitors of the University of Virginia*. June 26, 1854, pp 14 and 250.

[23] Index Rerum belonging to John Staige Davis, 1846. Accession #1912-a, Special Collections, University of Virginia.

[24] Annual Report of the Rector and Visitors of the University of Virginia, 1859, p 37.

[25] J. G. Waite Associates and University of Virginia, *The Rotunda, University of Virginia. Historic Structure Report.* 2008. Page 61.

[26] Annual Report of the Rector and Visitors of the University of Virginia, 1866, pp 4, 11 and Minutes of the Board of Visitors of the University of Virginia, June 27 1868, pp 225 and 227.
[27] *Engineering News*. Vol. 9, 21 January 1882, p 24.
[28] Annual Report of the Rector and Visitors of the University of Virginia, 1882, p 6.
[29] Minutes of the Board of Visitors of the University of Virginia, June 26 1882, p 140.
[30] M. Yengling. *Ragged Mountain Reservoir Dams Complex. Historic American Engineering Record.* 2011. See p 7ff.
[31] Melosi, (Note 2).
[32] Letter from Thomas Jefferson, (Note 1).
[33] Thompson, (Note 7).

The gap between theory, practice and regulations in design criteria for iron and steel structures in 19th century France: the example of train sheds

Hannah Franz [1,2], Mario Rinke [3], Emilie Lepretre [1] and Lamine Dieng [1]
[1] Université Gustave Eiffel, Bouguenais, France
[2] AREP Group, Paris, France
[3] University of Antwerp, Antwerpen, Belgium

Abstract

In the 19th century, the concept for designing metallic structures was to compare the stresses resulting from the loads with a working stress, a fraction of the ultimate strength of the material. The choice of the working stress depended mainly on the experience and theoretical knowledge of designers as early regulations left a lot of discretion to engineers. This paper traces the evolution of French design criteria used in practice for elements made of wrought iron or mild steel, working in tension or compression, based on an extensive survey of the French literature of the 19th century and the beginning of the 20th century. These design criteria are compared with original design reports of train sheds, which show that designers used working stresses higher than recommended in the literature and ensured buckling safety through constructive measures instead of calculations.

Introduction

The basic principle of structural design is to compare the internal forces of a structure with the capacity of the material constituting it. In the 19th century, the increasing use of cast and wrought iron, later of mild steel, as construction materials, went along with the development of the theory of structures. Kurrer's *History of the Theory of Structures* detailed the evolution of structural analysis methods, which allowed the calculation of internal stresses resulting from external loads [1]. As for the material's capacity, Timoshenko's *History of Strength of Materials* gave a historical overview of experimental studies on mechanical properties of materials, such as the ultimate or the yield strength, and of the theories deriving allowable stresses from those experiments [2]. In practice, safety factors were introduced to consider unknowns such as calculation errors, material inhomogeneities, imperfections related to manufacturing and construction, dimensional errors, etc. Schueremans et al. recently summarized design practices for iron and steel structures in 19th century Western Europe, mostly based on official regulations [3]. However, the choice of the allowable stress, the so-called *working stress*, depended a lot on the experience and theoretical knowledge of the designer and the 'risk-willingness' of the client. Early regulations gave little guidance [4]. The discrepancies between design criteria recommended in the literature or regulations and the ones effectively used in practice remain widely unexplored.

This paper aims to trace the evolution of French design criteria for wrought iron and mild steel based on an extensive survey of the French literature of the 19th century and the beginning of the 20th century. Beyond regulations, the survey draws on construction treatises, civil engineering periodicals and reports from the French Society of civil engineers. Some case studies of the literature highlighted the working stresses used for single constructions, such as the Garabit viaduct in France [5] or a dome in the Vienna Hofburg [6]. To illustrate more representatively the working stresses used in practice, this paper develops insight in the design criteria used for a large family of structures, namely train sheds. About 175 train sheds were constructed in France before 1950, 40% of which are still in service [7]. Train sheds are particularly relevant to study the gap between theory and practice, as regulations only came more than half a century after the first metallic

The gap between theory, practice and regulations in design criteria for iron and steel structures in 19th century France: the example of train sheds

train shed was built for the Gare St-Lazare in Paris in 1843 [8]. The first French regulation on metallic structures, published in 1869, concerned only bridges while train sheds were first covered in 1902 [9]. Archive materials on train sheds are centrally located at the National Center for Historical Archives of the French railway company SNCF in Le Mans, France [10]. Original design reports of extant train sheds have been gathered and design criteria used for the calculations compared with commonly recommended working stresses at the time of their construction.

Figure 1: Example of an existing historical train shed: Gare de Perpignan (built in 1896) before renovation of 2013. Photo: SNCF-AREP. D. Boy de la Tour.

Working stresses for elements in tension

Literature review

From the first half of the 19th century, the limit of 6 kg/mm² became the default working stress for iron, for elements working in tension. This value was first recommended by Navier in his *Résumé des Leçons* published in 1826 [11]. Poncelet, in his *Mécanique industrielle* published in 1829, set the same limit of 6 kg/mm², followed by Morin in his *Leçons de mécanique pratique* published in 1853 [12]. According to Vierendeel in his monograph on iron and steel construction published later in 1902, it was thanks to Poncelet and Morin that the limit of 6 kg/mm² was adopted by the French administration and became widely used in practice [13].

Authors often defined the working stress as a fraction of the ultimate strength or yield strength of the material. The ultimate strength remained for a long time the reference to define the working stress, mostly because the ultimate strength was easier to measure than the yield strength [14]. In 1826, Navier defined the working stress based on an average ultimate strength of 40 kg/mm² obtained from a comprehensive review of tensile tests conducted by other scientists. His safety factor of about 6 leading to a working stress of 6-7 kg/mm² became standard thereafter [15].

Recommended working stresses depended on the load combination used to calculate the stresses in the structure. Dead loads result from the weight of the construction, live loads correspond to the weight of trains, vehicles or pedestrians and climatic loads include snow and wind. In today's Eurocodes [16], dead loads are called "permanent actions" while live loads and climatic loads are grouped under the name of "variable actions". "Accidental actions" refer to explosions or impacts. In the literature of the 19th century, the words "permanent", "variable" and "accidental" were used in a much less straightforward manner. Holzer also showed that the refinement of load assumptions varied depending on their nature [17]. Several authors defined the working stress as a limit for "permanent" stresses, such as Bresse in 1859, but then some applied this working stress to examples including climatic loads, such as Ardant in 1840, or accidental loads, such as Collignon in 1869 and Brune in 1888 [18]. Navier indicated a limit of 6 to 7 kg/mm² for dead loads and 8 to 10 kg/mm² for stresses resulting from dead and "accidental" loads, without detailing their nature. The limit was set higher for combinations including several types of loads because they generated a lower level of uncertainty for the maximum calculated stress.

Other references were more explicit regarding load assumptions. The working stress of 6 kg/mm², recommended by the first French regulation on metallic road bridges published in 1869 and its revision published in 1877, applied to stresses resulting from dead loads and live loads [19]. In the first edition of his works *Stability of Constructions*, published in 1886, Flamand mentioned a formula for the working stress proposed by Séjourné:

$$\sigma_{lim} = \frac{6}{1 - 0{,}4 \frac{\sigma_{min}}{\sigma_{max}}} \text{ kg/mm}^2$$

σ_{min} was the minimum stress and σ_{max} the maximum stress in the element considered, depending on load combinations [20]. Vierendeel calculated that with this formula the working stress varied between 6 kg/mm² if the dead load was close to zero and 10 kg/mm² for permanent loads only. In the case of "light-weight roof structures, for which the dead load is low compared to accidental loads related to wind, snow or people", the working stress would lie between 6 and 7 kg/mm² [21]. The regulation for metallic bridges released in 1891 also gave formulae calculating the working stress depending on the ratio between live and dead loads, leading to values between 6 and 9 kg/mm² [22]. The first regulation for train sheds, released in 1902, recommended a working stress for iron of 8 kg/mm², corresponding to load combinations including dead load, snow and wind [23]. The next revision of the regulation on metallic bridges, published in 1915, introduced a wider range of load combinations including live loads, snow, wind and temperature [24].

The working stress of 6 kg/mm² for iron was a default value. This limit could be increased according to the type of structure, the quality of the material or the experience of the contractor. Poncelet stated that "contractors specialised in the construction of iron suspension bridges, guided by a long experience and sure of a consistent manufacturing" may use a higher stress limit. Regulations also explicitly allowed engineers to choose higher working stresses according to their individual judgement. Brune stated that "the safety load commonly accepted for iron is of 6 kg/mm² for public constructions, 8 kg/mm² for private constructions, and 10 kg/mm² for industrial constructions". Ardant indicated working stresses between 6 and 12 kg/mm² "depending on the quality" of the material. Morin allowed a working stress of 8 kg/mm² for roof trusses, arguing that the rigidity of connections and the friction of girders on their supports, which were not considered for determining the stresses, played in favour of stability. Moreover, Morin stated that roof trusses were made of "selected materials". The same idea was presented in the "General study on iron roof structures" of the periodical *Nouvelles Annales de la Construction* in 1863, thus recommending working stresses between 8 and 10 kg/mm² [25].

The gap between theory, practice and regulations in design criteria for iron and steel structures in 19th century France: the example of train sheds

In the 1880s, authors began to propose working stresses for steel. The recommended values in the theoretical literature varied more than those for iron, which may be due to fluctuations in the carburization level of the steel. Flamand suggested applying Séjourné's formula to steel, with a 50% increase compared to iron. The International Congress for construction processes, gathered in Paris during the World Exhibition of 1889, favoured an increase of 40%. Brune recommended working stresses between 6 and 10 kg/mm² for iron and 15 and 20 kg/mm² for steel. Résal, in his construction treaty published in 1892, gave working stresses between 5 and 8 kg/mm² for iron and between 7 and 9 kg/mm² for steel. The formulae in the bridge regulation of 1891 led to working stresses between 8 and 12 kg/mm² for steel. The train shed regulation of 1902 prescribed 10 kg/mm² [26]. In his lecture on material strength published in 1900, Novat stayed more conservative with recommended working stresses between 7 and 10 kg/mm² [27]. Flamand, in the third edition of his works *Stability of constructions* in 1909, cited both Séjourné's formula and the regulation of 1891, thus clearly showing that engineers remained free in their choices [28]. In his lecture on metallic bridges published in 1917, Résal stated that in practice a working stress of 12 kg/mm² for steel was commonly used. The bridge regulation of 1915 prescribed that stresses resulting from dead and live loads should not exceed 12 kg/mm² while stresses including also the effect of wind should stay below 12.5 kg/mm² [29].

Table 1 summarises the sources discussed above and indicates in which engineering school the authors were teaching, to enhance the potential impact of their knowledge in practice.

Table 1: List of sources used to establish the evolution of working stresses of iron and steel between 1820 and 1930.

Publication year	Author	Engineering school	σ_{lim}(iron) [kg/mm²]	σ_{lim}(steel) [kg/mm²]
1826	NAVIER C-L	Ecole des Ponts et Chaussées	6-10	-
1840	ARDANT P.-J.	Ecole d'Application de l'Artillerie et du Génie (Metz)	6-12	-
1841	PONCELET V.-J.	Ecole d'Application de l'Artillerie et du Génie (Metz)	6	-
1853	MORIN A.	Conservatoire des Arts et Métiers	6-8	-
1857	BRESSE J.	Ecole des Ponts et Chaussées	6	-
1863	MATHIEU E.	-	8-10	-
1869	COLLIGNON E.	Ecole des Ponts et Chaussées	5-6	-

1869	Circulaire du 15 juin 1869 relative aux épreuves à faire subir aux ponts métalliques destinés aux voies de terre		6	-
1877	Circulaire du 9 juillet 1877 relative aux épreuves des ponts métalliques		6	-
1886	FLAMANT A.	Ecole Centrale des Arts et Manufactures, Ecole des Ponts et Chaussées	6-7	9-10.5
1888	BRUNE E.	Ecole des Beaux-Arts	6-10	15-20
1891	Circulaire du 29 août 1891 relative aux épreuves des ponts métalliques		6-9	8-12
1892	RESAL J.	Ecole des Ponts et Chaussées	5-8	7-9
1900	NOVAT J.	Société d'enseignement professionnel du Rhone	6-8	7-10
1902	Règlement du 25 janvier 1902 sur les halles à voyageurs et à marchandises des chemins de fer		8	10
1909	FLAMANT A.	Ecole Centrale des Arts et Manufactures, Ecole des Ponts et Chaussées	6-9	8-12
1915	Circulaire du 8 janvier 1915 relative aux épreuves des ponts métalliques		-	12-13
1928	ARAGON E.	-	6-8	8-12

Data from design reports of train sheds

To complement the values from the theoretical debate with those used in practice, the working stresses used for the design of nine train sheds built between 1852 and 1931 were collected, either from original design reports preserved in the archives of SNCF or from articles of the periodical *Annales des Ponts et Chaussées* (APC) [30]. This journal regularly published short technical and economic data as well as technical drawings regarding major structures such as train sheds. Table 2 presents the collected values of the working stress, or of the maximum calculated stress (*), when the working stress was not explicitly indicated.

The gap between theory, practice and regulations in design criteria for iron and steel structures in 19th century France: the example of train sheds

Table 2: List of train sheds for which working stresses were collected.

Date of construction	Train shed	Code	Contractor	Source	σ_{lim}(iron) [kg/mm²]	σ_{lim}(steel) [kg/mm²]
1852	Paris St-Lazare (halle Flachat)	PSL	Joly	APC, 1855	7.6*	-
1868	Bayonne	BYN	Rigolet	Arch. SNCF, 1868	9.53*	-
1869	Paris Austerlitz	PAZ	Schneider	APC, 1871	6	-
1879	Hendaye	HND	A. Moisant	Arch. SNCF, 1880	6	-
1892	Marseille St Charles	MSC	Sénès et Arnal	Arch. SNCF, 1892	-	14.38*
1898	Bordeaux St Jean	BSJ	Daydé et Pillé	Arch. SNCF, 1896	-	13
1902	Bédarieux	BED	Daydé et Pillé	Arch. SNCF, 1902	-	11
1908	St Germain des Fossés	SGF	unknown	Arch. SNCF, 1908	-	12.62*
1931	Paris Gare de l'Est	PGE	Schmid, Bruneton, Morin	Arch. SNCF, 1929	-	13

Comparison between literature and design reports of train sheds

Figure 2 graphically brings together the working stresses obtained from the literature and the values used for train shed designs. The bars show the lower and upper limit for the working stress proposed by various authors, while the dots indicate the working stresses used for specific train sheds. The 3-letter codes are referring to Table 2. These charts highlight that the default working stress for iron stayed quite constant throughout its period of use, while the upper limit fluctuated, and that the working stress recommended for steel varied much more than for iron. They also reveal that the working stress values used for train sheds were mostly above the upper limit recommended in the literature.

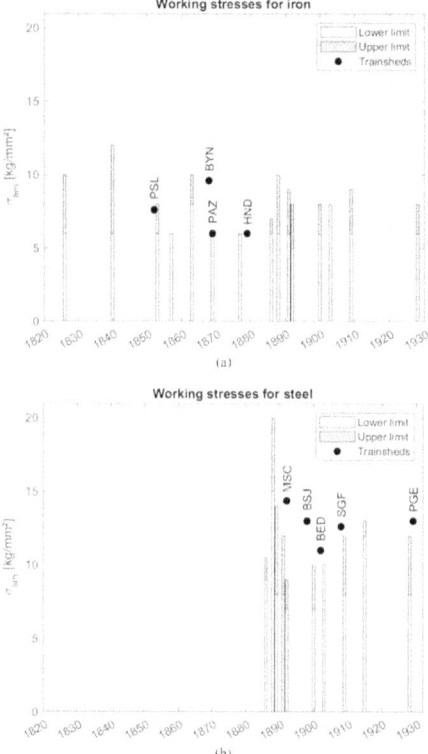

Figure 2: Evolution of the working stresses recommended in the literature for (a) iron and (b) steel between 1820 and 1930, compared with working stresses used for train sheds.

Working stresses for elements in compression

Unlike cast iron, the yield strength for wrought iron and mild steel was the same in compression and tension. However, elements working in compression were subjected to buckling and therefore necessitated a different approach to determine working stresses.

Evolution of the state of knowledge on buckling

The first studies on buckling of structural elements in compression date back to the 18th century. Around 1730, Van Musschenbroeck carried out experiments from which he concluded that the resistance of a column did not only depend on the material, but also on its geometry. In 1744, Euler developed a formulation of the critical load that a column could admit without bending [31]:

$$\sigma_{cr} = \frac{\pi^2 E}{\left(\frac{L}{r}\right)^2}$$

With σ_{cr} the critical stress, E the Young modulus, L the buckling length and r the radius of gyration, depending on the moment of inertia and the section of the bar. The ratio L/r defines the slenderness λ of a bar.

However, in further experiments, such as Hodgkinson's in 1840, instabilities occurred for compressive loads much lower than the critical load calculated by Euler. The idealized assumptions behind Euler's theory were unravelled progressively. Firstly, Euler assumed that bars were perfectly straight, with a load applied in a perfectly centred manner. The influence of geometrical imperfections (eccentricity of the load or initial curvature) was described at the beginning of the 19th century, for example by Young in 1807 and Navier in 1826. Secondly, Euler's formula necessitated bars to remain elastic. Navier in 1826 defined ranges of slenderness for which Euler's formula was valid but Lamarle was the first in 1845 to link this validity domain to the yield strength. The first theories of inelastic buckling were proposed by Engesser and Considère in 1889. Finally, Euler's theory was valid only for a homogeneous material. The fluctuation of the strength within the section as well as the residual stresses were accounted for from the 1950s onwards [32].

As an alternative to Euler's formula, many authors strived to propose an estimate of the critical stress that would be more in line with experimental data. Instead of defining the equilibrium like Euler, they conceptualised the maximum axial stress of a compressed bar as a combination of compression and bending. The bending stress was derived by assuming geometrical imperfections or by assimilating it to a stress due to the critical load. The resulting formula yielded:

$$\sigma_{\lim} = \frac{a}{1 + b\lambda^2}$$

Where a and b were constants, whose values could vary depending on ranges of slenderness. The first author to give such a formula was Tredgold in 1822. In the 1850s, several authors such as Schwarz, Gordon and Rankine proposed different approaches leading to a similar result. This formula was convenient to use and became very popular in the following decades, known mostly as Rankine's formula [33].

Euler's formula was rehabilitated in the 1880s, thanks to the experiments of Bauschinger and Tetmajer in Germany and Considère in France. They proved Euler's theory right for very slender elements when the experimental setup reflected theoretical boundary conditions. Tetmajer proposed to give up the unification of all results in a single formula as Rankine's formula tried to do. For intermediate slenderness values, Tetmajer described the maximum stress as a function of slenderness using a straight line, which became widely used in German-speaking countries [34].

Design criteria for buckling in France

As theoretical and empirical approaches regarding buckling were very diverse, the buckling design criteria recommended in construction treatises varied accordingly. In France, the first reference on which we can assume designers relied on for their design of iron columns is Navier's Résumé des Leçons from 1826. For large slenderness values, Navier recommended using Euler's formula with a safety factor of 4 to 5. For smaller slenderness values, he gave isolated experimental stresses [35]. In 1851, Love submitted a memorandum to the French Society of Civil engineers in which he presented the experiments of Tredgold and Hodgkinson. Based on those experiments, he proposed a Rankine-type formula, which, according to Buchetti in 1888, became prevalent in France until the end of the 19th century. Love did not recommend any safety factor but Buchetti indicated that Love's formula was to be reduced by a safety factor of 6 [36]. The first bridge regulations from 1869 and 1877 did not mention buckling. They recommended a working stress of 6 kg/mm² for iron, both in tension and in compression. At the end of the 1880s, several authors such as Flamand and Résal proposed Rankine-type formulas with different constants. Brune preferred the use of Euler's formula with a reduced modulus of elasticity E = 80 GPa instead of 210 GPa [37]. The 1891 bridge regulation was the first to require that "elements in compression be not exposed to buckling" but it did not indicate any method on how to ensure it. The same line was adopted by the 1902 train shed regulation. In 1915, the new regulation for bridges finally favoured a Rankine-type formula but it stayed quite vague, as it left engineers free to decide which constants to use [38]. Fig. 3 represents the buckling criteria proposed by the authors cited above.

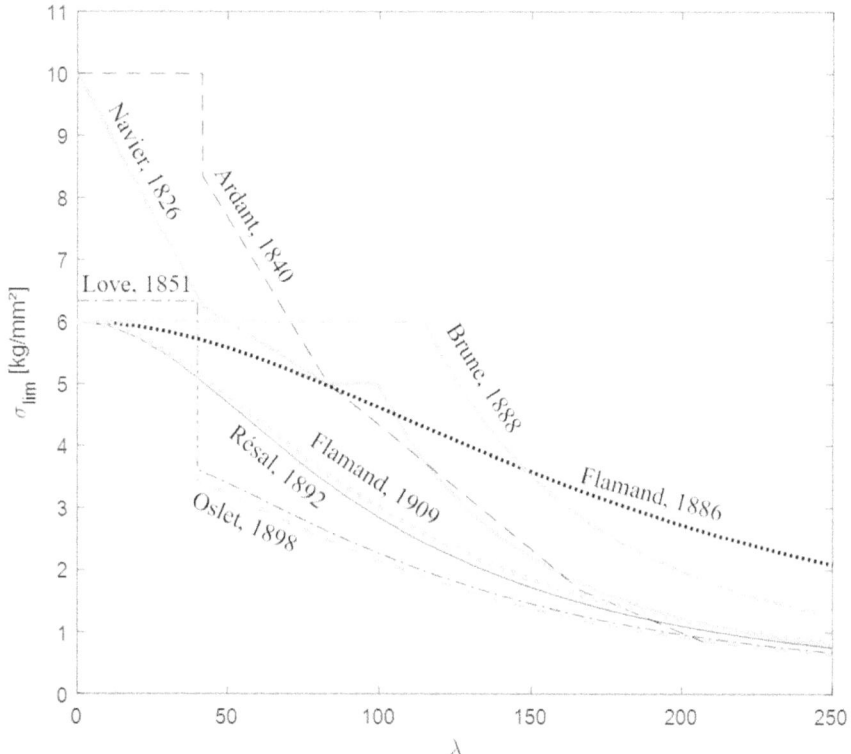

Figure 3: working stresses in compression as a function of slenderness λ in French literature

Buckling safety in practice

As pointed out by Gargiani in 2008, it was the search towards designing the "perfect column" that motivated engineers and physicists in the 18th and 19th centuries to progress in modelling the buckling problem. The acquired knowledge thus mostly benefited the design of structural columns. This was also reflected in the vocabulary used by authors dealing with buckling: in construction treatises, chapters dealing with buckling were usually entitled "Pièces chargées debout", literally "Standing members under loads". The risk of buckling for other elements working in compression, such as truss bars in bridges or roof structures, was neglected. Oslet, for instance, in his *Traité de charpente en fer* from 1898, referred to Love's formula for the design of columns only [39].

Several design reports of train sheds confirm this tendency. In a design report for the Gare de Marseille St-Charles from 1892, working stresses for Polonceau rafters in compression reached the extraordinarily high value of 14 kg/mm² while buckling was not discussed at all. In a design report from 1880 for the Gare d'Hendaye, also featuring Polonceau roof trusses, it was acknowledged that rafters could be subjected to buckling but their buckling length was reduced by clamping through the connected purlins. The slenderness of rafters was then low enough to disregard buckling, following Love's recommendations of 1851. In the design report for the Gare de Bordeaux St-Jean drafted by Daydé et Pillé in 1896,

The gap between theory, practice and regulations in design criteria for iron and steel structures in 19th century France: the example of train sheds

buckling was again not explicitly verified. For certain compression elements, though, the contractor pointed out that the maximum stress had been kept "voluntarily low".

For diagonal members in trusses, some authors argued that constructive measures were enough to ensure buckling safety. Collignon and Brune declared that truss diagonals were not exposed to buckling thanks to their clamped riveted connections. For elements in compression, other than columns, Novat recommended cross-sections shaped like an X, a T, a U or an L to avoid buckling [40].

Trussed beams used in train sheds for purlins or rafters also provide examples of constructive solutions. In some train sheds, one can observe differentiated cross-sections between truss bars in compression and in tension. For example, in the ridge purlin truss of the Gare d'Etampes, the diagonals in tension feature flat sections while the vertical bars in compression have a double L section (Fig. 4). As a common strategy to resist buckling, bars in compression were given a larger inertia than the bars in tension.

Figure 4: Trussed ridge purlin at the Gare d'Etampes (built in 1879). Photo: SNCF-AREP.

In trussed beams with diagonals crossing each other (Fig. 5 and 6), diagonals pointing upwards from the supports towards the centre of the beam usually work in compression while the diagonals pointing downwards work in tension. Compression diagonals therefore have a bigger cross-section. In the lower purlins of the Hall St-Etienne of the Gare de Lyon-Perrache, the compression diagonals close to the supports are reinforced by additional riveted plates (Fig. 5). In the purlins of the Gare de Montauban, compression diagonals consist of a double layer of flat plates while the tension diagonals only feature single flat plates (Fig. 6). Moreover, the intersection with tension diagonals provides another local stabilisation measure.

Figure 5: Trussed lower purlin at the Gare de Lyon-Perrache (halle St-Etienne, built in 1885). Photo: H. Franz.

Figure 6: Trussed upper purlin at the Gare de Montauban (built in 1903). Photo: SNCF-AREP.

The gap between theory, practice and regulations in design criteria for iron and steel structures in 19th century France: the example of train sheds

Conclusion

This paper traces the evolution of design criteria for wrought iron and mild steel structures in 19th century France and gives insight into the differences between literature, regulations, and practice. Authors of construction treatises or technical papers, who were often also professors in renowned engineering schools and practising engineers, recommended working stresses based either on experiments or on their practical knowledge. For elements in tension, the limits varied among authors, according to the load assumptions, the type of structure, or the quality of the material, and regulations followed the global trend. These approaches were compared with the design criteria used in practice for nine train sheds. Overall, designers chose working stresses higher than recommended. For elements in compression, design criteria were even more diverse in the literature, due to the theoretical struggle with the phenomenon of buckling, and regulations withdrew from the debate. Facing this disarray, designers ensured buckling safety with qualitative arguments and constructive measures, as it has been shown through examples of train sheds.

The presented debate among engineers did not only question the limits and strategies to be used for the design of structures but also the role of the designer within this process. What is surprising is that, while most narratives of the history of structures see an increasing influence of mechanical models and design procedures throughout the 19th century, the design practice still relied on an engineer as an experienced individual making deliberate design decisions. This apparent duality of a growing science and determinism on one side and an explorative practice and individual engineering agency on the other is a fascinating aspect of that period. This paper provides a basis for following research steps on French iron roofs designed and constructed in the 19th century.

Acknowledgments

This research project is funded by AREP, subsidiary of SNCF, and supported by the society Rails & Histoire.

References

[1] K.-E. Kurrer, *The History of the Theory of Structures: Searching for Equilibrium.* Berlin: John Wiley & Sons, 2018.
[2] S. Timoshenko, *History of Strength of Materials.* McGraw-Hill, 1953.
[3] L. Schueremans, H. Porcher, B. Rossi, I. Wouters, and E. Verstrynge, 'A Study on the Evolution in Design and Calculation of Iron and Steel Structures over the Mid 19th Century in Western and Central Europe', *International Journal of Architectural Heritage*, vol. 12, no. 3, pp. 320–333, Apr. 2018.
[4] F. Werner and J. Seidel, *Der Eisenbau: vom Werdegang einer Bauweise*. Berlin/Munich: Verlag für Bauwesen, 1992. p.72.
[5] Schueremans, (Note 3) p. 10.
[6] G. Hochreiner and G. Styhler-Aydin, '19th Century Iron Dome Structures in the Vienna Hofburg. An Insight into the Simplified Structural Assessment of that Period and Its Evaluation Using Modern Engineering Software', in *Structural Analysis of Historical Constructions*, R. Aguilar, D. Torrealva, S. Moreira, M. A. Pando, and L. F. Ramos, (Eds) Cham: Springer International Publishing, 2019, vol. 18, pp. 891–900.
[7] A. Emile and V. Veston, 'Les "Grandes Halles Voyageurs" : une architecture durable', *Patrimoine industriel,* no. 77, pp. 75–83, Dec. 2020.
[8] K. Bowie, *Les Grandes gares parisiennes au XIXe siècle*. Délégation à l'action artistique de la ville de Paris, 1987.
[9] B. Lemoine, *L'Architecture du fer: France ; XIX. siècle,* Collection milieux. Seyssel: Champ Vallon, 1986. p. 78.
[10] K. Bowie, 'La quête des sources : les différents types de documents et de fonds disponibles', *Revue d'histoire des chemins de fer*, no. 40, pp. 17–23, Nov. 2009.
[11] C. L. M. H. Navier, *Résumé des leçons données à l'Ecole des Ponts et Chaussées sur l'application de la mécanique à l'établissement des constructions et des machines*, 2nd ed. Paris: Carilian-Goeury, 1833. p. 118. (First published 1826).

[12] J.-V. Poncelet, *Introduction à la mécanique industrielle, physique ou expérimentale,* 2nd ed., Metz & Paris, 1841. pp. 356-357. (First published 1829) ; A. Morin, Leçons de mécanique pratique. Paris: Librairie de L. Hachette et Cie, 1853. pp. 52-53.

[13] A. Vierendeel, *La construction architecturale en fonte, fer et acier.* Louvain: Uystpruyst & Paris: Dunod, 1902. p. 404.

[14] E. Brune, *Cours de construction professé à l'Ecole des Beaux-Arts.* Paris: Librairie des Imprimeries réunies, 1888. p. 13.

[15] Navier, (Note 11) p. 19-34.

[16] British Standards Institution, *Eurocode 0: Basis of Structural Design.* London: BSI, Apr. 2002.

[17] S. M. Holzer, 'Kleine Geschichte der Schnee- und Windlastannahmen im 19. Jahrhundert', *Bautechnik*, vol. 83, no. 11, pp. 781–788, Nov. 2006.

[18] J. Bresse, *Cours de mécanique appliquée.* Ecole impériale des Ponts et Chaussées, 1857. p. 220 ; P.-J. Ardant, *Etudes théoriques et expérimentales sur l'établissement des charpentes à grande portée.* Metz: S. Lamort, 1840. p. 43, 84-87 ; E. Collignon, *Cours de mécanique appliquée aux constructions - Résistance des matériaux.* Paris: Dunod, 1869. pp. 34, 546-547 ; Brune, (Note 14) p. 13-14, p. 362.

[19] P. Regnauld, *Traité pratique de la construction des ponts et viaducs métalliques.* Paris: Dunod, 1870. pp. 539-543 ; Lemoine, (Note 9) p. 78.

[20] A. Flamand, *Stabilité des constructions. Résistance des matériaux.,* 1st ed. Paris: Librairie Polytechnique, 1886. pp. 227-230.

[21] Vierendeel, (Note 13) pp. 405-407.

[22] J. Résal, *Constructions métalliques, élasticité et résistance des matériaux : fonte, fer & acier.* Paris: Baudry et cie, 1892. pp. 526-534.

[23] 'Circulaire du ministre des travaux publics aux préfets du 25 janvier 1902 (Halles à voyageurs et à marchandises des chemins de fer)', in *Recueil de lois, ordonnances, décrets, réglements et circulaires concernant les différents services du Ministère des travaux publics - 2e série, Tome XII.* Imprimerie administrative Jousset, 1904, pp. 47–52.

[24] J. Résal, *Cours de ponts métalliques professé à l'Ecole nationale des Ponts et Chaussées.* Paris & Liège: Librairie Polytechnique Ch. Béranger, 1917. pp. 109-140.

[25] Poncelet, (Note 12) p. 357 ; Brune, (Note 14) p. 15 ; Ardant, (Note 18) p. 103 ; Morin, (Note 12) p. 402. E. Mathieu, 'Etude générale sur les charpentes en fer', *Nouvelles Annales de la Construction,* vol. 1, Jan. 1863, pp. 8–17.

[26] Flamand, (Note 20) p. 230 ; Vierendeel, (Note 13) pp. 414-416 ; Brune, (Note 14) p. 14 ; Résal, (Note 22) pp. 520-521, p. 532 ; Circulaire 1902, (Note 23) p. 50.

[27] J. Novat, *Cours pratique de résistance des matériaux professé à la Société d'enseignement professionnel du Rhône.* Paris: Librairie Polytechnique Ch. Béranger, 1900. p. 28.

[28] A. Flamand, *Stabilité des constructions. Résistance des matériaux.,* 3rd ed. Paris: Librairie Polytechnique, 1909. pp. 243-248.

[29] Résal, (Note 24) p. 112, 118.

[30] 'Note n°121: Sur les combles du chemin de fer de l'Ouest (rive gauche), à Paris', *Annales des Ponts et Chaussées,* 3e série, 1855, 2e semestre, pp. 81-85.
L. Sévène, 'Note n°1 : Sur la nouvelle gare des voyageurs du chemin de fer d'Orléans, à Paris', Annales des Ponts et Chaussées, 5e série, 1871, 1er semestre, pp. 1-8 ; SNCF Archives, Design reports :'Gare d'Hendaye, Comble de la Halle des Voyageurs, Calculs justificatifs', 9 January 1880 ; 'Gare de Marseille, Evaluation des charges', 1892 ; 'Gare définitive de Bordeaux St Jean, Halle métallique, Calculs justificatifs des résistances', 31 January 1896 ; 'Gare de Bédarieux, Halle métallique, Calculs justificatifs', May 1902 ; 'Gare de St Germain-des-Fossés, Halle à Voyageurs, Calcul des fermes', 22 June 1908 ; 'Chemins de fer de l'Est, Gare de Paris, Hall de banlieue, Calculs justificatifs', 17 mai 1929.

[31] R. Gargiani, 'La résistance des colonnes : expériences sur la qualité des matériaux et calculs de la forme parfaite au cours du XVIIIe siècle', in *La colonne: nouvelle histoire de la construction,* 1st ed., R. Gargiani, (Ed.) Lausanne: Presses Polytechniques et Universitaires Romandes, 2008.

[32] B. Nowak, *Die historische Entwicklung des Knickstabproblems und dessen Behandlung in den Stahlbaunormen.* Veröffentlichung des Instituts für Statik und Stahlbau der Technischen Hochschule Darmstadt, 1981, vol. Heft 35. pp. 21-25, 84, 144-148, 291-300.

[33] ibid., pp. 71-98.

[34] ibid, pp. 106-127.

[35] Navier, (Note 11) pp. 259-260.

[36] G.-H. Love, 'Mémoire n°27 : Résistance du fer et de la fonte, basée principalement sur les recherches expérimentales les plus récentes faites en Angleterre', *Mémoires de la Société des ingénieurs civils,* Vol. 4, 1851 ; J. Buchetti, *Manuel des constructions métalliques et mécaniques,* Paris, 1888. pp. 210-216.

[37] Flamand, (Note 20) pp. 443-445 ; Résal, (Note 22) pp. 507-511 ; Brune, (Note 14) pp. 183-197.

[38] Résal, (Note 22) p. 530 ; Circulaire 1902, (Note 23) p. 52 ; Résal, (Note 24) pp. 210-211.

[39] Gargiani, (Note 31); Flamand, (Note 28) p. VI ; G. Oslet, 'Traité de charpente en fer', in *Encyclopédie théorique & pratique des connaissances civiles & militaires.* Paris: Fanchon et Artus, 1898.

[40] Collignon, (Note 18) p. 563 ; Brune, (Note 14) p. 222 ; Novat, (Note 27) p. 241.

Timber Roof Structures of 19th-century Casinos in Switzerland

Kylie M. Russnaik
Institute of Construction History and Preservation (IDB), ETH Zurich, Switzerland

Abstract

In the early 19th century, the casino emerged as a new building type in Switzerland [1]. It originated from the Italian casino, a place of social gatherings for the bourgeoisie. In Switzerland these buildings were being founded by political, commercial, scientific, literary, and musical associations. Typically, the casinos had a foyer and a large hall with a span of up to 20 metres that was used for music, dance, or theatre. Corresponding to their neoclassical architecture these buildings mostly had a low-pitched hip roof. Their timber structures mark a break with the traditional Swiss carpentry of the baroque period. Five well-preserved casinos, erected between 1831 and 1876 are used as a case study to exemplify the changing building practices of this period in Switzerland. The buildings were documented by on-site surveys, using a laser scanner and hand measurements. Apart from analysing the construction systems of the roofs, a closer look at the surfaces of the timber elements gives insight into the tools that were used for the woodwork, such as the newly introduced circular saw. On this basis, the buildings are compared to each other as well as to the historic construction plans.

This study investigates the construction methods that were applied in the roof structures of the casinos and aims to understand their development from the early to the late 19th century.

Introduction

In the 19th century in Switzerland a large number of associations were being founded as new forms of sociability [2]. It is therefore not surprising that casinos emerged as a new building type satisfying the desire for a centre of social gatherings and entertainment. Up to now very little has been researched on the construction history of Swiss casinos. These buildings each had their particularities and evolved over the course of the 19th century. The casinos built in the first quarter of the 19th century are very typical examples of the then prevailing neoclassical architecture.

The casinos of Zurich (1807) and Schaffhausen (1805) by Hans Caspar Escher and the summer casino in Basel (1824) by Johann Georg von der Mühll were all small rectangular one-storey buildings with low pitched hip roofs and an accentuated main façade with a portico and a triangular pediment. The interior consisted of a foyer, a large event hall and further rooms for leisure. These three buildings were extensively modified and no longer have their original roof structure.

In the second quarter of the 19th century, the casinos grew vertically and usually had two to three storeys as can be seen in the studied examples of Aarau (1831, roof 1852), Herisau (1838), and La-Chaux-de-Fonds (1837). The main hall was mostly on the first floor, while the secondary rooms were on the ground floor.

The last examined casinos from the second half of the 19th century were larger and more complex buildings that were open to the general public. In the studied examples in Baden (1876) and Basel (1876), the halls have nearly twice the footprint and approximately three times the height of the halls in the older casinos. The five casinos that were built in in Aarau, Herisau, La-Chaux-de-Fonds, Baden and Basel (Table 1) between 1831 and 1876 were used as case studies to describe the development of wooden roof structures and timber craftmanship from the early to the late 19th century in Switzerland.

Timber Roof Structures of 19th-century Casinos in Switzerland

Table 1: Overview of the five examined Swiss casinos.

Location	Roof	Architect	Truss type	Traces
La-Chaux-de-Fonds	1837	Peter J. M. Felber	Queen-post truss	hewn, pit saw
Herisau	1838	Felix W. Kubly	Liegende Stuhl	hewn
Aarau	1852	unknown	Collar Beam Roof	hewn
Baden	1876	Robert Moser	Queen-post truss	gang saw
Basel	1876	Johann J. Stehlin	Queen-post truss	gang saw, circular saw

Casino Herisau

One of oldest preserved casinos can be found in Herisau. The casino association of Herisau was founded in 1836 by the merchant and chief magistrate of Appenzell Ausserrohden, Johann Heinrich Tanner [3]. The casino building was planned by the renowned architect from St. Gallen, Felix Wilhelm Kubly, and erected in 1838. The ground floor consisted of a restaurant, a billiard room, and a reading room, while the event hall and the library were situated on the first floor [4]. The rectangular two-storey building has masonry walls and a low-pitched hipped roof. The floorplan has an inner length of 18.1 metres and a width of 13.15 metres.

Roof Structure

The roof has two principal trusses and four half trusses set diagonally at the corners of the building. The principal truss consists of a so-called Liegender Stuhl (Fig. 1), a construction that was widely used in the baroque period in Switzerland. Two raking struts and a straining beam form a substructure under the rafters. The principal trusses are connected to each other with longitudinal beams on the upper end of the raking struts called collar plates. The collar plate has a pentagonal shape and is connected to the collar struts by mortise and tenon joints.

Longitudinal and transversal wind bracing is ensured by soulaces that are connected to the raking struts, the collar plate, and the straining beam. In between the principal trusses there are secondary trusses, only consisting of rafters, collar beams and tie-beams.

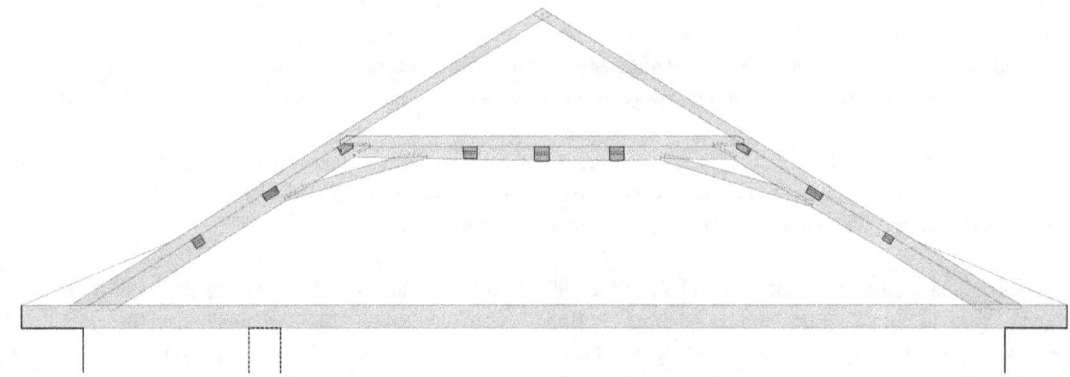

Figure 1: Liegende Stuhl of the casino in Herisau, built 1838 (K. Russnaik 2022).

The low-pitch roof has an angle of 31°, inducing an angle of only 21° at the diagonals of the hipped roof. A deflection of the Liegende Stuhl is noticeable at the top area of the collar struts resulting in a gap between the collar beam, the straining beam, and the raking struts. (Fig. 2) On the flattest part of the roof the gap measures 3 centimetres. This deformation is the result of the construction of a Liegende Stuhl for a low-pitched roof.

Craftsmanship

Figure 2: Top end of raking strut in the casino of Herisau (K. Russnaik 2021).

The timber roof structure of the building is mostly original. The timber beams are all of softwood and hand-hewn. All the connections are made with carpenter's joints, mainly mortice-and-tenon joints and abutting joints.

Casino Aarau

The casino in Aarau was commissioned by a literary society and built in 1831 [5]. The architect of this building is unknown. From 1842, the building was used by the singing society, later it served as a museum, and since 1930 the district court of Aarau has resided in this building. The low-pitched roof had a cement covering instigated by the founder of the first traceable cement factory in Switzerland Karl Herosé [6]. Because of leakage, the roof structure had to be reconstructed in 1852 by the contractor Daniel Schmutziger-Koller.

The rectangular two-storey building with its low-pitched hip roof has a length of 23.8 and a total width of 16 metres. The building can be divided into two parts, the original floorplan with a width 10.1 metres and an annex lightly set back with the width of 5.9 metres. The west-facing main façade is accentuated by four pilasters forming a slightly protruding central part that carries a triangular pediment. This neoclassical building is very sober and has almost no decorative elements.

Roof Structure

The purlin roof has three principal trusses and four half trusses on the diagonals. The timber structure was built with softwood that was hewn by hand. The roof has a ridge beam, four intermediate purlins and two inferior purlins. From the layout of the trusses, it can be assumed that originally there were four trusses with an axial distance of roughly 3 metres. The truss consists of a tie-beam, two principal rafters and a collar beam that was not accessible on site. Additionally, two posts support the principal rafters from underneath. Abutting joints are used for connecting the principal rafters to the tie-beam. At the ridge the rafters are connected with mortice-and-tenon joints and secured with a peg. Furthermore, the posts are attached to the tie-beam and the principal rafter with mortice-and-tenon joints. The purlins are connected to the principal rafters with notched joints.

Casino La-Chaux-de-Fonds

In the 1830s, the city of La-Chaux-de-Fonds was growing fast due to the successful watch industry [7] The casino association that emerged from the necessity of a social and cultural life raised money to build the theatre from 1836-37. The building was designed by the architect Peter Jakob Meinrad Felber of Solothurn and consisted of a restaurant, a foyer, and an Italian-style theatre [8]. This unique theatre is recognised as a monument of national importance in Switzerland. Together with the Teatro Sociale in Bellinzona, it is the only Italian-style theatre in Switzerland with its richly decorated ovoid shaped auditorium and three levels of galleries. The three-storey neoclassical building with a hip roof has a rectangular floor plan with an inner length of 31.5 and a clear span of 16.4 metres. The main facade on the north side is accentuated by a slightly protruding central part carrying a triangular pediment.

Roof Structure

The roof is supported by eight principal trusses that have a spacing of 3.8 metres. The main structure over the auditorium shows an Italian-style roof truss with a king-post flanked by two queen-posts. (Fig. 3) Furthermore, doubled collar beams positioned at mid height embrace the king-post, the queen-posts and the struts and are connected to them with iron bolts. The principal struts do not rest on the tie-beam but are attached to a short, elevated element with an abutting joint and secured by an iron strap. In this manner, space for technical installations is ensured. The struts are connected to the king- and queen-posts with mortice-and-tenon joints. Wrought iron straps secure the top and bottom ends of the king- and queen-posts. Suspender beams are positioned under the lateral queen-posts and secured to the tie-beam by wrought iron stirrup straps. The king-post is connected directly to the tie-beam with the same type of stirrup strap. The roof has a ridge beam that is held by the king-posts, four intermediate purlins that are positioned with purlin cleats and two inferior purlins. Longitudinal wind bracing is ensured by soulaces that are connected to the king-posts and the ridge beam by mortice-and-tenon joints.

At the eaves the bases of the trusses must have been altered at some point: empty mortices at the bottom of the outer struts and the way the struts end make it evident that the struts were shortened, while the supporting horizontal beam and the vertical post were elevated. The rolled steel straps that secure the struts with the horizontal beam were also added later.

The roof structure over the stage underwent many modifications over the course of time, including the shortening of the king- and queen- posts and the replacing of the original tie-beam with a modern beam at a higher level. Pictures showing the original state of the roof make it evident that the main structure was very similar. Only two minor differences can be noticed. Firstly, there were no beams between the trusses, thus leaving space for stage sets. Secondly the trusses had additional horizontal beams between the king- and queen-posts that presumably were used for stage installations.

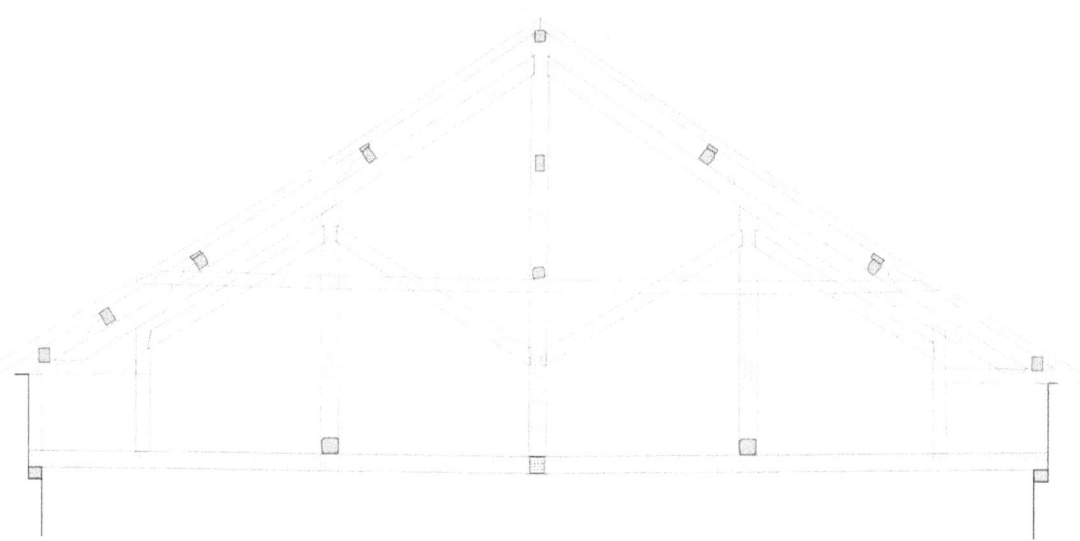

Figure 3: Queen-post truss of the casino in La-Chaux-de-Fonds, built 1837 (K. Russnaik 2022).

Craftsmanship

The structure was executed in softwood that was mainly hewn by hand. (Fig. 4) The beams of the primary structure are mostly full timber beams, including the doubled bracing collar beams. Only three vertical posts and two principal struts have rough and slightly irregular saw traces indicating the use of a pit saw. From the ten visible collar beams five display traces of a pit saw. (Fig. 4) Generally, traces of the saw could only be found on one side, the other three being hewn. Two of the collar beams are halved beams and have fine irregular traces of a pit saw. The sawn beams have coherent carpenters' marks which prove that they are original. The technique of sawing was used to avoid waste and obtain a larger number of timber beams from one log.

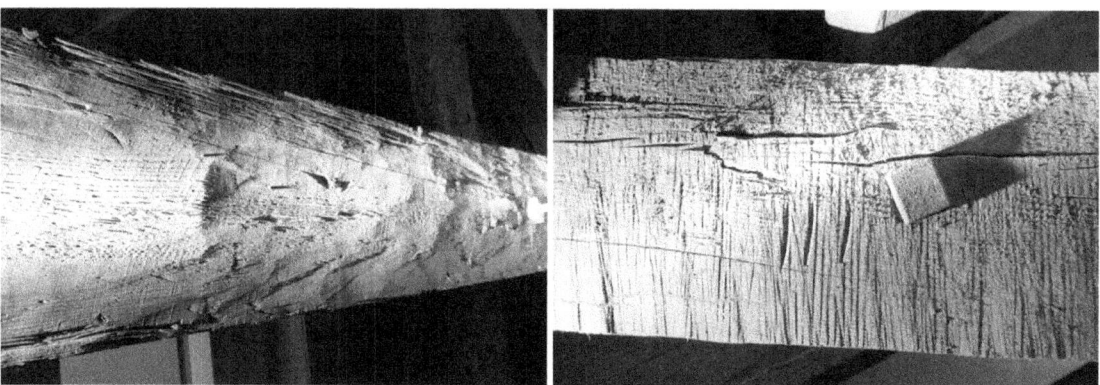

Figure 4: Hewing traces (left) and pit saw traces (right) in the casino of La-Chaux-de-Fonds, built 1837 (K. Russnaik 2021).

The original stirrup straps at the bottoms of the king-posts are made from wrought iron and have decorative curled endings at the top. The bolts used to fixate the strap have square 3x3 centimetre nuts. The same applies to the nuts of the iron straps at the top of the king- and queen-posts. Finally, an inscription at the top of the last king-post facing south gives us the year of the erection and the name of the carpenter: J.F.Seiler 1837. Additionally, an inscription on a doubled beam reveals more information on the carpenter: Jakob Friedrich Seiler from Bottmingen Basel worked here 1837.

Casino Baden

The thermal springs were widely cultivated in Baden since ancient times and gave the town its name [9]. With the opening of the railway line in 1847, more and more guests came to Baden and brought the desire for a centre of social gatherings and entertainment. The casino was commissioned by a corporation formed in 1871 and was built from 1872-75. The architect, Robert Moser, had studied in Karlsruhe and was taught by Friedrich Eisenlohr [10]. After his studies, he did an internship in Neuchâtel in the firm of Hans Rychner and travelled abroad to France, Belguium and Italy.

The casino was part of a large park complex with other buildings. It consisted of a central two-storey hall for balls and concerts. In front of the main hall there was a portico. On the south wing there was a café, a restaurant, and a billiard room. On the north wing there was a lady's salon and a reading salon. The main hall has a low-pitched hipped roof with an angle of 26° and measures 15x27 metres. The carpenter's work was executed by Leopold Garnin from Zug.

Roof structure

The main structure of the purlin roof consists of a king-post truss that is combined with two iron queen-posts. (Fig.5) Minor differences in the execution of the original plan were found on site. The roof has one ridge beam, two intermediate purlins and two inferior purlins. The principal rafters are connected to the tie-beam and the king-post by abutting joints. At the top end the king-post is secured to the struts with a V-shaped iron strap. The king-post is attached to the tie-beam by a bridge strap. Furthermore, a doubled collar beam is attached to the king-post, the struts and the rafters with iron bolts. Additionally, two shorter diagonal struts are installed between the king-post and the outer struts and connected with mortice-and-tenon joints. The two intermediate purlins are held by the doubled collar beam and secured by halved joints and iron bolts. Soulaces were installed between the struts and the purlins and between the king-posts and the ridge beam to ensure longitudinal wind-bracing and are attached by mortice-and-tenon joints. The heads of the bolts and the nuts are square and measure 5x5 centimetres. In contrast the stirrup strap on the bottom of the king-post has a large hexagonal nut with a diameter of 7 centimetres and a height of 6 centimetres. The vertical iron ties have a diameter of 2.5 centimetres.

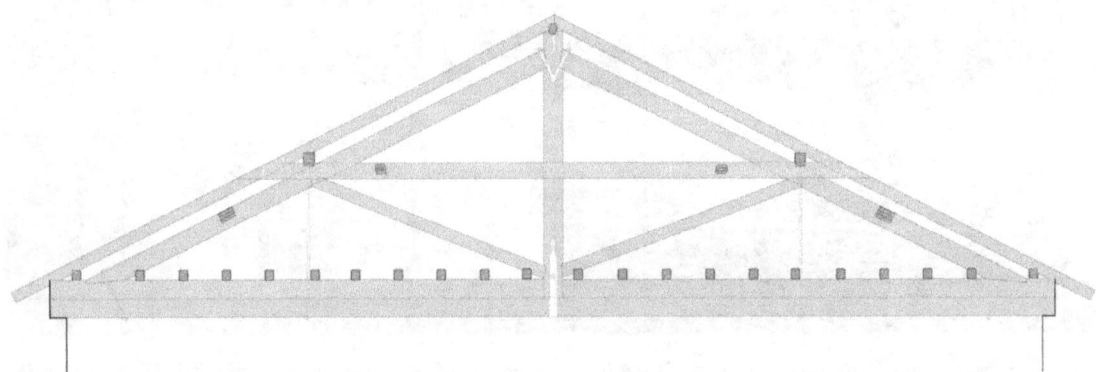

Figure 5: Queen-post truss of the casino in Baden, built 1876 (K. Russnaik 2022).

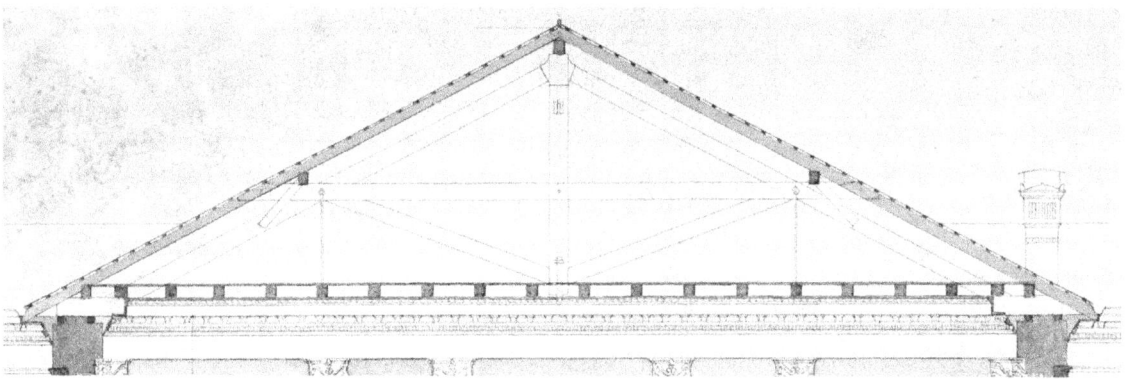

Figure 6: Historic Plan of the principal roof truss in the casino of Baden (City Archive Baden, Folder P.01.3.54).

Figure 7: Details at the top of the king-post (left) and the queen-tie (right) (K.Russnaik 2021).

Comparing the existing structure to the historic plan (Fig. 6), the main differences are the iron elements. In the original plan the queen-rods are attached to the collar beam and the struts at their intersection. In reality the queen-rods are attached to the intermediate purlin and run through the struts. (Fig. 7) Another difference can be seen in the connection of the king-post with the struts. In the historic plan, cast iron shoes are attached to the king-posts to hold the struts. This detail is solved with a v-shaped strap in the existing structure. In the original plan the diagonal struts are connected to the outer struts at the height of the doubled collar beam. In the existing structure the position of this connection is underneath the collar beam and has a metal plate to secure the struts from slipping away. This detail may be a later reinforcement.

Craftsmanship

The timber structure is made of softwood. Most of the beams have a very smooth surface with almost no traces of woodwork. Fine regular sawing traces can only be seen on some small areas of the beams. It can be assumed that the surfaces were planed after the beams were sawn in a gang saw. All the members of the principal truss are full beams except for the straining beams that consists of two slimmer half beams. Halved beams can be identified by the woodgrain and the knots on the surface. The diagonal struts have a different appearance from the other beams and seem to have had serious woodworm infestation. It thereby seems that a different timber or timber quality was used.

Stadtcasino Basel

The casino in Basel was designed by the architect Johann Jacob Stehlin and built in 1876. Stehlin was trained in the building company of his father and then studied in Mainz and at the Ecole des Beaux-Arts in Paris [11] This casino with large music hall was built as an extension of the former casino from Melchior Berri [12].

The building has a mansard roof covered in metal and slate. The hall of the casino has a length of 36 metres and a clear span of 21 metres. A unique feature of this building is the large skylight in the middle of the hall that is however no longer in its original state.

Roof Structure

The roof has ten principal trusses, a ridge beam and four purlins. The main structure consists of a queen-post truss. (Fig.8) The struts are connected to the tie-beam and the queen-posts by abutting joints. The doubled straining beams are connected to the queen-posts via halved joints and iron bolts. Longitudinal suspender beams are positioned under the queen-posts and secured by rolled iron stirrup straps. Soulaces are installed between the queen-posts and the purlins to ensure longitudinal wind-bracing and are attached by mortice-and-tenon joints.

A second type of truss that was constructed for the skylight of the hall also consists of a queen-post truss. In this case the tie-beam is interrupted in the centre with iron ties connecting the two ends. The straining beam is not doubled but placed right over the queen-posts and connected with mortice-and-tenon joints. A deflection of the structure is evident in this weaker area of the roof.

The original roof structure has been well preserved despite modern steel reinforcements that were added in 2016. The new steel elements are structurally detached from the original timber construction.

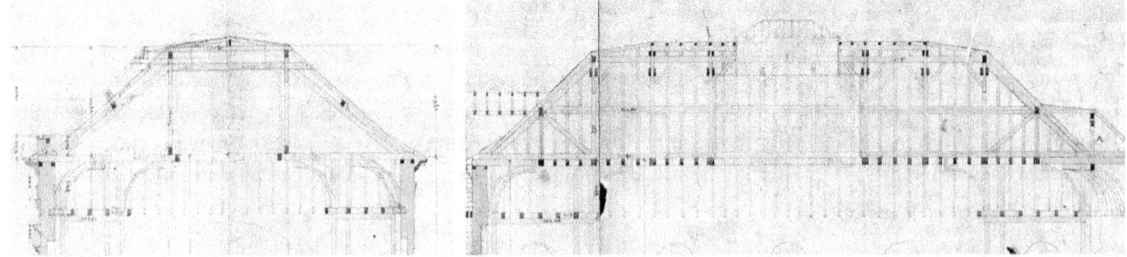

Figure 8: Historic Plan of the roof structure with skylight, casino in Basel, built 1876 (City Archive Basel-City, PLA 75, 2-22 [Stehlin Archiv: Planmappe B (IX) VIII 19a]).

There is a deflection of approximately 5 centimetres in the middle of the tie-beam causing the queen-posts to tilt outwards at the bottom. Furthermore, the iron ties were cut off at their ends and the former skylight is now covered. Light is brought into the hall with electric spotlights achieving a similar effect as the skylight.

Craftsmanship

The surface of most of the beams have rough traces of a circular saw with a blade that had a diameter of roughly 1 metre. (Fig. 9) In contrast the queen-posts have a very smooth planed surface that only in some areas still show traces of a gang saw. The difference between the vertical members and other members of the construction may be due to special timber requirements. The main material used in this structure is softwood, while iron is mainly used for securing the joints. At the bottom of the queen-post iron straps are attached to all four sides connecting the queen-post to the longitudinal suspender beam and the tie-beam. (Fig. 10) The flat iron straps evolve into iron bolts at the bottom and are attached to an iron plate and secured with nuts. The heads of the bolts and the nuts and have a diameter of 4 centimetres.

Figure 9: Circular saw traces in the casino of Basel (K. Russnaik 2022).

Figure 10: Rolled iron strap (K. Russnaik 2022).

Conclusion

This case study presents five buildings from the first quarter to the third quarter of the 19th century which allows us to draw a picture of the development of wooden roof structures and timber craftmanship of the 19th century in Switzerland.

Roof structures

The structures of the five casinos differ from one another making it apparent that the development did not only happen over time but was influenced by different construction traditions, namely, German and French carpentry traditions. The buildings did not follow a global reference or a unique source. The construction of a Liegende Stuhl in Herisau (1838) was very common for the Baroque period in the central and eastern regions of Switzerland and did not bring any innovations, but instead showed the failing of the structure for this type of neo classical low-pitched roof. The simple purlin roof of the casino in Aarau (1852) that was built 14 years later points towards the direction in which the roof construction was developing. Surely, purlin roofs were already being built much earlier, but particularly in Switzerland this development was not linear. The different cultural regions were being influenced by their close surroundings and neighboring countries specially in the first half of the 19th century. The casino in La-Chaux-de-Fonds built in 1837 appears much more advanced in comparison to the later examples in Herisau and Aarau. This queen- and king-post truss has similarities with the roof structure of the Grand Théâtre in Lyon (Fig. 11) and was clearly influenced by French carpentry. Another feature that stands out is the doubled collar beam that was widely established in the second half of the 19th century. This doubling of the horizontal beams can also be found in the Grand Théatre in Dijon built 1828[13].

On the other hand, the roof construction of the casino theatre in Bellinzona that was built in 1847 and replaced in 1993 originally had a traditional Italian king-post truss utilizing round timber beams.

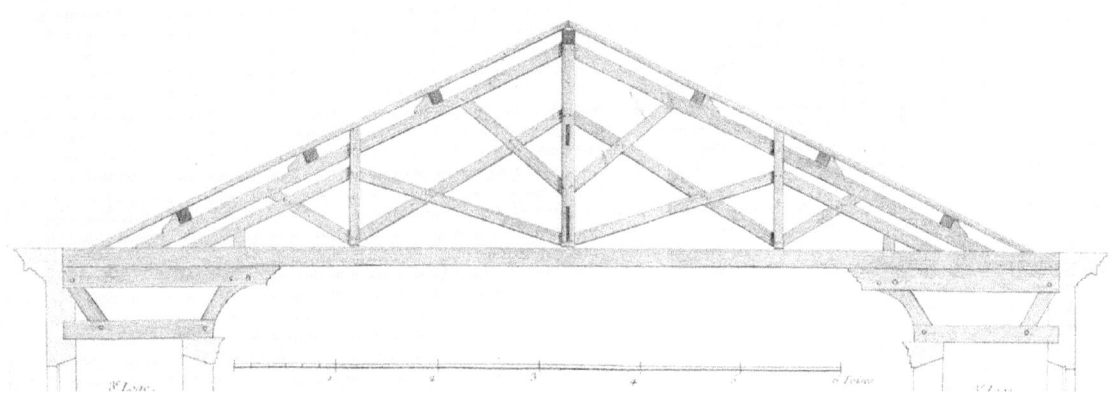

Figure 11: Historic Plan of roof structure of the Grand Théâtre in Lyon, built 1756 (Dumont 1765, between plate number 21 and 23).

Therefore, the influences for the roof structures were more regional and culturally determined.

Over the course of the 19th century the number of published books on construction theory increased significantly and ideas started to be spread more widely. At the same time the education of Swiss architects became more international and in this examples, they were being influenced by the architecture in Germany and France.

The casino in Baden (1876) was designed by Robert Moser, a Swiss architect who had studied in Karlsruhe and was taught by Friedrich Eisenloh [14]. The use of the vertical iron ties may have been influenced through the railway buildings of Eisenlohr [15]. Iron roof trusses such as the Polonceau system were already being published in the 1840s [16].

Mosers casino additionally had clear parallels the casino in Baden-Baden built 1824 by a famous architect in Germany Friedrich Weinbrenner. At the same time the city casino of Basel (1876) was designed by Johann Jacob Stehlin a Swiss architect who had studied in Germany and France. In this casino all the members of the principal queen-post truss were executed in timber. Iron horizontal ties were only used on two trusses as a substitute for the tie-beam under the skylight. Stehlin came from a traditional carpenter's family and may have relied more widely on timber as a building material. Hence in the 1870s Swiss casino roofs were still predominantly built in timber even though iron trusses were already being constructed in the 1860s such as the railway hall in Biel from J.Jenzer (translocated to Yverdon-les-Bains in 1922).

The roof of the casinos in Herisau and Aarau are strictly built with hand hewn timber and rely solely on the traditional carpenters' joints. The roof in La-Chaux-de-Fonds from the same period differs from the examples in the central and eastern regions of Switzerland. Although the beams were mainly hand hewn, there is a significant number of beams that show traces of a pit saw. This is specially the case for the doubled collar beams that consist of two relatively slim proportioned beams of 20x16 centimeters. The fact that most of the beams were hand hewn makes it evident that this technique was more efficient than sawing the beams by hand. On the other hand, it is apparent that wood had to be used economically and therefore large logs were divided with the saw to obtain more timber element [17]. Another particularity of this casino structure is the relatively extensive use of wrought iron straps at the bottoms and tops of the king- and queen-posts.

The later examples in Baden and Basel show completely different woodwork traces. The beams in Baden all have a very smooth surfaces and show fine regular saw traces in some areas. These traces correspond to a gang saw with a vertical alignment, additionally the timber was planned after being sawed. In Basel the same traces could be found on the queen-posts, while all the other members of the truss showed traces of a large circular saw with the large diameter of one metre. The circular saw traces were only discovered in the casino of Basel.

Although the circular saw that allowed longitudinal cutting of logs was introduced in the 1830s (Fig. 12), this technology was not widespread in Central Europe [18]. In the 1860s, circular sawmills were gradually being introduced. This technology had benefits when cutting logs of small diameters (< 48 centimeters). On the other hand, the circular saw was not material-efficient and created large kerfs. This technology was therefore mainly being used in countries that had large timber sources. Regarding the structure of the casino in Basel, this could mean that Basel had big wood resources during this period. On the other hand, it is possible that this important public building was being built with the most modern techniques of that time.

The multipurpose buildings under the umbrella term casino each had their particularities in the structure and craftsmanship of their roofs. Nevertheless, a development from the Liegende Stuhl towards the traditional French roof structure was traced and proved itself to be more suitable for this new building type.

Figure 12: Circular saw for cutting logs lengthwise, introduced in the 1830s (Braune,G: Anlage, Einrichtung und Betrieb der Sägewerke. Berlin, 1901).

Acknowledgements

This research was funded through the Swiss National Science Foundation (SNSF) as part of the project "Wide span timber roofs in Switzerland". A special thanks goes to Professor S.M. Holzer and Clemens Voigts for the valuable discussions and their feedback.

References

[1] Carl, B. *Casino*. 2005 [cited 2022 25.Feb.]; Available from: https://hls-dhs-dss.ch/de/articles/011003/2005-02-15
[2] Erne, E. and T. Gull. *Vereine*. 2014 [cited 2022 25. Feb.]; Available from: https://hls-dhs-dss.ch/de/articles/025745/2014-10-03/.
[3] Rebsamen, H., H. Oberli, and W. Stutz, *INSA: Inventar der neueren Schweizer Architektur, 1850-1920; Herisau*. Vol. Band 5. Gesellschaft für Schweizerische Kunstgeschichte, 1990.
[4] Ibid.
[5] Stettler, M., *Die Kunstdenkmäler des Kantons Aargau, Band 1: Die Bezirke Aarau, Kulm, Zofingen*. Die Kunstdenkmäler der Schweiz. Basel: Birkhäuser, 1948.
[6] schokke, E., *Die Laurenzen-Vorstadt in Aarau*. Aarauer Neujahrsblätter, 1932. **6**: p. 45-46.
[7] Tissot, Y. *Théâtre de La Chaux-de-Fonds, La Chaux-de-Fonds NE*. 2018 [cited 2022 04. Jan.]; Available from: http://tls.theaterwissenschaft.ch/wiki/Théâtre_de_La_Chaux-de-Fonds,_La_Chaux-de-Fonds_NE.
[8] Ibid.
[9] Birkner, O., *INSA: Inventar der neueren Schweizer Architektur, 1850-1920: Aarau, Altdorf, Appenzell, Baden*. Vol. 1. Gesellschaft für Schweizerische Kunstgeschichte, 1984.
[10] Ibid.
[11] Anselmetti, R. *Stehlin, Johann Jakob*. 2012 [cited 2022 25. Feb.]; Available from: https://hls-dhs-dss.ch/de/articles/019964/2012-11-07/.
[12] Fiechter, S., *1000 Jahre Basler Geschichte: Der Musiksaal und die Kulturmeile am Steinenberg*. Basel: Christoph Merian Verlag, 2020.
[13] Chalvatzi, A., Roofs over the action: Theatre construction in France from 1780 to 1862. (Ph.D. thesis, ETH Zürich, 2020).
[14] Birkner, O., *INSA: Inventar der neueren Schweizer Architektur, 1850-1920: Aarau, Altdorf, Appenzell, Baden*. Vol. 1. Gesellschaft für Schweizerische Kunstgeschichte, 1984.
[15] Eisenlohr, F., *Ausgeführte oder zur Ausführung bestimmte Entwürfe von Gebäuden verschiedener Gattung als Unterrichtsmittel für Gewerb- und technische Schulen, so wie für Baumeister*. Karlsruhe: J. Veith, 1852.
[16] Camille, P., *Notice sur un nouveau système de charpente en bois et en fer*. Revue Générale l'Archtecture et des traveaux Publics, 1840: p. 27-32.
[17] Voigts, C. *Beil oder Sägemühle? Über einen frühen Versuch, die Herstellung von Bauholz mit Maschineneinsatz zu rationalisieren*. p. 69-83. in *Jahrestagung der Gesellschaft für Bautechnikgeschichte*. Potsdam: Thelem 2019.
[18] Finsterbusch, E. and W. Thiele, *Vom Steinbeil zum Sägegatter: Ein Streifzug durch die Geschichte der Holzbearbeitung*. Leipzig: VEB Fachbuchverlag, 1987.

Pugin's role as Superintendent of Woodcarving

Jamie Jacobs
Department of Architecture and Planning, University of Kent, UK

Abstract

In his role as Superintendent of Woodcarving at the Houses of Parliament, Victorian architect and designer Augustus Welby Northmore Pugin guided craftsmen at the Thames Bank workshops, drawing upon a wide range of sources including a collection of medieval woodcarvings and casts to educate the workers and inspire them to find the "true thing" championed in his writings on Gothic architecture. To do so, Pugin utilised a combination of handicraft and manual skill alongside steam-driven machinery. This paper investigates these working methods to reveal practices relevant to future restoration works.

Introduction

Victorian architect and designer Augustus Welby Northmore Pugin's involvement at the Houses of Parliament encompasses a wide range of works, many undertaken in his role as Superintendent of Woodcarving. Through his association with architect Charles Barry and his command of the gothic style, Pugin was appointed to oversee the workers at the Thames Bank Workshops although his output extended far beyond the limitations of his title. Even today the exact nature of Pugin's role is unclear as it seems he outlined his own responsibilities, which involved collecting examples of medieval woodwork to educate the workers he was meant to supervise. He also drew upon his own background and training to create both fitted works and items of furniture. Examining Pugin's activities in this role is useful in understanding how goods were made and how they might be preserved and restored. Therefore, it is worth considering exactly what his position involved, how the work was completed, and the working methods, tools, and machinery involved.

Association with Charles Barry

While Charles Barry is credited as architect of the gothic revival Houses of Parliament, Pugin's involvement is undeniable and his influence is seen throughout the building. Phoebe Stanton notes how the collaboration evolved "as Barry fitted his building together and Pugin designed the parts of the decorative portions" [1]. Aside from building what Henry Russell Hitchcock regards as "cheap Commissioners' Gothic churches," Barry was not known for working in the Gothic idiom [2]. In cases where an understanding of the gothic was necessary, Barry looked to those more skilled than he, with one such occasion leading to his introduction to and collaboration with Pugin.

King Edward VI Grammar School

Barry's association with Pugin dates back to the pair's work on King Edward VI Grammar School in Birmingham (Fig. 1). Designed in 1833 by Barry in the perpendicular Gothic style and built between 1834-37, Barry employed Pugin to assist him in rendering his drawing plans for the project [3]. Pugin's work extended well beyond that point as furniture, fixtures, and fittings all fell under his remit, albeit outside his stated obligations. Following the completion of this structure, the two parted ways with Barry returning to his preferred neoclassical structures and Pugin to his gothic churches.

Figure 1: King Edward VI Grammar School, Birmingham, View of the front to New Street. Image from Alfred Barry, Memoir of the Life and Works of the late Sir Charles Barry (1870).

Fire at the medieval Palace of Westminster

The fire of October 1834 that destroyed the medieval Houses of Parliament set the stage for the two men reconnecting once again. Pugin opted not to submit a design for the rebuild, and instead accepted work drawing the plans for other entrants [4]. One of these individuals was Charles Barry, who once again called upon Pugin's encyclopaedic knowledge of gothic to fit the Commons Select Committee's stylistic guidelines [5]. Much like at the Birmingham Grammar School, Pugin prepared Barry's drawings but, once again, their working relationship would encompass much more.

Barry was awarded the contract and Pugin's involvement ended with the completion of the estimate drawings. However, as work on the building progressed, Barry found himself in need of assistance with the interiors [6]. He wrote to Pugin on 3 September, 1844 with the news that "I am in a regular fix respecting the working drawings for the fittings and decorations of the House of Lords" [7]. Barry flattered Pugin, stating that "I know of no one who can render me such valuable and efficient assistance" and requested that Pugin "enter into some permanent arrangement" regarding "occasional assistance for the future in the completion of the great work" [8].

Appointment as Superintendent of Woodcarving

In 1844 Pugin accepted Barry's invitation and was granted the government position of Superintendent of Woodcarving with a salary of £200. What Barry originally intended the role to encompass is unknown, as Pugin appears to have designated his own duties. In a letter from early 1845, Pugin writes to Barry wishing "to state exactly my views" on the role "to prevent any misunderstanding" regarding a task that "will occupy the greater part of my time" [9]. For the annual stipend, Pugin agreed to "furnish drawings and instructions for all the carved ornaments in wood that may be required" [10]. Additional payments covering travel expenses, casts and original models for the workers' instruction, and drawings for "glass, metal works, and tiles, &c." outside the scope of woodcarving, were also forthcoming [11]. Lastly, Pugin wrote that "I am only responsible to you in all matters connected with the work. I act as your agent entirely, and have nothing to do with any other person" [12].

Despite his desire to report only to Barry, word of Pugin's involvement spread and, in June 1845, he wrote to Barry, complaining about "exaggerated statements respecting the nature of my employment" [13]. Indeed, his work at the Houses of Parliament was not without great controversy. As an outspoken Catholic with polarising views, his involvement was met with a furore in the press and *The Artizan* of July 1845 published the article "Charles Barry and His Right-Hand Man" which declared that Barry "submitted to the indignity" of a "champion of Romanism in all its most besotted superstitions" [14].

Questions continued to circulate about the nature of their working relationship, prompting Pugin to publish a notice in *The Builder* on 6 September, 1845 to address "the misconception" surrounding his work with Barry [15]. Here Pugin describes how he is "engaged by him [Barry], and by him alone, with the approval of the Government, to assist in preparing working drawings and models from his designs of all the wood carvings and other details of the internal decorations" [16]. He finishes by noting that his "occupation is simply to assist in carrying out practically Mr Barry's own designs and views in all respects," reassuring readers that he is only assisting Barry [17].

Even with Pugin's efforts to delineate his role, the exact nature of his position as Superintendent of Woodcarving is unclear. Historian Michael Port feels his title is misleading, describing how Pugin's role was "to furnish Barry with designs for internal fittings and furniture, and to provide casts of medieval work for the carvers to use as models" while another individual, Richard Bayne, was Superintendent of Construction and tended to the day-to-day practicalities of the works along with "a 'woodcarver in chief, one Potts, described by Barry as an 'artist workman'" [18].

An account by the architectural sculptor J. Birnie Philip describes how "Pugin visited the works, averaging certainly not oftener than once in a fortnight, leaving a great number of sketches executed during the few hours he was with us" whereas Barry appeared more often [19]. This suggests a working arrangement mimicking Pugin's own undertakings with his collaborators John Hardman, Herbert Minton, John Gregory Crace, and George Myers where sketches and a brief description were provided with the understanding that each man would work out the full design. However, the historian Richard Cavendish suggests that both Barry and Pugin were hands-on in instructing their workmen. He states that "Barry was often seen climbing about on the scaffolding, with the ebullient Pugin laughing and capering cheerfully at his side" [20]. Whether a true depiction or just a charming anecdote, it appears that in his actions and his words, Pugin sought to educate workmen in his *true principles*. Regardless of how these works were completed, he ensured they exhibited "an extraordinarily consistent style and high quality" [21].

Past Experience

Pugin was not unfamiliar with supervising workers as tradesmen frequented his father's drawing school. Rather than being excluded from the practicalities of his father's business, Pugin "grew up in the workshop" [22] as his father "had connexions with the humbler fringes of the commercial art world" [23]. This familiarity would serve the younger Pugin well in the future when manufacturing his own goods.

Morel and Seddon at Windsor Castle

This opportunity presented itself when, in 1827 at the age of 15, Pugin was employed by the London cabinetmakers Morel and Seddon to create gothic designs for the refurbishment of Windsor Castle. In the course of his work Pugin spent time in the workshops, "overseeing the manufacture of furniture he was designing" [24] and it was on the shop floor that he was able to supervise the production of the work and observe "the constructional methods" involved therein [25].

In his autobiography, Pugin states that he "superintended the execution of" the furniture "at Mr. Seddons manufactory" [26]. This suggests that his work with Morel and Seddon encompassed all aspects of the project from start to completion. Indeed, Pugin exhibited some interest in creating items himself, as a boss in the collections of Oscott College is said to have been carved by Pugin in 1828 (Fig. 2). While Pugin was clearly more adept at drawing and designing, he was aware of the nature of the work required to produce his designs.

Figure 2: Wooden ceiling boss carved by Pugin in 1828. Architectural Museum, Oscott College, Birmingham, UK. Photograph by the author.

Self-employment in "carving and joinering"

Pugin drew upon this experience when, in November 1829 he "began business for myself in the carving and joinering line" in Covent Garden [27]. An article in *Blackwood's Edinburgh Magazine* of 1861 recalls this early venture as "a manufactory of carved work and Gothic decorative 'detail' of every kind, to execute which the young designer trained and collected a staff of art workmen" [28] with the goal to "supply all the ornamental portions of buildings which could by possibility be executed apart from the structure and be fixed afterwards" [29]. Initially this venture was successful with a large amount of items prepared and, once again, Pugin insisted on superintending the manufacture of his goods to "have all carved work, whenever possible, executed under his own eye" for fear that, as his biographer Benjamin Ferrey explains, his "reputation would suffer by the bungling way in which objects said to be taken from his drawings would be executed" [30]. The work soon became too demanding as he experienced difficulty directing his workers and his venture ended in bankruptcy and arrest. One can only assume that the knowledge gained from this event was applied to his role at the Houses of Parliament.

Interest in Medieval Examples

These past experiences gave Pugin the confidence to accept the job at the Houses of Parliament and the pragmatism to modify the position to utilize his strengths and avoid complications. Instead of superintending as his job title suggests, Pugin left these duties to Bayne and concentrated on securing examples of medieval woodwork to educate and inspire the workers. This was an activity well known to Pugin as he collected examples of medieval carvings both domestically and abroad which he then deposited in collections such as the Architectural Museum at Oscott College in Birmingham (Fig. 3). When he found architectural elements that were in situ but still particularly valuable for study, he employed antiques dealers to provide casts or "squeezes" of these elements. This was a common practice among craftsmen in the Victorian era when the "form, size, and depth" of extant carvings were otherwise "impossible to convey by a working drawing" [31].

Figure 3: Medieval woodcarvings collected by Pugin and displayed in the Architectural Museum at Oscott College, Birmingham, UK. Photograph by the author.

The use of casts

Pugin's correspondence with Barry makes reference to these collections to serve as carving models and a letter confirms that he will be reimbursed "for all the carved ornaments in wood that may be required" at the Houses of Parliament, and that he be "empowered to send persons to collect squeezes, etc., and all expenses connected with that object, or the purchase of original models, to be paid" [32]. With these arrangements in place, Pugin set about forming a collection of

Gothic woodwork – either original or plaster casts – of examples both at home and abroad with which to instruct the workmen under his employ.

In his book True Principles, Pugin talks of the importance of imbuing one's own creations with the "true thing" as evident in medieval works and by providing such examples, Pugin both educated and inspired the workmen. By referring to medieval examples, Pugin could divert workers away from the meretricious use of decoration, adhering to his belief that "all ornament should consist of enrichment of the essential construction" [33].

As Pugin expert Alexandra Wedgwood states, Pugin "wanted the carpenters to work surrounded by the best examples of the style he was aiming at [...] and to this end he built up in the Thames Bank Workshops a remarkable collection" [34]. In May 1845, The Builder reported that Pugin was collecting casts [35] as he requested a variety of designs from his suppliers, with instructions to "send the bill to me & the Casts to [the] Government Works Thames Bank London" [36].

Thames Bank Workshops

With supplies of building materials arriving by barge on the Thames to create an estimated two miles of moulded woodwork, the prospect of carving such a vast amount required a large supply of ready workers [37]. To this end, the Thames Bank Workshops opened in February 1845 and by December 1847, employed 335 men [38]. The bulk of wood carved at the Thames Bank was oak, a dense, firm wood suitable "for the use of experienced carvers but on account of its hardness is not so suitable for the beginner" [39]. Select areas, such as the ceiling in the House of Lords, are carved of softwood, a decision architect David Insall feels was made because it could be "easily carved" by less skilled workers "and could be done in a hurry by a machine" [40].

Regarding the specifics of the carving process, Wedgwood states that "[g]iven the outstanding quality of the work, it is particularly sad that it does not seem to be possible to give a full account of Pugin's views of how the carving was to be carried out and who did it" [41]. Indeed, very little documentation exists on the Thames Bank workshops overall; a project that lasted many years and cost large sums of money. Whether extant records were deemed unimportant and were destroyed at the project's completion, or if records were not initially taken, is unknown.

Carving Machinery

One aspect that has been well documented involves the use of carving machinery. Considering the quantity of work to produce, carving by hand was out of the question and other methods were required. Pugin acknowledged that he could work better "by adopting the best examples and getting them carried out in execution than by making a lot of drawings which could never be worked from," and he took advantage of the capability that machinery afforded [42]. Historian of engineering Denis Smith states how Barry set up steam-powered workshops "so that the fullest possible mechanisation could be employed" and facilities were quickly expanded to accommodate the necessary machinery [43].

Jordan's Patent Steam Carving Machine

An article in *The Civil Engineer and Architect's Journal* from March 1848 describes how "[t]hese premises were taken to facilitate the progress of the interior finishings of the new buildings, by the erection therein of carving machines, and the employment of carvers and other workmen" [44]. This machinery included Jordan's Patent Steam Carving machine, and the government leased five machines, powered by a ten-horsepower condensing steam engine and boiler [45] (Fig. 4). These machines allowed a worker to duplicate several copies based on the same pattern and Barry recommended their use at the Houses of Parliament, going so far as to publish a testimonial on the superiority of the machine [46]. Barry also gave testimony before the Office of Works, describing the working method employed. Briefly put, a guide follows the contours of the original piece while rotating cutters remove wood from the areas of negative space in the blank media to create a duplicate of the original (rather like an elaborate and sophisticated key-cutting machine). While carving machines could replicate detailed three-dimensional items, they were most effective in duplicating the low-relief linenfold panels used throughout the Houses of Parliament. (Fig. 5)

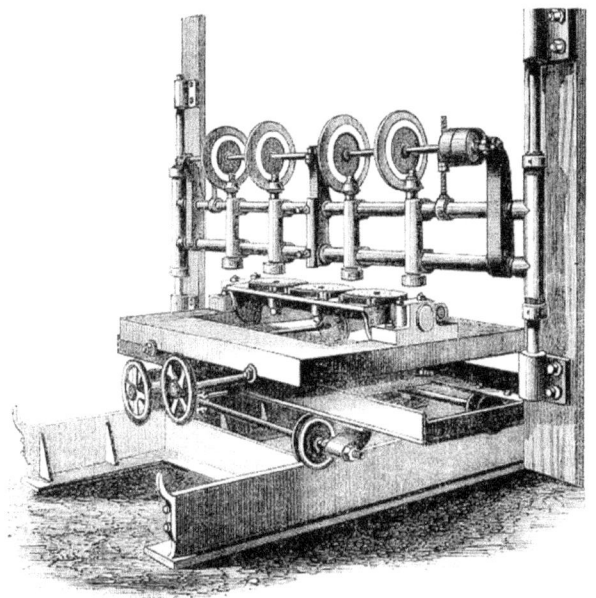

Figure 4: Jordan's Carving Machinery. Image from Scientific American, 22 April 1871.

Figure 5: Decorative paneling from the Palace of Westminster. Designer, Augustus Welby Northmore Pugin. The Metropolitan Museum of Art. Purchase, The James Parker Charitable Foundation and Friends of European Sculpture and Decorative Arts Gifts, and funds from various donors, 2015. Accession Number: 2015.675

Pugin's role as Superintendent of Woodcarving

Machine-made Controversy

The use of carving machinery at the Houses of Parliament was not without controversy and concerns surrounded the role of the craftsman in light of the repetitive duplication made possible by the machine. However, machines were only used to rough out shapes, known as 'bosting,' in the first phases of production, with hand work then required to finish the product. With this approach in mind, "even very large factories continued to depend on repetitive handwork to complete supposedly machine-produced articles" [47]. The English Victorian journalist George Dodd pointed out this discrepancy years earlier when he stressed that this sort of machine benefits the artist by "placing at his disposal machines that shall relieve him from the mechanical labour of roughing out, and fashioning the rude-sawn block, and placing it in the hands ready for the exercise alone of the mastery of the best talents at his command" [48]. Similar machinery was used in the stone carving department at the Thames Bank where the fear of being replaced by the "patent iron mason" played a part in an ongoing workers' strike [49]. There is no evidence that such insurrection took place amongst the wood carvers, but such fears must have been brewing. The perceived ease (and carelessness) surrounding machine carving also inspired debates about copyism [50]. However, in cases such as linenfold panels, a repetitive consistency is required to give the interior a uniformity and to allow the other features, be it the metalwork, stained glass, furniture, carpets, etc., to be the room's focal point (Figs 6, 7).

Figure 6: Example of linenfold panels lining the walls in the House of Lords. Detail from John Woods, active 1836–1860, after Read, c. 1816–1883, British, Her Majesty Proroguing Parliament - House of Lords, Engraving, Yale Center for British Art; Gift of Prof. William H. Dunham Jr., B1982.31.40

Figure 7: Oak cupboard at the Houses of Parliament. Note the repetitive use of linenfold panels in both the cupboard and the wainscoting. Historic Bookcases & Cupboards by Unknown © Historic Furniture POW 00163.

Furniture

Pugin is known for furnishing the Palace of Westminster, producing "various quantities of thirty-five different types of furniture" for the House of Lords alone [51]. Pugin himself writes to Barry, explaining that "[t]here will be upwards of 1000 detail drawings of ornaments for the carvers in the House of Lords" [52]. Considering the scope of Pugin's work, *A Report by the Victoria and Albert Museum Concerning the Furniture in the House of Lords* notes that the "design of every aspect of the interior decoration and furnishing" came from Pugin and, consequently, "hundreds of drawings in his hand survive" [53].

Production Companies

At the Thames Bank Workshops, production was limited to woodwork comprising mostly ornamentation, be it wall panels, door frames, benches, etc. These pieces were generally structural, *i.e.* affixed to the building, versus portable furniture items which were manufactured off-site by furniture makers. Therefore, it is uncertain whether Pugin's furniture pieces fall under the position of Superintendent of Woodcarving as they were fabricated off-site. Nevertheless, they show Pugin designing for production in wood, presumably drawing from the same casts and medieval samples acquired for the Thames Bank.

A variety of firms were used in the production of furniture for the Palace. One such manufacturer was Gillows, who produced the "Portcullis" chair found in both the Commons and Lords (Fig. 8). In her study of the company, Susan Stuart mentions how "Gillows were the first cabinet makers to win a contract to supply furniture for the New Palace Westminster which they carried out in 1851 to Pugin's designs" [54].

Figure 8: Portcullis chair – Historic Chairs by Augustus Welby Northmore Pugin © Historic Furniture, POW 00791.

Holland and Son, cabinet makers, upholsterers, and decorators, was another firm responsible for supplying huge quantities of furniture at the Palace and the pieces for the Lords' chamber "form the main body of furniture made by Holland & Sons for the functional areas, to designs by and after Pugin" [55]. Finally, the most recognizable pieces – the Sovereign's Throne and Chairs of State – were both produced by the "antique dealer and high-class cabinet-maker" John Webb [56] (Fig. 9). Pugin met Webb through the latter's trade in antiquities including the acquisition of casts for educating workmen, and he was responsible for supplying some of the medieval woodwork items at Oscott [57]. With each of these firms, there is no evidence to suggest Pugin had any involvement beyond providing the drawings, so it is uncertain as to whether these designs fall under his duties as Superintendent of Woodcarving, even though they are made of that material.

Figure 9: Sovereign's Throne and Chairs of State – Historic Chairs by John Webb, Augustus Welby Northmore Pugin and John Hardman & Co. © Historic Furniture POW 08031.

Houses of Parliament

The House of Lords was finally opened on 15 April, 1847 after Pugin completed the furniture and fittings for the space "together with those of the Peers Lobby and the Prince's Chamber to either side" [58]. This chamber, along with the rest of the structure, encompassed works in all media, making the Houses of Parliament a true *tour de force* of Pugin's work and one which *The House of Lords* descriptive survey calls "without doubt, the finest specimen of Gothic civil architecture in Europe" [59]. No one item is responsible for this impression, be it a single piece of furniture or a building element, and yet the overall effect is diminished by the removal of any part of the whole.

Conclusion: Restoration and Renewal

Examining Pugin's working methods as Superintendent of Woodcarving is vital in understanding how these goods were made and how they might be preserved. An historical investigation of this nature is highly relevant given the necessity of works at the Houses of Parliament, as craftspeople seek to repair and replace worn and damaged pieces. Indeed, by understanding the past, any future repair works may be assuredly addressed in the most historically accurate and stylistically sympathetic manner possible. An investigation into the workshops reveals details of how the initial work for the new Palace of Westminster was undertaken, including the equipment used and the methods employed.

Regarding his firm's work at the Houses of Parliament, Donald Insall of the London architectural firm of Donald W. Insall and Associates stresses how "[b]oth in the construction and decoration, we must honour the original work" by "relating new work to the original" [60]. This approach was undertaken in 1980 during Insall's repair of the Lords' ceiling as most of the structure, and indeed all of the damaged parts, were wood. Given that Pugin was the Superintendent of Woodcarving and the involvement of Crace on the decorative painting for the Lord's ceiling, Pugin would have been aware of, if not involved in, the ceiling's construction [61].

Regarding the woodwork, Insall points out how careful historical research was necessary before commencing the restorative efforts as it was only through this research that the firm was able to repair the ceiling to its original state [62]. Where modern intervention was necessary for the restoration efforts, these pieces were created "using the latest modern machinery, echoing its steam-driven predecessor […] to reproduce the mouldings exactly" [63]. This includes using machinery and working methods where indicated by historic precedent. With the looming Restoration and Repair project set to begin in the (hopefully not-so-distant) future, the investigation into Pugin's role at the Houses of Parliament, both as Superintendent of Woodcarving and outside of this position, is a timely endeavour.

Acknowledgements

Thank you to Matt James, Rosemary Hill, and Parliamentary Heritage Collections Information Assistant Lily Hosking.

References

[1] Phoebe B. Stanton, "The Collaboration Renewed: Barry and Pugin, 1844-52," in *The Houses of Parliament,* edited by M. H. Port (New Haven, CT: Yale University Press, 1976), p. 137.
[2] Henry-Russell Hitchcock, *Architecture: Nineteenth and Twentieth Centuries* (Harmondsworth: Penguin Books, 1958), p. 72.
[3] Alfred Barry, *Memoir of the Life and Works of the late Sir Charles Barry* (London: John Murray, 1870), p. 132.
[4] Margaret Belcher, *The Collected Letters of A.W.N. Pugin, Vol. 1 1830-42* (Oxford: Oxford University Press, 2001), p. 42.
[5] Barry, (Note 3), p. 236.
[6] Stanton, (Note 1), p. 129.
[7] Alfred Barry, *The Architect of the New Palace at Westminster: A Reply to a Pamphlet by E. Pugin Entitled "Who Was the Art-Architect of the Houses of Parliament?"* (London: J. Murray, 1868), p. 38.
[8] *Ibid.*, p. 39.
[9] Margaret Belcher, *The Collected Letters of A.W.N. Pugin, Vol. 2 1843-45* (Oxford: Oxford University Press, 2003), pp. 383-4.
[10] *Ibid.*, p. 384.
[11] *Ibid.*
[12] *Ibid.*
[13] *Ibid.*, pp. 393-4.
[14] "Charles Barry and his Right-Hand Man," *The Artizan* 3 no. 7 New Series (July 1, 1845), p. 137.
[15] "Decorations of the New House of Lords," *The Builder* 3 no. 135 (September 6, 1845), p. 426.
[16] *Ibid.*
[17] *Ibid.*
[18] M. H. Port, "Problems of the Building in the late 1840s," in *The Houses of Parliament,* edited by M. H. Port (New Haven, CT: Yale University Press, 1976), p. 69.
[19] Barry, (Note 7), p. 89.
[20] Richard Cavendish, "State Opening of the New Houses of Parliament," *History Today* 52 no. 11 (November 2002), p. 62.

[21] Alexandra Wedgwood, "The New Palace of Westminster," in *Pugin: A Gothic Passion,* edited by Paul Atterbury and Clive Wainwright (New Haven: Yale University Press in association with the Victoria & Albert Museum, 1994), p. 226.
[22] Michael Alexander, *Medievalism: The Middle Ages in Modern England* (New Haven: Yale University Press, 2007), p. 66.
[23] Rosemary Hill, "A.C. Pugin," *The Burlington Magazine*, Vol. 138, No. 1114 (January 1996), p. 12.
[24] Clive Wainwright, "A.W.N. Pugin and the Progress of Design as Applied to Manufacture," in *A.W.N. Pugin: Master of Gothic Revival,* edited by Paul Atterbury and Megan Brewster Aldrich (New Haven: Published for the Bard Graduate Center for Studies in the Decorative Arts, New York by Yale University Press, 1995), p. 163.
[25] Clive Wainwright, "Furniture," in *Pugin: A Gothic Passion* by Augustus Welby Northmore Pugin, edited by Paul Atterbury and Clive Wainwright (New Haven: Yale University Press in association with the Victoria & Albert Museum, 1994), p. 130.
[26] Alexandra Wedgwood, *A.W.N. Pugin and the Pugin Family, Catalogues of the Architectural Drawings at the Victoria and Albert Museum* (London: Victoria and Albert Museum, 1985), p. 27.
[27] Augustus Welby Northmore Pugin, "Autobiography," in Wedgwood, (Note 26), p. 28.
[28] [Margaret O. W. Oliphant,] "Augustus Welby Pugin," *Blackwood's Edinburg Magazine* 90 no. 554 (December 1861), p. 676.
[29] Benjamin Ferrey, *Recollections of A. N. Welby Pugin and His Father Augustus Pugin, with Notices of their Works* (London: Edward Stanford, 1861), p. 65.
[30] *Ibid.*, p. 65.
[31] Brian Hanson, *Architects and the "Building World" from Chambers to Ruskin: Constructing Authority* (Cambridge, UK: Cambridge University Press, 2003) p. 89.
[32] Belcher, (Note 9), pp. 383-4.
[33] A. Welby Pugin, *The True Principles of Pointed or Christian Architecture* (London: John Weale, 1841), p. 1.
[34] Alexandra Wedgwood, "The New Palace of Westminster," in *The Houses of Parliament: History, Art and Architecture,* edited by David Cannadine (London: Merrell, 2000), p. 123.
[35] "Decoration of Houses of Parliament." *The Builder* 3 no. 120 (May 24, 1845): p. 250.
[36] Belcher, (Note 9), p. 352.
[37] Donald W. Insall, "Restoration of the Lords' Ceiling at the Palace of Westminster," *Journal of the Royal Society for the Encouragement of Arts, Manufactures and Commerce* 134 no. 5360 (July 1986), p. 482.
[38] *The History of the King's Works, Volume VI, 1782-1851,* edited by J. Mordaunt Crook and M. H. Port (London: Her Majesty's Stationery Office, 1973), p. 613.
[39] Paul N. Hasluck, *Manual of Traditional Wood Caring: With 1,146 Working Drawings and Photographic Illustrations* (New York: Dover Publications, 1977), p. 17.
[40] Insall, (Note 37), p. 481.
[41] Alexandra Wedgwood, "The Throne in the House of Lords and Its Setting," *Architectural History* 27, Design and Practice in British Architecture: Studies in Architectural History Presented to Howard Colvin, (1984), p. 65.
[42] Robert Cooke, *The Palace of Westminster: Houses of Parliament* (London: Burton Skira, 1987), p. 113.
[43] Denis Smith, "The Techniques of the Building," in *The Houses of Parliament,* edited by M. H. Port (New Haven, CT: Yale University Press, 1976), p. 215.
[44] "New Palace of Westminster," *The Civil Engineer and Architect's Journal* 11 no. 126 (March 1848), p. 93.
[45] Akira Satoh, *Building in Britain: The Origins of a Modern Industry,* translated by Ralph Morton (Aldershot, UK: Scholar Press, 1995), p. 159.
[46] [Advertisement,] *The Builder* 8 no. 373 (March 30, 1850), p. 156.
[47] Glenn Adamson, *The Invention of Craft* (London: Bloomsbury Academic, 2013), p. 145.
[48] "Sketches of the Principal Manufactories of the Metropolis. No. 1 Patent Machine Carving Works," *Patent Journal and Inventor's Magazine* 4 no. 102 (May 20, 1848), p. 636.

[49] See Officinator, "The Patent Iron Mason," *The Builder* 1 no. 6 (March 18, 1843), 68; "Patent Iron Masons," *The Builder* 1 no. 5 (March 11, 1843), 54-55; "Patent Stone Cutting Machine and Patent Iron Masons!" *The Builder* 1 no. 4 (March 4, 1843), 41-42; P. M'Omie, "Patent Iron Masons," *The Practical Mechanic and Engineer's Magazine* 2 no. 3 (December 1842), 94-96.

[50] Robert Kerr, "Copyism in Architecture," *The Builder* 8 no. 406 (November 16, 1850): pp. 542-44; George Gilbert Scott, "Copyism in Gothic Architecture," *The Builder* 8 no. 375 (April 13, 1850), p. 42.

[51] Dorian Church, "'New Furniture of a Suitable and Proper Character': The Working Interiors, 1849-60," in *The Houses of Parliament: History, Art and Architecture,* edited by David Cannadine (London: Merrell, 2000), p. 172.

[52] Belcher, (Note 9), p. 384.

[53] Victoria and Albert Museum, *A Report by the Victoria & Albert Museum Concerning the Furniture in the House of Lords: Presented to the Sub-Committee of the Offices Committee on Works of Art in the House of Lords* (London: Her Majesty's Stationery Office, 1974), pp. 7, 9.

[54] Susan Stuart, "A Survey of Marks, Labels, and Stamps Used on Gillow and Waring & Gillow Furniture 1770-1960," *Regional Furniture* 12 (1998), p. 64.

[55] Church, (Note 51), p. 172.

[56] Wedgwood, (Note 34), p. 123.

[57] Judith Champ, *A Temple of Living Stones* (Oscott: St Mary's College Oscott, 2002), p. 42.

[58] Wedgwood, (Note 34), p. 127.

[59] *The House of Lords; A Description of that Magnificent Apartment, together with the Peers' Lobby and the Victoria Hall in the New Palace of Westminster* (London: H. G. Clarke and Co., 1852), p. 19.

[60] Insall, (Note 37), 485.

[61] Wedgwood, (Note 34), p. 125.

[62] Insall, (Note 37), 483.

[63] *Ibid.,* 491.

Early Iron Bridges in Switzerland 1850-1875: A Primer

Manuel Maissen
Institute of Construction History and Preservation (IDB), ETH Zurich, Switzerland

Abstract

Switzerland's natural geography, with its myriad mountains, valleys, and rivers, was predestined for a rich history of bridge building, from the covered timber bridges to the daring stone arch bridges, to the elegant concrete structures. For the history of construction, bridge engineering is particularly intriguing, as the actual structural design can be read so clearly on no other object. Nevertheless, particularly iron bridges, which were amongst the most prestigious engineering challenges in the second half of the 19th century, are hardly researched in Switzerland.

With the exception of a few suspension bridges built by prominent engineers in the first half of the 19th century [1], the heyday of iron bridges in Switzerland began shortly after the middle of the 19th century. The primary motor for the rapid emergence of iron as a new material in bridge construction was, of course, the railway, whose development was closely linked to the further development of iron bridges. At that time, however, there were only nine blast furnaces in Switzerland, which in 1854 were able to produce just over 12,000 tonnes of pig iron, covering only 42% of the actual demand [2]; the remaining material had to be imported from Germany, France, and England. This involved not only importing iron, but also attracting experienced engineers and companies who planned and built the earliest iron bridges. Thus, it is not feasible to speak of a domestic iron construction tradition shortly after the middle of the 19th century, but this was to change within the following years.

The present paper examines the early iron bridges in Switzerland and sheds light on their construction as well as the main protagonists involved. The study thus focusses on the genesis of a domestic iron construction industry whose development is based on a turbulent evolution of theory, curriculum, and practice. The relationship among these disciplines is not finally clarified, but it is the basis of an ongoing research project. Consequently, this paper serves as a basic introduction and a first chapter of the project; it is thus a primer.

Early suspension experiments

Whereas temporary and permanent bridges made of cast iron were built early on in England and France, e.g., the Iron Bridge by Abraham Darby III (1750-91) in Coalbrookdale (1779) or the *Pont des Arts* by Louis-Alexandre de Cessart (1719-1806) and Jacques Vincent de Lacroix Dillon (1760-1807) in Paris (1803), Switzerland never built bridges from cast iron. However, Switzerland was a pioneer in the early development of iron suspension bridges, at least in Europe. The idea of suspended bridges was already a reliable and widespread method of overcoming the many deep gorges in parts of East Asia and South America before the first suspension bridges were built in the Western world as chain bridges in the late 18th and early 19th centuries. For the European region, the Winch Bridge in northern England, built in 1741 for the workers of a nearby lead mine, is widely regarded as the first permanent chain bridge. Furthermore, the first proposal to use wire cables to suspend bridges came from England by Thomas Telford (1757-1834), who had already experimented with suspension bridges in the early 19th century. However, the use of wire cables remained a concept for the time being – at least in permanent constructions.

Early Iron Bridges in Switzerland 1850-1875: A Primer

The first permanent cable suspension bridge was then, as is well-known, built in Switzerland and has already been carefully studied and thoroughly published by Tom F. Peters [3]. Designed and constructed in Geneva by Guillaume-Henri Dufour (1787-1875) and Marc Seguin (1786-1875) between 1822 and 1823, the *Passerelle de Saint-Antoine* with a double span of 40 m each with six cables over a middle support [4] existed for about 40 years until its demolition. The *Passerelle de Saint-Antoine*, with its combined length of 82 m, was eclipsed a few years later by the *Grand Pont Supendu* in Fribourg, completed in 1834 by the French engineer Joseph Chaley (1795-1861): With its length of 273 m, this bridge was the longest in the world at that time. This suspension bridge, which remained until 1924, has also been published at length, with even a thorough contemporary publication by Louis-Joseph Schmid documenting the construction of the bridge [5]. Chaley also built in the region of Fribourg the 200 m long *Pont de Gottéron* over the Galtern gorge from 1838-40 as well as another suspension bridge near Corbièrs around 1836/37 [6].

Figure 1: Photograph of the 'Kettenbrücke' in Aarau taken by an unknown photographer before 1921 (ETH Library Zurich, Image Archive, Fel_003964-RE)

The last suspension bridge worth mentioning is less well known: After the previous timber structures were destroyed by floods in 1831 and again in 1843, the Mulhouse-born engineer Jean Gaspard Dollfus (1812-89) built a chain suspension bridge over the river Aare near Aarau. Completed in 1850 and inaugurated in 1851, the structure is commonly known as the *Kettenbrücke* (chain bridge) and spanned 96 m (Fig. 1). Two chains of flat iron links were arranged above each other on both sides and anchored to the gate structures; suspended from the chains was a roadway with timber cross beams, which were replaced in 1876 [7]. After a hundred years of service, the *Kettenbrücke* was finally replaced by a concrete bridge in 1949.

Age of Pioneers

The development of iron bridge construction after the middle of the 19th century was closely intertwined with the rise of the railway. The age of railway construction began late in Switzerland, partly because of the lack of a legal basis and disagreements between the cantons. The first contact with the railway came from outside when the city of Basel was connected from Strasbourg in 1844. The first railway line to be built entirely on Swiss territory was the 23 km long route from Zurich to Baden, which was opened in 1847 [8]. The hesitant development began to shift only after the adoption of the Swiss Federal Constitution of 1848 and the transition from a confederation of states to a modern federal state. This now laid the foundation for extending railway lines across cantonal borders. From 1849 onwards, the parliament debated whether the expansion of the railways should be state-owned or privatised. The resulting 'Federal Law on the Construction and Operation of Railways on the Territory of the Swiss Confederation' of 28 July 1852 ultimately confirmed in favour of private companies, whereby the cantons themselves could grant concessions [9]. The Railway Act immediately led to the foundation of several railway construction companies and fierce competition among private entrepreneurs such as the alleged 'Railway King' Alfred Escher (1819-89).

Already in 1850, the Federal Council began planning a route linking the three largest German-speaking cities in Switzerland, Basel, Bern, and Zurich, for which the British engineers Robert Stephenson (1803-59) and Henry Swinburne († 1855) were invited as experts. The contract then went to the recently founded *'Schweizer Centralbahn'* (SCB) in 1853, which at the same time had appointed the German-born engineer and architect Karl von Etzel (1812-65) as chief engineer [10]. Before his arrival in Switzerland, Etzel had already worked in the railway industry in France, Germany, and Austria [11]. Under his direction, the *Hauensteinstrecke* from Basel to Olten was built immediately from 1853, while at the same time he also organised the construction service of the SCB [12].

The extension of the Hauenstein line also required the construction of several bridges, of which two iron bridges designed by Karl von Etzel himself are particularly significant. In 1854, the *Frenkebrücke* at Liestal near Basel was built as probably the first continuous truss girder in Switzerland, over three spans of 18.6 m each. The bridge was decommissioned in 2007 and still exists largely in its original condition [13]. The second significant bridge was located at the other end of the railway line in Olten and crossed the Aare as the first Swiss arch bridge made of welded iron. The *Tannwaldbrücke* (Fig. 2) was built in 1854-56 by the Swiss engineer and head of the machine shop of the SCB Nikolaus Riggenbach (1817-99) and was 103 m in total length with three arches of 31.5 m span each. The Tannwald Bridge is thus about the same age as the *Pont d'Arcole* in Paris, which likewise opened in 1856. The landmark bridge regrettably no longer exists, having been replaced by a solid-web girder in 1952. Still preserved is a small bridge designed by Etzel near Läufelfingen north of Olten, which is regarded as the oldest solid-web girder in Switzerland dating back to 1856.

Figure 2: Photograph of the Tannwald Bridge near Olten, unknown photographer, approx. 1912-16 (SBB Historic, F_103_00001_012)

Concept of the incremental launch

What also has been preserved is a collection of plans with all the Swiss bridges designed by Karl von Etzel [14] as well as technical drawings of work processes, scaffolding and construction machinery used [15]. For instance, a detailed drawing of the Tannwald Bridge shows that each arch opening consists of five braced individual arches (Fig. 3) and further details such as the profiles and bolted connections. The collection also contains plans of other famous iron bridges, including the *Sitterbrücke* near St. Gallen of the *'Sankt Gallisch-Appenzellische Eisenbahn'* (SGAE), whose design he devised himself (Fig. 4). The bridge was built until 1856 by Jean Gaspard Dollfus, who had already built the *Kettenbrücke* in Aarau. The Sitter bridge was a 3.6 m high continuous lattice truss girder, which was supported on three almost 50 m high cast-iron columns and reached a total length of 165 m over four approx. 40 m spans. The same construction was implemented by Etzel for several bridges until 1856, including the Thur Bridge near Schwarzenbach as well as bridges near Bern, Burgdorf, Wil, Flawil, Derendingen, Solothurn or Lucerne. The bridges in eastern Switzerland (St. Gallen, Schwarzenbach, Wil and Flawil) were built by Jean-Gaspard Dollfus, while the bridges in Bern and Burgdorf were constructed by the German company Gebr. Benckiser [16].

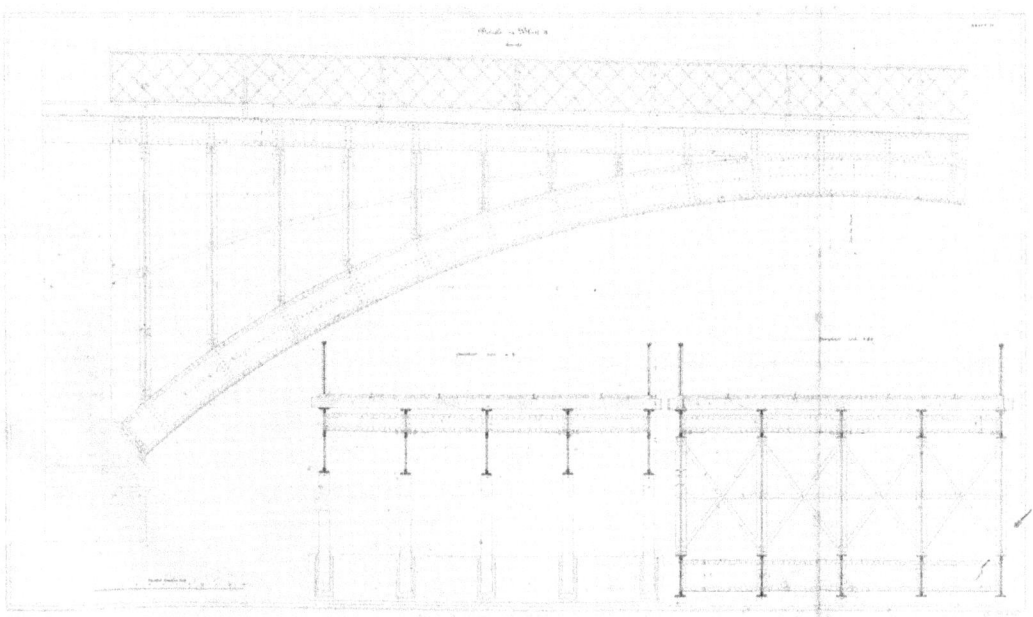

Figure 3: Details of the Tannwald Bridge drawn by Karl von Etzel and published in 1856 (ETH Library Zurich, Rar 10141)

Figure 4: The Sitter Bridge by Karl von Etzel and Jean Gaspard Dollfus, photographed by Otto Rietmann between 1900 and 1925 (Cantonal Library St. Gallen Vadiana, VSRG 51152)

Early Iron Bridges in Switzerland 1850-1875: A Primer

For three of the continuous lattice truss bridges in eastern Switzerland – the Sitter, Thur and Glatt Bridges – many details of the construction itself are known thanks to a detailed article by an unknown author in the '*Allgemeine Bauzeitung*' of 1856 [17]. Martin Trautz and Friedmar Voormann suggest that the author could have been associated with the Benckiser company [18], which could well be possible due to the company's involvement in the construction of the lattice truss bridges built shortly afterwards in the greater Bern area. The unknown author reports that the lattice truss bridges were transported as small welded-iron angles and flat bars and assembled on site in workshops. The finished lattice truss walls were then rolled onto the supports from the west on free-span auxiliary scaffolding (Fig. 5, Nr. 1) and then riveted to the transverse bars. The assembly of the bridge took a total of five weeks, although the author blames the cold and wet winter of 1855/56 for the prolonged time [19].

The three bridges were all assembled according to the same principle, whereby free-span scaffolds were always required for the roll-over. The unknown author criticises this costly and time-consuming process and provides a 'Proposal for the roll-over of the lattice walls without scaffolding' at the end of the article [20]. The author suggests that on the mainland the entire bridge, including the rails, is riveted together on pulleys or rollers, and then pulled or pushed over the piers from the other side with the help of a crane. (Fig. 5, Nr. 3) . The bridge is thus freely cantilevered without being supported by a scaffold, which conforms to the modern incremental launching method.

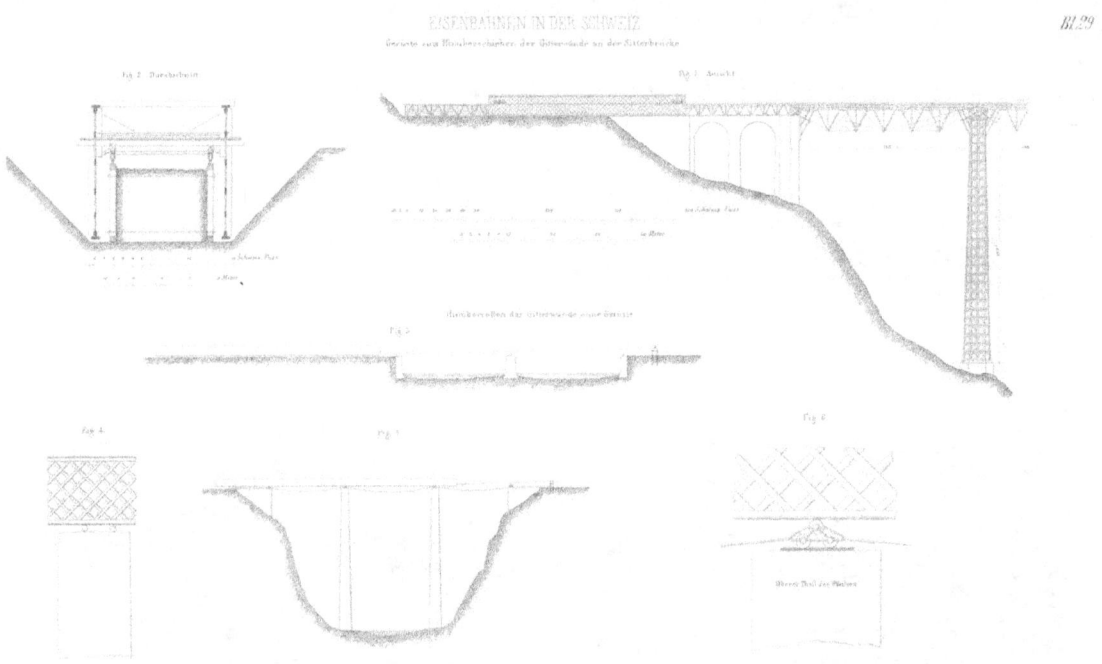

Figure 5: Construction of the Sitter bridge and proposal for the incremental launching method (Allgemeine Bauzeitung, note 17, plate 29)

This proposal was already realised in 1856 by the Gebr. Benckiser company at the bridge over the Worblaufen valley near Bern and at the *Thurbrücke* near Andelfingen, which is why the assumption of the unknown author's origin made by Trautz and Voormann seems reasonable. The first-mentioned bridge was again projected by Karl von Etzel, who produced a detailed drawing for the pulling of the lattice truss (Fig. 6), which confirms the procedure proposed by the unknown author. The same protagonists expanded the principle shortly afterwards when constructing the so-called *'Rote Brücke'* (Red Bridge) in Bern by 1858. Since the bridge with its total length of 168 m was too long to be prefabricated in one piece, an approx. 70 m long section was fully constructed, advanced over an auxiliary support onto the first pier and then the next stretch was added. To reduce the load on the girder, a wooden launching nose was attached at the front. The bridge was thus continuously advanced, and the auxiliary support could also be relocated in each step if necessary [21].

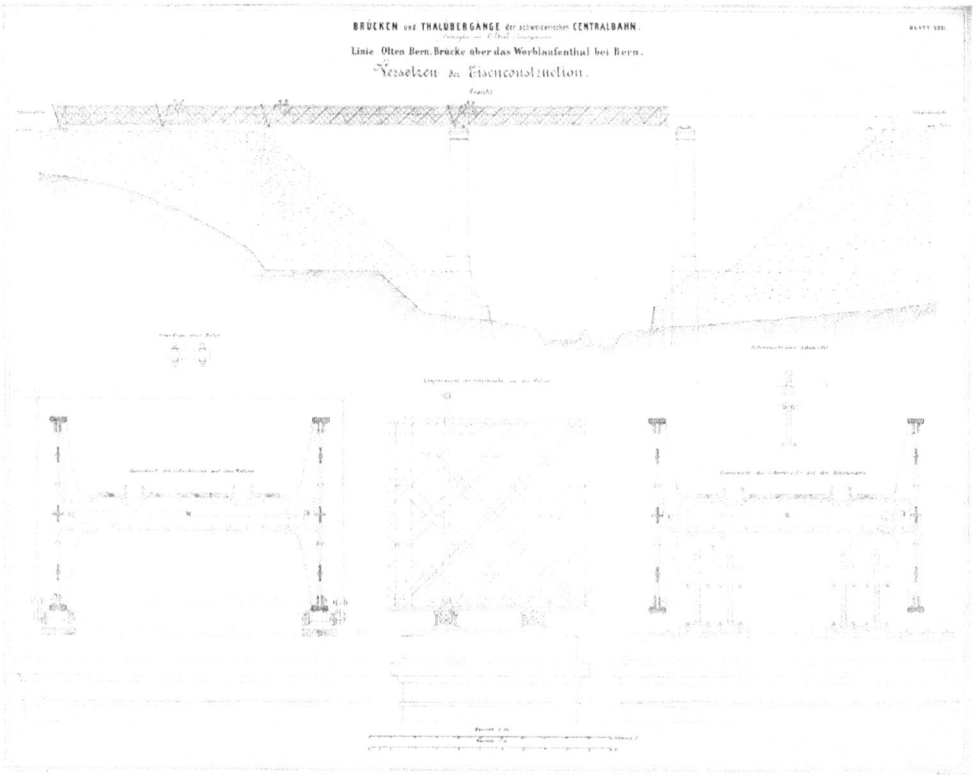

Figure 6: Incremental launching during the construction of the bridge over the Worblaufental near Bern, plan by Karl von Etzel and published in 1859 (ETH Library Zurich, Rar 10141)

Towards new shores and summits

The initial development of iron bridges in Switzerland is strongly associated with the person of Karl von Etzel, who already in 1857 transferred to Vienna, where he planned the Brenner Railway as construction director of the *'Südbahngesellschaft'* (Southern Railway Company) until his death in 1864. The Benckiser company continued to operate in Switzerland and built one of the most famous continuous lattice truss bridges still in use: The *Rheinbrücke* Waldshut-Koblenz. The Rhine Bridge was the first bridge to connect the Swiss and German railway networks and the first railway bridge ever to cross the Rhine. The bridge was built according to the same principle as the Red Bridge in Bern, whereby the lattice girder was pushed in from the German side over two supports (spans: 37 – 55 – 37 m) and was connected to a masonry viaduct on the Swiss side. The construction of the Rhine bridge was led by the Karlsruhe engineer Robert Gerwig (1820-85), who was also involved in the extension of the northern ramp of the Gotthard railway in the 1870s.

In western Switzerland, in the late 1850s, Jules Gaudard (1833-1917), a native of Arzier-Le Muids near Nyon, was perhaps the first Swiss engineer to build a series of iron solid-web girder bridges on the Yverdon-Vaumarcus and Lausanne-Villeneuve railway lines. Gaudard studied in Paris at the *École centrale des arts et manufactures* and became a professor at the *École spéciale de Lausanne* in 1865. During the same period, one of the most important iron bridges on the Bern-Lausanne railway line was built in Fribourg: The *Viaduc de Grandfey* (Fig. 7). The large-scale project was designed by the German engineer Wilhelm Nördling (1821-1908), Charles Jaquemin along with another engineer named Durbach, and constructed by Ferdinand Mathieu of the French company Schneider & Cie. from Le Creusot [22]. The 383 m long lattice truss bridge was built over six iron piers (spans 5 × 49 m, 2 × 42 m) through incremental launching. The extended end of the cantilevered bridge thereby also served as a crane for the construction of the piers made of prefabricated iron elements. Unfortunately, the bridge was becoming insufficient for the increasingly heavy trains and was replaced in 1925/26 by a concrete arch bridge designed by Adolf Bühler (1882-1951).

Figure 7: The Grandfey Viaduct of Fribourg, lithograph by Isidore Laurent Deroy, after 1862 (Swiss National Library, GS-GRAF-ANSI-FR-16)

In the 1860s, railway construction was temporarily slower, partly because the most important railway lines had been completed and were in operation. Iron bridges continued to be built, including, for example, the Reuss bridge in Lucerne built in 1864 from half-parabolic girders by the Benckiser company [23]. Five years later, Jules Gaudard built the first *Seebrücke* (lake bridge) in Lucerne as a shallow solid-web girder over six low piers for pedestrians and vehicular traffic (Fig. 8). Gaudard also engineered the *Viaduc du Day* near Vallorbe, completed in 1869, which was subsequently replaced by a concrete bridge in 1925. Involved in the construction of the Viaduc du Day was also the Swiss engineer Gustave Bridel (1827-84), who had been active in various railway projects in France in the 1850s. Bridel was responsible for the development of the *'Chemins de fer du Jura bernois'* (Bernese Jura Railway) in the 1870s and acted as chief engineer of the Gotthard line from 1879.

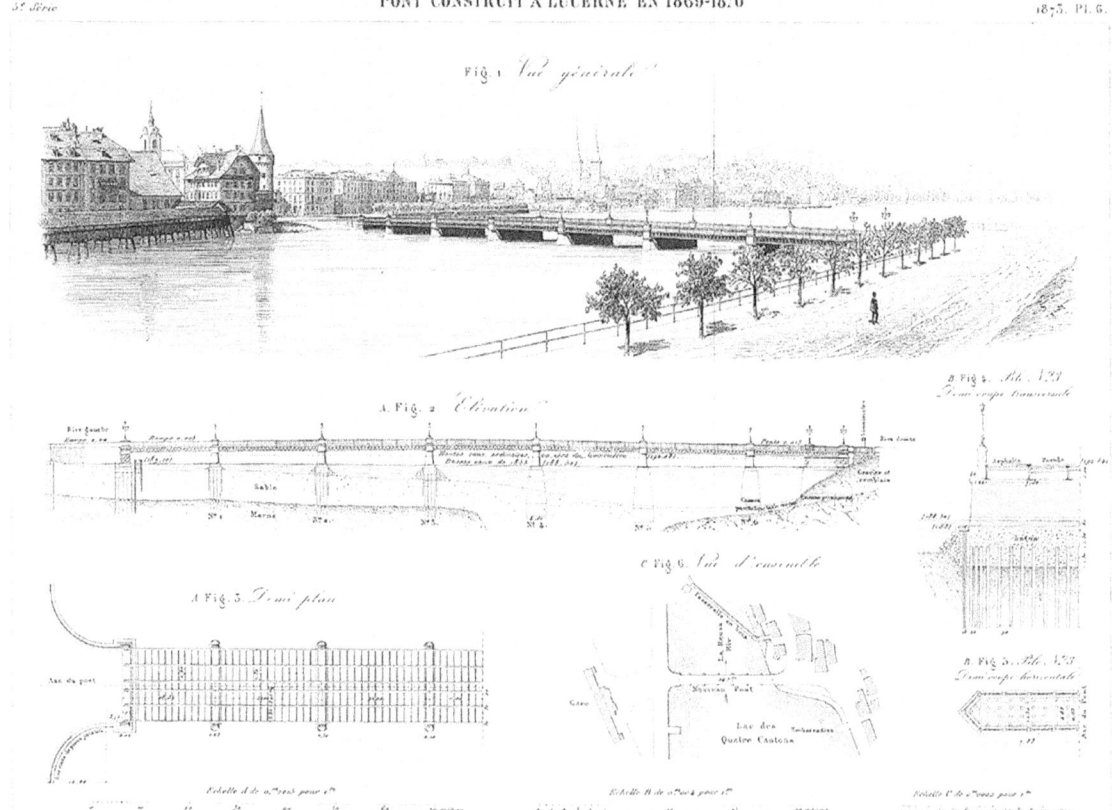

Figure 8: The 145 m long 'Seebrücke' Luzern by Jules Gaudard (1869), engraving by E. Pérot (Swiss National Library, G 8841/1)

The idea of constructing the transalpine Gotthard line arose already in the early 1860s after the success of the Semmering and Brenner railway. The German engineers August von Beckh (1809-99) and Robert Gerwig even prepared expert reports on this project shortly after 1860. However, the Gotthard Railway Company was only established in 1871 with Alfred Escher as its director, whilst the expansion of the transalpine route began shortly afterwards.

Genesis of a domestic iron construction tradition

The early years of industrial iron bridge construction in Switzerland were advanced by engineers from the neighbouring countries, especially Germany, as these engineers already had the benefit of many years of practical experience. Certainly, Swiss engineers were also involved in the construction of the early iron bridges before 1860, but hardly in leading positions. This only changed slowly during the 1860s through young engineers who studied mainly in Paris and then gained practical experience in France, Germany and in the Swiss railway projects.

The *École centrale* in Paris was particularly popular, where several later well-known engineers studied in the late 1840s. Among them were the already mentioned Jules Gaudard and Gustave Bridel, the latter studying together with Amédée von Muralt (1829-1909), Émile Burnat (1828-1920) and Henry Louis Oscar de Blonay (1826-1905) [24]. At that time Auguste Perdonnet (1801-67) was a professor at the *École centrale*, whose father Vincent came from Vevey on the shores of Lake Geneva and was married to a Françoise Bridel. Gustave Bridel was hence related to Perdonnet and worked with him on the first two volumes of the influential treatise *'Traité élémentaire des chemins de fer'* [25]. However, Bridel's name does not appear on the cover, a point that Perdonnet comments on in the introduction: "Telle a été sa coopération à ce travail qu'il aurait pu, s'il n'était aussi modeste que capable, revendiquer de droit de placer son nom avec le nôtre en tête de ce livre" [26]. Bridel would certainly have had a thriving future as an engineer in France, but he was drawn back to Switzerland by 1857.

Following the example and curriculum of the renowned schools in France, polytechnic schools were also founded in Switzerland after the middle of the 19th century. In 1853, modelled on the *École central*, the *École spéciale de Lausanne* was established, now known as the *École polytechnique fédérale de Lausanne* (EPFL). As previously mentioned, Jules Gaudard was appointed professor of construction, topography, and geodesy here in 1865. Two years after the Lausanne Polytechnic, the *Eidgenössische polytechnische Schule*, today's ETH, was founded in Zurich and began operations on 16 October 1855.

Among the first professors at the Zurich polytechnic school was Karl Culmann (1821-81), who together with Johannes Wild (1814-94), Professor of Topography and Geodesy, directed the Department of Engineering [27]. Culmann's significant contributions to the construction of iron bridges began after an extensive study expedition through England and North America from 1849 to 1851. Shortly after his return, he published two comprehensive travel reports in the *'Allgemeine Bauzeitung'*. In the first report on timber bridges in the United States of America [28], he developed his 'truss theory', which was published in 1851 more or less simultaneously with the theory of Johann Wilhelm Schwedler (1823-94). A year later the second report on the construction of iron bridges in England and America followed [29], containing analyses, calculations, and some drawings. As a professor of road, railway, bridge, and hydraulic engineering, Culmann taught a new generation of Swiss engineers the basics of building iron bridges and even visited with his students the construction site of the Sitter Bridge in St. Gallen in 1856 or the completed Grandfey Viaduct in Fribourg in 1862 [30]. From 1860, he also lectured for the first time on his main work *'Die graphische Statik'* (Graphic Statics), which he published in 1866 [31].

Several young outstanding minds studied under Culmann, who were later to excel in the various fields of engineering. Among Culmann's best-known graduates was Maurice Koechlin (1856-1946), who, under Gustave Eiffel (1832-1923), was instrumental as chief engineer in the construction of the Garabit Viaduct, the substructure of the Statue of Liberty and the Eiffel Tower. Also studying with Culmann in his sophomore year was Robert Moser (1838-1918) from 1856 to 1859, thus Moser was one of the students who was in the audience for the inspection of the Sitter Bridge. As chief engineer of the *'Schweizer Nordostbahn'* (NOB), he was responsible for the line extension from 1872 and designed several iron bridges, including the *Untere Limmatbrücke* near Wettingen, which was opened in 1877 (Fig. 9). Moser was also involved in the expansion of the Gotthard line and established his own engineering practice.

Figure 9: Construction of the *'Untere Limmatbrücke'* near Wettingen, photo by A. Bachmann c. 1875 (ETH Library Zurich, Image Archive, Ans_05444-025-AL-FL)

Figure 10: The Aare bridge near Brugg by Beat Gubser, photo by A. Bachmann c. 1875 (ETH Library Zurich, Image Archive, Ans_05444-003-AL-FL)

Nevertheless, Swiss engineers also attended polytechnic schools in neighbouring countries. The later iron industrialist Gottlieb Ott (1832-82) and the well-known bridge builder Beat Gubser (1836-82) both studied at the Karlsruhe Polytechnic and later built bridges together. Gubser was even a partner in the company Ott & Cie. for a time [32]. Beat Gubser built numerous iron bridges and iron roof trusses, as far away as Hungary. His most famous structure – and probably the most beautiful iron bridge ever to be built in Switzerland – was the *Aarebrücke* in Brugg with its wonderful 'Pauli girders' (Fig. 10). The Aare bridge existed from 1875 to 1905 when the Pauli girders were replaced by semi-parabolic trusses – this bridge is not preserved either as the iron superstructure was replaced in 1993-96.

Conclusion and perspective

The industrial construction of iron bridges began in Switzerland shortly after 1850 and was directly dependent on the development of railway lines. It is therefore not surprising that in the first phase until the early 1860s, almost exclusively iron railway bridges were built. Most of these iron bridges were designed by experienced engineers from Germany or France and built by companies from neighbouring countries. At that time, some young Swiss engineers trained in France and Germany were employed by these planners and companies and gained practical experience in iron construction.

A domestic iron bridge industry then developed in the 1860s and Swiss engineers shaped the industry by designing and building impressive monuments. In contrast to the first peak in iron bridge construction in the late 1850s, the second main phase from 1870 to 1892 involved significantly more Swiss engineers in leading roles – some of whom were also trained at the local polytechnic schools. The second phase was not as heavily dependent on the railway and thus road and pedestrian bridges made of iron were increasingly built. However, the railway remained the main client for the grandest and most prestigious iron bridge projects, for example on the Gotthard route. The second main phase continued until the 1890s, when the railway bridge at Münchenstein near Basel, built by Gustave Eiffel, collapsed on 14 June 1891. Subsequently, many of the existing iron bridges were modified and strengthened and new foundations for calculation and construction were created, for example by Culmann's successor Wilhelm Ritter (1847-1906).

A more profound study of the early development of iron bridge construction in Switzerland, the protagonists involved and their training and curriculum at the polytechnic schools in Lausanne and Zurich appears to have great potential. Especially the transition period of the 1860s and early 1870s deserves a closer look. And this is intended as a research project for the years ahead, very much in the spirit of Culmann, who wrote about the weighing of iron in industrial bridge construction: "[this], would be a fine task [...]. Let those who have the time set about it." [33]

References

[1] T. F. Peters, *Transitions in Engineering: Guillaume Henri Dufour and the Early 19th Century Cable Suspension Bridge*. Basel, Boston: Birkhäuser, 1987.
[2] E. Berninger, P.L. Pelet: '*Eisen'*, in: Historisches Lexikon der Schweiz (HLS), version of 10.04.2006, translated from French. Online: https://hls-dhs-dss.ch/de/articles/026231/2006-04-10/, consulted on 21.01.2022.
[3] Peters, Transitions (note 1), pp. 66-114.
[4] G.-H. Dufour, *Description du Pont Supendu en fil de Fer, construit à Genève*. Geneva: J.-J. Paschoud, 1824, pp. 28-42.
[5] L.-J. Schmid, *Description historique et technique du grand-pont, suspendu en fil de fer, à Fribourg en Suisse*. Fribourg: L.-J. Schmid, 1839.
[6] C. Mutter, 'Höhepunkte der Freiburger Brückengeschichte', *Kunst + Architektur in der Schweiz*, Vol. 46/2, 1995, pp. 144-154; Peters, Transitions (note 1), p. 156.
[7] E. Zimmerlin, 'Abschied von der Kettenbrücke', *Aargauer Neujahrblätter*, Vol. 23, 1949, pp. 66-71.
[8] SBB Fachstelle für Denkmalpflege (Eds.), *Schweizer Bahnbrücken*. Reihe Architektur- und Technikgeschichte der Eisenbahnen in der Schweiz. Zurich: Scheidegger & Spiess, 2013, p. 13.

[9] *Amtliche Sammlung der Bundesgesetze und Verordnungen der Schweizerischen Eidgenossenschaft*, Vol. 3. Bern: Stämpflische Buchdruckerei, 1853, pp. 170-176.

[10] There are different versions of his name, with both Karl and Carl. The title 'von' was conferred on him in 1853 after he was decorated with the Knight's Cross of the Order of the Württemberg Crown.

[11] A. Jursitzka, H. Pawelka, *Carl von Etzel: Ein Leben für die Eisenbahn*. Innsbruck, Wien: Tyrolia, 2017, pp. 9-18, 85-91.

[12] C. von Etzel, *Organisation des Baudienstes bei der Schweizerischen Centralbahn*. Basel: Schweighauser'sche Verlagsbuchhandlung, 1854.

[13] SBB, Bahnbrücken (note 8), p. 186.

[14] C. von Etzel, *Bruecken und Thaluebergaenge schweizerischer Eisenbahnen*. Basel: Bahnmaiers Buchhandlung, 1856.

[15] C. von Etzel, *Supplement zu den Bruecken und Thaluebergaenge schweizerischer Eisenbahnen*. Basel: Bahnmaiers Buchhandlung, 1859.

[16] Von Etzel, Bruecken (note 14), pp. 7-18.

[17] N. N., 'Eisenbahnen in der Schweiz: Das Aufstellen der Thur-, Glatt- und Sitterbrücken', *Allgemeine Bauzeitung*, Vol. 21, 1856 pp. 133-137, plates 28-29.

[18] M. Trautz, F. Voormann, 'Der Bau eiserner Brücken im Südwesten Deutschlands 1844 bis 1889 – Gitterträgerbrücken und Taktschiebeverfahren (Teil 2)', *Stahlbau*, Vol. 81/2, 2012, pp. 138-139.

[19] Allgemeine Bauzeitung (note 17), p. 135.

[20] Allgemeine Bauzeitung (note 17), p. 135-139.

[21] R. Merian, 'Gitterbrücke über die Aare bei Bern', *Schweizerische Polytechnische Zeitschrift*, Vol. 4/1, 1859, pp. 11-19.

[22] SBB, Bahnbrücken (note 8), p. 186.

[23] SBB, Bahnbrücken (note 8), p. 20-21.

[24] G. Bridel, 'Ingenieur Gustave Bridel (1827-1884)', *Berner Zeitschrift für Geschichte und Heimatkunde*, Vol. 14, 1952, pp. 55-71, here p. 56. This article was written by a descendant of Gustave Bridel with the same name.

[25] A. Perdonnet, Traité élémentaire des chemins de fer. Paris: Langlois et Leclercq, 1855-56.

[26] Perdonnet, Traite (note 25), Préface III. Translation by the author: "Such has been his cooperation in this work that he might, if he were not so modest as he is capable, have claimed the right to place his name with ours at the front of this book."

[27] C. Lehmann, B. Maurer, *Karl Culmann und die graphische Statik: Zeichnen, die Sprache des Ingenieurs*. Berlin: Ernst & Sohn, 2006, p. 96.

[28] K. Culmann, 'Der Bau der hölzernen Brücken in den Vereinigten Staaten von Nordamerika', *Allgemeine Bauzeitung*, Vol. 16, pp. 69-129.

[29] K. Culmann, 'Der Bau der eisernen Brücken in England und Amerika', Allgemeine Bauzeitung, Vol. 17, pp. 163-222.

[30] Lehmann & Maurer, Culmann (note 27), p. 99.

[31] K. Culmann, *Die graphische Statik*. Zurich: Meyer & Zeller, 1866.

[32] N.N., 'J. B. Gubser' (Orbituary), *Schweizerische Bauzeitung*, Vol. 1/2, 1883, p. 11.

[33] Culmann, Eiserne Brücken (note 29), p. 222.

Technical Writings as Political: Building Manuals and Pattern Books from British India (1880-1947)

Sarah Melsens [1], Chetan Sahasrabudhe [2]
[1] Postdoctoral Researcher, Faculty of Design Sciences, University of Antwerp
[2] College of Architecture (Savitribai Phule Pune University)

Abstract

This paper presents an analysis of building manuals and technical texts on construction authored in unofficial capacity by Indian engineers employed in British India's colonial Public Works Department (PWD). These texts were published between 1880 and India's independence in 1947, and thus emerged in parallel to the Indian nationalist movement. The paper aims to explore whether the two phenomena were related and, if so, seeks to reveal the specific nature of relationships between nationalist sentiments and technical writings on construction. In order to do so we examine a number of texts in terms of their intended audience, authors, content, and form, but also investigate the extent to which they borrowed or deviated from the government-published practical handbooks compiled for use in the colonial Public Works Department (eight editions between 1876 and 1931). While the latter were authored in English and have been well known, the former were also published in regional languages and have been largely forgotten.

Introduction

British India's colonial Public Works Department was formally established in 1854 around the time the territory of the East India Company came under Crown rule. It is well-documented and has featured extensively in scholarly research; yet, it is only in the last decades that attempts have been made to investigate the role of *Indian* engineers employed in this enormous organisation [1]. Accounts of the careers of legendary Indian PWD engineers such as Muncher Cowasji Murzban (1839-1917) and Ganga Ram (1851-1927) recently featured in English scholarship, and illustrate that by the end of the 19th century, certain Indian engineers were able to rise to posts where they could become 'intentional actors' who used their position not only to serve the British Raj but also their own community's interests (Fig. 1) [2]. Indeed, Murzban and Ram designed or organised the construction of some of the most prominent public buildings in colonial Bombay and Lahore and were even bestowed with imperial titles after their successful provision of temporary infrastructure for the royal visit of Prince Albert to Bombay (Murzban, in 1890), and for the Delhi Durbar (Ganga Ram for the 1903 durbar). However, in their nonofficial capacity, they also offered design-and-build services to Indian elites and financed welfare and educational projects for their own Parsee and Sikh communities. Far from being passive functionaries of the colonial regime, Indian engineers, thus, much like contemporary Indian mercantile elites and those engaged in upcoming law and medical professions, gradually accumulated agency in shaping the future of British India's cities and communities.

A contribution from these Indian PWD engineers which has remained overlooked so far is their technical writings directed at a general audience of laymen, craftsmen and contractors. Writing in an unofficial capacity and appropriating literary genres originating in the West, PWD engineers were prolific authors of technical texts on construction that took the form of articles in periodicals, building manuals, pattern books, and advice books, written in English and regional languages. What appears to be the earliest popular handbook by an Indian PWD engineer, is Ganga Ram's *Pocket book of Indian Engineering,* of which no less than four editions (in English and Urdu) were published between 1888 and 1906, with a fifth posthumous edition compiled in 1927 [3]. The first half of the book deals with mathematics, surveying, building

Technical Writings as Political: Building Manuals and Pattern Books from British India (1880-1947)

materials and civil engineering, but it also contains sections on sanitary, mechanical and electrical engineering as well as numerous practical tables and ready reckoners. Unique features are its 'technical dictionary' of building vocabulary from English to Hindustani (Punjabi in earlier editions), and the tables to convert India's regional measurement systems to European ones. Reflecting Ganga Ram's career trajectory – which included a short apprenticeship with an architect in London [4] – the second part of the book is a pattern book with drawings ranging from structural details to bridge designs, and from ornamental architectural details (historical and contemporary) to model plans of the sort of buildings on which the engineer himself was engaged, including houses of 'European' and 'Indian fashion'. Here, the engineer pioneered the wider circulation of knowledge of design aesthetics formerly only accessible to educated classes or those familiar with contemporary 'drawing portfolios' produced in art and architectural circles [5].

Figure 1: From left to right – Khan Bahadur Muncher Cowasji Murzban (1839-1917). Source: Fardunji Murzbanji, Leaves from the life of Khan Bahadur Muncherji Cowasji Murzban, C.I.E. Bombay: 1915; Sir Ganga Ram (1851-1927). Source: B. P. L. Bedi, Harvest from the Desert, Lahore: 1940; Rao Bahadur Vasudev Bapuji Kanitkar (1827-1904). Source: framed portrait in Pune's former Municipal offices, photographed by Vaidehi Lavand.

Ganga Ram's idiosyncratically collated book set the tone for a number of other books published in the interwar period including engineer Surendra Kumar Basu's books *Helps to building construction* (sic.) and *Specifications and other useful notes on building construction* printed in Bengal prior to 1924 [6]; several works by Bombay PWD engineer Raghunath Shripad Deshpande published in Marathi and English from 1930 onwards; and Bhavnagar State Engineer, Virendraray C. Mehta's book *Grihvidhan ('Statement on houseform'*, alternatively 'System and rules of architecture'*),* written in Gujarati in 1937 [7].

To shed further light on the ambiguous profiling and intermediary role of Indian engineers in late colonial power structures, this article focuses on two specific sets of publications produced in the Bombay Presidency before Indian independence in 1947. The first are the articles on building construction featured in the Marathi periodical Shilpa-Kala-Vidnyan (Construction-Art-Science) which was published monthly and continuously from 1887 until at least 1893. As far as we know, the journal has not been discussed in academic scholarship before and it does not feature in a recently compiled index of journals from British India [8]. These texts, as we will demonstrate, reveal how an emerging intertwinement of nationalism with technology in the late 19th century, a hotly debated topic amongst historians of science and technology in colonial India, also manifested itself in the field of construction [9].

The second set of publications are the advice books written by Bombay PWD engineer Raghunath Shripad Deshpande (1889-ca.1969). Almost all Deshpande's advice books, though to varying degrees, contain practical or technical advice on construction as well as model plans and elevations of residential buildings. This distinguishes them from the author's more 'scientific' publications intended for students of engineering or engineers, books which fall beyond the scope of this article [10]. A first duo of advice books are predominantly technical: the Marathi building manual *Sulabh Vastushastra* ('Simplified building science', 1930) [11], later substantially reworked and translated in English as *Build your own home* (1943). A second duo contains a larger number of pattern drawings and lays out practical advice on 'house planning' and how and when to economise through design and in construction: *Residential buildings suited to India* (1931), updated and republished as *Modern Ideal Homes for India* (1939). A fifth related yet somewhat distinct advice book by Deshpande is *Cheap and healthy homes for the middle classes of India* (1935) which is particularly concerned with affordable designs and (semi-vernacular) building technologies suited to the lower middle classes and 'poor'. As we will argue, these books reflect the author's efforts to cast construction knowledge in relation to the newly articulated and diverging positions of nationalists Mohandas Gandhi and Jawaharlal Nehru on the role of modernisation and industrialisation in the national project.

Delving into these technical publications and their conditions of emergence, we examine the social profile and networks of the authors, the texts' formats and intended audiences, their contents, and possible value judgments expressed in each. In addition, we will touch upon the extent to which authors borrowed or deviated from the official practical handbooks on construction compiled for use in the Public Works Department of the Bombay Presidency or felt the need to address issues raised in contemporary architectural discourse. The findings allow a shift to be discerned in popular writing on construction occurring between the late colonial and interwar period, a shift which we argue cannot be seen in isolation from the 'Indianisation' of many aspects of urban development and governance following the constitutional reforms of the Government of India Act in 1919 [12], and which draws attention to the changing way technology has served nationalist sentiments, also in the field of construction.

Shilpa-Kala-Vidnyan: modernising craftsmanship

In late 19th-century Pune (formerly Poona), a group of prominent English-educated Brahmins, employed in modern professional occupations such as teaching, law and medicine, were able to achieve an unseen level of organisation in their efforts for social reforms, modernisation and ultimately political self-rule. The unfairness of colonial policies and the denial of opportunities to the higher middle classes in upper levels of governance or public institutions, incited them to establish political organisations, educational organisations 'for Indians run by Indians', and an independent press critiquing current socio-political affairs (the *Kesari* and *Mahratta* newspapers). More than a decade before the Indian National Congress took up the question of technical education, 'both papers consistently argued for the need for the industrialization of India and for technical education [13]'. Only by gaining technical expertise, they believed, would they themselves be able to take control of their economy and future. Of the nine editors of the *Mahratta* prior to 1902, the editor 'most associated with industrial development' was Mahadev Ballal Namjoshi (1853-1896) [14].

A close associate of Bal Gangadhar Tilak (1856-1920), one of the leading figures in this nationalist movement, Namjoshi vigorously promoted technical education on various fronts. At his insistence, the curriculum of the New English school, a private high school he co-founded in Pune in 1880, included physics, chemistry, mechanics, and drawing [15]. He organised mixed-language vocational training at the Pune Native Institution Workshop in 1887 and at Pune's Victoria Jubilee Municipal Technical School in 1889 [16], and conceptualised the Poona Industrial Exhibition of 1888 [17]. He also edited two journals related to the sciences and industries: the English-language journal *The Industrial Quarterly Review of Western India* published from 1892, and the Marathi journal *Shilpa-Kala-Vidnyan*, published from 1887 (Fig. 2). While the former focused more on economic enterprise, the Marathi periodical was intended for artisans and dealt with such diverse subjects as cloth-weaving, machine mechanics, botanics, drawing techniques, carpentry, brickwork, and architecture. It was part of wider-spread efforts to publish technical knowledge in regional languages in late 19th-

Technical Writings as Political: Building Manuals and Pattern Books from British India (1880-1947)

century and early 20th-century India [18]. In keeping with the practice followed by many British periodicals, the content published in *Shilpa-Kala-Vidnyan* was serialised. The essays by various authors ran across several issues and had their own page numbering, a practice clearly meant to help the subscribers in binding the essays as separate topical handbooks.

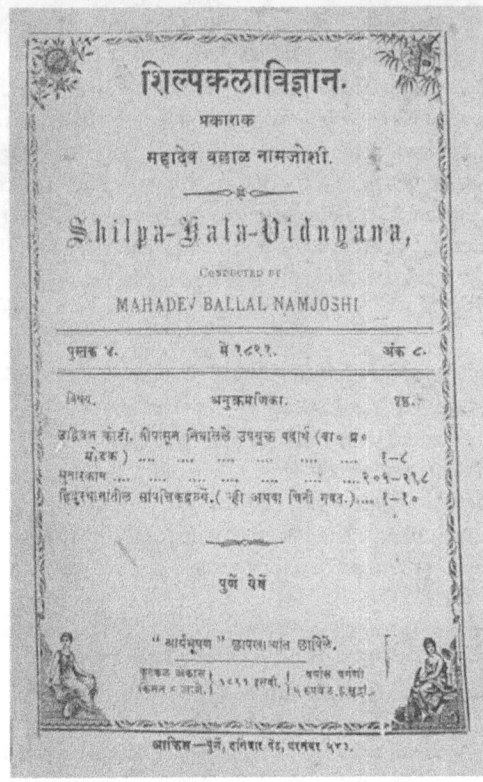

Figure 2: Cover page of the May 1891 issue of Shilpa-Kala-Vidnyan.

Authors who wrote on construction and architecture in *Shilpa-Kala-Vidnyan* included C. G. Bhanu on the planning of auditoria; J. V. Damle on woodwork and brickwork; Vasudev Bapuji Kanitkar on architecture; D. G. Kelkar with a well-illustrated serial article on carpentry, and G. G. Gokhale on horticulture and landscape design. All these contributors, just like Tilak and Namjoshi, belonged to the Chitpavan brahmin caste, a community which retained privilege in colonial power structures, and were well educated. Damle and Kanitkar were trained civil engineers. Bhanu had a bachelor's degree in Arts and Kelkar had a master's degree in Arts. By the end of the 19th century, the Chitpavan caste had not only become 'predominant and preeminent' in teaching, medicine, law, journalism, and arts [19], but also, as the profile of authors in *Shilpa-Kala-Vidnyan* shows, in science and engineering. Damle's and Kanitkar's essays are particularly interesting, because of their differing styles and approaches.

Vasudev Bapuji Kanitkar (1827-1904) was to Pune what his contemporaries Murzban and Ganga Ram were to Mumbai and Lahore respectively. He was a licensed civil engineer (Poona College, 1848), who built a successful career in the colonial PWD, and was appreciated both by the British rulers - he received the title of *Rao Bahadur (roughly 'Honoured Prince')* in 1876 - and the Pune nationalists for whom he built extensively after his retirement in 1879 [20]. Kanitkar's essay on architecture, titled '*Shilpakalechi Balyavastha',* or 'Architecture's childhood', was published in three parts beginning December 1887 and imagined as a series of weekly conversations between a teacher and student [21]. This traditional literary trope implies a superlative self-positioning that was in a way justified considering his substantial experience. In the first part of the essay Kanitkar wrote about the origins of architecture beginning from a tree house, and a pavilion, to a sloping roofed shelter with a plinth. The illustrations that accompany this text resemble those published in Laugier's 'Essay on Architecture' from 1753 (Fig. 3), which Kanitkar may have seen during his engineering education. Although Kanitkar was known for his imposing Neo-Gothic and Indo-Saracenic buildings in stone, the subsequent section of his essay is devoted to traditional brick nogging in teak posts, a construction technique which the contemporary PWD handbook described as 'excellent, cheap, and very desirable' without elaborating on its technicalities [22].

Figure 3: From left to right - a tree house, simple pavilion and sloping roof. Source: 'Shilpakalechi Balyavastha' ('Architecture's Childhood'), Pune, Shilpa-Kala-Vidnyan, vol. 1, no. 3, 1887, p.3-4.

All the descriptions and construction terms the author used in his writing on plinths, wooden frames, and floors are traditional. For example, the parts of a stone plinth are labelled with the terms 'bedari' ('bottom layer'), 'gunda' ('middle') and 'patthara' ('top layer') (Fig. 4). Even when English alternatives were available, he only used the traditional words: the components of a wooden frame are referred to as 'khamb' for 'columns', 'lag' for 'beams', and 'taktaposhi' for floor. For units of measurement, however, he switched between regional and British systems. The height of a plinth is quantified in tasu (a unit of linear measurement), but elsewhere he mentioned feet and inches.

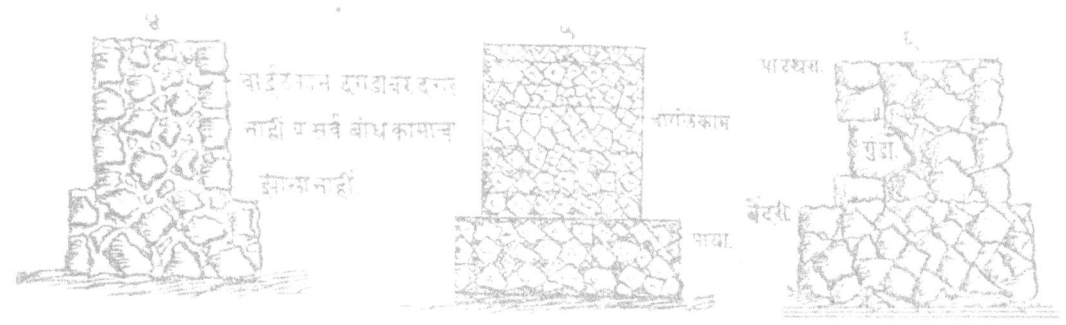

Figure 4: From left to right – 'bad work', 'good work', and 'parts of a stone plinth'. Source: Vasudev Bapuji Kanitkar, 'Shilpakalechi Balyavastha'('Architecture's Childhood'), Pune, Shilpa-Kala-Vidnyan, vol. 1, no. 3, 1887, p.12.

Technical Writings as Political: Building Manuals and Pattern Books from British India (1880-1947)

Kanitkar added two things to the traditional heuristics of building construction. One, is that he explained traditional construction practices using 'scientific' insights. For example, while addressing the width of the foundation wall, he discussed the need for distributing the loads of the building on a wider base. Second, Kanitkar used 'scientific' constructs such as tables and projected and isometric drawings to illustrate traditional practices. In a table establishing the relation between the span of a beam and its height and depth along with recommended wood type, Kanitkar used the term '*anumana*' or thumb rule [23]. This was probably the first time such information about traditional construction was put in print. The plans and sections clearly embrace an engineering language while representing traditional content (Fig. 5). Another noteworthy point, is that despite the objectives of Namjoshi, the intended audience of Kanitkar's essay is not just the craftsman but also 'the person wishing to build the house', to whom the author explicitly directed some instructions. Thus, Kanitkar's essay initiates a conversation between engineers and client-householders, something R. S. Deshpande's book would take further forty years to do.

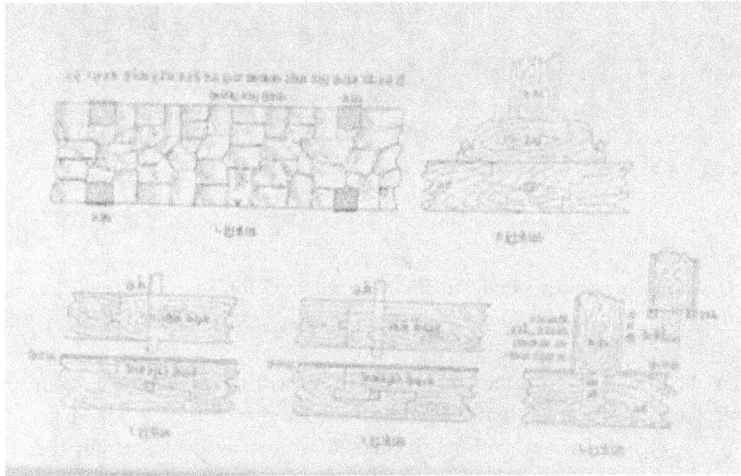

Figure 5: Wooden joinery details. Source: Vasudev Bapuji Kanitkar, 'Shilpakalechi Balyavastha', ('Architecture's Childhood'), Pune, Shilpa-Kala-Vidnyan, vol. 1, no. 3, 1887, opposite p.25.

In contrast to Kanitkar's essay, Jagannath Vishnu Damle's four-part essay on brickwork and woodwork, published from October 1888 onwards, is devoid of literary flourishes and perhaps more aligned to the objectives of the periodical [24]. In the introduction Damle mentioned the craftsmen as his intended audience. In his discussion of woodwork, he used traditional Marathi terms, while elaborating on why traditional sloping roof construction, which did not optimise triangular truss action, was less efficient than the '*navi reet*' or 'new system' consisting of Kingpost trusses (Fig. 6) [25]. In the second part of the essay, dedicated to brickwork, the author mentioned traditional wall construction only in passing: he referred to the traditional '*pustaki vit*', literally 'book-like brick', which was five to six inches wide and nine to ten inches long. Damle argued that building a one-and-a-half- brick-thick wall with these traditional brick proportions was impossible unless you broke the brick. Just like Kanitkar, he illustrated his article with modern engineering drawings and tables, such as a table relating wall thicknesses and the height and length of a wall reproduced *ad verbatim* from a document prepared by Molesworth, a consulting engineer for the railways [26]. Overall, Damle and Kanitkar's understanding of 'scientific' construction was not revolutionary, it was rather a natural evolution grounded in regional traditions.

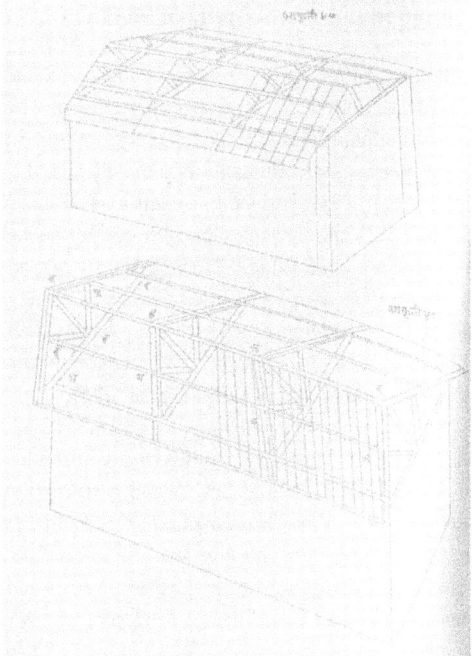

Figure 6: Truss used in traditional roof construction (top) and King post truss (bottom). Source: Jagannath Vishnu Damle, 'Imaratiche Lakudkam', ('Principles of woodwork'), Pune, Shilpa-Kala-Vidnyan, vol. 2, no. 12, 1889, p.8.

This moderation resonates with the stance Tilak and Namjoshi took on caste. As is well known, Tilak's nationalist group recognised the need for social reforms but maintained that the caste system was important for the survival of the 'industrial classes', a term used for the artisan and cultivator castes engaged in manual labour [27]. The same endeavour to retain but transform the caste order into a secular system with potential to protect artisans and farmers can be gleaned from *Shilpa-Kala-Vidnyan*. Arguing that those who understood English (belonging to educated higher castes) rarely made use of 'industrial knowledge', Namjoshi mentioned in an editorial that his reason for publishing in Marathi was to make industrial knowledge accessible to 'the carpenter or the farmer' [28]. The assumption was that manual workers would remain engaged in manual work but benefit from the improvement made possible by accessing modern knowledge. As a further illustration of this paradoxical stance on modernisation, Namjoshi declares in the same editorial, that 'the machine will never be able to produce a product that is comparable to a craftsman's work' [29].

Ross Bassett notes that 'Poona, with little industry to speak of, became the home to what was probably the largest campaign for industrialisation in India in the late 1800s'. This campaign not only called for 'Indians to become capitalists and enterprisers [30]' but also, as *Shilpa-Kala-Vidnyan* makes obvious, for artisan and farmer castes to reclaim (but remain in) their societal position by updating their craft skills with scientific knowledge. Paradoxically, this campaign was led by Chitpavan brahmins who had little experience either in business or in manual work.

Finally, it is noteworthy that a parallel crafts lobby had emerged slightly earlier amongst European(ised) architects and art critics with very different goals [31]. Appalled by what they considered to be substandard architecture and arts produced under imperial contact, their concern was to protect the 'mediaeval traditions' of Indian craftsmen from the degradation caused by forces of industrialisation to permit a revival of Indian styles. Their 'cult of the craftsman', to borrow Saloni Mathur's phrase, had its primary origin in aesthetic concerns that it shared with the Arts and Crafts movement [32]. Indian building craftsmanship was thus prominent in the discourse of both colonialist and nationalist elites, but ironicaly the voice of the craftsmen themselves remained unheard.

Technical Writings as Political: Building Manuals and Pattern Books from British India (1880-1947)

R.S. Deshpande's interwar building manuals and pattern books

In contrast to most articles on construction in *Shilpa-Kala-Vidnyan*, Deshpande's manuals, published from 1930 onwards, did not aim to provide readers with in-depth knowledge on a specific topic but with practical-level guidance on how to build a house, from site selection to creating plans and supervising construction. This was a current topic in the interwar period, as the devolution of urban planning responsibilities to municipalities and a growing Indian participation in the economy after the Government of India Act in 1919, had led to a significant rise in suburban housing construction. Both in their professional practice outside the PWD and through their writings in unofficial capacity, Indian PWD engineers took up a leading role in promoting such projects. Whereas Ganga Ram was one of the main actors involved in the planning and development of Lahore's 'Model Town', a co-operative suburban development of the 1920s financed and inhabited by Indian elites [33], Deshpande was amongst the first to implement such co-operative developments in Pune with the Saraswat Brahmin Colony built in 1928 [34]. Mehta's *Grihvidhan*, in turn, was "intended for those interested in building within a new suburban town planning scheme in Bhavnagar" [35].

The reason for Mehta and Deshpande to take up the writing pen was their confrontation with house commissioners' "lack of knowledge" of contemporary evolutions in residential design and construction or access to professional services beyond those offered by "the semi-literate *mistri*" (master craftsman) [36]. While new techniques, such as the use of steel reinforcement bars in both cement concrete elements and brickwork, had become more widely adopted in residential buildings as the result of a major growth in the domestic production of steel and cement after WWI, they were not necessarily well understood [37]. Reinforced concrete, according to Deshpande, was "very simple, but at the same time a most dangerous material to handle on the part of the layman" [38]. He had, for instance, "met several cases in which precast lintels were correctly prepared, but ... subsequently lifted and placed upside down in permanent position, with the natural result that they were badly cracked – some to a dangerous extent" [39].

Sulabh Vastushastra (1930), Deshpande's earliest advice book, not only aimed to "guide a layman in building his own home" [40] but to inform "even the *mistries [sic.]*, *karkoons* [clerks of works, sometimes also labour contractors] and artisans' [41]. The book proved so popular that Desphande was compelled to bring out a reprint within a few months as well as translations into Gujarati and Hindi. While there also existed demand for the book in Bengali and Kannada, Deshpande decided that an English version, eventually published as *Build your own home* (1943), "would reach more people and cause less bother and expense than publishing different editions in so many regional languages of India" [42]. However, the facts that traditionally-trained craftsmen were hardly conversant in English and that the number of 'plates' included in the books was far less than in PWD handbooks or Ganga Ram's *Pocket book of Engineering*, imply that the construction workers were not as significant an audience anymore as those planning to commission a house.

Just like contemporary PWD handbooks and Ganga Ram's *Pocket book of Engineering* (1927), Deshpande's manuals contained a section on building materials with tables of their characteristics, Deshpande's tables being, however, much less in number and restricted to standard steel sections used in house building. The books describe the building process organised per building part, from foundations to roofs, and address issues ranging from interior colour schemes to drainage. As in early editions of the Bombay PWD handbooks (prior to 1887) and Ganga Ram's book, Deshpande also elaborates on architectural drawing conventions. However, in Deshpande's books the focus lies on how to *read* drawings, whereas the former two describe how to *produce* them in terms of colour codes, paper sizes etc.

Deshpande's building manuals address several topics that had not been dealt with in earlier popular writings on construction, and which align more with PWD concerns of efficiency than taking pride in traditional building crafts. Firstly, he provided readers with plenty of design and construction suggestions to *save on building costs*. Secondly, and most expansively, Deshpande deals with the question of how to organise *the building process*. A principal decision was whether to get work done "by contract", being the item-rate or cost-plus-percentage contracts used in the PWD, or on "daily wages", the common way of remunerating craftsmen. Perhaps unexpectedly given his affinity with the PWD,

Deshpande recommended "a third system intermediate between these two". So as to obtain "a decent result at minimum cost", owners were advised to purchase materials themselves with the help of a *mistri* hired for overall coordination, then invite separate competitive tenders for each trade, and finally coordinate and supervise the construction with the guidance provided in the author's manuals [43]. The general contract system, as several of his contemporaries agreed, often led to wrongdoing [44]. They attributed this to the fact that 'engineers [operating as house designers] and [as] contractors were not clearly distinguished; neither were the [construction site] supervisors acting on behalf of owners or their engineers marked out from the class employed as overseers by the contractors themselves' [45]. As such, Deshpande advised engaging engineers only for their design services and directly employing *mistris* for the execution of the work. The appointment of an extra site supervisor or clerk of works working on the owner's behalf on a mere project basis was not a good solution, he claimed, because the person was sometimes bribed by the contractor to secretly work in his interest while being paid by the owner [46]. This stance, however, did not prevent Deshpande from stressing the importance of specifications and contracts, and even reproduce and translate standard templates for them, which appear to be the 'Standard Specifications', 'Specific Articles of Agreement', and 'General Conditions of Contract' issued by the Indian Institute of Architects (Fig.7).

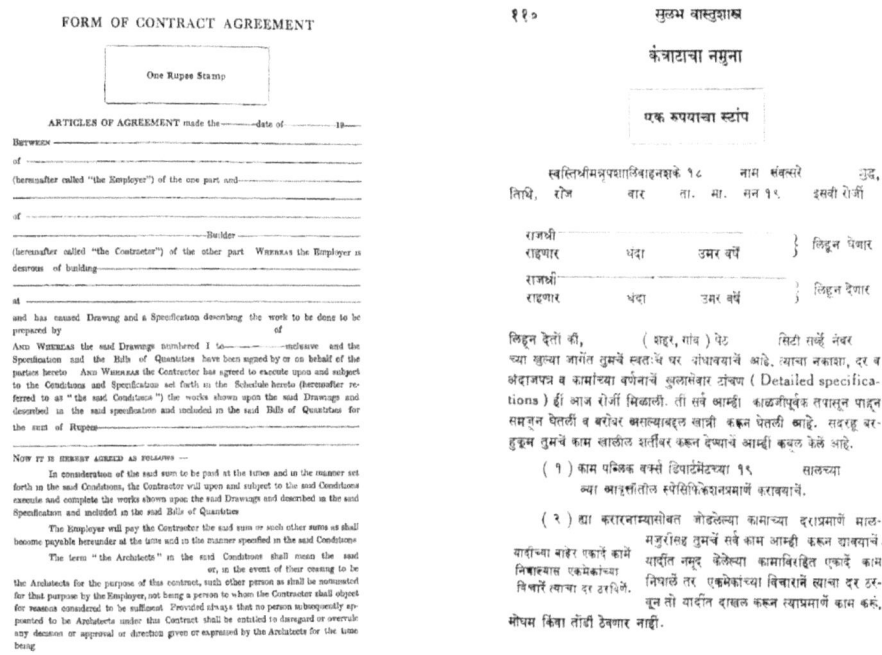

Figure 7: Template for a building contract agreement in English and Marathi. Source: Deshpande R. S., Build Your Own Home, Bombay : V.R. Sawant, 1943. p. 81. (left); and Deshpande R.S., Sulabha Vastushastra Athava Aadhunik Paddhatine Ghare Kashi Bandhavi (Simplified building science or how to build houses in the modern way), Pune : Raghunath Shripad Deshpande, 1930. p.110. (right)

Technical Writings as Political: Building Manuals and Pattern Books from British India (1880-1947)

Thus, Deshpande assigned educated house commissioners an active role, namely, to instruct the craftsmen of various trades with the help of 'modern tools' such as specifications and building manuals. This derived not only from his concerns for economy but also for poor workmanship. Throughout both the Marathi and English building manuals, Deshpande drew specific attention to the prevention of constructive mistakes. His elaborations on "how labourers scamp work" and "common faults made by masons and how to avoid them" illustrate that, leaving aside the question of its factual correctness, the narrative of a decline in Indian craftsmanship originating in late nineteenth-century art and architectural discourse had gained wider currency by the interwar period [47]. Unlike the revivalists, however, Deshpande, just like Namjoshi, saw the answer in promoting the *scientification and modernisation* of building crafts - he sought to do so not only through writing but also by intervening in the direction of the building site.

One can note a number of interesting differences between *Sulabh Vastu Shastra* (1930) and *Build your own home* (1943). Both books cover building with brick, lime, steel, and wood as well as steel-reinforced cement concrete, but in the Marathi book the use of steel is more closely evaluated against wood, the traditional alternative. And while in *Sulabh Vastu Shastra* concrete is proposed only for foundations, lintels, steps, wall corners, and floors, the 1943 book discusses its more extensive application in cantilevers, waffle slabs, and concrete-frame structures. According to Deshpande, by the late 1930s, reinforced cement concrete had become "within easy reach of the middle classes", which also may have had to do with the various financing options house builders had by then (private mortgage, bank loan, co-operative loan, etc.) [48]. In the Marathi book, in line with Ganga Ram's approach, Deshpande included a dictionary (Marathi-English). He insisted on using traditional terms when available ('*jote*' for 'plinth' and '*tulai*' for 'beams') while also providing English translations of certain words in brackets in the main body text. Deshpande even coined new Marathi words when the tradition did not supply them ('*chavicha dagad*' for 'keystone' and '*pahad*' for 'scaffolding'). Some of these terms such as '*guntava*' for 'bonding' are still in use today [49]. In the English book the dictionary is omitted but Deshpande used Marathi words to qualify workers – such as the *mistri, karkoon, coolie, bhistie* (water carrier), *chowkidar* (watchman), *mukadam* (foreman) or *wadar* (stone crusher) – and building materials – *murum* (soil), *surkhi* (pounded bricks), *chunam* (lime plaster), *khandki* (semi-dressed stones) – a practice which remained common in PWD handbooks too. The units of measurement mentioned in both books are exclusively British. Overall, both manuals suggest that radical changes in building culture had taken place, not only between the end of the 19th century and 1930, but perhaps even more so after the passing of the Government of India Act in 1935 and the corresponding uptake in economic activities.

Just before this Act, however, and in a departure from *Sulabh vastushastra* (1930) and *Build your own home* (1943), Deshpande wrote *Cheap and healthy homes for the middle classes of India* (1935), a book dedicated entirely to 'cheap' semi-vernacular building technologies and domestic sanitation, each covering approximately half of the book. Evidently influenced by the nationalist *swadeshi* movement, which promoted indigenous products rather than imported goods, and by Mahatma Gandhi's efforts towards relieving the plight of the 'common man', Deshpande wrote about "time-proven" construction methods with mud, stone, and wood, and occasionally on how they could be improved with the "advanced knowledge of the present day" [50]. He deplored "the craze for lime and cement", two relatively expensive materials, "for cottage building on the part of the poor" and the neglect of excellent vernacular materials, such as mud mortar made from cow dung, white earth, or *chopan* (a soil type found in the Deccan), by architects and engineers [51]. As his recommendations of corrugated iron sheets -"fortunately now manufactured in India at the same rates as those of foreign manufacture" [52] - or rammed earth work reveal, however, he was not adverse to the use of "the products of the modern science [sic.]" or Western methods *per se*. He simply believed, "that for the average Indian, who [was] very poor, [cement and lime] [we]re expensive luxuries." Deshpande's misleading use of the term 'middle-class' in the title might thus have more to do with the author recalibrating its meaning within the context of Gandhi's plea not to forget the plight of villagers and the urban poor.

In the part of the book on domestic sanitation Deshpande proposed *practical solutions* to achieve proper ventilation, natural lighting, water supply and drainage. Here again, a change in Deshpande's position that might have been influenced by nationalist thought becomes evident. Whereas in *Sulabh Vastushastra* Deshpande had been critical of the English practice to place a 'commode' in the dressing room, and considered kitchens found in English houses 'unclean', in *Cheap and healthy houses*, as Nikhil Rao describes elsewhere, he followed Gandhi's example by seeking to remediate "peculiar Indian social customs and religious prejudices", especially of upper-caste householders, which prevented the integration of toilets within the home [53]. Practical built solutions featured next to more general book sections on house cleaning, disinfectants and the prevention of epidemic diseases, "the most fundamental principles of hygiene", which Deshpande agreed with Gandhi, the masses needed to become acquainted with. Thus, the promotion of local building products, the fight against social prejudices, and an emphasis on sanitation were main themes of nationalist thought in the 1920s and 1930s that reflected in Deshpande's *Cheap and healthy homes,* yet in his technical writings on construction of the late 1930s and 1940s only the latter emphasis remained prominent.

Not all nationalists indeed fully agreed with Gandhi: they differed especially on his reservations with regards to industrialisation [54]. Renowned Indian engineer Mokshagundam Visvesvaraya (1860-1962) for instance, whom Deshpande must have known while teaching at the Poona College of Engineering, pleaded for rapid industrialisation through Indian capital and the need for Indians to plan their economy [55]. Before being replaced by Jawaharlal Nehru, Visvesvaraya headed the Indian National Congress's first National Planning Committee founded in 1938, a committee that started planning the first steps an independent government of an independent would have to take. This, together with Deshpande's nationalist orientation and dedication to the question of housing, might explain the appointment of Deshpande himself on the 11-member strong Housing Sub-Committee. In its early years, Gandhians who believed traditional technology and village industries served the common man better, critiqued the National Planning Committee but by 1945 "the political leadership had made a conscious decision to modernise and the dualism of the previous decades came to an end [56]". The latter suggests that Deshpande's increased support for 'modern' materials and techniques in Build your own home (1943) may not just have had to do with them becoming more available, affordable, or performant, than the traditional techniques he still discussed in 1935, but also with an increasing belief on his part that rather than merely applying scientific principles to traditional processes, a more radical change was needed.

Finally, it is worth noting that developments in Indian nationalism were not only reflected in the technical parts of Deshpande's books but also in the architectural type plans. In line with the more limited means of the middle-class audiences to whom PWD engineers increasingly catered, Deshpande's books do not include patterns for elaborate and expensive architectural ornaments like those still reprinted in Ganga Ram's 1927 book. They also focus on houses of moderate size, in which Deshpande argued, a large *diwankhana* (hall for entertaining guests), would hardly be in use, and could be dispensed with. The elevation drawings in his various publications since 1930, even though basic, reveal a stylistic evolution. Whereas *Sulabh vastushastra* (1930) and *Residential buildings suited to India* (1931) contain residential designs with pitched roofs in an everyday 'colonial' style (Fig. 8). Most designs in *Cheap and healthy houses* have flat roofs and facades embellished with Indian motifs such as diamond patterns and the swastika (1935, Fig.8). In 1936, provoked by what he had read on the Modernist Movement, Deshpande undertook an 8-month study tour of Europe and Japan. Convinced by what he had seen, his design discourse from *Modern Ideal Homes for India* (1939) onwards emphasised functionality, spatial efficiency, "flexibility", and "circulation", while type designs from then on almost all had flat roofs and modernist facades (Fig.8). The rather 'dry elevation drawings in earlier books made way for perspective views. This heralded a change in the purpose of pattern books published in India after independence in 1947, books which as Abigail McGowan notes, no longer focused on providing readers with technical information but increasingly "adopted a lighter tone, evoking comfort and sociability within depictions of the home as a site of leisure and consumption [57]".

Technical Writings as Political: Building Manuals and Pattern Books from British India (1880-1947)

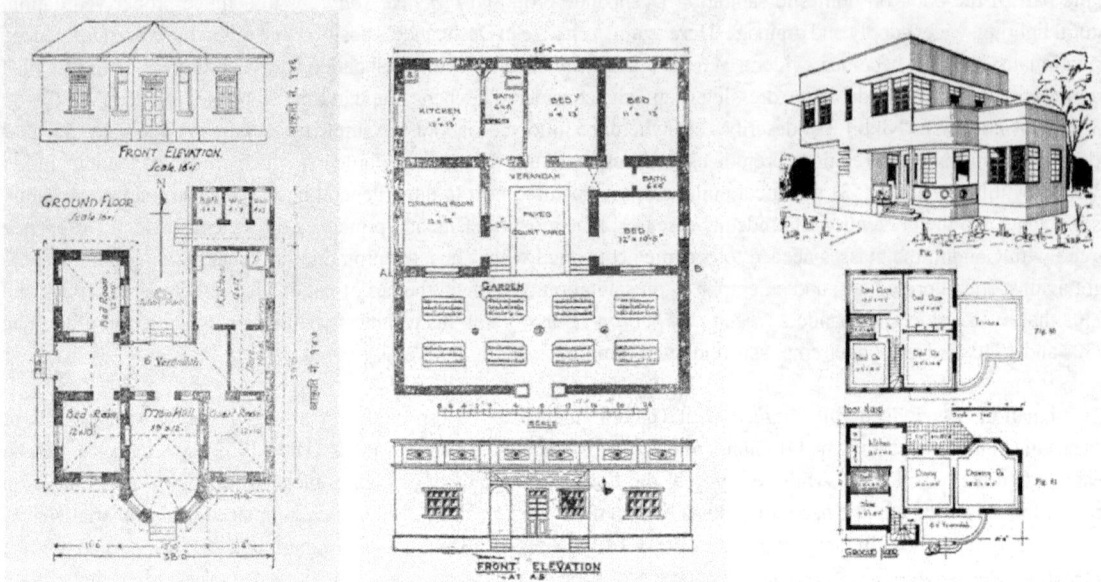

Figure 8: Pattern plans and elevations of houses in the colonial vernacular (left), modern vernacular (middle), and modenist style (right). Sources: DESHPANDE *R.S., Sulabha Vastushastra Athava Aadhunik Paddhatine Ghare Kashi Bandhavi (Simplified building science or how to build houses in the modern way), Poona: Raghunath Shripad Deshpande, 1932, p.303. (left);* DESHPANDE *Raghunath Shripad, Cheap and Healthy Homes for the Middle Classes of India, 1st ed., Poona, 1935, p.279. (middle); and* DESHPANDE *R. S., Modern Ideal Homes For India, 1st ed., Poona, 1939, p. 181 (right).*

Conclusion

The centrality of science and technology in Indian nationalist discourse emerging from the 1880s onwards influenced contemporary writings on construction by Indian PWD engineers. The ways in which it did so were far more nuanced than what simple binary frameworks of 'colonialism-nationalism' and 'modern-traditional', which long dominated Western as well as Indian views, suggest. The supposed decline of traditional construction practices through their replacement by 'British' building techniques has commonly been described as a social and technological rupture. However, evidence of the texts analysed shows that evolutions were much more gradual and hybrid. Vernacular practices merged into new ones, were resurrected or forgotten by particular social groups while, more often than is generally perceived, the catalyst for change was public aspiration rather than colonial oppression. As the views on how 'modern' science and technology were to serve India varied considerably and were at times internally contradictory, so too did the type of materials and construction techniques authors discussed, the value judgements they expressed, and even the vocabulary and literary style in which they wrote. Furthermore, it appears to have been evident to Indian nationalists and engineers alike that technical and social developments 'co-produced' each other. Thus, early writings influenced by Tilak's ideology focused on craftsmen and their re-education and were aimed at allowing them to retake their 'proper places' in the societal structure. In Deshpande's writings of the interwar period, the focus was on the emerging middle- and the lower-middle classes. While initially attempting to imbibe them with Gandhian values of frugality and practical thrift in the construction of their own homes, Nehruvian and more technocratic views on modernisation increasingly reflected in his later writings on construction.

References

[1] For research on Indian engineers, see Aparajith Ramnath, *The Birth of an Indian Profession: Engineers, Industry, and the State, 1900-47*, New Delhi: Oxford University Press, 2017; and the blog of the ENGIND Project, funded by the ANR (French National Research Agency), https://engind.hypotheses.org, (Consulted on 10th February 2022).

[2] William J. Glover, *Making Lahore Modern. Constructing and Imagining a Colonial City*, Minneapolis, London: University of Minnesota Press, 2007; Chopra Preeti, *A Joint Enterprise: Indian Elites and the Making of British Bombay*, Minneapolis, London: University of Minnesota Press, 2011.

[3] The full book's title varied slightly over time from *Pocket Book Of Engineering - in English and Urdu* (1888) to *Pocket Book Of Engineering for Sub-Divisional Officers, Mistrees, and Contractors* (1894). For brief discussions of the book, see Glover, *Making Lahore Modern*, (Note 2) p.84-85; and Shama Anbrine, 'The Co-Operative Model Town Society: History, Planning, Architecture and Social Character of an Indigenous Garden Suburb in Colonial Lahore', (Ph.D. thesis, University of Liverpool, 2014)

[4] William Glover, 'Making Indian Modern Architects', in *Colonial Frames, Nationalist Histories: Imperial Legacies, Architecture and Modernity*, ed. Mrinalini Rajagopalan and Madhuri Desai, Burlington: Ashgate Publishing Company, 2012, pp.27–46.

[5] For instance, Samuel Swinton Jacob's *Jeypore portfolio of architectural details*, London: W. Griggs and Sons Limited, 1890, indeed contains some very similar prints.

[6] A full bibliographic reference to these texts is missing so far.

[7] Other interwar building manuals and pattern books, not written by PWD engineers, include: A.V. Thiagaraja Iyer, Indian Architecture, 1920 (Madras); S. Douglas Meadows, Modern Eastern bungalows and how to build them, 1931 Calcutta.

[8] See 'The Rediscovery of India: Database of Periodicals, Magazines, Journals', http://ideasofindia.org (Consulted on 9th February 2022).

[9] Some of the pathbreaking works in this growing body of literature are: Kumar, Deepak. *Science and the Raj: A study of British India*, New Delhi: Oxford University Press, 1997; Prakash, Gyan. *Another Reason: Science and the Imagination of Modern India*. Princeton: Princeton University Press, 2020 (1999).

[10] For instance, Deshpande R. S. and Vartak G.V., *A treatise on building construction*, 11th ed., Poona : United Book Corp, 1968.

[11] The full title reads 'Sulabh Vastushastra athava aadhunik paddhatine ghare kashi bandhavit', literally 'Simplified building science or how to build houses in the modern way'. In his later English publications, Deshpande refers to the title as 'Building construction simplified' and 'Modern buildings and how to build them'.

[12] Rao notes how this Act meant that 'local self-government and public works were now "transferred" subjects to be administered by a minister chosen from by an elected provincial legislative council. Meanwhile on the municipal level, the franchise was enlarged, and again further widened in 1935. Nikhil Rao, *House, but No Garden: Apartment Living in Bombay's Suburbs, 1898-1964*, Minneapolis, London: University of Minnesota Press, 2013. p.9.

[13] Ross Bassett, *The Technological Indian*, Cambridge, MA and London: Harvard University Press, 2016, p.17.

[14] ibid., p.319.

[15] Jagadish Lanjekar, *Mahadev Ballal Namjoshi: Udyog Dhorani, ('Industrial Policymaker')* Pune: Vidyadeep Prakashan, 2021.

[16] Melsens Sarah, Mangaonkar-Vaiude Priyanka and Bertels Inge, 'The emergence and impact of vocational training in the building trades in Pune (India): an analysis of three institutes', *in Building Histories: The Proceedings of the Fourth Annual Construction History Society Conference*, Cambridge, Construction History Society, 2017, p. 27–39.

[17] Lanjekar, *Namjoshi*, (Note 15).

[18] For example, *Shilpakalasangraha* (शिल्पकलासंग्रह, 'Collection of construction and art') was a Marathi periodical published from Pune in 1877. It was intended for the 'good of the nation' as well as for artists, sculptors and *mistris*. The issues we accessed did not have essays on construction. Therefore, we have not dealt with it in detail. Similarly, the 1894 Marathi translation (and commentary) of E.L. Marryat and A.R. Seton's, *Specifications, Rates, and Notes on Work*, by

S.S. Deshpande has not yet been located by the researchers and could not be discussed here. Related texts in other languages are J. Kishen Singh's *Geometrical Patterns with Their Descriptions in English, Urdu and Gurmukhi*, from 1893. In 1896, Durga Charan Chakravorty authored '*Vishwakarma*' which as per Kumar, (Note 9), was the only Bengali publication on civil engineering from the nineteenth century.

[19] Maureen L. Patterson, 'Changing patterns of occupation among Chitpavan Bramhans', *The Indian Economic & Social History Review*, vol. 7, no. 3, 1970, pp. 375-396.

[20] Sarojini Vaidya, *Shrimati Kashibai Kanitkar: Atmacharitra ani Charitra (1861-1948)*, ('Shrimati Kashibai Kanitkar:Autobiography and Biography (1861-1948)'), Mumbai: Popular Prakashan, 1980.

[21] Vasudev Bapuji Kanitkar, 'Shilpakalechi Balyavastha', ('Architecture's childhood'), Pune, *Shilpa-Kala-Vidnyan*, vol. 1, no. 3, 1887, pp. 1-12.

[22] Ernest MARRYAT and A.R. SETON, *Specifications, Rates, and Notes on Work*, fourth edition, Bombay : Printed at the Government Central Press, 1887, p.256.

[23] Kanitkar, 'Shilpakalechi Balyavastha', Pune, (Note 21), pp. 18-25.

[24] There is not much information available on Damle other than the fact that he was a licensed civil engineer.

[25] Jagannath Vishnu Damle, 'Imaratiche Lakudkam', ('Woodwork in Building Construction'), Pune, *Shilpa-Kala-Vidnyan*, vol. 2, no. 12, 1889, pp. 9-26.

[26] Jagannath Vishnu Damle, 'Vitanche Bandhkam', ('Brick Construction'), Pune, *Shilpa-Kala-Vidnyan*, vol. 3, no. 1, 1889, pp. 1-10.

[27] Ravinder Kumar, *Western India in the Nineteenth Century*, Canberra: Australian National University Press, 1968. p. 311.

[28] Mahadev Ballal Namjoshi, 'Prastut Prayatna va tyachi disha', ('Present Efforts and their Direction'), Pune, *Shilpa-Kala-Vidnyan*, vol. 3, no. 1, 1889, pp. 1-8.

[29] Ibid.

[30] See Bassett, (Note 13), p.27.

[31] For instance, figures like Kipling, Swinton Jacob, Coomaraswamy and E.B. Havell.

[32] Mathur Saloni, *India by Design: Colonial History and Cultural Display*, Delhi : Orient Black Swan, 2007, p.42-51.

[33] Anbrine, 'The Co-Operative Model Town Society', (Note 3).

[34] The Deccan Gymkhana Co-operative Housing Society was built ca. 1924. See Arthur Edward Mirams, *Plans and Specifications of Houses Suitable for Occupation by the Working Classes*, Second edition (first edition 1919), Bombay: Bombay Government Central Press, 1925.

[35] Abigail McGowan, 'Consuming the Home: Creating Consumers for the Middle-Class House in India, 1920–60', in Bhattacharia B., Donner H. (Eds)*Globalising Everyday Consumption in India* (Routledge, 2020). p.143.

[36] R.S. Deshpande, *Modern Ideal Homes For India*, 1st ed., Poona : [s.n.], 1939, p.6.

[37] Descriptions of steel reinforced brickwork start featuring in PWD handbooks published from 1925 (7th edition) onwards, and Ganga Ram's *Pocket book of engineering*, includes new patents filed for reinforced brickwork slabs. For steel reinforced cement concrete, see Tappin Stuart, 'The Early Use of Reinforced Concrete in India', *Construction History*, vol. 18, 2002, p. 79–98.

[38] Deshpande, *Modern Ideal Homes,* (Note 36), p.128.

[39] R. S. Deshpande, *Build Your Own Home*, Bombay: V.R. Sawant, 1943, p.210.

[40] ibid., p.ii.

[41] ibid., p.3

[42] ibid.

[43] ibid., p.21.

[44] ibid., p.74.

[45] Batley Claude, 'The School of Architecture at the Government School of Art, Bombay', *Architectural Journal Being The Journal Of The Royal Institute Of British Architects*, XXXVII, 21 June 1930, p. 592–597, p. 592.; The quote is from Gadgil D. R., *Poona: A socio-economic survey. Part II*, Pune: Gokhale Institute of Politics and Economics, 1952.p.199-200.

[46] Deshpande, *Build Your Own Home,* (Note 39).p.74.
[47] ibid. p.II.
[48] Deshpande, *Modern Ideal Homes*, (Note 36), p.77. The first discussion of these financing options in Deshpande's writings is in *Build your own home,* (Note 39).
[49] Raghunath Shripad Deshpande, *Sulabh Vastushastra athava Adhunik paddhatine ghare kashi bandhavi*, (Simplified Building Science or How to Build Houses in the Modern Way), Pune: Raghunath Shripad Deshpande, 1930.
[50] Raghunath Shripad Deshpande, *Cheap and Healthy Homes for the Middle Classes of India*, 1st ed., Poona, 1935, p. 9.
[51] Ibid.,p. 8-9.
[52] Ibid., p. 163-164.
[53] Rao, *House, but No Garden,* (Note 12), p.131.
[54] Kumar, *Science and the Raj*, (Note 9), p.241-262.
[55] M. Visvesvaraya, *Planned Economy for India,* Bangalore, 1934.; see also Aparajith Ramnath, 'Engineers' Day: The Story of the Irishman Who Moulded Visvesvaraya's Alma Mater', *The Wire*, India, 15 September 2019. https://thewire.in/the-sciences/engineers-day-theodore-cooke-mokshagundam-visvesvaraya-civil-engineering-college. (Consulted on 14th February 2022).
[56] Kumar, (Note 9), p.250-251.
[57] McGowan, 'Consuming the Home', (Note 35). p.141.

Early Twentieth Century

Early Reinforced Concrete Shells in Russia

Vladimir Korensky
Research associate and doctoral candidate at the chair of Construction History (Prof. Dr.-Ing. David Wendland), Brandenburg Technische Universität Cottbus-Senftenberg, Cottbus, Germany.

Abstract

This paper discusses the development of shell structures in the context of the application of early reinforced concrete in the Russian Empire. Following a short discussion of the context and general conditions, the main construction methods are addressed. Different types of buildings are analysed in the paper, covering the period from the first structures in 1888 until the revolution of 1917. Special attention is given to shell structures and their supporting structures. As they are intricate and technically advanced, these structures arguably represent the highest point in the development of early reinforced concrete.

The research was based on Soviet era and later construction history publications, archival documents, and drawings as well as historical technical literature on the topic in Russian, French, German, and English. Such a broad overview has allowed the history of the development of early reinforced constructions to be seen from different perspectives.

Introduction

During the period under study, the Russian Empire expanded its territory to the northwest, into parts of Poland and the Baltic States, and to the southwest, into the regions of Ukraine and Georgia. The use of reinforced concrete in the Russian Empire as a new construction method was slightly staggered in comparison to its introduction in Europe. Nonetheless, particular local conditions in Russia — such as the well-developed iron and cement industry, presence of scientifically trained engineers, and skilled construction workers — resulted in a rapid spread of the technology. This accordingly led to the creation of various remarkable buildings.

Monier System

The knowledge and experience of the new construction methods were first brought to the country in form of a patent. The patent of French gardener Joseph Monier, also called the Monier system, was granted in 1880 and would become very influential in the Russian Empire. However, the patent was not applied in Russia and under local laws, expired within one year, allowing the new technology to be used unrestrictedly. Nevertheless, it took six years for the new construction method to first appear in the building industry [1].

Monier system was first used and tested in 1886 during the construction of slaughterhouses in Moscow. Samples of thin flat and vaulted slabs were loaded and investigated [2]. On the same construction site in 1888, a shell was integrated into the structure of a water tower. Its massive c. 22.5 m high octagonal masonry tambour supported a water tank. A 7.25 m wide and 8 cm thick dome with a rise of 85 cm was placed over the tank (Figure 1). The dome was composed of eight equal cylindrical segments to fit the geometry of the tower, [3].

Another water tower was constructed in 1902 at the Ekaterinodar Station on the Vladikavkazskaya Railway. A 243 cubic metre tank in reinforced concrete was built in accordance with the Intze principle on top of tambour built in double-wall masonry technique. The tank was enveloped by an additional structure in reinforced to protect it against frost. The thickness of the central and the peripheral wall of the tank as well as the wall of the envelope was 8 cm at the top and it was increased to 10 cm toward the bottom. A 6 cm thick segmental dome with a lantern at the center was constructed on top of the envelope to cover the entire structure.

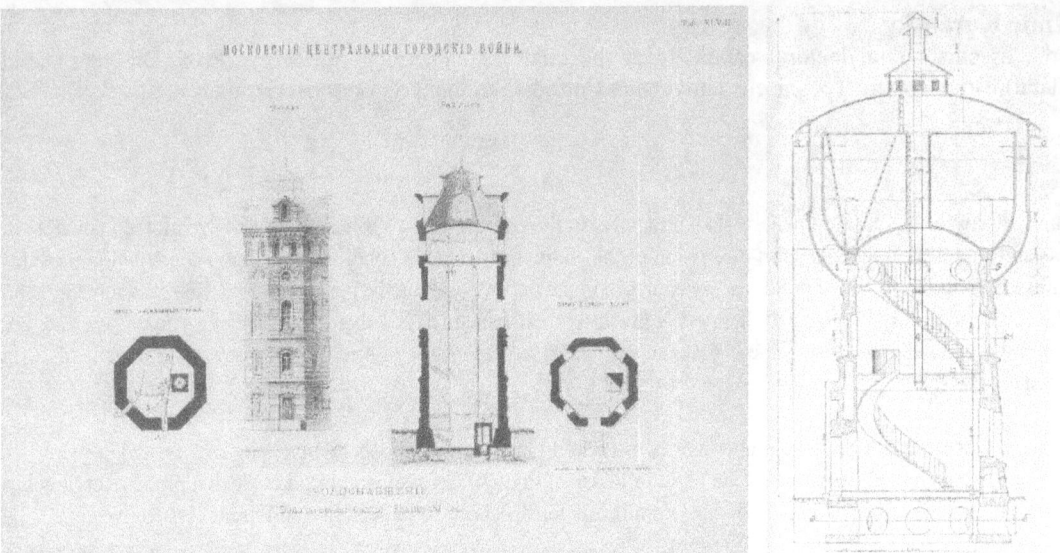

Figure 1: The first shell construction in the Russian Empire, water tower of slaughter houses in Moscow, 1888. Source: S. A. Podèrni, 1896 (Note 3). Water tower near Ekaterinodar station of Vladicaucas Railway, 1902. Source: S. D. Karejša, 1905 (Note 4).

In addition to tanks in water towers and tubes for canalisation, sedimentation reservoirs were an important application of reinforced concrete in water supply facilities. Round reservoirs were generally arranged in twos or threes. They were built on top of massive foundations made of unreinforced concrete. Five free-standing open reservoirs each designed to contain 340 cubic metres of water were constructed in 1900 at the Evlach and Poti Station on the Transcaucasian Railway. The reservoirs had an internal diametre of 13.44 m, were 2.45 m high and had 8.5 cm thick walls. Two reservoirs of larger diametre (16.22 m) and thicker walls (11 cm) were constructed at Evlach in 1901. Those were designed to contain 485 cubic metres. Tension rings atop of all those tanks were introduced to ensure their stiffness. Another reservoir constructed in 1903 (Station Železnovodsk) had an inner diametre of 8.5 m and 4.5 m high and 10 cm thick wall. It was fully submerged underground and was covered by a 5 cm thick spherical dome with a rise of 86 cm.

The influence of the Monier system on the local market and the local authorities in the Russian Empire was increased by the official loading tests held in Saint Petersburg in 1891. Different samples were tested in presence of important civil servants from different institutions and under the supervision of the Mechanical Laboratory of the Institute of Engineers of Ways of Communication. The variety of samples was limited to structures that could be deployed for the construction of railway infrastructure. Flat slabs, vaulted shells, octagonal tanks, and round tubes were built and loaded. The largest construction was a bridge consisting of a segmental vault with a span of 17 m stiffened by spandrels (Figure 2, left). One of the invited participants to tests was a very reputable Ministry of Ways of Communications which would influence the development of reinforced concrete in Russia in the following years and deploy the new method in its own constructions. As a result of this event, round, elliptical, and semi-elliptical tubes were laid under the trackbeds of the local railway lines.

After the experiments in 1892 by the authorities of the Moscow-Kasan'-Railway, a culvert of inner dimensions of 2.13 m in breadth and 2.56 m in height was constructed. The thickness of the shell of 13 cm at the crown was gradually increased to 18 cm to the base of the culvert. In 1903 a bridge over the railways track near Tiflis was constructed for the Transcaucasian Railway (Figure 2, right). The parabolic vault with a span of 12 m, a rise of 2 m, and a width of 9.17 m was stiffened by spandrels. The thickness of the vault was reduced from 35 cm at the springer to 16 cm at the crown. The vault was reinforced by one mesh of iron bars placed near the intrados and one near the extrados.

Figure 2: Experimental bridge in Saint Petersburg, 1891 and road bridge over the track of Transkavkazkaja Railway near Tiflis, 1903. Source: S. D. Karejša, 1905 (Note 4).

Shells were also deployed in the construction of engine sheds. Near the Sary-Jazy station of the Central Asia Railways, a 37.98 m long and 15.45 m wide shed for four locomotives was constructed in 1900. The foundations, the gable ends, the side base courses and the five frames of the lunettes on each side of the building were constructed in masonry. The building was covered by a single semi-circular barrel vault spanning 12.16 m. It was reinforced with two iron meshes made of 10 and 15 mm thick bars. The thickness of the vault at the crown was 14 cm and toward the springers where each reinforcement mesh was anchored in the base course, it was increased to 16 cm. Lunettes with upright side walls in reinforced concrete of 1.92 in span and 3.84 m in height were integrated into the main vault [4].

Shells were deployed to construct basement ceilings in residential and public buildings. The Upper Trading Rows built during 1892-93 are known because of their easily accessible arched bridges between the galleries in upper floors. But very little is known about the constructions above the basement. Those include rectangular double curved vaults with a span of 14.5 m are arranged along the building under the atriums. But a special element was built at the centre of the building at the cross-section of the main atrium and a crossway. The cut corners at the cross-section establish an octagonal. From each side of the octagonal a double-curved shell reaches the round skylight in the centre. A wine cellar of Deprez Company was constructed in 1900. Massive cross vaults spanning 6.5 m supported by masonry pillars and outer walls were designed to carry a live load of 1300 kg per square metre. A shallow segmental barrel vault was built in 1903 in the basement of the Museum of Fine Arts. With a span of 8.5 m, it was constructed to bear a live load of 540 kg per square metre. Along the springers, pitched lunettes were integrated and the vault was supported by massive pilasters constructed in masonry.

Shell structures were often deployed in religious buildings. In 1888 construction of the Choral Synagogue was completed. (Fig. 3, left) All the vaults in its structure were built as shells in reinforced concrete. The central nave has a span about 11 m ending by semi-circular apse for the altar (Bimah) was covered by barrel vault. The side aisles and the entrance narthex were covered by groin vaults. In 1901 a barrel vault of a span of 10.5 m over the nave and semi-dome of a span of 6.5 m was constructed over the altar in the Orphanage of Metropolitan Sergij (Prijut imeni Mitropolita Sergija). And an extraordinary configuration of the basket-handle vaults of 21 by 9 metres (Fig. 3, right) were constructed in 1903 in the church of St. Nikolaj Wonderworker (Nikolaj Čudotvorec) [5].

Figure 3: Vaults in religious buildings in Moscow: Choral Synagogue, 1888. Source: https://lechaim.ru/academy/kamni-pretknoveniya-horalnye-sinagogi-v-stolitsah/ (consulted on 23.01.2022). Church of St. Nikolaj, 1903. Source: Lopatto, 1969 (Note 5).

Reinforced concrete was also used to construct domes in religious buildings. The church on the Rjazansko-Ural'skaja Railway on the station Saratov II was constructed in 1896. (Fig. 4, left) The square crossing of 8.5 by 8.5 metres on the ground level was transformed into an octagonal tambour. The springers of the dome were embedded into the tambour. Following the configuration of the tambour, a dome of a span of 7 metres composed of 8 cm thick cylindrical segments was constructed [4]. Another dome with a span of 9.6 m composed of four double-curved shells was constructed in 1901 for the Peter Aleksander orphanage (Petrovsko-Aleksandrovskij Prijut) in Moscow. (Fig. 4, right)

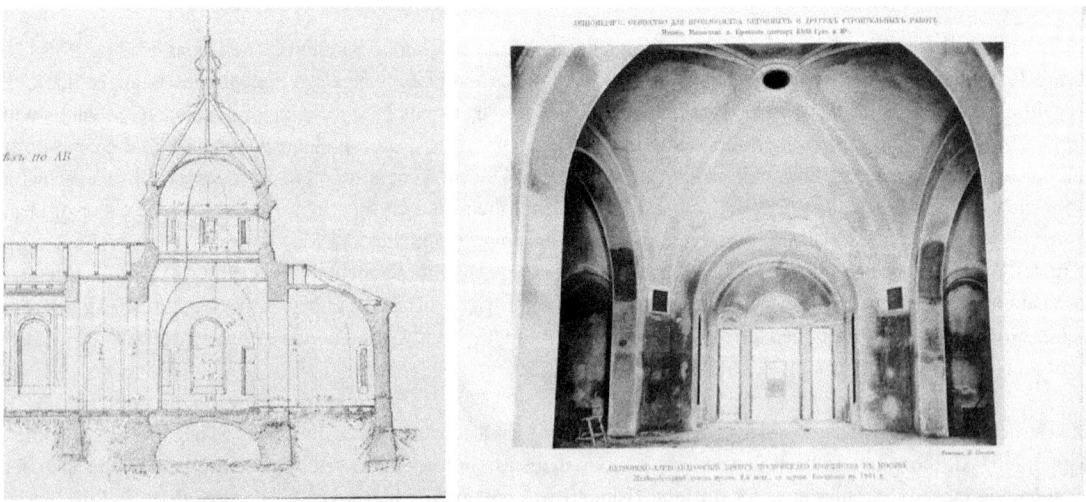

Figure 4: Dome in religious buildings: Church in Saratov, 1896. Source: S. D. Karejša 1905 (Note 4). Church in Moscow, 1901. Source: Akcionernoe obščestvo, 190- (Note 6).

Shells were also deployed in industrial buildings to cover large surfaces. One of the examples of this type construction is the two-storey bleaching building constructed in 1902 for the Joint Stock Company of Cotton Manufacture in Lodz. Its roof was composed of shallow vaults of a span of 4,6 metres oriented transversely to the roof consisting of two parts each inclined outward the building [6].

The peak of deployment of Monier system in shell constructions was marked by building of the 36 m tall lighthouse constructed near the city of Nikolaev on the Black Sea. The whole structure including the foundation was completely constructed in reinforced concrete. The cylindrical wall of the main structure was 20 cm thick at the bottom and was gradually reduced to 10 cm at the top. In order to increase the stiffness of the tower, the silhouette of the wall was in the form of a parabola. A single mesh of vertical bars of 22 mm and horizontal rings of 9 mm was embedded in the structure.

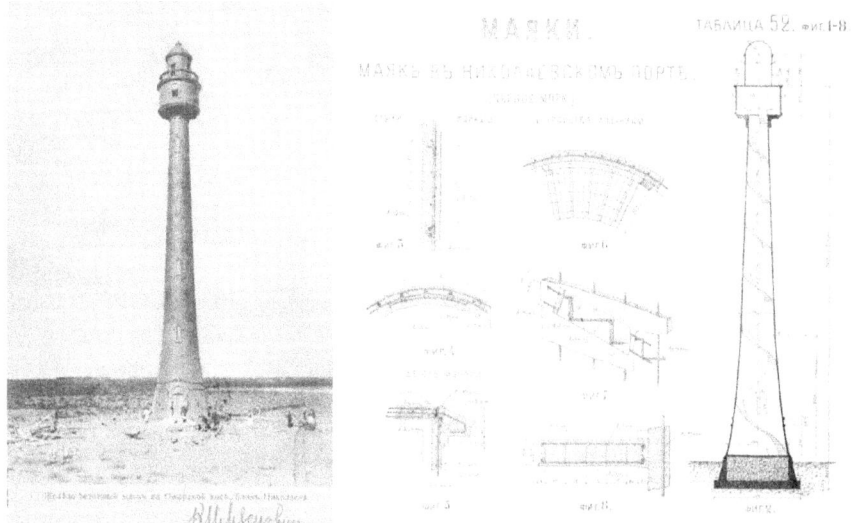

Figure 5: Light tower near Nikolaev, 1904. Source: http://img-fotki.yandex.ru/get/6432/97833783.153/0_99256_f09f8ee4_XXXL.jpg (Consulted on 15th May 2014) and B.N. Akimov, 1908 (Note 9).

Hennebique System

Another construction method, developed by the end of the 19th century by a French bricklayer, construction site supervisor, and the owner of world-renowned *bureau d'e*tudes François Hennebique, was used at this time in the Russian Empire. At first, only his European representatives applied the method in the country. Later on, Russian engineers were also able to apply it in various fields of the construction industry [7]. The system was first introduced in the southwestern part of the Russian Empire, in the region of Ukraine.

The first building deploying Hennebique system in shell construction was a water tower, built in 1902 in Ekaterinoslav. In this building, reinforced concrete tanks were created using the typical Hennebique skeletal structure. The tanks were put one above the other. [8] The lower was designed to contain 200 cubic metres and the upper 100 cubic metres of water. (Figure 6, left and middle) The structure of the water tower consisted of eight pillars arranged in a circle. The pillars were interconnected by four beams laid out as a hash. Additional short beams were added to the hash to support the tanks. (Figure 6, right) The shells of the 4.30 m high peripheral wall of the lower tank were constructed between the pillars. The peripheral wall of the upper tank of 2.23 m high and 10 cm thick was constructed as a free-standing structure. The upper edge of both tanks was stiffened by tension rings.

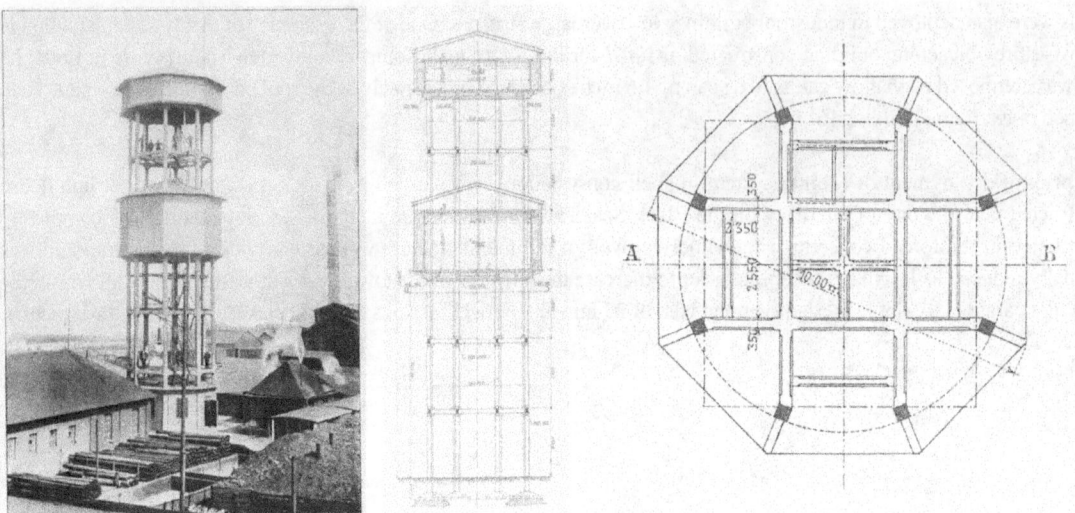

Figure 6: Water tower in Ekaterinoslav, 1902. Source: O. Lecocq, 1904 (Note 8).

According to the drawings, two examples following examples of sedimentation tanks can be attributed to the Hennebique system. Nevertheless, those were not listed in the catalogue of Hennebique construction company. This was because at that point of time the railway engineers in the southwestern part of the Russian Empire had studied the system and could apply it on their own [9]. In comparison to the previously described sedimentation reservoirs constructed according to the Monier system, the following examples are more elaborated. Through an introduction of ribs, the massive foundation could be eliminated and the stiffness of the cover could be increased. The first examples are the two round reservoirs of 667.5 cubic metres each constructed in 1903 to supply the station Sinel'nikovo on the Ekaterininskaja Railways. The outer diametre of the walls was 14.5 metres and their thickness was reduced from 40 cm at the bottom to 20 cm upwards. The covering domes were 12 cm thick and had a span of 14.1 m and a rise of 1.9 m. Each dome was stiffened by 15 ribs whose height altered from 40 cm at the wall down to 20 cm towards the centre. The width of the ribs was 18 cm. A round opening of 1 m was integrated at the centre of each dome. The domes were connected monolithically with the wall of the reservoir without any ring at the top of the wall. Another sedimentation reservoir was constructed in 1906 on the station Kavkazkaja of Vladikavkazkaja railway. The structure of the reservoir had a rectangular form in plan and inner dimensions of 25.6 by 17.5 m. A particularity of this construction was its 27 cm thick bottom that was composed of four concave slopes inclined to the centre and anchored in the peripheral 50 cm thick concrete wall. Within the walls, four rows of six columns of square section were arranged supporting the cover composed of grid of beams and slabs inclined outwards [10].

The Hennebique system was also deployed in constructions of public buildings. Rather a unique and exceptional application of this system was in construction of Roman Catholic cathedral in Kiev in 1902. Dome and vaults were built in Gothic style [11]. In further public buildings the Hennebique system was deployed in construction of domes which were supported in different manner. In some cases the supporting structure was built in reinforced concrete. As an example of the first category is the main hemispheric dome of the Armenian Church of Saint George built in Tiflis in 1903. It was constructed atop of 10.6 m high and 6.5 m wide tambour. The wall of the tambour was 11 cm thick and was placed on four beams arranged like a hash sign. All those elements were built in reinforced concrete supported by the masonry structure of the church.

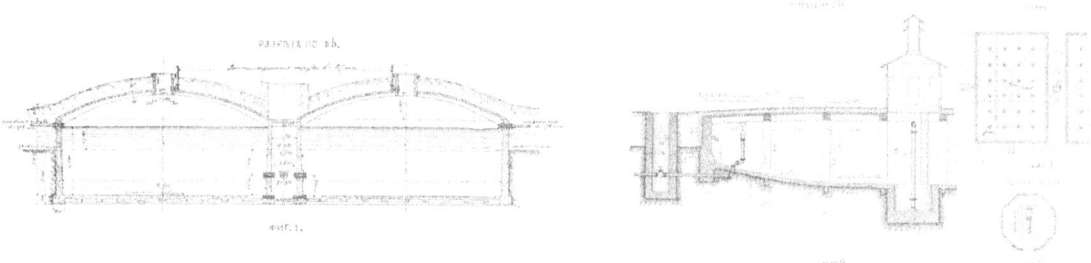

Figure 7: Sedimentation reservoirs at station Sinel'nikovo built in 1903 and station Kavkazkaja built in 1906. Source: B. N. Akimov, 1908 (Note 9).

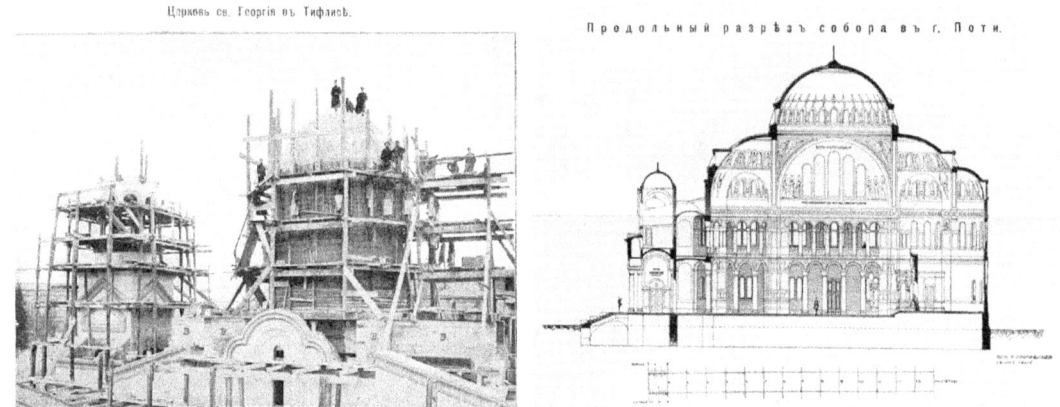

Figure 8: Domes supported by RC structures in Georgia: Armenian Church of Saint George, Tiflis, 1903 and Cathedral of Poti, 1907. Source: Černomorskoe stroitel'noe obščestvo, 1906, (Note 10).

The main structural feature of the following examples was the stiffening radial ribs arranged atop of the domes in order to obtain a smooth surface on the inner side. An elaborated complex of domes similar to the layout of Hagia Sophia was adopted in the design of the Cathedral in Poti, Georgia. It was built between 1906 and 1907 entirely in reinforced concrete. The main dome with a span of 12.8 m was constructed of 10 cm thick shell stiffened by 32 radial ribs. A window was integrated in the bottom of the dome between each two ribs. The main dome was supported by two semi-domes. The semi-dome in the east is intersected with three secondary semi-domes and the one in the west with two secondary semi-domes. All the semi-domes were stiffened by radial ribs and windows were integrated in between.

Further developments in terms of span occurred in domes of Hennebique system which were constructed on top of masonry tambours. Between 1903 and 1904 the dome of the Arena of the Imperial Stud reached a total span of 20 m. It was constructed on a 4-m-high dodecahedral tambour built in masonry. As the walls of the tambour were inclined inwards the span of the dome in reinforced concrete was reduced to 18.5 m. Exterior radial ribs were placed on the dome. Those were aligned with the corner of the tambour following the layout of the dodecahedral tambour. Since the radial ribs were spaced widely apart, two horizontal rings were added to the structure of the dome. The radial ribs as well as horizontal rings protrude visibly on the dome. A stylized lunette was integrated between the rings and between each two ribs. In order to integrate a lantern at the crown of the dome, an additional compression ring was added. And a disk shape ring was introduced to counter the tension forces at the bottom of the dome.

Early Reinforced Concrete Shells in Russia

The largest dome to apply the Hennebique system in the Russian Empire was built in 1905 over the Naval Cathedral of Saint Nicholas on the island of Kronstadt near Saint Petersburg. Like Poti, this cathedral adopted the layout of the domes of Hagia Sophia. The cathedral was constructed mainly in masonry. The integrated main dome with a span of 26,75 m and both large semi-domes of a span of 22.9 m were built in reinforced concrete. Elliptical domes were constructed to optimise the load transfer. The domes were stiffened by external radial ribs. The springers were constructed in masonry and the actual span of all the domes in reinforced concrete was slightly reduced [12].

 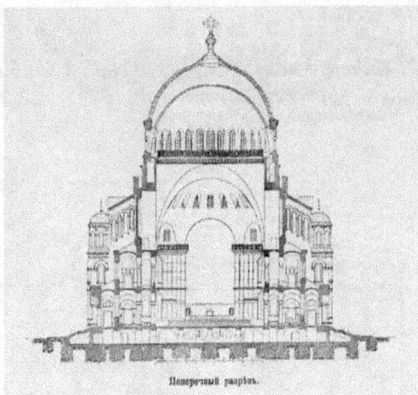

Figure 9: Hennebique system largest domes: Arena of the Imperial Stud in Saint Petersburg, 1904, Source: Černomorskoe stroitel'noe obščestvo, 1906 (Note 10). Naval Cathedral of Saint Nicholas, Kronstadt, 1905, V. A. Kosjakov, 1911 (Note 11).

No System

After an introductory period of successful implementation of reinforced concrete in the Russian Empire dominated by the Monier and Hennebique system the followed a period when the reinforced concrete became a generic term and these systems fell out of use. In this period, vaulting technology was further developed. The configuration of the supporting system of those constructions was directly related to the function of the building. As in the previously described dome structures, the inner surfaces of vaults in public buildings were kept clear of any supporting elements. One of the examples deploying vault construction is the church Our-Lady-of-Lourdes. According to the original design its interior space was divided into a nave and two-storey lateral aisles. While the plan of the lowest level was built according to the original design, the structure of the upper levels was modified. The nave and the aisles were unified into one single space covered by ca. 16 m wide vault. The eliminated buttresses were converted into arched girders built in reinforced concrete and placed transversely above the vault. The lower cords of the girders emerge as arched groins under the vault. Double-curved shells were introduced between the groins. The upper straight segments of the girders shape the gambrel roof of the church [13].

An elaborate double-shell structure was used int the construction in 1910 of the skating rink in Saint Petersburg. Its arena was covered by a long vault with semi-domes at each end. Three skylights were integrated at the crown of the vault. This three-centred vault had a span of ca. 21 metres and had a decorative function. It was held by hangers connected to the beams of a more complex vault structure above. The beams were supported by arches, the springers of which were connected by tension rods. An additional shell was constructed on those arches.

Figure 10: Vault constructions in public buildings in Saint-Petersburg: Our-lady-of-Lourdes Church, 1909. Source: Tovarišestvo Železo-Beton, 1911 (Note 12). Skating rink, 1910. Source: http://lobgott.livejournal.com/163665.html (Consulted on 27th December 2014).

Vaults were also used in industrial buildings as an optimal solution to obtain wide column-less spaces. In comparison to the previously described buildings, where the supporting system is hidden above the vaults, in the industrial buildings those features are visibly installed below. Two subcategories emerged in these buildings: plain curved shells and vaults with ribs. In both cases the structures of the vault took the form of a segmental circle and horizontal forces were restrained by tension rods. While the first was supported by masonry walls, the second was a part of a supporting skeletal structure.

Examples in Saint Petersburg include the plain vaults employed in the construction of Water Filter Plant. It was built between 1909 and 1910 on the riverbank of Neva with red brick walls. The thickness of segmental barrel vaults ranged between 10 cm at the crown and 16 cm at the springer. They spanned 15 and 16 metre wide rooms. Some of the vaults were supported by masonry walls and some by columns and beams in reinforced concrete. The springers of the vaults were connected by iron rods held by hangers.

The automobile factory Russkij Renault constructed in 1916 is an example of the second subcategory. The two rows of approximate 7.5 metre-high columns support the segmental arched ribs which had a span of 16.5 metres. The space between the ribs was filled with curved shells. Five skylights were integrated in the shell crowns of the roof. The tension elements and hangers made of reinforced concrete were placed between the springers of the ribs.

The last and most notable shell structure built in pre-revolutionary Russia was the seaplane hangar in Tallinn. Several structures were involved [14]. The Maritime Ministry of the Russian Empire commissioned three 50 m long, 30 m wide and 10 m high halls. The result was a building with exterior dimensions of about 123 by 50 m. Each hall was covered by a dome built above a square of 36.4x36.4 metres. 6.8 m long vaults of the same span were placed in front and behind the dome. An additional vault was constructed on the north side of the building in order to allow direct access to the water. The radius of the domes and of the vaults was 30.6 metres. The rise of the domes was 12 and of the vaults 6 metres. All the corner of the domes are supported by angle brackets composed of vertical and diagonal column. In each dome a round 10 metres wide lantern was integrated. The opening was stiffened by a compression ring 25x25 cm. The thickness of the dome around the ring was 8 cm and toward its edges it was increased to 15 cm. Towards the corners the dome thickness ranged from 40 up to 72 cm. The thickness of the vaults was 10 cm. The original structure was altered during renovation works. An additional layer of reinforcement and shotcrete was added on the interior side of the shells.

Figure 11: Vaults in industrial buildings in Saint Petersburg: Water Filter Plant, 1910 and Factory Russkij Renault, 1916. Source: M. S. Štiglic et al., Pamjatniki promyšlennoj architektury Sankt-Peterburga, Sankt-Peterburg: Č rnoe Beloe, 2005.

Figure 12: Seaplane hangars in Tallinn, 1917. Source: M. M ndel and O. Orro (Note 14).

Conclusions

The introduction of reinforced concrete in the Russian Empire was facilitated by the existing iron and cement industry. Merely two years after its first application in 1886, reinforced concrete was deployed in construction of a shell structure. At first, shells were mainly built according to the globally-known construction method invented by Joseph Monier. The shells constructed following this method were mainly plain vaults and domes. The construction method of François Hennebique was introduced later in 1898. The first shells built using this method appeared at the beginning of a 20th century. During the early period, shells were usually integrated in new buildings otherwise built using traditional construction methods and are thus difficult to identify. Only utilitarian structures such as reservoirs and tunnels, guided by principles of engineering rather than aesthetics, exposed their reinforced concrete structures.

Shells constructed during the second decade of the 20th century were not attributed to any system. During this period, liberation from the traditional architecture can be observed and the shells of reinforced concrete became visible. However, those changes took place mainly in industrial buildings where the shells were reduced to plain curved slabs.

Analysis of the shell structures built in reinforced concrete in the Russian Empire reveals a variety of different types of building. Those range from utilitarian, public, transport to industry buildings. The description of shell shapes has led to a classification according to geometric properties. Drawing on straight lines, complete and segmental circles those embrace: barrel vaults (with and without groins), cross vaults, segmental vaults, basket-handle vaults, hemispheric and segmental domes. In its turn, an analysis of supporting systems of the shell allows its categorisation according to static properties.

Particular local conditions in the Russian Empire resulted in construction of important structures that were globally discussed in the technical literature and played an important role in the development of reinforced concrete worldwide.

References

[1] V. Korensky, 'Impact of European Knowledge on the Development of Reinforced Concrete in the Russian Empire' pp.693-7 in J. Mascarenhas-Mateus and A. P. Pires, (Eds.), History of Construction Cultures, Proceedings of the 7th International Congress on Construction History (7ICCH 2021), Lisbon 2021, Lisbon: Creinforced concrete Press, 2021.
[2] Akcionernoe obščestvo dlja proizvodstva betonnych i drugich stroitel'nych rabot, 'Sistema Monier (beton s železnym ostovom) v ee primenenii k stroitelnomu iskusstvu' Moskva: Tipografija T.I. Gagen, 1891.
[3] S. A. Podėrni, 'Al'bom k techničeskomu opisaniju Moskovskich central'nych gorodskich boen' Moskva, 1896.
[4] S. D. Karejša, 'O primenenii vooružennogo betona na železnych dorogach v Rossii' Moskva, 1905.
[5] A. Ė. Lopatto, 'Artur Ferinandovič Lolejt. K istorii otečestvennogo železobetona' Moskva: Izdatel´stvo literatury po stroitel´stvu, 1969.
[6] Akcionernoe obščestvo dlja proizvodstva betonnych in drugich stroitel'nych rabot, 'Al'bom nekotorych ispolnenych Rabot' Moskva, 190-.
[7] V. Korensky, 'The Introduction of the Hennebique Reinforced Concrete System in the Russian Empire, 1898-1907', ICON: Journal of the International Committee for the History of Technology, vol. 26, pp. 112-129, France:CPI, 2021.
[8] O. Lecocq, 'Alimentation d'eau à Ekatérinoslav (Russie)', Beton und Eisen, pp. 152-153, Wien, 1904.
[9] Korensky, (note 7).
[10] B. N. Akimov, 'Železo-beton v praktike'. S.-Petersburg i Moskva: Izdanie T-va M.O. Wolf, 1908.
[11] Černomorskoe stroitel'noe obščestvo, 'Železo-beton sistemy Hennebique', S.-Peterburg: Tipografija A. O. Baškov, 1906.
[12] V. A. Kosjakov, 'Postrojka Kronštadskago Morskogo Sobora', Trudy IV S"ezda Russkich Zodčich, S.-Peterburg, 1911.
[13] Tovarišestvo Železo-Beton, 'Spisok važnejšich rabot, proizveděnnych tovarišestvom Železo-beton', Sankt-Peterburg, 1911.
[14] H. Onton, 'Investigation of the causes of deterioration of old reinforced concrete constructions and possibilities of their restoration' (Ph.D. thesis, Tallinn University of Technology, 2008); M. Mändel and O. Orro, 'The marvellous reinforced concrete shells of Tallinn seaplane hangars in the context of early concrete architecture in Estonia', Construction history, vol. 27, pp. 65-85, 2012.

The patent war between François Hennebique and Armand Considère: competing reinforced concrete systems in 'fin de Belle Époque' France

Nick von Behr
University of Kent, United Kingdom and ENSAPL/University of Lille, France.

Abstract

This paper examines the conflict between François Hennebique and Armand Considère, centred on competing patents for reinforced concrete systems in early 20th-century French structures. In the 1890s Hennebique first patented in Belgium and then France, key aspects of monolithic structural framing using the new combined material of béton armé. He rapidly grew a commercial empire in France and abroad, centred on his main design studios in the heart of Paris, and using a global network of agents and contractors. Considère patented his own reinforced concrete system, béton fretté, in 1901 but could only benefit financially from commercial activity five years later when he retired as a senior French state civil engineer setting up in private consulting. The two men were to confront each other in the French courts over aspects of their respective systems for foundation piling. The paper also references the work of the French Commission on reinforced cement and concrete, on which both men sat between 1901 and 1905, in addition to two non-monumental buildings in and near Paris, which provide exemplary material for the key technical issues. The content is derived from aspects of the researcher's current doctoral research on the influence of technical standards and associated regulations for steel and reinforced concrete on the development of modern architecture in Paris, Lille-Roubaix-Tourcoing and Brussels prior to WW1 [1].

Introduction

This paper explores the key role of patents and specifications for building systems using *béton armé* (invented by François Hennebique) and *béton fretté* (invented by Armand Considère), and their connections with theoretical and technical approaches to non-monumental building construction and architecture in pre-WW1 France. Considerable research by others has focused on the first use of reinforced concrete and cement in France at the turn of the twentieth century; in particular the development of a novel building framing system patented by Hennebique and adapted superbly by the Perret brothers and other constructors in Paris during the first decade of the 20th century. While there will always be new leads in this well-covered area, my own doctoral research is concentrating on the activities of Armand Considère, his business partners and his associates, records of which are held at the Archives Nationales du Monde de Travail (ANMT) in Roubaix near the University of Lille [2].

The protagonists

François Hennebique (1842-1921) was a dynamic Belgian contractor and entrepreneur who turned reinforced concrete into a worldwide product accepted by the construction industry. He ran a building contracting business in Belgium from the 1870s, but significantly for this paper, he began to develop a novel reinforced concrete system, *béton armé*, which he first patented in Belgium in 1886 – however, it was his August 1892 French patent (amended a year later) which would be of most significance to future developments with the material [3].

Armand Considère (1841-1914) was a highly-regarded French state civil engineer during the late nineteenth and early twentieth centuries. In 1902 Considère became Inspecteur Général at the Ponts et Chaussées, in effect head of the elite

The patent war between François Hennebique and Armand Considère: competing reinforced concrete systems in 'fin de Belle Époque' France

state civil engineering corps in France – the post had first been established by royal decree in 1716. He set up his own private business in 1906, having freely allowed the state to use his 1901 patent for *béton fretté*, in accordance with the then regulations for civil servants [4].

While Considère and Hennebique were almost the same age, they had very different personal attributes. Considère was an archetype of the French elite engineering system, well-educated and honourable, though also quietly spoken and thoughtful. By contrast, Hennebique was a very confident man, who had little evidence of formal education and was an outsider in French society; he appeared to hold a grudge against those who he thought spent too much time theorising about technical issues, rather than acting, as he did, based on many years of practical observation of on-site construction. This clash of personalities was to be at the heart of the commercial war between the two men. While there is some existing research on the wider technical impact of this rivalry in both France and Britain, there is still plenty of new material to uncover [5].

The French Commission on reinforced cement and concrete

The 'patent war' between the two inventors was sparked by a disagreement over the conception and application of technical standards when both were members of the French Commission on reinforced concrete and cement. The state-appointed group produced what it thought was final guidance in 1905 on the use of the new material in French national civil engineering projects. The Commission had been established in 1901 by the Minister of Public Works in response to concerns raised about the failure of reinforced cement and concrete structures in France. The distinction between cement and concrete is important as some systems used cement only, while others used cement with aggregates, and this together with the type of metal used, influenced the characteristics of the final combined building material [6].

Considère joined a majority of other eminent French civil engineers and theoreticians on the Commission, including his mentee Harel de la Noë, while Hennebique and Edmond Coignet were the only two contractors present, with two architects attending as well. Considère led a sub-strand of the Commission's investigations that undertook laboratory testing of reinforced concrete samples, focusing on the difference between his own newly-patented system, *béton fretté* and that of Hennebique, *béton armé*. He would eventually take over the main secretarial duties of the Commission, coinciding with his promotion to Inspecteur Général in 1902, and was the author of the final report to the Minister in 1905. It would seem that he fulfilled this role with his usual diligence; though given his close personal interest in *béton fretté*, patented in the first year of the Commission, it would be reasonable to question how objectively he operated [7].

Hennebique was sceptical about the dominant approach taken by the engineer-theoreticians on the Commission. To some extent this reflected the general view of the construction industry, which had relied on years of practical experience to develop new approaches, backed by the emergence of iron as a key building material in 19th century France. More importantly, Hennebique's main goal had been to market his brand of reinforced concrete as superior to every other type of such construction systems, particularly in terms of better economy, structural stability and greater fire-resistance. Already, in parallel with his membership of the Commission, he had begun to defend his patents for béton armé in legal suits about alleged breaches (see below) [8].

The final report of the Commission was referred on by the Minister to a special panel of the French Academy of Sciences, which produced its own set of recommendations. These were incorporated into the official guidance published by the Minister in late 1906. They weren't regulations *per se*, rather advice about the application of agreed national standards for reinforced concrete (now superseding cement), applied to those who worked on state civil engineering projects. This was a subtle but important distinction as other European countries, particularly Germany and Switzerland, had taken a more directive approach in applying their standards for the new building material [9].

The patents

Patents for béton armé and béton fretté were a vital part of technological innovation, giving French inventors up to 15 years in which to exploit their new products and processes before competitors could copy them. But more important than the date of their recognition by the state, was whether new patents were truly different from predecessors, and whether they were actually applied in industry within the two years allowed – if not, they ceased to exist [10].

In the construction industry the first patents for reinforced cement and concrete had been registered in the second half of the 19th century in and outside France. The key French and Belgian patents of relevance to the story outlined in this paper are listed in Table 1.

Table 1: List of key French and Belgian reinforced concrete and ciment patents

Years	Inventors	Patent description
1877-8	Monier	French patents for beams made from iron and cement
1886	Hennebique	Belgian patent for floors made from iron and cement or concrete
1889	Cottancin	French patent for ciment armé system
1892-3	Hennebique	8 February and 8 July 1892 Belgian patents for béton armé system. 8 August 1892 and 7 August 1893 French patents for béton armé system.
1894	Coignet & Coisseau	French patent for reinforced concrete piles
1897	Hennebique	French patents for béton armé monolithic structure and piles (the latter subsequently used in the Compressol system)
1901	Considère	French patent for béton fretté system

To provide some further explanation, the start of iron and cement as a *combined* building material in France originated with Joseph Monier at the end of the 1870s – though the most significant exploitation of this invention happened in the following decade under Monier's German patent, through engineer-contractors such as Matthias Koenen and Gustav Adolf Wayss. The French reasserted themselves through Paul Cottancin's invention of a new *ciment armé* system patented in 1889, using metal meshes and thinner layers of cement. While François Hennebique had preceded this in 1886 with his first Belgian patent, it was only in 1892-3 that his French patents for a *béton armé* system made a real difference to the French construction industry, initially in the north of the country. This system employed concrete rather than cement, and was the start of a monolithic construction approach which Hennebique would finesse in a further improved 1897 patent. As for reinforced concrete piling, while Edmond Coignet and a colleague had patented a new system in 1894, they didn't apply it, hence Hennebique's own patent for piling in 1897 became the predominant one in the industry. Indeed, Hennebique promoted a new mechanised process for installing reinforced concrete foundations under a separate business entity (Compressol) – this was to become relevant to the legal cases examined later in this paper [11].

The patent war between François Hennebique and Armand Considère: competing reinforced concrete systems in 'fin de Belle Époque' France

The contrast between Hennebique's and Considère's columnar systems is shown in Figure 1. In essence, *béton fretté*, on the far left and centre right of the diagram, had circular (initially octagonal) columns with more longitudinal metal bars, but most critically, because of a long spiral bar, it did *not* require the separate metal transversal ties found in *béton armé*, centre left and far right. Considère would later admit that the use of metallic spiralling wasn't a completely original idea; however his 1901 patent had developed the concept into a new system, using soft steel, and distinct from Hennebique's which had employed a four-sided cross-section [12].

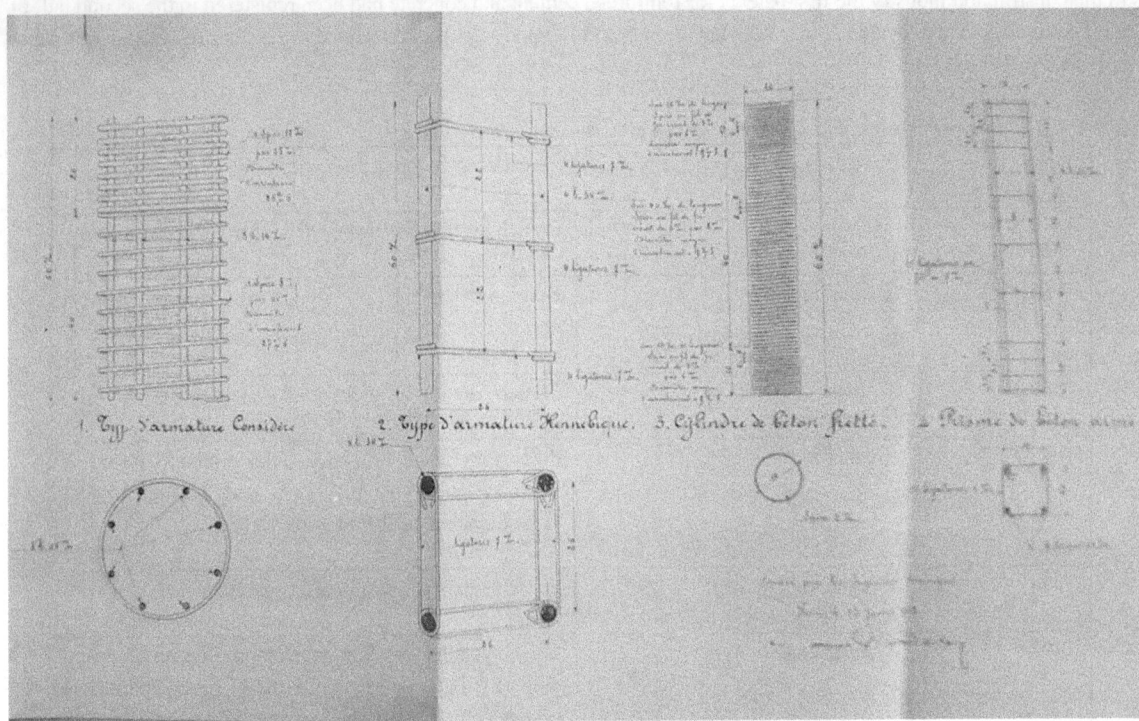

Figure 1: Comparison of Hennebique and Considère reinforcing systems. 1908. Pelnard-Considère-Caquot files, Archives Nationales du Monde de Travail.

The Menier case

La Cathédrale was an elegant, processing mill building at the Menier chocolate factory, Noisiel-sur-Marne near Paris completed in 1908. (Fig. 2) The original, and like *La Cathédrale* still extant, chocolate grinding mill was a famous 1872 iron-framed structure by the architect Jules Saulner, and Armand Moisant who had been the engineer for the concurrent *Bon Marché* iron-framed department store in Paris. The first building can be seen in the background of Figure 4.

The architect for the new mill building was Stephen Sauvestre, who had added architectural panache to the original technical designs for the Eiffel Tower, while the contractor was Jules Loup, who was very familiar with the Considère system of béton fretté employed for the building framing and foundations. In addition, an engineer called Viennot was used to assist with the reinforced concrete floors [13].

La Cathédrale had plenty of natural light entering the building through large windows. The Menier family were keen to admit visitors into the structure to witness their latest chocolate manufacturing technology in action from the safety of a special public gallery. This was another reason why Sauvestre and Considère designed and built an elegant arch-supported reinforced concrete *passerelle* across the River Marne from *La Cathédrale* to the rest of the factory complex – prior designs were by Hennebique and Eiffel, and there is a suggestion that the latter's metallic structure was the inspiration for the reinforced concrete approach finally used (Fig. 3) [14].

Figure 2: 'La Cathédrale' on right at the Menier factory, Noisiel-sur-Marne. Architect, Stephen Sauvestre. 1908. ©Mairie Noisiel.

The piling used in the foundations of *La Cathédrale* and the *passerelle*, as well as joining together two islands in the River Marne, was the subject of the main legal dispute between François Hennebique and Armand Considère between 1911 and 1914. (Fig. 4) In 1906 Hennebique had written to the head of the chocolate empire, Henri Menier, alleging that he was planning to use a piling system based on his own 1897 patent. Menier sought the advice of Considère, who reassured him that the piling used wasn't in breach of the patent, and so he replied to Hennebique to this effect – nothing was heard about the matter until five years later, when Henri Menier received a further letter from Hennebique demanding compensation equivalent to 10% of the project cost, with the threat of legal action if this wasn't resolved amicably (Fig. 5)[15].

The patent war between François Hennebique and Armand Considère: competing reinforced concrete systems in 'fin de Belle Époque' France

Figure 3: Construction of La Cathédrale and passerelle, Noisiel-sur-Marne. Architect, Stephen Sauvestre. 1907. ©Mairie Noisiel.

Figure 4: Considère piling process at the Menier Chocolate Factory, Noisiel-sur-Marne. Engineer, Armand Considère. 1907. Pelnard-Considère-Caquot files, Archives Nationales du Monde de Travail.

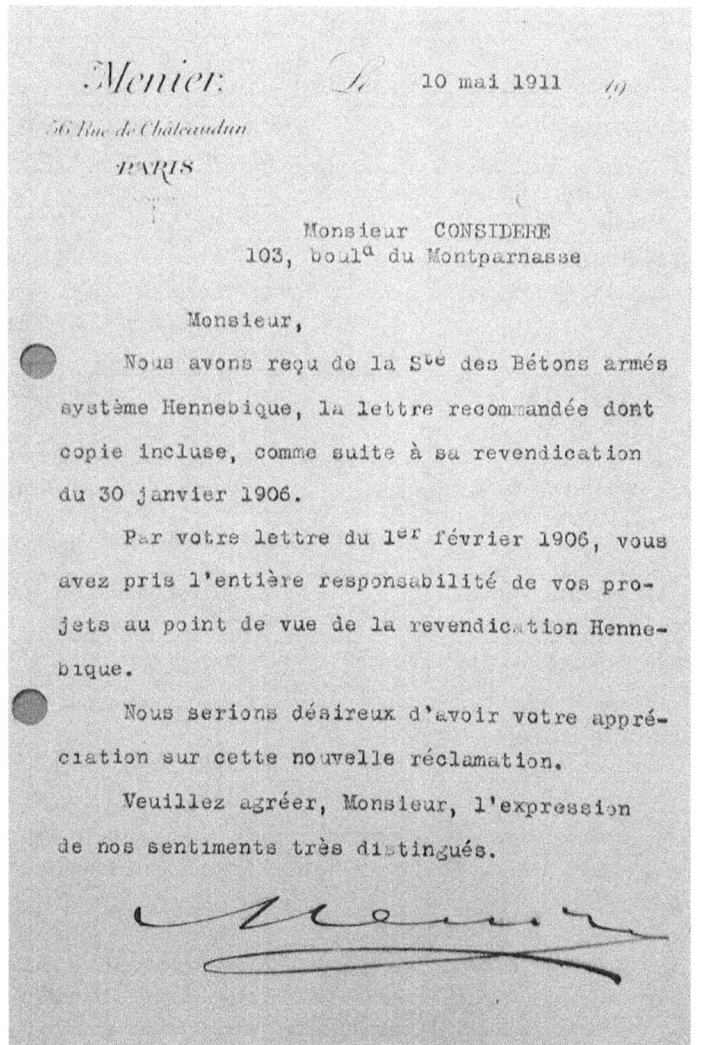

Figure 5: Letter from Henri Menier about Hennebique patent. 1911. Pelnard-Considère-Caquot files, Archives Nationales du Monde de Travail.

The other legal cases

Table 2 lists ten French legal cases involving François Hennebique or Compressol during the period 1902-14, either as plaintiff, accused or appellant. The principal source information is from the Pelnard-Considère-Caquot files held at ANMT, with some additions, hence it may not necessarily be entirely objective [16].

The patent war between François Hennebique and Armand Considère: competing reinforced concrete systems in 'fin de Belle Époque' France

Table 2: legal cases involving Hennebique or Compressol, 1902-14

Decision year	Litigants	Outcomes for Hennebique/Compressol
1902	Cottancin vs Hennebique	Cleared his name against accused breach of Cottancin's 1889 patent for ciment armé.
1903	Hennebique vs Mollet & Boussiron, Boussiron & Garrix et Picketty	His general patents for béton armé no longer applicable in France.
1909	Hennebique vs Picketty & Gittard; Coignet & Coiseau vs Hennebique	Lost his case for alleged breach of his 1897 piling patent. His breach of their 1894 piling patent recognised by the court.
1911	Hennebique vs Picketty & Gittard, Coignet & Coiseau. Considère vs Compressol. Hennebique vs Ministère de la Marine (Toulon)	Won his appeal against both 1909 judgements. Compressol cleared of defamation charges. Won his case for breach of his 1897 piling patent.
1912	Hennebique vs Considère, Menier, Combe, Société Générale d'Entreprises	Won his case for breaches of his 1897 piling patent.
1913	Ministère de la Marine (Toulon) vs Hennebique	Lost in an appeal against 1911 judgement.
1914	Considère, Menier, Combe, Société Générale d'Entreprises vs Hennebique	Lost in an appeal against 1912 judgement.

What was the rationale for bringing these cases to court and appeal? It appears there were three main reasons for undertaking what could become time-consuming and expensive legal action against a commercial competitor: the terms of a patent; defamation; politics.

The first reason was because the terms of an existing French patent for reinforced concrete was either being breached or was coming to the end of its 15 year life, hence the commercial protection it offered would cease – in certain cases it might be beneficial to accrue as much financially from competitors through the threat of legal action, or if ignored, by following through with, hopefully, court-imposed compensation. This would seem to have been a key reason behind most of the original cases, whether initiated by Hennebique or others. Once Hennebique led the way reinforced concrete had become a highly competitive part of the French construction market from the 1890s onwards.

Linked to the first reason, part of a product's value was connected to its producer's reputation, and litigators knew that they could employ (the threat of) legal suits as a weapon to undermine those of their competitors. Hence the second reason, defamation, applied to Considère's case against La Societe de Fondation par Compression Mecanique du Sol (which owned the Compressol mechanised piling system). This reinforced concrete foundation company was run by Hennebique from his Paris headquarters and had published text and photographs in an undated (probably 1908 or earlier) pamphlet criticising the *béton fretté* system. Considère lost his defamation case in 1911 because the judges were convinced that he had not sufficiently applied his system at the time of Compressol publishing their pamphlet; this was assumed to be within two years of Considère having established his new business [17].

Politics was also an impetus for legal action. This encapsulated the personal clashes between the main competitors, but also between their networks and alliances in industry and the ruling echelons of French society. When Hennebique threatened to sue such a highly respectable Frenchmen as Henri Menier, he was taking on more than just Considère as a business rival. The influence of the political factor broadened as cases entered the appeals system, but also as the prospect of war with Germany became more likely; it focused on the supremacy of French invention and innovation over foreign competition. In these circumstances it is difficult to understand why Hennebique, who always claimed to be a Belgian at heart, should have risked pursuing the French Ministère de la Marine in a case which he ultimately lost on appeal in 1913 [18].

A Considère retrofit to a Hennebique structure?

Another structure of relevance to this paper, but using both the Hennebique and Considère reinforced concrete systems, was an automobile company's office building in Levallois-Perret, a Parisian suburb, which was fully completed in 1907. (Fig. 6) The architect for the building was Edouard Arnaud and the contractor was Louis Roquerbe, two men who were probably the best known pairing of Hennebique system constructors in Paris, both having worked on the inventor's own new headquarters at 1, rue Danton completed in 1899, possibly as well as Hennebique's private villa in Bourg-la-Reine [19].

Figure 6: Le Garage des Automobiles de place, Paris. Architect, Edouard Arnaud. 1912. Postcard.

The patent war between François Hennebique and Armand Considère: competing reinforced concrete systems in 'fin de Belle Époque' France

The maison de rapport at 1 rue Danton in Paris contained the design offices of Hennebique reinforced concrete systems and was constructed in 1898 to demonstrate the new material's ability to fit within a traditional urban setting. However, probably against the wishes of the inventor, the facade included expensively-cast cement and ceramic mouldings hiding most of the concrete from view. Amongst other well-known buildings Roquerbe had contracted for were the immeuble at 9 rue Claude-Chahu (1902) by architect Charles Klein using the Hennebique system, and the immeuble at 6 rue Hanovre (1909) by the architect Adolphe Bocage, using the Perret Brothers' own reinforced concrete system [20].

Arnaud and Roquerbe began with the Hennebique system for constructing the three-storey car sales office by la Compagnie Française des automobiles de place in Levallois-Perret, a business with which Arnaud would seem to have had professional links. A further three storeys were added to the structure using the Considère system. It is not yet fully understood why the change of system for the extension, particularly by Arnaud and Roquerbe given their close links with Hennebique. Original sketches and diagrams held at the ANMT show that they and Considère were proposing to extend the storeys upwards by integrating the core of the Hennebique frame system into the béton fretté system. (Fig. 7) The work would involve removing concrete from the existing columns and retrofitting more metal reinforcement, both internally and through specially-designed armature banding at critical points on columns. Such was the complexity of the work that Roquerbe invited a senior representative from Considère's company to oversee it in person. Sadly, since the building has been demolished we can no longer examine exactly how the two different systems were combined, possibly uniquely [21].

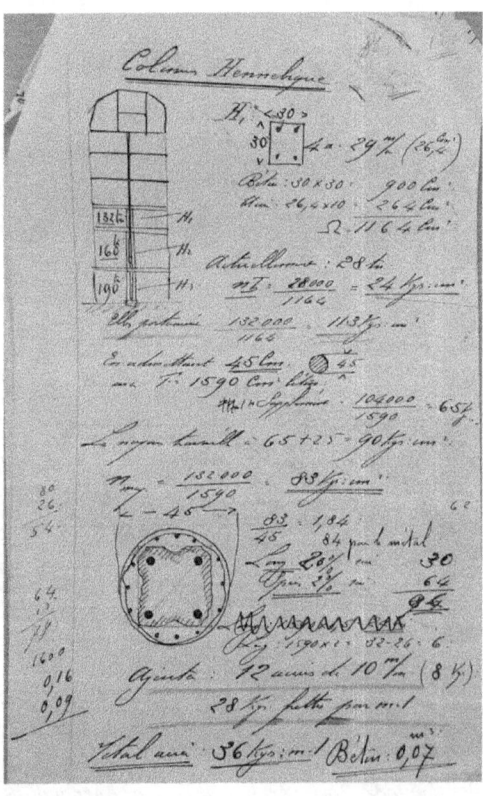

Figure 7: Sketch of frame and pillar at Levallois-Perret garage. Architect, Edouard Arnaud. 1906. Pelnard-Considère-Caquot files, Archives Nationales du Monde de Travail.

Conclusions

Does the patent war between François Hennebique and Armand Considère shed any light on the history of construction and architecture in pre-WW1 Paris? It is possible to highlight some tentative thoughts related to the contest between the two reinforced concrete systems and their inventors.

While the French Government did publish agreed standards for both *béton armé* and *béton fretté* in 1906, the year in which Considère first commercially exploited his 1901 patent, it was clear that this only applied to state civil engineering projects rather than all of the construction industry. Hennebique, however, wouldn't be deterred from competing forcefully with his new rival entrepreneur in any relevant context, but particularly in the use of reinforced concrete piling after 1906. This determined approach materialised first in the threat of legal action against a perceived breach of Hennebique's 1897 piling patent; then in the form of publicity aimed at undermining the reliability of *béton fretté*; and finally as actual litigation in the courts, and where this still failed, taking advantage of the appeals system to try to overturn judgements.

Considère had focused on testing reinforced concrete samples to support his scientifically-based work as a member of the French Commission. Hennebique had been dismissive of such an over-theoretical approach and was to continue to be so subsequently through the voice of his journal *Le Béton Armé*. It is somewhat ironic that ultimately Hennebique's case against Considère was rejected at appeal in part by the latter's self-commissioned and authenticated tests of samples of *béton armé* and *béton fretté*. The evidence from these tests indicated that Hennebique's original legal assertions about the originality and superiority of his reinforced concrete piling system were unfounded [22].

Both the Hennebique and Considère systems shared technical features in their use of the combined components of reinforced concrete to best advantage in French construction at the time – they emphasised economy of build, structural resilience and fire-resistance, all of which factors were aimed at industrial clients. They and their fellow inventors were less forceful, at least initially, on the advantages of a monolithic approach to building framing from an urban architectural perspective, despite respected advocates such as Louis-Charles Boileau and Anatole de Baudot. The cause was taken up by the next generation of early 20th-century Parisian builder-partners not least: Edouard Arnaud and Louis Roquerbe; Auguste and Gustave Perret; Henry Sauvage and Charles Sarazin; and Henri Deneux and Gustave Degaine. Their accrued knowledge of building non-monumental reinforced concrete structures prior to WW1 would be partially absorbed into the Modernist movement of the interwar years, led in France by leading architectural thinkers such as Le Corbusier and Robert Mallet-Stevens.

Acknowledgements

I would like to thank my supervisors at Kent School of Architecture and Planning, Professor Gerry Adler and Dr Alan Powers, and at ENSAPL (Lille), Professor Eric Monin, and Dr Gilles Maury, for their continual input into my PhD; others who have helped me with my research and thinking include Professor Gwenaël Delhumeau, Professor Bernard Espion, Dr Sabine Kuban, Dr Valentin Gillet, Professor Réjean Legault and Professor Henrik Schoenefeldt. Last but not least, my thanks go to the archivists at Archives Nationales du Monde de Travail (Roubaix), Archives du Ville de Noisiel-sur-Marne and the Archives Architecturales Contemporaines du XXe siècle (Paris).

References

[1] N. von Behr, 'The Influence of Standards and Regulations for Steel and Reinforced Concrete on the Development of Modern Architecture in Pre-WW1 Paris and Brussels', pp. 355-63 in J. Campbell et al, (Eds), The History of Building Trades and Professionalism, Proceedings of the Eighth Annual Conference of the Construction History Society, Cambridge: Construction History Society, 2021.

The patent war between François Hennebique and Armand Considère: competing reinforced concrete systems in 'fin de Belle Époque' France

[2] J. Abram, 'An Unusual Organisation of Production: The Building Firm of the Perret Brothers, 1897-1954', *Construction History,* Vol. 3, 1987, pp. 75–93; G. Delhumeau, L'Invention du Béton Armé: Hennebique 1890-1914, Paris: Éditions Norma, 1999 ; P. Collins, Concrete: The Vision of a New Architecture, Montreal: McGill-Queen's University Press, 2004; C. Simonnet, Le Béton: Histoire d'un Matériau, Marseille: Éditions Parenthèses, 2005 ; S. van de Voorde, 'Hennebique's Journal Le Beton Arme. A Close Reading of the Genesis of Concrete Construction in Belgium', pp. 1453–62 in K.-E. Kurrer, W. Lorenz & V. Wetzk, (Eds), Proceedings of the Third International Congress on Construction History, Cottbus, Berlin: NeunPlus1, 2009; A. Hellebois, 'Theoretical and experimental studies on early reinforced concrete structures' (Ph.D. thesis, Université Libre de Bruxelles, 2013); Pelnard-Considère-Caquot files at Archives Nationales du Monde de Travail: *1994 035 4191 Procès Hennebique: pièces de justice, assignations, conclusions, jugements, procès verbaux, notes de Monsieur Considère, notes diverses, imprimés, notices, lettres circulaires. 1910-1914 ; 1994 035 4192 Procès Hennebique: correspondance, brevets et croquis, marché-soumissions-contrats, plans photographies. 1909-1914.*

[3] Delhumeau, L'Invention Du Béton Armé, (Note 2) ; Hellebois, thesis (Note 2).

[4] A. Considere, 'Le Beton Frette et Ses Applications', *Le Génie Civil*, 1907 ; F. Sioc'han, 'Des effets de la houle sur les ouvrages d'art: application des moles du type 'Considère' dans la protection des ports', pp. 325–34 in G. Bienvenu et al, (Eds), Construire!: Entre Antiquité et époque contemporaine, Actes du 3e congrès francophone d'histoire de la construction, Paris: Éditions Picard, 2019.

[5] P. Cusack, 'Agents of Change: Hennebique, Mouchel and Ferro-Concrete in Britain, 1897-1908', *Construction History*, Vol, 3, 1987, pp. 61–74; S. van de Voorde, 'Bouwen in Beton in België (1890-1975): Samenspel van Kennis, Experiment En Innovatie' (Ph.D. thesis, University of Ghent, 2010).

[6] Delhumeau, L'invention Du Béton Armé, (Note 2) ; J. Christophe, Le Béton Armé et Ses Applications, Paris: Béranger, 1902.

[7] Delhumeau, L'invention Du Béton Armé, (Note 2) ; F. Sioc'han, 'Des effets de la houle sur les ouvrages d'art: application des moles du type 'Considère' dans la protection des ports', (Note 4).

[8] Delhumeau, L'invention Du Béton Armé, (Note 2).

[9] S. van de Voorde, S. Kuban, and D. Yeomans, 'Early Regulations and Guidelines on Reinforced Concrete in Europe (1900-1950): Towards an International Comparison,' pp. 345-56 in J. Campbell et al, (Eds), Building Histories, Proceedings of the Fourth Annual Conference of the Construction History Society, Cambridge: Construction History Society, 2017.

[10] Simonnet, Le Béton: Histoire d'un Matériau, (Note 2).

[11] ibid; Société de Fondation par Compression Mécanique du Sol, Problèmes des Fondations, n.d. .

[12] Pelnard-Considère-Caquot files, (Note 2).

[13] C. Cartier, H. Jantzen et R. Michel, Noisiel: La Chocolaterie Menier Seine-et-Marne, Ile-de-France: SPADEM, 1994.

[14] Ibid ; Archives du Ville de Noisiel-sur-Marne.

[15] Pelnard-Considère-Caquot files, (Note 2).

[16] ibid; Delhumeau, L'invention Du Béton Armé, (Note 2); Simonnet, Le Béton: Histoire d'un Matériau, (Note 2) ; Hellebois, thesis (Note 2).

[17] A. Considère, La Société de Fondation par Compression Mécanique du Sol contre le Béton Fretté, Paris: Considère, 1911 ; Pelnard-Considère-Caquot files, (Note 2) ; Société de Fondation par Compression Mécanique du Sol, Problèmes des Fondations, (Note 11).

[18] Pelnard-Considère-Caquot files, (Note 2).

[19] J.-F. Belhoste, 'Les debuts du beton arme et son introduction dans les ecoles d'ingenieurs et d'architecture', in M. Porrino, (Ed), Le béton armé. Histoire d'une technique et sauvegarde du 20e siècle, Gollion: Infolio éditions, 2019.

[20] P. Belle-Riz, 'Le Beton arme a la recherche d'un style', pp. 641–50 in R. Carvais et al, (Eds), Édifice et artifice: Histoires constructives, Paris: Picard, 2010.

[21] P. Smith, 'Édouard Arnaud (1888)', *Centralien*, Vol, 660, 2018, pp. 42–5; Pelnard-Considère-Caquot files, (Note 2).
[22] F. Hennebique, 'Theorie et Bluff', *Le Beton Armé*, Vol, 165, 1912, pp.41-2; Pelnard-Considère-Caquot files, (Note 2).

Capturing the Practice of Deconstruction in Brussels (1903-1939): Photographic Heritage Collections as A Starting Point for Construction History

Lara Reyniers, Stephanie Van de Voorde, Ine Wouters
Department of Architectural Engineering, Vrije Universiteit Brussel, Belgium.

Abstract

This paper uses the photographic collection created by the heritage organisation 'Comité d'Etudes du Vieux Bruxelles' to study deconstruction practices in Brussels between 1903 and 1939. An analysis of images just before, during and after buildings were taken down, allows insights into the demolition techniques that were used and the economic and heritage value of the materials that were dismantled. By doing so, the paper contributes to the research on the reuse of building materials in Brussels, while also illustrating the value of photographic reportages that documented buildings at the end of their lives.

Introduction

Throughout history, the reuse of building materials salvaged from ruins, abandoned or destroyed buildings was a common phenomenon, happening in different historical contexts, with a variety of motivations and in all parts of the structure. Recent developments in archaeological technology have facilitated the identification of reused materials, yet those findings reveal little information on the context in which deconstruction and reuse occurred. Namely, it does not provide insights into the actors that were involved and the preceding demolition, including the extraction, collection and treatment of materials [1]. In their article 'For a history of deconstruction', Phillipe Bernardi and Daniela Esposito argued that construction historians could pay more attention to the practice of deconstruction as it holds the promise to reveal many strategies in relation to the preparation of a site, the salvage of materials and the adoption of security measures to avoid damage to the materials [2]. As such, research into the process of deconstruction can contribute to a more thorough understanding of the building culture, including the handling of buildings at the end of their lives. However, whereas the festive inauguration of a building was often well documented, sources on the disappearance of the building's last remains are scarce, which makes the collection of information on deconstruction more complicated.

This paper draws attention to a source that particularly focusses on buildings at the end of their lives: the photographic collection commissioned by the Comité d'Etudes du Vieux Bruxelles in 1903-39. A detailed analysis of three types of photographs of this collection is complemented by a close reading of additional sources like textbooks, newspapers and local magazines to enrich the understanding of what is depicted. Six photographs are selected and discussed to understand what the photographic collection can reveal about demolition techniques and the economic and heritage value of deconstructed materials. As such, the paper provides new insights into the previously initiated research on the reuse practice in nineteenth- and twentieth-century Brussels by Ghyoot et al., Wouters and Dobbels [3]. In doing so, the analysis enables us to establish the (unintended) value of photographic reportages as a source of information on the deconstruction process in Belgium and beyond.

Capturing the Practice of Deconstruction in Brussels (1903-1939): Photographic Heritage Collections as A Starting Point for Construction History

Photography as an alternative to preservation

The emergence of photographic collections such as those of the Comité d'Etudes du Vieux Bruxelles corresponded to a twofold international trend. During the second half of the nineteenth century, in line with the growing historical consciousness in Western Europe, photographers like Henri Le Secq (1818-82) and Edouard Baldus (1813-89) in France, and Edmond Fierlants (1819-69) in Belgium, were commissioned to document important monuments and to set up a catalogue of national heritage [4]. This interest in the photograph as a documentary tool was stimulated by improvements in photographic technology, enabling shorter exposure times and price drops. Therefore, photography became the medium par excellence not only to document the heritage that was to be preserved, but also what was about to be lost or threatened to disappear. As the historic city centre of many European cities was subject to large-scale infrastructure works and renewal, photographic reportages were an efficient and instantaneous tool to capture fast-paced urban transformations in the nineteenth and twentieth century [5].

At the turn of the century, new and often local conservation organisations were actively engaged in preserving buildings with an 'old' and 'picturesque' character. In addition to their attempts to physically preserve buildings, which all in all had relatively little impact, they committed themselves to ensure an alternative existence of the built fabric through photographs. Entire parts of the city were inventoried systematically, street by street, by capturing them on camera. For example, in London, the Society for Photographing Relics of Old London was founded in 1875. In Paris, it was one of the core tasks of the Commission Municipale du Vieux Paris, created in 1898. The development of their photographic inventory took place simultaneously with the rising fame of the photographer Eugène Atget (1857-1927) and his work dedicated to the Old Paris. Furthermore, in Berlin, the Märkische Provinizial Museum published three volumes of a photo publication 'Das malerische Berlin: Bilder und Blicke' (Picturesque Berlin: Images and Views) between 1911 and 1914 [6].

The Brussels' Comité d'études du Vieux Bruxelles (from here onwards referred to as 'the Comité') fits into this list of organisations. Similar to the organisations in Paris, London and Berlin, it was established in response to the large-scale renewal of the historic centre of the capital city, that was taking place since the second half of the nineteenth century. The Comité started its activities in 1903 and contacted their Parisian counterpart, established only five years before, to use their approach as a source of inspiration for their own activities. One of the major achievements of the Comité was the creation of an extensive photographic collection of Brussels' quarters and lesser-known heritage that were threatened to disappear. They appointed several photographers, who remained anonymous, to complete this work. By 1939, the collection contained around 1,500 photographs, mainly of buildings constructed between the sixteenth and eighteenth century that were considered to have an 'artistic' character. A considerable part of the buildings were taken down not long after they were photographed, and some structures were already in the process of demolition. Only 278 buildings that correspond to the 1,200 photographed civil houses were preserved throughout time. Today, a major part of the collection is easily consultable via the online library of the Académie Royale des Beaux-Arts de Bruxelles (ArBA-EsA) [7].

The photographic collection from a construction history perspective

Whereas construction history research is often used as a source for heritage studies and renovation projects, this collection enables the opposite approach. The collection of the Comité was initially established (and is mostly praised) for documentary purposes, as it is often the only remaining iconographic source of some remarkable Brussels' monuments that have disappeared [8]. Yet, as a number of these pictures depict heritage just before, during, and after it was taken down, the collection gives an idea of the extent of the destruction of Brussels' architectural heritage since the beginning of the 20th century. As such, it becomes a valuable and rare source that documents the deconstruction process. The 'end-of-life' pictures can be divided in three categories, each showing different aspects. The first type captures buildings just before they were taken down and give an idea of the buildings' state right before the end of its life. A second type of photograph focused on buildings in the process of demolition and contains information on demolition techniques and tools, the workers involved and their working conditions. A third type of image depicts the materials that were salvaged during demolition works and illustrates which materials were considered valuable from an economic and heritage perspective.

One of the most interesting photographs that catches the eye, because it combines the three afore mentioned categories in one picture, is the image of the former seat of the Université Libre de Bruxelles, Palais Granvelle, taken around 1930 (Fig. 1). Some parts of the building are still standing while others are already in the process of demolition. The façade of the courtyard can still be observed in all its glory, and it is clear that this part of the building was in a good condition – indeed, the façade had only recently been constructed of high-quality materials during a renovation in 1860 [9]. On the other hand, the clearance of the interior parts was already in progress, as can be observed from the many old materials gathered in the courtyard. These large piles of already sorted brick and timber would probably be transported by the truck, visible at the back of the courtyard, which tells us that the materials were of significant economic value to the demolition contractor. Moreover, when zooming in on the panel that is hanging on the front left façade of the building, it is possible to read the words "matériaux façade à vendre". A publication in a magazine of local history gives insights into the heritage value of this façade, as it explains that it was purchased in its entirety in 1931 by the administration of a nearby municipality, who wanted to reconstruct it as the front façade of their new town hall [10].

Figure 1: Demolition of the of the former seat of the Université Libre de Bruxelles, Brussels, 1930. Photo: Comité d'Etudes du Vieux Bruxelles. © KIK-IRPA.

Capturing the Practice of Deconstruction in Brussels (1903-1939): Photographic Heritage Collections as A Starting Point for Construction History

Before-and-after images of demolition

The combination of photographs before and after demolition can give information about the deconstruction process that happened in between. An example of this are the images of Caserne Sainte-Elizabeth, a building complex that was built several centuries earlier on the sloping terrain of Montagne de Sion and that was photographed by the Comité just before as well as immediately after its demolition. In the 2018 publication by Ghyoot et al., the demolition of the buildings of Caserne Sainte-Elizabeth in 1912 was perceived as a turning point for the reuse of building materials in Brussels. The complex needed to be demolished to make room for infrastructure works, yet the state had difficulties in finding a demolition contractor who could meet the conditions of the building specifications. The authors concluded that from then on, the value of second-hand materials decreased and the timeframe to demolish increasingly became shorter due to an accelerating economy [11]. However, in the research by Wouters and Dobbels such a trend was not visible [12]. At this point, the Comité's photographs can add another dimension to this history of the Caserne Sainte-Elisabeth, which may explain the demolition contractors' concerns.

Because the barracks were documented before their demolition in 1912 (Fig. 2), the photographs provide rare information about the state of the monument at the time, with implications for its material value. The photo of 1912 pictures a building in a poor condition. The outer walls are peeling off, windows are broken, the roof seems unstable and lacks several tiles…. In short, the building is depicted as a ruin in a bad state. That there was no place or time for a ruin in the rapidly changing city of Brussels was confirmed by several newspaper articles, which announced with relief that the state finally decided to take down the centuries-old, dilapidated barracks [13]. However, the photo of 1913 from the site after demolition (Fig. 3) indicates that despite the condition of the buildings, they still contained valuable materials. The image gives an overview of the site where the buildings were located. The terrain is closed off from its surroundings by the remains of the outer walls of the old buildings at one side (at the right), and wooden panels at the other side (in the back). Materials such as timber and tiles can be observed on the site, sorted and ready to be sold. This sale was also confirmed in a newspaper article, although the journalist described it as a sad *bric-a-brac* business for bidders "competing for the remains of the dilapidated building" [14]. Further studies are necessary to determine if the difficulties in finding a demolition contractor were linked to an accelerating economy and changes in the profession. In any case, the before-and-after photographs of the Comité show that the building was in a bad condition, yet still yielded economically valuable second-hand materials.

Figure 2: The Caserne Sainte-Elisabeth before it was demolished, Brussels, 1912. Photo: Comité d'Etudes du Vieux Bruxelles. © KIK-IRPA.

Figure 3: The site of Caserne Sainte-Elisabeth after demolition, Brussels, 1913. Photo: Comité d'Etudes du Vieux Bruxelles. © KIK-IRPA.

Picturing the demolition site

Another type of photograph by the Comité that is of interest, are the images taken during the demolition. The Comité had to act quickly to record certain buildings before their disappearance, and in some cases the demolition was already in progress. These images provide insights into the organisation of the site, the workers, and the tools and techniques they used. Typically, demolition contractors paid a certain amount of money for taking a building down. In return, they became the owners of the materials that were released while doing so. Therefore, it was important for them to take down the building carefully and to damage the materials as little as possible. Furthermore, they had to deal with an imposed timeframe that varied from a few weeks to months [15]. This meant that demolition contractors had to look for strategies and technologies that allowed them to achieve the desired balance between speed and caution. To get a better understanding of the common techniques, two of the photographs of the Comité are deciphered by comparing them with the information given in Edgar Lucas' 1944 textbook 'Building repairs and maintenance', in particular the chapter on 'Demolition. Shoring'. As the textbook was mainly instructive for small demolition works as a part of a renovation, including the salvation of some important materials, it contains valuable information on common demolition techniques and procedures in the first half of the twentieth century. Furthermore, Lucas' drawings can easily be compared with the photos of the Comité, resulting in the identification of specific demolition techniques [16].

A first technique was applied by contractor Henri Elsoucht in 1913 during the demolition of a number of adjacent houses in the city centre (Fig. 4). Therefore, the demolition contractor placed a row of inclined shores against the façades, to prevent the walls from collapsing. Lucas described how these shores had to consist out of one to four struts each and had to be placed at certain intervals along the wall. The shores were attached to the wall with a wall plate, and the angle of the shores needed to be around 60 degrees, depending on the available space (Fig. 6). The photo also shows that the workers dismantled the windows in the early stages of the demolition. To strengthen the wall and prevent distortion, the window openings were strutted as in the drawings by Lucas.

Capturing the Practice of Deconstruction in Brussels (1903-1939): Photographic Heritage Collections as A Starting Point for Construction History

Figure 4: Shored façades and windows during the demolition works in rue de la Madeleine, Brussels, 1913. Photo: Comité d'Etudes du Vieux Bruxelles. © KIK-IRPA.

Figure 5: The use of fans during the demolition works in rue Montagne du Parc, Brussels, n.d., Photo: Comité d'Etudes du Vieux Bruxelles © Bibliothèque artistique, ArBA.

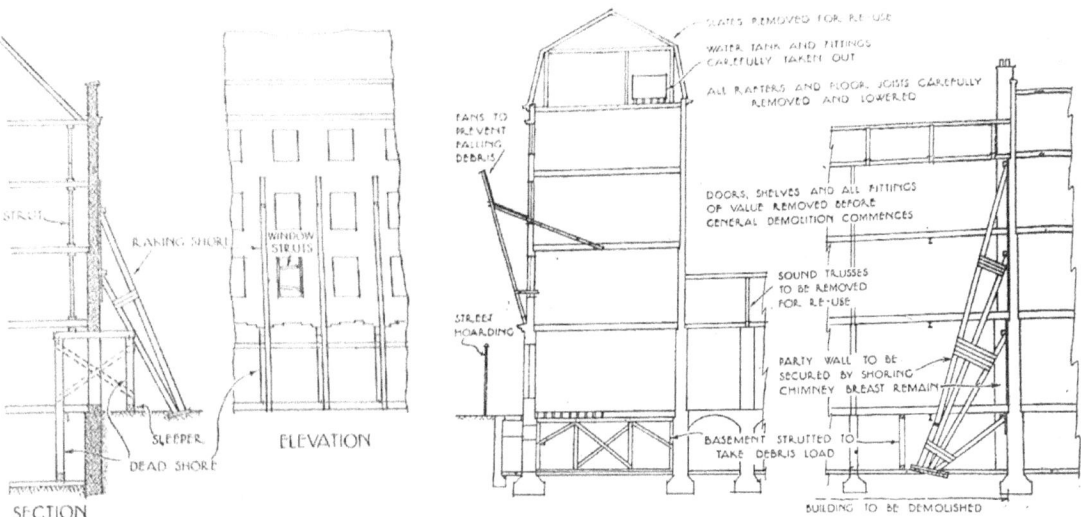

Figure 6: The execution of deconstruction works, 1944, Illustration: Edgar Lucas.

Another interesting technique described by Lucas and visible in the photographs of the Comité is the placement of fans (Fig. 5). This wooden structure was used to prevent materials and debris from falling into the street. Lucas described how such fans could be constructed, using old timbers that projected outward, through the window openings, and upward, so that they rested on the sill and could be secured to the floor, as is visible in the section in Figure 7. The fans were tied to scaffold poles that rested on a cornice, a sill, or a hole in the wall. Afterwards, strong boards had to be secured to the fans. Demolition started at the top of the building, so fans could be removed and re-erected lower after each part of the works [17].

Beside these two techniques, the photos of the Comité show that the demolition contractors used a handcart to transport materials and a pulley for hoisting (Fig. 4). Furthermore, they used a long tool to carry out their works, possibly a shovel or a crowbar. Moreover, the large number of people in the photo could be an indicator for the labour intensity required for this kind of work (Fig. 5).

The salvage of architectural objects

The collection of photographs not only provides insight into the practice of deconstruction, but also into the broader participation of organisations such as the Comité itself in this practice. Remarkably, several photos of buildings before their demolition correspond to drawings of objects that were salvaged from these buildings. These drawings were part of an inventory that describes how a variety of salvaged architectural elements were stored in the city depot of Brussels, that was established around 1850 [18]. The strong resemblance between the photographs and the drawings (Figs 7-8), suggests that the Comité was involved in the dismantling of objects, the drafting of the inventory, and the production of the corresponding drawings.

Figure 7: Door in rue des Tanneurs 73, Brussels, n.d., Photo: Comité d'Etudes du Vieux Bruxelles © KIK-IRPA.

Figure 8: Corresponding drawing of the door in rue des Tanneurs 73 that was salvaged and stored in the city depot, n.d., Brussels, City Archive Brussels, ARCH808.

The inventory of objects contains a list of 231 elements that were salvaged between 1877 and 1931 from different quarters in transformation. The list was supplemented by 58 drawings which match the inventory and several of the featured objects were formerly present on the façades or in the interiors of the houses photographed by the Comité. Furthermore, the inventory mentioned the address of the buildings from which the objects were salvaged (including the year of demolition), the material characteristics of the objects, and sometimes an additional observation [19]. Could this imply that the Comité inspected Brussels' quarters threatened by demolition to photograph objects with a certain heritage value to them, thus encouraging their salvage and eventual storage at the city depot?

Indeed, most of the objects stored in the city depot were architectural elements with a distinctive character, such as (partial) staircases in oak, marble mantlepieces, sculpted panels and stones, columns, parts of balconies, decorations, etc. To most of the objects an architectural style was ascribed, such as Louis XV, Louis XVI, or Henri II. This reflects the Comité's desire to physically preserve at least some distinctive elements of the buildings that were to be demolished, thus encouraging their dismantling. This desire was also pointed out in the reports of the departments and services of the city of Brussels from 1920. Here it was stated that the Comité wanted to find the missing coping stones of the dismantled entrance of the former Arbalétriers garden that was transported to the city depot [20].

The comparison between the photos of the Comité and other archival sources thus illustrates how different actors with different motivations were engaged in the process of deconstruction. The city administration of Brussels, probably encouraged by the Comité, took possession of certain elements of houses in the process of demolition. That the city administration did not do this out of economic considerations is confirmed by a letter in which an alderman gave a negative answer to the request to sell one of the stored staircases to a company. To them, the dismantled objects had probably more of a heritage value, as a souvenir of the Old Brussels. However, a journalist once called the city depot a 'museum without visitors', because all these stored objects and curiosities reminiscent of a past city were not presented to a wider audience [21].

Conclusion

Deconstruction is an understudied part of the construction sector involving unrecorded organisation and skills. This study demonstrates that the photographic reportage of the Comité d'Etudes du Vieux Bruxelles is helpful to understand the practice of deconstruction, certainly in combination with other sources. First, the images allow us to identify the state of a building just before it was taken down, with implications for the economic value of the building materials. Second, they reveal insights into the demolition site, the techniques that were used and other details about the deconstruction process. Finally, the photos illustrate an involvement of the members of the Comité in the extraction of elements with heritage value from demolished buildings, making clear that they took an active role in the deconstruction practice themselves. The insights from the collection of the Comité show that there is useful information to find in photographic reportages created by heritage organisations in response to urban transformations that took place from the second half of the nineteenth century. Therefore, collections similar to those of the Comité are possibly a valuable source in further studies on the deconstruction practice and the life cycle of building materials in general.

References

[1] S. Büttner, 'The Use of the "Already There": Reuse and Recycling for Monumental Building in the West in Late Antiquity and the Medieval Period' pp.461-68 in R. Carvais, A. Guillerme, V. Nègre, J. Sakarovitch, (Eds), *Nuts & Bolts of Construction History: Culture, Technology and Society, Proceedings of the Fourth International Congress on Construction History,* Paris 2012, Paris: Picard, 2012.; J. F. Bernard, P. Bernardi, D. Esposito, P. Dillmann, L. Foulquier, R. Mancini, (Eds), *Il Reimpiego in Architettura*, Rome: Ecole française de Rome, 2009.

[2] P. Bernardi, D. Esposito, 'For a History of Deconstruction' pp.453-60 in R. Carvais, A. Guillerme, V. Nègre, J. Sakarovitch, (Eds), *Nuts & Bolts of Construction History: Culture, Technology and Society, Proceedings of the Fourth International Congress on Construction History,* Paris 2012, Paris: Picard, 2012.

[3] M. Ghyoot, L. Devlieger, L. Billiet, A. Warnier, *Déconstruction et Réemploi. Comment Faire Circuler Les Éléments de Construction*, Lausanne : Presses polytechniques universitaires romandes (PPUR), 2018. pp. 15-38.; I. Wouters, J. Dobbels, 'Salvaging Construction Materials in Brussels, 1900-1925' pp. 487-493 in J. Mascarenhas-Mateus, A. P. Pires, (Eds), *History of Construction Cultures: Proceedings of the Seventh International Congress on Construction History. Lisbon 2021*, Leiden: CRC Press, 2021.

[4] S. Hughes, 'Imag(in)Ing Paris for Posterity', *Future Anterior: Journal of Historic Preservation, History, Theory, and Criticism,* vol10, no. 2, 2013, pp.1–15.; I. Bertels, 'Picturing Construction. Photographical Documentation of Belgian Construction Sites by Late Nineteenth and Early Twentieth-Century Contractors.' pp.25-36 in J. Campbell, N. Bill, Y. Pan, (Eds), *Further Studies in the History of Construction: the Proceedings of the Third Annual Conference of the Construction History Society*, Cambridge 2016, Cambridge: Construction History Society, 2016.

[5] M. Paeslack, 'High-Speed Ruins: Rubble Photography in Berlin, 1871-1914', *Future Anterior: Journal of Historic Preservation, History, Theory, and Criticism,* vol.10, no. 2, 2013, pp. 33–47.

[6] F. Bourillon, '"Paris Se Met En Scène", l'administration Parisienne à l'Exposition Franco-Britannique de 1908', *Synergies Royaume-Uni et Irlande*, no. 2, 2009, pp. 33–45.; R. Fiori, *L'invention Du Vieux Paris. Naissance d'une Conscience Patrimoniale Dans La Capitale*, Wavre: Mardaga, 2012. p. 88. A. H. Mayor, 'Old London. The Metropolitan Museum of Art Bulletin', vol.3, no. 9, 1945, pp. 220–223.; M. Paeslack, 'Inventing Tradition: The Märkische Museum and Picturesque Berlin' in M. Paeslack, *Constructing Imperial Berlin. Photography and the Metropolis*, Minneapolis: University of Minnesota Press, 2019.

[7] G. Meyfroots, 'Het comité d'études du vieux Bruxelles (1903-1937). Vier decennia in de marge van de monumentenzorg', *Monumenten & Landschappen*, vol. 20, no. 2, 2001, pp. 8–33.; P. Ingelaere, 'De fotocollectie van het Comité d'Etudes du vieux Bruxelles', *Monumenten & Landschappen*, vol. 20, no. 2, 2001, pp. 34–37.; The collection is consultable via the website of the Bibliothèque artistique de l'Académie Royale des Beaux-Arts de Bruxelles https://photos-vb.bruxelles.be/index.html (Consulted on 12th February 2022).

[8] Ingelaere, *De fotocollectie,* (Note 7), p. 34.

[9] Municipal Archives Woluwe-Saint-Pierre, Conseil Communal, 1930, p.380. ; Municipal Archives Woluwe-Saint-Pierre, Conseil Communal, 1931, pp.387-388.

[10] G. Chabeau-Poels, C. Temmerman, 'L'Hôtel Granvelle à Woluwe-Saint-Pierre', Wiluwa. *Cercle d'histoire, d'archéologie et d'architecture Des Woluwe.*, December 1996, pp. 7–38.

[11] Ghyoot, *Déconstruction*, (Note 3), p.29.

[12] Wouters, *Salvaging*, (Note 3), p.492.

[13] Le Soir (27 September 1912), p.1. ; Le Peuple (31 October 1912), p.3.

[14] Le Peuple (21 November 1913), p.3.

[15] Wouters, *Salvaging*, (Note 3).

[16] E. Lucas, *Building Repairs and Maintenance, Dealing with the Survey of Premises, Demolitions and Repairs to Structure and Supply Services of Buildings*, London: Newnes, 1944. pp.25-31.

[17] ibid.

[18] City Archives Brussels, ARCH 808, 'Inventaire de modèles déposés au magasin de la Ville – Impasse Cail et Halot'.

[19] ibid.

[20] City Archives Brussels, Bulletins communaux, 1920, Tome I2.

[21] La Lanterne (31 January 1950), p.4.

National, traditional, scientific – the formation of a multifaceted early glulam identity

Roshanak Haddadi [1], Mario Rinke [2]
[1] ETH Zürich, Zurich, Switzerland
[2] University of Antwerp, Antwerp, Belgium

Abstract

This paper demonstrates the identity-shaping process of glulam in its formative years in Switzerland and sheds light on the role of different actors of the projects in the early networks of glulam. Periodicals, newspapers, and archival materials documenting different projects provide material to discuss how glulam was conceptualized and how its identity was shaped throughout the early decades of the 20th century.

Introduction

Since its introduction in Switzerland in 1909 and due to its broad acceptance, wide-range application, and in most cases visible penetration of the public space, glued laminated timber (glulam) was from the very beginning deeply anchored in what was then modern building culture and practice. Modernism in construction, however, has most commonly been associated with steel: the mass production of steel and later reinforced concrete were important ingredients of modern architecture, establishing a new way of building, and consequently a "new architecture" [1]. Aesthetic-related accounts of modernism observing "simple, austere form and clear organization", have been largely understood as the result of a new technical setting, derived from the use of "new building materials such as iron, concrete, and glass", the main materials that have historically supported the modernist discourses [2].

Wood, in contrast, not having a leading role in this context and being almost absent in the narratives of modern architecture, has nevertheless been in some respects highly influenced by this movement. Glulam can be seen as the result of the modernization of timber, both as a structural material and in its building tradition, and also contributed to those aesthetic-related accounts of modernism. However, it took some decades before glulam entered the focus of the modernists. Giedion, for instance, mentions in 1943 "curved laminated wooden arches", besides light metal structures as modern materials [3].

Unlike steel and concrete that have been subject of intense, critical, and passionate debates, mainly over their architectural and representative use, glulam did not raise critical arguments [4]. It always enjoyed an aesthetic sense conditioned by the centuries-old natural timber.

At the beginning of the 20th century, various structural types of timber construction had been developed, mostly for large-span structures, but it was the new glulam system that could compete within and at times even dominate the market of large-span timber structures. This early role led to a Swiss building culture today in which glulam is an evident material for large-span structures. One of the reasons for this pioneering role was that its fabrication and assembly were industrialized and standardized before other timber structures of that time. However, another reason for that, which is proposed in this paper, is that it was the offspring of a new aesthetic and a technical identity for timber. It allowed the overcoming of local and semantic references, which were too established to be 'modern'.

National, traditional, scientific – the formation of a multifaceted early glulam identity

The identity of glulam in its historical context is complex and multilayered with notions of nature, technology, modernity, culture, craft, or industry. The identity of glulam in its early years was shaped by both the builders and the audiences of projects alike. Different perceptions of the new material, in fact, shaped different associations between the material and the actors. Understanding these identities could explain a constantly shifting network of relationships between actors in the formative years of this young material. Materials convey meanings, and it is through the attributions of material expressions and the appropriation and claiming of their meanings, that the social relations, value systems, and decision-making processes in a building project can be understood. In articles and advertisements in technical and trade journals of the time, different parties and various actors shaped the image and identity of early glulam through semantic attributions and cultural appropriations. National exhibitions held in the early decades of the 20th century were important platforms to mediate both professional and public perceptions of the new material. Through these exhibitions particularly, authorities and public institutions reframed timber within a larger cultural narrative on a national scale.

Using various case studies, this article aims to shed light on the identity shaping process of glulam in Germany and in Switzerland in its formative years. Different projects, as well as their representations in periodicals, newspapers, and reports of the time and archival materials documenting these projects and different exhibitions, provide the subtext to a discussion of how glulam was conceptualized, its identities shaped, and how different networks of stakeholders in Switzerland and in Germany claimed glulam differently in these two contexts.

Glulam as rational and modern timber

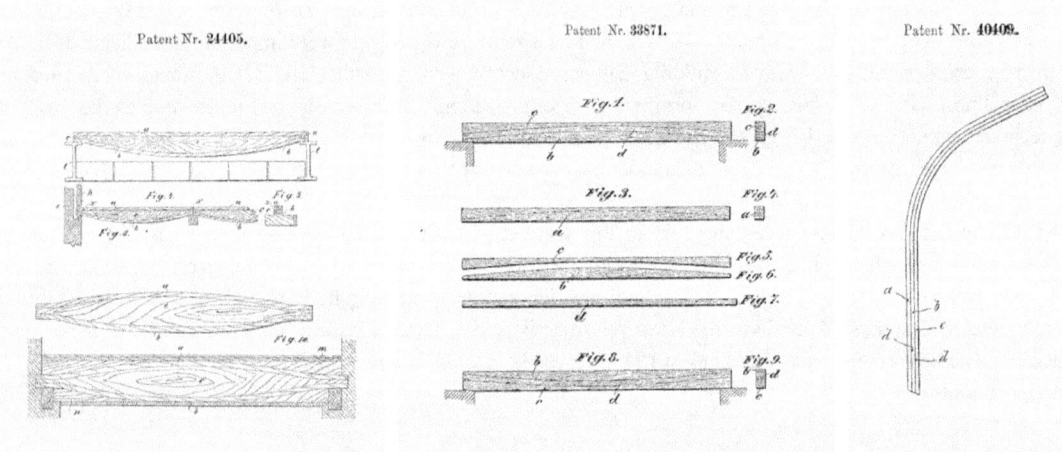

Figure 1: Otto Hetzer patents in 1900, 1903, and 1906, for 3 different types of wooden beams by laminating and gluing timber

Glulam was patented in 1906 after successive efforts to produce more economic timber alternatives by combining and gluing smaller pieces of wood to make a "rational beam" out of timber. Otto Hetzer, German grand-ducal master carpenter (1846-1911), registered his concepts in 3 patents. Figure 1 shows his first patent in 1900 for a composite beam of varying cross-sections, the second, patented in 1903, is a reinforced beam with a wooden inlay, and his third patent in 1906 presents a curved glue-laminated wooden girder.

The core idea of Hetzer's successive patents was material economy. Hetzer was a master carpenter and not an engineer, nor an architect. However, his concepts for a revised use of wood as a structural material are described in technical journals as a way to depict a scientific image of a new, engineered material. Multiple comparisons with iron and reinforced concrete were effective ways to deliver this message, materials with which timber was in competition at the time, as timber was commonly regarded as a less reliable and efficient for structural purposes.

In those articles, Hetzer's beams reinforced with wood inlays were compared with reinforced concrete beams to imply the use of scientific method, choosing material properties for the actual stresses. Other comparisons of glulam with steel beams of variable cross-sections suggested that by having the opportunity to shape the cross-section, glulam could be designed as efficiently as steel beams. In this context, the central journal of the building administrations "Zentralblatt der Bauverwaltung" should be mentioned. Published by the Prussian Ministry of Public Works, the journal reports the Hetzer patents in various articles. Hetzer, from 1891 on, was honoured with the title "the grand-ducal master carpenter", and his works were then repeatedly reported in the high-profile journal and promoted in professional circles, e. g. Architects' Associations of different cities. That way, he could readily organize a network of architects, engineers, politicians, and authorities around his construction efforts. These articles described a new concept of construction with timber, which brought back "rationality" to timber as a material and to timber construction in general [5]. In this context, two criteria can be pointed out: first, glulam became as calculable as other structural materials, especially for curved glue-laminated timber, and second, the relation between material, form, and function of the structural elements became rational. As a consequence, glulam structures could be demarcated from traditional timber structures which were referred to as "unclear, old, king and queen post timber trusses" [6].

Glulam, although initially a material economy concept, had its greatest significance and most important feature through its formability. Glulam made it possible to give theoretically any form to the wooden girders. This feature had the immediate advantage of freeing space in timber structures. Glulam was consequently disconnected from the image of bulky trusses in dusty and dark attics, and rather celebrated as an elegant solution in light and exposed structures.

The early two patents of Hetzer in 1900 and 1903, which concerned flooring and resulted in the new brand of a parqueting system called "German Floor", should be understood in the context of Wilhelmine Prussian state propaganda for design and increasing the quality of German products for the export purposes. It was the state's goal to push for a qualitatively superior "German-Style" in global commerce, and these efforts made it a true sponsor of modernist design principles through its economic development policies [7]. Hetzer's products, complying with the new reformist agenda of the Wilhelmine Prussian State, had the advantage of being circulated in networks of prominent architects and industrial designers. One of those circles was the Deutsche Werkbund, the German association of artists, architects, designers, and industrialists, established in 1907, a state-sponsored effort to integrate traditional crafts and industrial mass-production techniques. The Wilhelmine Prussian State, as John Maciuika demonstrates, is associated with the birth of the 20th century modern German design, and its Ministry of Commerce and Trade became an "unlikely sponsor of path-breaking modernist design principles through its economic development policies" [8].

Another goal of the Werkbund was to promote Germany's progress in the arts and crafts and architecture among foreign countries through effective propaganda. For this goal, special attention was given to exhibitions and illustrated periodicals as the best means of achieving this. In 1910 the Werkbund participated in the World Exhibition in Brussels, with the topic "Germany's interior architecture and decorative arts", strongly supported and promoted by the Prussian State. In this division, Otto Hetzer collaborated with prominent architects of Werkbund on flooring and parqueting projects [9]. However, the most important collaboration took place on the occasion of the glulam pavilion for the German Railways (see below).

Exhibitions and public advertising

Although the history of exhibitions at the end of the 19th century and the beginning of the 20th century is largely connected to the history of iron and steel, rare exceptions show the significance of some timber projects in the history of these exhibitions. They reveal the ambitions of both the timber industry and the authorities to raise the status of the material and promote its use as a modern structural material.

1910, Brussels

The World's fair of 1910 was held in Brussels. In the whole exhibition, two halls were dedicated to the railway industry - one for international and Belgian exhibitors, and another for German exhibitors which showcased the latest technology of German locomotives. Glulam was chosen for the structure of the pavilion of German Railways, a project resulting in two awards for its "solid and innovative design" [10].

This pavilion was the result of the collaboration of the Otto Hetzer company (for this project his son Otto Alfred Hetzer was responsible), architect Peter Behrens, and the engineer Hermann Kügler, while the execution of the girders was carried out by Otto Steinbeis & Co sawmill. The two-hinged glulam girders with a total height of 14 m spanned a hall of 43m width [11]. The space was lightened by glass-covered openings in the roof.

Figure 2: German Railways glulam pavilion for the World's fair of 1910 in Brussels.

Via Behrens as the architect of the project and co-founder of the Werkbund, the exhibition offered the first opportunity for a major international presence to the German Werkbund.

The fascination for this structure was mainly thanks to the appreciation of the slenderness of the glulam girders. This was technically possible by using a material that shattered the centuries-old relation of the mass and volume of traditional timber structures with the span:

> "[the pavilion] expresses the power of these iron organisms [locomotives and engines]. This is done through the shape of the arched girders […]. Starting at the foot and slowly bending inwards, the force of each girder rises steeply, takes with it the energy of the stiffener sitting there in the angle of rotation, then flows in a wide, safe arch under the roof, meets the opposing flow of force coming from the other side and returns, released, to earth. […]. Viewed as a whole, the hall is of the greatest unity" [12].

An attempt was made to reduce the effect of iron elements, by painting them in a wood tone, in order to emphasize the timberness of the structure [13].

Those slender glulam girders in such a long span structure gave a "dematerializing quality" to the structure, which was intended by the architect Peter Behrens, whose steel-framed structures for AEG Turbine Factory in Berlin, constructed the year before, was a milestone for the modern design of industrial buildings. This new appearance of timber, which was achieved by reducing the joints to a minimum, eliminating complexity, and associating timber with the unity of the form of the structure, the roof, and the space and light, was then largely unfamiliar.

Although at that time, most of the timber pavilions were clad to hide their timber structures, the glulam structure of the Railway hall remained unclad. This project marked a milestone for glulam on an international scale and introduced glulam to the European stage, and this thanks to an unprecedented span for a timber structure, and to its architectural qualities.

The German Werkbund saw one of its core duties, alongside influencing and guiding contemporary design, as promoting aesthetic education. At this exhibition, for which Germany aimed at "creating a new taste destined for world domination" by introducing "modern forms for modern purposes", glulam was chosen to present the latest achievements of the railway industry. Germany defined and presented its own national style under the auspices of the Werkbund as a distinctly modern one [14]. Like the triumph of structural iron, celebrated at the Paris World Exposition of 1889 with the Eiffel Tower and the Galerie des Machines, and the reinforced concrete of François Hennebique at the World Exposition in 1900, Glulam celebrated its public identity as modern timber in the International Exhibition of Brussels in 1910.

This famous collaboration of Behrens and Hetzer happened to be the last one. Hetzer died in 1911 shortly after the exhibition ended in November 1910. After this exhibition, several other buildings have been made in glulam in different exhibitions, but none of them could gain the significance that this building had for the building industry.

1910, Lausanne

In the same year, the National Agriculture Exhibition was held for 10 days in Switzerland in the city of Lausanne. It was on this occasion that the first glulam structure in Switzerland was built. It was a footbridge, located outside of the exhibition site and near the main entrance, passing over the tram lines. [15].

Figure 3: Glulam foot-bridge on the occasion of the National Agriculture Exhibition of 1910 in Lausanne

The bridge was constructed by the engineers Terner and Chopard, who received the exclusive right to exploit the glulam patent of Hetzer in Switzerland, in collaboration with one of their licensed contractors Edouard Bugnion. By then, Bugnion was a member of the City Council of Lausanne, one of the main organizers of the exhibition, and also the president of the Sawyers Association of the French-speaking part of Switzerland. As this network did not give glulam a larger role beyond this footbridge, it might be concluded that glulam was not promoted by the local timber industry to have a larger spotlight.

The project was reported in the local journal "la revue" which appreciated the "very elegant footbridge" recalling the aesthetic of iron bridges: "two wooden arches imitating the curve of iron bridges" [16]. However in the publicity booklet of the exhibition, the name glulam was not even mentioned in the description of the project, being simply referred to as "*le pont en bois*" or "the wooden bridge".

The network of early stakeholders of glulam made a timid step towards the public presentation of the new material, and the very limited coverage of the project by the media demonstrates that there had very likely been no intention from the professional circles to promote the new and hardly known glulam.

1914, Bern

The third Swiss National Exhibition in Bern opened in May 1914 and soon became the center of pilgrimage for domestic and foreign visitors wishing to view the finest products of Swiss industry. The presence of glulam in this exhibition, however, shows again a significant difference from the celebrated presence of German glulam in the Brussels' Exhibition.

In Bern, three glulam structures were standing at different places of the exhibition site. The pavilion for Building Construction and Interior Design was dedicated to the novelties in the building industry. Archival documents show that glulam was most probably the first and the only material candidate for this pavilion. The architect Otto Ingold and the licensed contractor Zöllig agreed to use tried-and-trusted form and proportions, very similar to those of the hall for the Gymnastics Festival held in Brugg in 1913, constructed by the same contractor. Following visits to the construction site, journals reported on this building, whose bare and slender structural elements evoked an unexpected and skeptical feeling towards a timber structure: "The hall for the Building Industry is still under construction, whose imposing Hetzer girders offer an unfamiliar look" [17].

In this project, glulam girders were left in their natural wood color. Another report comments on the pleasing association of elegant curves with the timberness of glulam: The yellowish, elegantly curved Hetzer girders stand out clearly from the [background]" [18].

Figure 4: Pavilion for Building Construction, Swiss National Exhibition, Bern, 1914.

The second glulam structure was erected for the pavilion for the Chemical Products, Paper, and Graphic Industry. For this purpose, a series of three-hinged girders with a span of 21meters were proposed by the contractor Gribi who manufactured very similar glulam girders, in terms of form, span, and proportions for the locomotive depot in Bern in 1911. The contractor's previous experience with this type of glulam structure resulted in another tried-and-tested design. Here, the choice of glulam over another truss-girder structure, was very likely not based on the architectural features of glulam, since the plans reveal the intention of the architect to cover the collar tie and the crown post with canvas hanging from the roof, almost entirely hiding the glulam structure.

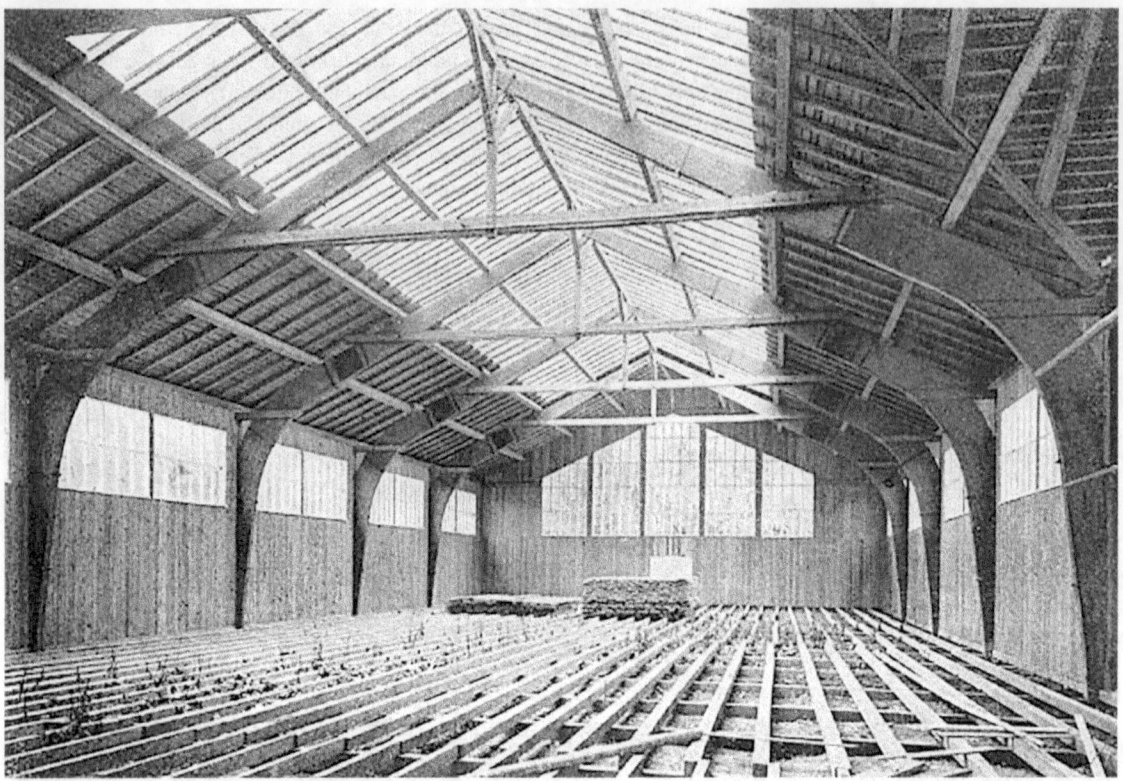

Figure 5: Pavilion for Chemical Products, Paper, and Graphic Industry, Swiss National Exhibition, Bern, 1914.

It might be argued that the most outstanding glulam structure of this exhibition was the Food industry Hall, with a central cupola of 30 m diameter, the result of the collaboration of architects Polak & Piollenc of Montreux and Bugnion, the contractor responsible for the foot-bridge in the exhibition of Lausanne in 1910. The initial choice for the Food Industry hall has been a triangulated truss-girder timber frame. However, the plans show that the architects have been then facing difficulties in shaping a true curve for the dome, and the search for an integral wooden structure for defining the central space of the dome found no pleasing result and remained a challenge. At this stage, the compelling offer of Bugnion was considered for the dome and the lateral galleries, consisting of a series of slender and elegantly curved glulam girders that followed the form of the dome. Here once again, glulam won over usual timber trusses, being a practical, functional, and efficient solution for shaping the space.

Terner and Chopard had aimed earlier at involving glulam in this exhibition for reasons beyond its structural advantages, referring to its architectural features the engineers said that, "[…] as an elegant hall construction, [glulam] should also find advantageous use in the buildings of our forthcoming national exhibition" [19]. This study, however, demonstrates that glulam stepped onto the scene of the exhibition mainly thanks to the practical advantages and pragmatic solutions that it could offer compared to the usual timber truss-girder frames of the time.

Although the bare structures attracted the attention of visitors, delighting and astonishing them, there was limited coverage by the press. Succinct reports with photographs in which the focus was mainly on the products and goods exhibited in these halls, while the structure could hardly be recognized in the background, show that glulam was not planned to exercise any influence beyond its pure functional purposes and temporary existence.

Figure 6: Pavilion for Food Industry, Swiss National Exhibition, Bern, 1914.

Journal advertisements

Tracing the development of advertisements of early glulam in the journals can help to give an image of how the engineers and the licensed contractors wanted glulam to be perceived and their preferred identity to be recognized by the public, a trustable material and building technique.

These early advertisements, appearing as early as 1910, depict a construction site, hardly distinguishable from a usual timber structure construction site considering the size of glulam girders, the assembly process, and the role of the craftsmen, with glulam girders partially replacing timber structural elements (Fig. 7). The image was then coupled with a text, describing the advantages of different patents of Hetzer for glue-laminated beams.

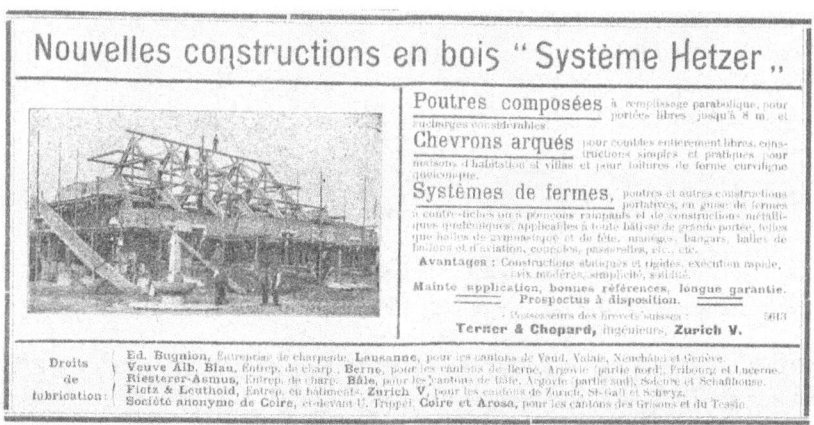

Figure 7: Advertisement for glulam, Bulletin technique de la Suisse romande, 1910.

National, traditional, scientific – the formation of a multifaceted early glulam identity

From the moment when the Swiss Federal Railways became a client of glulam structures in 1911, these federal projects very soon appeared in the advertisements. The message communicated by the early advertisements was adjusted to the new identity of the material, following the successive glulam projects of the Swiss Railways. These projects allowed the engineers Terner and Chopard to accredit their technology and to associate them with the authority and credit of the Federal institution (Fig. 8). No image of the exhibition constructions of 1914 appears among the advertisements.

Figure 8: Advertisement for glulam, Schweizerische Bauzeitung, 1913.

Figure 9: Advertisement for glulam, Schweizerische Bauzeitung, 1918.

Later, and with the outbreak of World War I, glulam was used more and more for the structures of the army mainly as hangars for its equipment and aeroplanes. In the photos appearing in the advertisements of these years, glulam is usually associated with the power of the locomotives and aeroplanes of the Federal institutions, without any particular focus on the construction site or the structural capacity. Using the Federal institutions as a reference helped to identify glulam as a trustable and legitimate material and construction concept (Fig. 9).

After the decline of glulam in the Interwar Period, glulam was back to the building market and advertisements, mainly reflecting its new identity as a regular modern building material. Glulam was then no longer referred to as break-through technology, army hangars, large-span depots, etc (Fig. 10).

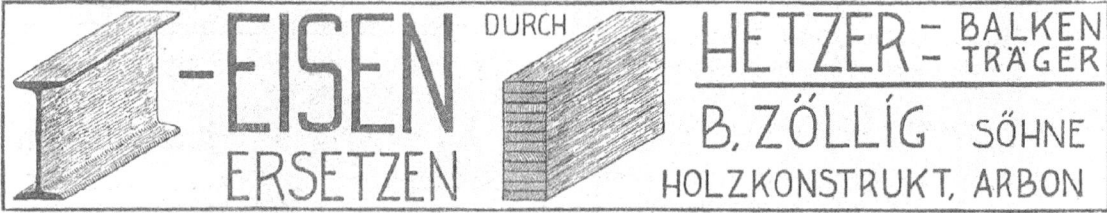

Figure 10: Advertisement for glulam, Schweizerische Bauzeitung, 1942.

A material surrogate

In order to identify an entity, one may refer to a similar product. However, not all involved saw this new material, glulam, in the same way. When in 1916, Le Corbusier proposed a glulam structure for the roof of the cinema Scala in La Chaux de Fonds, the city authorities asked for a loading test to prove the capacity of the girders. Le Corbusier, in turn, opposed this decision by claiming that "the structure has been calculated by the engineer's specialist in reinforced concrete, based on the rules dictated by the federal law, which are very strict and imply absolute security" [20]. By referring to concrete, a material that had already at that time been established through technical regulations, Le Corbusier saw glulam as an equivalent or even identical to concrete. The cantonal authorities backed the city in requiring a loading test, emphasizing that not only the calculation but "it is the execution of the work which plays an important role" and considering it basically a "new material".

It also seems that workers on the construction site did not associate glulam with timber. They identified timber by the way they understood it: by the scale and dimensions of the structural member, the way they handled it, by the tools they used, and by the process of assembly on the construction site. These criteria of "timberness" differentiated glulam from regular wood. Glulam, for them, was not a new timber, rather a new material. For example, the workers of the construction site of the Bern Exhibition in 1914 seemed to hardly identify glulam as a natural part of their work. When the Bern Carpenters' Section staged a group photo at the Swiss National Exhibition, the proud craftsmen posed in front of the wooden construction of the scenery railway instead of in the large open halls of the new timber construction technique (Fig. 11).

National, traditional, scientific – the formation of a multifaceted early glulam identity

Figure 11: Association of Carpenters of Switzerland, Bern Section, at the National Exhibition 1914, Wooden construction scenery railway, (Photo Fr. Büttikofer, expoarchiv.ch)

Conclusion

Different sources, archival materials as well as general and technical journals, covered the presence of early glulam in the public projects of different types, in the scale of a city to national and international exhibitions. Besides the projects themselves, the coverage with its reflections of early glulam, were part of this identity-shaping process of the new material.

In the early publications on glulam, the concentration was on that type of value that was related to the inherent properties of this construction medium, such as functionality, material composition, structural logic, etc. Although these concepts contributed to the image of glulam as an engineered material, competitive with other modern materials of the time, they however were not in line with the development of the manufacturing process aiming at an ever more industrialized fabrication. The passage from an engineered to an industrial material is traceable in projects, articles, and advertisements that shifted their focus away from the presentation of the patents as distinct ideas to an integral constructional concept.

Over time, and in parallel with regarding glulam as a modern material, glulam was also attributed with new meanings through its appearance in particular social, cultural, economic, and political situations, as in the case of exhibitions. Individuals and institutions were engaged in the process of shaping the identity of the new material. This was a politically mediated process, such as the organization of national and international exhibitions. Those exhibitions were among the most important stages where new meanings emerged.

Different exhibitions in Germany and in Switzerland served here as illustrative examples to demonstrate how architects, engineers, carpenters and contractors, authorities, politicians, and the press, in different contexts, combined to mediate various identities for the young glulam.

While the Brussels' exhibition gave a unique opportunity to the Werkbund to express the modernity of new timber, in Switzerland in contrast, glulam was at this time in the hands of local carpenters, who were responsible for design, manufacturing, assembly and even the ownership of their glulam structures in an un-centralized coopetition system.

In the identity shaping process of early glulam, the young material featured a spectrum of references; referring to nature for its timber side, referring to the chemical industry for its glue, referring to handicraft and industrial processes at the same time, referring to concrete and to steel for the professionals, and referring to the local timber for private clients. This broad and diverse range of references, allowed different interested parties and audiences of the project to readily identify with glulam: sometimes as a new timber, other times as a new material, as a modern material, as a local and national one, as an equivalent for steel or concrete. This specific feature of glulam has a decisive role in its early and rapid development in Switzerland, where it became a "tool of the best modernity and a link between it and good tradition" [21].

References

[1] As Karl Bötticher was convinced that iron represented the emergence of a new architecture and a new historical level: *Das Prinzip der Hellenischen und Germanischen Bauweise hinsichtlich der Übertragung in die Bauweise unserer Tage,* 1846.
[2] W. C. Behrendt, *The Victory of the New Building Style,* Los Angeles: Getty Research Institute, 2000.
[3] Giedion et. al., 'Nine points on Monumentality', 1943, in Sigfried Giedion, *Archtiecture, you and me: the dairy of a development,* Massachusettes: Harvard University Press, 1958. p. 50.
[4] This was not the case for iron for example. Semper had a negative attitude toward the extensive architectural use of iron. Gottfried Semper, *Der Stil in den technischen und tektonischen Künsten oder praktische Ästhetik*, Frankfurt am Main: Kunst und Wissenschaft, 1860.
[5] *Zentralblatt der Bauverwaltung*: 05.11.1892 (p. 476), 17.02.1894 (p. 69), 09.03.1907 (p. 147).
[6] *Rheinische Baufach-Zeitung*, 1909.
[7] John V. Maciuika demonstrates the influence of this State on the early modern movements in design. Sources used for this paper are: "Werkbundpolitik and Weltpolitik: The German State's Interest in Global Commerce and "Good Design" 1912-1914", in *German Politics & Society*, 2005(23), Berghahn Books, pp. 102-127. *Before the Bauhaus: architecture, politics, and the German state, 1890-1920,* New York: Cambridge university press, 2005. "Art in the Age of Government Intervention: Hermann Muthesius, Sachlichkeit, and the State, 1897-1907", in *German Studies Review*, on behalf of the German Studies Association, 1998 (21), pp. 285-308.
[8] ibid., 1998 (21).
[9] Collaborating with Bruno Paul, co-founder of Werkbund, and with Wilhelm Thiele, a leading voice in early Werkbund.
[10] W. Rug, '100 Jahre Hetzer-Patent', in *Bautechnik : Zeitschrift für den gesamten Ingenieurbau,* Vol. 83, 2006, pp. 533-540.
[11] Ch. Kersten, *Freitragende Holzbauten*, Berlin: Springer, 1926.
[12] F. Mannheimer, 'Eisenbahnhalle', in *Der Industriebau,* 1910 (9), pp. 206-216.
[13] V. Manikowsky (Royal Architect), 'Die Deutsche Abteilung auf der Brüsseler Weltausstellung 1910', in *Zentralblatt der Bauverwaltung*, 28.05.1910, n° 43, p. 288.
[14] R. Breuer, 'Deutschland auf der Brüsseler Weltausstellung', in *Moderne Bauformen, Monatshefte für Architektur und Raumkunst*, 1910 (7), pp. 301-414.
[15] R.Haddadi & M.Rinke, 'Early glulam timber for large scale temporary structures in Switzerland', *The Proceedings of the Seventh Annual Conference of the Construction History Society*, Lisbon, 2020, pp. 477-488.

[16] La Revue is a non-discipline-specific journal. 27.08.1910, n° 201, p. 1.

[17] 'Die Bauten der Schwizerischen Landesausstellung in Bern', in *Illustrierte schweizerische Handwerker-Zeitung*, 1913 (24), p. 402.

[18] 'Von der Schweizerischen Landesausstellung in Bern', in *Illustrierte schweizerische Handwerker-Zeitung*, 1913 (29), p. 866.

[19] 'Die Hetzersche Holzbauweise', in *Schweizerische Bauzeitung*, 1911 (57), p. 218.

[20] Le Corbusier, Correspondences with the authorities, dated 21.8.1916, Library of the City of Neuchâtel, archival fonds: LC102-1090. Neuchâtel: unpublished.

[21] P. Meyer, 'Die Architektur der Landesausstellung, kritische Besprechung', in *Das Werk*, 1939, pp. 321-352.

Contribution of Early Women Architects in North Macedonia

Vladimir B. Ladinski
University American College Skopje, North Macedonia

Abstract

The emergence of women architects in the territory of present Republic of North Macedonia can be traced back to the 1920s. The paper seeks to identify the early women architects in North Macedonia and their contribution to construction related activities, as well as to look into their experiences on entering the profession and throughout their careers. This is expected to provide a useful insight into this area of research, as well as encourage further and more in-depth exploration in the future.

Introduction

The Republic of North Macedonia is a small land-locked country centrally located within the Balkan Peninsula. The geo-strategic location of its territory has made it an area of overlapping influences that generated an ongoing struggle between the Great Powers and the countries that they support, to take and maintain control over the area throughout the history. From around the 1390s until the First Balkan War (1912-1913) the territory of the present-day country was under control of the Ottoman Empire, and since then has remained a hotspot for conflicts and ongoing changes. In the current study, the term North Macedonia is used to define the territory of the country since it became, initially, post-World War II (WWII) a republic within former Yugoslavia and since 1991 an independent country, as well as the territory it occupies now when discussing the period up to the end of the WWII period.

This paper looks into the emergence of women architects on the territory of North Macedonia, aims to identify them and understand their contribution to the construction industry and associated activities whilst exploring the challenges and opportunities they experienced throughout their professional careers.

Materials and Methods

Definitions of terminology

Considering the limited data available, in the context of this paper the term 'architect' is used to describe women who have graduated in architecture regardless of whether they have passed the State (professional) exam and gained a license to practice or not.

Search Methodology

The initial list of early women architects was established from the prime source on architects in North Macedonia, the three volumes of *Graditelite na Makedonija* (Architects of Macedonia) by the late Prof. Georgi Konstantinovski. Subsequently, this initial list was expanded with other examples of early women architects identified from other sources. The process of identifying further early women architects was affected by the pandemic and is still ongoing and is expected to yield additional names for inclusion on the list. The early female landscape architect, Ms Mira Halambek-Wenzler, was excluded from this study as her background was not in architecture.

Scope and categories

Considering that the first programme in architecture in the country was established at the University of Skopje in 1949, the scope of this research aims to cover those women architects who graduated abroad up to and including 1955, and were:

- Born in North Macedonia but practised abroad;

- Born abroad but practised in North Macedonia on short- or long-term basis; and

- Both born and practised in North Macedonia.

The results are presented over three distinct periods:

- Under the Ottoman Empire,

- The Interwar (WWI to WWII), and

- Post WWII.

Data collection

Within this paper only the highlights of the lives and careers of the women architect are presented with emphasis on those who have left a lasting contribution through the buildings they designed either in person or as a part of a team. Information about other team members on the project were either identified if available or highlighted if a particular project was delivered as a team effort. Considering how sensitive the issue of origin and nationality in the Balkans is, the early women architects presented in this paper are mainly identified by their place of birth.

Only the current country of any place mentioned in the paper is indicated, and the educational establishments are identified by their location as there was only one school of architecture available in each location. For places outside North Macedonia, the name of the country is stated at the first occurrence of the place within the text, either in full or by using the ISO 3166 alpha-2 codes within the tables. In the paper, all of the original Cyrillic words have been Romanised using the British Permanent Committee on Geographical Names (PCGN) system.

The paper presents early findings from an ongoing research based on the use of primary and secondary sources with inclusion of selected grey literature where necessary to inform the results in a greater detail. Where insufficient literature was available, sources from other neighbouring countries or other professions were used to present the experiences of early women on entering and practising professions. The early women architects, notably, Ms Vera Ćosevska, Member of the Academy of Architects (AA) at the Association of Architects of Macedonia (AAM), as well as their descendants and past colleagues kindly provided valuable data and information for this study.

The Ottoman Empire Period (c. 1392-1912)

The research carried out to date did not identify any women architects born in or working in North Macedonia during this period, despite the fact that programmes in architecture became available since the second half of the 19th Century, both within the Ottoman Empire and the neighbouring Serbia. Under the Ottomans the level of literacy was generally quite low throughout the Empire and access to primary and especially secondary education was quite limited in North Macedonia.

However, there were examples of early professional women from North Macedonia but in other disciplines. Ms Rajna Aleksova (1883-1959) from Bitola, then Monastir, a sister of a local pharmacy owner, graduated in pharmacy in Lausanne, Switzerland, in 1906 and is considered to be the first woman pharmacist both in North Macedonia and in the Balkans. However, her graduation just marked the beginning of her struggle to get the right to practice within the Ottoman Empire. After three years working in Bulgaria in various roles and following an intervention from an Ottoman nobleman, she was eventually able to return to Bitola and commence practising as pharmacist under special permission [1]. Less fortunate was the first woman doctor Ms Zaharina Velova-Dimitrova (1873-1940), born in Resen, who graduated in medicine in Nancy, France, in 1901. Apparently at the time, the Ottoman Empire did not allow women to practice medicine, and, as a result, she had to move to neighbouring Bulgaria where she was allowed to practice and remained there until her death [2].

The earliest woman architect in the Balkans is probably Ms Jelisaveta Načić (1878-1955), born in Belgrade, Serbia, where she graduated in 1900. Because of her gender, she was not permitted to enter employment within the Ministry of Construction, but was eventually able to get employment within the Municipality of Belgrade few years later after passing her professional exam in 1902. Unfortunately, her productive professional career was cut short during WWI when she was interned in a camp in Hungary by the Austro-Hungarian Empire occupying forces in 1916 [3].

The Interwar Period (1918-41)

The emergence of women architects on the territory of present North Macedonia has been documented in this period. Konstantinovski identified Ms Elena Bokus as probably the earliest woman architect working in North Macedonia, then part of the Kingdom of Serbs, Croats and Slovenes (Kingdom of Yugoslavia from 1929), who worked on private houses in Skopje in the 1920s [4]. The information about her appears to be limited and research is ongoing to establish what happened with this early woman architect. Namely, her work was apparent only for a short period of time without any further information being available on her origins and whereabouts, either before or after her period of practice in Skopje.

Ms Marija Šulentić, *née* Pavlović, is the only other woman architect mentioned by Konstantinovski, as someone who was assisting her spouse, engineer Mr Pajo Šulentić, in his private practice in Skopje, and was working on private houses and small buildings in the 1930s [5]. The research also identified Ms Jelica Gazikalović (*née,* Ganović), a University of Belgrade graduate architect, who lived in Veles (1933-36) but did not practise at the time [6].

Entering and practising a profession was not easy for women within the Kingdom, although it appears to have been somewhat less restrictive in comparison with that of the Ottoman Empire period. The main restriction on entering a profession was focused on those seeking employment in the public sector at state level, e.g., Ministry of Construction, where initially permanent appointments were open only to those who had completed the military service which was not an option for women at the time. As a result, the professional women had to seek either a contract-based employment or an appointment within a private practice.

A good indication of the position of the women architects towards the end of this period is the interview with architect Ms Milica Krsić, an Inspector at the Ministry of Construction at the time, for the newspaper Vreme (Time) in 1940 [7]. In the interview, she pointed out that within a period of four decades the number of women engineers and architects in the Kingdom of Yugoslavia had grown from the first one, Načić, in 1900 to about 220 in 1940. In her view, women engineers and architects were still finding it difficult to establish themselves fully within the profession despite their results and recognition of their professional achievements, since employers still gave preference to their male counterparts despite being equally qualified.

Post WWII Period (1945-1955)

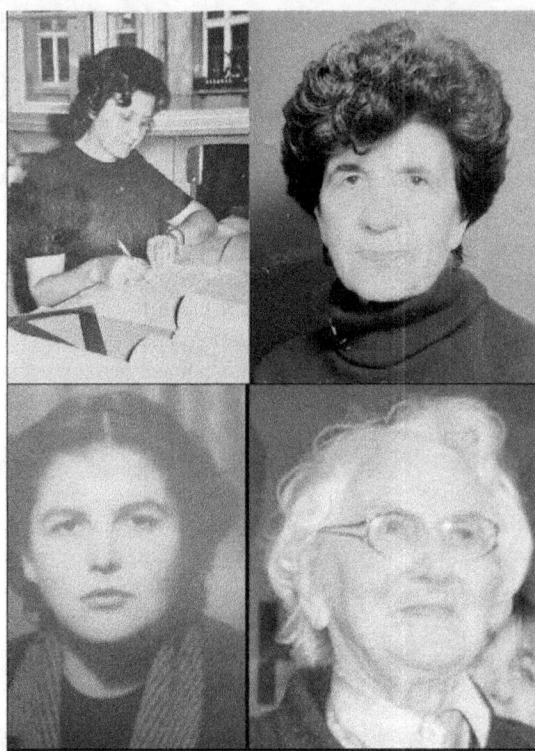

Figure 1: (a) Ms Cvetanka Roškova-Krepieva (upper left, Source: Mukaetov), (b) Nada Župan (upper-right, Source: Overholt), (c) Dragoslava Tomova-Serafimova (lower-left, Source: Ivanonvska), (d) Lidija Folonova-Markova (lower-right, Source: Porta 3).

The study identified an increased number of women architects in the post WWII period. The data about those identified and processed to date are presented within Tables 1 and 2 that cover the key personal data of these early women architects, their areas of work, as well as highest position held, and distinctions received where available.

Women architects born in North Macedonia but who practised abroad

So far only two women architects born in North Macedonia who practised abroad have been identified: Ms Danica Milosavljević-Jovanović and Ms Cvetanka Roškova-Krepieva (Figure 1a). Both graduated in the post WWII period in Belgrade, and Sofia, Bulgaria, respectively, where they remained to practice. Milosavljević-Jovanović, a sister of the well-known polymath, the Serbian Academician Predrag (Peđa) Milosavljević, became a prominent architect especially in the field of pre-school, educational and residential buildings. When she passed away aged 98, she was the oldest woman architect in Serbia [8]. For Roškova-Krepieva, the breakdown of relationships between the Eastern Bloc, led by the USSR, and Yugoslavia known as *Informbiro* Period (1948-55) and the resulting blockade prevented her from returning home. As a result, she practiced in Sofia as an urban planner with focus on the industrial zones [9].

Women architects born outside North Macedonia who practised in North Macedonia

The data gathered to date has identified six women architects born abroad who came to work in North Macedonia and seven born in North Macedonia who returned home to practise after qualifying abroad.

Table 1: List of key personal data of post-WWII women architects identified and processed to date. Abbreviations: BG, Bulgaria; HR, Croatia; SR, Serbia. (Sources: Compiled by the author from cited sources within this paper)

Name and Surname	Born	Year	Died	Year	Alma Mater	Year	Active in MK
Born in North Macedonia but practised abroad							
Danica Milosavljević-Jovanović	Skopje	1919	Belgarde, SR	2018	Belgrade, SR	1946	N/A
Cvetanka Roškova-Krepieva	Prilep	1925	Sofia, BG	?	Sofia, BG	?	N/A
Born abroad but practised in North Macedonia							
Ruža Paulić	Crikvenica, HR	1922			Zagreb, HR	1949	1956-60
Bosiljka Krstić-Novaković	Pirot, SR	1926			Belgrade, SR	1952	1952-?
Nada Župan (*née* Gazikalović)	Belgrade, SR	1927	Skopje	2008	Belgrade, SR	1952	1953-86
Ratomirka Anđelković (*née* Cvetković)	Tulare, SR	1928			Belgrade, SR	1953	1954-83
Rosanda Minčeva (*née* Cvetković)	Tulare, SR	1928	Skopje	2001	Belgrade, SR	1953	1953-84
Vera Ćosevska (*née* Rotman)	Osijek, HR	1929			Belgrade, SR	1953	1953-55 & 1959-89
Born and practised in North Macedonia							
Dragoslava Tomova-Serafimova	Skopje	1924	Skopje	2017	Zagreb, HR	1954	1954-82
Lidija Filonova-Markova	Strumica	1927	Skopje	?	Zagreb, HR	1954	1954-87
Ljubinka Malenkova	Ohrid	1927	Skopje?	2011	Belgrade, SR	1951	1951-87
Granka Zlatković-Džunova	Gradsko	1929	Skopje?	2006	Belgrade, SR	1955	1959-81
Vasilka Ladinska (*née* Petrovska)	Kumanovo	1928	Skopje	2013	Belgrade, SR	1954	1954-87
Mimoza Nestorova-Tomić	Ohrid	1929			Belgrade, SR	1953	1953-89
Vera Ušinska-Žežova	Štip	1930			Belgrade, SR	1954	1954-79

Table 2: List of key areas of work, highest position and distiction held by post-WWII women architects identified and processed to date. Abbreviations: Acad – Academia / Teach – Teaching / Arch – Architecture / Cons – Construction / Int A – Interior Architecture / Plan – Urban Planning. (Sources: Compiled by the author from cited sources within this paper)

Name and Surname	Areas of Work						Highest Post	Highest Distinction
	Acad	Teach	Arch	Cons	Int A	Plan		
Born in North Macedonia but practised abroad								
Danica Milosavljević-Jovanović		X	X		X			
Cvetanka Roškova-Krepieva			X			X		
Born abroad and practised in North Macedonia								
Ruža Paulić			X			X		
Bosiljka Krstić-Novaković	X				X			
Nada Župan (née Gazikalović)		X				X		
Ratomirka Anđelković (née Cvetković)				X			Technical Head (Cons. Group)	SFRY 'Order of Labour'
Rosanda Minčeva (née Cvetković)			X					'11th October' Award (Project)
Vera Ćosevska (née Rotman)			X			X	Head of an Architectural Team	'Andrej Damjanov' Award
Born and practised in North Macedonia								
Dragoslava Tomova-Serafimova	X		X			X	Professor of Urban Planning	
Lidija Filonova-Markova			X	X		X	Head of various groups	'11th October' Award (Project)
Ljubinka Malenkova			X			X	Head of an Architectural Team	'Andrej Damjanov' Award
Granka Zlatković-Džunova			X	X				
Vasilka Ladinska (née Petrovska)			X				Head of an Architectural Team	'Andrej Damjanov' Award
Mimoza Nestorova-Tomić	X		X		X	X	Director	'Andrej Damjanov' Award
Vera Ušinska-Žežova			X	X	X		Head of Municipal Service	

Ms Ruža Paulić is among those who came from Croatia to practice briefly in North Macedonia (1956-60) at the State Institute for Urban Planning in Skopje, mainly in the area of urban planning and residential architecture [10]. The other five settled in the country; four of them came from Serbia but they pursued different career paths. Ms Krstić-Novaković devoted her career to interior architecture and furniture design in combination in part with an academic career [11]. Ms Nada Župan (Figure 1b), is the only example of a second-generation woman architect. She also trained as Environmental Health Engineer (Architecture) in Zagreb. Following a period of teaching at the Secndary Medical School in Skopje, she devoted her career to urban planning [12]. Similarly, the twin sisters, Ms Ratomirka Anđelković [13] and Ms Rosanda Minčeva [14] pursued different careers. The former one devoted her career to site management and site architect roles, whilst the latter worked on architectural design with an emphasis on residential and educational buildings. Minčeva is known for her *Vardar Uvoz-Izvoz* (Vardar Export-Import, 1975) offices in Skopje (co-designed with Mr Dimitar Dimitrov), as well as for the residential complex *Porta Vlae* (1984) in Skopje (as one of the co-designers).

Ms Vera Ćosevska is probably the oldest living woman architect in North Macedonia. She moved from Croatia to join her colleague and spouse Mr Vladimir Ćosevski. Inspired by her architect uncle, she excelled in her professional career mainly in the field of architecture and urban planning. Some of her most prominent work include the Court in Ohrid (1961, Fig. 2), a residential tower with department store in Kisela Voda (1964, Fig. 3) in Skopje, the mixed use complex (1975) in Kumanovo, the Hotel Jugo (1977, Fig. 4) in Gevegelija and the Hotel Panorama in Radoviš (1978) [15].

Figure 2: The Court in Ohrid, Architect, Vera Ćosevska, 1961, Photo: N/A, Source: Porta 3.

Figure 3: Residential tower with department store in Kisela Voda, Skopje, Architect, Vera Ćosevska, 1964, Photo: N/A, Source: Porta 3.

Figure 4: Hotel Jugo in Gevgelija, Architect, Vera Ćosevska, 1977, Photo: N/A, Source: Private Archives of Vera Ćosevska.

Women architects born in North Macedonia and who practised in North Macedonia

The same divergence of roles and professional focus are also observed among the women architects who were both born and practised in North Macedonia. Two of them, Prof. Dragoslava Tomova-Serafimova (Fig. 1c) and Ms Lidija Filonova-Markova (Fig. 1d) were educated at the University of Zagreb. Tomova-Serafimova devoted her career to academia whilst maintaining practice in the fields of architecture and urban planning. She is probably the first woman professor at the University Ss Cyril and Methodius Faculty of Architecture in Skopje, and had a particular interest in children's playgrounds design [16]. Filonova-Markova had a similar level of professional versatility, starting her career as site manager and site architect, before becoming a Head of Construction, followed by Head of Design and ending her career as Head of Building Inspections. Her lasting legacy is the co-design of the *Gradski Trgovski Centar – GTC* (City Shopping Centre, 1969) in Skopje [17].

The remaining five women architects were educated at the University of Belgrade. Among them, Ms Granka Zlatković-Džunova and Ms Vera Ušinska-Žežova successfully transitioned between roles. The early part of Zlatković-Džunova's career was focused being a site manager / site architect before moving into the architect's design role with an emphasis on residential construction [18]. In contrast, Ušinska-Žežova, started her career as a design architect working on residential builings before moving into client and building inspection roles, combined with some interior architecture too [19].

Figure 5: Residential tower in Karpoš IV, Skopje, Architect, Ljubnika Malenkova, 1965, Photo: Vladimir Ladinski, Source: Private Archives of Vladimir Ladinski.

Ms Ljubinka Malenkova and Ms Vasilka Ladinska, instead, devoted their careers to architectural design work covering a variety of building types and leaving lasting legacies. Malenkova was also engaged in urban planning. The residential towers in Karpoš IV (1965, Fig. 5) in Skopje, the Main Post Offices in Prilep (1975), Tetovo (1977), Kumanovo (1978), Strumica (1981) and Kočani (1982), and mixed-use complex *Porta Bunjakovec* (1985) in Skopje with architect Mr Lj. Andreev, are some of her major architectural achivements [20]. Similarly, among Ladinska's most prominent buildings are *Komunalna Banka* (1964) bank in Kumanovo, the five residential towers on Ilinenska Street (1953), the residential block on Makedonija Street (1962), the Grammar School Joisp Broz-Tito (1968, Fig. 6) with architects Mr Živko Gelevski and Mr Slavko Đurić, the University Hospitals for Infectious Disases, and Surgery (1979) with architect Mr Blagoja Babamov, the residential block on the corner of Boulevard Partzanski Odredi and Boulevard St Kliment Ohrdiski (1982) with architect Mr Blagoja Micevski, as well as the two urban villas on Ilindenska Street (1986 and 1987), all in Skopje [21].

Figure 6: Grammar School 'Josip Broz-Tito' in Skopje, Architects, Vasilka Ladinska, Živko Gelevski and Slavko Đurić, 1968, Photo: N/A, Source: Grammar School Josip Broz-Tito (Public Domain).

Ms Mimoza Nestorova-Tomić, had a wider level of versatility covering academia, urban planning, conservation, architecture and interior architecture during her professional career. Among her most prominent buildings are the *Muzeji na Makedonija* (Museums of Macedonia, 1972, Fig. 7) with architect Mr Kiril Muratovski, and the recently lost department store *Beko* (1973), as well as the residential blocks in Kapištec (1985, Fig. 8), all in Skopje [22].

Some of the early women architect established great working partnerships that resulted with even more remarkable buildings. For example, the Malenkova~Ćosevska collaboration produced the *Gradski Dzid-Blok* (City Wall Residential Block, 1966, Fig. 9) in Skopje with others, as well as the *Teatar na narodnosti* (The Ethnic Groups Theatre, 1974, Fig. 10) in Skopje [23]. Similarly, the Ladinska~Minčeva partnership resulted in the *Gradski Dzid-Kula M* (City Wall Tower M, 1966, Fig. 11) in Skopje working with other colleagues, and the mixed development on the corner of Makedonija and Dame Gruev Streets (1966) in Skopje [24].

Figure 7: Museums of Macedonia in Skopje, Architects, Mimoza Nestorova-Tomić and Kiril Muratovski, 1972, Photo: Rumen Čamilov, Source: MArh, https://marh.mk/wp-content/uploads/2016/11/20161101_112105-768x759.jpg

Figure 8: Residential blocks in Kapištec, Skopje, Architect, Mimoza Nestorova-Tomić, 1985, Photo: Vladimir Ladinski, Source: Private Archives of Vladimir Ladinski.

Figure 9: Grdski dzid – Blok (City Wall Block) in Skopje, Architects, Vera Ćosevska, Ljubinka Malenkova, Aleksandar Serafimovski, Slavko Đurić, Nikola Bogačev, and Simo Simoski, 1965, Photo: N/A, Source: Porta 3.

Among all of the identified early women architects probably the highest level of prominence was achieved by the four laureates of the *Andrej Damjanov Nagrada* (*Andrej Damjanov* Award) awarded by the Association of Architects of Macedonia: Ljubica Malenkova (2000, Fig. 12a), Vasilka Ladinska (2005, Fig. 12b), Mimoza Nestorova-Tomić (2011 Fig. 12c) and Vera Ćosevska (2014, Fig. 12d). This is the country's highest award that the profession can bestow in recognition of lifetime achivements and contribution to architecture. All recepients become lifetime members of the Academy of Architects at the Association of Architects of Macedonia [25]. Most of the recepints of the Andrej Damjanov Award, as well as Anđelković, were also honoured by the state of the Socialist Federal Republic of Yugoslavia (SFRY) generally with the Order of Labour with Silver Wreath.

Figure 10: Teatar na narodnosti (The Ethnic Groups Theatre) in Skopje, Architects, Vera Ćosevska and Ljubinka Malenkova, 1965, Photo: N/A, Source: Private Archives of Vera Ćosevska.

The acceptance of early women architects in North Macedonia

In response to the question of how women architect were treated by their colleagues, profession and the society, the Doyenne of the women architect in North Macedonia, Vera Ćosevska replied (26):

"I graduated on the 25 July 1953, and was employed a week later, on the 1 August 1953. I was among the first women graduate architects in the post Second World War per anod. In that period there was no gender differentiation between the members of a profession, only the professional education was respected. We were equally treated by our colleagues, and within the profession projects were allocated to those who have passed the state professional exam for design and construction of all types of buildings. The progression within the profession was based on incremental grades and dependent on the work related results. Designs for projects were prepared in large state design organisations that had professionals covering all aspects of construction. The profession of architect was respected by the society during my working life. The opinions and projects by professionals were discussed and were subject of polemics, but they were never ignored."

Figure 11: Grdski dzid – Kula M (City Wall Tower M) in Skopje, Architects, V. Ladinska, R. Minčeva, A. Serafimovski, S. Đurić and S. Dimitrov, 1966, Photo: Vladimir Ladinski, Source: Private Archives of Vladimir Ladinski.

Figure 12: (a)Ms Ljubinka Malenkova (upper left, Source: Porta 3), (b) Vasilka Ladinska (upper-right, Source: Ladinski and Ladinski), (c) Mimoza Nestorova-Tomić (lower-left, Source: Porta 3), (d) Vera Ćosevska (lower-right, Source: Ćosevska).

The above statement provides an important insight of an early woman architect's acceptance within the profession. However, it has not been possible to identify particular studies covering the post-WWII experiences of women architects, hence it was necessary to focus on more generic studies covering women's issues in former Yugoslavia. Based on those, the conditions for women architects, in general, including their access to education and the entrance to profession and professional practice, significantly positively changed in the post-WWII period in comparison to the Interwar period. The 1946 Constitution of the Socialist Federal Republic of Yugoslavia gave equal rights to women in all fileds of state, economic and social-political life, thus at least in theory opened the way for their full integration in the society [27]. The author's experince of studying architecture in North Macedonia in the late 1970s recalls women students representing over 50 per cent of the student body. Equally, in professional practice during the 1980s the majority of architects and architectural technicians in the design office were women. This was also the case for other professions at the time, i.e. medicine, education, etc.

However, there was probably a 'glass ceiling' limiting the extent to which a woman architect could progress, especially in management, leadership and outside the profession on political positions. Out of the identified early women architects, Nestorova-Tomić achieved the highest position becoming the Director (1986-89) of the City Institute of Town Planning and Architecture in Skopje at the end of her professional career, whilst Ušinska-Žežova became the Head of the Communal Serivice (1963) within the town of Štip. Anđelković and Filonova-Markova held various management positions, whilst Malenkova, Ćosevska and Ladinska, became heads of Architectural Teams. The latter were responsible for managing up to about 50 professionals each. Equally, Tomova-Serafimovska seeems to be the first woman to achive a full Professorship at the Faculty of Architectre in Skope.

However, these (limited) achievements need to be considered in the wider context. For example, Malenkova and Čoseva were both employed by the construction company Pelagonija that had its own in-house design office and employed about 12,800 people in the 1980s [28]. Similarly, Anđelković and Filonova-Markova, worked for the construction company Beton that also had an in-house design office and employed around 8,700 people in the 1980s [29]. These very large companies had their branches spread around North Macedonia and construction sites much wider.

Conclusions

The ongoing research has so far identified 17 early women architects educated abroad by 1955 who were born in and/or worked in North Macedonia. No examples were identified from the time period when the territory of North Macedonia was under the Ottoman Empire, although two women architects were identified in the interwar period and 15 in the post-WWII period based on the period when they practiced. Out of the 15 women architects from the post-WWII period, two were born in North Macedonia but never practised in the country, six were born abroad and practiced in North Macedonia and seven were born and practiced in North Macedonia. Out of the 17 early women architectural graduates, 12 were graduates from the University of Belgrade, three from the University of Zagreb, one from the University of Architecture, Civil Engineering and Geodesy in Sofia and the Alma Mater for one is unknown. Only one of the identified 17 women architects is known to be a second-generation woman architect.

Considering that about 220 women engineers and architects existed in 1940 in the Kingdom of Yugoslavia, it is possible that the already identified two women architects may be an underestimate of the actual number of practicing women architects in North Macedonia at the time. A similar issue applies in relation to the number of identified women architects practising in the post WWII period in North Macedonia, hence ongoing research should focus on identifying as many of them as possible.

This research found that the early women architects were involved in various roles ranging from academia and design to urban planning and construction related activities, leaving a lasting legacy in their own field of work. Equally, the research identified varying societal attitudes towards the early women architects. The level of acceptance appears to be grater in the post-WWII period in comparison with the Interwar period. The most prominent women architects in this period of their professional activity received both professional and societal recognitions for their achievements. Although some of them gained more senior and managerial positions it is difficult to say if they were really allowed to achieve their full potential and meet their personal aspirations in a deeply rooted patriarchal society where probably the government policies and objectives were never quite met. Similarly, it is not possible to be sure if the early women architects' professional ambitions were stifled by their peers and the wider society or whether they were indeed content with less prominent roles in order to maintain a better work-life balance considering their families. This can probably also be said even for the most advances societies anywhere in the world. Regardless, these women's achievements mostly still remain to be both seen and used by the public, as well as to inspire the generations to come.

Acknowledgements

The author expresses his gratitude to Ms Vera Ćosevska, Ms Sanja Rađenović, Ms Stanislava Župan-Overholt, Dr Ivanka Stefanovska, Mr Slobodan Mukaetov, Mr Boris Roškov, Mr Aleksandar Ladinski, and to the *Porta 3* magazine and the MArh Portal for their kind access to information and images used in the preparation of this paper. The author is son of Ms Ladinska.

References

[1] R. Bojadžieva-Cvetkova, 'Aptekarskite Dnevnici od Aptekata na Rajna Aleksova', *Farmacevtski Informator*, vol.10, no.25, 2011, pp.62-65.
[2] S. Gilgenkrantz, 'Les premières étudiantes étrangères en médicine à Nancy (1894-1914)', http://professeurs-medecine-nancy.fr/premieres_etudiantes_etrangeres.htm (Consulted on 13 Feb. 2022).
[3] B. Ibrajter Gazibara, 'Talentovana Graditeljka Beograda Jelisaveta Načić', CAB-Centar za arhitekturu Beograd, https://cab.rs/blog/talentovana-graditeljka-beograda-jelisaveta-nacic (Consulted on 13 Feb. 2022).
[4] G. Konstantinovski, Graditelite vo Makedonija XVIII-XX vek, *Skopje: Tabernakul*, 2001, p.62.
[5] Konstantinovski, (Note 4), p. 110; Pravda, (15 Dec. 1931), p.12, http://istorijskenovine.unilib.rs/view/index.html#panel:pp|issue:UB_00042_19311215|page:10|query:%D0%BF%D0%B0%D1%98%D0%BE%20%D1%88%D1%83%D0%BB%D0%B5%D0%BD%D1%82%D0%B8%D1%9B (Consulted on 13 Feb. 2022).
[6] S. Overholt, Correspondence, Feb. 2022.
[7] Vreme, (26 May 1940), p.19, http://istorijskenovine.unilib.rs/view/index.html#panel:pp|issue:UB_00043_19400526|page:19|query:%D1%98%D0%B5%D0%BB%D0%B8%D1%81%D0%B0%D0%B2%D0%B5%D1%82%D0%B0%20%D0%BD%D0%B0%D1%87%D0%B8%D1%9B (Consulted on 13 Feb. 2022).
[8] G. B. Anđelković, 'Arh Danica Milosavljević (Skoplje 1919 – Beograd 2018)', *Arhitekt*, October 2018, pp.61-62.
[9] B. Roškov, Telephone interview, Jan. 2022; S. Mukaetov, Correspondence, Feb. 2022.
[10] Konstantinovski, (Note 4), p.214.
[11] Konstantinovski, (Note 4), p.179.
[12] Overholt, (Note 6); Konstantinovski, (Note 4), pp.154-155.
[13] Konstantinovski, (Note 4), pp.126-127.
[14] Konstantinovski, (Note 4), pp.176-177.
[15] V. Ćosevska, Correspondence, Dec. 2021 – Feb. 2022.
[16] I. Stefanovska, Correspondence, Dec. 2021 – Feb. 2022; Konstantinovski, (Note 4), pp.198-199.
[17] S. Rađenović, Correspondence, Feb. 2022; Konstantinovski, (Note 4), pp.174-175.
[18] Ćosevska, (Note 15); Konstantinovski, (Note 4), pp.234-235.
[19] Konstantinovski, (Note 4), pp.222-223.
[20] Ćosevska, (Note 15); S. Rađenović, (Note 17).
[21] A. Ladinski and V. Ladinski, Vasilka Ladinska Personal Archive.
[22] Architectuull, Mimoza Nestorova-Tomić, http://architectuul.com/architect/mimoza-nestorova-tomic (Consulted on 13 Feb. 2022); Konstantinovski, (Note 4), pp.206-207.
[23] Ćosevska, (Note 15).
[24] A. Ladinski and V. Ladinski, (Note 21).
[25] S. Rađenović-Jovanović, '25 Dobitnici na Nagradata Andreja Damjanov', PresIng, vol.IV, no.25, 2015, pp.57-59.
[26] Ćosevska, (Note 15).
[27] C. Bonfiglioli, Becoming citzens: the politics of women's emancipaction in Socailist Yugoslavia, CITSEE Research Project, https://www.citsee.eu/citsee-story/becoming-citizens-politics-women%E2%80%99s-emancipation-socialist-yugoslavia (Consulted on 13 Feb. 2022).
[28] Konstantinovski, (Note 4), p.248.
[29] Konstantinovski, (Note 4), p.249.

Voices from the Post-War Belgian Building Industry: A Study of a General Contractor and its Involvement in Building Practices via Oral History

Jelle Angillis, Inge Bertels
Henry Van de Velde Research Group, Faculty of Design Sciences, Antwerp University, Belgium

Abstract

Contractors are key actors in the construction process and take a leading role in the finalisation of a building. Researching the history of these contractors, therefore, not only provides information on the actor and their close involvement with the construction site, but also on the entirety of building practices within the site boundary. However, the preservation and accessibility of the contractors' archives is a stumbling block, and the builders themselves have also left very little source material. By including oral history in the research on a Belgian contractor Van Laere (°1938), this case study aims to show how this gap in source material can be bridged to some extent. Interviews with five former employees of the company provide information about the historical evolution of the company, the interaction between different company actors and their activity on the site, allows the recognition and positioning of this actor within post-war Belgian building practice.

Contractors, tough to trace actors in construction practice

It is well known that general contractors and their workforce played a prominent role in the realisation of the built environment. Within their corporate structure, contractors provide capital to translate design and mathematical concepts into practice and built results. They call on organisational skills to organise the site in a thorough manner and use their equipment and machinery to shape construction layer by layer. Their workforce includes all kinds of craftsmen, who translate the drawn lines into reality. Although they are usually on the lowest hierarchical level of this economic sector, bricklayers, formworkers, carpenters and countless other specialised occupations rely on indispensable commitment and expertise. Their hands, knowledge and interaction on the building site are the final step in the realisation of the construction, and ensure the synthesis of the entire building process.

Because of their position and involvement, the building contractor is therefore an important player for studying, through their legacies, firstly the actor, but also the building site and subsequently the entire building practice. However, a major challenge remains the lack of historical evidences to develop and reconstruct their history. Although in the Belgian context there are a few companies such as Blaton (°1865), Entreprises Louis De Waele (°1866) or Entreprises Générales Henri Ruttiens (°1878-2000) that have left a considerable amount of consultable archival material, this is not representative of the entire research field [1]. Previous research on the Belgian construction sector has already indicated that contractors' archives are often not disclosed, inaccessible because they are still stored in the company itself, fragmentary, or simply non-existent [2]. In the Anglo-Saxon context, it was Christine Wall, among others, who pointed out the problem of dealing with contractor archives when, for example, a company loses its identity through a takeover or ceases to exist. It is also an undeniable fact that both workers and contractors have left far fewer sources than the other actors involved in the building practice [3]. An additional challenge that arises when archival material can nevertheless be found is that the actual building practice on the site and especially the surrounding building culture is only fragmentarily documented.

Voices from the Post-War Belgian Building Industry: A Study of a General Contractor and its Involvement in Building Practices via Oral History

With her research into the construction of the Southbank Centre (London 1961-1967) and the Barbican (London, 1965-1982), among others, Wall was able to show how interviews with the people who actually carried out the work in the field could provide an important addition to this gap in the available source material. The application of oral history provides, she says, "immediacy to the building process, only guessed at from examining archival photographs and drawings". Where the latter two types of sources only give a static and summary picture of the activities on the site and the actors such as the contractors and the workers who were active there [4]. This immediacy is otherwise important for understanding the underlying attitudes and traditional social, technical and industrial relations in building practice that shape the culture of building but also the culture of the construction company [5]. It was, moreover, the British architectural historian John Summerson who as early as 1986 advocated placing these relationships at the centre of the study of historical building practice [6].

Following on from this research, this article aims to show what the application of oral history can mean for a study of post-war building practice in Belgium, and more specifically for the identification of the contractor as an important actor. For example, what aspects of construction practice emerge during the interviews, how do they fit within the operations of the construction company, and above all, what information is revealed through these interviews about the evolution of the contractor and their activities?

Over a period of almost two years, witnesses were traced and several interviews were conducted of five persons with various responsibilities who worked between 1945 and 2018 for the East Flanders construction company Van Laere (°1938), based in Kruibeke/Burcht. This company, which was a family business from 1938 to 1989, is still active within a holding company today. The focus was the period during which the company was owned by the Van Laere family, and the following people were approached: a former shareholder and manager (Herman Van Laere, active in the company from 1962 till 1989), a clerk/archivist (Rudi Gyselinck, active 1969-2018), an engineer (André Hauman, active 1971-2009), a carpenter/trade union delegate (Louis Anné, active 1978-2008) and a joiner (Frans Anné, active 1945-1987).

Figure 1: Construction of the 'King Boudewijn highway' by Van Laere, circa 1958. Flemish Architecture Institute - Flemish Community Collection, image archive Van Laere.

A pre-structured list of questions was prepared for the witnesses, which on the one hand asked for information about the company itself, and on the other hand about the nature of their own activities in the firm. For example, they were asked about their knowledge of how the firm operated, how they saw themselves within this corporate structure, what relationships they could observe between the various actors and branches of the firm, what their own specific job description was and how they experienced their activities. After an analysis of the content of the interviews, three main themes in the narratives could then be distinguished, which also shape the structure of this paper. First, there was the evolutionary aspect with a historical framing of the company and its archive, and how this related to the broader historical context of the construction industry in Belgium. Second there were the human interactions that determined the company's operation and its practices, and finally its activities on the construction site that formed the very essence of its existence. (Fig.01)

Unravelling the history of the company and its archives

It was just after the First World War, in 1919, that Leopold Van Laere (1880-1946) founded a small enterprise. In the aftermath of the global conflict, the demand for (emergency) housing had grown, which this cabinetmaker anticipated. In a shed, behind a small popular pub in rural Kruibeke, the contracting company took shape during the interwar period. However, the construction company Van Laere, which became a successful business after the Second World War, was not officially founded until 1938 when Leopold's five sons entered the business. Albert (1907-1969), Florimond (1909-1980), Gérard (1911-1999), Réne (1913-1973), Léon (1919-2018) and Cyriel became shareholders and each occupied a different position, from architect to construction site supervisor. Between 1938 and 1939, Van Laere realised, among other things, a social housing complex comprising a total of 160 flats (Luchtbal, Antwerp), until a new global conflict from 1940 onwards would largely keep the company in chains and limit its activities [7].

When a new housing shortage manifested itself at the end of the Second World War, the company had again anticipated the crisis and was positioned to respond. In the first months after the German capitulation, for example, they erected emergency wooden houses in Kruibeke [8]. Gradually, contact grew again with the social housing companies with whom they had already worked regularly before the conflict. The post-war housing shortage was so great, however, that it became an important political agenda item in the 1950s, which would mean a major growth spurt for the company. In cooperation with the city of Antwerp and its social housing companies, Van Laere was thus able to realise the Jan De Voslei social housing project between 1952 and 1961, and parts of the revolutionary, in both its architectural and construction aspects, social district of Kiel between 1955 and 1958. In a context of tense international relations, military construction was also an important part of their activities in that period. In 1946, for example, they built 36 troop blocks in the military Beverloo Camp (Kamp van Beverloo). Between 1951 and 1952, they subsequently realised a large part of the buildings in the Stockem Camp (Kamp van Stockem). At Beverloo, Van Laere met Harry Steegmans (1919-2001), who at the time had been appointed by the Ministry as superintendent of military buildings. Close contact remained between the company and Steegmans, after which he eventually started working for Van Laere. From 1948 he was the only non-family member to hold a management position within the company, and he was also to play an important role in the further development of the company [9]. (Fig. 02)

The further evolution of the company, in the successive two decades, can also be framed by the external societal factors that would influence the construction sector. In short, according to Herman Van Laere, the company always knew how to ride the waves of the political, economic and social conditions in the country [10]. After the housing problems in the forties and fifties, the country subsequently invested heavily in road construction, water engineering and other public works and bridges. The slogan '100 kilometres of motorway per year' of Minister Omer Vanoudenhove, among others, represented this ambition, which was finally realised by his successor Jos De Saeger in the early 1970s [11]. For Van Laere, this resulted, for example, in the construction of a large part of the E3/A21 motorway (1969-1973) and a large-scale viaduct in Gentbrugge between 1969 and 1970. During that period, water works also became an increasingly important part of this contractor's range of tasks. Among other things, they realised the Fourth Dock in Antwerp in 1966, and between 1971 and 1979 they gained national and international fame with the construction of the Kallo lock complex. An important note here is that Van Laere continued to offer a total package for all types of works, which required major investments in terms of equipment and technology. While civil engineering formed a significant part of their activities between the 1960s and 1980s, in the context of the emerging tertiary sector they also focused on office and flat construction. The realisation of the Antwerp Tower office complex between 1970 and 1975, a skyscraper of 24 floors and 87 metres in height, is a good example of this [12].

Figure 2: Construction of three tower blocks by Van Laere in the Jan De Voslei social housing area, circa 1960. Flemish Architecture Institute - Flemish Community Collection, image archive Van Laere.

It was during this period of growth for the company, between roughly 1955 and 1985, that the company archives also grew and developed. When Van Laere moved to its current facility in Burcht at the beginning of the seventies, a separate room was provided for the ever-growing archive. In a room on the ground floor of the main building with a surface area of approximately 70 square metres, current files were kept. In the basement, a room twice this size was used as extra storage space for the files of completed works. From 1977, Rudi Gyselinck was responsible for the archives in these rooms, which had been made fireproof. He developed his own archival system in which each site was given a serial number. Under these serial numbers he filed some 20 sub-folders in which, per category, building plans, building studies, correspondence, but also all construction site diaries were kept [13]. (Fig. 03)

According to Rudi Gyselinck, maintaining a substantial archive for the company was valued at senior levels of management. The management of the company, and especially Harry Steegmans, stressed the importance of the archive as it was seen as the guiding thread running through the company. The Belgian legal retention period of 10 years for project files was therefore often exceeded, with the archives of some projects being kept for up to 40 years after completion. The interview also revealed that pragmatism was the most important criterion for assessing the value of archive documents. The number of hours spent preparing a project, the know-how it contained, but also the risks involved after completion, for example, were important factors in determining the storage period. Yet, also more personal elements played a role. As such, the family involvement, translated mainly into a large quantity of photographic material, which was kept as a souvenir of each construction site, and which often survived its paper counterpart [14].

Figure 3: The new Van Laere company site in Burcht around 1971. In the middle the office building, surrounded by workshops. Flemish Architecture Institute - Flemish Community Collection, image archive Van Laere.

However, the handling of the archives and the overall strategy of the company changed dramatically when the Van Laere family left the company in 1989 and a professional manager took over. It is this critical point of transition, which Wall, among others, pointed out, that can be seen as decisive for the legacy left by the company [15]. The personal ties to the earlier completed projects faded, but emerging digitalisation also had an impact on the company's inheritance. The new management generally aimed to destroy project files after a maximum period of 15 years. The remaining files were digitised and, due to internal restructuring, the position of archivist was also called into question [16]. A major clearing operation in 2019 resulted in what was left of the historical archive disappear, with only the extensive photo collection being spared. The last written traces of 81 years of construction were thus erased, with only the photographic material and human memory making it possible to understand the internal workings of this actor on the one hand and its activities on the other. All this means that today these interviews are even more crucial for analysing and documenting the past.

The company's internal structure and associated business culture

With regard to the internal structure and the business culture that developed between 1938 and 1989, the interviews showed very clearly that the involvement of the Van Laere family was very decisive for the functioning of the company and its activities. In this sense, three generations of Van Laere's followed one another throughout its existence, the number of shareholders almost multiplying with each generation. When Herman Van Laere was asked about the family's attitude towards their representation in the company, he replied, for example, that it was almost a foregone conclusion that the male descendants would join the company. Especially the second generation, to which Herman belonged, who were supposed to take up studies that could be useful for the company at that time. They were employed from architect to estimator or site manager, which meant that family members were represented in every branch of the company. A striking fact here is that only male successors were allowed to join the company. Nevertheless, the involvement of women with the company was never far away, since most female Van Laere's were married to men who were active within the company [17]. This internal structure of the company can be framed within what the American business philosopher William Gibb Dyer Jr. calls a paternalistic corporate culture [18]. With the exception of Harry Steegmans, the company managers were all Van Laere family members and, within a strong hierarchical structure, kept a firm grip on the reins. Lived-in traditions were therefore central. Importantly, a certain path dependence within the company strategy was also linked to this. An important example of this is that Van Laere tried to keep the entire execution process under their own control. For example, on the company premises, they had their own carpentry shop, their own garage, their own smithy and their own painting department, but also the contracting of different types of works led to substantial investments and a large machine park [19]. The branching out of the family members into the company structure, especially the presence and direct control on the construction site by the site managers, was an important element in keeping a grip on its activities [20].

While, according to the interviewees, this company structure and strategy had a certain strength and commanded authority, its market orientation and position were threatened, especially from the late 1970s onwards. It was Harry Steegmans, who had held an important position at Van Laere since 1948, who wanted to steer the company more in the direction of administrative downsizing, specialisation and subcontracting. On the managerial level, the involvement of the family and the division of the shares had become too great, which did not benefit the management. In the mid-1980s, for example, there were no less than 19 employed associates in the family. On the other hand, the competition from more specialised companies with more favourable pricing became too strong, so the company had to evolve towards subcontracting. However, this met with resistance from Florimond Van Laere, the manager at the time, whereby after his sudden death in 1980 the torch was nevertheless handed to Harry Steegmans, who tried to translate his own vision into practice. Despite Steegmans' appointment, the company structure remained very paternalistic with a strong family influence, and he emerged, nonetheless, as a strong leader figure who still endorsed a hierarchically oriented company [21]. Rudi Gyselinck, characterised him as a workaholic, a special character, but one who enjoyed great respect within the company: "He had a lot of knowledge, power and influence, also politically. As an ex-military man of high rank, he also knew his way around government contracts. When Van Laere missed out on some tenders, he got into his car and drove to Brussels. He was not afraid to punch in closed doors in order to move the company forward" [22].

These family and trust ties were not only important to the management of the company, but, according to the testimonies of Frans and Louis Anné, also to the workforce. Although the company's activities spread over the whole of Belgium over time, it remained very much rooted in the local community. The vast majority of its workforce therefore consisted of people living in a radius of less than 10 kilometres. It was therefore not unusual for mutual communication and word-of-mouth advertising to result in a vacancy being filled within the company or in people being brought in. It was also a fact that several members of different families were employed by the company, often from generation to generation. The Anné family from Kruibeke, for example, was well represented among the carpenters with three generations, but several people from the Lesire family from Kruibeke were also engaged. Van Laere also put a lot of effort into this embedding and tried to maintain these close connections with the neighbourhood. With its own football team, composed of both managers and employees, it frequently took part in the local competition, which reflected its representation in the local scene [23]. (Fig. 04)

Figure 4: The Van Laere football team, during a tournament in 1954. Flemish Architecture Institute - Flemish Community Collection, image archive Van Laere.

Voices from the construction site, the company and its activities

It was within this internal structure and surrounding corporate culture that its activities at the construction site developed. According to Herman Van Laere and André Hauman, the company's wide range of construction work over the years has led it to focus strongly on innovation and new techniques, which were introduced at the site. As much as the company was interspersed with family ties, the family was also interspersed with a far-reaching interest in the construction sector and its technological aspects. During the construction of the Kiel neighbourhood in the south of Antwerp (1955-1958), for example, they were among the first in Belgium to use prefabrication on a grand scale, which was to become a trend in large-scale construction in the following decades. In doing so, the company also tried to build lasting relationships with other actors such as public clients, architects and engineering firms, who were involved in the building practice and knew the company's operation and capabilities [24]. (Fig. 05)

Figure 5: Van Laere active at the 'Theatre Building' construction site in Antwerp, 1964. Flemish Architecture Institute - Flemish Community Collection, image archive Van Laere.

For the people involved in the work on the site, this meant that they were also subject to these developments both within the company and on the site. Training, personal development and craftsmanship were therefore often recurring elements in the interviews with people such as Frans Anné, Louis Anné and André Hauman, who themselves have a great deal of experience of working on the construction site. The National Fund for Vocational Training in the Construction Industry (*Fonds voor Vakopleiding in de Bouwnijverheid*, FVB) only came into being in 1965, so that on-the-job training was the norm, certainly in the early period [25]. Employees were thus gradually trained while they worked within the company. The local embeddedness and the attraction of people from the neighbourhood, where personal relationships sometimes had more weight than qualifications in recruitment of new personnel, possibly played a role in this. People with no real experience were given the chance to develop within the firm. Frans Anné, for example, started as a 14-year old with no experience or education in the carpentry shop in 1945, and after his activities in the company he also attended night school to learn the trade. Rudi Gyselinck too, who as a young school leaver in 1969 started in the reproduction department of the drawing office, had to learn everything on the job. "Back then there was still time for it," Frans told us. "It didn't come at an hour, as long as it was done well" [26].

An important factor here is the hierarchical structure and the division of labour that applied within the company. Because the family business offered a wide range of work, and furthermore tried to carry it out in-house as much as possible, there was a certain specialisation within the various tasks. New people were therefore welcomed in an organisation where the division of labour and tasks was still well-defined and where the know-how of a particular trade was present. Especially when the Van Laere family still owned the company, there was still a recognisable distinction between the various specialities. "In those days, carpenters were still carpenters, shuttering was still shuttering and bricklayers were bricklayers", emphasised Louis Anneé [27].

Notwithstanding the fact that this factor was closely linked to the business strategy and corporate culture of the family business, the interviewees noticed, in particular from the 1980s onwards, a certain blurring of the job description. This evolution continued, especially after the takeover in 1989, when the Van Laere family left the company, and the phenomenon of subcontracting became more and more prevalent within the new business strategy. Increased bureaucratisation and the introduction of new players on the construction site also played a part. While the Van Laere's still tried to maintain a close involvement with the activities on site and with supervision, this dropped significantly after the takeover. "The site supervisor used to be on site and knew every stone that was being moved. This person increasingly disappeared into the site offices, where the entire building process was monitored from behind a computer", Rudi Gyselinck told us [28]. The tasks changed in this way and the division of labour became hybrid. One of the interviewees would even have experienced this as 'the downfall'. Although this statement certainly has to take into account the influence of nostalgic feelings, it says a lot about how certain developments helped to determine working conditions, methods and, to a certain extent, job satisfaction on the construction site.

It is, among other things, working conditions and job satisfaction that are important core values promoted by trade unions. Traditionally, social dialogue has a strong presence in the Belgian labour market, where, in the compartmentalised political landscape, trade union activities are linked to the dominant ideologies. Since October 1958, the national statute of the trade union delegate in the construction industry has been in force, with Van Laere counting up to eight trade union delegates in its peak years (more than 1,000 employees around the 1960s and 1970s). According to Louis Anné, who was a representative of the socialist trade union, the work of the trade union within Van Laere could be seen as an example for many other construction companies. The family management recognised its functioning, respected the position of the delegates, and met with them every month to discuss the situation on the construction site [29].

A recurring element in the interviews was how trade unionism functioned as an important intermediary between the company on the one hand and its activities on the other. While the employer, whose activities were determined by political, economic and social impulses, controlled, as it were, the operations of the site, the agency of the workers also had a reciprocal effect, which was expressed by the trade unions. For example, long before safety measures such as fall protection or compulsory parapets were cast in a legal framework, these were already, based on these interviewees, points of contention for the trade unions that were derived from the experiences of workers on the site. The resulting legal framework in turn had an influence on all stages of construction practice, making clear also the agency of the workers as the lowest ranked actors.

Reflection

The knowledge that the witnesses had about the evolution of the company allowed us first of all to map out its history, which had not been written down before. Former company manager Herman Van Laere (1937-2021) was able to tell us about this through surviving family stories. The employees, who had grown up in the area, and where the locally embedded Van Laere was an established value, could also contribute. When this information is then compared with the general post-war evolution in the Belgian building industry, it forms a good basis to examine the company and its activities on the site. An interview with the former archivist Rudi Gyselinck furthermore gave a look at how the company's archives evolved, how the company dealt with its inheritance and what the consequences are today for the study of the company and its involvement in the building industry.

By subsequently questioning the witnesses about their position within the company structure and the relationships between the various actors, the core of the company was exposed. It created the possibility to get an insight into its functioning, the structures and the surrounding corporate culture that manifested itself at the different levels of the company. The fact that Van Laere was a family business with very local roots determined the development of the company, its strategy and its activities. The strong family ties and traditional business strategies that had made the company great, however, no longer proved resilient to the changing economic conditions in the construction industry at the end of the 1980s. A first step towards reorientation was taken by Harry Steegmans, which was then drastically implemented when the family left the company in 1989.

How the internal structure and surrounding corporate culture determined activities at the construction site was finally revealed by filtering out three key themes from the interviews. A look at the evolution of training and craftsmanship, division of labour and hierarchy, and the position of the trade union revealed part of the underlying soul of working on the site. Here again, the underlying corporate culture and path dependency were decisive factors, which were reciprocated by, among others, the trade union and its representative role of the construction site worker. Specialisation and downsizing then saved the company and made it market-oriented again, but this also had an impact on how the workers experienced work on the site. The close connection with the trade diminished to some extent and the tasks became more hybrid. Van Laere became a manager-driven construction company where family traditions faded away, and which today is navigating its way through the political, economic, social and technical conditions that determine today's construction industry.

References

[1] M. Culot and Y.Pesztat, eds., *Blaton, une dynastie de constructeurs* (Bruxelles: Éditions AAM : Civa-brussels, fondation/stichting, 2017); J. Dobbels, 'Aannemersarchieven, Een Belangrijke Bron Voor de Monumentenzorg- En Erfgoedsector' (Masters thesis, Antwerp University, 2017).
[2] J. Dobbels, 'Aannemersarchieven Onder de Loep: Analyse van de Bruikbaarheid Voor de Erfgoedsector', *M&L - Monumenten, Landschappen En Archeologie* 1 (2020): 4–26.
[3] C.Wall, 'Recording the "Building World": How Oral History Transforms Construction History' (The First Construction History Society Conference & Annual General Meeting, University of Cambridge: Construction History Society, 2014).
[4] Wall, (Note 3).
[5] B. Addis and A.Schlimme, 'Editorial: Oral History', *Construction History* 31, no. 1 (2016): i.
[6] J. Summerson, 'What Is the History of Construction?', *Construction History* 1 (1986): 1–
[7] Herman Van Laere, interview by Jelle Angillis, 1 October 2020.
[8] Frans Anné, interview by Jelle Angillis, 23 December 2021.
[9] D.C., 'Aannemersbedrijf N.V. Van Laere (Burcht) Blijft in Vlaamse Handen', *Het Vrije Waasland*, 6 May 1988; Van Laere, interview, 1 October 2020.
[10] Herman Van Laere, interview by Jelle Angillis, 3 November 2020.
[11] Piet Lombaerde, Bouwen Is Leven, Leven Is Bouwen (Nationale Confederatie van het Bouwbedrijf (NCB), 1996, 48.
[12] Van Laere, interview, 3 November 2020.
[13] Rudi Gyselinck, interview by Jelle Angillis, 15 February 2022.
[14] Gyselinck, interview; See also: Jelle Angillis, 'The Post-War Construction Site in Photographs : The Photographic Collection of the Belgian Contractor Firm Van Laere (°1938)', History of Construction Cultures : Seventh International Congress on Construction History, Proceedings, 2021, 447–57.
[15] Wall, (Note 3), 3.
[16] Gyselinck, interview.
[17] Van Laere, interview, 3 November 2020.
[18] William Gibb Dyer, 'Culture and Continuity in Family Firms', Family Business Review 1, no. 1 (March 1988): 18–20.
[19] Van Laere, interview, 3 November 2020.
[20] André Hauman, interview by Jelle Angillis, 29 November 2020.
[21] Van Laere, interview, 3 November 2020.
[22] Gyselinck, interview, 15 February 2022.
[23] Frans Anné, interview, 23 December 2021; Louis Anné, interview by Jelle Angillis, 12 January 2022.

[24] Van Laere, interview, 1 October 2020; Gyselinck, interview.
[25] Lombaerde, Bouwen Is Leven, Leven Is Bouwen, 62.
[26] Frans Anné, interview; Gyselinck, interview.
[27] Louis Anné, interview.
[28] Gyselinck, interview.
[29] Louis Anné, interview.

The Livestock Auction Hall in Riedlingen – Regional Timber Construction in the 1930s in the South-West of Germany

Sabine Kuban
Landesamt für Denkmalpflege Baden-Württemberg im Regierungspräsidium Stuttgart

Abstract

At the beginning of the twentieth century, a number of German timber engineering companies specialised in industrialised timber construction and patented individual systems, using modern iron and steel fasteners. The years between 1910 and 1940 were particularly a time of innovation. Unfortunately, some of the larger companies including Hetzer, Stephan and Tuchscherer did not remain in business after an economic crisis in the 1920s.

This paper summarises the development of German timber construction in this period with a focus on a selected number of companies, before discussing the livestock auction hall in Riedlingen – an example of German timber construction built in 1936, a time when innovative ideas were still very much present. However, the political developments of that time also needs to be put into perspective, when analysing the structure.

The livestock auction hall in Riedlingen is a decorative remnant of German carpentry of the 1930s, and at the same time an anachronistic example. Designed in a traditional architectural style, it combines traditional carpentry and modern joint design within its timber load-bearing structure. Only fragmented details of the architects and engineers responsible for the structure are available, meaning that the true motivation to make use of traditional ideals and designs remains unclear. However, an analysis of the structure also has to consider the political developments of that time.

In conclusion, this paper aims to contribute to a better understanding of the development of industrial timber construction in Germany in the first half of the twentieth century. The roof structure of the Riedlingen livestock auction hall is an interesting example of this development.

Introduction

Building with timber has a very long history in Germany, as elsewhere. Often medieval timber frame houses and shed structures come to mind when talking about historic timber construction in the south-west of Germany.

The state of Baden-Württemberg, located in the south-west of Germany, was founded in 1952 by merging the post-war states of Württemberg-Baden, (South) Baden and Württemberg-Hohenzollern, three original states of the German Empire created by unification in 1871. In this part of Germany, additional boundary conditions apply (building law, local authorities, etc.) due to different social and political developments. However, in terms of building regulations Prussia was something of a role model and other German states generally quickly introduced regulations published by Prussian authorities.

Wood as a natural resource in the south-west of Germany

Historically, the Black Forest offered large resources of oak and fir trees to be used as timber and firewood in the south-west of Germany. In the seventeenth century, a large amount of wood was also sold to the Netherlands to build ships. In fact, the overall demand was so great that by 1800 the Black Forest showed significant signs of overexploitation. In order to convert the fallow lands and to propagate a more sustainable forestry, fast-growing spruce trees were planted.

In the nineteenth century, due to industrialisation and population growth, the need for firewood was not the sole demand. The demand for wood for the production of charcoal, to fire brick-kilns and furnaces also increased greatly. In addition, the use of wood in construction diversified. For example, the so-called Grubenholz (mine wood) was not only used for coal mine pitprops and machinery, but also as the expansion of the railway required large amounts of wooden railway sleepers and timber structures for stations, bridges, etc., at the same time that wood also became a major resource in the production of paper [1].

Challenges of timber construction in the nineteenth century

Around 1910 the annual wood consumption of the German Empire was about 45,000,000 cubic metres, of which 30,000,000 cubic metres were harvested within the German Empire and about 15,000,000 cubic metres imported from different countries [2]. Wood was a natural resource used in different industries, of which building was only one small part [3].

Wood as a naturally grown resource shows a variety of material characteristics, which depend on the species as well as growing conditions in the forest, during harvest and handling. This makes it not only difficult to use as part of an industrialised production process [4], it also requires larger safety factors when calculating timber structure strengths [5].

In Germany, carpentry is still a craft with an institutionalised education based on the condition that a journeyman/-woman is trained by a master carpenter over several years to pass down his/her experience. Besides the varying characteristics of wood as material, this is surely also one reason why timber construction in Germany underwent a rather unspectacular adaptation to the changing conditions brought about by industrialisation. By the end of the nineteenth century the use of timber had been somewhat reduced as iron and reinforced concrete structures became much more common [6].

The non-homogeneous material characteristics of wood that result from its natural growth led to different developments. One was a more organised material testing system. In the late nineteenth century, different material test institutions carried out tests on different types of wood [7]. However, even results from the same tree still varied since climatic conditions during storage or the moisture content of specimens differed somewhat depending on the institution where the test was carried out. In order to overcome the variety of results when comparing, for example, material strength, in 1906 unified testing methods for wood were published by Max Rudeloff (1857–1929), then head of the material testing institution in Berlin. This publication greatly improved the comparability and reliability of test results [8].

Another way of dealing with the material characteristics of wood made use of the benefits brought by developments in the mechanisation and production of artificial adhesives in synthetic resins. For example, Plywood, chipboards and fibreboards had been introduced in German construction by the end of the nineteenth century [9]. All of these products show somewhat balanced material characteristics. Industrialised production, and particularly the use of artificial adhesives, eventually revolutionised the development of wood-based materials (for example glue-laminated timber elements).

A third way to overcome the varying characteristics of the material was the introduction of a system that combined smaller timber parts to form a larger structure by using metal connectors. This idea originated in the sixteenth century. Philibert de l'Orme (1500/14–1570) a French architect well-known for his timber arches made of upright standing and overlapping timber boards connected with nails, was the first to publish this construction method [10]. Later on, this idea taken up by David Gilly (1748–1808), a Prussian master builder, and again by Armand Rose Emy (1771–1851) and his student Paul Joseph Ardant (1800–58) [11, 12]. The idea of combined timber beams was not new to German master carpenters and timber engineers. In fact, around 1900 German architects and engineers published a number of high-quality publications focussing on timber construction including these combined arch structures [13].

Developments in timber construction before 1930

The German Carpenters' Association

It was also during this time that German carpenters decided to centralise and organise their efforts to gain more political and professional influence, to coordinate publications and generally to revive the motivation to build in timber [14]. Thus, in 1903 184 carpenters from all over the German Empire founded the German Carpenters Association in Hannover [15]. One of the main aims was to tackle the competition between timber and the more fabricated and industrialised materials such as iron. There was an especially strong competition with iron, for building structures with large (column free) spans, structures that needed a certain level of design and engineering.

Still, it took some time before things started to change. The Prussian regulations for building construction, published in 1910 [16], included values for allowable stresses for timber that were quite close to the numbers later published in the first timber engineering standards [17].

The shortage of building materials during the First World War led to the construction of a number of wide-span timber structures, such as airship hangars and bridges. These experiences, and the Post-War shortage of building materials, led to a strong revival of timber structures [18].

After 1918 new methods were available, as were elaborate theories of structures and a number of high quality material-testing institutions. Concurrently it was a time of depression and shortage. The First World War had demanded great sacrifices from all sides. In Germany, the period of reconstruction lasted until the 1920s. By then, the German timber construction industry had noticeably developed. Besides traditional carpentry, it now included not only industrialised production factories, but also specialised construction engineering companies. The latter would generally concentrate on roof structures with large spans and an explicit load-bearing structure. They would also use metal fasteners and adhesives rather than mortise and tenon joints.

The Stephan-Bogen

One of the earliest ideas for a new approach to timber construction came from Philipp Stephan (?), a carpenter and architect from Düsseldorf. He introduced his idea for widespan timber arches around 1895 [19]. A *Stephan-Bogen* is a combination of upright standing boards that form a curved lattice truss. (Fig. 1) One of his earliest patents (issued in Great Britain), from 1903 describes the *Stephan-Bogen* as follows: "This invention relates to a method of constructing trussed arches or arches girders with large span for roofs and the like. ... these constructions are exceedingly strong and always completely retain their shape ... twisting or warping is impossible" [20].

The Hetzer-System

Also around 1900, Otto Hetzer (1846-1911) started to work on his construction method. In 1906, he issued a patent for "Composite Wooden Structural Elements applicable for Roofs, Barns, Ladders, Lattice Work, Furniture and other Structures" [21], which was the basis for his later success [22, 23]. Hetzer was not the first to combine timber elements by using adhesives. In fact, Benjamin Green presented his designs for laminated timber roofs to the British Institution of Civil Engineers as ago as 1846. The oldest known structure is the Holy Trinity Church in Cambo, Northumberland, England, built in 1840. It has a span of 9 metres (29 feet) [24, 25]. Nonetheless, it seems that Hetzer was the first to present a practicable, standardised production process and applicable solutions for larger dimensions. (Fig 2)

The Livestock Auction Hall in Riedlingen – Regional Timber Construction in the 1930s in the South-West of Germany

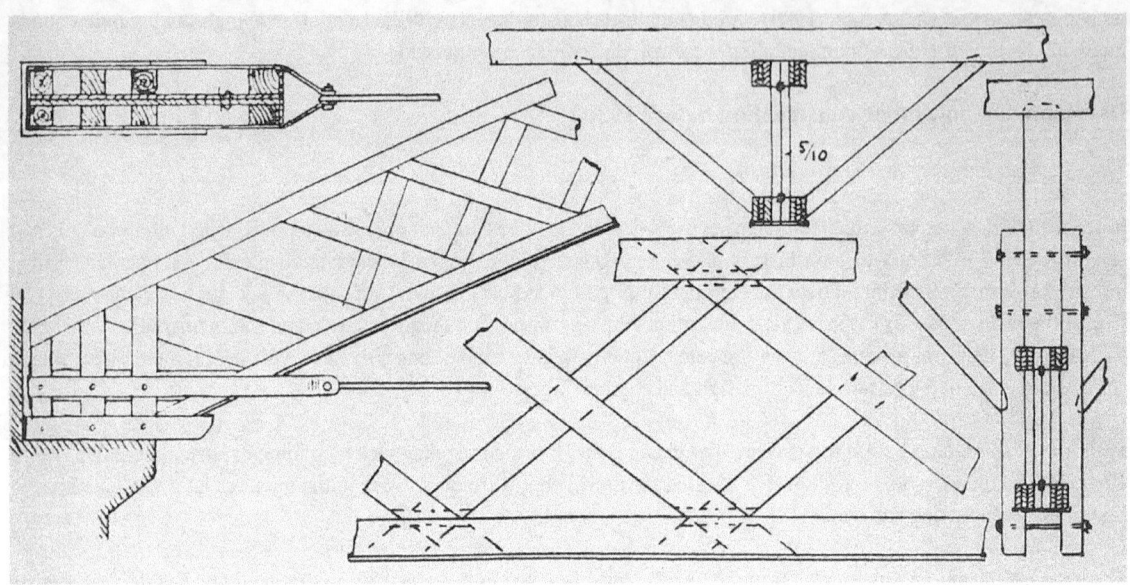

Figure 1: Details of the Stephan-Bogen. Drawing: Nenning, August: Moderne Holzbauweisen. München: Max Steinebach, 1921, p. 11.

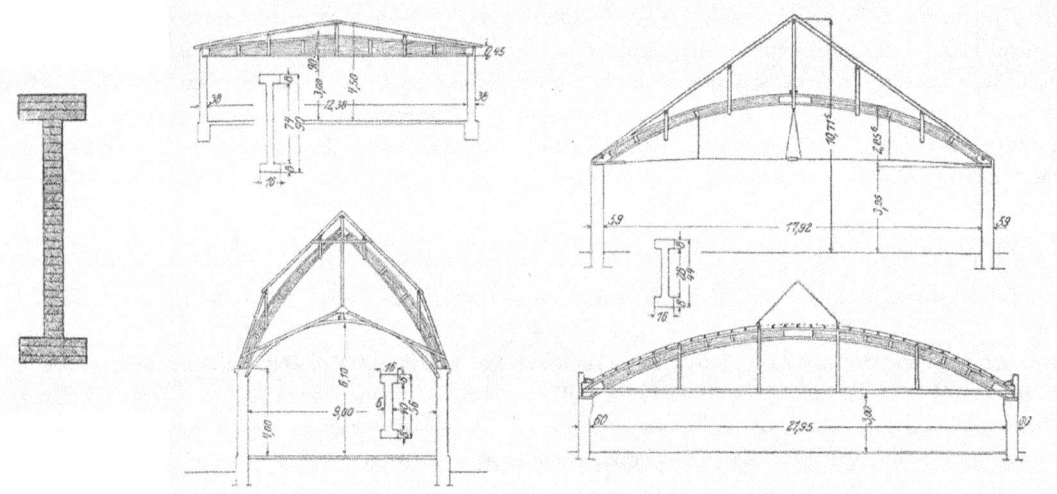

Figure 2: The Hetzer-System. On the left a typical cross section with glue laminated boards and on the right different applications as girder. Drawing: Kersten, Carl: Freitragende Holzbauten. Berlin: Springer, p. 69.

Sabine Kuban

The Meltzer-System

By 1914, another way to overcome the main problem: how to properly join timber elements without significantly minimising the cross-section – that is providing enough material to transmit compressive and tensile forces, was available in German timber construction. This method was invented by Paul Meltzer (1869–1953) a German engineer living in Darmstadt. He used timber boards to build larger structures by joining them with aglets, thus creating large lattice frames. (Fig. 3)

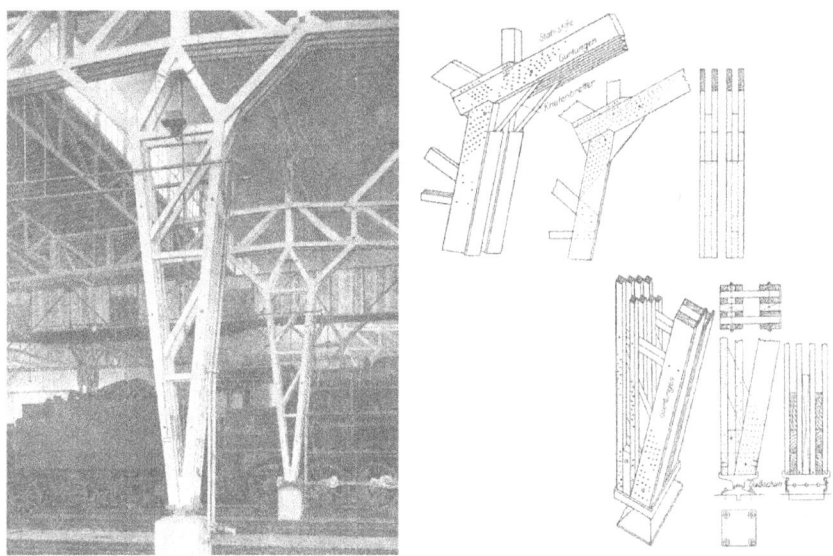

Figure 3: Details of the Meltzer-System, railway engine shed in Kornwestheim, built in 1916. Collage: Kersten, Carl: Freitragende Holzbauten. Berlin: Springer, p. 98–99.

Originally, this construction was used to cover large spans (for example, for airship hangars), but as it was very adaptable, it was also used to build towers and even small family homes. (Fig. 4)

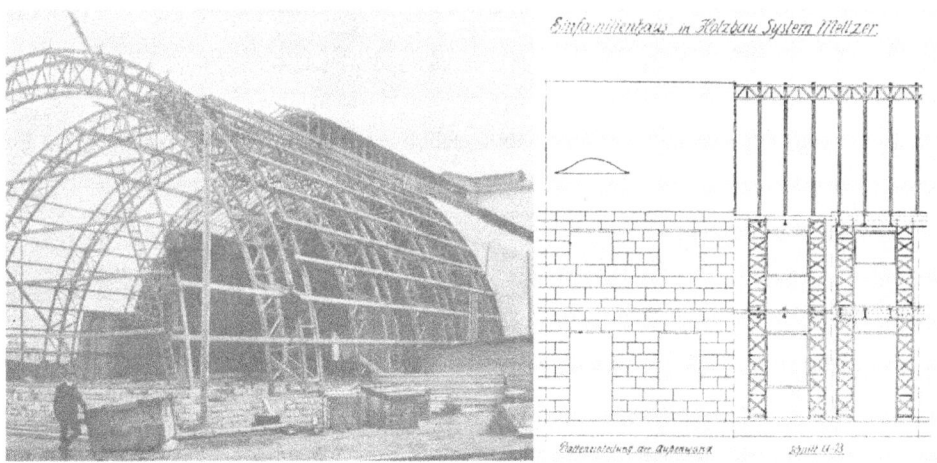

Figure 4: The Meltzer-System on the left covering a span of 27.5 metres, right as part of a family house. Collage: Zipkes, Simon: Holzbauweise System Meltzer. In: Deutsche Bauzeitung 1914; Nenning, August: Moderne Holzbauweisen. München: Max Steinebach, 1921, p. 41.

The Livestock Auction Hall in Riedlingen – Regional Timber Construction in the 1930s in the South-West of Germany

Cabröl and Greim metal fasteners

The years between 1910 and 1940 were a time of innovation in German timber engineering [26], especially in the construction of lattice trusses and frame structures, which benefited from developments in structural calculation and metal fasteners [27].

As for metal connectors, the company C. Brösel (Kassel) patented a pipe-shaped dowel and used this as a specific element within their Cabröl-System [28], whereas the Greim company (Berlin) worked with a claw fastener, somewhat similar to *Bulldog* fasteners that are still used today. (Fig. 5)

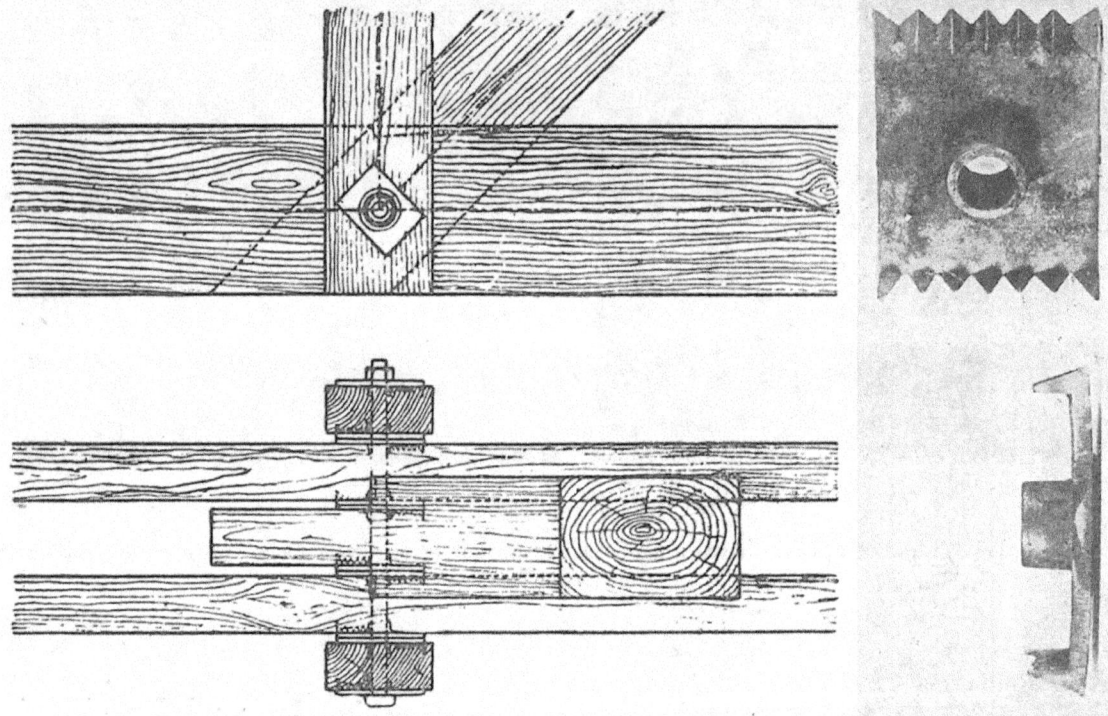

Figure 5: Details of the claw fastener by Greim. Collage: Kersten, Carl: Freitragende Holzbauten. Berlin: Springer, p. 178.

The Tuchscherer company

The construction company Karl Tuchscherer AG started in Breslau, its early repertoire including curved parabolic trusses and two-hinged arches. From 1919 onwards, their company's name stood for a specific type of joint. Based on a patent developed by then chief engineer Samuel Voss, Tuchscherer used round dowels or ring connectors positioned according to structural calculations. The transmission of forces was much more effective – loads could increase by 1.5 to 1.75 and the typical shrinkage of wood had fewer effects on joints [29].

The Karl Kübler AG

Around 1918/19 another company introduced a different kind of ring connector. Based on an idea of Alfred Jackson, then chief engineer at Karl Kübler AG (Stuttgart), this dowel had a double-cone shape and was made of hard wood, cast iron, iron or steel. The transmission of forces required a combination of dowels and a double-ended stud. (Fig. 6)

 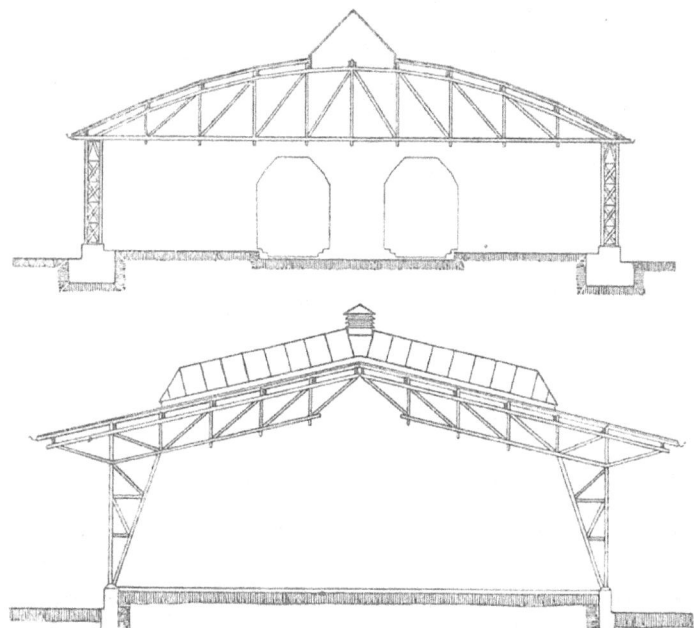

Figure 6: On the left details of the double-cone shaped dowels and the joints, on the right shed structures with a span of about 22 metres using the Kübler-System. Collage: Kersten, Carl: Freitragende Holzbauten. Berlin: Springer, p. 123, 129.

Companies such as Sommerfeld (Berlin) or Christoph & Unmack (Niesky) are also known to have realised large structures in timber [30]. In general, all of these companies introduced new design principles based on an industrialised production process and using standardised prefabricated timber elements. As a result of a national economic crisis in 1926, some of these companies (including Hetzer, Stephan and Tuchscherer) had to terminate their business.

The livestock auction hall in Riedlingen

Riedlingen is a small country town located in the south-west of Baden-Württemberg, halfway between Stuttgart and Lake Constance. The town is situated on the Danube River, with the historic town centre on its north-western shore. This part of town has a long history going back to 835AD. The town features a grid layout of streets orientated to a market square and is enclosed by fortifications. In 1994 a large part of the historic town centre was listed as a cultural monument [31].

Between 1291 and 1806, Riedlingen belonged to the Austrian Habsburg dynasty. During that time, the town, including the number of inhabitants, changed only very moderately. In 1852 around 1900 people lived in Riedlingen. In 1806 Riedlingen became part of the Kingdom of Württemberg and in 1870 the town was connected with the railway line from Munich to Freiburg im Breisgau. These developments improved the economy, and by 1933 the number of inhabitants had grown to 2500 [32].

The Livestock Auction Hall in Riedlingen – Regional Timber Construction in the 1930s in the South-West of Germany

A large number of guest- and roadhouses still indicated the importance of Riedlingen as a market town. This included regular markets for livestock even in the early twentieth century [33]. Besides wheat growing and dairy farming, the Riedlingen area was known for breeding Simmental cattle, horses and pigs.

After the international financial crisis in 1929, the German economy eventually recovered following a recovery of prices and a large economic stimulus programme introduced by the Nazi regime in 1936. At the same time, new laws and regulations governing the examinations for breed certification were introduced, which required new market conditions.

Local breeding associations had frequently asked the town council in Riedlingen to provide adequate market buildings to present their livestock and to hold markets. In October 1936, with the new regulations in mind the town council decided to support the idea of a large showroom and auction hall, not only for sale of breeding animals but also for livestock in general. It assigned the local building authority to carry out the design and to take care of the management of the construction [34]. The location of the planned auction hall along with a stable and administrative building part is outside the historic town centre on the south-eastern shore of the Danube River, next to the town's slaughterhouse and a large gym (built in 1884). The administrative building part with the stables, built at the same time as the auction hall, is a one-story timber-frame structure with a gabled roof.

The design team

In November 1936, the town council initiated a committee that included the town master builder "Maier" and the council master builder "Reck" [35]. In November, the architect Dr. Ernst Schwaderer (1899-1944) from Stuttgart additionally became a member of the design committee. Schwaderer had been involved in previous building projects carried out by the town council. For the auction hall, he apparently gave very good instructions, especially on the urban design of the overall layout, and showed a way forward that had significant advantages to what had been planned [36].

It is not clear how detailed Schwaderer's input into the design of the new auction hall really was. However, his previous work included a project, *Haus Nr. 5* within the *Kochenhof Siedlung* (Stuttgart), a traditionalist counterpart to the famous *Weißenhof Siedlung*.

In 1933, the *Kochenhof Siedlung,* coordinated by lead architect Paul Schmitthenner (1884-1972), included model family homes made of timber and aimed to contribute to an upswing in timber construction and to convince building professionals of the economic efficiency and durability of timber buildings. Schmitthenner emphasized that any further development of timber construction technology must be based on traditional experience.

Another of Schwaderer's projects was the *Wolfsbuschschule*, a school complex in Stuttgart-Weilimdorf built in 1936. Schwaderer, at that time an NSDAP city councillor and state director of the Reich Chamber of Fine Arts in Württemberg, was a very influential person in the state's cultural politics. With the *Wolfsbuchschule* he designed a model school, which later was published as an ideal school building type. The building still shows a high level of traditional craftsmanship [37].

The Building Design

The design process in Riedlingen was comparatively quick. Just one year after it was agreed to actually build an auction hall, it was opened to the public in November 1937. The architecture embodies a conservative style. It features a conventional hipped roof and dormer windows on the long sides of the roof, of which only the ones facing north-east are preserved. The actual building is made of a reinforced concrete skeleton frame filled with masonry and a circumferential running window band to provide light. The reinforced concrete columns are visible from the outside and the walls on the inside are covered with plaster. (Fig. 7)

Figure 7: The auction hall in Riedlingen from the outside, north-eastern façade. Photo: Sabine Kuban LAD, 2020.

The stands for spectators and auctioneers have been preserved unchanged and thus convey a vivid picture of traditional livestock shows and auctions. Originally, the timber roof structure was visible, but since 1975 a ceiling made of pressboard and insulation panels has covered the overhead view. (Fig. 8)

Figure 8: Interior of the auction hall in 2020. Photo: David Grüner, Andreas Stiene LAD 2020.

The Livestock Auction Hall in Riedlingen – Regional Timber Construction in the 1930s in the South-West of Germany

The original design drawing showed a tilted beam, probably to enhance the height of the room. The latest investigation showed that the realised roof structure differs from the original design. (Fig. 9)

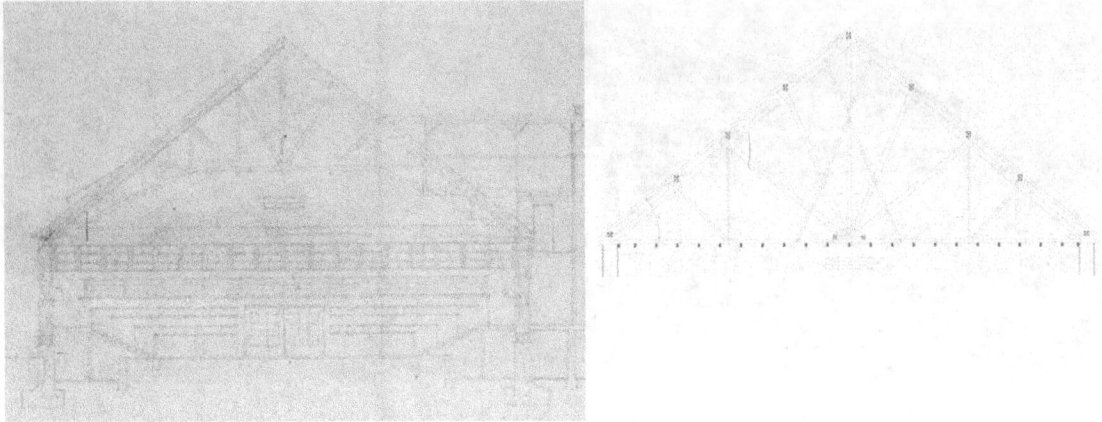

Figure 9: Comparison of the roof structure: left a historical design drawing and on the right, the as built design. Drawing: Town Archive Riedlingen 1936; CAD drawing: David Grüner LAD 2020.

Five large triangular lattice girders made of softwood (probably fir) span about 22 metres. (Fig. 9) The distance between the trusses is 5 metres and each truss is numbered consecutively, starting in the north. The construction of each truss features a central fan-like bundle of beams. Each beam has a cross-section of 20 x 20 centimetres. The vertical beam in the centre acts as a king post. Two smaller diagonal elements pointing upward connect the king post with the rafters, and two diagonal elements pointing downwards connect to the tie beam. The diagonals are made of two boards (2 x 12 x 3 centimetres) each. Next to the king post, four inclined beams act as struts and support the principal rafter (i.e. the purlins and the common rafters). Five purlins sit on the principal rafter on a separate timber element that connects to the rafter with two stud bolts. Next to this structure, the purlins sit levelled on the principal rafter, making it easier to support the common rafters. Underneath the middle purlin an additional tension element, an iron bar with a cross-section of 2 centimetres, connects the rafter with the tie beam. From here, an additional strut connects the tie beam with the rafter. The outmost vertical element connecting the rafter and the tie beam is made of two boards, similar to the ones connecting to the king post.

The tie beam is made of two individual beams that meet underneath the king post. Here, level with the tie beam, a clamp connection provides enough stability for the joint. (Fig 11) At the end of each tie beam, above the walls, an additional timber element (probably oak) again acts as support for the rafters. The foot of the rafter connects to it with a step joint and a stud bolt. The support timber then connects to the tie beam via a scarf joint with several knees.

Almost all wooden structural elements show tool marks, by which the construction process is still readable. (Fig. 10)

Figure 10: The building site of the Riedlingen livestock auction hall in 1937. Photo: Winfried Aßfalg, Riedlingen

Figure 11: Details of the central joint within the roof structure of the Riedlingen auction hall. Photo: David Grüner, Andreas Stiene LAD 2020; CAD drawing: David Grüner LAD 2020.

Unfortunately, as historical information is scarce, it remains unclear whether any structural calculation was carried out. However, it is clear that the *Reichsarbeitsdienst* carried out the construction under the supervision of the local building authority [38].

From 1935 onwards, young men between 18 and 25 were obliged to attend fatigue duty for six months to carry out unpaid work. The *Reichsarbeitsdienst* affiliated to the Ministry of Interior was part of a nationwide education programme [39].

Based on this information, one can assume that some of the workers were untrained and obviously, the level of mechanisation was rather low. (Fig. 10) It seems that the timber was prepared and cut before transportation to the building site. Here the erection of the actual truss was probably from a platform within the building and effected by using a hoist and winches.

Nevertheless, as the truss was designed to be visible from underneath, the quality of the joints is remarkable. The construction accurately combines different techniques. For example, traditional step joints are complemented with a number of metal fasteners and additionally include threaded bars as well as nails and bolts. (Fig. 11)

Conclusion

Before 1920, a number of innovative approaches to spanning a moderate distance of about 22 metres with timber were published in Germany. Specialised companies also had developed loadbearing structures (beams, lattice girders etc.) as well as metal fasteners that signify a more industrialised timber construction. Prefabrication, as with glue-laminated elements by Hetzer, was also part of that development.

However, everyday construction took time to adapt to these developments. With the livestock auction hall in Riedlingen an example of timber construction in the 1930s is preserved. Its design and building process took place within the limits of a small country town, changed ideology and politics as well as restricted finances and resources. The conservative architectural style seen from the outside finds it equivalent on the inside. It represents an interesting variant within roof truss structures that evidently does not acknowledge ideas popular about ten years before its construction. In fact, it is a rather anachronistic example. For example, the prefabrication was on a smaller scale here compared to the Meltzer System. It includes large timber elements and fasteners that were almost prepared as an assembly kit. The combination of traditional joints with metal fasteners seems simple and easy to handle. Nevertheless, the details of the structure are of good quality and very accurately done. Thus, the auction hall's timber roof structure is still an impressive and decorative remnant of carpentry from the 1930s. Additionally, it seems that compared to other building projects undertaken by the *Reichsarbeitsdienst*, it is one of only a few buildings of that size, but this idea needs further research.

Acknowledgements

I would like to thank my colleague Sabine Kraume-Probst for her initial research on the buildings history, as well as my colleagues Andreas Stiene and David Grüner for providing the photographs and the CAD drawing.

References

[1] Max Scheifele, *Als die Wälder auf Reisen gingen. Wald, Holz, Flößerei in der Wirtschaftsgeschichte des Enz-Nagold-Gebiets*. Karlsruhe: Braun, 1996, p. 281.
[2] S. Michalski, Die wirtschaftliche Lage des Holzmarktes. in Carl Kersten (Ed.) *Freitragende Holzbauten*. Berlin: Springer, 1921, S. 2.
[3] Carl Kersten (Ed.), *Freitragende Holzbauten*. Berlin: Springer, 1921.
[4] Joachim Radkau; Ingrid Schäfer: *Holz. Ein Naturstoff in der Technikgeschichte*. Orig.-Ausg. Reinbek bei Hamburg: Rowohlt, 1987, p. 242.
[5] Kersten, (note 3), p. 26.
[6] Mathias Seraphin, Zur Entstehung des Ingenieurholzbaus. (Ph.D. Thesis Technische Universität München, München. Fakultät für Architektur / Lehrstuhl für Tragwerksplanung, 2003).
[7] Wolfgang Rug, '100 Jahre Forschung für den Holzbau. Die Erforschung der Grundlagen/Entwicklung der Holzbauforschung/Berechnungsvorschriften' in *Bauen mit Holz* 50 (4), 2003, p. 50.
[8] Kersten, (note 3), p. 26.

[9] Radkau; Schäfer, (note 4), pp. 233–235.

[10] Philibert de L'Orme, *Nouvelles inventions pour bien bastir et à petits fraiz, trouvées n'a guères par Philibert de l'Orme. Lyonnois, architecte, conseiller & aulmonier ordinare du feu* Roy Henry & abbé de S. Eloy lez Noyon. Paris: De l'imprimerie de Frederic Morel, 1561. Available online: www.cesr.univ-tours.fr/architectura/Traite/liste.asp.

[11] David Gilly, *Ueber Erfindung, Construction und Vortheile der Bohlen-Dächer: mit besonderer Rücksicht auf die Urschrift ihres Erfinders*. Berlin: Vieweg, 1797. Available online: https://www.digitale-sammlungen.de/de/view/bsb10048356?page=5;.

[12] Paul Joseph Ardant, *Theoretisch-praktische Abhandlung über Anordnung und Construction der Sprengwerke von grosser Spannweite*. Hannover: Hahn, 1847.

[13] Franz Stade, *Die Holzkonstruktionen*. Reprint of 1904. Holzminden: Repr.-Verl. Leipzig, 2002, p. 38ff. For additional publications see the list in Klaus Erler, *Kuppeln und Bogendächer aus Holz. Von arabischen Kuppeln bis zum Zollinger-Dach*. Stuttgart: Fraunhofer IRB-Verl, 2003, p. 17.

[14] Fördergesellschaft Holzbau und Ausbau mbH (Ed.), *100 Jahre Bund Deutscher Zimmermeister. 100 Jahre Verband, Holzbau, Holzbauforschung ; 1903 - 2003*. In cooperation with Annette Ciré, Peter Kuhweide and Helmhard Neuenhagen. Bund Deutscher Zimmermeister; Zentralverband Deutsches Baugewerbe. 1st edition. Karlsruhe: Bruderverlag, 2003, p.17.

[15] Ibid.

[16] 'Minister der öffentlichen Arbeiten. Runderlaß betreffend die Bestimmungen über die bei Hochbauten anzunehmenden Belastungen und die Beanspruchungen der Baustoffe sowie Berechnungsgrundlagen für die statische Untersuchung von Hochbauten' in *Zentralblatt der Bauverwaltung* 30 (16), 1910, pp. 101–110.

[17] See Erler, (note 12), p. 253. A first draft of the DIN-1052 was published in 1921. However, it was only in 1933 that the DIN 1052 was officially introduced in German construction.

[18] Kersten, (note 3).

[19] o.A. 'Holz-Fachwerksbogen von Ph. Stephan in Düsseldorf' in *Deutsche Bauzeitung* 36 (30), 1902, p. 195. Stephan is known to be one of the pioneers for combined timber structures, see also Erler, (note 12), p. 224.

[20] Philipp Stephan 'Improvements in the Construction of Arches with Considerable Span for Roofs and the like' patent application by Stephan, Philipp am 04.12.1903. Application no.: 26600, publication no.: GB000190326600A.

[21] Carl Friedrich Otto Hetzer, 'Improvements in Composite Wooden Structural Elements applicable for Roofs, Barns, Ladders, Lattice Work, Furniture and other Structures', patent application through Jensen & Son Charted Patent Agents am 18.09.1906. Application no.: 20,684. Publication no.: 20,684.

[22] Wolfgang Rug 'Innovationen im Holzbau - Die Hetzerbauweise' in Die Bautechnik 71 (4), 1994, pp. 213–219;

[23] Wolfgang Rug, 'Innovationen im Holzbau - Die Hetzerbauweise' in Die Bautechnik 72 (4), pp. 231–241.

[24] Paul W.R. Bell, '19th CENTURY LAMINATED TIMBER ROOFS IN ENGLAND' in: Brian Bowen, Donald Friedman, Thomas Leslie und John Ochsendorf (Eds.), *Proceedings of the Fifth International Congress on Construction History*. June 2015, Chicago, Illinois. Chicago, IL: Construction History Society of America, 2015, pp. 179–186.

[25] Paul W.R. Bell, 'The work and professional status of John (1787–1852) and Benjamin Green (1813–58), architects and engineers' in Ine Wouters, Stephanie van de Voorde, Inge Bertels, Bernard Espion, Krista de Jonge und Denis Zastavni (Eds.), *Building Knowledge, Constructing Histories. Proceedings of the sixth International Congress on Construction History* (6ICCH), Brussels, Belgium, 9-13 July 2018. 2nd Vol. Brussels: Taylor & Francis Group, 2018, pp. 357–364.

[26] Erler, (note 12), p. 253.

[27] Rug, (note 21), p. 233.

[28] Kersten, (note 3), p. 143.

[29] Fritz-Ulrich Buchmann 'Carl Tuchscherer: 1911–1934. An Innovative German Timber Construction Company. in Bowen et al, proceedings (note 23) pp. 247–254.

[30] Kersten, (note 3); Rug (note 21); Seraphin (note 6); for the history of Christoph & Unmack see also Museum Niesky Konrad-Wachsmann-Haus (Ed.) 'Holzbauten der Moderne. Die Entwicklung des industriellen Holzbaus [Dauerausstellung. Unter Mitarbeit von Claudia Wieltsch und Eva-Maria Bergmann' Sandstein Verlag, 2015.

The Livestock Auction Hall in Riedlingen – Regional Timber Construction in the 1930s in the South-West of Germany

[31] Sabine Kraume-Probst, 'Riedlingen. Die Altstadt als Denkmal' in *Nachrichtenblatt der Landesdenkmalpflege Baden-Württemberg* 24 (1), 1995, pp. 9–14.
[32] https://www.leograph-bw.de/public/doGraph.php?ONDB_ID=17487&T=V052&doTable (11.02.2022)
[33] Kraume-Probst, (note 28), p. 13.
[34] Stadtgemeinde Riedlingen town archive, minutes of the town council meetings. 20.11.1936. Stadtarchiv.
[35] ibid, p. 259.
[36] ibid, p. 275.
[37] Kerstin Renz, *Schule als Denkmal. Stuttgarter Porträt : Begleitbroschüre zur Ausstellung.* Esslingen am Neckar: Landesamt für Denkmalpflege im Regierungspräsidium Stuttgart, 2014, p. 30.
[38] Winfried Aßfalg, *Ziegelhütte – Reichsarbeitsdienstlager – Studienheim*, Riedlingen: Altertumsverein, 2013.
[39] https://www.dhm.de/lemo/kapitel/ns-regime/ns-organisationen/reichsarbeitsdienst-rad.html (13.2.2022).

Technical manuals in the years of Reconstruction after World War II in Italy: Mario Ridolfi and the "Manuale dell'Architetto"

Roberta Lucente, Giuseppe Canestrino
Department of Civil Engineering, University of Calabria, Rende, Italy

Abstract

The debate on the role of construction techniques in post-World War II Reconstruction in Italy was articulated between advanced positions proposing the renewal and industrialization of building processes and positions closer to more settled, and perhaps traditional, construction techniques. The latter positions, widespread in the area of Rome, proposed the creation of a typology of constructional elements to be disseminated through manuals, such as the 1946 "*Manuale dell'Architetto*" with Mario Ridolfi as editor-in-chief. This paper investigates the contribution provided by this manual to the post-war reconstruction effort and to Italian architectural design culture, questioning how the creation of the typology conveyed in the manual was able to strengthen and spread specific construction techniques that, eventually, led to a recognizable architectural canon diffused throughout the entire national territory.

Introduction

The post-World War II period in Italy is remembered as "La Ricostruzione", a significant word that declares what was "the central problem of all national activities" [1] at that time and that reveals the deep involvement of architects and engineers in the related intensive debate. It led to the foundation of magazines, such as *Metron* and *Cantieri*, and of associations such as the *Movimento Studi per l'Architettura* (MSA) in 1944 in the Milan area and the *Associazione per l'Architettura Organica* (APAO) in 1945 in Rome.

This debate was characterized by a general delay in industrialization, by the inability of politics to correct this drift and by the role claimed by private entrepreneurship [2]. One of the main issues in this debate was a recognized need to reorganize and redefine the technical standards that were supposed to regulate and guide the Reconstruction. The Milan area saw a possible solution to the housing problem in the industrialization of the construction processes, while the Rome area manifested a will to recover a constructive tradition that was never forgotten, before or during the years of fascism. Technical manuals played a significant role in this debate and they could be closer to the Milan area, such as "*Il problema sociale costruttivo ed economico dell'abitazione*" [3] written by Irenio Diotallevi and Franco Marescotti, or closer to the Rome area, such as "*Manuale dell'architetto*" [4] edited by the Consiglio Nazionale delle Ricerche (CNR), United States Information Agency (USIS) and Mario Ridolfi as editor-in-chief. The debate took place with various controversies, even with positions that today appear as harsh, as in Manfredo Tafuri's [5] critics who denigrated Ridolfi's manual to an "abacus of the 'small technique'" and Marescotti and Diotallevi's manual as mere "ideological populism". In response to these criticisms, Bruno Zevi [6], involved in the development of the *Manuale dell'Architetto*, accused Tafuri of "critical nihilism".

Two technical manuals in the period of Italian reconstruction

These two manuals had to respond to the need for new technical sources given the inadequacy of existing manuals to be used in the Reconstruction, such as that of Daniele Donghi [7]. Also, a translation for the widespread *Bauentwurfslehre* by Ernst Neufert was missing [8].

Technical manuals in the years of Reconstruction after World War II in Italy: Mario Ridolfi and the "Manuale dell'Architetto".

The manual by Diotallevi and Marescotti was based on the social dimension behind construction and on the awareness felt in the Milan area of the significant number of houses missing in the aftermath of World War II. Therefore, it faced the problem of the house first with a typological codification subsequently completed by a technological codification, thinking in terms of seriality and types, both functional and constructive. This manual was edited in large landscape plates (35.5 x 24.5 cm) and it was conceived as a useful tool to be sold in instalments, which could be increased or updated over time.

The idea of an "open" tool also inspired the *Manuale dell'Architetto,* coordinated by Mario Ridolfi, which consisted of 264 portait plates equipped with punched holes to be collected in a normal ring binder. This manual was different from that of Diotallevi and Marescotti since it ignored typological themes and was focused on the study and illustration of construction elements. The social dimension was, however, taken into account throgiuh the process of selecting and representational techniques, materials, and construction components as they were closely reflected the actual practices of the construction sector in Italy at the time. This state-wide vision of the construction relected to the ideas behind *INA casa* [9], the Italian State's public residential construction program

Ridolfi's contribution to the Reconstruction, between tradition and industrialization.

Mario Ridolfi (1904-1984) was central figure as his way of dealing with architectural design was characterized by a close understanding of construction which was seen as one possible source design ideas. His role in the Reconstruction debate is also interesting and multifaceted in relation to his personal history. Ridolfi had been a rationalist in the last years of fascism when he designed the memorable *Palazzo delle Poste* in Piazza Bologna (Fig.2). Then he joined the Communist Party after the war and was also elected municipal councillor in Terni. He directed *Metron* together with Cesare Ligini and was among the first members of APAO. In those years he supported the attention to the psychological dimension of architecture, drawn from Northern European neo-empiricism, which he knew thanks to his subscription to *Byggmasteren* journal, as testified by his son Massimo [10]. Furthermore, for similar reasons, he has also been considered one of the main protagonists of the so-called *Neorealism* in architecture.

 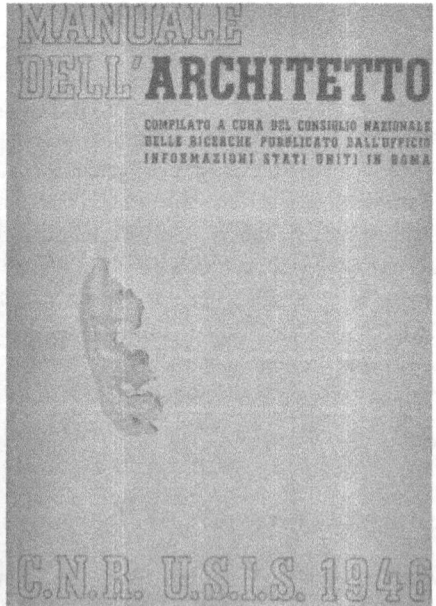

Figure 1: Covers of Il problema sociale costruttivo ed economico dell'abitazione (1948) and Manuale dell'Architetto (1946).

Figure 2: Palazzo delle Poste in Piazza Bologna, Rome. Mario Ridolfi, 1933-1935. Photo: Wikimedia Commons.

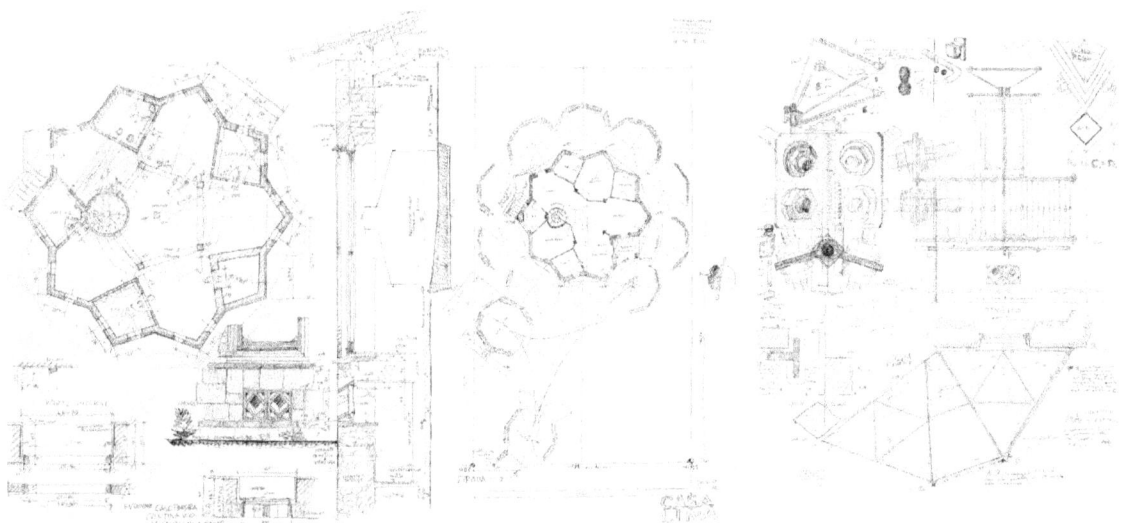

Figure 3: Casa Lina a Marmore, Terni. Mario Ridolfi, 1964-1967. Fondo Mario Ridolfi [15].

Ridolfi started his involvement in the Reconstruction architectural debate by taking a firm stance in favour of the industrialization of building construction in the first *Convegno Nazionale per la Ricostruzione Edilizia* [11] as he felt the recovery and the general housing problem were paramount. In the early 1940s, he also declared an interest in unification and normalization, as Giò Ponti [12] noted in an article dedicated to the "style" of Mario Ridolfi.

Technical manuals in the years of Reconstruction after World War II in Italy: Mario Ridolfi and the "Manuale dell'Architetto".

Ridolfi's interests were mainly aimed at the normalization and standardization of building components and were driven by the desire for meticulous control of construction as he traced in it the ability of the designer and the value of the project. This explains how the endorsement of industrialization can be reconciled with the craftsmanship that is recognizable in his work and which is documented by his numerous and splendidly detailed drawings, as in the subsequent season "*Ciclo delle Marmore*" (Fig. 3) [13] that bring together his hand drawings for private clients in the city of Terni. This also justifies the apparent contradiction of the declarations of the 1940s when, in a 1983 interview, Ridolfi himself declared "I tremble when I think of prefabrication, of the lack of creativity with which it is used, of building regulations" [14].

Returning to the years in which the manual was written, Ridolfi had already claimed to have produced "an appreciable study in a sector where he was particularly well prepared, that of doors and windows and their connected parts such as walls, coatings, glass and wood"[16]. On standardization, he also stated that when it is "done on a scientific basis it allows the maximum economy of use of raw materials minimizing wastes and it gives a conventional meter for measuring the construction parts to be built" [17].

Notes on the content of the *Manuale dell'Architetto*

The Manuale dell'Architetto, as already mentioned, was edited by CNR and USIS with the aid of Ridolfi as editor-in-chief together with Cino Calcaprina, Aldo Cardello and Mario Fiorentino. The organizing committee consisted of Gustavo Colonnetti (president), Biagio Bongioannini, Pier Luigi Nervi, Bruno Zevi and again Ridolfi (Fig. 4), and some other additional collaborators such as Carlo Cestelli-Guidi and Luigi Piccinato.

Figure 4: The organizing committee behind the Manuale dell'Architetto working on the ferrofinestra drawings. From left to right: Biagio Bongioannini, Mario Ridolfi, Pier Luigi Nervi and Bruno Zevi.

The manual is organized into individual plates and is divided into eight sections: summary of standards and data; urban planning; building materials; structural design; structural elements; finished construction elements; technical systems; and characteristic data and overall dimensions. Within the sections, identified by a capital letter, the individual plates, identified by lowercase letters, are organized into groups, identified with a progressive numbering. This particular organization system may have been chosen not just to produce an easy to consult manual, as stated by Ridolfi [18], nor just to make the manual expandable over time. It may be assumed that the organization system adopted also derived from the need to complete the drafting of the manual in just six months, as required by USIS [19]. Furthermore, its division into single plates, most of which are self-contained, minimized the editing times and aided the division of tasks in a collaborative working group.

From the very first pages, the manual is free from theoretical approaches and, in the first section, proposes a design handbook where technical drafting rules for building and urban design, equivalences between units of measurement, geometric rules, function and mathematical tables can be found.

The next section dedicated to urban planning is very limited as it contains general notions and applications.

The section of building materials is also presented as a small design handbook containing the characteristics of the main building materials available in Italy. There is ready-to-use information on the various cement mixtures, on Italian stones, on the commercial sizes of wood and, finally, data of metal profiles. The next section introduces notions of statics and structural mechanics useful for structural design.

After the first four sections, the structural elements are addressed and they are supposed to be handled by Pier Luigi Nervi. In those sections, various elements are anticipated by suggestions for their dimensioning, design, and structural verification and subsequently their various technological alternatives are illustrated. Foundations, retaining walls, load-bearing masonries, reinforced concrete, and prestressed concrete follow the same scheme. Wood constructions are dealt in a particular way since the manual provides numerous constructive insights while indications for structural design are limited. Only for the balloon frame, which will be discussed later, and slabs are are provided with indications of their dimensions. The section closes by addressing the dimensioning of the most common types of slabs, roofs, and stairs. This section prefers the discussion of common use construction technologies and gives minimumal space for technologies with a higher level of prefabrication that saw a relatively limited use in Italy.

The subsequent technical systems section deals with the issues of sanitary, heating, lighting, water and sewer systems.

The final section provides characteristic data and measurements such as the various equipment of the house, the dimensions of fixed furniture, door and window fixtures. The manual closes by superficially addressing some architectural typologies, such as schools, offices and fields for various sports. The typologies, as well as the different parts of the house, are studied in their dimensional aspects without ever reconstructing their relationship with the entire building.

Purposes of the "finished construction elements" section.

Ridolfi's contribution to the Manual went beyond the traditional responsibilities of an editor-in-chief. Ridolfi, in fact, drew 60 plates out of 264 total [20], dedicating himself in particular to the section "finished construction elements" (Fig.5). The content and the level of depth of this section distinguish the *Manuale dell'Architetto* from other manuals, not just for the particularization of the construction techniques with respect to Italian building practice, but also for the surprising decision to give ample space to traditional and artisanal techniques, despite the USIS hoping for a push towards a general modernization of the construction sector in Italy.

Technical manuals in the years of Reconstruction after World War II in Italy: Mario Ridolfi and the "Manuale dell'Architetto".

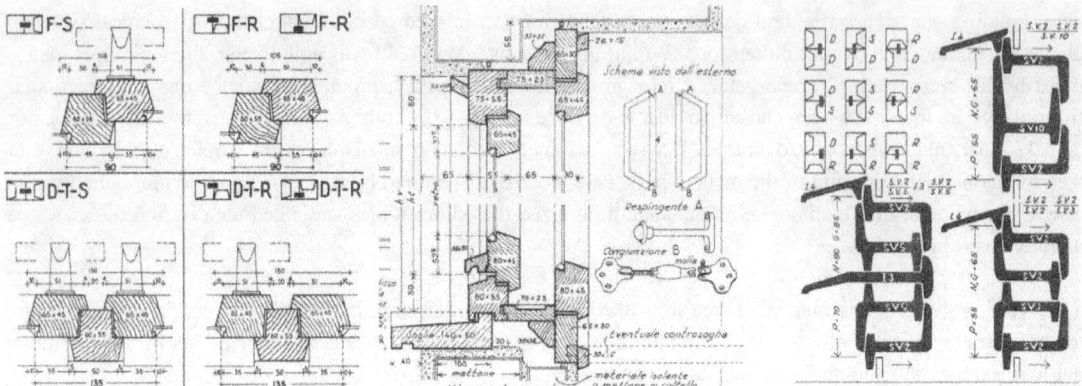

Figure 5: Drawings with the involvement of Mario Ridolfi: Wooden and "ferrofinestra" fixtures. Manuale dell'Architetto.

The criticicism the manual received, which were chiefly focused around tits preceived regressive approach to construction, probably arose from the contents of this section. The harsh accusations that it focused on "small technique", was a "workshop handbook" and "nationalist" [21] made by Tafuri [22] are reflected in the space given to building site, to design precautions able to minimize material waste and to optimization of the construction process. Elements such as vertical and horizontal coatings, waterproofing, fixtures, false ceilings, railings, movable walls are covered in an unusual level of depth for Italian manuals, with scales up to the 1:1 scale being employed to illustrate how to avoiding leakage, incorrect combinations of materials, dust deposits, material waste and other construction errors.

The debt to German manuals

Although the manual is mainly interested in Italian building practice, its editorial choices, from the layout to the arrangement, show international influences. Among these influences were German manuals and the declared link with the USIS. It is possible to trace how Ridolfi became influenced by German manuals to his association with Wolfgang Frankl and the availability in Italy of the German edition of the *Bauentwurfslehre*. Its influence is explicitly stated in the notes and references in the plates of the manual [23]. However, when we make a comparison between the two texts, the absence of a section dedicated to Building Types in the Italian manual is noticeable together with omission of all those German technologies that were not applicable in the Italian context.

A further possible German model behind the Italian manual was Adolf Breymann's *Allgemeine Baukonstruktionslehre*, published in 1884, which Ridolfi [24] had hoped for an update with the respect to novel technologies. The German influence is also confirmed by statements made by Ridolfi and Frankl [25] regarding their use of Alexander Klein's research in their professional activities.

The debt with US manuals

The US influence on the manual can be traced in the relations between USIS and Zevi to whom we owe the credit for creating the editorial opportunity. In this partnership, USIS saw a general improvement of the construction sector in Italy in the approach to standardization and industrialization.

In this regard, the Architectural Graphic Standards (AGS), published in the US in 1932, became as Zevi stated one of the models behind the Italian manual [26]. It is reasonable to assume that the Italian manual derived its ratio between graphic and textual information from the AGS, as well as the layout organized in self-contained plates or pages. When the two manuals are compared we can even see ijnstances of direct copying. This is the case for the plate showing balloon framing (Fig. 6) where the plate in the Italian manual [27] is clearly redrawn from the AGS [28] model despite this not being Italian practice at the time. Because of this divergence in practice, some details are modified such as the foundation which in the plate in the AGS is masonry, while in the Italian manual is shown as either masonry or concrete. Furthermore, the balloon frame in the Italian manual contains several simplifications or omissions from the AGS, such as the absence of diagonal sheathing.

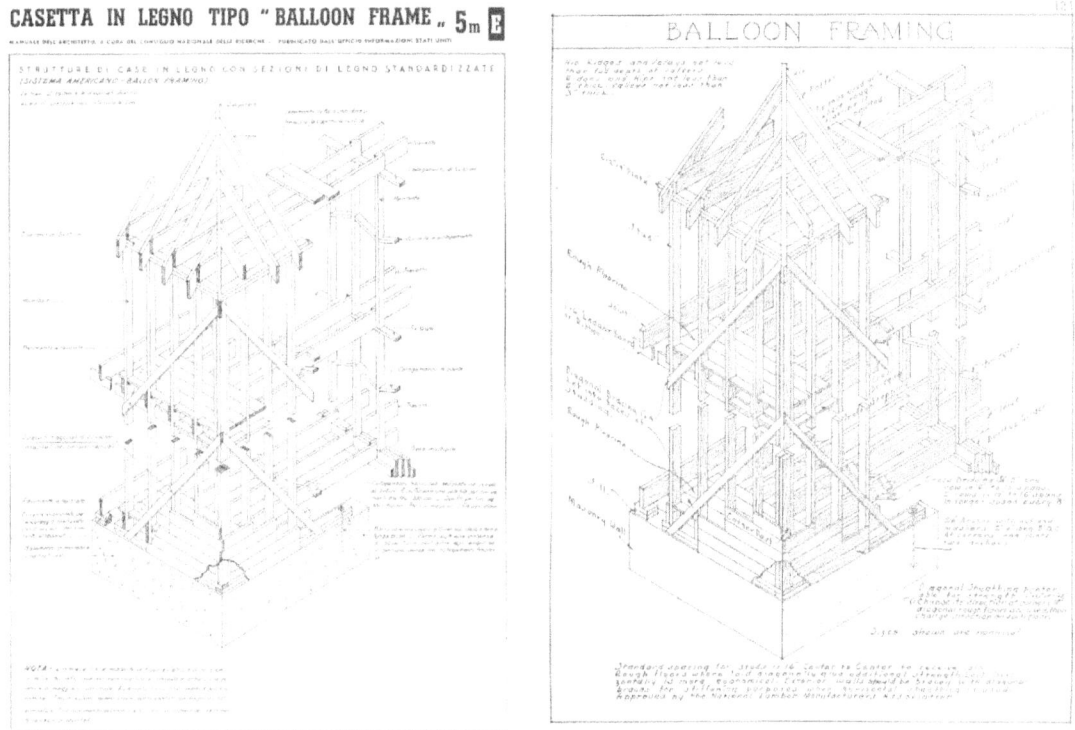

Figure 6: Balloon frame in the Manuale dell'Architetto (left) and in the Architectural Graphics Standard (right).

Aspects of innovation and improvement of design and construction practices

The manual did find space for some references to design and construction methods which were innovative in the Italian context. This included the various plates dedicated to wooden houses which included a "Wachsmann-type wooden house" (Fig. 7)[29], although it is much simplified compared to the experiments of Konrad Wachsmann [30]. A two-floor house made of wooden panels stiffened by metal profiles (Fig. 8) [31]is also proposed and can be traced back to some projects by architect Erik Friberger. These two cases, although they did not fit into the Italian construction tradition, allowed the introduction of themes such as modular designing, the limitation of the number of technical elements, volumetric expansion over time, demolition at the end of the lifecycle of the building and designing with "catalogue" systems.

Technical manuals in the years of Reconstruction after World War II in Italy: Mario Ridolfi and the "Manuale dell'Architetto".

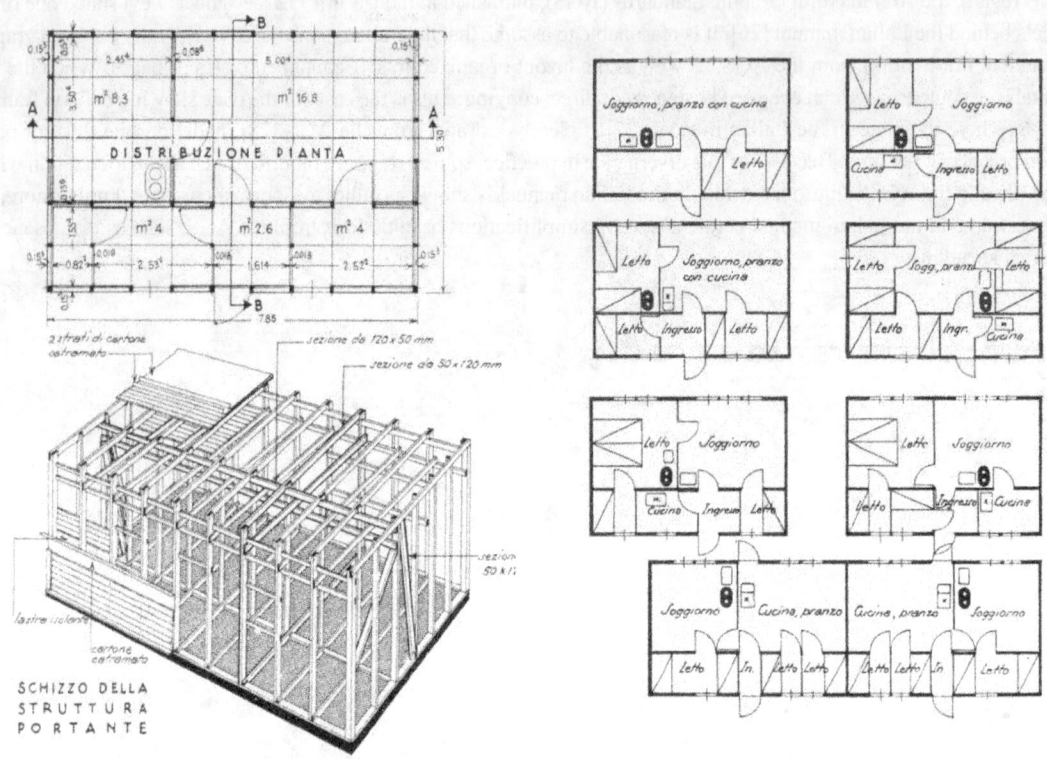

Figure 7: Wachsmann-type wooden House. Manuale dell'Architetto.

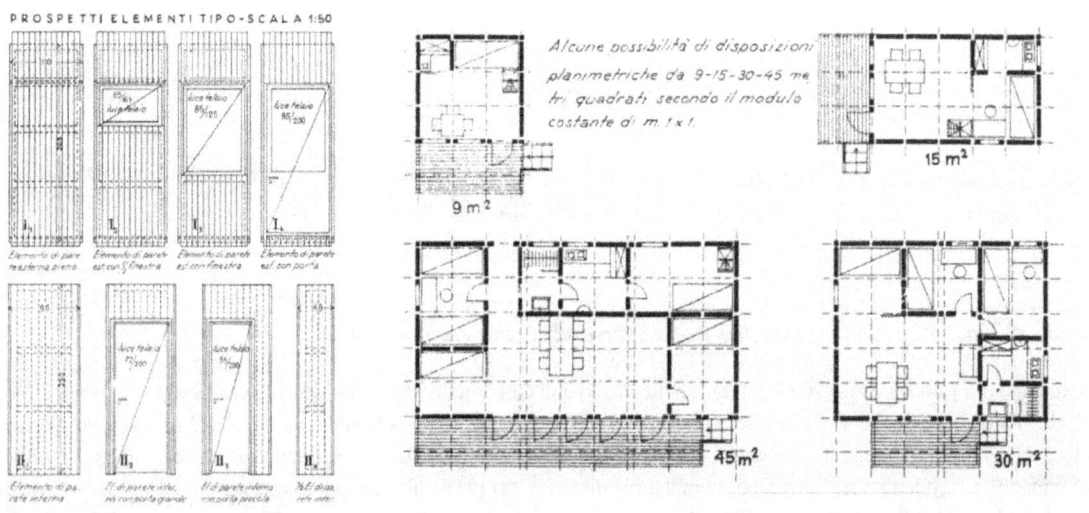

Figure 8: Elevation of prefab load-bearing wooden panels stiffened by metal profiles and plans solutions. Manuale dell'Architetto.

In terms of traditional technologies, the manual offered illustratutions to demonstrate that show the relationship between good construction and good design reflected Ridolfi's principles. This is the case for kitchens and bathrooms where the illustratiosn highlight the imrpotance of designing using tiling modules to minimize waste [32]. Modular designing is also shown as a method of organising the architectural space of an entire apartment. The manual proposes the plan of a *Casa in Linea* [33] (Fig. 9) whose architectural space, as well as construction elements such as internal and external fixtures, walls, stairs and even the furnishings, are linked to elements discussed in other boards of the manual and to the dimension of a chosen module. This showed how it was possible to conceive of an architectural synthesis, optimized with respect to a precise module, starting from the elements of the manual.

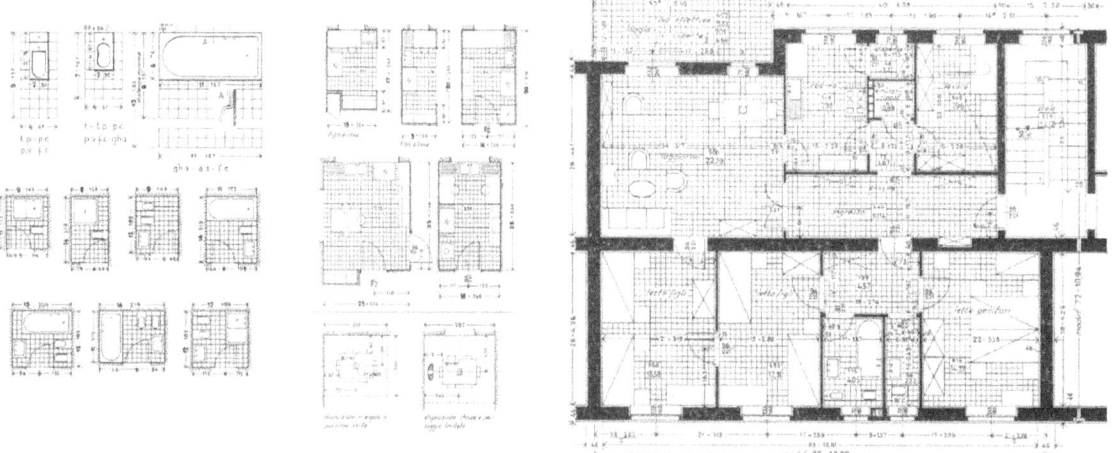

Figure 9: Bathrooms (left) and kitchens (centre) designed with modular dimensions. Modular plan (right) designed with element discussed in the Manuale dell'architetto

The role of construction techniques in the development of an Italian neorealism poetic.

A specific role is played by construction techniques and by the *Manuale dell'Architetto*, in the poetics of the so-called *architectural neorealism*, of which Ridolfi himself was one the absolute protagonists. Critics gave different visions of neorealism in architecture over time that were based on a return to traditional construction techniques and on the use of building elements reminiscent of previous periods of construction history that, all together, constitute the characteristics of the Italian 20th-century building practice. More generally, looking at the Italian construction culture from the beginning of the 20th century until the 1950s, we may assume that it derived from an economic system of small and medium-sized enterprises that were unwilling and unable to adopt large-scale industrial building processes. The construction culture, therefore, was more inclined to develop and disseminate traditional construction methods, with the further attended result of also having a strong visual and expressive impact on architecture so that in the Italian experience of that period techniques, materials, form, and expressiveness would appear at last to be intimately linked together [34].

The *Manuale dell'Architetto* described and handed down this tradition, developed on the basis of what Tafuri called "small technique", whose origins could also be found in the construction details of the "minor" Baroque and of Roman eclecticism of the early 20th century, as suggested by Bruno Reichlin [35].

Technical manuals in the years of Reconstruction after World War II in Italy: Mario Ridolfi and the "Manuale dell'Architetto".

The return to the past and perhaps to vernacular construction, defined in the most derogatory opinions as *strapaese* [36], spread in Italy thanks also to the INA casa program buildings. This diffusion may be traced to another awareness that will underlie the *Manuale dell'Architetto*: the 1949 Fanfani law, that informed the INA Casa program, had among its objectives not just the construction of the houses that people needed but also the creation of jobs in the construction sector. At the bottom of this was the awareness that there were a large number of unskilled workers needing to be trained. In fact, the manual was distributed by USIS free of charge to 250,000 architects, engineers, surveyors and building experts.

This recognized building *praxis* explains and feeds the fact that experiences such as APAO and Neorealism coexisted but were not expressly connected. Thanks also to the dissemination provided by the Manual they gained the upper hand in Milan, safeguarding the legacy of rationalist abstractionism and promoting the industrialization of the construction processes. The Milan area still managed to demonstrate and to diffuse its ideas in buildings such as those in the QT8 district and in the manual by Diotallevi and Marescotti, which, however, had a lower circulation and more limited impact.

Figure 10: Harar Housing, Milano. Luigi Figini and Gino Polini, 1951-1955. Photo: Wikimedia Commons.

The two different constructive visions underlying the two manuals inspired different declinations of INA casa: the Milanese manual is reflected in the Harar district (Fig. 10), while the *Manuale dell'Architetto* finds its most emblematic application in the Tiburtino district, with Ridolfi as the author. Ridolfi produced the famous towers of Viale Etiopia (Fig. 11) in which, faithful to the logic outilined in the manual, he based the architectural expression "on the configuration of the wall" confirming his "meticulous analytical knowledge of construction procedure" accumulated since the debate "to question the ideological identification between autarchy and traditional technique" [37]. This is how he built a poetic "description" of the construction system in the towers of Viale Etiopia [38] pillar, string course, the infill wall, lintel, roller shutter, threshold, parapet, together with the unmistakable "*a cappa*" roof, an element typical of Ridolfi, placed "on the head" of many of his buildings like the hat on the head of "every self-respecting man" [39].

This finally demonstrates that Ridolfi's relationship with architecture was intense, physical, all-embracing. In fact, despite the centrality of his cultural role and his civic commitment, he declared that he "did not attend much" of the APAO meetings and did not write too much for Metron because he believed that "architecture, done as a profession" required "a lot, day and night", so much that it required "sacrificing everything else" [40].

Figure 11: INA towers in Viale Etiopia. Mario Ridolfi, 1949-1955. Photo: Wikimedia Commons.

Conclusions

The relevance of the role of manuals in Italy in the post-war II period is demonstrated by the many issues they encapsulated, such as the relationship between tradition and innovation in construction and architectural design, the need to achieve a normalization of construction techniques and processes, and the differences between Milan and Roman experiences. The "Manuale dell'Architetto", in particular, thanks to its wide distribution on a national scale, encompasses some specific issues such as the centrality of the figure of Mario Ridolfi, the relationship with international manuals, the USIS soft-power, the social question of the unskilled workforce and the effect on the INA casa program. The large space dedicated in this manual to traditional technologies also suggests a position taken by Italian architectural culture concerning the improvement of the construction processes in the Reconstruction: optimization and in-depth knowledge of those technologies that had already proven their reliability and safety were preferred to the industrialization of the building process. Therefore, it is possible to identify in this "realist" vision of construction a predominant role in the definition of a certain aesthetic imaginary of Italian architectural culture, with an impact that goes beyond the temporal boundaries of Reconstruction.

The reinterpretation in historical perspective of the *Manuale dell'Architetto* coordinated by Ridolfi, therefore, highlights an approach to traditional techniques combined with the dimensional rigour typical of prefabricated construction. This implies cultured and committed professionalism, a connoisseur of construction but also sensitive to the most intricate questions of the building site. A professionalism represented in an admirable and emblematic way by Ridolfi as it is reflected in his poetics and in the care and attention he deserved for every project, through his ability to "take into account an infinite number of things, insulation, water infiltration, resistance of materials, ease of attachment, installation of coatings to avoid waste" in order to "do things well" [41]. In this manual, there is also a didactic ambition, as it attempts to refine the training of the professionals involved in the Reconstruction. This is a process that Ridolfi will not consider completed, as in 1983 he continued to question whether "the scholars who teach at universities" [42] bother to address those minute aspects of construction in which the manual was interested.

References

[1] M. Ridolfi, 'Provvedimenti urgenti per la ricostruzione', in *Rassegna del Primo Convegno Nazionale per la Ricostruzione Edilizia*, fasc. 3, Milan s.d. 1946, pp. 24-27. Also see F. Brunetti, *L'architettura in Italia negli anni della ricostruzione*. Firenze: Alinea, 1986. pp. 221-223.

[2] Cfr. Brunetti, (Note 1).

[3] I. Diotallevi and F. Marescotti, *Il problema sociale, costruttivo ed economico dell'abitazione.* Milan: Poligono, 1948.

[4] Consiglio Nazionale delle Ricerche and United States Information Service (Eds), *Manuale dell'Architetto*. Rome: CNR-USIS, 1946.
[5] M. Tafuri, 'Architettura italiana 1944- 1981', in F. Zeri (Ed.), *Storia dell'arte italiana, II. Dal Medioevo al Novecento, 7. Il Novecento*, Torino: Einaudi, 1982, pp. 14-17.
[6] B. Zevi, '«La veritàaaa» arrogante del nichilismo critico', *L'architettura – cronache e storia*, n. 325, 1982.
[7] D. Donghi, *Manuale dell'Architetto*. Turin: Unione Tipografico-Editrice, 1893.
[8] E. Neufert, *Bauentwurfslehre*. Berlin, 1936.
[9] Cfr. INA Casa (Ed.), *Piano incremento occupazione operaia, case per lavoratori. 1. Suggerimenti, norme e schemi per l'elaborazione e presentazione dei progetti. Bandi dei concorsi*. Roma: Damasso, 1949 and INA Casa (Ed.), *Piano incremento occupazione operaia, case per lavoratori. 2. Suggerimenti, esempi e norme per la progettazione urbanistica. Progetti tipo*. Roma: Danesi, 1950.
[10] Cfr. F. Bellini, *Mario Ridolfi*, Roma: Laterza, 1993.
[11] Ridolfi, (Note 1).
[12] G. Ponti, 'Stile di Ridolfi', *Lo Stile nella casa e nell'arredamento*, n. 25, 1943, p.15.
[13] F. Cellini and C. d'Amato, *Mario Ridolfi: Manuale delle tecniche tradizionali del costruire. Il ciclo delle Marmore*. Milano: Electa, 1996. p. 16.
[14] F. Cellini and C. D'Amato, 'Intervista a Mario Ridolfi', in Cellini and D'Amato (Note 13), pp. 246-247
[15] Fondo Mario Ridolfi, CD 146/I/1 and CD 146/III/32.
[16] Cfr. M. Ridolfi, 'Contributo allo studio sulla normalizzazione degli elementi di fabbrica. Proposta di un sistema per la normalizzazione degli infissi in legno', *Architettura*, fasc. V, 1940. Cited in Brunetti, (Note 1).
[17] Ibid.
[18] M. Ridolfi, 'Il Manuale dell'architetto', *Metron*, n. 8, 1946, pp. 35-42.
[19] A. Imperiale, 'Modularity, Prefabrication + Building Manuals In postwar Italy: Scenes from America' pp. 246-250 in J. Quale, R. Ng, R. E. Smith, (Ed.), *OFFSITE: Theory and practice of architectural production. Proceedings of Association of Collegiate Schools of Architecture 2012 Fall Conference*. Philadelphia: ACSA Press, 2012.
[20] Bellini, (Note 10), p. 53.
[21] "Nazional popolare" when used with a reductive value indicates everything that represents the stereotypes and the more superficial aspects of a taste and a presumed national identity.
[22] Tafuri, (Note 5).
[23] CNR-USIS, (Note 4), A1a, G4e.
[24] Ridolfi, (Note 18).
[25] M.Ridolfi and V. Frankl, 'Due interviste', *Controspazio*, 1974c, pp, 2,97-101; M. Ridolfi and V. Frankl in *Hinterland*, 32 and 34. See B. Reichlin, A. Shugaar and B. W. Joseph, 'Figures of Neorealism in Italian Architecture (Part 2)', *Grey Room*, No. 6, 2002, pp. 110-133.
[26] M. C. Ghia, A lightning bolt. The activity of Bruno Zevi in post-war Italy, ZARCH, no. 10, 2018, pp. 166-177.
[27] CNR-USIS (Note 4), E5m.
[28] C. G. Ramsey and H. R. Sleeper, Architectural Graphic Standards. New York: John Wiley & Sons, 1947, p. 121, 3rd Edn.
[29] CNR-USIS (Note 4), E5o
[30] Cfr. Herbert, G., *The Dream of the Factory-Made House: Walter Gropius and Konrad Wachsmann*, Cambridge: MIT Press, 1984.
[31] CNR-USIS (Note 4), E5q, E5r.
[32] Ibid., H1m, H1n.
[33] Ibid., H1p.
[34] S. Poretti, 'La costruzione', in F. Dal Co (Ed.), *Storia dell'architettura italiana. Il secondo Novecento*, Milano: Electa, 1997. p. 272.
[35] B. Reichlin, A. Shugaar and B. W. Joseph, 'Figures of Neorealism in Italian Architecture (Part 1)', *Grey Room*, No. 5, 2001, pp. 78-101.

[36] "Strapaese" indicates trends inspired by the purely rural tradition, against any form of cosmopolitanism or xenophilia. See *strapaese*, in Treccani.

[37] Poretti, (Note 34). On the relationship between constructive elements and the form of the facade in Italian Architecture of the post-war years see also: R. Lucente and L. Greco, '1950s housing in Milan: Façade design and building culture' pp 93-99 in J. Mascarenhas-Mateus. A. P. Pires, M. M. Caiado and I. Veiga (Eds), *History of construction culture. Proceedings of the Seventh international congress on Construction History (7ICCH)*, Lisbon 2021, London: CRC Press, 2021.

[38] Poretti, (Note 34).

[39] C. De Seta, *L'architettura del Novecento*, Torino: UTET, 1981, p.119. See also R. Lucente, *L'architecture de la "palazzina" à Rome*, 1945-1960, Lille: Presse Universitaire du Septentrion, 2000.

[40] M. Ridolfi, 'Intervista', *Controspazio,* 1974b, pp. 2, 97-100.

[41] F. Cellini and C. D'Amato, 'Intervista a Mario Ridolfi', in Cellini and D'Amato (Note 13), pp. 246-247.

[42] Ibid.

Late Twentieth Century

Alfred Picardi and the Tubular Structure of Chicago's Standard Oil Building: Engineering for Holistic Efficiency

Giorgio Marfella
Faculty of Architecture, Building and Planning, University of Melbourne, Australia

Abstract

The Standard Oil of Indiana Building (today AON Centre) is one of the most discernible skyscrapers in Chicago's skyline. Albeit not the only one of its kind, the structure of the Standard Oil Building is a remarkable example of the earliest pure tubular structures in steel. Its structure relies on an uninterrupted perimeter frame as the primary and practically stand-alone element for resisting lateral loads during service and construction. The case of the Standard Oil Building demonstrates the seminal role played by its structural engineer, Alfred Picardi, and the American steel construction industry in the historical development of tubular skyscrapers.

Introduction

The Standard Oil of Indiana Building is one of the most underrated and understudied skyscrapers of the 'Second Chicago School' of Architecture [1]. The building was designed in the late 1960s by a New York architect, Edward Durell Stone, in collaboration with the architecture and engineering firm of Perkins and Will. Once completed in 1974, its tall structure was, for a short time, the tallest building in Chicago and one of the tallest in the world. (Fig.1) The lack of recognition accrued by this landmark derives most likely from its overshadowing from the critical accolades earned by two other skyscrapers of the Second School, the John Hancock Centre and the Sears Tower, the two supertall modernist towers designed and engineered by the local branch of Skidmore Owings and Merrill (SOM).

Figure 1: Standard Oil of Indiana Building (now AON Center), Chicago (Illinois). Edward Durell Stone in collaboration with Perkins and Will, 1969-1974. External view, 2019. Photo by the author.

Alfred Picardi and the Tubular Structure of Chicago's Standard Oil Building: Engineering for Holistic Efficiency

Before joining Perkins and Will in 1967, the structural engineer of the Standard Oil Building, Egidio Alfred Picardi (1922-2010), was the chief engineer in charge of the structural engineering department of SOM in Chicago. Picardi's collection of professional papers held at the Ryerson and Burnham Library of the Chicago Art Institute reveal first-hand evidence of the critical role held by this engineer, not only in the conception, development, and construction of the Standard Oil Building, but more generally for his contributions to the development and understanding of tubular structures. The legacy of Picardi's work, which is embodied in the Standard Oil Building, helps to understand tubular structures, not only from a structural engineering standpoint but also as a result of a holistic motivation to integrate structure, architecture and construction processes efficiently in tall buildings of the late 1960s and 1970s.

Alfred Picardi (Fig.2) was introduced to the construction business from a young age by his father, an Italo-American general contractor active in the New York area. After graduating in civil engineering in 1947, and a period of service in the war with the US Army Corps of Engineers and the Navy Office of the Chief of Naval Operations, Picardi worked his way as a young engineer in Boston, gaining experience in leadership and responsibilities on industrial and marine facilities, bridge design, oil refinery and chemical plants. In 1954, Picardi moved to Toledo, Ohio, where he joined the architectural and engineering firm of Bellman, Gillett & Richards and worked as the head of the structural engineering department in commercial and institutional building projects. Having established himself as a senior engineer in the architectural engineering business of the Mid-West, Picardi moved to Chicago in 1959 to join the local branch of SOM [2].

At SOM, Picardi quickly rose to the role of associate and chief structural engineer leading several commercial projects, including, among others, the Brunswick Building, the Equitable Building and, most notably for this paper, the Dewitt-Chestnut Apartments, and the John Hancock Center, two projects which are generally recognised as quintessential examples of high-rise structures conceived as 'tube' and 'braced tube' type, respectively.

Figure 2: Egidio Alfred Picardi (Art Institute Chicago, Ryerson Burnham Library, A. Picardi Papers). Photographer and date unknown.

The tubular skyscraper: precedents in Chicago

Before the late 1960s, most high-rise structures were designed to resist lateral loads with column and girder skeletons assembled with moment-resisting connections. Under the effect of lateral actions, rigid frames distort by combining the bending of windward and leeward columns with floor-to-floor drifting, resulting in a characteristic S-shaped lateral deformation.

A tubular system approximates, better than a rigid skeleton system, the structural behaviour of the entire building to that of a simple vertical cantilever. In other words, a tube is a vertical structure that eliminates or at least minimises the effects of the drift component, deforming under lateral stress like a pure vertical cantilever of a hollow section. By concentrating the primary lateral-resisting structure on the perimeter of the floor plate, the tube offers the architectural benefit of freeing the interiors and the core of a tower from the encumbrance of large internal columns. The architectural trade-off to be paid for the gain of internal flexibility is the substantial reduction of freedom and space available for the façade's design.

Tubular structures gained popularity in the late 1960s for providing more efficient use of structural materials, especially steel, lowering structural cost per square foot, thus allowing the design of skyscrapers which would otherwise have been too costly and unfeasible to be built with traditional moment-resisting skeletons.

Tubular structures also brought benefits to architects for concentrating the primary structure of tall buildings at the perimeter of floors, thus providing freedom from major internal columns and shear walls.. At the same time, architectural expectations required to maximise the size of openings for windows while coexisting with the perimeter structure.

The concrete structure of Dewitt-Chestnut Apartments building in Chicago is credited as the 'first' tubular structure in the history of skyscrapers [3]. The conception of the tubular concept at the Dewitt-Chestnut apartments has been described at length before. It is generally ascribed as fruit of the 'genius' of Fazlur Rahman Khan (1929-1982), Bangladesh-born structural engineer who worked in the structural engineering team of SOM in Chicago [4]. The exact origin and authorship of the 'first' tubular idea may be, however, not so easy to attribute to one individual only. Tubular structures were already understood and employed, for example, in silos. The tube was a logical step forward realised by several American architects and engineers of the 1960s, who faced the common challenge to design tall buildings of unprecedented height and lightness. In 1962, Architect Minoru Yamasaki and engineer Leslie Robertson, while working independently from SOM's Chicago professional circle, conceived the twin towers of the New York World Trade Centre clearly along the lines of a pure tubular system [5]. In many regards, the World Trade Centre may be considered an archetypical example of tubular skyscrapers, and arguably a much more eloquent demonstration of its structural principle than the aforementioned example in Chicago.

Without reducing the merits of Khan's contribution to the historical development of innovative high-rise systems, it is worth noting that historical records from contemporary media and news coverage indicate that Picardi was the key leading figure of the structural engineering team of SOM Chicago in the late 1960s. When Picardi joined SOM in the late 1950s, he was a senior civil engineer with considerable experience. Picardi's role at SOM is rarely acknowledged, perhaps due to the much more celebrated fortune accrued by Khan. After Picardi left SOM to join Perkins and Will, Khan took leadership of the engineering department at SOM Chicago, becoming the chief engineer in charge of many renowned projects of the 1970s, like the Sears Tower, and continuing to work at SOM as a partner until his premature death in 1982.

Historical records from Picardi's archive reveal that his leadership was instrumental in shaping a new culture in tall structural engineering design in the 1960s. In 1965, speaking about the dynamics that led to the conception of the Dewitt-Chestnut, Picardi emphasised the advantages computers bring in engineering practice. He stressed that the benefits of data processing did not consist of eliminating human resources in engineering departments but rather in the possibility to test several options rapidly until the most efficient balance between architectural and engineering could be found. The

Alfred Picardi and the Tubular Structure of Chicago's Standard Oil Building: Engineering for Holistic Efficiency

use of computers ultimately liberated engineers from the burden of menial tasks allowing them to attend 'creative activity' outside of otherwise repetitive structural computations [6].

Picardi's team-based approach to computer-aided design at SOM transpired from the vicissitudes of the 100-storey-high John Hancock Center, (Fig.3) for which the use of computers was a vital instrument to resolve the nodes of a tapered tube strengthened by tiers of diagonal bracing. The tapering imposed complicated stress analyses. Furthermore, the engineers were required to test several iterations before the optimal massing of the tall building could be found to the satisfaction of the mixed-use brief imposed on the architects. The indeterminate nature of the rigid nodes that gave shape to the tower required the stress analysis of approximately 1,500 simultaneous equations, a task that could only be overcome by the 'combination of men and machines working together' [7]. One journalist described the computational burden lifted by the computer as equivalent to the employment of 'one mathematician working regular hours for several hundred years.' Others went as far as crediting altogether the engineering authorship of the John Hancock Center to an IBM machine [8]. Leaving aside the mediatic overstatements of the times, Picardi explained that the critical advantage of electronic data processing was not merely a time-saving device but a tool to optimise the cost and construction of complex structural systems:

> '[We were able to] speed up design work, eliminate errors associated with manual computation, explore all possible solutions to the design problem, and then refine the final solution for maximum economy and efficiency in construction. Effective use of the computer's speed helped to compress perhaps three years' work into five months.'[9]

The use of computers at SOM was, according to Picardi, not an 'experimental' affair, but rather a staple of the firm's innovative approach to high-rise building design, which his department had implemented progressively in previous projects under his leadership in Chicago, like the Brunswick Building, the Equitable Building and the Gateway Center [10].

Figure 3: John Hancock Center, Chicago, Skidmore Owings and Merrill (Art Institute Chicago, Ryerson Burnham Library, A. Picardi Papers Collection). Photographer unknown, 1969 circa

Work on the construction of the John Hancock Centre began in 1965. The tapered braced tube conceived by Graham and Picardi with the aid of Khan's talent and the power of electronic data processing at their disposal, was planned to be built like a 'construction handbook' using four crawler cranes adapted to skyscraper building from bridge construction [11]. The construction job was awarded Tishman, a reputable general contractor company with a most respectful track record of successful high-rise projects in America. [12], but the erection of the hollow braced tubular structure had to wait longer than expected due to the slow completion of a USD2million contract for the foundations marred by the inadequate pouring of concrete inside steel caissons. The delays were so substantial as to force the developer, builder-sportsman Jerry Wolman, to face bankruptcy, leaving the anchor tenant, John Hancock Mutual Life with no other choice but to take over the ownership of the project [13].

Picardi's professional records do not indicate if the troublesome ground-breaking of the John Hancock Centre may have put him under undue pressure. It is plausible, although not certain, that such difficulties may have contributed to encouraging his career move in 1967 from SOM to Perkins and Will when he decided to join the latter as a partner. At any rate, his decision at that time has led to significant historical consequences. On the one hand, Picardi left a vacant leadership position in the engineering team of SOM, which accelerated Khan towards a brilliant career of posthumous stature and designer stardom that a structural engineer rarely achieves [14]. On the other hand, by joining Perkins and Will, Picardi could embrace a position of responsibility for the realisation of the most important project of his career, the engineering of the tubular structure of the Chicago headquarters of the Standard Oil of Indiana Building.

Big John versus Big Stan

Plans for the construction of the Standard Oil Building were disclosed in January 1970, accompanied by considerable public relations efforts by John Swearingen, the Chairman of Standard Oil Company of Indiana (today Amoco), starting with a press conference held in the office of Chicago's Mayor Richard Daley [15]. Daley endorsed the project for adding 'luster' to the Chicago skyline, swelling employment and property tax revenue. Standard Oil committed to the project as an owner-occupier, purchasing land to relocate 5,400 employees scattered in twelve different locations [16].

Edward Durell Stone, was engaged to design the tower in collaboration with the architecture department of Perkins and Will, with Alfred Picardi as the structural engineer in charge. Stone responded to the task with a simple unadorned, slender, shaft. He gave vertical emphasis to windows intermitted by the direct expression of the structure on the façade with marble-clad columns. The free-standing, 80-storey high tower provided 3.3 million square feet (300,000 square metre) space, occupying with its footprint only a quarter of the site in Randolph Street, overlooking Grant Park (today's Millennium Park) to the south, and dwarfing the adjacent Prudential Building, which until then had dominated the Eastern fringe of the Chicago's skyline.

The floor plate of the skyscraper was a conventional 194 feet (60 metre) square plan with workspace served by forty lifts divided into five groups of double-deck elevators, one of the largest installations of the kind supplied by Otis. Double-deck elevators saved space for shafts, thus providing more rentable space and resulting in a narrower footprint and more slender tower [17].

Newspapers in Chicago reacted to the announcement and design of the Standard Oil Building with contrasting comments. Some read the project as a sign of the city's self-confident tradition of commercial architecture and building, whereas others voiced pessimistic outlooks on the urban implications of rampant vertical developments. The *Chicago Daily News* reacted to the announcement of the Standard Oil with a vignette and editorial that dubbed the new structure 'Big Stan', portraying the newly announced skyscraper as a contending rival of 'Big John', the John Hancock Centre [18]. An undertone of criticism accompanied most reactions, targeting the will of the *grandeur* of their patrons to 'outdo' one another by pointlessly racing for height [19]. (Fig.4)

Alfred Picardi and the Tubular Structure of Chicago's Standard Oil Building: Engineering for Holistic Efficiency

Figure 4: 'Big John, Meet Big Stan', caricature comparing John Hancock Center and Standard Oil Buildings, Chicago Daily News, 15 January 1970.

The *Chicago Tribune* remarked on the confident civic aspirations embodied by the two buildings, [20] transposing to the present the 'city of big shoulders' [21], as poet Carl Sandburg described Chicago in the 1910s. Others were more concerned to voice the fear of an ever-growing 'race to the top' with building fuelled by corporate ego unwary of urban design consequences. Harry Chadwick, the director of the Chicago Zoning Board expressed public criticism of the giant downtown towers, for their contesting consequences on vehicular and pedestrian traffic and on 'the shutting off of air and light' [22].

Responding to popular misconceptions that identified the conception of skyscrapers as the product of corporate grandeur, architect Robert Sullan, partner and colleague of Picardi at Perkins and Will, responded bluntly, suggesting that economics, and not ego, drove the determination of the height of the Standard Oil Building. Building height, he said, is a 'matter of arithmetic' driven by simple brief parameters, like the client's need for a certain of space, the optimal floor area of typical floors, and the optimal distance, 40 to 45 feet (12 to 14 metre), from the core to the external wall to allow executive offices with outside views [23].

Once the building works for Standard Oil took shape on the Chicago skyline, the economic design imperatives that informed the conception of the headquarters began to emerge with clarity. *Dodge Construction News*, a periodical less concerned with architectural aesthetics than construction activity, exalted the technological and engineering qualities of 'Big Stan' calling it a 'true skyscraper' and reporting its citation for excellence in high-rise construction awarded to Picardi and his engineering team at Perkins and Will [24].

Refining the 'Hollow Tube'

The Standard Oil Building was a refinement in developing the 'hollow tube' typology. Compared to the earliest tubes that Picardi implemented with Khan at SOM, the Standard Oil was conceived to be simpler in design and easier to build.

Departing from the braced structural expressionism of the John Hancock Center, Picardi devised a structural concept without the need for overly complex stress analysis. His design integrated an effective structural solution with the simplicity of Durell's neo-art Deco verticalism of the façade, marked by 5 feet (1.5 metre) wide windows separated by 5 feet (1.5 metre) triangular columns clad in Italian marble. (Figs. 5,6)

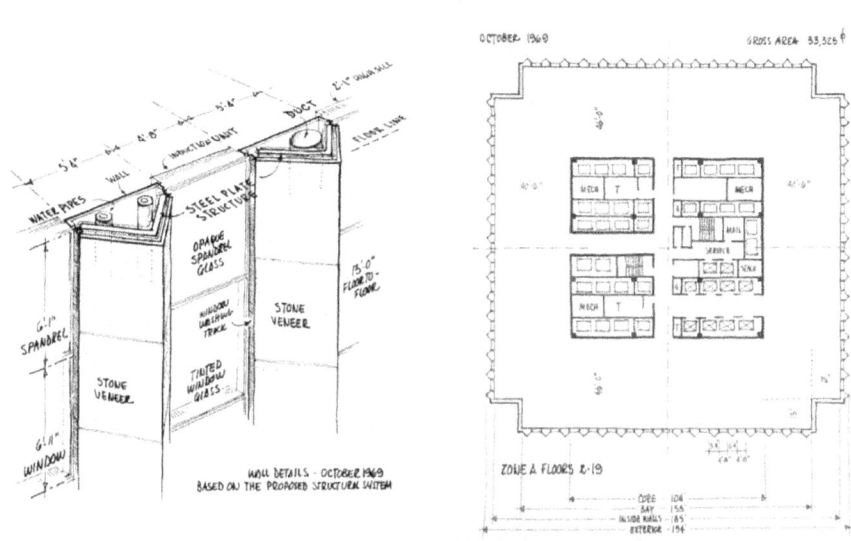

Figure 5: Standard Oil Building, Chicago. Perkins and Will, Wall detail and typical floor plan, 1969 (Art Institute Chicago, Ryerson Burnham Library, A. Picardi Papers Collection).

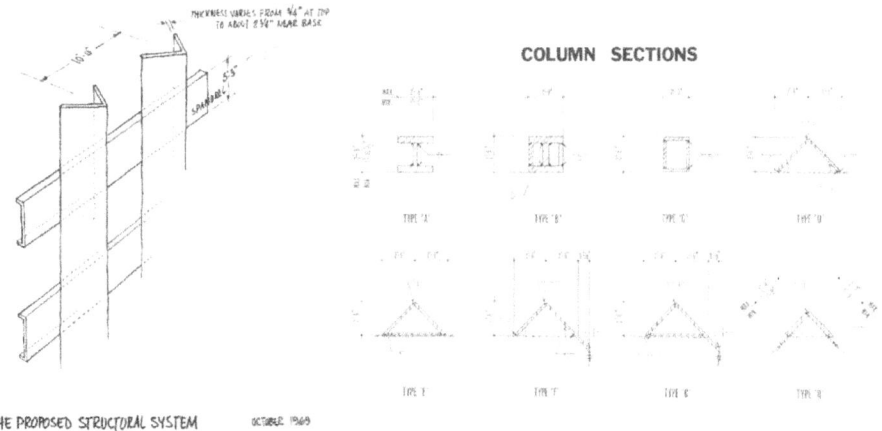

Figure 6: Standard Oil Building, Chicago. Perkins and Will, Diagram of the tubular structural system and schedule of structural column types, 1969 (Art Institute Chicago, Ryerson Burnham Library, A. Picardi Papers Collection).

Alfred Picardi and the Tubular Structure of Chicago's Standard Oil Building: Engineering for Holistic Efficiency

The structural analysis of the tube began with simple hand calculations and then proceeded with the verification by an electronic analytical model set in collaboration with a research team from MIT led by Robert J. Hansen. Wind tunnel studies at the Colorado State University were also used to determine cladding pressures and ascertain aerodynamic effects from vortex shedding. The computer-aided analysis was instrumental in verifying that the structure, overall, did accurately act as a pure tubular system [25]. The team utilised a structural model of finite elements subject to parametric studies that allowed them to optimise the tube for the most economical solution [26].

The tube consisted of 64 chevron columns, built with vee-shaped steel plate columns spaced at 10 feet (3 metre) centres and connected by 5 feet 3inches (1.6 metre) high C-shaped spandrels. The chevrons wrapped around the tower like a rigid skin of steel able to withstand all the lateral loads acting on the tower, disengaging the internal core from any contribution to the lateral resistance. Four re-entrant corners of solid-steel plate completed the structure, serving as stiffeners that connected the four perforated faces of the tube.

Picardi conceived the chevron arrangement of the tube to simplify as much as possible the methods of fabrication and installation, aiming to erect the entire structure in just over one year. The tube also integrated services along the façade, thus freeing valuable rentable space inside the tower, following an integrated approach of structural and mechanical engineering used in other American tall building projects of the 1960s.

The tube was broken down into three-storey-high and two-column-wide sections. The chevron columns were fabricated off-site by welding two plates forming the sides of a triangle with the base stiffened by a continuous C-shaped spandrel beam. (Fig.7)

Figure 7: Standard Oil Building, Chicago, Views of steel tube under construction, 1971 (Art Institute Chicago, Ryerson Burnham Library, A. Picardi Papers Collection). Photographer unknown.

The engineering of the chevrons was a pre-cursor of 'design for manufacturing' principles, based on repetitive use of jigs and the simplification of factory and site assembly procedures. For example, only two bolt sizes were utilised for the connections of the chevron columns to minimise the risk of mistakes on site.

The quest for economic savings involved design considerations that went holistically beyond the primary resisting element of the tube. Similar considerations of construction efficiency were applied to the design and fabrication of the floor systems, which besides supporting the office gravity loads with a column-free span of 45 feet (14 metre), also served as a diaphragm to stabilise the tube on the perimeter. (Fig.8)

Figure 8: Standard Oil Building, Chicago. Perkins and Will, Model of typical structural bay, 1969 (Art Institute Chicago, Ryerson Burnham Library, A. Picardi Papers Collection).

The floors were a composite steel-concrete decking, supported by 3 feet 2 inches (0.95 metre) deep trusses spaced 10 feet (3 metre) apart, following the structural module dictated by the chevron columns and a 5 feet (1.5 metre) modular ceiling grid. Overall, the construction of the tower required the fabrication of 4,000 trusses, where the principles of economic efficiency adopted throughout the building led to the establishment of a mass production assembly line [27].

A welded wire mesh was used in place of traditional steel bars to reinforce the steel-concrete decking system. The mesh allowed the steel deck to remain exposed due to its ability to hold the concrete topping in place in case of fire and failure of the corrugated steel decking. The welded mesh brought direct savings on the cost of materials and labour by eliminating sprayed on fireproofing and requiring only a small crew of five men to install the fabric on each floor on a two-day cycle [28].

Alfred Picardi and the Tubular Structure of Chicago's Standard Oil Building: Engineering for Holistic Efficiency

The job for the construction was awarded to the general contractor Turner Construction Company for a total cost of more than USD100 million, a figure that set a new record for the scale of investments in Chicago supertall construction, as inaugurated by the John Hancock Centre built on a USD95 million contract. Works commenced on 6 April 1970, not long after the first announcement of the project, with Mayor Daley and John Swearingen breaking ground under a helicopter hovering overhead at 1,136 feet (346 metre), the planned final height of the building [29].

The pure cantilever of the SOB was anchored to the ground by 40 concrete-filled steel caissons, transferring the vertical loads of the chevron columns on a capping beam and reaching to bedrock 100 feet (30 metre) below [30]. Another 16 internal caissons completed the 'egg crate' of the foundation system, receiving the vertical loads of the lift core. Applying the lessons learnt with the troubles of the John Hancock Centre, the concrete inside the caissons was fitted with sonic transmitters at the base, which sent a signal to receivers located on the ground. The sonic signals allowed Picardi and his team to detect voids or water penetrations that could compromise the strength of concrete [31].

The steelwork of the Standard Oil Building was rolled, fabricated and erected by the American Bridge Company, a local steel manufacturer with an impressive pedigree of high-rise structures built in Chicago, such as the Chicago Tribune, the Prudential Building, the Civic Center and the Sears Tower. Responding with tongue in cheek to media headlines that emphasised the growing role of computers and automation in the design of skyscrapers, the public relations manager of American Bridge advertised the weight of his company in the construction of the Standard Oil, reminding the public that '… machines don't build skyscrapers - men do [32]'.

An average of 600 men worked on the project over 36 months, with peaks of 1,200 men in the busiest stages of construction. The three-storey high chevron elements of the tube were progressively transported to the site and erected by one lift into position and then connected with high-strength bolts, minimising site-welding and its associated risks and demands for quality control on the field. All the steel was erected by four crawler cranes, each located at mid-points of the tower with overlapping zones served by derricks that covered every corner of the floor. The cranes were lifted into new positions once a portion of four floors of their work was completed [33]. (Figs. 9,10)

Figure 9: Standard Oil Building under construction, Chicago, 1970-71 (Art Institute Chicago, Ryerson Burnham Library, A. Picardi Papers Collection). Photographer unknown.

Figure 10: Standard Oil Building, Chicago, Views of steel tube under construction, 1971 (Art Institute Chicago, Ryerson Burnham Library, A. Picardi Papers Collection). Photographer unknown.

The perimeter structure was fire-proofed with a sprayed-on cementitious material to achieve a four-hour fire-rating meant to provide insulation to mitigate the effects of thermal stresses induced by Chicago's extreme weather conditions [34].

In October 1972, after sixteen months of steelworks, Turner and American Bridge reached the top of the structure. Daley and Swearingen did not miss the opportunity for another public display for the occasion, attending the traditional ceremony of 'topping-out' by signing their names on one of the last beams [35].

Creative engineering

Following completion of the works, the architecture of the Standard Oil Building attracted more criticism than praise [36]. Some years later, the owner, Amoco, had to face considerable embarrassment and cost of rectification due to failures of the façade marble slabs, which led to an entire recladding in the 1990s [37]. The remarkable design structure of 'Big Stan', however, did not pass unnoticed. In the mid-1970s, Picardi was awarded a prize by the James F. Lincoln Arc Welding Foundation for his 'contribution to the significant efforts being made to conserve material and reduce costs' shown in the design of the building [38].

Picardi refined the application of the tube for high-rise, transforming its theoretical idea into a configuration that did not merely express the structure on the façade of the building. The Standard Oil Building fully integrated the primary elements of its architecture, structure, and even mechanical services into a single skin. By applying lessons learnt in previous projects at SOM, he took the tubular concept to its extreme, achieving a pure tubular action, yet by simplifying procedures

Alfred Picardi and the Tubular Structure of Chicago's Standard Oil Building: Engineering for Holistic Efficiency

for fabrication and erection of steel members, overcoming the somewhat troublesome and compromised X-braced approach of the John Hancock Center.

Overall, the primary structure of the Standard Oil, counting the perimeter frame, floor trusses and girders and internal core columns, required approximately 50,500 tons (46 million kilogram) of steel. By comparison to other high-rise steel structures built in the US before and after 1945, the tubes of the Standard Oil Building and John Hancock Centre proved the economic efficiency of their structural approach. While exceeding by far in height and size most tall building precedents, they proportionally used much less tonnage than other notable skyscrapers of the post-war years, such as the Pan Am Building and Chase Manhattan Bank in New York. They consumed an amount of steel per square foot that until then had been used, typically, in much shorter buildings, only twenty to forty storeys high [39]. (Fig.11)

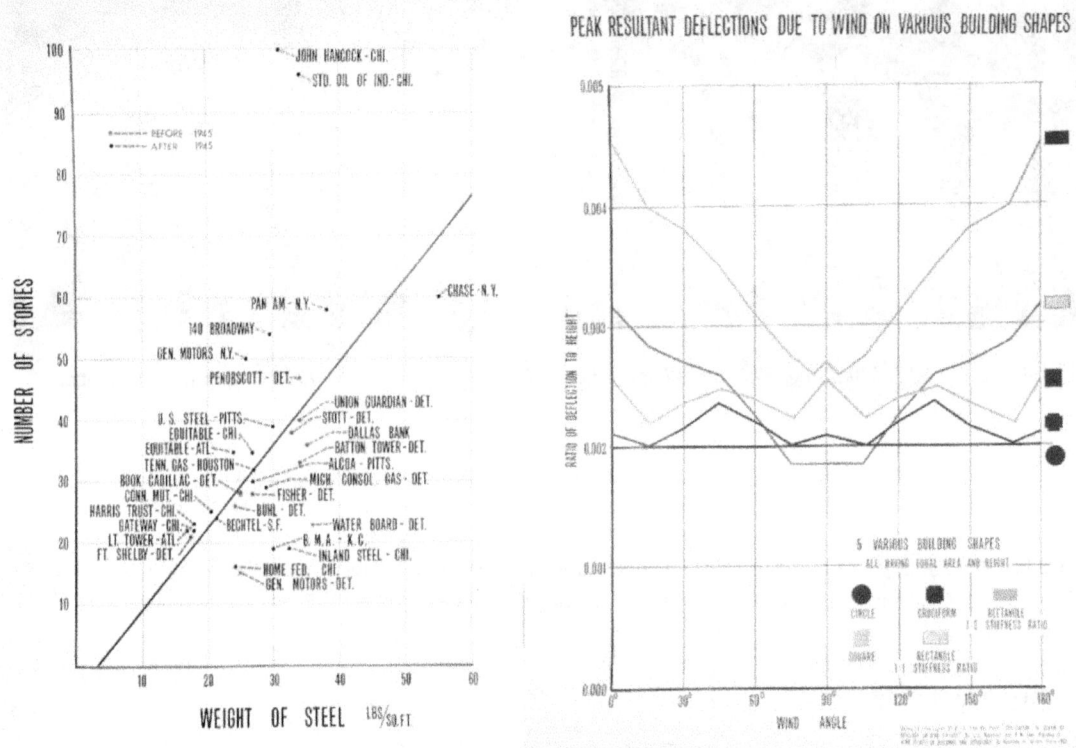

Figure 11: Standard Oil Building, Chicago. Perkins and Will, Charts showing comparison of steel tonnage in American high-rise buildings and effect of floor plan shape on wind-caused deflections (Art Institute Chicago, Ryerson Burnham Library, A. Picardi Papers Collection).

Nevertheless, the main objective pursued by Picardi was not the mere realisation of a pure tubular concept with a minimal amount of steel per square foot. The objective was to find the optimum point where the economy of the material allowed by the tube meets the practicality and economies of scale needed by high-rise construction.

Although quantities of materials did have an important effect on the cost of structures, optimising the quantity of materials alone were not sufficient to provide the most efficient outcomes. In an article published in 1973, Picardi clarified that the main achievement of the Standard Oil Building structure was not the mere reduction of steel tonnage; just as importantly, it was the achievement of striking a balance with the economies imposed by fabrication and erection procedures [40].

In the mid-1980s, at the end of his career, Picardi further clarified his design philosophy as 'creative' structural engineering. The premise for a successful outcome in structural design is *in primis* a close collaboration with the architect, from which a 'truly creative structural concept may well dictate the form of an architectural solution [41]'. The structural engineer can achieve these results if given the contractual responsibility to work directly for the client, and not the architect [42]. Referring explicitly to the experience of the Standard Oil Building, Picardi described the design process that led to its conception as a fortunate 'unusual instance' and explained:

> 'In most instances, today, we find the structural engineer labouring to make the architect's concept of some formed mass structurally competent often when the form is not rational structurally or ideally functional for its intended purpose. [...] I do not make this charge lightly as I have seen it time and again where architectural design inconsistent with the client's objectives was defended by the engineers. Too often the engineer's attitude has been to make the architect's design work, in spite of his better judgment, and the client objectives [43]'.

According to Picardi, interdisciplinary collaboration is the most important ingredient for the successful delivery of high-rise projects. The fundamental premise is that both architects and engineers understand the role of the client and that architects accept the premise that 'good architecture must also be good engineering [44]'.

Conclusion

In 2002, in the aftermath of the terrorist attack on the New York World Trade Center, Alfred Picardi wrote an unpublished note [45], from which he appears compelled to respond to a television documentary on 911 and explain the historical mechanisms that led American cities to develop super tall projects with tubular structures. Picardi explained how large tubular towers like the Standard Oil Building and the World Trade Center came into existence as the response to entrepreneurial demands that expected, above all, design efficiency to offset risks caused by inflationary trends on the cost of labour and materials. His letter declared scepticism about the future of megastructures due to the apparent vulnerability shown by the New York terrorist attack. The collapse of the World Trade Center showed the Achille's heel of tubular skyscrapers for lack of structural redundancy due to the concentration of all lateral resistance on the skin of the tower. His questioning stemmed primarily from an emphatic imperative to safeguard the lives of people occupying such buildings.

This late note from Picardi, helps to contextualise the legacy and relevance of the Standard Oil Building as a remarkable - and after the loss of the World Trade Center perhaps unique - surviving example of the earliest and most pure tubular tall building structures in America. Ultimately, the Standard Oil Building responded to the never out-of-date economic imperatives of large-scale tall construction. In periods of high inflation - like the 1970s - economics imposed austere design decisions and holistic considerations about material quantities and construction labour from the very initial stages of a project. Looking beyond the vertical emphasis and geometric simplicity of its appearance, the Standard Oil Building is an eloquent exemplar of such integration of economics, architecture, engineering and construction methodology, and a demonstration of the critical role played by structural engineers to the design and construction history of tall buildings.

References

[1] F. Schulze, 'Architecture: the Second Chicago School.' *Encyclopedia of Chicago History*, 2005. Available on https://encyclopedia.chicagohistory.org/pages/64.html

[2] Art Institute Chicago, Ryerson Library Archival Collections, E. Alfred Picardi Papers, 1949-2011 (herafter Picardi Papers). Box 1, Folder 6, Professional Records, E. Alfred Picardi, 1985 circa.

[3] S. Wilson, "Dewitt Chestnut Apartments: the First Tubular Skyscraper" in *First Skyscrapers – Skyscraper Firsts: Considerations of Critical Buildings and Technologies in Skyscraper History*, edited by Lee Gray, Antony Wood and Daniel Safarik. Chicago: Council on Tall Buildings and Urban Habitat – Society of Architectural Historians, 2020, pp.175-183.

[4] Mir. M. Ali. Art of the Skyscraper: the Genius of Fazlur Khan. New York: Rizzoli, 2001.

[5] Ibid., p. 43.

[6] Picardi Papers, "Skyscraper in Chicago," p. 99.

[7] "The Computer in Structural Design," Computers and Automation, July 1965, p. 37.

[8] Picardi Papers, Box 1, Folder 3, Newspaper Clippings, Pat Murphy, "Computer Designs Skyscraper: 'Brain' Spits Out Data for 100-Story Building," *Chicago Daily News,* May 28, 1965. Printed also as "Computer Given Credit for New Building in Chicago" in Columbia S.C. Record, May 28, 1965.

[9] Ibid.

[10] Picardi Papers, Box 1, Folder 3, Newspaper Clippings, "Architects, Engineers Use IBM 1620 in Designing Chicago's Hancock Center." BEMA News Bulletin, May 31, 1965.

[11] Picardi Papers, Box 1, Folder 3, Newspaper Clipping, Alvin Nagelberg, "Hancock Building's Journey Toward Sky Starts Tomorrow," 1965.

[12] J.L. Tishman, *Building Tall: My Life and the Invention of Construction Management*. Edited by Tom Schactman. Ann Arbor, Michigan: University of Michigan Press, 2011.

[13] B. Hughes, "'Big John' Gets Off to a Tipsy Start', *Chicago Tribune*, March 24, 1985.

[14] See for example the documentary trailer 'Reaching New Heights: Fazlur Rahman Khan and the Skyscapeper', available at https://www.frkdocumentary.com/

[15] J. McMullen, "New Tallest Building for Chicago," *Chicago Daily News*, January 14, 1970. See also, E. Schreiber, "100 Million Dollar Tower Announced," *Chicago Tribune*, January 15, 1970.

[16] Ibid.

[17] "It's Standing Room Only … Piggy-back Elevators: Double-Deckers Installed by Otis for Standard Oil," *Dodge Construction News,* July 3, 1970, p. 7.

[18] Picardi Papers, Box 1, Folder 4, Newspaper Clipping, "Big John Meet Big Stan," *Chicago Daily News*, January 15, 1970.

[19] "Chicago Plan Signed in Mayor's Office," *Dodge Construction News,* January 16, 1970; "City's Tallest Skyscraper!" *Chicago Today*, January 17, 1970.

[20] Picardi Papers, Box 1, Folder 4, Newspaper Clipping, "Reflecting Confidence in Chicago," Chicago Tribune, January 16, 1970.

[21] C. Sandburg, "Chicago", originally published in *Poetry* 3, no. 6 (March 1914): 191.

[22] M.W. Newman, "Call This the Age of High-Rise Man," *Chicago Daily News*, January 15, 1970, p. 22.

[23] A. Nagelberg, "Simplicity is Key to Standard Tower," *Chicago Tribune*, February 8, 1970, 3A.

[24] "A True Skyscraper," *Dodge Construction News*, June 18, 1973.

[25] E. Alfred Picardi, "Structural System: Standard Oil of Indiana Building*,"* *Journal of the Structural Division*, ASCE 99, no. 4 (April 1973): 42-51.

[26] P. K. S. et al. 'Computer Aided Design - Standard Oil of Indiana Building' *Journal of the Structural Division,* ASCE 99, no. 4 (April 1973): 621-635.
[27] Picardi, "Structural System,": 45
[28] "Wire Mesh Eliminates Sprayed-On Fireproofing in Composite Floors," *Building Design & Construction* (December 1972): 47.
[29] "Turn for the Better," *Chicago Tribune*, April 7, 1970.
[30] Picardi, "Structural System,": 45-46
[31] Ibid.
[32] T. E. Ward, "Steel Heads for the Sky in Chicago," *Dodge Construction News*, December 18, 1972, p. 54.
[33] Picardi, "Structural System,": 49.
[34] Ibid.: 43-44.
[35] "New Standard Oil Building Rises in Chicago," *Advertisement in Adventure Road*, May 1973, p. 19.
[36] T. Leslie [?], "One Last Tube Structure: Standard Oil," in *Architecture Farm: Architecture and the Ivory Tower in the Great Mid-West,* September 2021, available at https://architecturefarm.wordpress.com/2021/09/.
[37] Greg McMillan, "Two Buildings, Two Cities, One Problem," *The Globe and Mail*, December 6, 2007.
[38] Picardi Papers, Box 1, Folder 7, correspondence, Richard S. Sabo [Secretary of the James Lincoln Arc Welding Foundation] letter, May 1975.
[39] Picardi, 'Structural System,": 49.
[40] Picardi, 'Structural System,": 50.
[41] Picardi Papers, Box 1, Folder 10, "The Evaluation of Structural Concepts for Buildings: the Client's Perspective," p. 3.
[42] Ibid, p. 2.
[43] Ibid., pp. 4, 24.
[44] Ibid., p. 25.
[45] Picardi Papers, Box 1, Folder 10, writings, "High Rise Buildings and 911", May 5, 2002, unpublished.

From physical to digital – the form-finding and measuring models of the *Mannheim Multihalle*

Benjamin Schmid, Christiane Weber
Department of building history and preservation, University of Innsbruck, Austria

Abstract

The *Mannheim Multihalle*, built as a temporary structure for the 1975 *Bundesgartenschau* (Federal Horticultural Show), is an iconic lightweight construction and as the largest free-span wooden grid shell listed as construction history monument. To determine the geometry of the hall the international planning team had to build physical models, first made of wire-mesh and then of hanging-chains. For the measurement of the models, photogrammetry was used and the structural calculations were carried out with the help of model tests. Of the models produced, the elaborate model made of hanging-chains on a scale of 1:98.5 has been preserved at the *Deutsches Architekturmuseum* (DAM) in Frankfurt. This paper investigates the preserved model regarding manufacturing processes and measuring methods to clarify the significance of physical models for the planning and implementation of the innovative wooden construction.

Introduction: The Federal Horticultural Show and Frei Otto

The *Bundesgartenschau* (Federal Horticultural Show) is a six-month exhibition that took place every two years in Germany. In a large park, with flower shows specially designed for the exhibition, events such as concerts, theatre, sporting competitions, etc. are organised in temporary exhibition spaces. The Federal Horticultural Show has been very popular, especially in the early days after the Second World War, as it offered the opportunity to redesign and revitalise the destroyed urban landscapes with different gardens, lakes, kiosks and restaurants. For this, the hosting cities received considerable financial support [1].

The architect Frei Otto had already attracted attention with buildings for Federal Horticultural Shows, for example with a tent for the music pavilion in Kassel in 1955 or the so-called *Tanzbrunnen* (dancing fountain) in Cologne in 1957. Frei Otto always pleaded for light, changeable and transparent buildings instead of monumental, massive and representative architecture. In his designs for his lightweight constructions, such as tents, grid shells or pneumatic envelopes he used physical models to simulate the forms, optimise them and even carry out measurements to calculate the load-bearing structure [2]. Frei Otto began his research and project work at his *Entwicklungsstätte für den Leichtbau* (Development Centre for Lightweight Construction), founded in Berlin in 1958. With his appointment to the University of Stuttgart and the creation of the *Institut für Leichte Flächentragwerke* (Institute for Lightweight Structures/IL) in 1964 which he headed with the help of his deputy Berthold Burkhardt, he moved his office to Warmbronn in 1969, where he mainly worked on the realisation of his projects with the help of his long-time colleague Ewald Bubner [3].

Competition and design for the Federal Horticultural Show in Mannheim

As the decision to hold the Federal Horticultural Show in Mannheim in 1975 had already been made in January 1970, the *Bundesgartenschau Mannheim GmbH*, was able to announce a nationwide architectural competition. The architectural office Carlfried Mutschler and Partners and the landscape architect Heinz H. Eckebrecht won the competition for this project in the *Herzogenriedpark* in Mannheim. The architects structured the exhibition site with an axis and a multifunctional hall should serve as centre. Parts of the exhibition were to be covered with large umbrellas arranged in rows, which were to be suspended from floating gas balloons. Due to construction difficulties and building law objections, this idea, like several other design proposals, was soon abandoned [4]. Thus, after winning the competition in 1971, the architects Joachim Langner and his brother Winfried Langner made their way to Frei Otto's Atelier Warmbronn in autumn 1972 to discuss alternative constructions. In this cooperation the idea of a wooden lattice dome was finally born. A first model made of a wire-mesh was built to roughly determine the shape of the domes, containing the hall, the restaurant, the entrances and connecting passages [5]. In this process, the planning team also benefited from a Japanese-German funded research project on grid shells at the IL [6]. The client, the *Bundesgartenschau Mannheim GmbH,* finally accepted the participation of Frei Otto with his Atelier Warmbronn, where Frei Otto himself, as well as Ewald Bubner, Matthias Banz, Jean Goedert, Alf van Lieven and Georgios Papakostas worked on the project and immediately began with further model studies. Thus, the shape of the roof was elaborately generated in the Atelier, while the architectural office worked predominantly on the development of the floor plans [7]. The hilly landscape of the multifunctional hall was to cover an area of approximately 7,400 square metres and the structure was to reach a total length of 160 metres and a width of 115 metres. The larger dome was planned with a height of 20 metres and a span of 85 metres [8].

The participation of the engineers

Frei Otto's involvement brought his Stuttgart networks at the Faculty of Civil Engineering into the project: the *Institut für angewandte Geodäsie im Bauwesen* (Institute for the Application of Geodesy in Civil Engineering/IAGB) at the University of Stuttgart under the direction of Klaus Linkwitz was responsible to measure the physical models photogrammetrically. The determined data could already be used to draw the production plans by means of an automatic drawing machine. The Mannheim engineers Ludwig Bräuer and Heribert Späh with Rüdiger Spring were commissioned with the structural calculations to prove the stability. However, the commissioned engineers soon realised that their office had neither the facilities nor the capacity for the calculation of such an innovative and experimental shell. As a result, the engineering company Over Arup & Partner from London, in particular the Division Structures 3 with Edmund (Ted) Happold and Ian Liddell, was commissioned with the structural calculations of the grid shell. Frei Otto's contact and collaboration with the London engineers had already been established several years earlier [9].

The beginning of a long-term relationship between Frei Otto and the office of Ove Arup & Partner began back in 1967 in the desert of Saudi Arabia. As Ove Arup & Partner won there a competition for a conference centre in Riyadh and Frei Otto and Rolf Gutbrod were commissioned for buildings in Mecca, they immediately engaged Arup's office for the structural design. This initial contact developed into a long-term collaboration. How inspiring Frei Otto's methods were, can be seen in the establishment of the Lightweight Structures Laboratory within the Arup Group in 1973, modelled on the IL. A model workshop was set up in this laboratory under the direction of Ted Happold (and nominally Frei Otto), to investigate cable nets, membranes and grid shells. In 1976, Ted Happold set up his own office and became a professor at the University of Bath. He continued to work regularly with Frei Otto [10].

However, the Arup office already used physical models before: as structural and measurement models were already produced by the engineers for the Sydney Opera House project. This included a large 1:60 scale Perspex model on which load tests were carried out at the Structural Laboratory at Southampton University in 1960, as well as tests on models in the wind tunnel at the National Physical Laboratory in Teddington. Despite the still limited possibilities, the pioneering work with computers in Arups office in the context of this project saved years of calculation time [11]. Frei Otto and the *Mannheim Multihalle* project undoubtedly benefited from these early experiences with computer technology in construction practice held by the Arup office. For structural modelling the British engineers used the Univac 1108 with extended core memory and magnetic tape drives for data input and output [12].

The grid shell construction

The construction of grid shells is based on the inversion principle, which means that hanging up a flat grid structure it will be deformed into a double curved shape. The inversion principle is based on the fact that the tensile stress in a suspended object becomes compressive stress when the structure is inverted. Structures developed in this way are thus free of tensile and bending stresses under dead load, a basic requirement for material-saving, lightweight constructions. The inversion principle was not first discovered by Frei Otto but was yet formulated by Robert Hooke in 1676. In the field of architecture Antoni Gaudí perfected the use of suspension models as a design and form-finding tool. Frei Otto used various textiles such as medical plaster patches, rubber membranes or chains and nets for his experiments with hanging models from 1946 onwards. Chain nets are particularly suitable for designing grid shells, and the shape of the suspended shell can be influenced by adjusting the edges and the length of the suspended chains. For the constructions itself, grid shells are made of flat slatted grids with square meshes whose crossing points are rotatably connected by bolts. By pushing them upwards, the slats are bent and the angles of the meshes are changed so that they become rhomboids. This creates the desired double-curved surface, which is held in shape by fixing the edges and stiffening the crossing points. The advantages of such grid shells are the low material costs, the simplicity of the construction, the low number of details and the fast construction process. Before the project in Mannheim, Frei Otto had already realised grid shells for the 1962 German Building Exhibition (*Deubau*) in Essen, as well as for a conference room under the tent of the German Pavilion at the 1967 World Exhibition in Montréal [13]. The grid shell in Essen was the first to be designed by Frei Otto and the shape of this shell with a base area of 15 metres x 15 metres, was also generated using a model of hanging chains [14].

During a design process, different types of models can be used. Depending on the intended use, different materials, accuracies and shapes are possible, whereby one model can also fulfil several purposes. The already mentioned German-Japanese research project on grid shells at the IL, came to the conclusion that four model types are distinguished and defined as follows:

Design models: models that are as realistic as possible and are made of mouldable or rigid materials.

Form-finding models: Suspension models made of materials that are flexible in bending, such as textiles, meshes, rubber skins, chains, etc. Models with low dead weight can be manipulated by weights. Determining the forces is possible to a limited extent.

Measurement models to determine the exact geometric shape: Suspension models made of flexible chain or element meshes. Measuring the forces is not possible due to unavoidable geometric changes.

Measurement models for measuring forces and deformations due to loads: Models made of materials that are stiff in bending with the closest possible elastic and geometric similarity for transferring the measurement results [15].

Models for the Multihalle

First form-finding models

In order to define the basic shape of the two main domes and the connecting corridors, a model on a scale of 1:500 was made in the Atelier Warmbronn [16]. This simple model was created as a first concept model in collaboration with the architects using wire mesh, similar to the material used in kitchen sieves, which was attached to the base plate of balsa wood with threads and pins. From this first model, a series of similar wire mesh models were created to develop and refine the shape of the multifunctional hall. These models were partly photographed outdoors and from different perspectives to get a better impression of the exterior and spatial impression of the design [17]. (Fig. 1)

From physical to digital – the form-finding and measuring models of the Mannheim Multihalle

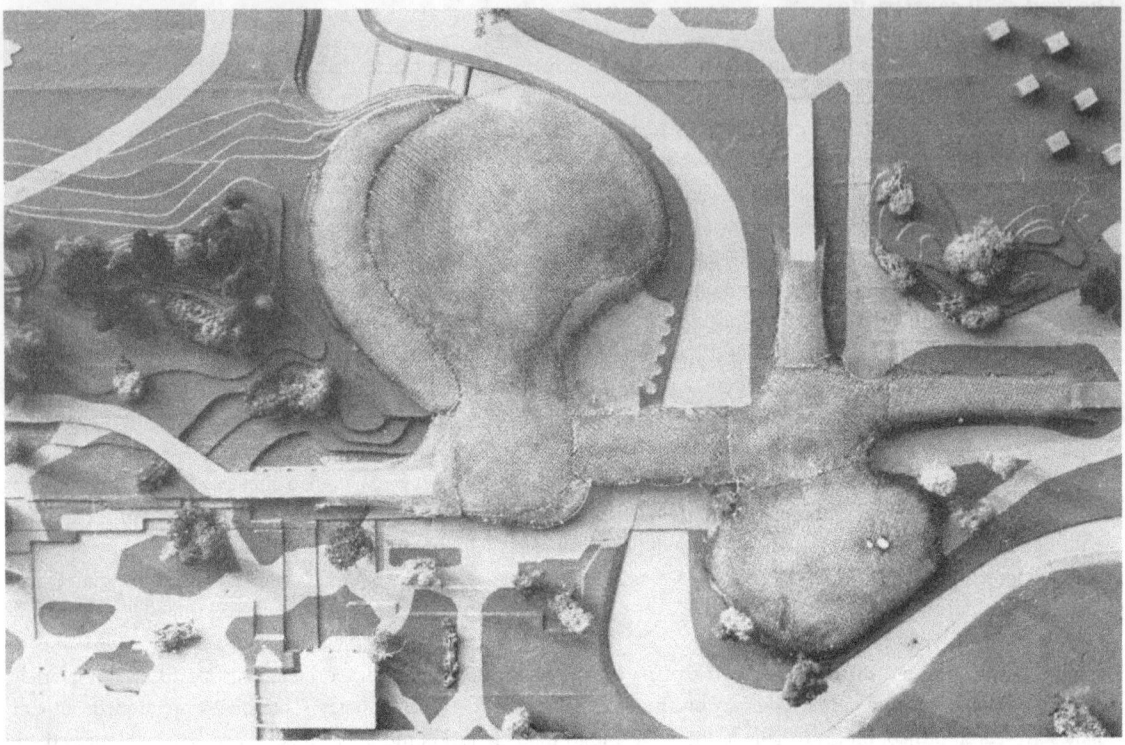

Figure 1: Form-finding model out of wire mesh on a scale of 1:500. Image from private collection of Berthold Burkhardt.

The preserved form-finding and measurement model

By measuring these first form-finding models, with the help of threads which were stretched over the models and unwound, a detailed hanging model on a scale of 1:98.5 could be produced: The grid was made of 15 millimetres long chain links with cranked eyelets on both sides and rings with a diameter of 2.5 millimetres [18]. The ring wire was thicker than that of the links, which was intended to prevent the links from slipping out of the rings. Despite the machine production of the elements, the desired accuracy was not achieved, i.e. the links were not all exactly the same length, which was due to the tolerance in production and the abrasion of the tools. This resulted in the scale of 1:98.5 instead of 1:100 [19]. In order to produce the three-dimensional form of the model, the first parts of the knotted net were suspended in a provisional frame made of balsa wood. The provisional frame was removed once the shape was finalised, so that the hanging net was only suspended from brass supports with an adjustable head in the form of a cantilever and acrylic glass strips. To reduce the already considerable effort in the production of the model, only every third mesh of the later grid shell was represented. In addition, thin chains, twine, brass wire and small springs were used in the model to fix the mesh. The brass wire was roughened to prevent the twisted threads from sliding on it, partly this was also done with liquid glue. To obtain a pre-tension in the net and to stabilise it, the hanging chain net was weighted down with commercial nuts suspended by filigree threads. After removing the wooden frame, the model had to be fine-adjusted with the help of pliers and tweezers (Fig. 2), especially in the boundary areas, in order to correct the last irregularities. Measuring points in the model are marked by glued-on blue dots [20]. The base plate was made of marble, as this guaranteed high dimensional accuracy, was insensitive to temperature and humidity changes and did not change its position due to the heavy weight when working on the model [21].

Figure 2: Fine-adjusting the hanging model. Image from private collection of Berthold Burkhardt.

The final shape of the *Multihalle* was derived from this hanging model: the dome-shaped openings at the entrances, for example, were the result of the self-finding process of the hanging chains. The final shape was photogrammetrically measured with the help of the IAGB under the direction of Klaus Linkwitz by the engineers Hans Dieter Preuß, Lothar Gründig and Ulrich Hangleiter. Frei Otto was already familiar with this team and their photogrammetric method from the projects for the German Pavilion for the 1967 World Exhibition in Montréal and the Olympic buildings for the 1972 Summer Games in Munich [22]. The advantages of photogrammetric measurement compared to direct measurement on a measuring table using solders were the possibility of capturing the entire model in one moment, the non-contact measurement method on the sensitive model and the transportable measuring equipment, so that the model did not need to be transported. The model could therefore be photographed in the Atelier Warmbronn with a close-up measuring camera (f = 115 millimetres) suspending from the ceiling for vertical images and with tripods. (Fig. 3) The negatives were measured with a Zeiss PSK precision stereo comparator [23].

Finally, the IAGB produced a digital spatial model on the data gained by these measurements, adding the missing nodes **and** correcting inaccuracies such as different long chain links or excessive kinks in the boundary areas. This cleaned model was calculated on the large computer CDC 6600 at the University of Stuttgart and could then be converted into plans with the help of an automatic drawing machine, which served as the basis for the construction planning and the cutting of the slats [24]. In addition, the determined data served as the basis for the further digital static calculations in the Arup office, because the geometric information for the complex shell shape could not be described without the produced model at this time. The other static models produced in the Arup office were also based on the drawings produced by the IAGB [25].

From physical to digital – the form-finding and measuring models of the Mannheim Multihalle

After the project was completed, the model remained in Frei Otto's possession and was probably kept in the Atelier Warmbronn. Together with a further nineteen models, the model of the *Multihalle* was handed over to the DAM in Frankfurt between 1980 and 1982, which in return had to finance the restoration work on the models. The model was loaned by the Architecture Museum of the Technical University of Munich in 2005 for the exhibition "*Frei Otto: Das Gesamtwerk – leicht bauen, natürlich gestalten*" together with thirteen other exhibits of the DAM in Frankfurt. During the return transport, the model was badly damaged, parts of the knotted chain net came loose, rods, threads and springs were partially broken. Finally, the model was restored on the occasion of the exhibition "*Das Architekturmodell: Werkzeug, Fetisch, kleine Utopie*" in 2011 and 2012. In the process, the parts of the destroyed chain net were restored, and new feathers and coloured threads (instead of the original white threads) were inserted [26]. Today, the model is kept protected under a covering in the archive of the DAM in Frankfurt (Fig. 4) and may no longer be transported. Despite the restoration, individual chain links or springs are still unhinged, not in their intended position or are missing altogether.

Figure 3: Carrying out the photogrammetric recordings at the Atelier Warmbronn. Image from B. Burkhardt, (Ed.), IL 13: Multihalle Mannheim, Stuttgart: Institut für leichte Fl chentragwerke (IL), 1978. p.45.

Figure 4: Preserved form-finding and measurement model at the archive of the DAM in Frankfurt under a covering. Photo by B. Schmid at the archive of the DAM in Frankfurt

Measurement models out of Perspex

In order to test the behaviour of the grid shell under load, assuming linear elastic behaviour, a model out of Perspex laths was made. However, as there was no experience in building models of this material and the transferability of tests to the complex grid shell was without precedent, it was decided to first build such a model for an already executed smaller grid shell, to test and check the correspondence with the real construction. The production of a 1:16 scale model of the grid shell for the *Deubau* 1962 in Essen, made of Perspex laths with a cross-section of 3.0 millimetres x 1.7 millimetres, was to provide the necessary experience in model making and confirm the suitability of the material. The model was tested in four versions, with loose and stiff connections in the nodes of the slats and with and without diagonal stiffening cables in the meshes, so that the critical failure load could be determined. The test results were compared with the real behaviour of the grid shell to determine conversion factors. These tests already indicated that a two-layer grid would be necessary for the design of the *Multihalle* in Mannheim, as well as diagonal tension bands made of steel cables. Based on this preparing model tests, a 1:60 scale model of the main dome of the *Multihalle* was made from Perspex laths with a cross-section of 1.4 millimetres x 2.6 millimetres on a wooden base plate. The model was loaded by attaching bundles of 100 millimetre long nails and the deformation was determined with the help of dial gauges. (Fig. 5) The measurement results enabled an understanding of critical areas of buckling in the shell and confirmed the results of the computer model for the complex three-dimensional structure [27].

From physical to digital – the form-finding and measuring models of the Mannheim Multihalle

Figure 5: Model of the main dome made of Perspex laths on a scale of 1:60 with bundles of nails and dial gauges. Image from B. Burkhardt, (Ed.), IL 13: Multihalle Mannheim, Stuttgart: Institut für leichte Fl chentragwerke (IL), 1978. p.81.

Models for wind tunnel tests

In order to obtain realistic values for the wind loads for the structural calculations, several hollow measurement models were produced at a scale of 1:200 and tests were carried out on them by the British Hydrodynamics Research Association in the wind tunnel at the Cranfield Institute. The scale of 1:200 was chosen because the size of the surrounding area was determined by the size of the turntable in the wind tunnel. For the production of the vacuum-formed models with a shell thickness of approx. 2 millimetres, a model was produced from urethane foam according to a contour drawing by Frei Otto, on which the models could be moulded. This was used to create the transparent, rigid models firmly attached to the base plate with the required openings on the sides. To carry out the tests, the models were equipped with 150 measuring points on the top and bottom and connected to a manometer: the results were photographed after each test. In this way, wind pressure and suction could be determined for different wind directions and wind speeds and plans with the occurring pressures on the shell could be generated with the help of computer programmes. In order to observe wind streams and turbulences, additional experiments with smoke were carried out in the wind tunnel [28]. (Fig. 6)

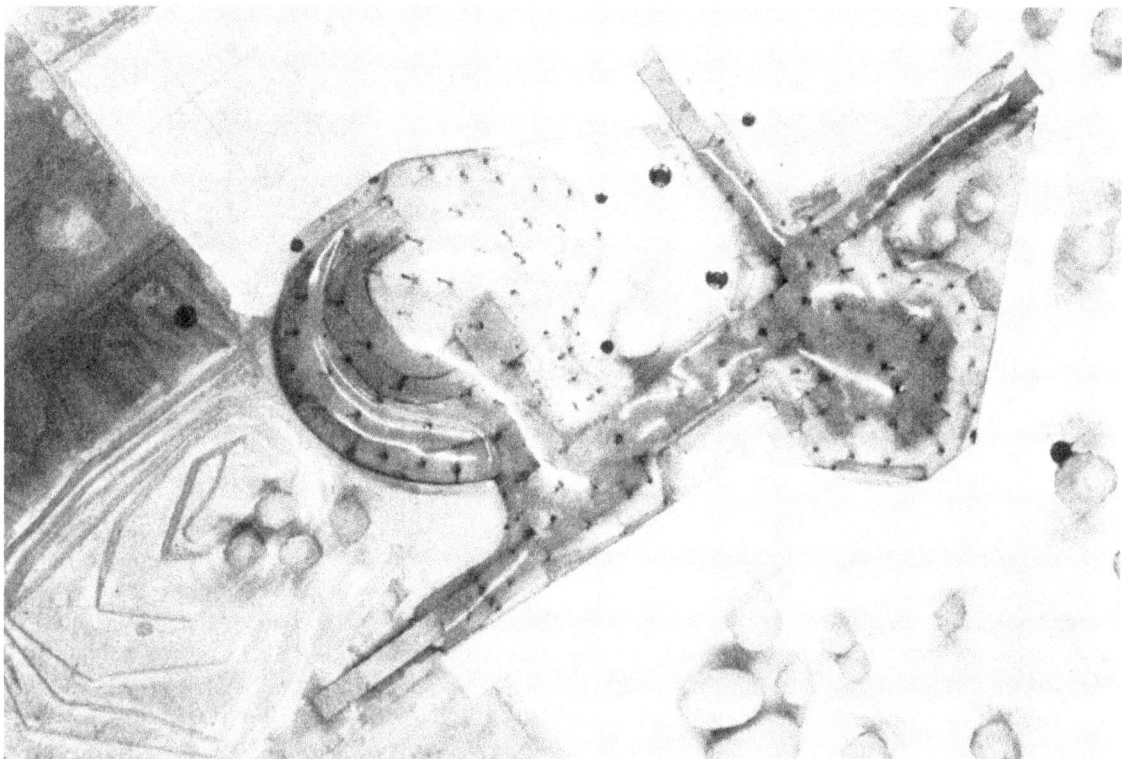

Figure 6: Fig. 6. 1:200 scale model for wind tunnel tests. Image from private collection of Berthold Burkhardt. Image from B. Burkhardt, (Ed.), IL 13: Multihalle Mannheim, Stuttgart: Institut für leichte Fl chentragwerke (IL), 1978. p.66.

The *Multihalle* today

After its completion, the *Multihalle* was consistently praised in contemporary national and international architectural criticism, and the technical innovations of the lattice shell construction were acknowledged. The people of Mannheim also compared the shell to a stranded whale or a lush, sluggish snake, but the building nevertheless won various awards in the years that followed. Despite being planned as a temporary structure, the hall was used as a venue for exhibitions, concerts, sports competitions, meetings and conferences after the Federal Horticultural Show. In 1980, the first repairs had to be carried out on the grid shell and in 1981 the roof skin had to be renewed for the first time. It was not until 1999 that major deformations and settlements of the shell were detected and in 2008 it became necessary to attach a supporting scaffold to the hall. Since 2011, part of the hall has been closed to the public, whereupon the restoration of the structure in accordance with the preservation order was discussed internationally. This is because the *Multihalle* was already included in the list of monuments in 1998 and has also been a cultural monument of special importance in the monument book of *Baden-Württemberg* since 2019. After the sensational announcement in 2016 to demolish the iconic lightweight construction [29], the renovation of the *Mannheim Multihalle* was finally started in 2021.

Conclusion

As this paper has shown in detail, the form-finding, shape-optimisation, static calculation and finally the construction of the *Mannheim Multihalle* as an iconic grid shell would not have been possible without the use of various models and with the help of a multi-diciplinary planning team. It was mainly the interaction between architects, university institutes with experience in model surveying and engineers who were already able to use the latest digital technologies that led the project to its success. The photogrammetric survey of the elaborately produced form-finding model at the IAGB resulted for the first time in a completely digital model, which could subsequently be used in planning. This hybrid use of physical and digital models is groundbreaking for the following developments in architectural production, in which the digital model takes centre stage and physical measurement models are no longer absolutely necessary. The precondition for this was that Arup already had experience with digital calculation methods but had to adapt them to the requirements of the curved grid shell and could only verify them by using further measurement models. For these reasons, it is of great importance to locate and preserve the last preserved models of this almost forgotten engineering practice and to document their significance for innovation in civil engineering and architecture. Currently, a research project funded by the German Research Foundation (*Deutsche Forschungsgemeinschaft*/DFG) is being carried out at the Universities of Innsbruck, Munich and Karlsruhe within the framework of the SPP *Kulturerbe Konstruktion*, to ensure the preservation of the objects and to proof their relevance to the management of built heritage, for example by retro-digitisation of the models into digital twins and their use in damage mapping [30] and restoration practice.

References

[1] E. Happold and W. I. Liddell, 'Timber lattice roof for the Mannheim Bundesgartenschau', *The Structural Engineer*, vol.53, no.3, 1975, p.103.
[2] W. Nerdinger, 'Frei Otto – Arbeit für eine bessere „Menschenerde"' in W. Nerdinger, (Ed.), *Frei Otto: Das Gesamtwerk – leicht bauen, natürlich gestalten*, Basel: Birkhäuser, 2005. pp.9-16.
[3] E. Bubner, 'Die Entwicklungsstätte für den Leichtbau und das Atelier Warmbronn' in W. Nerdinger, (Ed.), *Frei Otto: Das Gesamtwerk – leicht bauen, natürlich gestalten*, Basel: Birkhäuser, 2005. pp.81-90.
[4] E. Möller, 'Dach der Multihalle in Mannheim' in W. Nerdinger, (Ed.), *Frei Otto: Das Gesamtwerk – leicht bauen, natürlich gestalten*, Basel: Birkhäuser, 2005. p.283.
[5] Bubner, (Note 3), p.88.
[6] F. Otto 'Gedanken zum Bau der Gitterschale in Mannheim' in G. Vrachliotis, (Ed.), *Frei Otto, Carlfried Mutschler, Multihalle*, Leipzig: Spector Books, 2017. pp.168-187.
[7] Möller, (Note 4), p.283.
[8] ibid., p.288.
[9] ibid., pp.283-288.
[10] C. Brensing, 'Frei Otto und Ove Arup – Szenen einer gegenseitigen Inspiration' in W. Nerdinger, (Ed.), *Frei Otto: Das Gesamtwerk – leicht bauen, natürlich gestalten*, Basel: Birkhäuser, 2005. pp.103-108.
[11] https://vam.ac.uk/articles/computers-and-the-sydney-opera-house (Consulted on 7th December 2021)
[12] I. Liddell, 'Models for the design development, engineering and construction of the Multihalle for the 1975 Bundesgartenschau in Mannheim' in B. Addis, (Ed.), *Physical models – Their historical and current use in civil and building engineering design*, Berlin: Wilhelm Ernst & Sohn, 2021. p.654.
[13] R. Barthel, 'Naturform – Architekturform' in W. Nerdinger, (Ed.), *Frei Otto: Das Gesamtwerk – leicht bauen, natürlich gestalten*, Basel: Birkhäuser, 2005. pp.24-27.
[14] Happold and Liddell, (Note 1), p.100.
[15] B. Burkhardt, (Ed.), *IL 10: Gitterschalen*, Stuttgart: Institut für leichte Flächentragwerke (IL), 1974. p.46.
[16] B. Addis, 'Physical Modelling and Form Finding' in S. Adriaenssens, P. Block, D. Veenendaal and C. Williams, (Eds), *Shell Structures for Architecture – Form Finding and Optimization*, London/New York: Routledge, 2014. p.40.
[17] G. Vrachliotis 'Die Multihalle. Experimentalbau, Gesellschaftsutopie und Diskursobjekt' in G. Vrachliotis, (Ed.), *Frei Otto, Carlfried Mutschler, Multihalle*, Leipzig: Spector Books, 2017. pp.38-167.
[18] Bubner, (Note 3), p.88.
[19] E. Bubner 'Die Formfindung der Gitterschale' in B. Burkhardt, (Ed.), *IL 13: Multihalle Mannheim*, Stuttgart: Institut für leichte Flächentragwerke (IL), 1978. p.34.

[20] Vrachliotis, (Note 17), pp.38-167.
[21] Bubner, (Note 19), p.36-40.
[22] C. Weber 'Frei Otto: Dach der Multihalle Mannheim, 1970-75' in O. Elser and P. C. Schmal, (Eds), *Das Architekturmodell: Werkzeug, Fetisch, Kleine Utopie*, Zürich: Scheidegger & Spiess, 2012. p.178.
[23] L. Gründig, U. Hangleiter and H. D. Preuss, 'Berechnung des Hängenetzes und Zuschnittsermittlung' in B. Burkhardt, (Ed.), *IL 13: Multihalle Mannheim*, Stuttgart: Institut für leichte Flächentragwerke (IL), 1978. p.44.
[24] Weber, (Note 22), p.178.
[25] Happold and Liddell, (Note 1), p.108.
[26] Information via email from the model restorer of the DAM Christian Walter on 22.11.2021
[27] Addis, (Note 16), p.41-42.
[28] Happold and Liddell, (Note 1), pp.108-110.
[29] M. Mertens, 'Der gestrandete Wal – Das Baudenkmal Multihalle', *Denkmalpflege in Baden-Württemberg – Nachrichtenblatt der Landesdenkmalpflege*, vol.49, no.1, 2020. pp.9-14.
[30] C. Kayser and I. Kovacevic, 'Unter Gittern – Exemplarische Schadensaufnahme an der Mannheimer Multihalle', *Denkmalpflege in Baden-Württemberg – Nachrichtenblatt der Landesdenkmalpflege*, vol.49, no.1, 2020. pp.15-20.

Systems for Standardised Precast Concrete Elements: The Case of the Larsen & Nielsen System

Jørgen Burchardt
Museum Vestfyn

Abstract

Many systems for large-scale industrialised building in precast concrete were developed in the beginning of the post-war period after the Second World War. One of the most important systems was constructed by the Danish company Larsen & Nielsen.

Thanks to intensive development work, it was possible to switch to full industrial construction of houses in just 15 years, so that the annual output of built square meters could be quadrupled compared to pre-war figures.

This innovation involved not only the use of new technology but also a complete transformation of organizational forms, company constellations, education, public administration, and financial management. This development was supported by courageous politicians.

The L&N system became one of the leading building systems for houses in Denmark, and since 1956 the company has held export to and production licenses in many other countries. The export first went to nearby countries and later to Asia, America, and Africa.

The use of large-scale elements had some weak points. One was a vulnerable construction and the construction fraud of unskilled workers on skyscrapers, as seen with the Ronan Point accident in Great Britain in 1968. Another was the need for steadily high production volume to keep the production facilities alive. This was lost due to energy crises and the collapse of state administrations in many countries, and the company went out of business in 1997.

Industrialised building systems

Production in large quantities takes place by industrial production of standardised elements. Bricks and timber with fixed dimensions have been used for centuries in the construction industry.

However, the assembly of these relatively small elements was costly and often carried out on the construction site by skilled workers. It was laborious and thus expensive. A new generation of businesspeople after World War II saw that one could learn from the manufacturing of cars. Houses could be built on assembly lines if parts of the assembly work moved to an industrial production plant. This happened with the manufacture of doors and windows, and for the more significant constructions came entire staircases cast in concrete and long elements for flooring [1].

France became the leading country in industrial building, as it had long been with other pioneers in the field of concrete, after the engineer Raymond Camus developed a complete building system. He had experience from the car factory Citroen, and he developed a building system based on prefabricated concrete elements. He applied for a patent in 1948, and his ideas were realised quickly. Houses were not built in France alone. In 1977, a census showed that

350,000 apartments were built in 20 different countries. Of these, 300 factories existed in the USSR inspired by his ideas and some based on his approximately 42 patents [2].

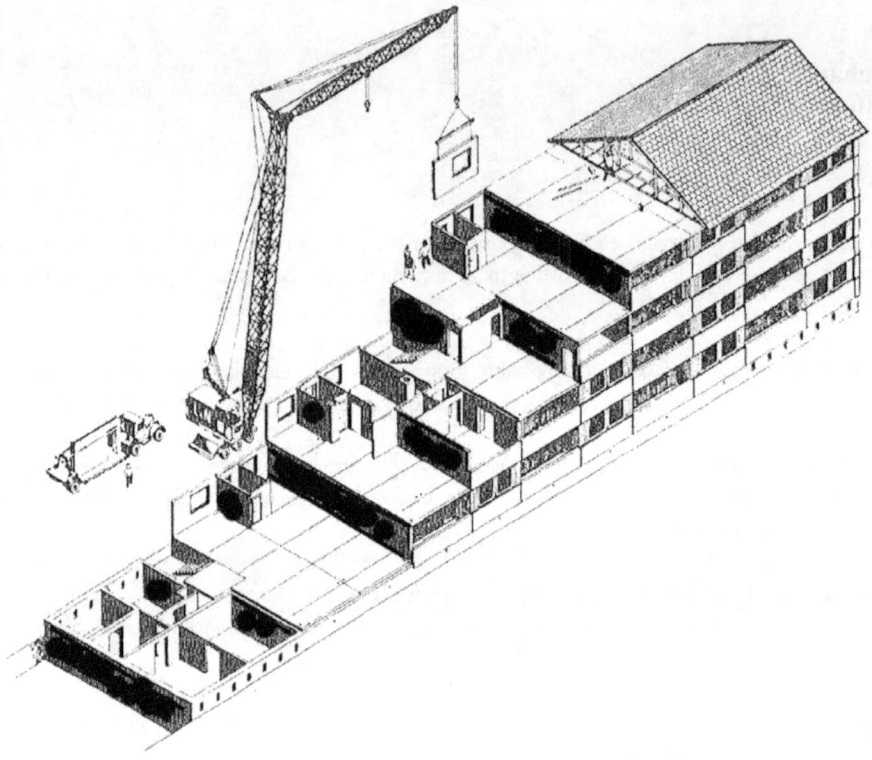

Figure 1: The over 400 m long Vesterbo building in Værløse created an international breakthrough for LN in 1959. Many countries were impressed by the LN-BO system, including the delivery of elements with everything mounted (Nissen, p. 283) [3].

This article mentions another of the important developers of building systems, the Danish company Larsen & Nielsen (LN), Copenhagen (in some English literature spelled Larson & Nielson) [4]. The civil engineers R.A. Larsen (1905-1983) and Axel Nielsen (1906-1989) established the company in 1931. It started using elements in the facade when building a hospital in 1948, and after a few years of experience it developed a complete system for assembly construction [5].

Larsen & Nielsen's first system and its subsequent improved systems had a great advantage. Columns could be avoided by letting walls bear the building. Many other systems had facades as a load-bearing element, but the systems from LN had the advantage that only the internal transverse walls carried the building. This gave the architects a more significant opportunity to unfold their abilities to decorate the facade, which could otherwise become monotonous through the constant repetition of similar elements and small windows.

Jørgen Burchardt

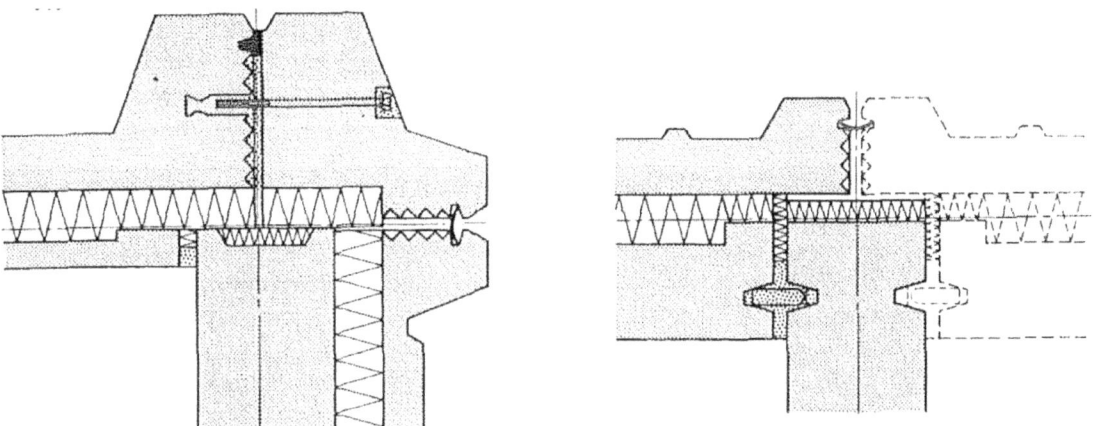

Figure 2: The assembly of elements was continually improved. Here are two of LN's solutions. On the left is an assembly of a corner from the Hareskovvej building in 1958; on the right is an assembly from Bellmansgade from 1962 (Nissen Note 3, p. 47).

Figure 3: Povl Egon Malmstrøm (1917-1985) helped, through his own consulting engineering company, several companies plan almost all the most important Danish assembly systems (Photo: The Royal Library).

In total, LN designed more than 25 factories around the world, and the company's worldwide importance in spreading expertise within the industry was significant. In total, the company entered into 53 licensing agreements in 25 countries.

The company had many competitors. In 1965 at least 120 building systems for industrialised construction existed on the English market; however, probably only 40 were usable. A simultaneous description of systems for the heavy panel concrete buildings counted 71 systems. Most systems were developed in countries where World War II had created a great need for renewal. In the English inventory, 19 were British, 11 French, and 10 German. In fourth place came Scandinavia with eight systems [6].

In Denmark, LN had competition from two companies. One was Jespersen & Søn, a system that ended up being licensed in 1980 at 14 factories in seven different countries, and more than 80,000 homes were built according to the system. Jespersen & Søn used a so-called open system, to which other companies could also supply elements. Thus, 80% of its construction was done by tire and wall production standard components [7].

Another important Danish company was Højgaard & Schultz, founded in 1918. It had already established a cement foundry in 1950. It also became one of the country's huge companies, and its systems also developed towards an open system.

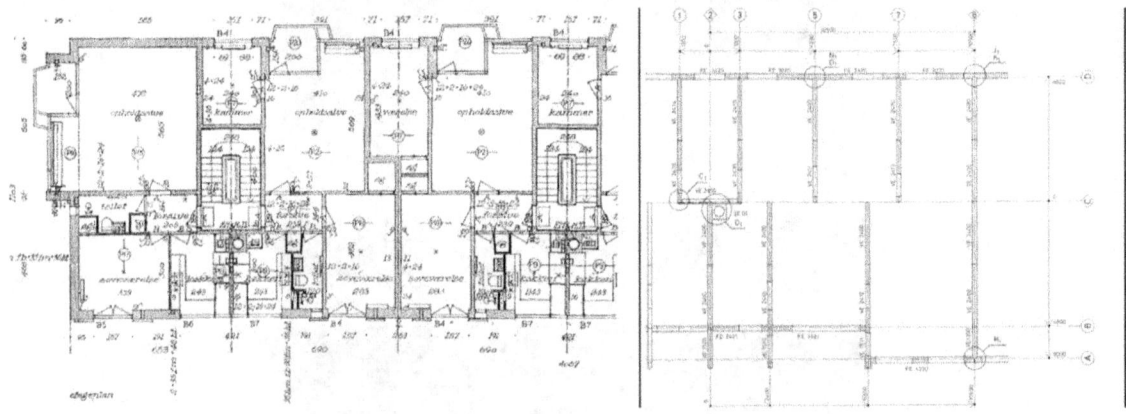

Figure 4: Construction with elements changed the drawings at the workplace. At left a drawing from traditional construction with information for all subjects, while in element construction, it was only a drawing of the assembly (Nissen Note 3, p. 152 and 154).

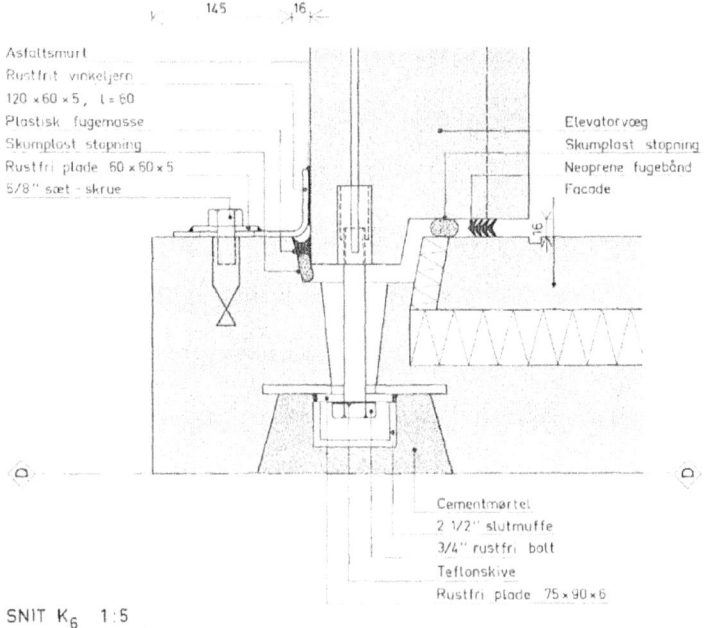

Figure 5: Horizontal section in joint between facade and exterior elevator tower in the LN-BO system. Many parts had to be mounted accurately to avoid later construction damage. Poorly instructed unskilled workers and failing control was the weakness of industrialized construction (Nissen Note 3, p. 301).

The need for housing

At the liberation in 1945, the housing situation in Denmark was critical. House construction had stalled and in the following years the redevelopment properties of the big cities deteriorated further due to a lack of materials [8].

The influx of apprentices to the construction trades was minimal during the limited construction of the war years, and with continued limited construction in the post-war years the number of skilled masons continued to decline. Seasonal unemployment was high. For example, 17,000 out of the nearly 53,000 (32%) unskilled construction workers were unemployed in January 1950.

Therefore, desire rose to spread construction throughout the year. Here, element construction had many advantages: it could be completed in a very short time when elements were cast in parallel with earthworks and load-bearing foundations. It was possible to build during the winter period, as the elements could be installed in almost any weather, and with the house under one roof, the other craftsmen had controlled working conditions.

Wood was especially in short supply, which was a problem when an average of approximately 10 m³ of wood was used for an apartment around 1950. The former major producers, the Soviet Union and the Baltic countries, supplied almost nothing, which is why Denmark introduced strict restrictions.

The best solution was to completely replace wood with factory-made concrete building elements. Elements for floor separations could be the basis for casting a cement floor. Unskilled people could assemble many of the elements, which was an advantage with the lack of skilled workers. These were all reasons behind the desire for prefabricated construction.

The nature of the element factories

It took many years to learn how to use concrete for building houses. Only a few building parts were cast at the many concrete foundries across the country, which otherwise mainly supplied road tiles and sewer pipes.

Entire houses were cast in concrete as early as 1900. Although the first element houses were assembled in the United States in 1918 and in Germany in the 1920s, the first many years were spent casting in the traditional way: carpenters built a form of wood, and in this formwork the load-bearing walls or columns were cast.

As early as the 1940s, the City of Copenhagen made plans for pilot building, but it took some years before construction on the high-rise buildings at *Bellahøj* began (words in italics are names of important building projects). LN built some of the high-rise buildings erected using climbing formwork, while partitions were cast on site [9].

A large number of forces worked together to rationalise the construction: a new Ministry of Housing was established in 1947, and a new state research institute for construction got started and worked with the Engineers' Association, the Standardization Council, and many private companies. The work of rationalizing the construction also came to include the standardization of building elements. The initiative was taken by the Engineers' Association's Rationalization Committee, which published a report on the simplification of construction in 1951. In it, a "vertical modularity" was proposed, with a ceiling height of 280 cm, which was introduced as a requirement for state-subsidised housing construction in 1953.

Element construction was not yet mature, but it gave LN an opportunity to work, as the Danish military had to build extensive barracks buildings. It received such large orders that it was worthwhile to build a permanent element factory in a suburb of Copenhagen, Glostrup, in 1951, thanks to support from Marshall Aid. In the first years, 20,000 tons of items per year were produced by 60-70 men. The factory was expanded in 1954 in connection with delivery for construction for the City of Copenhagen. In 1954-1961, production increased to 50,000 t/year. In its best year in 1971, production exceeded 200,000 tons.

Much development work took place in the offices of the rapidly growing company. However, one person should be mentioned in the development of LN's systems: P.E. Malmstrøm. He not only helped LN but also helped develop other Danish companies' building systems [10].

LN's first building system

The first building system, LN-BO, was a closed system. "Closed" means that the geometric configuration of the elements was brand-specific. The connection detail was unique for the company, where one element of one system was incompatible with those of other systems [11].

It was a complete system because all elements and components for an entire building were included in the package. The design and construction process was included.

Reinforcement bars and hooks that facilitate transporting, handling, and joining the panels were provided beforehand, as well as frames for doors and window openings.

The moulds were the bottleneck of an element factory. They were expensive to manufacture and had a limited life. Eventually, they were made of steel, but were expensive and therefore had to be used many times. For the first building systems a dwelling type consisted of approximately 60 different concrete elements, which could then be assembled into four or five different apartment types.

Torveparken in Gladsaxe became the first of LN's buildings constructed by elements. In 1957 the company went ahead with hollow core elements produced in moulds with inserted tubes, which were pulled out the day after casting. This construction used less concrete and reduced the weight.

Completely finished bathrooms with all accessories - including toilet paper holders - were delivered in finished units. Initially, they presented a logistical problem with their weight of 6-7 tons, but later they were replaced by lighter constructions made of fiberglass-reinforced polyester.

LN's first type house was built on *Hareskovvej* in Copenhagen. It was the first eight-story building, which became the starting point for LN's multi-story type house.

The first large project with all parts manufactured at the factory was the *Vesterbo* building in Værløse, built in 1954-1959. Here, sandwich elements with insulation between two concrete slabs were used for the first time. The elements were even finished with glazed windows. The 400 m long house became Denmark's longest house. It was used for a long time as a reference when the company had to sell solutions abroad.

The experiences led to the development of a building system called LN-BO (bo means 'to live' in English). The was first used was on the *Søbækgaard* building in Espergærde in 1963.

A building was typically constructed with floor plates of 2.4 m broad elements, whereas most other Danish companies used 1.2 m. The hollow cover elements were laid on the 15 cm solid load-bearing transverse walls of unreinforced concrete. The decks, normally 18 cm thick, were usually sufficiently rigid for the limited spans of up to 4½ m. Non-load-bearing walls were 6.4 cm thick with solid, unreinforced elements supplemented with carpentry walls around cabinet sections. Non-load-bearing partitions were traditionally carried out of wooden partitions with sheet metal cladding. They were replaced by 64 mm concrete elements with surfaces ready for painting work. The painting work was also rationalised, as it was reduced to a spray treatment of ceilings and walls, as the majority of the furniture and installations were supplied with finished surfaces.

Kitchen furniture and cupboards went through a long development from semi-finished products that were processed and assembled on the building to fully finished components ready for installation in the raw house.

This system became a success. More than 9,000 apartments of this type were built in Denmark in 1980.

New systems

There was constant development in the industry, and LN continuously improved its systems. Production techniques were developed at the company's element factory in the 1960s, so tolerances were reduced. This meant that joints could be made without giving jumps and unevenness in the surface during assembly.

A new system, LN-NYBO (NY-BO = new live), was introduced in 1969. Slabs of 23 cm thickness were delivered in spans of 6.6 m, which gave a much freer division of the area between the load-bearing transverse walls [12].

The new type was not developed for a specific building, but rather made after commercial and production considerations, as well as on a large resident survey (later translated into English by the Canadian Building Research Institute, as it was the only survey of its type at that time). The series length was at least 4,000 apartments, with a minimum of 100 apartments.

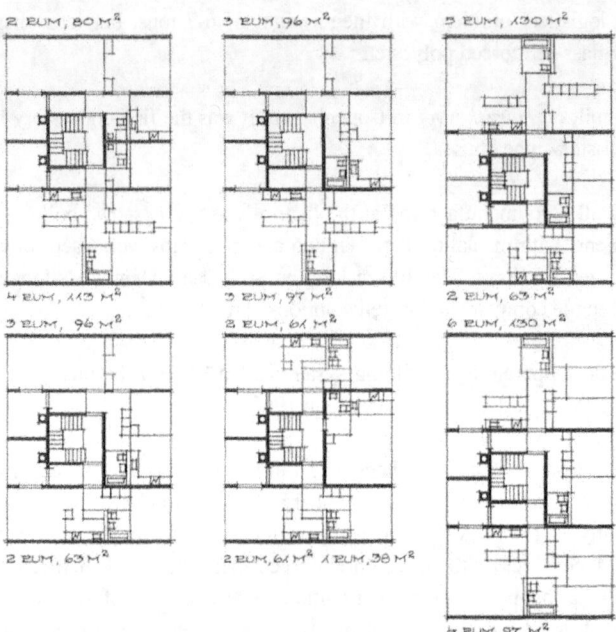

Figure 6: A new developed system, LN-NYBO, was launched in 1968. Its apartments had improved facilities, elements with even more installations built-in, and there were 14 possible combinations of apartments with a net area of 33 to 117 m² (Nissen Note 3, p. 289).

The planning for the element factory in Glostrup in the 1970s was based on the goal that LN-NYBO ran on the two production lines. The third production line ran at a new element factory in Taastrup, which was to run *Brøndby Strand* since it was a "foreign project" and not based on one of the company's series.

The company expected to develop new housing types based on a planning period of three years. However, a new project, LN-73, was hit by the Ministry of Housing in 1972 when it demanded a decline in the cost of new social housing. The quality had to deteriorate and the maximum size of the apartments was reduced to 80 m² on average. It was announced in a circular, popularly called the "Tiled stove Circular". The average LN apartment in social housing in 1966 was 74 m², while it had risen to 100 m² by 1971. At the same time, equipment and materials were improved with more built-in cabinets, flooring from extra-flamed beech to ash or oak. The refrigerator grew from a 125 l to 350 l fridge and freezer. At the same time, there was better ventilation and double-glazed windows. In addition, there were many improvements outside the apartment with more and larger hobby rooms; the playground equipment increased as well. Parking spaces were increased from 1 to 1½ per. apartment. Traffic segregation had been introduced, and more was sacrificed on gardens.

The desire for the sharp cuts meant the LN-BO system had a revival, and 2,000 apartments were built with certain modifications.

However, the time of the high-rise building was over, and thus the efficient mass production also stopped. It became low-density buildings instead. A new system was launched in 1974, LN-Hylde Bo, which was first used for the residential development *Hyldespjældet* in Albertslund. The current demand for low-density buildings meant a new development. The insulation layers were nine cm thicker, and PEX hoses were used for water pipes. It was a heavy construction with large elements on spans for up to 6 m. The load-bearing elements weighed more than 5 t, and tires even 5.7 t.

In the period 1962-1974, 7,751 LN-BO type apartments were manufactured. During the same period, one-off projects were built on 9,286 apartments, of which included *Brøndby Strand, Valby Gasværk,* and *Stjernen*. In *Brøndby Strand*, LN's design department was only involved as an assistant in the planning. The planning period was ten years, which is why it was not easy to plan an optimal production rate at the element factory.

Element export

During periods of surplus capacity at the element factories, employment could be maintained through the export of elements. Although the transport costs naturally amounted to a fairly high extra cost, it could pay to bid on construction projects far from Denmark.

Hamburg was in dire need of housing after a flood disaster in 1962, and finished elements were delivered on 1,000 *Bellmansgade*-type apartments. The great need meant that a dispensation was granted from the strict German building regulations.

Many elements for Germany were also supplied by an element factory in Hjallese on Funen, which was produced under license. The railway in Funen had a direct connection to Germany, so the elements did not have to be transported to ships along the way, as was the case with the occasional deliveries to Sweden and Norway.

In 1966 it was delivered to Berlin in connection with the start-up of a new licensed factory in Berlin.

Figure 7: Institutions, office buildings, and, as here, the factory hall type LN 02 were a large part of LN's building activities. Despite standard types, the customers' individual wishes reduced the possibility of a significant system export (LN archive, Danish National Archives).

Commercial buildings, schools, etc.

Construction of factories, offices, and warehouses was also on LN's building program based on typified, prefabricated projects. The majority of the constructions were in the Nordic countries and England. It was a rational construction with a high degree of completion. It also developed into type houses, although there was rarely mass construction, as in the case of large construction projects, but often tailor-made projects for each company's fabrication based on one type.

However, warehouses were produced in large numbers in two types. One type had a main girder across the neck vessels, while the other type had main girders with roofing sheets between the facade and the main girder in the centreline of the building.

Similarly, types were also developed for schools, care centres, and skating rinks. Schools became somewhat widespread based on a type first built on Funen in 1963 (hence the Funen Plan). A number of architects set up a design studio in collaboration with a number of schools, the "Central Office for Practicing Architects on Funen". The state supported the construction, and in the first years more than 100,000 m^2 of schools were built. In 1983, a total of 110 schools were built with a total floor area of 477,000 m^2 in Denmark. The construction was based on 12 different building types.

The company tried several times to produce single-family houses, but it was usually only for a few experimental houses. Among other things, a villa was built in Switzerland.

Purchased licenses for manufacturing abroad

The first licensing agreement occurred in 1956 with Ungdomsbyg in Oslo, Norway; the first contracts followed in Sweden, Germany, the Netherlands, and England soon after. These agreements were with existing companies that wanted to mechanise and systematise their housing production.

Figure 8: One of the factories based on license was opened in 1965 in Sunderland, Great Britain, by Taylor & Woodrow – Anglia (LN archive, Danish National Archives).

No guarantees were given in relation to the quality of the construction, but the licensees could see the quality from the factory in Glostrup and from the finished homes in Denmark. The agreements went on a percentage charge of future sales.

Demand abroad grew, and in 1966 a special department was set up to take care of sales abroad: Larsen & Nielsen Consultor.

In Hungary and Czechoslovakia, factories were built with a desire for a high production rate. LN supplied Europe's largest element factory to the state-owned construction group, Stavebni Zavody Praha, in Czechoslovakia. The Malešice factory had seven production lines for horizontal moulds. Here, LN had to guarantee a production capacity of a promised quality. Governments did not trust a local licensee to provide this service.

Germany became the biggest market. The need was great, but tight and outdated local building codes prevented large success. By 1980, more than 24,000 homes were built under the LN system. The first licensee factory was built in 1959, and later element factories were built in Schleswig-Holstein, Hessen, Berlin, and North Rhine-Westphalia.

Figure 9: Collaboration with local licensees was necessary to handle, among other things, the many different local building regulations. Betonfertigbau West did it in Cologne with the complex Neue Heimat (LN archive, Danish National Archives).

In the United States, the RELBEC consortium in Puerto Rico was merged with the International Basic Economy Corporation and the Rexach Construction Company. The factory opened in 1972 after two years of preparation. One- and two-story single-family houses were produced, but only a few elegant high-rise buildings were built, and in 1975 a planned municipal housing development fell away, RELBEC went bankrupt, and the factory closed [13].

Licensing in the first years was mostly based on 10-year contracts. In recent years, the contracts were based on the payment of direct services. All in all, however, the sale of licenses abroad comprised only a tiny part of LN's revenue.

LN never succeeded in developing international housing types. The building regulations and traditions of the individual countries were too different from the Danish ones. It also meant that no additional components could be sold.

In 1960s Spain a number of buildings were built in Barcelona with the Construccion Industrial de Edificios S.A. (CIDESA). However, the raw house was cast on-site and provided with prefabricated facades of concrete sandwich elements. In 1972, a new element factory was built in a suburb of Barcelona to manufacture 100% LN constructions. Another factory was built in 1974 in the Alcala de Henares in the province of Madrid. As a result, the annual capacity was approximately 3,000 apartments.

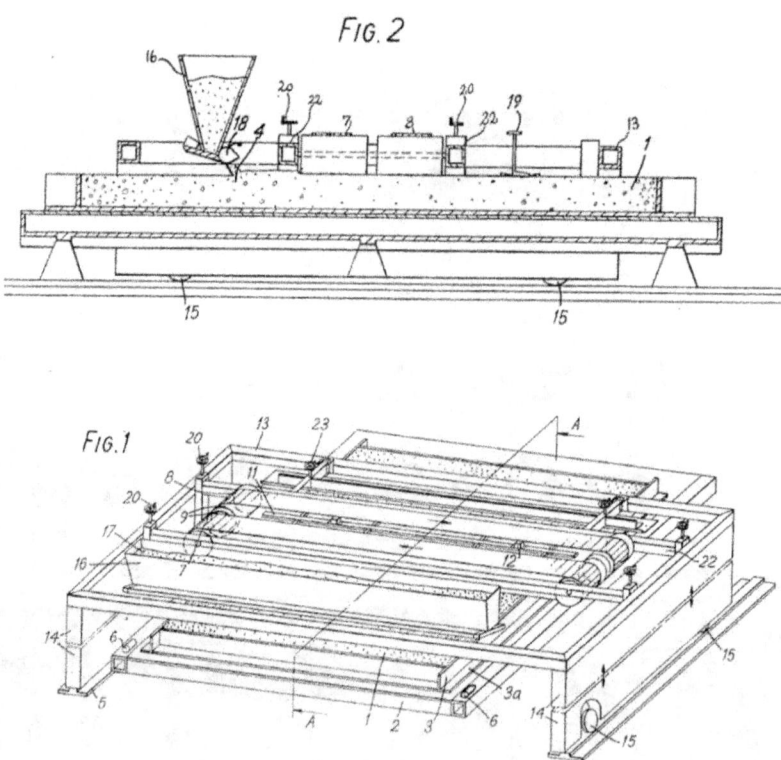

Figure 10: Patents were essential to LN for the company to maintain its position as one of the world's leading suppliers of finished element foundries. This casting machine for smooth slaps was patented in 1971 (patent GB1402317A).

Jørgen Burchardt

The Anglo-Danish engineer Ove Arup arranged contact with one of England's largest construction companies, Taylor Woodrow-Anglian, and since 1963 a number of significant buildings have been built in the London suburbs. Later, construction continued in Sunderland.

One of the English buildings has become world-famous in a tragic way. The 1968 *Ronan Point* accident became a critical event for not only LN, but for the entire industry. Two months after construction, part of a 22-story high-rise collapsed after a gas explosion, and four people were killed after a cascading collapse. In England alone there were 600 buildings of that same type. Restrictions were immediately placed on the use of gas in high-rise buildings. The accident gave rise to a revision of building regulations around the world so that high-rise buildings were better equipped to withstand unforeseen events and strong winds. When new technical problems arose, investigations showed heavy construction fraud in the *Ronan Point* building, leading to nine high-rise buildings being demolished in 1991 [14].

Figure 11: A gas explosion in a 22-storey house, Ronan Point, near London, showed that high-rise buildings were not designed to withstand extreme impacts. Building authorities worldwide then had to revise their building regulations (LN archive, Danish National Archives).

International technology transfer

LN was active in technology transfer. The company thus exchanged knowledge with the Soviet Union and other Eastern European countries, which had extensive experience in assembly construction. In 1966, a visit was arranged by a reciprocal visit with the Soviets. For 20 days a strong group of actors of industrialised construction studied assembly construction in Moscow, Leningrad, and Sochi on the Black Sea. Similarly, Russian engineers gained access to Danish factories and construction sites. The co-operation also took on a formal character in 1972-1973, when the Ministry of Housing signed agreements with both the Polish and Soviet ministries on co-operation.

Outside Europe

Following the first licensing agreements in highly industrialised countries, LN sought customer potential for package-deal deliveries in middle-developed countries. The least developed countries were avoided as industrialised construction required a certain infrastructure level.

One of the first projects outside of Europe was realised in Asia. In 1966 a partnership was formed with Gammon Southeast Asia Berhad Ltd. to build housing for the city government of Kuala Lumpur in Malaya. An element factory was established in order to build 3,000 apartments. In 1969 the buildings were completed at a very modest price, which is why everything should be cheap in the 40 m² apartments. For example, there was no flooring.

Figure 12: Brøndby Strand became one of the country's largest construction projects between 1969-1974, with 2,850 apartments spread over buildings in two, four, and 16 storeys. Other firms carried out the work of engineers and architects. The oil crisis stopped LN's large projects in Denmark (Suburban Museum).

The oil crisis of 1973 dampened construction in Europe, and interest in construction exports grew in the industry. The trend was supported by various government measures through fund support and export credits. There were also a number of bilateral agreements with other countries in the form of agreements on technological cooperation and arrangements for construction symposia. These were mainly held with countries in Eastern Europe, the Middle East, and the Far East. LN hosted nine international congresses with broad exchanges of technical information during the 1970s and 1980s.

The Middle East became an important area of work for many years. Major construction projects resulted from a lengthy diplomatic effort by the Danish government. The foundation was laid when the Iranian shah visited Denmark in 1959, where he visited companies such as LN. In 1974, the Iranian finance minister visited the country and signed a series of supply agreements, including the construction of 20,000 homes a year for five years.

In a wave of enthusiasm for industrialization in the Middle East and Asia, there was great interest in receiving know-how. LN offered the Egyptian Ministry of Housing a staff member free of charge to thoroughly analyse the entire issue surrounding industrialised construction. The ministry established a department to assist the country's 11 element factories.

LN offered a total "package" to Egypt, Iraq, Saudi Arabia, and South Korea. In addition to the actual construction of a factory, training programs and management services were included. Until the mid-1980s, 12 of these packages were delivered. Despite the war between Iraq and Iran, LN continued to build a number of element factories in Iraq.

Conclusions

The construction company LN moved early into element construction and quickly gained a leading position in Denmark. When the state started supporting large construction projects in the 1940s, LN had the opportunity to become one of the most significant participants.

The technique was based on transverse walls as load-bearing elements, whereby the facades gave the architects an opportunity for creative expression. In this way, the technique had an advantage over systems, where the facade as a supporting element limited the architectural possibilities both aesthetically and spatially.

Establishing their own element factories in combination with the logic of element construction for planning all details and tight time management meant organizational change for LN. The company became a system supplier, and for many large building projects LN also became a total supplier with many permanent employed architects and engineers. It could deliver buildings at a fixed price and at the agreed time in a turnkey contract.

The construction method was rational in continuous production, and at the same time the transport of the heavy elements gave a natural boundary at a distance of 200 km between the factory and construction site. These conditions were met in the years after the war when the need for new housing was great. There was also a great deal of political attention at the same time, so public authorities provided conditions for the large number of new buildings.

Thanks to the good conditions in Denmark, the Danish company had developed good systems that were continuously replaced by improved versions. It provided exports to many European countries. The company's technology became important with production in 25 countries. In addition, the company was important through effective exchange of knowledge with other countries, e.g., in Eastern Europe.

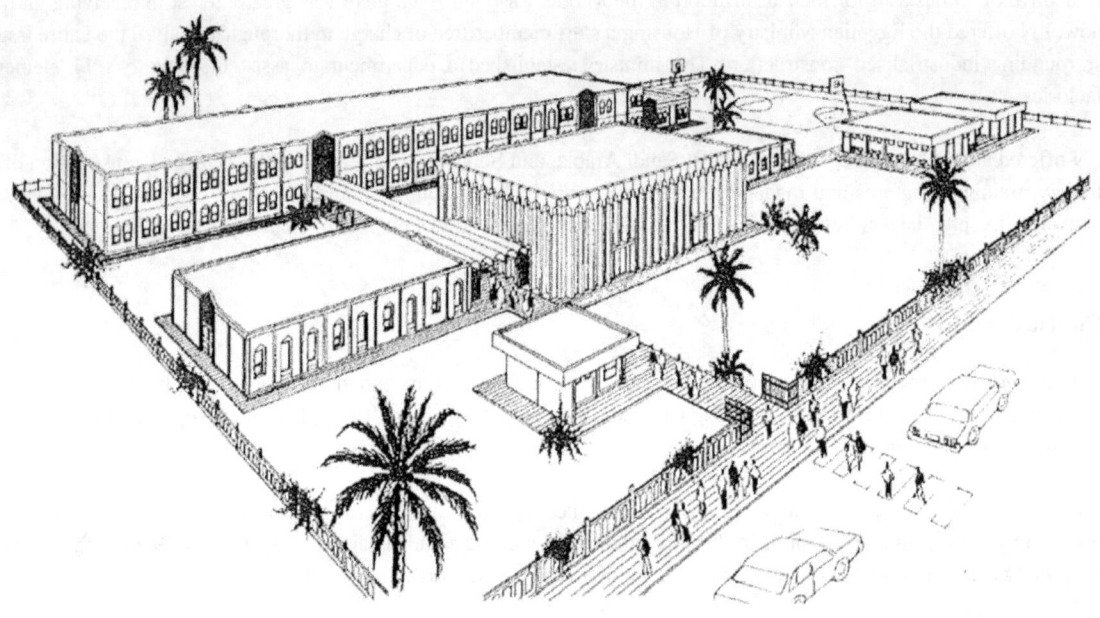

Figure 13: LN built 216 schools in Baghdad on a total of 715,000 m^2 based on the model from the Danish Funen Plan. The project did not become a faithful copy, as conditions had to be adapted to local conditions and the possibilities of an existing element factory (Nissen Note 2, p. 401).

References

[1] Jørgen Burchardt, 'Vejen til det industrielle byggeri: 15 års forceret teknologiudvikling 1945-1960', *Fabrik og bolig* 2018, pp. 9–33.

[2] Yvan Delemontey,'Raymond Camus et l'avènement de la préfabrication lourde en France: Vers un nouveau paradigme structurel', *Centraliens* (625) 2013, pp. 57–62, Raymond Camus, "Camus throughout the world" in B. Campbell, *Housing from the factory*, London: Cement & Concrete Association, 1963, pp. 9-16 and Johs. F. Munch-Petersen, *Fransk og britisk byggeri: Indtryk fra en studierejse for udvalget i 1956,* København: Teknisk Forlag, 1957. The factories in USSR are mentioned only inspired by Camus but are not exact types, according Nikolay Erofeev, 'The I-464 housing delivery system: A tool for urban modernisation in the socialist world and beyond', *Fabrications* 29 (2), 2019, pp. 207-230. See also Christel Frapier, "The circulation of technical knowledge between France and Eastern Europe, 1945–1975", *The Journal of Architecture*, 14:2, 2009, p. 185-196.

[3] Henrik Nissen, *Montagebyggeri,* [3. edn.], Lyngby: Polyteknisk Forlag, 1984.

[4] For instance R. M. E. Diamant, *Industrialised building 1: 50 internat. Methods,* London: Iliffe Books, 1964.

[5] I. Vaarby Laursen, *Larsen & Nielsen, 1951-78.* IFH-rapport 152, Lyngby: Institut for Husbygning, Danmarks Tekniske Højskole, 1980 and L&N, *L&N gennem 60 år,* Birkerød: Larsen & Nielsen, 1991.

[6] Diamant (Note 2), R. M. E. Diamant, *Industrialised building 2: 50 international methods: second series,* London: Iliffe Books, 1965 and R. M. E. Diamant, *Industrialised building 3: 70 international methods: third series,* London: Iliffe Books, 1968. On the French Coignet system, see Edouard Fougea "The Coignet system", in Campbell Note 2, pp 17-24. On German systems see: Karoline Terlau-Friemann, 'Industrielles Bauen in Europa - 75 Jahre Grosstafelbauweise', in Günther Peters *Geschichte und Zukunft des industriellen Bauens,* Tagungsmaterialien, Berlin: NORA 2002, pp. 47–66 and Christine Hannemann, *Die Platte. Industrialisierter Wohnungsbau in der DDR,* Berlin: Springer, 2000.

[7] Morten Lind Larsen and Troels Riis Larsen, *I medgang og modgang: Dansk byggeri og den danske velfærdsstat 1945-2007,* Ballerup: Byggecentrum, 2007.

[8] Burchardt Note 1 and Larsen and Larsen Note 7.

[9] Sven Bertelsen, *Bellahøj, Ballerup, Brøndby Strand: 25 år der industrialiserede byggeriet,* Hørsholm: SBI, 1997, and Burchardt Note 1.

[10] *Ingeniøren*, 1959, 48, p. 1.

[11] Nissen Note 3, Vaarby Laursen Note 5, L&N Note 5, Burchardt Note 1, articles from *Ingeniøren* and letters in the L&N Archive, Danish National Archives.

[12] Frits Gravesen, *Analyse af byggesystemer*, IFH-rapport nr. 147, Lyngby: Institut for Husbygning, 1981.

[13] Evans K. Essienyi, *Prefabricated housing, a solution for Ghana's housing shortage*, Boston: Massachusetts Institute of Technology, 2011.

[14] *Failure of a high-rise system.* Reprint from Architectural Record, November 1968 and Cynthia Pearson and Norbert Delatte, 'Ronan Point apartment tower collapse and its effect on building codes', *Journal of Performance Construction Facilities* 19 (2) 2005, pp. 172–177.

Algorithm or experience – The search for objective design methods for serial structures in the GDR

Konrad M. Frommelt
Brandenburgische Technische Universität Cottbus-Senftenberg

Abstract

The creation of standardised methods for the systematic creation and selection of feasible solutions for prefabricated structural systems had an important role in the industrialisation in the GDR building construction industry. The predominance of mass-produced structures demanded streamlined design processes that provided variants of highly efficient solutions and methods for their evaluation. This paper explores concepts conceived in academic research for design and evaluation of structures by revisiting some relevant contemporary doctoral theses dealing with these problems. The results show that a generalised, easy to use, and accurate methodology could not be achieved in GDR research.

Introduction

A large majority of building construction in the German Democratic Republic (GDR) for both residential and non-residential building was carried out with serial systems, utilising parts prefabricated in only a few specialised factories (Fig. 1). The decision to concentrate the whole building sector on industrialised methods was made in 1955. The intended technocratic approach to industrialisation encompassed the methods of production and assembly, as well as design procedures [1]. While the industrialisation of building production itself made huge leaps forward in the following years, the 'scientification' of the creative design process lagged behind. This was considered a significant problem since the creation of detailed alternative variants as the basis for a substantiated decision, as required for mass production, was very labour-intensive [2].

Figure 1: In-line assembly of prefabricated steel roof segments of the 'Ruhland' type (Büttner & Stenker, 1986)

Algorithm or experience – The search for objective design methods for serial structures in the GDR

In the contemporary literature, two strategies were considered to boost planning output: the work of a considerable number of engineers and architects with non-localised, pre-planned *Typenprojekte* (type projects) – with the whole GDR as a vast 'building site' – and the automation of design, with computers taking over a lot of routine tasks. This approach was consistent with the postulate of an incremental shift of creative activities away from physical labour in the course of the 'scientific-technical revolution': an increased significance of mental work, before routine tasks were gradually taken over by machines and finally computers [3]. Additionally, the gains in productivity were to free up valuable labour time that was made available for research and development, unleashing more creative potential in the building industry [4].

At the end of the 1970s, the design of standardised structures was at a high level while a synthetic overview was still lacking [5]. In the GDR, building research was carried out at industrial research facilities, at the institutes of the *Bauakademie*, a public institution for building related research under the aegis of the Ministry for Building, as well as at the *Ingenieurhochschulen* (engineering colleges), which focused on training skilled engineers and providing research rapidly applicable in the industry [6]. One of these colleges, the relatively small *Ingenieurhochschule Cottbus* (IHC), centred entirely upon structural engineering and building research. Of the theoretical research done there, some works that dealt with the engineering design process itself are of special interest.

As Bill Addis has pointed out, engineering design can be described as a process with two main objectives: providing a sufficiently concise description of the design, and creating the confidence to begin building it by proving that the selected solution accomplishes the pursued task [7]. Analogously, a suitable design strategy would have to pursue two principal aims: (a) guiding paths – setting up an appropriate workflow that ensures the schematic creation of standardised designs, and (b) evaluating alternatives – providing a method to measure the fitness of the obtained engineering solution. To prove this point, we will have to take a look at selected methods and evaluate how they achieved these two goals.

Guiding paths

Building systems are usually not designed entirely from scratch, but are iterations on existing solutions, often only altered in selected aspects. Standardised workflows for engineering design can help integrate the design process into an industrialised environment by achieving a consistent quality in the results, levelling the impact of individual experience and subjective decisions.

A quest for automated design processes

Proposals for methodologies for more schematic design processes for industrial buildings were discussed in the GDR and West Germany from the 1960s. The creation of schematised algorithms for the design process itself was seen as an appropriate means towards more material-efficient and cost-effective designs [8]. A considerable amount of research targeted algorithmic optimisation methods that could be used with computer systems, often confined to predetermined structural topologies and a limited number of constraints [9]. Beyond that, automated design procedures proved suitable for the 'manual' design of type projects as well. Different levels for this kind of design process have been proposed: the totally determined design, with only a few modifications necessary; an assemblage of pre-planned building segments; or the independent, individual design, possibly made of standardised and prefabricated elements. However, individual projects in particular posed limits on what could be objectively achieved with design algorithms [10].

The significance of individual and collaborative knowledge in the design process had initially been acknowledged by calling for interdisciplinary cooperating design teams – an honourable, but unspecific suggestion, considering that the actual nature of interdisciplinary work remains a subject of much debate to this day [11]. The underlying body of knowledge, especially of tacit knowledge as a significant contributing factor, only shifted into research focus in more recent years [12].

A cyclical algorithm for light metal structures

Individual institutions like the *Metalleichtbaukombinat* (MLK, the largest state-owned conglomerate of steel construction companies) had already established guidelines for workflows for type-project design as early as 1969. In research, development and production, the MLK pursued the concept of *Leichtbau* (light building). Working efficiently with material proved to be a vital driver in structural design, especially with the backdrop of the scarcity of resources in the GDR. Beyond the demand for material efficiency, *Leichtbau* called to a new approach to design itself: an integrated collaboration of all participating disciplines, knowledge and consideration of cutting-edge new developments, and the verification of the design with the help of practical experiments [13]. More general and centralised guidelines were established in the following years with the *Projektierungsordnung* (design guideline) issued by the Ministry for Building in 1972 and with a standardised nomenclature for the different phases of a development project issued by the Ministry for Science and Technology in 1975 [14].

At that time, Dieter Golembiewski and Peter Schmalzried, both working in the research and development department at MLK in Leipzig, put forward a schematic workflow for the design of segmented steel roofs in their 1975 doctoral thesis at *Hochschule für Bauwesen Leipzig*, splitting the development cycle into three major phases including two distinct phases of optimisation (Fig. 2) [15]. They aimed to create feedback loops between production, use and development, without specifying exact feedback methods. They had been aware of the fact, though, that design had to balance contradicting targets, for example flexibility and material efficiency. This dilemma was again to be solved by working on the projects in interdisciplinary teams.

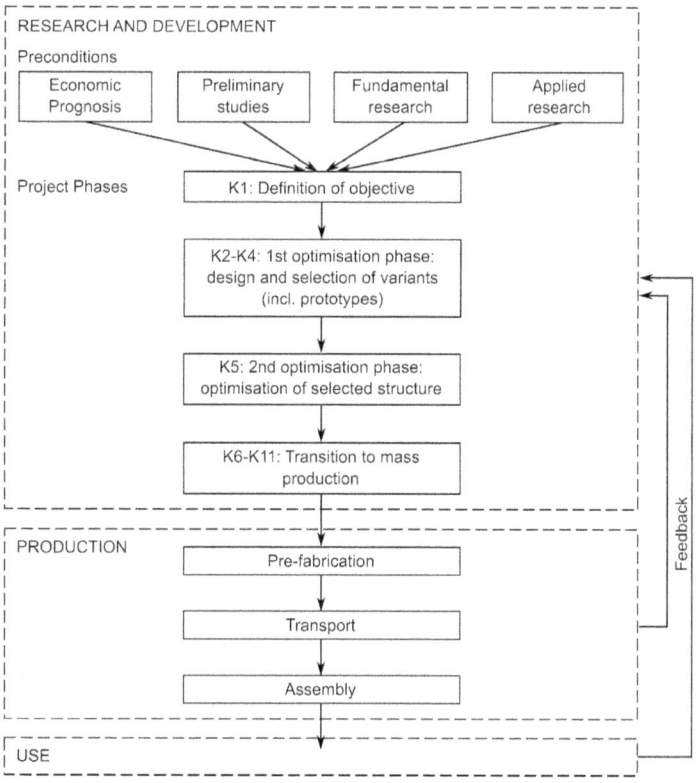

Figure 2: Design algorithm proposed by Golembiewski & Schmalzried, Golembiewski &Schmalzried 1976,177/author).

Algorithm or experience – The search for objective design methods for serial structures in the GDR

The method was later adopted by Dietmar Grünberg and Siegfried Thomas, two engineers associated with the production facility of MLK in Ruhland and at the research and development department of *Bau- und Montagekombinat Kohle und Energie* (BMK K+E, the company responsible for building design, production and assembly of power plants and industrial buildings) in Dresden, respectively. In their 1981 proposal, submitted as a dissertation to IHC, they shifted the whole algorithm more towards *fertigungs- und montagegerechte Gestaltung* (suitability for production and assembly), opening a space of optimisation with three poles: material efficiency, production efficiency and assembly efficiency (Fig. 3). As 'the authors [were] convinced that the choice of the structural solution is still of highest importance in the development cycle', they proposed to start the algorithm with a material-efficient solution as baseline, before introducing aspects of production and assembly in consecutive loops. At the end of each loop, the result is evaluated regarding the fulfilment of predefined thresholds – the loop of redesign had to be started if the criteria had not been fulfilled. Finally, an economic evaluation of the design had to be carried out, as well as an addition of some kind of aesthetic design [16].

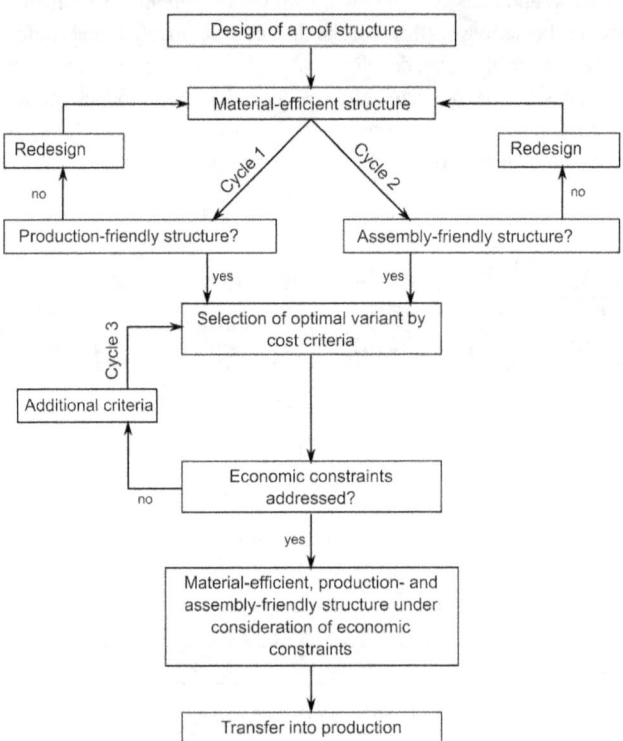

Figure 3: Proposed algorithm for the design of structures in Grünberg & Thomas (Grünberg &Thomas 1981, 69/author).

This algorithm implied two things: optimization was conceived as something that could be measured with a set of yes/no criteria. This provokes the obvious question, how these criteria were to be defined in advance, and how the process should react to thresholds that kept on shifting during the design process (e.g. prices and availability of raw materials). Secondly, the algorithm dealt with a single solution maturing on its way through the algorithm, while the problem of comparing alternative designs was not addressed.

A more general algorithm incorporating the selection of variants

Another researcher directly affiliated with the department of engineering construction at IHC, Horst Bark, acknowledged and confirmed the Grünberg/Thomas algorithm, and added another, easier algorithm, pursuing the goal of describing a linear selection process (Fig. 4). This process consisted of three principal steps: (1) the creation of a number of variants, (2) a first narrowing of possible results by selecting preference variants, (3) the final decision about the variant to realise. In the first and second stages, external conditions interacted with the variants still being considered. This appears relatively trivial, however Bark admitted the effects of the structural solution on certain boundary conditions such as maximum maintenance and usage costs, while other, general economic constraints were considered 'imperative' [17].

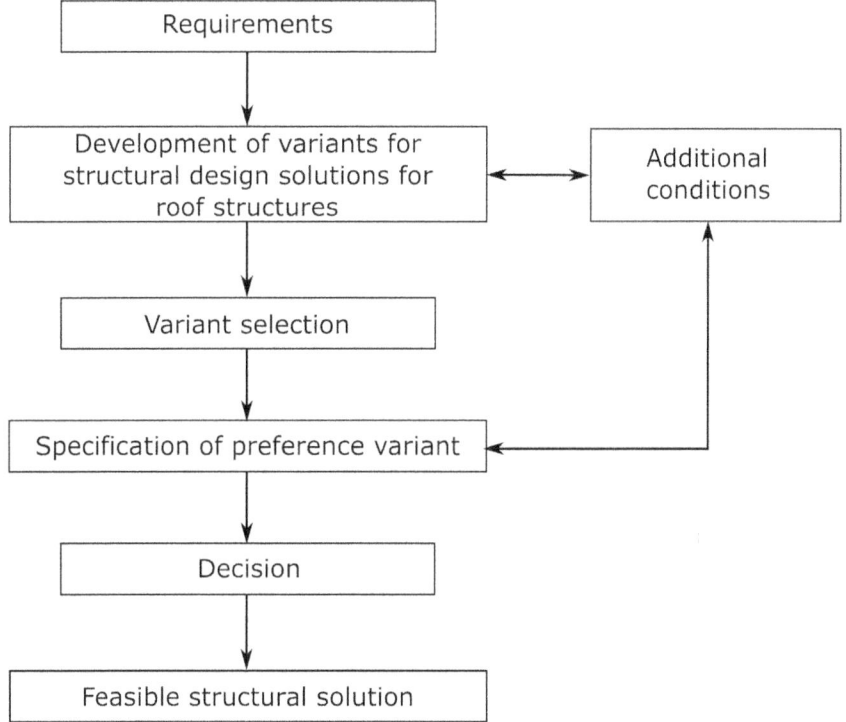

Figure 4: Algorithm describing the creation and selection of design variants as proposed by Bark (Bark 1987, 136/author).

Bark acknowledged that the conditions of structure, manufacturing and assembly were usually considered in a quite detailed way in a design, while those of use, maintenance, recycling etc. were drastically underrepresented due to their more speculative nature. Although good arguments could be made for the GDR economy having an interest in the reuse and recycling of scarce materials, it is worth noting that the significance and perception of labour-intensive repair works – being very individual and defying schematic analysis – generally decreased with extended mass production of a product [18].

At the same time, design practice shows that a large share of principal decisions about the progress of a project were still heavily dependent on individual experience and informal networks. For instance, this was very apparent in the development cycle of the *Riegellose Bauweise Cottbus* building system (RBC, a prefabricated concrete flat-slab ceiling structure), which was developed in the 1980s in a collaboration between IHC and several partners in the industry [19].

Algorithm or experience – The search for objective design methods for serial structures in the GDR

A majority of engineering design work carried out in the 1970s and 1980s aimed at making structural design and optimization accessible for computerised tools. The algorithms made for 'manual' usage as described here represent only a smaller part of that work and are interesting for their broader and more generalised nature. In this regard, the question of evaluation of competing designs is interesting – not only considering quantitative differences, but also qualitative contrasts, where computerised algorithms may hit technological limits.

Evaluating alternatives

Designing means comparing alternatives. Bark has pointed out that this process should involve first the creation and then the comparison of variants. Although this task of selecting the fittest alternative should happen as early as possible in the project, a clear understanding of the fitness of variants was often hampered by only vaguely determined benchmark values at that point [20].

Evaluating the applicability of design variants in principle means the weighting of criteria of utility against criteria of effort. Utility can mean either usability, efficiency or target goals, whereas effort could be quantified in multiple dimensions, namely as function of cost, material or time. As Grünberg and Thomas observed, the comparison of costs would have been sufficient if all the variants equally fulfilled the utility requirements. However, this was very rarely the case [21]. Weighting the different criteria against one another was anything but an easy task: 'Currently, quantity, efficiency and quality are often in contradiction to each other,' Hans Fritsche, the *Bauakademie*'s last president, admitted [22].

The twin terms *Effektivität* and *Effizienz* (effectiveness and efficiency) of a structural solution are of particular significance in this discourse. *Effektivität* describes the qualitative ability of a solution to meet predetermined goals, while *Effizienz* is a quantifiable metric for the effort it takes to reach this goal. In the context of structural design, these two terms allow a wide range of interpretations: technocratic ones – for example manifesting parameters such as the capabilities of the material itself, of the structural system, or of the manufacturing process – but also socio-economic ones, meaning the ability to contribute to society in a useful way (e.g. by optimised workflows in the planning process) [23]. This corresponds to the 'utilization of all material and creative resources' to 'increase the national income' on the way to the 'scientific-technical revolution' [24].

In the early 1970s, the industry code TGL 29 432 (General Methods for Evaluation of Quality of Industrial Products) tackled exactly this problem, using instead of 'effectiveness' the term 'quality' of a product, described as 'a category that can only be evaluated by comparison with a baseline value defined in quality or quantity'. This standard provided some guidelines about how to compare a technological solution against a predefined target rather than comparing variants with each other, thus requiring a sufficiently clear grasp of the target product. The guideline recommended the use of coefficients to describe the percentage of fulfilment of these goals, thus transforming parameters to dimension-less evaluation values [25].

Each evaluation strategy has to deal with the challenge of making very different things (like the rebar use per square metre, the assembly effort and the flexibility of use) comparable. As the way to find an optimal solution, the use of quantifiable parameters was a widely accepted standard. These parameters stemed from both the realms of effort and of usability, that is, the variants were rated against each other according to the gains they offered as well as the expenses they entailed. The rating systems for efficiency discussed here accordingly used mixed collections of parameters.

The dilemma of selecting parameters

Obviously, the choice of parameters was vital to getting useful results from the selection process. Dietrich Zeidler, then head of the department of industrial building technology at IHC, approached this problem in his 1980 research thesis. He proposed grouping the multitude of potentially useful parameters into six categories with broader implications:

- Functionality
- Load bearing capacity
- Resilience
- Variability of form
- Ease of production
- Exploitability (incl. adaptability and reusability)

The nature of the parameters varied considerably. On the one hand, there were quantifiable, scalar parameters, which could be correlated with a design goal in a positive or a negative way, meaning the higher the value, the better, or vice versa. On the other hand, there were parameters that could not be quantified, but only judged in a qualitative way. Several strategies were conceivable to make these accessible by transformation into evaluation values: for example, using simple patterns like [1;0] for [goal met; not met], or more differentiated scales like [0;1;2;3] for [bad fit; medium fit; good fit; optimal fit].

To make sense, a narrow choice of parameters had to be made, and they had to be weighted, which meant that the relative priority and importance of parameters had to be defined. This process, however, was in principle a very manual task susceptible to subjective biases. This contrasts with the aspiration of objectifying design by employing a 'technocratic' selection process. Thus, the ultimate result of the process was still highly determined by experience and personal preferences. Therefore, Zeidler also reflected on the choice of suitable criteria, regarding to which he emphasized that that one has to keep in mind:

- the selection,
- description,
- competent use of weighting factors,
- useful categorisation and
- concise presentation [26].

That Zeidler's proposal was only one way to set up a categorisation scheme is illustrated by a later proposal by the *Bauakademie*. Having supported Zeidler's dissertation project, and therefore certainly aware of his work, they issued a guideline in 1983 defining six very different parameter complexes with a more technocratic undertone: Function, Transport, Design, Area efficiency, Recycling, and Overall efficiency [27].

Four years later, Bark also confirmed that the process was highly determined by individual influences: the kind and number of criteria, the choice of weighting factors, the assignment of evaluation points [28].

To dampen the influence of individual decisions, the *Bauakademie* guideline paper suggested using an expert vote on the weighting, involving a number of experts who would independently make votes on the percentage weight of the parameters which were subsequently combined into an average value. An alternative method would be the use of the half-matrix method [29].

The suggestions in the guideline for comparison methods itself included two methods: the so-called *Bestwertmethode* ('best-value method'), which included normalising the comparison value per parameter of the best solution to 1.0, and a more complex *Methode zur Vergleichbarmachung und Aggregation heterogener Kriterien* ('method for the comparison and combination of heterogenous criteria') [30].

Two examples of comparison methods for reconstruction projects and industrial roofs

During the 1980s, refurbishment and conversion of older industrial buildings – many still dating from the era before the Second World War – gained more significance. For the development of projects in this context, which typically combined traditionally constructed fabric with prefabricated additions like new floors or roof structures, Johann-Christoph Kröhan developed a comparison methodology in yet another doctoral thesis from 1985. He had made a choice of thirty-six parameters, which were all equally weighted and grouped into parameter groups oriented more towards technical categories: Geometry, Loads, Structure, Technology, System, Function and Design, Benchmark Numbers. Not all of the criteria he made use of, however, were precisely quantifiable, for example 'openness' or 'flexibility'. The scale used was also very simple: the conformity of a solution with the parameters was evaluated with values between 0 and 3, with 3 indicating high conformity. The resulting basis for the decision was a single numerical value, the sum of the points awarded to each parameter [31].

In the context of finding economic solutions for prefabricated, segmented steel roof structures, Bark developed another, more specialised evaluation scheme in his 1987 dissertation. Such design tasks typically consist of the development of competing solutions for both the structure itself and the manufacture and assembly processes. As suggested by the *Bauakademie* guideline paper, Bark proposed a comparison of benchmark numbers created from parameter values multiplied with weighting factors. He recommended the use of typically only five to fifteen distinct parameters, as many criteria would have the same value for all variants and thus could be ignored due to their limited validity. To facilitate the comparison, a simple scale with evaluation points with possible values [0; 1; 2; 3; 4; 5] was to be used for each parameter, with the ascending steps meaning [not applicable; insufficient; OK; sufficient; good; very good]. The most important parameters were to be assigned the weighting factor 1.0, but all weighting factors were to be normalised in a further step to add up to 1. An evaluation benchmark for each variant was to be created by adding up the benchmark numbers for all parameters. While the transposition of parameters and weighting factors to normalised scales greatly improved the handling of the numbers, it depended on subjective assignment of evaluation points and was thus sensitive to bias [32].

A demonstration of the evaluation method

An example of this evaluation method in practice was provided by Bark in his thesis after having described several new solutions for prefabricated steel roof structures. Roof segments 6.00 m or 12.00 m wide, with common spans of 18.00 m, 24.00 m or 30.00 m, had become the standard for industrial developments and were offered off the shelf by MLK. At this time, segments made up of spatial trusses, like the 'Berlin' and 'Ruhland' types, had already been phased out by systems composed of planar trusses like the 'Fachwerk 80', with worse material efficiency, but lower production costs than the older systems [33].

Bark proceeded to prove the viability of his method by comparing three of his possible solutions (out of the nine he had described) as a retrospective view of a design project that had already been finished at this time: the construction of a textile industry facility in Upper Lusatia, with around 56,000 m² of roof area, arranged in five naves with segments spanning 18.00 m and 24.00 m [34]. Three variants were considered for the comparison: (1) Type 3, a *Pfetten-Binder-System* (truss-purlin system); (2) type 7, another truss-purlin-system; (3) type 9, a spatial truss (Fig. 5).

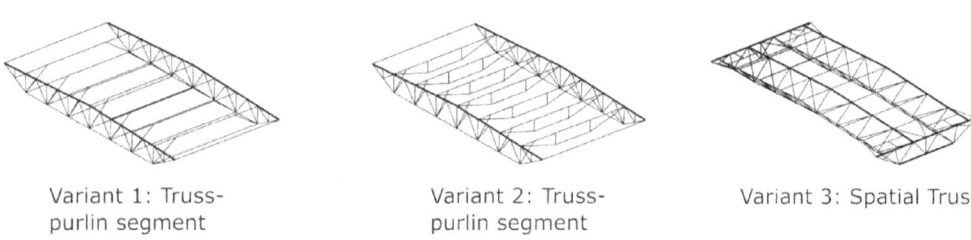

Variant 1: Truss-purlin segment

Variant 2: Truss-purlin segment

Variant 3: Spatial Truss

Figure 5: Variants of segmented roof structures used for comparison (Bark 1987/ author).

The alternative variants based on the principal systems contained the structure of the roof segments, the building envelope, the connection points and the assembly concept. For the comparison, Bark used twelve criteria, representing main differences between the variants [35].

The criteria were derived from actual parameters such as the amount of steel per square metre or assembly duration per segment, but the method itself used only rating points between 0 and 5 for each parameter. The criterion weighted the most important was material efficiency, followed by criteria for manufacturing and effort for pre-assembly. The effort for auxiliary assembly tools was considered of lesser importance.

The assigned weighting factors w_i were scaled into normalised factors $\bar{w}_i$, with $\sum \bar{w}_i = 1.0$. The value $G_k = \sum \bar{w}_i \cdot P_i$ then served as a benchmark number describing the fitness of each of the variants. In a final step, normalisation of these values lead to a benchmark number $\bar{G}_k$. According to this evaluation, variant 2 seemed the best fit for the posed construction task. This was in contrast to the actual construction project, in which variant 3 had been chosen for implementation (Table 1).

This academic demonstration shows some of the limitations and problems of such a formalised evaluation algorithm. It is especially unsuitable for the development of new variants as the basis for decisions. The three variants here had not been developed from scratch, but taken from an already existing pool of proven technologies, and then modified. That meant that the selection process was already simplified due to the groundwork. At the same time, the algorithm made no statement about how to lay the ground with the development of alternatives.

Additionally, this method lacked transparency about how criteria were gathered and weighted, and it raises the question of how the rating points were derived from the actual parameters, which might be quantifiable as well as non-quantifiable. Bark made no note about how this step could be carried out objectively, obscuring the fact that this introduced a significant element of subjectivity into the evaluation process. The benchmark numbers from this comparison process therefore promised an accuracy that did not actually exist.

Algorithm or experience – The search for objective design methods for serial structures in the GDR

Table 1: Comparison of evaluation criteria for three structural variants (Bark 1987, 163)

	Evaluation criteria g_i	Weighting factor		Evaluation points for variants P_i			Values $\bar{w}_i \cdot P_i$ for variants		
		w_i	$\bar{w}_i$	1	2	3	1	2	3
1	Material efficiency	1.0	0.128	5	4	3	0.641	0.513	0.385
2	Manufacturing effort	0.8	0.103	4	5	2	0.410	0.513	0.205
3	Level of prefabrication	0.5	0.064	4	5	2	0.256	0.321	0.128
4	Transport effort	0.6	0.077	4	3	5	0.308	0.231	0.385
5	Labour effort for pre-assembly	0.8	0.103	4	5	2	0.410	0.513	0.205
6	Effort for assembly tools	0.4	0.051	2	5	4	0.103	0.256	0.205
7	Lifting gear occupancy	0.7	0.090	4	3	5	0.359	0.269	0.449
8	Technological quality of assembly processes	0.5	0.064	3	5	4	0.192	0.321	0.256
9	Employment of workforce	0.7	0.090	5	2	4	0.449	0.179	0.359
10	Assembly duration	0.6	0.077	2	5	2	0.154	0.385	0.154
11	Effort for coordination of various companies	0.6	0.077	3	5	3	0.231	0.385	0.231
12	Effort for in-situ-completion	0.6	0.077	2	5	4	0.154	0.385	0.308
	Σ	7.8	1.000	42	52	40	3.667	4.269	3.269
	$\bar{G}_k$						0.859	1.000	0.766

The strength of this method – Bark has argued that the very limited number of criteria reduces complexity in usage – could therefore turn into a weakness when it came to making a qualified and definitive choice. Arguably, this approach of over-simplification was a bit too optimistic and trivialised the complex issue of structural design.

The parameter of material efficiency had been assigned the maximal weight in this comparison. However, in the real project setting the precedent for this investigation, a solution similar to variant 3 had been selected for execution, representing a system of inferior material efficiency compared to the winning variant 2. These differences could be due to the influence of additional, less palpable, factors in design, but it might also show the sensitivity of the outcome towards the assignment of evaluation points. In fact, a very strong alteration of weighting factors in this example would be necessary to produce an outcome other than variant 2, which indicates that the evaluation points had a greater impact on the evaluation result.

While this methodology might not have served the static purpose of yielding definitive structural solutions, it might instead have been understood and put to use as a dynamic design tool to explore interdependencies between parameters in the course of the design process, and to make transparent what parameters really mattered.

Conclusions

The examples discussed in the paper originated from different dissertations linked to various development projects in metal roof design as well as precast concrete construction. They show that the question of standardised design workflows and evaluation methods has been an integral part of the development of serial structures in the academic context. The models for development processes achieved a good compromise between defining project phases while still leaving sufficient freedom for the individual interpretation of partial processes and feedback procedures. The evaluation models showed uneven tendencies, with the procedure presented by Bark aiming toward an easy to use reduced parameter palette, while Kröhan's model used a more differentiated catalogue of criteria.

The models display a principal conflict between two opposing challenges in these models: objectification and 'intended irritation' – and a struggle to find a fine balance. On the one hand, a technical process like the creation and evaluation of structural design variants could be heavily compromised by the influence of factors such as individual experience, preoccupation, and bias. On the other hand, the developers and researchers had to face the problem of creating methods that were too schematic, ultimately impeding 'out-of-the box' thinking. The academic models, with varying scope and complexity, reacted with the use of empirical evaluation strategies and looping algorithms.

As straightforward methods, the proposed strategies might not have resulted in definitive design tools – the influence of very subjective approaches and networks remained strong. However, such methods might still have the potential to be put into use as dynamic tools to aid manual design by making transparent suggestions for the selection of structural solutions. At the same time the fact that these strategies were still a subject of investigation in 1985 and 1987 suggests that the aspiration to objectify creative processes – an established motif of High Modernity – remained attractive in GDR innovation culture well into the 1980s.

Acknowledgements

The paper has been prepared as part of a research project funded by the DFG research training group 1913 at BTU Cottbus-Senftenberg. The author wants to thank particularly Elke Richter, Karen Eisenloffel, Werner Lorenz, Dietrich Zeidler and Johann-Christoph Kröhan, for valuable talks and suggestions.

References

[1] G. Kosel, *Unternehmen Wissenschaft: Die Wiederentdeckung einer Idee,* 1st ed. Berlin: Henschelverlag Kunst und Gesellschaft 1989, pp. 169, 172.
[2] Z. Turán, 'Über die Automatisierung der Bau- und Organisationsplanung', *Periodica Polytechnica Architecture*, vol.18, no.3–4, 1974, pp. 216–217.
[3] Ibid., p. 221.
[4] Kosel, Wissenschaft, (Note 1), p. 169.
[5] D. Grünberg, S. Thomas, *Beitrag zur Entwicklung von materialsparenden, fertigungs- und montagegerechten Dachkonstruktionen in Metallleichtbauweise* (Dissertation A, Ingenieurhochschule Cottbus, 1981), p. 3. Besides the *Dissertation B*, which is comparable to a habilitation, the *Dissertation A* represented one of the doctoral levels of academic research in the GDR.
[6] The term *Ingenieurhochschule* has no adequate translation into English; they were higher education institutions with a strong focus on doctoral research.
[7] B. Addis, 'Inventing a history for structural engineering design' p. 114 in S. Huerta, (Ed.), Proceedings of the First International Congress on Construction History, Madrid 2003, Madrid: Instituto Juan de Ferrera, 2003.
[8] O. Jungbluth, G. Pegels, W. Zwanzig, 'Konzept für Entwurf und Fertigung im Stahlbau', pp. 40, 43 in IABSE, (Ed.) *In Serien gefertigte Stahlbauten: Symposium, Prag 1971*, Zurich 1971.

[9] Notably: G. Vanderplaats, F. Moses, 1973, 'Structural optimization by methods of feasible directions', *Computers and Structures*, vol.3, no.4, 1973, pp. 739–755. N.S. Khot, L. Berke, V.B. Venkayya, 'Comparison of Optimality Criteria Algorithms for Minimum Weight Design of Structures', *AIAA Journal*, vol.17, no.2, 1979, pp. 182–190.

[10] As acknowledged by Turán, Automatisierung, (Note 2) pp. 218, 220.

[11] O. Büttner, H. Stenker, *Metalleichtbauten: Band 1: Ebene Raumstabwerke*, Berlin: Verlag für Bauwesen 1971, pp. 10–11. See also S. Schregel, 'Interdisziplinarität im Entwurf: Zur Geschichte einer Denkform des Erkennens in der Bundesrepublik', *NTM*, vol.24, 2016, pp. 1–37.

[12] D. Baxter, J. Gao, K. Case, J. Harding, B. Young, S. Cochrane et al., 'An engineering design knowledge reuse methodology using process modelling', *Research in Engineering Design*, vol.18, no.1, 2007, pp. 37–48, https://doi.org/10.1007/s00163-007-0028-8 (Consulted on 17th January 2022).

[13] Büttner & Stenker, Metalleichtbauten, (note 11) p. 10. Based on principles laid out by W. Günther, 'Die Prinzipien des Leichtbaues', *IfL-Mitteilung* vol.3, no.4, 1964, pp. 97–105.

[14] H. Bäumler, 'Einheitliche Grundsatzregelungen in der Projektierung des Bauwesens', *Bauplanung Bautechnik*, vol.26, no.11, 1972, p. 561; H. Reuss, & I. Röder, 'Projektierungskonferenz des VEB Metalleichtbaukombinat', *Bauplanung Bautechnik*, vol.27, no.4, 1973, p. 168. See also Spezialarchiv Bauen in der DDR, Informationszentrum Plattenbau, sig. 01384, VEB Wohnungsbaukombinat Berlin, 'Richtlinie zur Ausarbeitung von standortunabhängigen Wiederverwendungsprojekten'; Spezialarchiv Bauen in der DDR, Informationszentrum Plattenbau, sig. 04200, Ministerium für Wissenschaft und Technik, 'Nomenklatur der Arbeitsstufen und Leistungen von Aufgaben des Planes Wissenschaft und Technik', 28 May 1975. The *Staatsplan Wissenschaft und Technik* was an instrument of central scientific planning supporting projects of outstanding economic importance.

[15] D. Golembiewski, P. Schmalzried, *Beitrag zur Entwicklung optimaler Konstruktionssysteme eingeschossiger Mehrzweckgebäude in Metalleicht- und Mischbauweise, vorzugsweise für die Industrie und Landwirtschaft* (Dissertation A, Hochschule für Bauwesen Leipzig, 1975).

[16] Grünberg & Thomas, Dachkonstruktionen (Note 5) p. 68.

[17] H. Bark, *Effektives Bauen mit Metalleichtkonstruktionen unter besonderer Berücksichtigung der Segmentbildung bei Dachkonstruktionen* (Dissertation B, Ingenieurhochschule Cottbus, 1987), pp. 136–137.

[18] This was observed in D. L. Edgerton, *The shock of the old: Technology and global history since 1900*, London: Profile Books, 2019, p. 83.

[19] E. Richter, K. Frommelt, 'The RBC building system - How to innovate between central planning and personal networks in the late GDR' pp. 766–773 in J. Mascarenhas-Mateus, A.P. Pires (Eds.), *History of Construction Cultures: Proceedings of the Seventh International Congress on Construction History (7ICCH), Lisbon, Portugal, 2021*. Boca Raton: CRC Press, 2021.

[20] Bark, Metalleichtkonstruktionen, (Note 17) pp. 134–135.

[21] Grünberg & Thomas, Dachkonstruktionen (Note 5) p. 8.

[22] Fritsche on the 39th plenary session of the Bauakademie, December 1978, Grundsatzreferat, 'Grundrichtung der Entwicklung von Wissenschaft und Technik im Bauwesen und Schwerpunkte der Bauforschung im Zeitraum 1981-1990'. Cited in D. Zeidler, *Beitrag zur Auswahl und Weiterentwicklung rationeller und effektiver Tragstrukturen für Dächer von ausgewählten eingeschossigen Mehrzeckgebäuden des Industriebaues bei hinreichender Erfüllung komplexer Anforderungen* (Dissertation B, Bauakademie der DDR, 1980), p. 2.

[23] For the general economic targets see R. Kühnert, 'Leichter und ökonomischer bauen – Metalleichtbau', *Bauplanung Bautechnik* vol.2, no.3, 1969, p. 148. In contemporary literature, the term *Effektivität* – as ability to meet these goals – has been used more widely.

[24] H. Elze 1967, 'Metalleichtbau und Rationalisierung', *Bauplanung Bautechnik*, vol.21, no.4, 1967, p. 157.

[25] TGL 29 432: 1974-01, pp. 1, 7–10.

[26] Zeidler, Auswahl und Weiterentwicklung (Note 22), pp. 63–64, 68–69, 131. Zeidler himself recurs to C. Zangemeister, *Nutzwertanalyse in der Systemtheorie*, München, 1970, who has defined rules to deal with valuation scales.

[27] Bauakademie der DDR (Ed.), *Methode zum Variantenvergleich*, Entwurfsgrundlagen für die Industriebauplanung No.6. Berlin: Institut für Industriebau, 1983, pp. 9-10. The *Institut für Industriebau* (institute for industrial building) was

only one of the research institutes associated with the *Bauakademie*. The proposed variant complexes targeted the design of entire industrial complexes and not primarily the design of roof structures.

[28] Bark, Metalleichtkonstruktionen, (Note 17) p. 142.
[29] Bauakademie, Methode, (Note 27) pp. 14, 35.
[30] Ibid., pp. 15, 37.
[31] J.-C. Kröhan, *Weiterentwicklung von Bausystemen im Industriebau am Beispiel des Einsatzes der Riegellosen Bauweise Cottbus, zur Aufwandssenkung und Nutzenserhöhung* (Dissertation A, Ingenieurhochschule Cottbus, 1985).
[32] Bark, Metalleichtkonstruktionen, (Note 17) pp. 140–142.
[33] D. Grünberg, S. Thomas, 'Entwicklungsstand und Tendenzen der Montage von Dachkonstruktionen in Metalleichtbauweise', *Bauplanung Bautechnik*, vol.36, no.12, 1982, pp. 562–565.
[34] Bark, Metalleichtkonstruktionen, (Note 17) pp. 149–150.
[35] Ibid., p. 163.

The Palazzo Galbani by Eugenio and Ermenegildo Soncini and Pier Luigi Nervi (1956-59). A case of building prefabrication in Milan

Laura Greco, Francesco Spada
Department of Civil Engineering, University of Calabria, Cosenza, Italy

Abstract

The paper refers to the research field on the evolution of construction techniques in Italy in the twentieth century and is part of the study that the authors are conducting on the building industrialisation in the country.

In Italy, the development of building industrialisation principles and prefabrication techniques affected the office sector in the 1950s, thanks to inventive structural solutions, such as those of the Pirelli skyscraper and the Galfa tower, and to the use of the curtain wall. The development of structural typologies suitable with the functional needs, the adoption of the curtain wall and movable internal walls, as well as the concentration of the system ducts, were some of the technological design topics used to ensure the functional flexibility of these buildings.

The study enriches – thanks to bibliographic sources and archival documents – the state of the art on construction evolution in the office sector in the 1950s, currently based on the analysis of the most famous office skyscrapers. The case study is Palazzo Galbani (1956-59) designed by the Milanese architects Eugenio and Ermenegildo Soncini, Alberto Mazzoni and Giuseppe Pestalozza, with the structural design by Pier Luigi Nervi. Reinforced concrete structures were realized by the company Nervi e Bartoli.

The building presents several interesting aspects. In methodological terms, it is useful to investigate the collaboration between the architects and the engineer, highlighting the Italian master's habit to work with architects, as evidenced by Nervi's best-known cooperation with Marcel Breuer, Luigi Moretti and Gio Ponti. From a construction point of view, the Galbani headquarters is an example of the designers' efforts towards the structural concept, evident above all in the enterprising solutions of tall buildings. The reinforced concrete structure designed by Nervi guaranteed functional flexibility to spaces and connoted the architectural features of the interior spaces in a singular way. It consisted of perimeter pillars and prefabricated ferrocement beams with a wavy section, arranged on a single span of 15 meters and with a thickness of a few centimetres. The beams, prefabricated on site, were placed side by side and combined with hollow bricks and with concrete slab cast on site. Nervi's solution was part of the series of works such as the warehouse of the Nervi & Bartoli company in Rome (1946), the shed roofing of the hemicycle building of the Milan Fair (1947) and, finally, the Palazzo delle Esposizioni in Turin (1948), which after the war enhanced the intuitions of the master builder in the use of ferrocement structural elements prefabricated on site. Therefore, the analysed case is useful to investigate the prefabrication and assembly process of the structural elements, relating them to Nervi's research on ferrocement elements prefabricated on site, and to evaluate the influences of the main works of the Italian engineer on this little-known construction.

Introduction

Palazzo Galbani is a good example of the efforts made in Italy, and in Milan in particular, in the 1950s, to evolve construction process techniques and strategies for site organization. Palazzo Galbini is a little-known building within Italian construction history, obscured by the proximity of two contemporary masterpieces of office architecture, the Pirelli

The Palazzo Galbani by Eugenio and Ermenegildo Soncini and Pier Luigi Nervi (1956-59). A case of building prefabrication in Milan

skyscraper (by Gio Ponti with Fornaroli, Rosselli, Valtolina e Dall'Orto, 1956-58) and the Galfa tower (by Melchiorre Bega, 1956-59). In Milan, the interest in experiments in construction involved architects and engineers, who were involved in the design of buildings that stood out for the originality of the structural solutions, for the elegance and quality of the curtain walls and for the evolution of the organization of the construction site. In the case of the Galbani headquarters, the structure and curtain wall contributed to reinforce the image of the building. The structure was notable for an effective system of ferrocement corrugated floors, prefabricated on site, according to a technique developed by Pier Luigi Nervi (1891-1979).

In the mid-1950s, foreign prefabrication systems had not yet been imported and domestic production of prefabricated components struggled to advance, due to the artisan nature of the construction sector. On-site techniques were still preferred and reinforced concrete was the favoured technique. On the other hand, the transformation of the construction site began, thanks to the rationalization and mechanization of operations, with the on-site prefabrication of structural elements. In this context, Nervi's work stood out for its authority and originality thanks to his major works, the effects of which were felt even in his minor ones, such as the Galbani headquarters in Milan. Prefabrication in Nervi's approach was mainly related to the construction of buildings with complex geometry and/or regular and modular dimensions. The procedure developed by Nervi in the most complex cases involved the separation of the structure into small parts precast on site, and assembled by connecting them with parts cast in-situ. Under conditions of less geometric complexity he preferred the prefabrication on site of individual structural elements (i.e. beams and trusses). This on-site prefabrication procedure, called structural prefabrication (prefabbricazione strutturale), often combined with the use of ferrocement, was prominent in the experiments with reinforced concrete techniques conducted by Nervi, notably in the masterpieces of the Italian engineer such as the vault of the Palazzo delle Esposizioni in Turin (1947-48), the roof of the Kursaal restaurant in Ostia (with the architect Attilio La Padula, 1950) and of the dome of the Palazzetto dello Sport in Rome (with the architect Annibale Vitellozzi, 1956-57), and many other buildings including the Palazzo Galbani in Milan. Structural prefabrication was based on the production of parts of a structure that only works globally. The individual pieces therefore do not have a precise static function, unlike a prefabricated beam already produced with a defined section and length [1]. According to Nervi, prefabbricazione strutturale guaranteed the elimination of the formwork necessary to cast structural parts with complex geometry (vaults) or with large dimensions (floors and beams). The first building which benefitted from the results of research into the ferrocement and prefabbricazione strutturale was the Palazzo delle Esposizioni in Turin. This building introduced a new type of on-site prefabrication, based on the use of ferrocement precast elements to build large concrete roofs and floors quickly. It was an important step in the Italian development of building techniques and prefabrication.

This study aims to analyse the building of the Palazzo Galbani underlining the role of Pier Luigi Nervi in the project and its construction processes and the influence of his major works on this office building.

The protagonists of the design process

The Palazzo Galbani project (Fig. 1) was the result of a fruitful collaboration between architects, including the Soncini brothers, and the engineer Pier Luigi Nervi, who at the same time was involved in the construction of the Pirelli skyscraper. The brothers Eugenio and Ermenegildo Soncini were both architects and skilled designers, who were well known in Milanese architectural and construction circles. Eugenio Soncini (1906-1993), graduated from the Polytechnic of Milan in 1929 and after professional practice in the studio of Emilio Lancia, from 1934 to 1945 was part of the Ponti-Fornaroli-Soncini design office. The collaboration with Gio Ponti allowed him to acquire familiarity with the design of office buildings, the use of modern techniques and materials, and to develop an interest in a global design approach that impacted all scales and phases of the project. In 1947 he opened an office with his brother Ermenegildo (1918-2013) in the Lombard capital. They specialised in the residential and office sector. Among their major works are the Michelin Italia headquarters (1946-47), the Breda tower (with L. Mattioni 1952-1954), the Tirrena tower (1956-57), the Madonnina health clinic (1957-59), the headquarters of the Compagnia di Assicurazioni di Milano (1958-65), the Palazzo della

Serenissima (1966-68). Their projects were characterised by a common design approach based on construction accuracy, technological innovation, and the quality of the details. They were exponents of cultured Lombard professionalism and were engaged in the urban and architectural transformation of Milan in the 1950s-1960s. They applied a balanced synthesis between building practice and attention to the domestic and international cultural theoretical debate, whose themes they experimented with in their everyday professional life. [2]. In their major works, the Soncini brothers preferred reinforced concrete structures, as evidenced by the Breda tower (1947-48), the Tirrena tower (1956) and the Palazzo Galbani. The relevance of the structure in their works was shown by the fact that in the most demanding cases, the two architects were supported by structural consultancy from the masters of concrete technique in Italy, such as Arturo Danusso for the structure of the Breda tower and Pier Luigi Nervi for the structure of the Galbani headquarters.

Figure 1: Palazzo Galbani in Milan. Project: Eugenio and Ermenegildo Soncini and Pier Luigi Nervi, 1956-59. Source: Vitrum, no. 135, 1963 (Subsequent citations Vitrum 1963).

By the time of the construction of the Galbani headquarters, Pier Luigi Nervi had already established an international reputation thanks to his project for the Palazzo delle Esposizioni in Turin. In Milan, whilst he was working on the structure of the Galbani headquarters, he joined Gio Ponti in the design of the Pirelli skyscraper, dealing with the innovative reinforced concrete structure. In both buildings, the skill of the engineer interpreted the functional program and the symbolic value of the architecture in the design of the structural system.

From the beginning of his career Nervi worked with architects showing that he understood the synthesis between aesthetic-formal values and technical-structural solutions, for example at the Augusteo Cinema theatre and the central station of the funicular in Naples (1926-27) with Arnaldo Foschini, the Arco Monumentale for the Universal Exposition of Rome E42 (1938-39) with Adalberto Libera, the Conte Trossi shipyards (1947-48) with Carlo Daneri, the Kursaal restaurant at Lido di Castel Fusano (1950) with Attilio Lapadula, the Unesco headquarters in Paris (1952-1967) with Marcel Breuer and Bernard Henri Zehrfuss. In the Pirelli skyscraper, the Kursaal restaurant and the Unesco headquarters in Paris, Nervi developed iconic structures that became the signature of the works. In other cases, such as the Palazzo

The Palazzo Galbani by Eugenio and Ermenegildo Soncini and Pier Luigi Nervi (1956-59). A case of building prefabrication in Milan

Galbani, the structural solution - even without having the symbolic value of the major works - satisfied the functional requirements of the project. At the Galbani headquarters Nervi could also count on a fruitful understanding with the Soncini brothers and their interest in the evolution of construction site organization, as evidenced by their work on the Breda tower (with Luigi Mattioni 1952-1954), for which prefabricated pillars and mechanization techniques of the construction site were used to make the façade [3].

At the Palazzo Galbani, Nervi's ability to participate at the architectural concept phase was clear. This predisposition allowed him - sometimes - to design projects in which his aesthetic mark emerged with strength and independence. This was generated by the close connection between architectural form and structural form, which informed Nervi's method [4], which he used when working with other professionals and as he experimented with building techniques. In the Milanese office building, to solve the question of the functional flexibility of the plan, Nervi used prefabricated ferrocement beams with a curvilinear profile that he had experimented with in the Palazzo delle Esposizioni. Moreover, in the definition and in the development of new construction solutions, Nervi was helped by his collaboration with Nervi & Bartoli a company that he directed together with his brother-in-law and was involved in many of his works. At the Palazzo Galbani, Nervi could count on Nervi & Bartoli, who built the reinforced concrete structure, developing the prefabrication of the ferrocement beams, their installation and connection with the structure cast on site.

The project

The Galbani headquarters, located at the corner of via Pirelli and via Fabio Filzi - between the Pirelli skyscraper to the south-east and the Galfa tower to the north - is an example of the work done in Milan on structural typologies suitable for the functional layouts of office buildings. These were developed as inventive solutions in the tall buildings, but were also appropriate for use in smaller buildings. [5].

Egidio Galbani s.p.a., leader in Italy in the food manufacturing sector, entrusted Eugenio and Ermenegildo Soncini, Alberto Mazzoni and Giuseppe Pestalozza with the project developed in 1956. The reinforced concrete construction was completed in 1958 [6]. The design and construction supervision of the reinforced concrete structure was entrusted to Pier Luigi Nervi and the construction to Nervi & Bartoli.

The complex was developed in three parts: a block of twelve floors above ground and two underground; there were two low elements (of two and three floors) at the sides. The main block (Figs 2-3) was intended for the Galbani offices (fifth-twelfth floors) and affiliated companies (first-fourth floors). The ground floor housed the hall and the offices of a bank, whose headquarters extended into one of the two side blocks. The basement floors were reserved for archives, a systems area and a garage. The two-story block was destined for shops.

The main block has the elements of greatest construction interest. Architects derived the polygonal plan, tapered on the extremities, by the study of circulation flows in the typical floor. This choice was inspired by experience gained in Milan, for example with the project of the Pirelli skyscraper, whose plan was defined on the base of the circulation flows [7].

Architects arranged the plan on a functional and construction module, to which the organization of the structure and the façade was related. In general, the designers of office buildings considered different values of the module; sometimes it was a narrower step (for example 75 cm in the Galfa tower and 95 cm in the Pirelli skyscraper in Milan), in other cases the module increased (180 cm in the Breda tower in Milan and, in the best known international cases, 122 cm in the headquarters of the United Nations and 147 cm in the Chase Manhattan Bank, 106 cm in the Seagram Building in New York), due to the design requirements that referred to the arrangement of the structure, of the façade, and of the functional layout. In the Palazzo Galbani the module was 92x92 cm (Fig. 4). It regulated the composition of the façade.

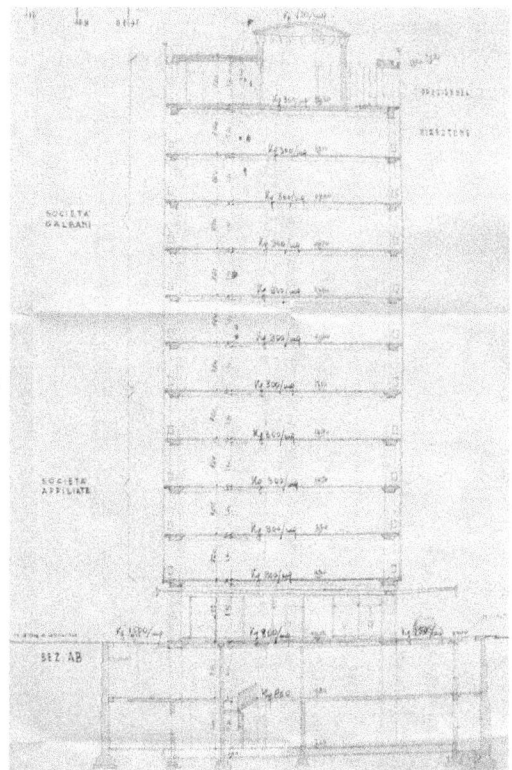

Figure 2: Section of main block destined for the Galbani offices. Source: Archivio di Stato of Milan, Prefettura di Milano-Opere in cemento armato Collection, (Subsequent citations ASMI)

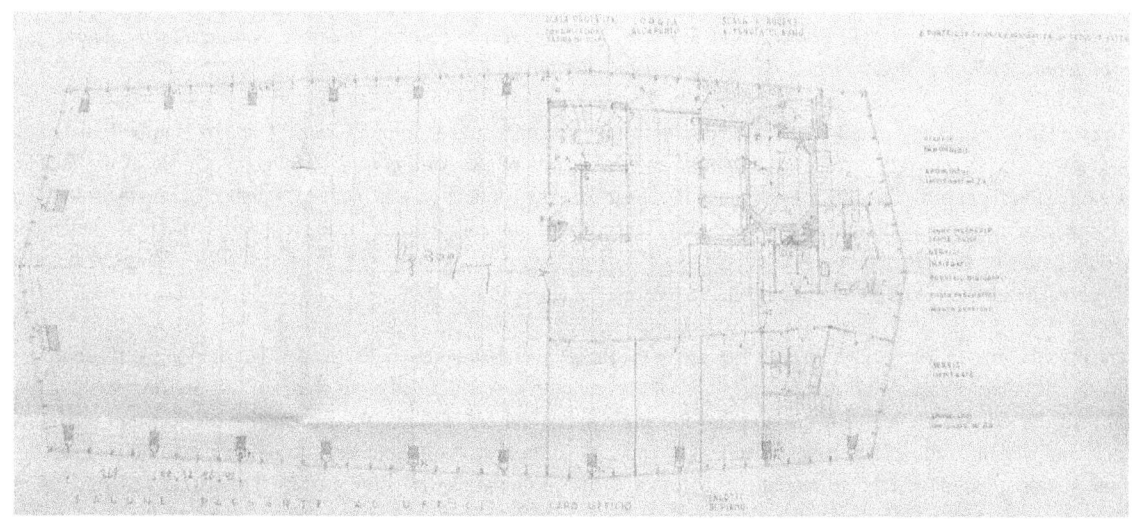

Figure 3: Plan of a typical floor (5°-9° floors) destined for Galbani offices, 27 February 1956. Source: ASMI

The Palazzo Galbani by Eugenio and Ermenegildo Soncini and Pier Luigi Nervi (1956-59). A case of building prefabrication in Milan

The building had a reinforced concrete structure (Fig. 4) placed on plinths and foundation beams [8]. An open area of approximately 300 square meters (15x21 meters), which could be sub-divided into different configurations thanks to the use of moveable walls, (Fig. 4), was provided for floors first to ninth. The remaining area on each floor was intended for individual offices and services.

Figure 4: The main block under construction. In evidence the reinforced concrete structure, Source: R. Aloi, Nuove architetture a Milano, Milan: Hoepli, 1959 (Subsequent citations Aloi 1959).

The walls of the building were formed by a curtain wall with an anodized aluminium frame, made by Bombelli of Milan. A reinforced concrete slab of reduced thickness and variable depth, according to the polygonal profile of the façade, provided the support for the curtain wall's metallic structure. The connection was made by a plate cast into the floor slab to which the curtain wall uprights were anchored (Fig. 5). The organization of the façade was based on a typical element (coinciding with the 92 cm module) divided into a square parapet-pane, which could be opened with a pantograph and a fixed rectangular top (Fig. 5).

The model of the building shows an early design for the façade which was later redesigned. (Fig. 6). In this early solution, the façade, although arranged with a parapet and an upper element, was defined on the basis of two narrow elements (92 cm) side by side with a double main module with single pane (184 cm) [9]. During construction production constraints (size and weight of the glazed panes, loadbearing capacity of the metallic framework, economic costs) determined the final solution, based on a 92 cm module. The design of the curtain wall was completed by the black aluminium string courses set beyond the façade. On the eleventh floor, destined for the offices of the president of the Galbani company, there was a roof garden protected by a glass window with aluminium frame. The width of the frames and the small size of the parapet module worked against the effect of lightness and transparency of the façade, which was included by the designers in their initial ideas as a linguistic and technological reference to the International Style.

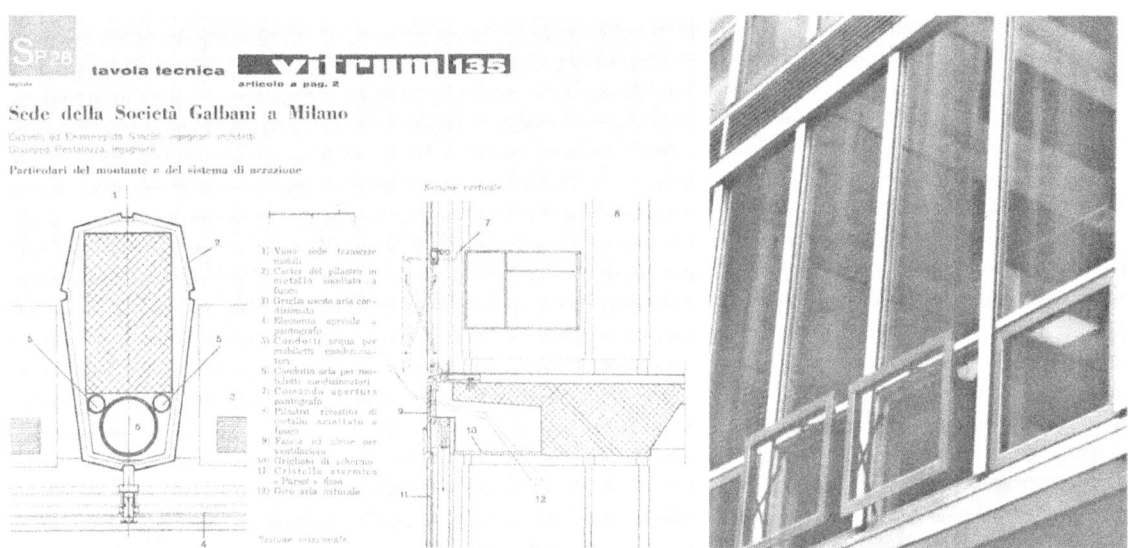

Figure 5: Details of the façade, In evidence the connection between the reinforced concrete structure and the curtain wall and the natural ventilation solution (on the right). Source: Vitrum 1963

Figure 6: Preliminary model of the Palazzo Galbani with the initial curtain wall solution. Project: Soncini and Nervi, 1956-59. Source: Aloi 1959

The Palazzo Galbani by Eugenio and Ermenegildo Soncini and Pier Luigi Nervi (1956-59). A case of building prefabrication in Milan

The building was equipped with an air conditioning and heating system, while an air extraction system was provided for the toilets. Nevertheless, the designers focused on natural ventilation of the offices. The opening in the parapet module allowed air to enter, while an outlet, positioned in the string course and protected by a grid with horizontal aluminium strips, allowed air to be expelled (Fig. 5). The string course hid the Venetian blind boxes and the depth of the perimeter beam. This solution was inspired by the Pirelli headquarters and the Galfa tower, where similar schemes were used to minimize the visual impact of the structure and the Venetian blinds.

The Galbani headquarters appears to have been more influenced by the Galfa tower in its search for lightness and transparency of the curtain wall, although in both examples there was a determination to conceal the structural elements behind the curtain wall. In the built project, a polygonal-shaped enamelled aluminium casing clad the reinforced concrete pillars. The air conditioning duct was inside the metal casing, while on its faces, where necessary, holes for the insertion of the internal movable walls were provided (Fig. 5).

The role of Pier Luigi Nervi

The reinforced concrete structure, designed by Nervi to meet the functional requirement for flexibility, consisted of a series of rectangular-section pillars arranged around the perimeter at 3.70 metre centres (Fig. 3). The V-section prefabricated ferrocement floor beams had a thickness reduced up to 2.5 cm; they covered spans of 15 meters with overloads of 300 Kg/m2. The beams were placed side by side, to form an undulating intrados (Fig. 7). The hollow bricks were arranged on the prefabricated beams and then there was the reinforced concrete slab cast on site (Fig.8). The height of the beam was 38 cm, while the total thickness of the floor was 50 cm, according to the maximum height of floors allowed by the Milanese building laws.

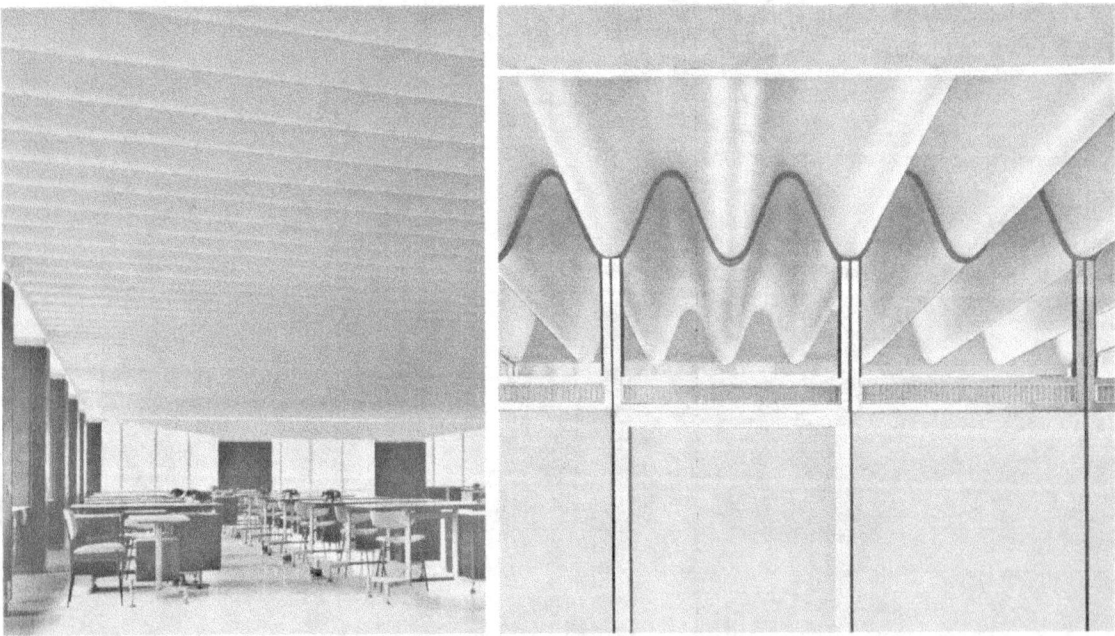

Figure 7: Internal views of the undulating intrados of the floor. Source: P.L. Nervi, Nuove strutture, Milan: Edizioni di Comunità, 1963 (Subsequent citations Nuove Strutture)

The undulate section was stiffened at the extrados by the hollow bricks and the slab. At the intrados, the stiffening was guaranteed by the concrete nucleus of the section. This concrete core had variable thickness (8 cm in the middle and 12 cm at the edge) giving support to the concrete elements that support the perimeter structure. The φ 6 mm bend steel bars were placed in this concrete core; to these metal reinforcement two layers of metal mesh (0,600 Kg/m2) arranged according to the geometry of the beam section were added (Fig. 8). Cement mortar was applied to these layers of mesh. The upper extremities of the bars φ 6 mm to be embedded in the concrete slab, were bent on site to allow the placing of the hollow bricks (Fig. 8). These brick tiles had a thickness of 3.2 cm and the overlying slab, cast in two phases, had a thickness of 8.3 cm [10].

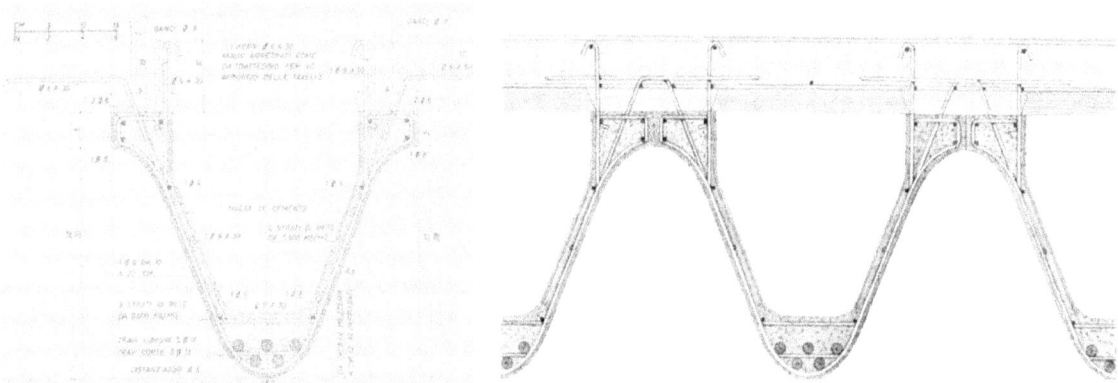

Figure 8: Detail of the V-section prefabricated ferrocement floor beams (left) and the floor section with the hollow bricks and the slab cast on site (right) Source: L'architettura, no. 75, 1962

It should be noted that these prefabricated beams took advantage of Nervi's 1930s studies on ferrocement. Nervi's work was part of an evolutionary line that included the research of Joseph-Louis Lambot, pioneer of the reinforced concrete technique, who introduced the term *fer ciment* to define the material, patented in 1855, for the construction of boats and based on a combination of iron and concrete. The metal trusses were modelled according to the desired shapes and then covered with a thin layer of concrete. Subsequent studies were conducted by Joseph Monier who, in 1867, registered a patent for iron and concrete containers to be used in horticulture, while in Italy the Roman manufacturer Carlo Gabellini developed building applications for thin concrete slabs reinforced with a metal mesh at the end of the XIX century [11]. Against this background Nervi began to consider a further development of reinforced concrete technique. He registered patent n. 163733 of 18 December 1917, concerning the use of a concrete mix reinforced with iron shavings that constituted a widespread reinforcement of the cement section. From the mid-1930s Nervi showed further developments in his research on ferrocement, as testified by a series of patents and his first achievements. Patent n. 410202 of 1943 was for the construction of slabs and other reinforced concrete elements. This was the beginning of the use of ferrocement in the building sector, allowing the positioning of concrete elements without the use of expensive and laborious wooden formworks [12]. The first tests developed by Nervi on ferrocement had concerned thin slabs (thickness ≤ 10 cm) reinforced by overlapping wires of variable diameter (0.5-1.5 mm) and reinforcement rods (6-10 mm) covered by a thin layer of concrete [13].

Nervi's solution for the Galbani headquarters was one of a number of developments that had been made since the end of the second world war. These included the warehouse of the Nervi & Bartoli company in Rome (1946), the shed roof of the hemicycle building of the Milan Fair (1947) and finally, the Palazzo delle Esposizioni in Turin (1947-48), and encouraged Nervi to describe the use of ferrocement as a "decisive factor, both from the technical and architectural point of view" [14].

The Palazzo Galbani by Eugenio and Ermenegildo Soncini and Pier Luigi Nervi (1956-59). A case of building prefabrication in Milan

As might be anticipated, the undulating beams of the perimeter floors of the roof of Hall C of the Turin complex inspired the solution adopted in the Palazzo Galbani. In fact, the vault of the Turinese hall was formed by the union of precast ferrocement elements connected through the reinforced concrete ribs which had been cast on site. [15]. Another reference, which inspired Nervi for the floors of Palazzo Galbani, was in the Conte Trossi shipyards (1947-48) in San Michele di Pagana, near Rapallo, whose project was developed together with the architect Luigi Carlo Daneri (1900-72). The design called for the creation of a large column free space for the storage of boats. Nervi solved the structure with a series of reinforced concrete arches of 30 meters of span, arranged at 10 meters centres. A continuous structure, which substituted the typical frame of floor beams, and the overlapping ferrocement tiles – used to obtain the horizontal extrados – made up the floors. They were supported by the arches and had a wavy profile [16]. The elements were prefabricated on site, using masonry moulds, and then moved with a crane. There was a strong visual impact which anticipated that of the Palazzo Galbani, about which in 1962 Renato Pedio observed that "these floors, given the transparency of the glass curtain wall, are an important factor in the figurative consistency of the building" [17]. As with the Turin exhibition complex and the Conte Trossi shipyards, the intrados of the floors of Palazzo Galbani were characterized by the sinusoidal profile, confirming the functional and architectural potential that in Nervi's work enriched the structural intuition and the evolution of the construction procedures.

The construction site

On-site prefabrication involved the meticulous planning of time and resources to be used on the construction site. Nervi, taking advantage of the experienced gained with Nervi & Bartoli, arranged an area for the production of prefabricated components within the construction site. The organization of the production of prefabricated elements showed the value of Nervi & Bartoli's contribution. The success of the development was down to the collaboration between the Italian engineer and Nervi & Bartoli. The two areas - that of construction and that of on-site prefabrication - were separated and each provided with the necessary equipment and manpower. The times of the prefabrication and the integration of the parts cast on site were scheduled to optimize the programme. Nervi developed the first experiments on the organization of on-site prefabrication during the construction of the Palazzo delle Esposizioni and perfected it in the construction sites of the Fiat-Mirafiori factory complex [18]. At the Galbani headquarters, Nervi and Nervi & Bartoli drew on their experience. The production of ferrocement beams was organized in a specific area of the construction site and was arranged to complement the overall programme prepared for prefabrication on site in accordance with Nervi's method. The construction of ferrocement elements was started by stretching the wire mesh on the moulds (made of masonry placed on the ground) and then coated with a thin layer of concrete. There were three lines of moulds in the Milanese prefabrication area to stretch the wire mesh of the ferrocement beams (Fig. 9).

Figure 9: The prefabrication on site of the V section ferrocement beams, the handling and assembly process of components of the floors. Source: Nuove Strutture

Once cast, the beams were raised and placed on a transport carriage to transfer to them from the prefabrication area to the storage area. Here the beams were stacked and prepared to be craned up to the various floors as and when required. The construction site machines were designed by Nervi & Bartoli to fit in with the requirements of prefabrication, handling, storage and assembly of the components. Once the beams had been placed side by side, the floor was completed with hollow bricks and the casting of the reinforced concrete slab was undertaken in two phases (Fig. 9). The first phase was cast after the hollow bricks had been positioned and the second was cast to connect the beams to the perimeter structure and to incorporate the steel reinforcement of the prefabricated beams.

Conclusions

In the Galbani headquarters Nervi demonstrated how ferrocement could be introduced into the main works. This was an important step in the evolution of prefabrication techniques. It showed how structural components could be made economically with respect to both tools and materials, whilst harmonizing the construction choices with design research that was both essential and elegant. This interest in the development of concrete construction and structural prefabrication distinguished Nervi's work. Thanks to the activity of both himself and his company it was an important step in the transformation of the Italian construction site in the 1950s, foreshadowing the spread of prefabricated systems produced in factories in the early 1960s. In fact, Nervi's method reconciled Italian craftsmanship with the requirements of economy and speed of construction in the post-world war period without waiting for the prefabricated systems developed in factories.

Nervi's method, fully supported by Nervi & Bartoli, allowed him to design and build numerous buildings guaranteeing their design quality and performance. It was a key aspect in the success of Nervi's work that thanks to the close relationship between engineer and contractor they were able to develop a prefabrication process based on handcrafted operations, rigorously designed to maximise construction quality and economy.

References

[1] P.L. Nervi, 'Le strutture in cemento armato', Il Cemento, no. 959, 1962, pp. 12-15.
[2] R. Lucente & L. Greco, '1950s Housing in Milan: Façade design and building culture' vol. 1, pp. 93-99, in J. Mascarenhas-Mateo & A. P. Pires (Eds), *History of Construction cultures*, Leiden: CRC Press Balkema. Taylor & Francis Group, 2021.
[3] L. Mattioni, 'Il grattacielo di Milano', Edilizia Moderna, no. 56, 1955, pp. 9-30.
[4] P.L. Nervi, 'Concrete and structural form', The structural engineer, no. 5, May, 1956, p. 55; P.L. Nervi, 'The place of structure in architecture', The Architectural Record, no. 7, 1956, p. 189; P.L. Nervi, *Aesthetics and technology in Building*, Cambridge MA, USA: Harvard University Press, 1965.
[5] L. Greco, 'Sapienza costruttiva e innovazione tecnologica negli edifici per uffici in Italia. Note sull'esperienza dell'area milanese negli anni Cinquanta' p. 623-632, in A. Cottone, T. Basiricò, S. Bertarotta, G. Vella (Eds), *Benedetto Colajanni. Opere, Progetti e Scritti in suo onore*, Palermo: Fotograf, 2010.
[6] See 'Relazione della visita di controllo delle opere in calcestruzzo armato' 16 June 1958, Archivio di Stato of Milan, Prefettura di Milano-Opere in cemento armato Collection, (Subsequent citations ASMI).
[7] G. Ponti, 'Analisi di un progetto', Edilizia Moderna, no. 55, 1955, pp. 25-38.
[8] "Denuncia delle opere in c.a.", 21 June 1956 (ASMI)
[9] R. Aloi, *Nuove architetture a Milano*, Milan: Hoepli, 1959, pp. 223-228.
[10] R. Pedio, 'La nuova sede della Società Galbani in Milano', L'architettura. Cronache e Storia, no. 75, 1962, pp. 593-601.
[11] C. Greco, *Pier Luigi Nervi. Dai primi brevetti al Palazzo delle Esposizioni di Torino 1917-1948*, Lucerna: Quart Edizioni, 2008, pp. 189-192.
[12] See Note 11, p. 196.

[13] P. L. Nervi, *Costruire correttamente*, Milan: Hoepli, 1955, p. 29.
[14] See Note 13, p. 31.
[15] See Note 13, Tav. XIII; See Note 13, pp. 227-245.
[16] See Note 11, pp. 255-258.
[17] See Note 9.
[18] L. Greco, 'Pier Luigi Nervi and Fiat. The expansion of Officine Mirafiori in Turin' vol. 2, p. 699-706, in I. Wouters & S. Van de Voorde Inge Bertels et al (Eds), *Building Knowledge, Construction Histories*. Leiden: CRC Press Balkema. Taylor & Francis Group, 2018 ; L. Greco, 'Machine à batir: standardisation de la construction et préfabrication structurelle dans le projet de Pier Luigi Nervi pour la création de l'usine Cromo de Venaria Reale (1962-1964)' p. 995-1003, in G. Bienvenu, M. Monteil, H. Rousteau Chambon (Eds), *Construire! Entre antiquité et époque moderne*, Paris: Picard, 2019.

Fibre Cement Slates: An Industry Reinventing Itself (1970-2000)

Marylise Parein [1,2], Ine Wouters [1], Stephanie Van de Voorde [1]
[1] Department of Architectural Engineering, Vrije Universiteit Brussel (VUB), Belgium
[2] Public Service Urban, Brussels, Belgium

Abstract

Roof slates have featured prominently in the residential architecture of Western Europe for several centuries. Artificial slates made from fibre cement, and asbestos-free fibre cement slates in particular, are more recent, however. This paper will examine the transition towards asbestos-free fibre cement slates that was initiated following the controversy concerning asbestos in the 1970s to determine the impact of that transition upon architecture in Western Europe. The majority of our research has been performed by studying (inter)national architecture journals and manufacturer documentation. Its aim is to supplement the knowledge of the construction history of the recent past, which is largely unexplored [1].

Introduction

At the end of the twentieth century, many countries inside and outside Europe were shifting to asbestos-free products. In this paper, we will focus on the particular case of the fibre cement slate in Western Europe. Not only have slates been used there for centuries as roof covering material, but significant quantities of (asbestos) fibre cement slates have been produced and deployed since the early twentieth century.

The main objective of this paper is to analyse the impact of the transition towards non-asbestos technology on fibre cement slates and consequently on West-European architecture. We will investigate the legal framework governing the use of asbestos and its impact on the production method, the connection method and the appearance of the individual fibre cement slate. The impact will be viewed from different angles and on the basis of diverse sources. The study into the architectural applications of asbestos fibre cement slates was performed by referring to the International asbestos-cement review, now '*AC*', which was published until 1985. In addition and with regard to the period after 1985 in particular, manufacturer documentation was consulted, mainly in the form of advertising sheets, product leaflets and archival information [2]. These sources provided detailed information on specific products, which is often not specified in architectural journals such as *AC*. The scope of the analysis therefore varies between the international level (such as with regard to changes within the legislative framework and applications) and the national level (e.g. in relation to specific products).

The paper consists of four parts. After an introduction on the origin and evolution of the fibre cement slate up to 1970, the applications of asbestos fibre cement slates are analysed by referring to the journal *AC*. Next, the transition towards asbestos-free products is studied from the perspective of legislation and, finally, asbestos-free fibre cement slates are analysed by referring to manufacturers' documentation. This research not only generates knowledge concerning the fibre cement slate in particular, but also about the transition towards asbestos-free fibre cement products. This research therefore contributes towards the broadening of existing knowledge on the subject of building materials and building culture in the period 1970-2000.

Fibre Cement Slates: An Industry Reinventing Itself (1970-2000)

Origins and evolution of the (fibre cement) slate up to the 1970s

In many parts of Europe, clay slates and clay roof tiles had been the most commonly applied roof covering materials since the Middle Ages. As a result of the Industrial Revolution, significant changes took place, not only in the process used to manufacture (these) existing roofing materials, but also in the introduction of new materials, such as cement. In 1844, the German Adolph Kroher used a type of cement he had developed himself to produce roof tiles, one of which he called the slate-type. However, it was only after production had been rationalised at the end of the nineteenth century that cement sheets could be made available in greater quantities. The material became quite popular because of its low cost and its high water- and frost resistance, which made it possible to construct shallow roof pitches. At the turn of the century, it was discovered that by adding fibres to the cement matrix, the material was even further enhanced with regard to its fire resistance, thermal properties and bending strength [3].

The process of manufacturing fibre cement was developed by the Austrian industrialist, Ludwig Hatschek, at the end of the nineteenth century. At the time, the main components were (Portland) cement, water and asbestos fibres. The manufacturing process was patented and, as a reference to the alleged 'eternal' lifespan of the material, the trademark 'Eternit' was adopted [4]. Licences were rapidly granted in many countries, including Belgium, France, Great Britain and Switzerland and the United States. Even though the asbestos fibre cement slate has since taken a prominent place as roof covering, the quantities manufactured over the years were not constant and fiercely decreased since the 1940 onwards [5]. During the war, the supply of asbestos was limited and was mainly reserved for military use, while during the '*trentes glorieuses*', slates became largely incompatible with the typically flat roofs of modern architecture. The comeback of the pitched roof in Western Europe at the end of the 1960s, gave rise to a renewed interest in roofing materials and therefore in fibre cement slates [6].

Figure 1: Dark fibre cement slates as roof covering material in holiday camp in Bretagne, France. Source: AC103 (1981), p.18.

Applications in buildings

The architectural applications of fibre cement slates were analysed by means of the International asbestos-cement review (1956-85) (also called *Revue internationale d'amiante-ciment*). This journal presented asbestos fibre cement products in the context of current international architectural and engineering projects. Although Eternit is not mentioned in the title, it is clear that there was a direct link between this leading company and the journal [7]. From 1980 onwards, the subtitle of the journal changed into '*La Revue du Fibreciment*', yet the slates that were promoted through these pages probably still all contained asbestos fibres, as Eternit only started to produce asbestos-free slates around 1986 [8]. Since the journal abruptly stopped publishing in 1985 – whether this was related to the asbestos debate of the 1970s is not stated – only applications from the 1970s and the first half of the 1980s were analysed in this part. However, certain findings might be extrapolated to the late 1980s and 1990s as well.

A systematic browsing of all issues of *AC* between 1970 and 1985 allows us to identify a total of 277 buildings in which asbestos fibre cement slates were used. These buildings were mainly located in Western Europe, including Germany (27 per cent), Switzerland (17 per cent), the United Kingdom (14 per cent), Belgium (9 per cent) and France (9 per cent). Over half of the buildings (52 per cent) were residential buildings. In addition, educational (10 per cent), cultural (10 per cent) or religious (8 per cent) buildings were depicted. The prevalence of certain building types, such as educational buildings, is clearly a result of the typical thematic approach of the journal. Nevertheless, the diversity of building types in which fibre cement slates were used is clearly illustrated within this overview.

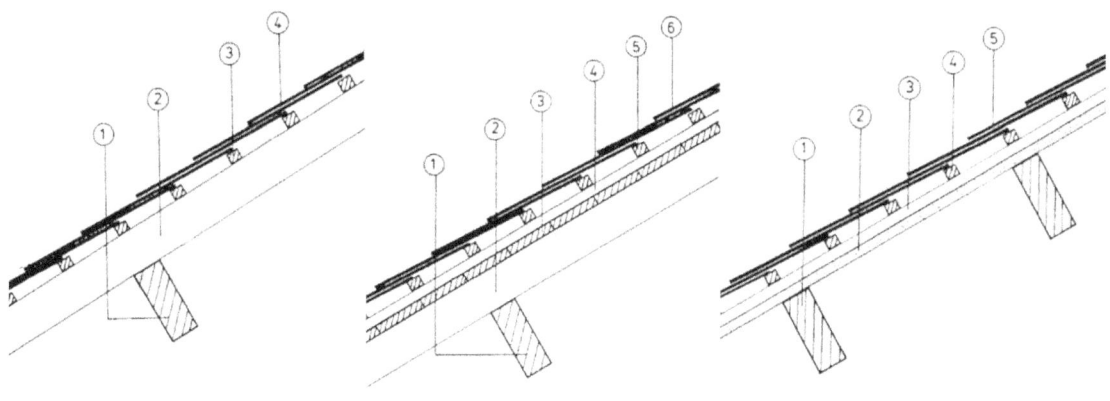

Figure 2: Slates on battens fixed on rafter (left), fixed on boarding (middle) and fixed on plates (right). Source: NBN B 44-001 (1983), 3-4.

Focusing on the most popular category depicted in *AC*, many residential projects illustrate the contemporary tendency to increase the roof surface, either by extending it downwards or by using the same material in the façade to obtain a similar visual effect (Figs 1, 3). This increased use of roof slates, on inclined as well as vertical surfaces, was enabled thanks to the typical connection method, which consisted of fixing the slates directly on battens by means of nails and hooks [9]. The battens could be fixed directly onto the rafters, or intermediate layers could be used (Fig. 2). This connection detail remained unchanged in the late 1980s and 1990s [10].

Fibre Cement Slates: An Industry Reinventing Itself (1970-2000)

The journal *AC* made no direct reference to Eternit as no product names were mentioned, except in a few individual advertising spreads. Only the format, colour, shape or pattern of the slates were occasionally evoked. Those data show that the most commonly applied formats were 60 by 30 cm and 40 by 40 cm. As for the colours, the most popular colour tone was grey. However, variations in this colour differed from country to country. In Belgium, for example, purplish grey ('rose nuit') slates were often used, but this colour was never mentioned in other countries (Fig. 3). Blue-black, on the other hand, is a colour that was only mentioned in the U.K. and Ireland.

Figure 3: Les Venelles, Brussels. Architectes Urbanistes Sociologues Ingénieurs Associés (AUSIA). Built between 1975 and 1977 (Left) ; Asbestos fibre cement slates in the colour 'rose nuit' and double overlap pattern (Right). Photos: Marylise Parein, September 2021.

Research and Legislation

In the 1970s, the public debate on the health hazards associated with asbestos emerged. The legislation concerning asbestos did however not evolve in the same way and at the same speed in all countries. The earliest official measures were aimed at minimising the dangers by implementing strict safety measures and controls for the production and processing of asbestos products [11]. The first proper bans usually did not concern all types of asbestos. Sweden, for example, introduced a ban on blue asbestos as early as 1975 [12]. Blue asbestos, also known by the scientific name of crocidolite, was primarily used for the production of pipes. It only represented a very small share of the asbestos market compared to white asbestos or chrysotile, which represented 90 per cent of the market. This ban had therefore mainly the aim of calming the spirits with regards to the asbestos polemic. Overall bans on the use of all types of asbestos only appeared in the mid-1980s. Before that date, some countries, such as Denmark in 1980, prohibited asbestos, but made some major exceptions, such as for asbestos cement. In 1986, Denmark and Sweden established an overall ban on all types of asbestos (including asbestos cement), making them the first European countries to do so. The two countries were followed by Austria (1990), the Netherlands (1991), Finland (1992), Italy (1992), Germany (1993), France (1996), Belgium (1998), United Kingdom (1999), Ireland (2000), Spain (2002), Luxembourg (2002), Greece (2005), Portugal (2005) and all other member states of the European Union from 2005 [13]. Outside the European Union, however, there are many nations, such as the United States, China, Russia and Canada, in which asbestos has not been banned (yet) [14].

In anticipation of an upcoming ban, some fibre cement companies, such as the Swiss Eternit Group, started to sponsor research into substitute fibres [15]. Laboratory research was launched from 1976 onwards [16]. Over several years, different types of fibres (glass, carbon, polyvinyl alcohol, etc.) were tested and various matrix modifications (reducing alkalinity, changing the curing conditions, etc.) were performed to obtain a material with properties similar to those of asbestos fibre cement.

Gradually, the first asbestos-free fibre cement products appeared on the market. By 1990 at the latest, the Eternit factories in Switzerland and West Germany planned to have implemented asbestos-free technology in their complete range of building materials [17]. In the meantime, in order to further improve the properties of the fibre cement and verify the harmless character of the substitute fibres, research was carried on. In 1999, the Medical Research Council Institute for Environment and Health of the University of Leicester (UK) published an article concluding that it was not justifiable anymore to use chrysotile in fibre cement products, as the substitute materials proved to be less harmful than chrysotile [18]. On 26 July 1999, the EU Commission issued a Directive banning the use of asbestos for any purpose from 1 January 2005 onwards [19].

Strikingly, despite the substitution of the main component, the production technique remained largely unchanged. Most factories continued to use Hatschek's machine, at least a modern version of it. Because of the similar production process and material properties, one could expect that the impact of the transition to asbestos-free technology at production level, on the product range and its implementation was limited. Research indeed shows that manufacturers tried to protect their market share, yet, because of the negative perception and controversy, they only partially succeeded.

Belgian manufacturers and their slates

Belgium was one of the major international manufacturers and consumers of asbestos products. Proportionally speaking, the country was even the largest consumer of asbestos products of all industrialised countries in the 1960-70 period [20]. In fact, public awareness of asbestos-related health risks remained low until the late 1970s [21]. The first restriction, concerning the use of sprayed asbestos, was issued in 1978. At the time it was assumed that if asbestos was contained in a matrix, as is the case for asbestos cement, it was not harmful [22]. In 1986, a Royal Decree was issued, stipulating that industries should replace products containing asbestos with less harmful products if the technical possibility existed. Only over a decade later, in 1998 was a Royal Decree on the use of asbestos issued prohibiting the (re)use, manufacture and advertising of all types of asbestos, with some exceptions for chrysotile. The Royal Decree of 2001, which abrogated the Decree of 1998, also banned chrysotile [23].

In order to identify the main Belgian fibre cement manufacturers and to gain an insight into how they managed the transition towards non-asbestos technology, the architectural journals *A+ Architectuur* and *Nieuw/Neuf* from the period 1975-2000 were systematically consulted. As such, three manufacturers were encountered: Eternit nv, Scheerders van Kerchove's Verenigde Fabrieken nv (SVK) and Johns-Manville Balmatt Industries nv. In addition to these journals, a search on the Belgian Building Research Institute (BBRI) website enabled us to detect a fourth manufacturer of fibre cement slates, namely Cembrit.

Fibre Cement Slates: An Industry Reinventing Itself (1970-2000)

First and foremost, Eternit is by far the most important manufacturer of fibre cement in Belgium. At the beginning of the twentieth century, Eternit factories were erected in several European countries, including Belgium. By the end of the second World War, the Belgian and Swiss Eternit branches (founded in 1905 and 1903 respectively) had become the most influential [24]. They held interests in several other national firms. In the 1970s, the Belgian Eternit Group strengthened its position, mainly because a lot of companies, including the Swiss Eternit group, started to withdraw from the production of fibre cement due to the emerging controversy [25]. The Belgian group continued to produce and export asbestos products until 1997, i.e. one year before the national ban on asbestos. The production of asbestos slates in particular stopped in 1996 [26]. Yet, at the same time they also invested in alternative asbestos-free products: in 1986 for example, in an advertisement for the Stonit slate (Fig. 4), they highlighted the "New composition. Without asbestos".

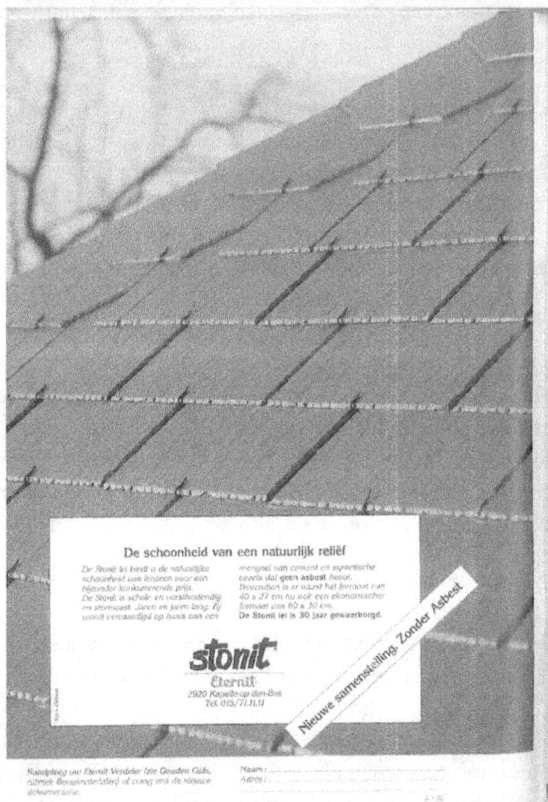

Figure 4: Advertising sheet for Eternit's Stonit slates. A sticker highlights the new composition 'without asbestos' ('Zonder asbest' in Dutch). Source: A+Architectuur 93 (1986).

In 1987, on the occasion of the largest annual construction fair in Belgium 'Batibouw', Eternit announced two new ranges of products based on the 'New Technology without asbestos (NT)' [27]. They clearly stated that these new NT ranges would not replace existing ranges of products in asbestos cement. Visually, the new NT slate and NT Stonit slate did not, according to that publication, differ from their asbestos twins, the Alterna slate and the Stonit slate. Unlike the Alterna slate, the Stonit and NT Stonit slate had a structured surface as to imitate natural slate (Fig. 4). Flat and structured surfaces were thus both available in NT technology. The number of formats and colours for the new NT ranges, however, remained quite limited. By 1996, the NT ranges had extended to include the diamond range, and a larger variety of formats and colours were available [28].

The second company, Scheerders van Kerchove's Verenigde Fabrieken, was founded in 1905 in Sint-Niklaas (near Antwerp). As its original name '*Pannen en Steenbakkerijen van Sint-Nicolaas*' (English: 'tiles and brickwork factory') implies, this family business started out as a producer of tiles and bricks. The production of fibre cement products only began in 1923 [29]. Over the years, this family business continued to grow, even though no additional factories were erected in Belgium or abroad. Today, the company is selling its products worldwide, but mainly in Western Europe [30].

SVK experienced approximately the same transition period as Eternit: the first asbestos-free slates, which they called the 'New Generation (NG)' slates, were marketed from 1988, while the slates containing asbestos were sold until 1998 [31]. The company archive does not mention particular product names until 1992: until then, SVK was mainly selling slates of different sizes and colours with either a smooth or textured surface. In a technical sheet of 1992, SVK mentions the asbestos-free Ardonit product range, which became their main product line for slates [32]. An advertising sheet from 1998 also mentions another range of slates: Fasonit [33].

The third manufacturer is J.M. Balmatt. The company commenced operations in 1928, when a small family business situated in Mol, initially called 'N.V. Beton en Mollith', was acquired by the well-known American asbestos group Johns-Manville and was renamed [34]. In 1962, J.M. Balmatt opened another production site in Ghent. Due to a lost asbestos-related lawsuit, filed exactly half a century earlier, the American Johns-Manville group went bankrupt in 1982 [35]. In consequence, the factory in Mol was sold to board members in 1983. Although the American Group emerged from bankruptcy in 1988, the factory in Mol, on the other hand, went bankrupt in 1998, i.e. the same year of the Belgian ban on asbestos. The factory in fact completely stopped the production of asbestos products only six months prior to the bankruptcy [36].

Whether the factories in Mol and Ghent continued to produce slates under the name of J.M. Balmatt as from 1982 is not clear, as very few sources concerning these two sites could be found. Some advertisements in *Neuf* (1985, 1987) demonstrate, however, that J.M. Balmatt slates were still being sold on the Belgian market in the years that followed. These advertisements do not mention whether the slates were asbestos-free and only allude to an asbestos-free coating in 1985 (Fig. 5).

Figure 5: Advertising sheet for J.M. Balmatt's Structural slates. The text mentions a coating without asbestos ('Couche superficielle sans amiante' in French). Source: Neuf 117(1985).

Finally, as a fourth company, Cembrit Belgium is one of the subsidiaries of the eponymous main company, located in Denmark since 1927 [37]. Initially, the company was called Dansk Eternit, as they were working with Hatschek's patent. Unlike most other Eternit firms, Dansk Eternit was not controlled by the Swiss or Belgians, but became one of the major companies in Scandinavia [38]. In 1938, Dansk Eternit started exporting under the name 'Cembrit' [39]. It is however only since 1995 that Cembrit has been active on the Belgian market, selling products manufactured in a Czech factory [40]. As the prohibition of asbestos cement products had already been established in 1986 in Denmark, Cembrit had some advances in New Technology products compared to Belgian manufacturers [41]. Its entire production of fibre cement products was asbestos-free from 1988 onwards [42]. As this brand is not mentioned in any of the Belgian periodicals or archives consulted, its role within the Belgian market for fibre cement slates in the period from 1970 to 2000 remains uncertain.

In summary, the 1970-2000 period witnessed two generations of fibre cement manufacturers in Belgium. From the first half of the twentieth century until the 1990s, Eternit, SVK and the Belgian branch of the Johns-Manville Group together clearly controlled the Belgian market. They can be considered as the first generation of manufacturers. They were well-known as a result of the fact that they had marketed asbestos products for years, yet that reputation worked to their disadvantage when the asbestos debate emerged, especially in the case of Eternit. They needed a transition period of approximatively 10 years to switch entirely to asbestos-free alternatives. Cembrit, for its part, only entered the Belgian market after the debate had broken out, and, as the transition towards non-asbestos technology did not occur simultaneously in all countries, it had a head start over Belgium's first-generation manufacturers.

Conclusion

Following the increasing insight and debate concerning the health risks related to asbestos fibres, a ban on asbestos products was imposed in several countries from 1975 onwards. This ban was declared step-by-step, often depending on the type of fibres and their application. During the following decades, manufacturers of asbestos fibre products largely invested in finding a substitute material and production technology. They tried to minimise the impact of the new technology: the new products were often similar to existing product ranges, with a view on replacing their asbestos twins by the end of the transition period. When focusing on one particular product, namely fibre cement slates, the impact can indeed be considered limited, at least from a technical point of view. Besides the substitution of its basic component, the production process remained largely unchanged and the resulting products were also similar, in their formats, colours and textures, to their predecessors that contained asbestos (although the variety was much more limited at first). The connection method was not impacted either. Yet, although the visual impact seems limited, the effect on the implementation of asbestos-free fibre cement slates in West-European architecture is more difficult to grasp for three reasons. The first reason concerns the sources. Because the journal *AC* was discontinued in 1985, no complete overview of (international) applications of fibre cement slates is available for the period from 1970 to 2000. Due to the controversy surrounding asbestos, the amount of literature on fibre cement products was quite reduced and fibre cement manufacturers today are still reluctant to open their doors to researchers. Secondly, the impact on architecture has to be evaluated for each country separately as the transition did not happen in precisely the same way throughout Western Europe as a whole. Moreover, this transition was influenced by legislation, but also by increasing import and export activity between countries. The third, quite obvious reason that explains why evaluating the impact of the asbestos-free fibre cement slates on the architecture is a complicated matter has to do with the architecture itself. While the 1960s and the 1970s architecture was marked by the presence of slates on the roof and on a building's façades, this was far less the case in the two subsequent decades. A decrease in use is therefore not completely or necessarily related to the new slate product itself but is also a result of the architectural trends in existence at the time.

Acknowledgements

This research has been carried out within the framework of the project 'The Brussels building stock (1975-2000): materiality and heritage value' funded by the Brussels-Capital Region through Innoviris. The research project was carried out in close collaboration between the Vrije Universiteit Brussel and the Public Service urban.brussels, Belgium' (https://urban.brussels/fr).

References

[1] J. Mascarenhas-Mateus and A. Paula Pires, (Eds), *Proceedings of the 7th International Congress on Construction History* (7ICCH), Lisbon 2021, Lisbon: CRC Press, 2021.
[2] Document library of UCLouvain (BAIU-Bruxelles) and Archives of Scheerders van Kerchove's Verenigde Fabrieken (Sint-Niklaas).
[3] E. Schunck, H.J. Oster, R. Barthel and K. Kiessl, *Roof Construction Manual: Pitched roofs,* Basel: Birkhäuser, 2003. pp. 10-14.
[4] L. Hatschek, 'Verfahren zur Herstellung von Kunststeinplatten aus Faserstoffen und hydraulischen Bindemitteln', AT5970B, 25 November, 1900.
[5] R.F. Ruers and N. Schouten, *The tragedy of asbestos. Eternit and the consequences of a hundred years of asbestos cement*. The Netherlands: Socialistische Partij, 2006. pp. 4-6.
[6] F.F. Adler, O. Riege, A. Oeschger and Y. Greutert, 'Nous nous posons des questions et cherchons les réponses', *AC: Revue internationale de l'amiante-ciment,* vol.1, no. 89, pp. 4-7, 1978.
[7] S. Van de Voorde, R. Devos, 'L'histoire d'un héritage matériel non-durable : l'auto-promotion internationale de l'amiante-ciment par le revue AC (1956-1985)', In G. Bienvenu, M. Monteil, & H. Rousteau-Chambon (eds.), *Construire! Entre l'Antiquité et époque contemporaine : Actes du 3e congrès francophone d'histoire de la construction,* Nantes, 2017, pp. 661-671.
[8] Eternit (Belgium), 'Stonit. De schoonheid van een natuurlijk reliëf', *A+ Architectuur,* no.93, 1986.
[9] Ministère des Travaux publics e.a., 'Couvertures en tuiles et en ardoises', in STS 34. Couvertures de bâtiment, vol. 1, 5 vols. Feluy: C. Crappe, 1971. p. 8.
[10] *Fiber-cement slates. Roofcoverings*, NBN B 44-001, Belgisch Bureau voor Normalisatie (NBN), Brussel, 1983; *Fiber-cement slates. Roofcoverings,* NBN B 44-001/A1, Belgisch Bureau voor Normalisatie (NBN), Brussel, 1997.
[11] J.B. Studinka, 'Asbestos substitution in the fibre cement industry', The International Journal of Cement Composites and Lightweight Concrete, vol.11, no.2, 1989, pp. 73-78.
[12] R.F. Ruers and N. Schouten, (Note 5) p. 19.
[13] K. Müller, 'Protecting workers from asbestos. European added value assessment accompanying request for a legislative proposal 2019/2182(INL): in-depth analysis', European Parliamentary Research Service (EPRS), November 2021. Accessed on 5 January 2022. [Online]. Available: https://op.europa.eu/en/publication-detail/-/publication/1ac1d795-5321-11ec-91ac-01aa75ed71a1/language-en; 'Commission Directive 1999/77/EC', 26 July 1999. [Online]. Available: https://eur-lex.europa.eu/LexUriServ/LexUriServ.do?uri=CELEX:31999L0077:EN:HTML. [Accessed on 5 January 2022].
[14] Environmental Working Group (EWG), 'Asbestos bans around the world', 2022. [Online]. Available: http://asbestosnation.org/facts/asbestos-bans-around-the-world/. [Accessed on 5 January 2022].
[15] J.B. Studinka, (Note 11) p. 76.
[16] Ibid., p. 74.
[17] Ibid., pp. 73-78.

[18] P.T.C. Harrison, L.S. Levy, G. Patrick, G.H. Pigott and L. Smith, 'Comparative Hazards of Chrysotile Asbestos and Its Substitutes: A European Perspective', *Environmental Health Perspectives*, vol.107, no.8, 1999, pp. 607-611.
[19] Environmental Working Group (Note 14).
[20] E. de Kezel, 'Asbest, gezondheid en veiligheid. Ontwikkelingen in het aansprakelijkheisrecht, 2013' (Ph.D. thesis, Antwerpen: Intersentia, 2013), p.123.
[21] E. de Kezel, (Note 20) pp. 41-60.
[22] Ibid, p. 137.
[23] Ibid, pp. 150-151.
[24] R.F. Ruers and N. Schouten, (Note 5), pp. 6-7; P. Carrard, M. Hanak and B. Maurer (dir.), *Eternit Suisse. Architecture et culture d'entreprise depuis 1903*, Zürich : ETH Zürich, 2003.
[25] R.F. Ruers and N. Schouten, (Note5), pp. 36-37.
[26] Eternit Belgium, 'Asbestverleden', n.d. [Online]. Available: https://www.eternit.be/nl-be/asbestverleden/. [Accessed on 7 September 2021].
[27] F. Logist, (Ed.), 'Batibouw 87, 20 nouveautés', *Eterflash*, n.d.
[28] Eternit (Belgium), *Eloge de l'ardoise*, Kapelle-op-den-Bos, 1996.
[29] SVK, 'Geschiedenis', n.d., [Online]. Available: https://svk.be/nl-BE/geschiedenis. [Accessed on 11 February 2022].
[30] SVK, 'Verdelers', n.d., [Online]. Available: https://svk.be/nl-BE/verdelers. [Accessed on 11 February 2022].
[31] SVK, 'Asbesthoudend of asbestvrij', Kapelle-op-den-Bos, n.d.
[32] SVK, 'Ardonit. Technische gegevens,' Kapelle-op-den-Bos, July 1992.
[33] SVK, 'Een leven vol schwung', *A+ Architectuur*, no. 152, 1998.
[34] Urbex, 'Johns-Manville Balmatt. The abandoned factory in Belgium', 2021. [Online]. Available: https:// urbex.nl/johns-manville/. [Accessed on 11 February 2022].
[35] J. De Wit, 'Het asbestproces in Brussel', *Gazet van Antwerpen*, 24 October 2011. [Online]. Available: https:// gva.be/cnt/aid1086997/. [Accessed on 11 February 2022].
[36] Urbex, (Note 34).
[37] Cembrit (Belgium), 'Ons Verhaal', n.d. [Online]. Available: https:// cembrit.be/nl/over-cembrit/ons-verhaal. [Accessed on 4 February 2022].
[38] R.F. Ruers and N. Schouten, (Note 5), p. 40.
[39] Cembrit (Belgium), (Note 37).
[40] Belgische Unie voor de technische goedkeuring in de bouw (BUtgb), 'ATG 03/2548. Dakbedekking met Dolmen leien van vezelcement', 30 January 2003. [Online]. Available: https://butgb-ubatc.be/nl/technical_approval/atg-2548/. [Accessed on 11 February 2022].
[41] The Danish Working Environment Authority (WEA), 'AT guide. Asbestos', July 1st, 2005. [Online]. Available: https://at.dk/regler/at-vejledninger/asbest-c-2-2/. [Accessed on 11 February 2022].
[42] Cembrit (Belgium), 'Al sinds 1988 asbestvrij', n.d. [Online]. Available: https:// cembrit.be/nl/thema/asbest. [Accessed on 11 February 2022].

A Joint of Many Worlds: Entangled Stories in Battaile en Ibens's 78+ Construction System in Timber

Eric Ferreira Crevels
Department of Architecture and the Built Environment, Delft University of Technology, NL

Abstract

This paper explores the distinct networks of technical and embodied knowledge present in the development of the 78+ construction system in timber, designed in the 1970-80s by Flemish design office Battaile Ibens. It develops the history of the *knooppunt,* a joint of a particular material and technical complexity that structures the system's wooden beams and cross-shaped columns, and argues for the understanding of architecture and construction as complex constellations of different crafts and skills, including but not limited to architectural design and engineering. Design and technical decisions are traced in parallel to economic and marketing strategies, weaving together social and material phenomena that shaped the system's history. From the initial designs and prototyping, through publicity decisions and appearances in international expositions, until its idealization in the office's approach, the history of the *knooppunt* exemplifies the interplay between different stakeholders and knowledge orbiting the technological development of construction systems.

Introduction

Amongst the dozens of models in the archive of the *Vlaams Architectuurnstituut* (VAi) in Antwerp, one finds what is expected in an architectural collection, from private houses to new urban developments. Sitting on a high shelf, however, a large wooden model contrasts with the landscape [1]. (Fig. 1) Four sets of mitred butt-joints surround a cross-shaped axle – their edges sitting in the recesses and their ends extruding outwards in a larger, doubled-lined shape resembling a military medal or heraldic symbol. The inner corners are filled with triangular blocks, which gives the assemble a robust, solid appearance. The central axle protrudes outwards on one side, and the ends of large rods are visible on the faces of the corner pieces, fastened with washers and nuts. It is clear that the model represents no building.

Figure 1: Wooden model of the 78+ knooppunt. circa 1980. Source: VAi

A Joint of Many Worlds: Entangled Stories in Battaile en Ibens's 78+ Construction System in Timber

The piece is a true-scale model of the *Knooppunt* ("joint" or "node", in Dutch), a joint that connects the beams and columns of the 78+ construction system developed by Claire Bataille and Paul Ibens's design office (B&I), working with International Design Constructions (IDC). Named after the year of its instalment, the 78+ is designed as a modular system, intended to be an "original, flexible, and above all economical prefabricated system [2]". The cross-shaped axle on the model, sitting horizontally at the VAi's shelf, represents the column of the system, while the eight long profiles, conjoined in four mitred butt-joints, are the beams. The entire piece is traversed diagonally by two large perpendicular threaded rods, running slightly off centre, so as not to collide in the middle. The rods act as tethers and, with the help of the corner blocks, lock everything in place.

A microhistory of design development

The *knooppunt* appears almost fully developed in the VAi's archives, already presenting its main components and general form in the earliest documents. Given the complexity of the assembly, however, it is likely to be the result of an exploration with many earlier versions, through careful consideration and iterative processes, as common in design [3]. Unfortunately, there are no sketches showing this initial progress but, despite the lack of recorded changes, traces of the design's development can still be recovered from the archived documents. Specifically, by comparing the existing technical drawings, photographic material and the model, some partial conclusions about the *knooppunt*'s design and the knowledge behind its production can be drawn.

The intention behind the model's construction seems to be experimental, meant to test the joint assembly rather than being used for exposition. The model was shown only once in later media articles, in October 1980, and it was not included in the IDC's catalogue (Fig. 2) nor presented in the *De Wereld van het Design* exhibition in the same year [4]. This absence is rather significant, given that the *knooppunt* is almost always featured, be it in exploded views or through the prototype building's pictures, and it appears to have become the main publicity element of the 78+.

Figure 2: Advertising material of the 78+ Construction System in timber. Source: VAi

As a crafted artefact, the model is rather unimpressive. Its pieces are loosely bound, the mitred joints are not flush and do not match exactly the angle of the cross-shaped column. The pieces are not *square*, as a carpenter would say. Several gaps can be seen, in sizes not expectable from its age. From a craft point of view, it was not particularly well made. This low quality matches what is expected of a test model, built without the utmost care for precise fitting, but maintaining key aspects of its composition.

The existence of two different configurations of the corner blocks in the model attests to this interpretation. In one solution, the corner blocks possess a square angled chamfer and sit in a recess carved in the beam, matching its geometry. This configuration would prevent the piece from moving backwards, which is a common feature in many carpentry and woodworking joints. Yet, its application in the *knooppunt* is misplaced. The bolt which crosses and tethers the pieces acts by pulling the corner block towards the joint, not away from it. Accordingly, the alternative configuration is far simpler, with the corner block sitting flush on the surface of the beams, without any recess or other complications.

The use of both versions in the model suggests that the matter was not resolved at the point of its development. (Fig 3a) Indeed, this detail can offer some clues on where temporally it sits in the whole story. The patent files of the 78+, submitted in June 1980 (Fig 3c), also show the two solutions [5]. Whereas one illustration in the file shows the flush version, another depicts the carved one, accompanied by a description that translates to "Figure 3 shows a solution in which the blocks 9 are incorporated into the beams 8", presenting an "execution variant [6]". Moreover, in an exploded view with the carved solution, dated June 1978, it is possible to see a small ink marking made over the original drawing, (Fig 3e) hinting at the possible use of a flush configuration [7]. In the later (September 1980) and much more complex exploded view, the flush version is the only one employed, notably with the addition of two pegs between the corner blocks and the beams, this time acting in accordance with the forces at play. From these documents, it is possible that the alternative, flush method, was suggested in 1978, but only tested at around the same time as the patenting process, *via* the wooden model – most probably, in preparation for the construction of the prototype pavilion around 1980 (discussed below).

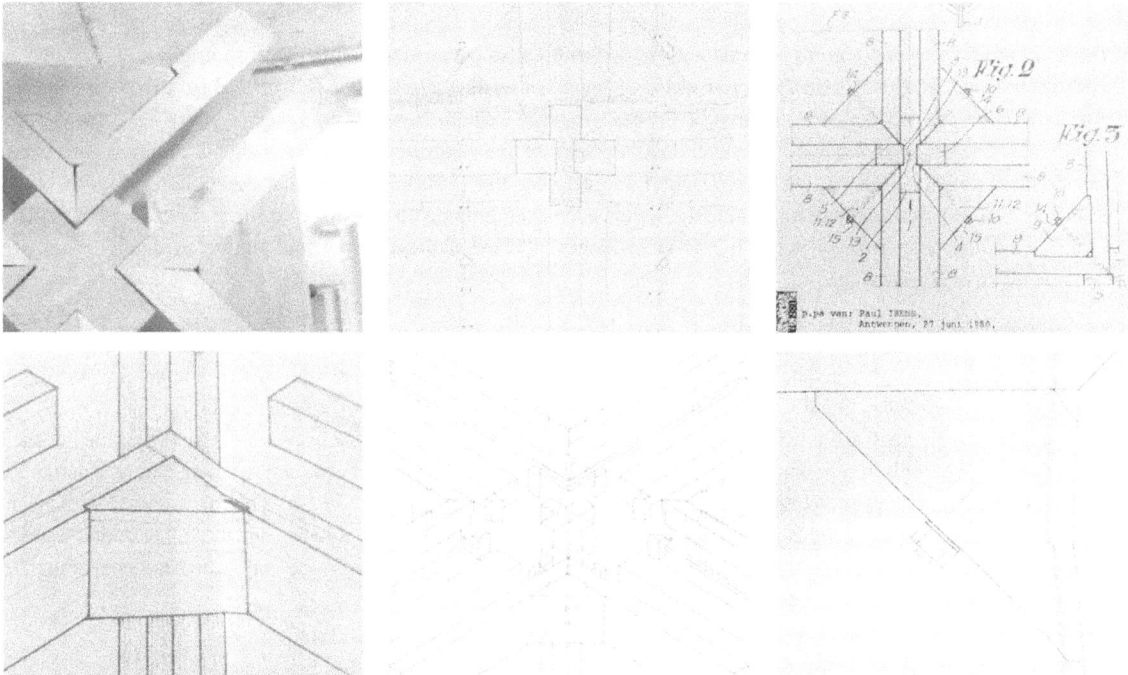

Figure 3: Variation in the solutions for the corner block. Source: VAi

A Joint of Many Worlds: Entangled Stories in Battaile en Ibens's 78+ Construction System in Timber

While not useful in the 78+ specific case, the proposal of the carved solution requires some knowledge of carpentry techniques and it suggests that the craft's *savoir-faire* had already made its way into the project. Minute as they may seem, such tales of technical development present traces of practical knowledge regarding the properties of wood and the techniques of its employment when confronted with the specific requirements and contingencies involving the development of a new way of building. This story sketches a picture of iterative development, indicating little nudges from craft knowledge that usher the design towards a more applicable and practical form, a story of epistemic interference between different fields. B&I, together with IDC, were treading a path that connected industry, craft and architecture, balancing the many aspects surrounding its development. The *knooppunt* model is part of the process. As an experimental tool, it connects the conceptual and constructive sides of architectural productions by materializing ideas in the complex contingencies of physical reality. This phenomenon is akin to what is described by Gibson as *Material Inheritance*, a concept that refers to the traces of craft knowledge and rationality that make their way into and influence the ways of making and thinking of a particular industry, without being formally recognized or easily brought to surface [8].

However, an examination of the 78+ construction system through the *knooppunt* model, while significant in terms of understanding the tectonic values of the system's design, fails to put in evidence the complete picture behind the system's material inheritance. The representational character of technical drawings, sketches, and models present in architectural archives can often be misleading to understand the practical, *hands-on* dimension that governs craft knowledge and skill. Additionally, despite the material and technical entanglements exposed so far, the logic behind the design of the 78+ and the particular form of the *knooppunt* remain rather unclear. According to Brazilian scholar Sérgio Ferro, mysteries in architecture are often related to a logic that is specific to the construction site [9]. Therefore, in order to fully understand the knowledge at play in the development of the 78+ system, it is necessary to investigate its *chaîne opératoire* [10].

The concept of *chaîne opératoire* is particularly significant for studies of technology because it tells a story detached from its products and particular characteristics – technical or aesthetic – and focuses instead on the conditions and processes within the production of artefacts. In the case of the 78+ and the *knooppunt*, these operations have even greater importance. The design of modular systems follows a discourse that advocates for rationality in construction, thriving on industrial maxims of efficiency, mass production and affordability [11]. In the system's description provided by the architects, there was a great focus on making the system adequate for numerous applications (from residences to industrial villages) and different sites (including "third-world villages") [12]. This flexibility would require, evidently, a similarly versatile mode of construction.

One could argue that this was precisely the *knooppunt*'s *raison d'être*, but that is not the entire story. There is, in the 78+, another particular arrangement that works in favour of these premises, and a single written source provides some explanation on this matter. In a text provided by the architects to the *Wereld van het Design* exhibition, it is stated that the 78+ is "based on cross sectioned vertical columns that are joined by *horizontal square frames* that form the floor and roof supports [13]." This description is accompanied by a step-by-step erection procedure instructing that "the horizontal frames are installed" after the columns, and directing builders to see "the *model joint*" [14]. In stark contrast to the technical drawings, the instructions do not mention the *knooppunt*, but refer to the columns and these 'horizontal frames', never mentioned elsewhere. Notably, in a photographic series depicting the system's assembly, where a model of the 78+ is constructed in steps, the square modules are missing [15]. (Fig. 4)

Eric Ferreira Crevels

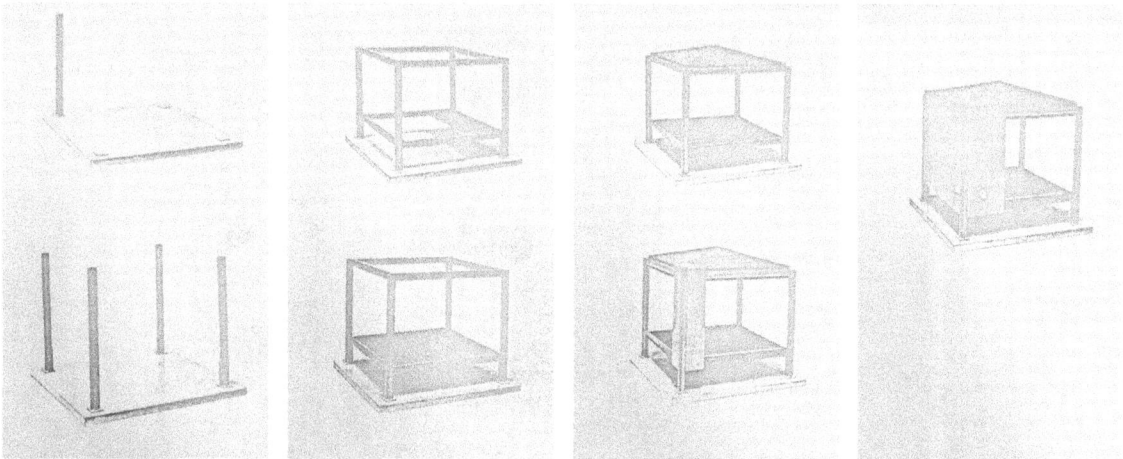

Figure 4: Montage model depicting the 78+ assembly. Source: VAi

Fortunately, some clues of this arrangement come from the photographs depicting its use. The archives of the VAi include a photographic collection showing the assembly of a prototype building using the 78+ system, built for J. Ibens, Paul's brother [16]. (Fig. 5) The prototype consists of a pavilion of approximately 70 m², whose designs are dated from November 1979. The plan was developed over a four-square grid formed by nine of the 78+ cross-shaped columns. An isometric perspective of the design can be found in the patent documents, but the pictures (themselves undated) appear in other printed materials only in May 1981, meaning that its construction probably occurred around the same time as the patenting process – from the vegetation and clothing seen in the pictures, sometime in the warmer months of 1980.

Figure 5: Pictures of the prototype's building process. Source: VAi

As can be seen from these photographs, the beams are previously joined together along with the corner blocks in a square-shaped module. The module is then raised and fastened to the previously positioned columns. From the perspective of the construction site, the employment of the square modules with the *knooppunt* locking mechanism has significant advantages. Being the corner piece glued to the beams in a frame, the ensemble is easy to position and secure in place. Rather than dealing at once with several pieces that must converge in a single point, with their leveraged ends hanging on the back, the builders would deal with only one piece. Additionally, the cross shape section of each column houses the square modules, keeping them in place and guiding them along the vertical axis.

A Joint of Many Worlds: Entangled Stories in Battaile en Ibens's 78+ Construction System in Timber

Figure 6: The finished prototype. Source: VAi

This small, almost unseen, detail of the system's assembly affords an important consideration regarding the relationship between the knooppunt, the square module, and the 78+ system. Instead of understanding the knooppunt as the main element supporting the system, both structurally and in terms of design logic, perhaps the definition of the square module has a similar importance. Indeed, the 78+ system only works as it does because of the square module and the joint, and they can be seen as complementary negatives of each other [17]. It is possible to envision a scenario in which both were developed simultaneously, each element participating in the other's formation, as symbiotic counterparts that work together constructing the design, both in terms of the production process and of the final product.

Phase Shifts – the other sides of technical developments

The mutual interference between the *knooppunt* and the modular square frames imbues the 78+ systems with a superimposed, *dialogic* modularity that merges the rationalities of the design office and the construction site. In other words, it represents a combination of intellectual and operative ways of thinking, and different communities of practice – namely, design, engineering and carpentry [18].

Unfortunately, as can be attested from the archival collection on the 78+ system and the literature around it, this dialogic modularity remains unspoken of. While the *knooppunt* is represented not only in the model, but in several other media and in different formats (particularly with exploded isometrics), the assembly logic of the square frames is never portrayed visually in any technical drawing, in the IDC's 78+ catalogue, or the media articles. Taking into consideration its constructive rationality and possible importance for the very constitution of the *knooppunt*, the lack of representation of the square module in most of the 78+ documents is intriguing, as it goes against the system's advocacy for Do-It-Yourself (DIY) and simplicity [19].

The shift makes sense from a marketing perspective, however; a realm in which the 78+ system was particularly successful. It was featured in several exhibitions organized by the *Design Centre*: the *De Wereld van het Design* exhibition, in late 1980, after which the 78+ was awarded the Sigle d'Or prize; the *Design and Export* exhibition in the spring of the following year; and the *Belgica Hoy*, in November 1982, in Barcelona. The system was featured in the *Biënnale Interieur* in Kortrijk, also in 1982, with the construction of a red barn-like two-stories pavilion. (Fig. 7) Following the exhibitions and prize, it appeared in several press articles [20], including the cover of *neuf* magazine [21].

Figure 7: The 78+ pavilion of the 1982 Biennale Interrieur Kortrijk. Source: VAi

Besides the media attention, the designers worked on urban development projects in the Belgian cities of Vielsalm, Virton, and Manderfeld, in addition to many private commissions. Furthermore, in late June 1980, Clarie Bataille and Paul Ibens formed the *Preewood Construction Company* in the United States, in partnership with Robert Huckins and Walter Van Elven, meant to "carry the trade or business of General Contractor" [22]. Not long after, they were engaged in projects for neighbourhoods in Ruidoso, New Mexico, and in Rifle, Colorado, designing several different residential types, in many shapes and sizes.

Along with so much development and growth came the associated demands. As such, it would be reasonable for the designers to choose a method of representation most familiar to their practice. It is no secret that the work of architects involves the production of advertising material for both their own marketing and their client's. Architecture and construction are economic practices that sell specific products, which, in the specific case of the 78+, converge into one. In this scenario, the marketing promotion of the system corresponded directly to the promotion of the design.

A Joint of Many Worlds: Entangled Stories in Battaile en Ibens's 78+ Construction System in Timber

Figure 8: Design for a neighborhood in Viesalm. Source: VAi

When starting the design of the 78+ system, B&I had existed for about 10 years and had designed many different things – an impressive collection ranging from furniture, with many tables, stools, chairs, couches, *dressoirs, canapés, commodes* and so on, to cutlery, glasses, dinnerware, doorknobs and even some sinks [23]. Claire Bataille and Paul Ibens did not hold architecture diplomas, but were trained as *interieurarchitecten* at the Hoger Instituut voor Bouwkunst en Stedenbouw, in Antwerp, and their embraced cross-disciplinarity was reflected in their chosen name "*Studiebureau Bataille-ibens Designers*" [24]. This multi-faceted aspect of the office's origin and work meant that B&I, intentionally or not, carried into their architectural work the modes of representation and practices from other fields of knowledge, effectively blurring the divide "between architecture and design, between garden and interior, between the ideal plan and the compromise of living, between art and craft" [25].

The representation choices for the 78+ system were surely connected to the office's involvement with interior and furniture design. As seen from B&I's other projects, the isometric and exploded views used to depict the *knooppunt* are common in their representative repertoire [26]. These are methods of drawing frequently used to detail the assemblage of furniture, particularly customary in woodworking manuals. Favoured by makers because of their capacity to depict tridimensionality while maintaining the true dimension of lines, they require little knowledge of drawing technique, in contrast to perspectival drawing, and are easily understood by laymen.

Therefore, it is reasonable to believe that the focus on the knooppunt as a representative element of the system is an emergent condition. While the joint's design seems to derive not from marketing or visual quality's sake, its form greatly resonates with the modes of representation commonly employed in B&I's professional environment. In the exploded view, the tectonic intricacy of the joint's assembly is shown on a symmetric, ordered composition – from the empty edges inwards, the elements progressively appear, orbiting the column, and their angled lines converge at the drawing's centre, culminating in the knooppunt. It is a powerful picture, able to maintain the ideal of technical prowess in a language of design and aesthetical quality. (Fig. 9)

Figure 9: Exploded isometric view of the knooppunt. Source: VAi.

When compared to the square module, the *knooppunt* is far more appealing from a *commodity* point of view. While both elements share much of the same technical rationality, they possess specific qualities with opposite affordances in the dialectics of product and production. The *knooppunt* is easily portrayed as an independent object while maintaining its complex appearance and technical appeal. The qualities of the square module, on the other hand, can only be seen *in movement*, while it is being installed. Thus, the two elements tend to operate, discursively, in different realms – and, again, for different publics. The logic behind the square modules is that of the construction site, particularly significant to builders and contractors, but the *knooppunt* better portrays the product offered by the 78+, ultimately what most concerns potential clients.

By focusing on the element that represents the final assemblage instead of the *chaîne opératoire*, B&I aligned the 78+ with a commodity-oriented aesthetics. In this framework, the depictions of the *knooppunt* not only serve to inform but, and even more prominently, they deploy a particular discourse, with a specific lexicon and aiming at an intended target. Through this process, the *knooppunt* can be interpreted as akin to a *dispositif,* as Michel Foucault would put it [27]. Echoing a movement from the medieval *codex* to the *theatre des machines* [28], the focus on the *knooppunt*, especially through exploded isometric views, represents a progression towards a commercial logic of exposition, prioritizing elements that portray a technological product as a commodity. In other words, the *knooppunt* was elevated as the avatar of the 78+ because it represents the product of the assembly rather than its process, a quality that resonates well with a market-oriented environment.

A Joint of Many Worlds: Entangled Stories in Battaile en Ibens's 78+ Construction System in Timber

None of this means, however, that the *knooppunt* is inefficient from a constructive and processual point of view. If the elevation of the *knooppunt* as the avatar of the 78+ system perhaps finds a better explanation in its visual power, its form is still a result of deep technical exploration. A great testimony to this double value can be found in the way the *knooppunt* was further explored in later projects by B&I. Developed for serial production under the *Bulo* brand, B&I's design for the H20 table makes use of cross-shaped elements as its legs [29]. While not identical, the similarity with the 78+ is pointed out by many scholars [30]. (Fig. 10) In architectural works, solutions resembling the *knooppunt* can be found in the metal structure of *Brants-Voets* house in Dwerp, and in an extension of a residence in Sint-Niklaas [31]. Finally, the 78+ was further developed in the 98+ construction system [32]. This revision presented a version of the system without the modular square frames and replaced the corner blocks with aluminium L-shaped profiles. These modifications further simplified the assembly process and drastically reduced the amount of wood required for its construction.

Figure 10: H20 table. Source: VAi

The recurrence of the knooppunt in many different designs accounts for its visual, technical, and conceptual appeal, but also for the joint's capacity to bridge together different domains. As seen from the stories in this paper, the knooppunt carries knowledge from many communities of practice, including the savoir-faire of carpentry, construction site logistics, and market strategies. Behind this repetition, however, lies yet another phase of the knooppunt's history. As Christian Kieckens notes, the knooppunt reverberated with the designer's approach on a deeper level.

> An important part of their oeuvre - not immediately visible and yet clearly present - deals with mastering this detail, with the materiality of the construction. It is part of their attitude that this mindset is transformed into a kind of wordless knowledge, a knowing 'how to deal with things [33]'.

The slow, re-iterative coming back to the *knooppunt* can be perceived as a way the designers related to materiality. B&I found in it a tool that allowed them to navigate the many agencies involved in material productions while maintaining their attentiveness to functionality and efficiency, and fostering their transdisciplinary stance [34]. Abstracted into a design approach, the *knooppunt* became a concept underlying the office's work, a way in which the network of different epistemic regimes was accessed.

Forged across many phase shifts – from experimental model to design concept – the knooppunt weaved threads of craft, market practices, and design processes and subverted the roles of creator and creation, blurring the expected boundaries of knowledge in architectural production. Moving between concrete and abstract dimensions, the joint carries forward the processes of its development, in a renewed material inheritance wedged in architectural history and the shelves of the VAi.

Conclusion

The investigation in this paper attempted to appraise the connections between the built environment and the processes involving its material constitution, using the 78+ construction system and its *knooppunt* as case study. Through the microhistories of the joint's design and its employment in the construction site it becomes clear that, as Glenn Adamson points out, technological development is never fully independent of craft skill [35]. As a constructive analogue to Joseph Kosuth's *One and Three Chairs*, the 78+ system is one but many at the same time. This multiplicity reflects the many fields involved in its formation and their specific directionality – some oriented towards the system's assembly in the construction site, while others focus on the aesthetic appeal for marketing material. In the 78+, market, industry, design and craft come together in an enmeshed artefact. These are all different dimensions of what can be understood as a single phenomenon – each representing, nonetheless, a specific skill set and way of knowing, and the values inscribed in an episteme. Beyond modern discursive schisms between intellectual and operative, conceptual and constructive ways of thinking, the constellations of skill, knowledge and agency in the 78+ reveal a shared environment of material, practical and discursive horizons.

Metaphorically and literally, the *knooppunt* connects the many worlds surrounding the craft of architecture, forming and being formed by the different elements involved in its history. These entangled stories shape the way timber is employed and understood, being embedded into and giving rise to the particular way in which the material relates to society [36] – what, from a Foucauldian perspective, could be called a *discursive materiality* [37].

References

[1] Wooden model of Bataille en Ibens' 78+ construction system joint "knooppunt", BE/653717/0101-BI/0299, Archief van Claire Bataille en Paul Ibens Desgin, Vlaams Architectuutinstituut archief, Antwerp, Flanders, Belgium.
[2] Documents from Bataille en Ibens' 78+ construction system, BE/653717/0101-BI/0299, box 47- 49, Archief van Claire Bataille en Paul Ibens Desgin, Vlaams Architectuutinstituut archief, Antwerp, Flanders, Belgium.
[3] Donald A Schön, *The Reflective Practitioner* (Basic Books, 2013), https://doi.org/10.1017/CBO9781107415324.004.
[4] Archief van Claire Bataille en Paul Ibens Desgin, Vlaams Architectuutinstituut archief.
[5] Ibid.
[6] Ibid.
[7] Ibid.
[8] Chris Gibson, "Material Inheritances: How Place, Materiality, and Labor Process Underpin the Path-Dependent Evolution of Contemporary Craft Production," *Economic Geography* 92, no. 1 (2016): 61–86, https://doi.org/10.1080/00130095.2015.1092211.
[9] Sergio Ferro, *Arquitetura e Trabalho Livre* (São Paulo: Cosac Naify, 2006).

A Joint of Many Worlds: Entangled Stories in Battaile en Ibens's 78+ Construction System in Timber

[10] Heide W Nørgaard, "Technological Choices," in *Bronze Age Metalwork: Techniques and Traditions in the Nordic Bronze Age*, 2013, https://doi.org/10.4324/9781315887630. Carl Knappet and Lambros Malafouris, *Material Agency: Towards a Non-Anthropocentric Approach*, Journal of Chemical Information and Modeling, vol. 53 (New York: Springer, 2019). Lambros Malafouris, *How Things Shape the Mind: A Theory of Material Engagement*, American Anthropologist, vol. 117, 2015, https://doi.org/10.1111/aman.12210.

[11] Koen Van Synghel et al, *Claire Bataille, Paul Ibens : Projets et objets 1968-2002* (Brussels, Ludion Distributie, 2003).

[12] Archief van Claire Bataille en Paul Ibens Desgin, Vlaams Architectuutinstituut archief.

[13] Ibid, my highlights.

[14] Ibid, my highlights.

[15] Ibid.

[16] Koen Van Synghel et al, *Claire Bataille, Paul Ibens : Projets et objets 1968-2002*

[17] Alfred Gell, "Vogel's Net: Traps as Artworks and Artworks as Traps.," *Journal of Material Culture* 1, no. 1 (1996): 15–38.

[18] Etienne Wenger, Richard Mcdermott, and William M Snyder, *Cultivating Communities of Practice* (Boston: Harvard Business School Press, 2002).

[19] Koen Van Synghel et al, *Claire Bataille, Paul Ibens : Projets et objets 1968-2002*

[20] Archief van Claire Bataille en Paul Ibens Desgin, Vlaams Architectuutinstituut archief.

[21] Vol. 6, n 95, 1981 – from Bataille en Ibens' 78+ construction system, BE/653717/0101-BI/0299, box 47- 49, Archief van Claire Bataille en Paul Ibens Desgin, Vlaams Architectuutinstituut archief, Antwerp, Flanders, Belgium

[22] Archief van Claire Bataille en Paul Ibens Desgin, Vlaams Architectuutinstituut archief.

[23] Koen Van Synghel et al, *Claire Bataille, Paul Ibens : Projets et objets 1968-2002*

[24] Ibid.

[25] Ibid.

[26] Archief van Claire Bataille en Paul Ibens Desgin, Vlaams Architectuutinstituut archief, Antwerp, Flanders, Belgium.

[27] Michel Foucault, *The Archaeology of Knowledge* (New York: Vintage Books, 2010).

[28] Keller, Alex. Review of *Renaissance Theaters of Machines*, by E. S. Ferguson, M. T. Gnudi, Agostino Ramelli, and Giovanni Branca. *Technology and Culture* 19, no. 3 (1978): 495–508. https://doi.org/10.2307/3103380.

[29] Archief van Claire Bataille en Paul Ibens Desgin, Vlaams Architectuutinstituut archief.

[30] Koen Van Synghel et al, *Claire Bataille, Paul Ibens : Projets et objets 1968-2002*

[31] Ibid.

[32] Ibid.

[33] Ibid.

[34] Ibid.

[35] Glenn Adamson, *The Invention of Craft* (London: Bloomsbury Visual Arts, 2013).

[36] Tim Ingold, "The Textility of Making," *Cambridge Journal of Economics* 34, no. 1 (2009): 91–102, https://doi.org/10.1093/cje/bep042.

[37] Foucault, *The Archaeology of Knowledge*.

www.ingramcontent.com/pod-product-compliance
Lightning Source LLC
Chambersburg PA
CBHW081754300426
44116CB00014B/2109